Virginia Historic M

D0887994

Mecklenburg County Marriages, 1765 - 1853

John Vogt
&
T. William Kethley, Jr.

Iberian Publishing Co.

Athens, Georgia

Published by the Iberian Publishing Company.
548 Cedar Creek Drive Athens, GA   30605-3408

ISBN 0-935931-46-5

Printed in the United States of America

CONTENTS

ABBREVIATIONS

b-	bondsman (party granting surety to the clerk that marriage can be held without any legal impediment)
con-	consent (usually given by a parent or guardian)
d-	daughter of
(dec.)-	deceased
gdn-	guardian of
lic-	license,followed by date of license when available
min-	minister performing ceremony, followed by date of return when available
s-	son of
test.-	witnesses in a sworn oath
wid-	widow
wit-	witness

Introduction

The origins of Mecklenburg County, Virginia, begins properly in 1765 when the Virginia Assembly passed legislation to establish two new counties from the western part of Lunenburg County. The area which lay within the bounds of Cornwall Parish became Charlotte County and the county's lands within St. James Parish now became the independent county of Mecklenburg. Both new counties were named in honor of Charlotte of Mecklenburg-Strelitz, who became Queen of England upon her marriage to King George III.

The new county of Mecklenburg reflected the swell of frontier migration occurring all along the western edge of the Virginia colony. New plantings of tobacco were opening up the western lands. And the ending of the conflict with the French and their Indian allies marked a new beginning of frontier expansion, despite the attempts of British leaders to control western migrations. Mecklenburg County quickly became an important political element in the Virginia Southside.

USING THE VIRGINIA HISTORIC MARRIAGE REGISTER

Designed so that the reader may quickly search by name both husband and wife, this ready reference guide has an additional master frequency listing of all last names to account for variations in spellings by the recording clerks or ministers. The record arrangement should assist in searching through a large volume of marriages with relative facility. Yet, by no means is this guide to be an ending point for inquiry on the particular marriage under search. For the beginning genealogist, an excellent reference is Norman Edgar Wright's *Building an American Pedigree* (Provo, Utah: Brigham Young University Press). Among current periodical literature, the most extensive source listing may be found in The *Genealogical Helper* (c/o The Everton Publishers, Inc., P.O. Box 368, Logan, UT 84321). Another major reference for genealogical titles in print is Netti Schreiner-Yantis, *Genealogical & Local History Books in Print* (2v., fourth edition, 1985). In addition, the authors have published *Marriage Records in the Virginia State Library: A Researcher's Guide* (2nd edition--1988); this volume contains a complete listing of extant Virginia marriage records arranged by counties and independent cities.

In this volume's master listing of all last names (Part 1), which also shows the frequency of their occurrence, the researcher must utilize his creativity in searching all the possible variants of a name. County clerks often spelled the names according to their own phonetic whims, and versions of the same family name may occur pages apart in the husband/wife listings. English county clerks were wont to record names phonetically in the absence of literate couples, and frequently the surnames appear slightly altered in the surname frequency of this volume. Whenever possible, the names given by clerks on a document were checked against the signatures of the persons concerned (where it was evident that the signatures were true and not merely notations of a signer's mark); in each case where there was a discrepancy, the signature was used in preference to the clerk's notation. Where surnames are at odds between the clerk's recording and the minister's return, both entries have been retained and a note of the variation has been placed in the marriage record (e.g., 'Minister's return spells name as 'Armontrout'. It is usually clear from the date and other data that this in fact is a single marriage. However, the researcher is left to decide on the proper name spelling. Similarly, where the names are identical, but the year varies, both entries have been retained.

Arranged in triple columns for speed in searching, each unique last name is followed by two numbers. These represent the number of husbands and wives respectively by that name occurring in the register. Once the researcher has determined the various names desired, he can proceed to the alphabetical listings of marriages first by husband's last name (Part 2), and then by wife's last name in a separate listing (Part 3).

Both of these listings contain identical information--only the names have been reversed. In all instances, the first names of the two marriage partners are fully spelled out to facilitate indexing. Thus, 'Abm.' was rendered 'Abraham' in all cases and not 'Abram,' which in itself represents an abbreviation. Similarly, 'Eliz.' became 'Elizabeth,' etc. However, names such as 'Polly', 'Eliza', and 'Lucy' were retained.

In most instances the date of the marriage bond varies from the actual return by several days to a week or more, and both are recorded whenever available. Whenever a bondsman (b-) is cited, it may be assumed that the date following the name of the couple in the record is that of the bond's issuance; if a minister's return (min-) was also recorded for that couple and incorporated in the record, the date of the return follows the name of the minister.

If only a minister's return is recorded, the date is omitted after the minister's name, and any of the normal comments found in a bond (bondsman, consent, permission) are absent, then the date following the couple's name is that of the actual marriage ceremony as reported by the minister.

The first appendix consists of a statistical analysis of the recorded marriages for Mecklenburg County by each month of the year. A quick glance demonstrates the early years where only a few records have survived.

The second appendix is a listing of all the ministers who are recorded in Parts 1 and 2 of the Register. A beginning and ending date, as well as the number of marriages reported, are provided for each minister. This should be of considerable value in linking related families together by religious affiliation or by areas of the county.

Finally, a chart of the administrative origins of Mecklenburg County are provided. In this way, a reader who is seeking an ancestor earlier than the date of Mecklenburg's formation (1765) can determine what parent county needs to be researched for that record.

DEFINITION OF TERMS

Marriage Bond

Mecklenburg County followed the rubrics of regulations for marriages which dated from the colonial period. In 1660/1661 the law requiring a bond was first enacted. Because of a scarcity of ministers, the colony required that all persons wishing to be married by license must go to the county court clerk and give bond with sufficient security (usually $150 by the nineteenth century) that there was no lawful cause to prevent the marriage. Bonds were formal legal documents and often hand-transcribed with appropriate spaces left for names to be inserted. It is interesting to note that the bondsman was not usually the parent of the bride, as might be expected. Often a brother, uncle, or other male relative would sign the contract. Only very rarely does a woman's name appear on the bond as a signatory.

The license was then prepared by the clerk and presented to the minister who would perform the ceremony. Because many of the bonds were secured on the same day of the marriage, or else dated by the clerk with the marriage date, a system of conventional notation has been adopted in this volume to avoid unnecessary repetition (see above).

Another option was to perform the ceremony 'by banns', that is, after publicly announcing or 'publishing' the intentions of the parties at three congregational meetings. Such marriages avoided the necessity of a bond or license from the clerk. This custom predominated in several religious denomination, including the Church of the Brethren. Consequently, ministers of this denomination rarely reported such marriages to secular court authorities.

Consent

Parties seeking a license to marry were required to show evidence of their legal age to enter such a contract or else to have a consent from their parent(s) or guardian if under the age of twenty-one years. Unlike the formally prepared marriage bonds, a written consent was at the discretion of the writer and therefore a very individualistic document. Most consents were mere scraps of paper with a brief permission signed by a parent or guardian. Occasionally a parent would also designate themselves as guardian, implying perhaps that the other parent was deceased. Other surviving consent documents reveal a wealth of information for the researcher.

For the genealogist, such records as the above can provide a treasure-trove of information. Unfortunately, not all consents are quite so detailed. However, it can never be emphasized enough that the proper research should also "GO BACK TO THE ORIGINAL WHENEVER POSSIBLE." Nuances of a signature or a casual phrase can often open new doors to the careful researcher who is familiar with the parties involved.

Marriage Records; Marriage Register

During the colonial period, the law required that every marriage be recorded in a true and perfect parish register. After 1780, ministers were required to report within three months all marriages to the court clerk whose duty it was to see that the returns were entered in a book kept for that purpose. The time requirement was only rarely observed, and occasionally years passed before a minister turned in a complete and, by then, somewhat sketchy list of returns.

The county record books which have survived, such as that of Mecklenburg County, are sometimes titled "Marriage Registers," although true 'registers' as defined by law did not begin until 1853. At that time a new record-keeping system was begun by the clerk of Mecklenburg County and all other county clerks which standardized the record and provided much more family data than the older system of bonds, consents, and returns.

SOURCES

The current volume of Mecklenburg County marriages is compiled from a number of primary sources available in the Virginia State Library, Archives Division, and from Mecklenburg County court records. The two most important collections consisted of the bonds (with their accompanying consent papers) and the ministers' returns. The bonds were collected first; then they were sorted by year and alphabetical within each year to provide a data file into which the ministers' return could easily be included. After all the primary source material collection was completed, secondary sources were then consulted and a date sampling made to ascertain the validity of the data.

Primary sources (Virginia State Archives)

Marriage Bonds and Consents, 1770-1860, ca. 4 cu. ft.

Marriage Certificates and Consents, 1850-1861, .9 cu. ft.;
  Certificates [of age], 1836, 2 items; and, Consents, 1890-1891,
  2 items

Marriage Licenses, 1862-1905, ca. 9.8 cu. ft.

Marriages and Returns of Ministers, 1785-1854, 1 vol.

Returns of Ministers prior to 1854, compiled by N.G.
  Hutcheson, Clerk of the Circuit Court, 1939, 1 vol.

Index to Marriages and Ministers' Returns, 1785-1854, 1 vol.

Microfilm sources (Virginia State Archives)

Reel No.	Description
47	General Index to Marriages, A-Z, Males, 1854-1929.
47	General Index to Marriages, A-Z, Females, 1854-1929.
48	Marriage License Bonds, 1765-1810. 71pp. Typescript, arranged alphabetically.
48	Marriage Returns of Ministers, 1785-1854. Unpaged index, 164 pp.
53	Marriage Bonds and Consent Papers, 1770-1810, A-C.
54	Marriage Bonds and Consent Papers, 1770-1810, C-G.
55	Marriage Bonds and Consent Papers, 1770-1810, G-J.
56	Marriage Bonds and Consent Papers, 1770-1810, J-Mc.
57	Marriage Bonds and Consent Papers, 1770-1810, M-N.
58	Marriage Bonds and Consent Papers, 1770-1810, N-S.
59	Marriage Bonds and Consent Papers, 1770-1810, S-T.
60	Marriage Bonds and Consent Papers, 1770-1810, T-Y.
61	Marriage Bonds and Consent Papers, 1800-1820, A-H.
62	Marriage Bonds and Consent Papers, 1800-1820, F-P.
63	Marriage Bonds and Consent Papers, 1800-1820, N-Y.

Published Sources.

Bell, Landon C. *The Old Free State, A Contribution to the History of Lunenburg County and Southside Virginia.* 2 vols. Richmond: William Byrd Press, Inc., [1927] (reprinted 1974 by Genealogical Publishing Company, Baltimore, Md.). 1267 pp.

Elliott, Katherine B. (comp.). *Marriage Records, 1765-1810, Mecklenburg County, Virginia.* South Hill, Va., 1963. 190 pp.

Nottingham, Stratton (comp.). *The Marriage License Bonds of Mecklenburg County, Virginia, from 1765 to 1810.* [Onancock, Va., 1928]. 71 pp.

Prestwould Chapter, Daughters of the American Revolution (Katherine B. Elliott, comp.) *Marriage Records, 1811-1853, Mecklenburg County, Virginia.* South Hill, Va., 1962. 235 pp.

Virginia Genealogical Society. *Virginia marriages in Rev. John Cameron's Register and Bath Parish register, 1827-1897.* [Richmond, 1963], 57 pp., index.

A total of 4,120 marriages are recorded in this present Virginia Historic Marriage Register for Mecklenburg County.

-----... 1.. 2
Abernathy... 5.. 3
Adams... 7.. 6
Aigner... 0.. 1
Akin... 1.. 2
Alderson... 0.. 1
Aldridge... 1.. 0
Alexander... 3.. 6
Allen... 26.. 16
Allgood... 17.. 12
Almand... 1.. 1
Alston... 1.. 0
Alvis... 0.. 1
Ambrose... 0.. 1
Anderson... 4.. 6
Andrews... 7.. 12
Apperson... 5.. 8
Archer... 1.. 0
Armistead... 1.. 0
Arnold... 7.. 17
Arrington... 2.. 1
Arthur... 1.. 0
Ashton... 1.. 0
Atkins... 2.. 1
Atkinson... 2.. 7
Avary... 0.. 1
Averett... 7.. 7
Avery... 8.. 8
Avory... 4.. 2
Baber... 1.. 0
Bacon... 2.. 1
Bagley... 1.. 0
Bagwell... 2.. 0
Bailey... 13.. 14
Baird... 4.. 4
Baisey... 1.. 2
Baker... 2.. 9
Ballard... 0.. 5
Baptist... 4.. 6
Barbee... 1.. 0
Barber... 1.. 0
Barbour... 1.. 0
Barham... 1.. 0
Barker... 2.. 0
Barlow... 0.. 2

Barnard... 0.. 1
Barner... 4.. 2
Barnes... 11.. 7
Barnett... 9.. 5
Barron... 1.. 0
Barrow... 2.. 0
Barry... 2.. 2
Basey... 1.. 1
Baskervill... 7.. 9
Baskerville... 1.. 0
Bass... 3.. 2
Batte... 1.. 0
Baugh... 6.. 6
Baynham... 1.. 0
Beasley... 4.. 3
Beauford... 1.. 0
Beaver... 1.. 0
Beckley... 0.. 1
Beckwith... 1.. 0
Beddingfield... 0.. 1
Bedford... 3.. 0
Belcher... 1.. 1
Bell... 1.. 0
Benford... 2.. 5
Bennett... 14.. 10
Bently... 0.. 1
Berry... 2.. 4
Bevil... 0.. 1
Bevill... 3.. 3
Bigger... 0.. 1
Bignal... 0.. 1
Bilbo... 4.. 7
Billups... 0.. 1
Binford... 3.. 1
Bing... 5.. 9
Birchett... 0.. 2
Birtchett... 0.. 4
Bishop... 2.. 1
Black... 2.. 0
Blackbourn... 1.. 2
Blackbourne... 1.. 0
Blacketter... 2.. 4
Blackwell... 2.. 1
Blair... 1.. 1
Blake... 1.. 1

Blanch... 1.. 0
Bland... 2.. 4
Blane... 1.. 0
Blankenship... 2.. 2
Blanks... 7.. 11
Blanton... 1.. 2
Bolling... 1.. 0
Booker... 7.. 3
Booth... 4.. 6
Boothe... 0.. 1
Boswell... 6.. 5
Bottom... 3.. 2
Bouldin... 1.. 0
Bowen... 23.. 21
Bowers... 2.. 3
Bowler... 1.. 0
Bowman... 1.. 0
Boyd... 12.. 26
Boyland... 1.. 0
Boynton... 1.. 0
Bozwell... 0.. 1
Bracey... 3.. 1
Bracy... 0.. 1
Bradley... 4.. 2
Bradshaw... 1.. 0
Bragg... 4.. 0
Brame... 25.. 25
Branch... 2.. 1
Brandon... 3.. 9
Brasley... 0.. 1
Brawner... 0.. 1
Bressie... 1.. 0
Brewer... 2.. 0
Bridgewater... 1.. 0
Bridgforth... 0.. 3
Briggs... 2.. 1
Brightwell... 1.. 0
Broadfoot... 0.. 1
Brodie... 1.. 0
Brogdon... 1.. 1
Brook... 0.. 2
Brooke... 0.. 1
Brooking... 1.. 1
Brooks... 4.. 7
Browder... 5.. 3

Brown... 13.. 15
Brummell... 3.. 5
Brydie... 1.. 1
Buckner... 1.. 0
Buford... 1.. 0
Bugg... 21.. 20
Bullington... 1.. 0
Bullock... 3.. 0
Burger... 1.. 0
Burks... 0.. 3
Burnes... 0.. 1
Burnett... 10.. 12
Burney... 1.. 0
Burns... 1.. 3
Burrows... 0.. 2
Burrus... 0.. 4
Burt... 1.. 0
Burton... 15.. 16
Burwell... 3.. 19
Butler... 8.. 13
Butterworth... 1.. 0
Byasee... 1.. 1
Byassee... 0.. 1
Byers... 1.. 1
Cabaniss... 0.. 1
Cabiness... 3.. 1
Callis... 8.. 1
Calloway... 1.. 0
Calltharp... 1.. 0
Camp... 4.. 2
Campbell... 1.. 1
Cannon... 2.. 0
Cardin... 2.. 1
Cardwell... 3.. 2
Carless... 0.. 1
Carleton... 1.. 2
Carlin... 0.. 1
Carlton... 0.. 1
Carpenter... 2.. 3
Carrier... 1.. 0
Carrington... 0.. 2
Carroll... 10.. 5
Carter... 14.. 20
Cary... 1.. 0
Cater... 1.. 0

Cattiler... 0.. 1
Caveniss... 1.. 0
Caviness... 1.. 0
Cazy... 1.. 0
Certain... 1.. 0
Chamberlain... 0.. 2
Chambers... 3.. 5
Chambliss... 5.. 5
Chandler... 10.. 8
Chappell... 1.. 1
Charlton... 1.. 0
Chatman... 1.. 0
Chavous... 17.. 16
Cheatham... 9.. 9
Childers... 0.. 1
Childress... 3.. 6
Childrey... 1.. 0
Childry... 0.. 1
Christian... 2.. 0
Christmas... 1.. 0
Christopher... 2.. 8
Church... 1.. 0
Cirkes... 1.. 0
Clack... 2.. 1
Claiborne... 2.. 2
Clanch... 0.. 1
Clardy... 1.. 0
Clark... 14.. 15
Clarke... 2.. 3
Claunch... 4.. 1
Clausel... 3.. 7
Clay... 3.. 7
Clayton... 1.. 0
Cleaton... 11.. 15
Clements... 4.. 0
Clemmonds... 2.. 0
Clemonds... 0.. 1
Cliborne... 2.. 1
Cobb... 1.. 0
Cobbs... 1.. 0
Cocke... 3.. 0
Cogbill... 1.. 0
Cola... 0.. 1
Cole... 13.. 7
Coleman... 25.. 29

Coles... 1.. 0
Coley... 5.. 1
Colley... 3.. 9
Collier... 9.. 11
Collins... 2.. 0
Comer... 0.. 1
Conley... 1.. 0
Connaway... 2.. 0
Connell... 4.. 1
Conner... 1.. 1
Cook... 7.. 10
Cooper... 2.. 2
Copley... 1.. 0
Coppedge... 0.. 2
Corn... 0.. 1
Corpier... 2.. 0
Couch... 3.. 2
Courtney... 0.. 3
Cousen... 0.. 1
Cousins... 2.. 1
Couzens... 1.. 0
Covington... 0.. 1
Cowan... 1.. 0
Cowen... 0.. 1
Cox... 21.. 22
Craddock... 5.. 3
Crafton... 1.. 0
Craig... 1.. 0
Crawley... 0.. 2
Creath... 2.. 4
Creedle... 4.. 6
Crenshaw... 2.. 12
Crew... 2.. 2
Crews... 7.. 3
Crook... 2.. 3
Crow... 6.. 3
Crowder... 33.. 38
Crutcher... 1.. 1
Crutchfield... 9.. 6
Crute... 1.. 3
Crymes... 1.. 0
Culbreath... 7.. 6
Cumbia... 2.. 1
Cunningham... 5.. 9
Curtis... 14.. 10

Cutts... 2.. 1
Cypress... 1.. 0
Dabbs... 1.. 0
Dacus... 1.. 0
Dailey... 0.. 1
Daley... 3.. 0
Daly... 8.. 11
Dance... 2.. 0
Daniel... 12.. 18
Daves... 4.. 3
Davis... 27.. 42
Daws... 3.. 7
Day... 3.. 1
DeGraffenreid... 1.. 1
DeGraffenreidt... 1.. 0
Decker... 1.. 1
Dedman... 8.. 4
Delk... 0.. 1
Delony... 0.. 4
Dennis... 1.. 1
Denton... 0.. 1
Dew... 2.. 0
Dewes... 1.. 0
Dickerson... 1.. 0
Dickins... 1.. 0
Dixon... 1.. 0
Dodson... 7.. 7
Doggett... 0.. 4
Dortch... 13.. 19
Douglas... 5.. 3
Doyle... 2.. 0
Draper... 1.. 5
Drew... 4.. 5
Drummond... 1.. 2
Drumwright... 15.. 16
Duffee... 2.. 0
Dugger... 3.. 0
Duncan... 0.. 1
Dunn... 2.. 0
Dunnavant... 3.. 3
Dunnavon... 0.. 1
Dunnington... 1.. 0
Dunston... 1.. 5
Dupree... 2.. 1

Duprey... 2.. 1
Durham... 1.. 3
Duty... 1.. 0
Earles... 1.. 0
Easley... 2.. 0
Easter... 0.. 4
Eastham... 0.. 1
Eastland... 0.. 2
Eaton... 1.. 3
Eddins... 0.. 1
Edmonds... 2.. 1
Edmondson... 3.. 1
Edmonson... 3.. 5
Edmunds... 4.. 0
Edmundson... 4.. 4
Edwards... 5.. 8
Elam... 18.. 25
Elder... 1.. 0
Elibeck... 1.. 0
Ellington... 4.. 0
Elliott... 2.. 3
Ellis... 0.. 4
Elvin... 1.. 0
Emery... 0.. 2
Epperson... 3.. 4
Eppes... 1.. 2
Epps... 0.. 1
Erby... 0.. 1
Erskine... 0.. 1
Estes... 2.. 3
Eubank... 6.. 5
Evans... 33.. 32
Ezell... 8.. 13
Fagins... 1.. 1
Fain... 0.. 1
Fargeson... 2.. 1
Farley... 2.. 0
Farmer... 1.. 1
Farrar... 21.. 24
Farris... 1.. 0
Faulkner... 1.. 0
Fausett... 1.. 0
Feagins... 2.. 1
Feagons... 0.. 1
Featherston... 1.. 1

Feggin... 1.. 0
Feggins... 0.. 1
Feild... 13.. 6
Feilder... 0.. 1
Fennell... 2.. 0
Ferguson... 3.. 4
Ferrell... 9.. 3
Field... 4.. 2
Fielder... 0.. 1
Finch... 16.. 4
Finn... 0.. 3
Finney... 0.. 1
Fisher... 1.. 0
Fitts... 5.. 0
Fitzackerly... 1.. 0
Fleming... 1.. 0
Flinn... 1.. 2
Flood... 1.. 0
Floyd... 3.. 7
Flynn... 1.. 0
Flynne... 1.. 0
Fontaine... 1.. 0
Foote... 1.. 0
Fore... 2.. 0
Forlines... 2.. 0
Forman... 1.. 0
Foster... 2.. 1
Fowler... 1.. 2
Fowlkes... 1.. 3
Fox... 4.. 7
Francis... 1.. 0
Franklin... 0.. 1
Frasar... 1.. 0
Fraser... 1.. 0
Frazer... 3.. 1
Frazier... 1.. 0
Freeman... 8.. 6
French... 1.. 0
Fuller... 1.. 0
Furham... 0.. 1
Gabard... 1.. 0
Gafford... 1.. 0
Gaines... 1.. 0
Gardner... 1.. 0
Garey... 1.. 0

Garland... 2.. 0
Garner... 9.. 12
Garrett... 7.. 3
Garrott... 1.. 3
Gary... 0.. 2
Gayle... 5.. 2
Gee... 16.. 6
Geoghegan... 0.. 1
George... 2.. 1
Giles... 5.. 4
Gill... 5.. 0
Gillespie... 7.. 4
Gilliam... 0.. 1
Glasgow... 3.. 0
Glasscock... 6.. 5
Glidewell... 1.. 0
Glover... 1.. 3
Gober... 0.. 1
Godsey... 1.. 0
Goen... 3.. 0
Goff... 1.. 0
Gold... 6.. 6
Gooch... 1.. 0
Goode... 18.. 25
Goods... 0.. 1
Goodwin... 2.. 2
Gordon... 2.. 6
Graham... 1.. 0
Granger... 1.. 0
Grasty... 1.. 0
Graves... 13.. 21
Gray... 1.. 0
Green... 17.. 20
Greenwood... 6.. 15
Greer... 0.. 1
Greffies... 0.. 1
Gregory... 28.. 46
Gresham... 1.. 1
Griffin... 15.. 25
Griffith... 1.. 0
Grigg... 7.. 3
Grimes... 1.. 0
Grymes... 1.. 0
Guy... 6.. 5
Gwaltney... 6.. 2

Hagerman... 1.. 0
Hagood... 1.. 0
Haile... 6.. 5
Hailestock... 0.. 1
Hailey... 6.. 6
Hailstock... 1.. 0
Haley... 3.. 0
Hall... 9.. 12
Halm... 0.. 1
Halton... 0.. 1
Hamblen... 0.. 1
Hamblin... 2.. 8
Hamilton... 11.. 1
Hamlett... 1.. 0
Hamlin... 2.. 1
Hamme... 1.. 1
Hammond... 1.. 0
Hamner... 3.. 2
Hanbury... 1.. 0
Hancock... 1.. 0
Hansard... 0.. 1
Hanserd... 4.. 2
Hardie... 2.. 1
Hardin... 1.. 0
Hardy... 4.. 4
Hargrove... 4.. 0
Harper... 8.. 14
Harria... 0.. 1
Harris... 39.. 30
Harrison... 6.. 8
Harriss... 0.. 1
Harwell... 5.. 9
Harwood... 1.. 1
Haskins... 7.. 8
Hasten... 0.. 1
Hastin... 5.. 0
Hasting... 0.. 2
Hastings... 1.. 0
Hatch... 0.. 1
Hatchell... 4.. 4
Hatcher... 4.. 0
Hatsel... 1.. 1
Hatsell... 3.. 4
Hawkins... 12.. 2
Hawks... 1.. 0

Hawthorne... 1.. 0
Hayes... 13.. 10
Hayles... 1.. 0
Haynes... 1.. 0
Hazelwood... 3.. 1
Hazlewood... 1.. 0
Hearn... 1.. 0
Heathcock... 0.. 2
Hedderly... 1.. 0
Heggie... 1.. 0
Helm... 1.. 0
Hendrick... 10.. 9
Henly... 0.. 1
Henry... 0.. 2
Hepbourne... 1.. 0
Hepburn... 1.. 0
Hester... 16.. 23
Hethcock... 1.. 0
Hewes... 1.. 0
Hickman... 0.. 1
Hicks... 11.. 4
Higgerson... 0.. 2
Hightower... 5.. 2
Hill... 9.. 3
Hilton... 1.. 0
Hines... 1.. 1
Hinton... 4.. 3
Hite... 8.. 1
Hix... 5.. 3
Hobsin... 0.. 1
Hodge... 1.. 1
Hodges... 0.. 1
Hogan... 2.. 4
Hogwood... 0.. 1
Holcomb... 2.. 0
Hollins... 0.. 1
Holloway... 13.. 20
Holmes... 17.. 29
Holt... 2.. 0
Holtsford... 1.. 0
Homes... 1.. 1
Hood... 3.. 1
Hooper... 1.. 0
Hopkins... 2.. 2
Hord... 3.. 1

House... 6.. 3
Howard... 1.. 1
Howerton... 1.. 0
Hubbard... 2.. 4
Huddleston... 0.. 1
Hudgins... 1.. 4
Hudson... 30.. 34
Hughes... 6.. 3
Hull... 0.. 1
Humphress... 0.. 1
Humphries... 1.. 4
Hundley... 2.. 5
Hunt... 7.. 12
Hunter... 1.. 1
Hurst... 1.. 0
Hurt... 5.. 5
Hutcherson... 11.. 8
Hutcheson... 14.. 35
Hutson... 0.. 1
Hutt... 0.. 7
Hutton... 1.. 0
Hyde... 1.. 4
Hynt... 1.. 0
Inge... 1.. 2
Ingram... 2.. 4
Insco... 5.. 5
Irby... 0.. 2
Isham... 1.. 0
Ivey... 1.. 4
Ivy... 0.. 2
Jackson... 18.. 18
James... 2.. 1
Jarrott... 1.. 0
Jefferson... 1.. 0
Jeffress... 3.. 3
Jeffreys... 1.. 0
Jeffries... 19.. 22
Jenkins... 2.. 0
Jerman... 1.. 0
Jeter... 2.. 4
Jewell... 1.. 0
Jiggetts... 1.. 2
Johns... 1.. 0
Johnson... 41.. 47
Johnston... 3.. 4

Jones... 78.. 69
Jordan... 2.. 3
Joyce... 0.. 2
Justice... 1.. 0
Keeling... 2.. 0
Keen... 3.. 2
Keeton... 15.. 23
Kelley... 2.. 0
Kelly... 3.. 2
Kendrick... 1.. 1
Kennedy... 1.. 0
Kennon... 4.. 5
Kersey... 2.. 2
Keys... 1.. 0
Kidd... 4.. 2
Kimball... 0.. 1
Kimbrough... 1.. 0
King... 14.. 9
Kinker... 1.. 0
Kirk... 5.. 0
Kirkland... 3.. 2
Kirks... 3.. 6
Kiser... 0.. 1
Kittrell... 1.. 0
Knight... 1.. 1
Knott... 1.. 1
Knowell... 1.. 0
Knox... 0.. 3
Lacy... 0.. 2
Ladd... 10.. 4
Laffoon... 2.. 1
Laine... 1.. 0
Laird... 2.. 0
Lamay... 1.. 0
Lamb... 0.. 1
Lambert... 9.. 15
Lamkin... 1.. 0
Land... 2.. 3
Langford... 0.. 1
Langhorne... 1.. 3
Langley... 5.. 2
Lanier... 5.. 5
Lark... 0.. 5
Lawrence... 1.. 1
Lawson... 2.. 0

Lawton... 1.. 0
LeNeve... 0.. 4
Leach... 1.. 1
Leaker... 1.. 0
Lear... 1.. 0
Leckie... 0.. 1
Lee... 3.. 0
Leftwich... 1.. 0
Leigh... 4.. 0
Leneve... 4.. 0
Lester... 2.. 1
Lett... 9.. 11
Leverman... 0.. 1
Lewis... 19.. 12
Lidderdal... 0.. 1
Lifford... 1.. 0
Light... 0.. 1
Lightfoot... 0.. 1
Ligon... 8.. 7
Lindley... 0.. 1
Lisk... 1.. 0
Lloyd... 0.. 1
Loafman... 1.. 1
Lockett... 4.. 11
Loftis... 2.. 0
Lollis... 1.. 0
Lomax... 1.. 0
Lonnon... 1.. 0
Love... 6.. 4
Lovingston... 0.. 1
Lowery... 2.. 0
Lowry... 0.. 1
Loyd... 1.. 2
Lucas... 4.. 5
Lukes... 1.. 0
Lumpkin... 1.. 0
Lumsdon... 1.. 0
Lunsford... 2.. 2
Lydick... 0.. 2
Lyle... 1.. 0
Lynch... 1.. 1
Mabry... 2.. 4
MacCarter... 0.. 1
MacGowan... 1.. 0
Mackecy... 1.. 1

Maclin... 4.. 9	Meredith... 1.. 0	Nelson... 5.. 10
Major... 1.. 0	Merritt... 2.. 0	Nethery... 1.. 0
Mallett... 7.. 6	Merryman... 5.. 4	Newman... 2.. 0
Mallory... 1.. 0	Michaux... 0.. 1	Newsom... 1.. 0
Malone... 12.. 18	Middagh... 1.. 1	Newton... 17.. 15
Manley... 2.. 0	Miller... 2.. 0	Nicholas... 0.. 1
Mann... 1.. 0	Mills... 6.. 5	Nicholson... 5.. 3
Manning... 4.. 3	Mimms... 3.. 0	Nipper... 2.. 0
Marable... 3.. 0	Mims... 1.. 0	Noblin... 1.. 0
Markam... 1.. 0	Minor... 1.. 2	Noel... 3.. 3
Marks... 0.. 1	Mise... 1.. 1	Nolley... 5.. 4
Marriott... 0.. 1	Mitchell... 13.. 5	Norman... 1.. 1
Marshall... 8.. 22	Mize... 4.. 0	Norment... 3.. 12
Martin... 5.. 1	Monday... 1.. 0	Northcross... 1.. 0
Mason... 10.. 11	Monroe... 1.. 1	Northington... 3.. 14
Massey... 2.. 2	Montague... 1.. 0	Norvell... 5.. 1
Matthews... 3.. 7	Montgomery... 1.. 0	Norwood... 2.. 0
May... 2.. 1	Moody... 12.. 12	Nowell... 3.. 1
Mayes... 4.. 3	Moon... 1.. 1	Nuckols... 0.. 1
Mayfield... 1.. 0	Moore... 21.. 31	Nunn... 2.. 0
Maynard... 1.. 3	Morgain... 0.. 1	Nunnelly... 0.. 1
Mayne... 1.. 3	Morgan... 15.. 10	Nunnery... 0.. 2
Mayo... 10.. 4	Morris... 11.. 10	O'Brian... 0.. 1
McAden... 2.. 1	Morton... 4.. 4	O'Briant... 1.. 0
McCargo... 0.. 3	Moseley... 4.. 1	Ogburn... 1.. 5
McCarter... 3.. 1	Moss... 18.. 15	Oliver... 9.. 6
McCraw... 1.. 0	Mountcastle... 1.. 0	Organ... 1.. 0
McCutcheon... 2.. 5	Mullins... 5.. 9	Ornsby... 0.. 2
McDaniel... 8.. 4	Munford... 0.. 1	Osborn... 1.. 0
McDearman... 1.. 0	Murdock... 0.. 1	Osborne... 2.. 3
McDowell... 1.. 0	Murfey... 0.. 1	Oslin... 9.. 5
McGowan... 1.. 0	Murphey... 1.. 0	Osling... 0.. 1
McHarg... 0.. 2	Murray... 8.. 8	Outland... 1.. 0
McKinney... 4.. 2	Murrell... 1.. 0	Overbey... 0.. 1
McLaughlin... 0.. 1	Murrill... 0.. 1	Overby... 24.. 26
McLin... 2.. 2	Mustian... 1.. 0	Overton... 5.. 9
McNeal... 2.. 1	Naish... 0.. 2	Owen... 12.. 14
McQuie... 1.. 1	Nance... 13.. 13	Pace... 1.. 0
McRilon... 1.. 0	Nanney... 12.. 3	Page... 0.. 2
Meacham... 2.. 1	Nash... 14.. 7	Paine... 1.. 0
Mealer... 4.. 4	Neal... 10.. 11	Palmer... 6.. 8
Mealey... 1.. 0	Neathery... 4.. 3	Parham... 3.. 3
Mealler... 0.. 1	Neathry... 1.. 0	Paris... 1.. 0
Medley... 4.. 1	Neblett... 1.. 0	Parish... 1.. 0
Meldrum... 1.. 2	Neely... 1.. 0	Parker... 1.. 4

Parrish... 4.. 5
Parrott... 1.. 0
Parsons... 0.. 1
Paschall... 0.. 1
Patillo... 8.. 2
Patrick... 1.. 2
Patterson... 2.. 0
Paul... 1.. 0
Paulette... 1.. 0
Paull... 1.. 0
Paylor... 1.. 0
Payne... 1.. 0
Pearce... 0.. 1
Pearcy... 1.. 1
Pearson... 5.. 0
Peebles... 3.. 0
Peek... 1.. 0
Peete... 1.. 2
Penn... 0.. 2
Pennington... 9.. 23
Pentecost... 0.. 1
Penticost... 1.. 0
Peoples... 2.. 0
Perkins... 1.. 3
Perkinson... 6.. 2
Perry... 1.. 0
Persize... 0.. 1
Pescud... 1.. 0
Pettiford... 1.. 2
Pettipool... 1.. 0
Pettus... 9.. 20
Pettway... 1.. 0
Petty... 1.. 0
Pettyford... 0.. 2
Pettypool... 12.. 4
Phillips... 26.. 20
Piemont... 0.. 1
Pierce... 0.. 1
Piller... 1.. 0
Pinson... 3.. 1
Pitts... 0.. 1
Plummer... 1.. 0
Poarch... 3.. 0
Poindexter... 4.. 10
Pointer... 0.. 1

Pool... 1.. 4
Poole... 2.. 3
Pope... 1.. 0
Portwood... 1.. 0
Potter... 2.. 0
Potts... 2.. 1
Powell... 2.. 1
Power... 0.. 1
Powers... 3.. 4
Poynor... 2.. 4
Poythress... 8.. 2
Prather... 1.. 0
Preston... 1.. 0
Prewitt... 0.. 1
Price... 3.. 0
Prichett... 1.. 3
Pride... 2.. 0
Pritchett... 5.. 0
Pryor... 1.. 0
Puckett... 2.. 4
Pugh... 1.. 0
Pulliam... 4.. 2
Pullian... 1.. 0
Pully... 4.. 9
Puryear... 41.. 47
Quarles... 1.. 1
Quincey... 0.. 1
Quinchett... 2.. 1
Quincy... 0.. 1
Rachael... 1.. 0
Ragland... 1.. 0
Ragsdale... 10.. 7
Rainey... 21.. 27
Ramsey... 1.. 0
Ransom... 1.. 0
Ravenscroft... 1.. 0
Read... 4.. 5
Reader... 4.. 2
Reagan... 1.. 0
Reamey... 6.. 6
Reams... 2.. 0
Reamy... 2.. 1
Reaves... 0.. 1
Redd... 4.. 4
Redding... 1.. 0

Redford... 1.. 0
Reekes... 5.. 6
Reese... 4.. 0
Renn... 1.. 1
Reynolds... 2.. 0
Rhodes... 0.. 1
Rice... 3.. 0
Richards... 1.. 4
Richardson... 3.. 4
Richeson... 0.. 1
Ricks... 0.. 1
Ridley... 0.. 1
Ridout... 1.. 0
Riggans... 0.. 1
Riggin... 0.. 1
Riggins... 4.. 0
Ripley... 0.. 1
Rives... 1.. 0
Roach... 1.. 0
Robards... 3.. 3
Roberts... 25.. 28
Robertson... 11.. 8
Robinson... 2.. 2
Roffe... 12.. 15
Rogers... 4.. 6
Rook... 0.. 3
Roper... 0.. 1
Rose... 2.. 0
Ross... 1.. 0
Rottenberry... 3.. 2
Rottenbury... 0.. 1
Rowland... 2.. 0
Rowlett... 1.. 6
Royal... 3.. 3
Royer... 1.. 0
Royster... 20.. 24
Rudd... 2.. 5
Rudder... 1.. 1
Ruffin... 1.. 1
Russell... 11.. 15
Ryan... 1.. 0
Ryland... 8.. 6
Sadler... 1.. 1
Salley... 1.. 2
Sally... 0.. 2

Sammons... 1.. 0
Samuel... 1.. 0
Sandifer... 1.. 0
Sands... 0.. 1
Sandys... 1.. 4
Saulsberry... 0.. 1
Saunders... 6.. 10
Savage... 2.. 0
Scott... 6.. 8
Scruggs... 1.. 0
Sculthorp... 1.. 0
Selden... 1.. 0
Seward... 6.. 3
Shackelford... 0.. 1
Shackleford... 1.. 1
Shanks... 1.. 0
Sharp... 2.. 0
Shaw... 2.. 1
Shearer... 1.. 0
Shell... 3.. 0
Shelton... 6.. 2
Short... 9.. 14
Simmons... 24.. 17
Simpson... 1.. 0
Sims... 2.. 2
Sinclair... 0.. 1
Singleton... 7.. 7
Sizemore... 2.. 2
Skelton... 0.. 1
Skinner... 0.. 1
Skipwith... 0.. 2
Slate... 1.. 0
Slaughter... 2.. 0
Small... 3.. 4
Smelley... 2.. 1
Smith... 53.. 57
Smithson... 6.. 3
Snead... 1.. 0
Somervill... 1.. 3
Somerville... 0.. 1
Sommervill... 1.. 0
Soward... 2.. 1
Spain... 17.. 9
Sparks... 1.. 1
Speaks... 1.. 0

Speed... 7.. 17
Spence... 1.. 1
Spencer... 5.. 1
Spraggins... 1.. 0
Spurlock... 2.. 3
Stainback... 3.. 4
Stalcup... 1.. 0
Stamps... 1.. 0
Standley... 1.. 4
Stanfield... 2.. 0
Stanley... 1.. 1
Steagall... 0.. 1
Steel... 0.. 2
Stegall... 5.. 2
Stembridge... 3.. 2
Sterling... 0.. 1
Stevens... 1.. 1
Stewart... 16.. 36
Stigall... 0.. 1
Stiner... 0.. 1
Stith... 1.. 2
Stokes... 2.. 2
Stone... 17.. 27
Stovall... 1.. 0
Strange... 4.. 0
Straub... 1.. 0
Stroud... 3.. 0
Strum... 1.. 0
Stuart... 4.. 2
Sturdivant... 4.. 0
Suggett... 0.. 3
Sullivan... 2.. 2
Sullivant... 0.. 1
Swepson... 3.. 5
Sydnor... 1.. 2
Tabb... 2.. 4
Talley... 12.. 14
Tandy... 0.. 2
Tanner... 13.. 15
Tansley... 0.. 1
Tarry... 8.. 4
Tarwater... 2.. 1
Tatum... 0.. 2
Taylor... 46.. 42
Temple... 2.. 1

Terrell... 1.. 0
Terry... 1.. 0
Thacker... 1.. 0
Tharp... 1.. 0
Thellis... 0.. 1
Thomas... 23.. 25
Thomason... 11.. 8
Thomerson... 0.. 1
Thompson... 27.. 25
Thomson... 3.. 0
Thornton... 1.. 2
Threadgill... 1.. 0
Throgmorton... 1.. 0
Thrower... 1.. 0
Tibbs... 0.. 1
Tillotson... 9.. 11
Tindal... 0.. 1
Tinsley... 0.. 1
Tisdale... 4.. 4
Tompkins... 1.. 0
Toone... 12.. 14
Totty... 0.. 2
Towler... 0.. 5
Townes... 6.. 7
Townsend... 1.. 0
Travis... 1.. 0
Traylor... 1.. 0
Trice... 1.. 0
Tucker... 29.. 29
Tudor... 2.. 1
Tunstall... 3.. 2
Turnbull... 1.. 0
Turner... 13.. 13
Tutor... 3.. 1
Underwood... 0.. 2
Vaden... 0.. 1
Valentine... 7.. 4
Vaughan... 50.. 44
Venable... 3.. 3
Vercer... 1.. 0
Vowell... 1.. 0
Wade... 6.. 10
Wagstaff... 5.. 7
Walden... 6.. 5
Walker... 44.. 51

Wall... 16.. 12
Wallace... 1.. 2
Waller... 6.. 8
Walthall... 1.. 0
Walton... 2.. 3
Ware... 1.. 1
Warren... 6.. 4
Wartman... 4.. 4
Wartmen... 0.. 1
Watkins... 14.. 10
Watson... 12.. 11
Watts... 2.. 2
Weatherford... 3.. 5
Weaver... 2.. 0
Webb... 6.. 4
Webster... 1.. 0
Weekes... 0.. 1
Wells... 11.. 7
Wesson... 2.. 0
Westbrook... 4.. 2
Westmoreland... 1.. 2
Whitby... 0.. 1
White... 10.. 14
Whitehead... 0.. 5
Whitlow... 5.. 5
Whitt... 1.. 1
Whittemore... 3.. 3
Whittle... 1.. 0
Whitworth... 1.. 0
Whoberry... 1.. 2
Whobry... 1.. 1
Wiggins... 1.. 0
Wilborn... 0.. 1
Wilbourn... 0.. 1
Wilbourne... 1.. 0
Wilburn... 4.. 1
Wiles... 5.. 5
Wiley... 1.. 0
Wilkerson... 13.. 9
Wilkes... 1.. 0
Wilkins... 1.. 2
Wilkinson... 3.. 6
Willard... 1.. 0
Williams... 28.. 15
Williamson... 10.. 10

Willis... 7.. 6
Wills... 1.. 1
Wilmoth... 2.. 1
Wilson... 20.. 21
Wiltse... 1.. 0
Wimbish... 2.. 0
Winckler... 3.. 1
Winfield... 2.. 4
Winfree... 3.. 0
Wingfield... 3.. 2
Winkfield... 0.. 1
Winkler... 0.. 1
Winn... 7.. 9
Winstead... 1.. 0
Wood... 3.. 3
Woodall... 0.. 1
Woodruff... 2.. 0
Woodson... 2.. 0
Woody... 2.. 0
Wootton... 10.. 11
Worsham... 5.. 11
Wortham... 6.. 3
Wray... 0.. 1
Wrenn... 0.. 1
Wright... 34.. 20
Wyatt... 2.. 0
Wynn... 0.. 1
Wynne... 0.. 1
Yancey... 30.. 31
Yates... 1.. 2
Yeargen... 0.. 2
Young... 7.. 10

----- & Mary Brame 11 Apr 1796; son of John and Martha Smith b-James Norment min- William Richards- 21Apr1796

Abernathy

David H & Jane Warren 16 Feb 1824; b- Samuel H Warren min- J. Carson- (Lunenburg County)- 16Feb1824

John E & Martha C Smith 5 Nov 1842; b- Robert Scoggin con- Henry Wilson, grandfather of Martha

Thomas & Martha Moore 29 Oct 1814; b- Richard H Edmonson con-John J Moore, gdn of Martha min- Charles Ogburn- (Methodist) 30Oct1814

Thomas & Martha Waller 4 Jan 1813; b- John Waller con- John Waller, father

Tignal & Martha Holmes 8 May 1796; b- John Holmes min- John Loyd-12May1796

Adams

Isaac & Judith Carroll 30 Dec 1786; b- William Parish

James & Jane Allen 8 Jan 1835; b- Benjamin Bugg con- Lucy Allen, mother

John & Permelia Johnson 10 Feb 1840; b- Phillip Johnson con- Polly Johnson, mother

Richard & Sally Allen 28 Oct 1808; b- Fielding Noel min- John Meacham- 17Nov1808

Sackfield & Betsy Daly 23 Jun 1795; b- William Dailey min- John Loyd-4 August 1795

William & Mary Mallett 11 Jul 1839; b- Pleasant Burnett min- Benjamin R. Duval-

Wyatt & Mary G Chambliss 2 Dec 1823; b- John T Barner con- John Chambliss, father

Akin

Joseph & Mary Eastland 10 Oct 1774; b- William Eastland

Aldridge

John & Agnes Baugh 20 Jan 1800; b- E Macgowan min- Ebenezer McGowan- 22Jan1800 widow of James Baugh

Alexander

Lawson Henderson & Lucy Jane Alexander 2 Oct 1823; b- Nathaniel Alexander con- Mark Alexander min- James Smith

Mark & Nancy Eaton 18 Oct 1804; b- William Baskervill

Mark & Elizabeth Q McHarg 19 Jan 1797; b- Robert Baskervill min-John Loyd- 26Jan1797

Allen

Abel W & Ann Daly 14 Oct 1835; b- Cuthbert Wagstaff

Alexander G & Martha C Townes 12 Aug 1822; b- William Bedford con- Joseph Townes, father

Arva & Polly Clarke 1 Aug 1786; b- Bolling Clarke min- John Marshall-(Baptist)- 19Aug1786

Charles & Sarah Smith 28 Apr 1781; b- David Royster con- Drury Smith, father

Darling & Judith Nance 19 May 1783; b- Robert Nance s of William

David & Catharine Chavous 17 Nov 1836; b- Jacob Chavous min- William Steel- (Episcopal)-

Ephraim & Patsey Skelton 13 Feb 1792; b- Thomas Allen min- James Read- (Baptist)

Gray & Molly Nance 16 Dec 1791; b- William Drumwright con- Robert Nance, father con- Darling Allen, brother of Gray Gray s of William Allen

James & Frances Comer 13 Apr 1795; b- Burwell Russell min- William Richards- 15 Apr1795

John & Elizabeth Bugg 3 Oct 1791; b- Thomas Langley John Allen from Buckingham County min- Edward Almand- 6Oct1791

John & Martha Colley 12 Nov 1798; b- William Brown min- Charles Ogburn- (Methodist)- 22Dec1798

John & Patsey Cox 14 Jan 1793; b- Thomas Cox min- William Creath- 22Jan1793

John & Constant Marriott 3 Mar 1806; b- Thomas Marriott

John & Nancy Morgain 15 Dec 1783; b- Frederick Rainey s of William Allen

Jones & Nancy Lewis 8 Jan 1810; b- Robert Lewis

Joseph P & Lucy Ann Adams 18 Dec 1832; b- Richard Adams

Leroy P & Virginia Anne Allen 8 Feb 1845; b- John T Wootton con- Martha C Allen, mother

Matthew & Mary Brawner 8 May 1797; b- James Thompson

Meredith & Nancy Cooper 9 Aug 1788; b- John Bailey con- William Allen, father

Pleasant & Rebeccah Watson 8 Aug 1787; b- John Allen con- William Allen, Sr., father

Richard M & Mary Wynne 8 Dec 1814; widow b- Thomas Rowlett

Richard & Elizabeth B Blacketter 6 Nov 1809; b- David Blacketter

Robert Jones & Caty Hollins 1 Dec 1786; b- Thomas Richardson

Ruel & Mary Pulliam 13 Jan 1794; b- James Norment min- William Creath- 21Jan1794

Thomas & Lucy Adams 13 Dec 1796; b- John Freeman min- William Richards- 22Dec1796

Young & Sarah Poole 27 Feb 1786; b- Darling Allen Young s of William Allen

Allgood

Benjamin L & Mary Ann Bevil 15 Oct 1851; min- George W. Andrews- 16Oct1851

Creed A & Emily Parrish 3 Aug 1843; b- Alexander Pritchett

David & Panthea Hayes 28 Nov 1840; b- Joseph Averett

Edmund & Frances Talley 20 Dec 1813; b- Samuel Bugg con- Elizabeth Talley, mother

Edward & Eliza Akin 24 Nov 1828; b- Thomas Atkins con- Nancy Akin, mother min- John B. Smith- 27Nov1828

Edward & Elizabeth Hudson 28 Nov 1788; b- Bartlett Cox

George & Dicey Hudson 23 Jan 1806; b- Thomas Mallett min- William Richards- 29Jan1806

James P & Mary Owen Graves 6 Jun 1853; con- Thomas Graves, father min- James S. Kennedy- 9Jun1853

James & Elizabeth Stewart 13 Dec 1842; b- James Stewart con- John Stewart, father

Jeremiah & Dicey Harris 13 Dec 1802; b- James Harris d of James Harris

John & Jinsey Blake 31 Dec 1798; b- Edward Goodrich min- William Creath- 3Jan1799

Robert W & Ava H Parrish 6 Mar 1848; b- Benjamin S Allgood con- Peter Parrish, father

Samuel & Jinny Claunch 29 Dec 1804; b- Matthew Claunch

Samuel & Mary Royal 4 Oct 1786; b- Edward Clarke

William T & Eliza K Covington 15 Feb 1836; b- Edmund Young

William & Polly H Hamilton 16 Aug 1813; b- Samuel Bugg con- Joseph Hamilton, father con- Edward Allgood, father min- James Meacham- 26Aug1813

William & Sarah Royal 5 Mar 1790; b- Manley Allgood

Almand

David & Rebecca W Green 20 May 1824; b- Archibald Green min- James Smith-

Alston

John & Jane H Davis 14 Dec 1799; b- Thomas H Davis min- Ebenezer McGowan- 19Dec1799

Anderson

Athelston & Sally A Irby 27 May 1825; b- John W Irby con- Peter Irby, father min- Pleasant Gold- (Baptist)- 2Jun1825

Charles & Sally Thornton 11 Sep 1787; b- James Thornton Charles from Amelia County

Jordan & Margaret Easter 6 Jun 1785; b- Lewis Rolfe Jordan from Prince Edward County

Joseph & Martha Edmondson 12 Aug 1794; b- William Phillips min- William Creath-

Andrews

Allen T & Martha J Oslin 12 Oct 1835; b- James Oslin min- James McAden-

Anderson & Sally Gee 28 Nov 1816; min- Charles Ogburn- (Methodist)- 28Nov1816

Ephraim (Jr) & Stacy Humphress 15 Feb 1786; b- Thomas Humphress

Robert & Julia Royster 20 Aug 1827; b- Clark Royster min- Allen D. Metcalf- 24Aug1827

Thomas & Margaret Broadfoot 29 Mar 1791; b- Frederick Andrews

William A & Nancy G Arnold 7 Sep 1827; b- Joseph A Arnold min- James McAden-

William A & Rebecca L Smith 27 Dec 1830; Rebecca test. that she is 22 b- David Oslin min- James McAden-

Apperson

David & Martha Speed 30 May 1778; b- Richard Hanserd

Richard & Jane E Maclin 26 Sep 1821; b- William Townes con- James Maclin, father min- Alexander M. Cowan-

Samuel & Polly Worsham 1 Oct 1801; b- Archibald Clarke con- John Worsham, father

Thomas & Martha Gregory 21 Sep 1829; b- Alexander Blankenship con- Mary Gregory, mother

Thomas & Kitty Wynn 6 Aug 1791; b- Holeman Rice min- James Read- (Baptist)- 12Aug1791

Archer

Edwin B & Edney W Davis 9 Dec 1833; widow b- Amos Roberts con- John Nance, father of Edney

Armistead

John & Elizabeth Royster 17 Jul 1777; b- John Farrar con- William Royster, father

Arnold

Edwin & Prudence Carter 16 Aug 1830; min- William Steel- (Episcopal)-

Elisha & Mary Drumwright 19 Dec 1831; con- William Drumwright, father min- James McAden-

Hartwell & Mary M Harper 20 Dec 1830; b- Roberty Moore min- James McAden-

Isaac & Anne Andrews 16 May 1795; b- George Hightower Walker con- George Andrews con- John Arnold min- Charles Ogburn- (Methodist)- 21May1795

Joseph & Mary Bennett 2 Nov 1837; b- Joseph Bennett Jr min- James McAden-

Joseph & Frances Drumwright 24 Sep 1800; b- William Drumwright

Joseph & Martha Harper 18 Dec 1820; b- Thomas Farrar min- Thomas Adams- (Lunenburg Co.)-

Arrington

John & Elizabeth Jones 18 Aug 1825; b- Mark Wilkinson con- Richard Jones, father min- Pleasant Gold- (Baptist)- 24Aug1825

John & Susanna Vaughan 30 Apr 1790; married in Granville County, N.C.

Arthur

Thomas S & Nancy Lewis 6 Aug 1844; b- Robert C Nelson

Ashton

Henry & Elizabeth Hanner Barbara Watts 31 Mar 1788; b- Richard Watts min- Thomas Scott-

Atkins

James & Saluda W White 10 Dec 1835; b- William R Mason con- Jane white, mother

Thomas & Sally Johnston 8 Jan 1810; b- Caleb Johnston

Atkinson

Arthur C & Elizabeth Pinson 12 Sep 1791; b- Thomas Pinson min- James Read- (Baptist)- 29Sep1791

Richard & Susanah Davis 4 May 1815; widow b- William Bilbo

Averett

Beverly & Peggy Spence 25 Jan 1820; b- Richard Dunson con- Thomas Spence, father min- William Richards- 25Jan1820

Edwin & Prudence Carter 26 Aug 1830; b- Robert Carter con- James M Averett, father

James & Elizabeth MacCarter 21 Jun 1813; b- Wingfield Averett min- William Richards- 1Jul1813

Joseph James & Phybie H Homes - Sep 1848; b- George Holmes

Thomas & Rebecca Allen 13 Jul 1807; b- Joel Averett min- William Richards- 23Jul1807

Washington & Joybe Hailey 13 Nov 1817; b- Josiah Gold con- Thomas Hailey, father

Wingfield & Mary Avery 15 Nov 1813; b- Matthew Averett con- Langston Avery

Avery

Henry W & Missouri Avery 21 Nov 1835; con- John Nelson, gdn of Missouri min- John B. Smith-

Henry & Martha Owen - Dec 1839; min- John B. Smith- Dec1839

Henry & Rutha Stewart 9 Jan 1823; b- Thomas Spence min- John S. Ravenscroft- (Episcopal)- 15Jan1823

Joel & Franky Puryear 12 Dec 1808; b- Elijah Puryear min- William Richards- 29Dec1808

Matthew & Obedience Crowder 12 Sep 1803; b- John Wagstaff min- William Richards-

Matthew & Leah Jeter 15 Dec 1843; b- Thomas Hayes

William & Lucy Noel 16 Jul 1817; b- James Avery min- William Richards- 17Jul1817

Wingfield & Mary Avery 1 Dec 1813; min- William Richards-

Avory

Brown & Elizabeth Royster 27 Jan 1810; b- Miles Hall

Elijah Evans & Delia Crew 12 Jun 1809; b- Leeman Haile

James & Polly Spain 12 Dec 1808; b- Abraham Reamy min- William
  Richards- 20Dec1808
Jarrott & Rebecca Worsham 17 Dec 1810; b- Daniel Jones

Baber

William & Polly King 19 Aug 1817; b- Diggs Poynor

Bacon

Drury A & Elizabeth Jones 16 Aug 1817; b- Thomas P Pettus
James E P & Martha P Gregory 20 Jun 1825; b- William Hicks min-
  James McAden-

Bagley

William & Phebe Marshall 16 Mar 1812; b- Daniel Middagh con- Dancy
  McGraw min- William Richards- 26Mar1812

Bagwell

Henry & Lucinda Simmons 21 Mar 1818; b- Edward Simmons
Samuel & Catherine Brown 12 Nov 1788; Samuel from Brunswick County
  b- Richard Edmondson

Bailey

Benjamin & Patsy Durham 11 Jun 1798; b- Valentine McCutcheon min-
  William Richards- 28Jun1798
Francis Baker & Evalina Hill 4 May 1819; b- John Clark min- Alexander
  M. Cowan-
George & Duannar Hicks 21 Oct 1799; b- Bartholomew Medley min-
  William Creath-
Henry & Jessie Curtis 17 Feb 1802; b- Jesse Curtis
Henry & Polly Edwards 9 Dec 1793; b- Thomas Edwards con- John
  Edwards, father
Howard & Elizabeth Vaughan 3 Dec 1783; b- John Bell
John & Anne Allen 2 Mar 1791; b- Elisha Arnold min- Henry Ogburn-
  5Mar1791
Peter & Sarah Baker 27 Aug 1792; b- Thomas Jeffries Sarah daughter
  of Zachariah Baker and Jane Baker
Richard & Anne Brown 12 Jan 1795; b- William Brown
Thomas J & Elizabeth O Goode - --- 1842; b- J T Williamson
Thomas & Orpy Robertson 22 Oct 1825; b- James Robertson con- John
  Robertson, father min- George Petty-
William H & Mary Johnson 27 Nov 1820; b- Thomas Atkins min-
  Alexander M. Cowan-
William & Martha Holloway 21 Nov 1801; b- Henry Bailey

Baird

Charles W & Fanny D Gregory 6 Dec 1808; b- West Gregory con-
  Richard Gregory, father
Charles W & Mary A Phillips 23 Sep 1812; widow b- John Gregory
  min- James Meacham- 24Sep1812
John & Sally Cunningham 3 May 1805; b- Jesse Johnson
William & Sylvia Bass 29 Nov 1802; b- Independence Poarch min- John
  Meacham- 1Dec1802

Baisey

Jesse & Jane Perrin Giles 19 Dec 1791; b- Isham Eppes con- Henry
  Edward Giles, father min- John Loyd- 21Dec1791

Baker

James & Polly Holmes 4 Oct 1804; b- Richard Crowder
William & Leah Hendrick 12 May 1800; b- George Baker min- Matthew
  Dance- 17May1800

Baptist

John G & Eliza T Maclin 10 Sep 1813; b- Thomas Hill con- James
  Maclin

Matthew & Aphia W Clausel 11 Dec 1809; b- Benjamin W Jeffries min-George Micklejohn-

Richard H & Sally Goode 28 Feb 1818; d of Samuel Goode b- John W Lewis min- John S. Ravenscroft- (Episcopal)-

William G & Mary Ann Green 27 Dec 1831; b- Hilliard J Manning con-G B Green, father min- William Steel- (Episcopal)-

Barbee

Edward & Sarah E Fielder 3 Dec 1846; b- Dennis R Fielder

Barber

Edward & Jincey Williamson 9 Dec 1799; b- James Greenwood con-Robert Williamson, father

Barbour

Shadrach & Fanny C Higgerson 22 Aug 1851; con- Charles Higgerson, father min- S.G. Mason-

Barham

Burwell B & Ellen Puryear 25 Dec 1850; con- John G Puryear, father min- Robert Burton-

Barker

Benjamin W & Amanda C Cleaton 13 Nov 1853; con- Margaret Cleaton, mother min- James McAden-

Charles & Barbara Walton 15 Aug 1791; b- John Walton Charles from Nottoway County min- James Read- (Baptist)- 18Aug1791

Barner

Antilochus J & Elizabeth Walker 20 May 1833; con- John Connell, gdn, who test. he has raised Elizabeth since childhood b- John C Jones

Harrison & Polly Jones 17 May 1786; b- Theophilus Harrison

John F & Elizabeth L Chambliss 3 Jul 1821; b- John Chambliss

Lafeyette & Amanda C Tanner 12 Mar 1842; b- Tatnal Ellis con-Elizabeth Tanner, mother

Barnes

Brackett & Jane Jeffries 8 May 1797; b- Swepson Jeffries, Sr. min-William Richards- 11May1797

Daniel R & Mary A B Marshall 17 Feb 1812; b- William G Pettus min-William Richards- 4Mar1812

George T & Elizabeth Burnett 1 Mar 1821; b- Lewis Winn

John F & Ellenor G Marshall 17 Apr 1826; b- William Marshall con-Thomas Marshall, father

John J & Mary B Pettus 19 Oct 1846; b- Samuel F Barnes con- C H Pettus, father min- S.G. Mason- 27Oct1846

John & Polly R Birtchett 1 Apr 1822; widow b- Enoch Jones

John & Rebecca Winkfield 15 Jan 1794; b- Joshua Winkfield John from Brunswick County min- John Loyd- 23Jan1794

Ludwell B & Margaret T Osborne 16 Nov 1824; b- Abner A Lockett con- Thomas Goode, gdn (?), who gives consent min- William Richards-

Phillip & Mary White 8 Jan 1798; b- William Naish min- William Richards- 20Jan1798

Reps & Mary B Hutcheson 22 Dec 1812; b- John A Speed con- John Hutcheson, father min- James Meacham- 24Dec1812

Thomas & Jane Willis 20 Dec 1830; b- Samuel Dedman con- Anne Willis, mother min- John B. Smith- 24Dec1830

Barnett

Campbell & Mary E Scott 16 Sep 1852; con- R M Scott, father min-F.N. Whaley-

German B & Lucy Taylor 17 Oct 1822; b- Pennington Barnett con-David Taylor, father

John & Sally Merryman 7 Aug 1805; b- Richard Hailey

Pennington & Clarissa Gee 5 Jan 1820; b- William C Creath con- James
     Gee, father
Robert S & Virginia A Smith 22 Mar 1852; con- William Smith, father
     min- Adam Finch- 8Apr1852
Thomas & Hannah Rook 10 Jun 1790; b- William Walker con- Anna
     Thompson
William & Frances Y Daniel 12 Jan 1836; b- Charles H Yancey con-
     Stark Daniel, father William Barnett from Granville Co., N.C. min- John
     B. Smith-
William & Mary Thellis 9 Jan 1844; b- Thomas Lambert con- Lucy
     Thellis, mother min- James McAden-
William & Judith Thomason 10 Jan 1793; b- William Bowen min- John
     Loyd- 15Jan1793

Barron
John & Charlotte Watson 2 Dec 1809; b- James Standley

Barrow
William & Polly King 21 Sep 1817; min- Charles Ogburn- (Methodist)
William & Susannah Marshall 2 Oct 1801; b- Dennis Marshall daughter
     of Samuel min- John Phaup- 22Oct1801

Barry
James Harwell & Patsy Thompson 20 Jan 1808; b- William Crow
Joseph & Mary Massey 30 Dec 1795; b- Drury Andrews con- Thomas
     Massey and Mary Massey, parents min- Matthew Dance- 31Dec1795

Basey
Isaac & Ann Cole 27 Sep 1832; b- R Temple con- Isaac Cole, father

Baskervill
Benjamin & Ann Stewart 15 Sep 1851; min- Hartwell Arnold-
Charles & Lucy Goode 25 Jun 1823; b- Thomas Goode min- John S.
     Ravenscroft- (Episcopal)-
Edward & Susannah Holmes 4 Mar 1800; daughter of Samuel b- John
     Dortch min- Ebenezer McGowan- 5Mar1800
George H & Elizabeth Tabb 16 Dec 1791; b- Robert Baskervill George
     s of George Baskervill, Sr. min- John Loyd-
George T & Lucy H Goode 11 Dec 1849; b- William Baskervill Jr con-
     William O Goode
John & Martha Burton 30 Jul 1765; s of George Baskervill b- Samuel
     Young
William & Susanna R Jiggetts 13 Mar 1839; b- Daniel T Hicks con- D
     E Jiggetts, father min- F.H. McGuire-

Baskerville
William R & Sarah T Dortch 16 Feb 1824; b- Charles Baskerville min-
     James Smith- 19Feb1824

Bass
Elijah & Milly Walden 28 Nov 1829; b- Frederick Nowell min- William
     Steel- (Episcopal)-
Joel & Peggy McNeal 8 Dec 1828; b- Charles Mills
Peter & Rebecca Rainey 9 Aug 1823; b- William Rainey con- William
     Rainey, father min- Stephen Jones- (Lynchburg, Va.)- 14Aug1823

Batte
Edward S & Martha Maria Taylor 2 Dec 1819; b- George E Powell con-
     Thomas Taylor, father min- James Smith- 9Dec1819

Baugh
Daniel & Lucy Brooks 10 Oct 1780; b- John Eppes
James & Peggy Smith 22 Dec 1800; b- John Smith Jr. con- John Smith,
     Sr., father min- Ebenezer McGowan- 31Dec1800

James & Susanna Stone 19 Jul 1813; b- Martin Phillips con- John Hutcheson, gdn of Susanna

Richard & Elizabeth P Harwell 28 May 1800; b- Edward Patrick Davis con- James Harwell, father min- Ebenezer McGowan-

William B & Martha Minge Bilbo 15 Nov 1804; s of James Baugh, dec. b- William Baskervill con- John Aldridge and Agnes Aldridge

William B & Elizabeth B Lewis 27 Aug 1815; b- William B Simmons con- Ann Lewis, mother

Baynham

John & Rebecca Tillotson 20 Feb 1832; b- James Yancey con- William Tillotson, gdn for Rebecca, who test. she is under 21

Beasley

James & Rebecca Jones 10 Sep 1800; b- Uriah Hawkins min- Ebenezer McGowan-

John & Martha N Insco 15 Jun 1801; b- William Insco

Thomas & Sally Jackson 22 Dec 1800; b- Mark L Jackson min- Ebenezer McGowan- 26Dec1800

William & Rebecca Vaughan 19 May 1804; b- Reuben Vaughan

Beauford

Daniel & Sarah Hightower 24 Mar 1787; b- Thomas Jones

Beaver

William & Elizabeth Hutcheson 28 Dec 1789; b- James Jones

Beckwith

Josiah & Pamela Ann Barnett 18 Dec 1843; b- Joseph Connell con- P Barnett, father

Bedford

Henry M & Virginia Clark 9 Jul 1840; min- D.B. Nicholson-

James & Frances Maynard 14 Nov 1786; b- William Maynard

John & Mary Ann Marshall 10 Sep 1787; John from Charlotte County son of Thomas Bedford, Sr. and Mary Bedford min- James Watkins-

Belcher

Burwell & Amey Murray 15 Dec 1835; b- William Malone

Bell

John & Mary Butler 12 Jan 1785; b- William Lucas

Benford

Asbury & Eliza Drumwright 6 Aug 1838; b- Gee Drumwright con- William Drumwright, father min- James McAden-

Isaac & Martha A Pennington 28 May 1850; b- Robert Malone min- Richard E.G. Adams- (Lunenburg County)-

Bennett

Anthony & Susanna Davis 13 Dec 1779; b- John Brown

John & Mary A Boyd 30 Nov 1829; b- Alexander Boyd min- William Steel- (Episcopal)-

Jonathon H & Mary A M Moody 11 Sep 1832; b- Henry Moody con- Arthur Moody, father min- William Steel- (Episcopal)- 20Sep1832

Jonathon & Sarah Tanner 17 Dec 1793; b- Thomas Tanner

Jordan & Nancy Murfey 15 Dec 1795; b- Thomas Tanner min- John Loyd- 17Dec1795

Jordan & Mary Ann Tanner 14 Mar 1791; b- Anthony Bennett min- John King- 17Mar1791

Joseph (Jr) & Julia Tanner 15 Oct 1827; b- Benjamin Tanner

Joseph & Elizabeth Burrus 9 Apr 1787; b- Anthony Bennett

Joseph & Nancy Lanier 24 May 1785; b- Ingram Vaughan

Joseph & Mary Towler 6 Sep 1821; b- Edward Deloney min- J. Nolley-

P A & Mary Nelson 12 Jan 1835; b- C R Kennon con- N Nelson, father

Thomas & Betsy T Paschall 6 Jan 1817; b- Philip Rainey con- Anderson Paschall, father

William M & Louisa F Rowlett 8 Nov 1841; b- Isaiah Jackson con- Steven D Rowlett, father min- James McAden-

William & Tabitha Lanier 1 Oct 1807; b- Philip Roberts

Berry

Henry B & Jane T Langhorne 7 Feb 1840; b- Alexander Langhorne min- Edward Wadsworth-

James G & Eleanor Frances Tucker 23 Feb 1841; b- William Hendrick con- William Tucker, father

Bevill

Thomas & Nancy Keeton 24 Jan 1797; b- Hutchins Burton min- William Creath- 26Jan1797

William & Rebecca Harris 3 Mar 1829; b- William Graves min- John B. Smith- 5Mar1829

William & Nancy Prewitt 22 Dec 1800; b- Thomas Johnson

Bilbo

Allen Moss & Martha Farrar 15 Dec 1810; b- Benjamin Whitlow min- James Meacham- 20Dec1810

John & Mary Clemonds 28 Sep 1786; b- Nicholas Bilbo

John & Mary Nicholson 2 Apr 1807; b- George H Baskervill

Joseph & Jane Greer 11 Sep 1780; b- Zachariah Bevers con- Joseph Greer, father

Binford

Thomas & Susanna Finch 2 May 1795; b- William Finch min- John Loyd- 3May1795

Thomas & Elizabeth Oslin 25 Dec 1786; b- John Oslin con- Jesse Oslin, father

Thomas & Rebekah Thompson 16 Jan 1804; b- Edward Thompson

Bing

Edmund & Lucy Johnson 5 Oct 1812; b- Daniel Tucker con- Phil. Johnson, father min- James Meacham- 8Oct1812

George & Mary A Curtis 15 Sep 1827; b- David B Johnson con- Zachariah Curtis, father min- Charles Ogburn- (Methodist) 20Sep1827

James & Patsy Short 8 Jan 1789; b- Daniel Tucker min- Thomas Scott-

John & Patsy Day 9 Jan 1816; b- Edmund Bing min- Charles Ogburn- (Methodist) 11Jan1816

Spencer & Elizabeth Johnson 16 Jun 1828; b- Philip R Johnson con- Phillip Johnson, father min- Charles Ogburn- (Methodist) 19Jun1828

Bishop

Jeremiah & Elizabeth Colley 8 Feb 1802; b- Charles Colley min- William Creath-

William & Louisa Maria Talley 22 Dec 1852; con- Robert Talley, father min- P.F. August-

Black

Frederick & Elizabeth Lockett 11 Jan 1790; b- Royal Lockett min- John Williams- Frederick from Campbell County marriage celebrated 12Jan1790

Stephen & Temperance Clay 8 Jan 1793; b- Britain Clay min- John Williams- 10Jan1793 Stephen from Campbell County

Blackbourn

Clement & Mary Lewis 21 Oct 1784; b- Francis Lewis Clement son of Thomas Blackbourn

Blackbourne

Francis & Nancy O Roffe 18 Dec 1816; b- Melchior Roffe con- Hannah O Roffe, mother min- Richard Dabbs- (Lunenburg County)- 19Dec1816

Blacketter
 David & Mary F Cox 13 Dec 1796; b- Edward Cox
 William & Elizabeth Allgood 24 Dec 1793; b- Bartlett Cox

Blackwell
 Benjamin E & Elizabeth Jones 15 May 1820; b- William T Oslin con-
  Wood Jones, father min- Thomas Adams- (Lunenburg Co.)-
 Robert & Jane Northington 30 Sep 1822; b- John W L Northington con-
  Nathan Northington, father

Blair
 William G & Mary House 9 Nov 1843; b- Daniel J Morris

Blake
 Benjamin & Sally Whobry 3 Apr 1809; b- George B Hamner min- James
  Meacham- 6Apr1809

Blanch
 William & Mary C Rogers 16 Sep 1834; b- A C Dugger con- George
  Rogers, father min- William B. Rowzee-

Bland
 John & Sally Burnett 22 Apr 1794; b- Anselm Bugg con- Elizabeth
  Burnett, mother min- Charles Ogburn- (Methodist)- 26Apr1794
 Williamson & Dorcas Williams 17 Nov 1806; b- James Bugg min- James
  Meacham-

Blane
 John & Sally Tillotson 2 Dec 1829; b- Edward Tillotson min- E.
  Hollister-

Blankenship
 Alexander & Martha Apperson 15 Jan 1821; b- George Williams con-
  W S Apperson, father min- Pleasant Gold- (Baptist)- 25Jan1821
 Armistead & Martha Hailey 11 Jun 1822; b- William H Jones con- John
  Hailey, father min- Pleasant Gold- (Baptist)- 14Jun1822

Blanks
 James & Margaret Owen 21 Jun 1830; b- Evan Owen con- Thomas
  Owen, father min- Pleasant Gold- (Baptist)- 2Jul1830
 John & Mary Wilkerson 14 Aug 1821; min- Pleasant Gold- (Baptist)-
 John & Tabitha Worsham 20 Feb 1815; b- Stephen Worsham
 Joseph & Rebecca Pettypool 15 Jan 1827; b- Stephen Pettypool min-
  Pleasant Gold- (Baptist)- 18Feb1827
 Thomas & Sally Talley 2 Mar 1818; b- Stephen Pettypool
 William F & Elizabeth Jane Blanks 10 Dec 1853; con- John A Blanks,
  father min- John E. Montague- (Granville County, N.C.)- 15Dec1853
 William & Dolly Jones 13 Dec 1830; b- William Yancey con- Daniel
  Jones, father min- Pleasant Gold- (Baptist)- 22Dec1830

Blanton
 Green & Nancy D Overby 15 Feb 1810; b- Adam Overby min- James
  Meacham- 22Feb1810

Bolling
 Royal & Eliza Brandon 23 Aug 1832; b- John Stewart min- William
  Steel- (Episcopal)- 25Aug1832

Booker
 Jonathon & Lucy Simmons 10 Aug 1795; b- Thomas Jones min- William
  Creath-
 Lowry & Phebe Cox 11 Dec 1780; b- John Clay con- John Cox, Sr.
  (relation not cited)
 Reuben & Judy Bowen 19 Jun 1801; b- Daniel Tucker Jr.
 Richard T & Ronsey Ann Quincy 23 Dec 1829; b- William A Quincy
  con- Elizabeth Quincy, mother

Samuel D & Mary Jane Daniel 6 Oct 1837; b- Henry M Spencer con- James Daniel, father

William & Martha Bozwell 14 Jan 1799; b- Benjamin Bozwell min- William Creath- 17Jan1799

William & Polly Finch 10 Nov 1802; b- John Puryear Jr min- William Richards-

Booth

John & Lucretia J Davis 3 Jan 1814; b- Hugh Davis min- John Allen- 4Jan1814

John & Elizabeth Mabry 29 Dec 1810; b- Edward Giles

John & Sally Read Marshall 9 Apr 1805; b- John Johnson con- Richard Marshall, father

Reuben & Rebecca Malone 21 Sep 1812; b- Charles D Cleaton

Boswell

John & Elizabeth B Bigger 13 Feb 1840; b- J W Yates, Jr con- John Bigger, father

John & Mary Coleman 16 Feb 1784; b- James Coleman con- Cluverius Coleman, father John son of Joseph Boswell

Joseph & Susanna Pettus 9 Dec 1805; b- Samuel Pettus, Sr. s of Ransom Boswell and Martha Boswell min- Thomas Hardie- 24Dec1805

Thomas T & Martha Walker Nelson 7 Jul 1846; b- T E Burton con- William Nelson, father

William C & Mary A Burwell 31 Jul 1851; con- P R Burwell, father min- Adam Finch- 20Aug1851

William C & Ann Eliza Taylor 16 Nov 1822; b- Richard E Walker con- Thomas Taylor, father min- James Smith- 24Dec1822

Bottom

Anderson & Sally Hatchell 30 May 1809; b- William H Bugg min- James Meacham- 31May1809

Bolling & Martha Harper 14 Mar 1796; b- Wyatt Harper Bolling from Brunswick County min- John Neblett- 16Mar1796

Wilson & Elizabeth Richardson 20 Dec 1806; b- Nathaniel Moss min- James Meacham-

Bouldin

James B & Martha Goode 5 Feb 1825; b- William Townes min- William Steel- (Episcopal)- 17Feb1825

Bowen

Allen & Elizabeth Tillotson 23 Jul 1829; b- James Tillotson con- Thomas Tillotson, father

Asa & Charlotte Bowen 6 Dec 1796; b- Charles Bowen Asa son of Charles Bowen and Amey Bowen min- John Loyd- 13Dec1796

Benjamin & Martha Sparks 12 Sep 1803; b- Zachariah Yancey

Briant & Tabitha Bing 27 Jul 1839; b- Zachariah Curtis con- John Bing, father min- Benjamin R. Duval-

Charnel & Omea Bowen 15 Oct 1805; b- Berry Bowen

David & Nancy A Bowen 24 Dec 1838; b- Grandison Glasscock

Edwin H & Martha L Meldrum 27 Sep 1827; b- Robert Moore

Elisha & Magdalene Salley 24 Aug 1803; b- John Turner Jr min- William Creath-

Henry & Sally Murray 14 Jan 1818; b- Charles Carter con- Catharine Murray, mother

Hugh & Jincy Finn 30 Nov 1801; b- Littleberry Bowen

James E & Martha Overbey 21 Jun 1847; b- S P[etty]pool con- James Overbey, father

James & Nancy Newton 29 Nov 1831; b- David Vaughan con- Mary Newton, mother min- Pleasant Gold- (Baptist)-

John & Nancy Murray 8 Jan 1816; b- Christopher Singleton
Jordan & Nancy Pearcy 25 Mar 1804; b- John Hudgins
Lowry & Lucy Barnett 19 Nov 1818; b- Salathiel Bowen con- William Barnett, father
Ranson & Elizabeth Owen 16 Sep 1822; b- Joseph Owen min- Pleasant Gold- (Baptist)- 17Sep1822
Richard Jones & Betsy S Kirks 22 Nov 1808; b- James Bowen
Salathiel & Lively Bowen 18 May 1811; b- Littleberry B Kirks
Wesley W & Elizabeth Kirks 22 Dec 1835; b- Anderson Overby
William & Catharine G Bowen 17 Dec 1849; b- John W Nicholson
William & Mary Glasscock 7 Dec 1846; b- William Yancey con- Thomas Glasscock, father
William & Martha Overby 22 Dec 1817; b- Zachariah Glasscock
Zachariah & Mavel Drummond 2 Oct 1795; b- Thomas Drummond Zachariah son of James Bowen and Susannah Bowen min- Charles Ogburn- (Methodist) 8Oct1795

Bowers
Sandefer & Elizabeth Vaughan 14 Dec 1790; b- Richard Edmondson
William & Elizabeth Ann Lett 17 Jul 1826; b- Waddy J Jackson con- Joseph Lett, father min- John B. Smith- 19Jul1826

Bowler
William O & Delilah Walker 19 Sep 1836; b- Ben F Williamson

Bowman
Archer & Priscilla Stewart 8 Feb 1819; b- Charles Stewart min- Alexander M. Cowan-

Boyd
Alexander S & Sarah D Young 25 Jan 1847; b- Philip Rainey, Sr. con- Dianita M Young, mother min- William A. Smith- 26Jan1847
Alexander & Matilda Burwell 10 Oct 1803; b- John Dortch Matilda daughter of Lewis Burwell, dec. con- Armistead Burwell, guardian for sister min- John Cameron-
Alfred & Elizabeth Townes 24 Aug 1836; b- William Townes min- William Steel- (Episcopal)-
Armistead G & Ann V Hendrick 25 Apr 1848; b- N M Thornton con- William Hendrick, father
Francis W & Isabella H Townes 2 Nov 1837; b- William Townes
Richard (Jr) & Lucy Ann Goode 5 Dec 1821; b- Beverly Sydnor con- John C Goode, guardian of Lucy min- Alexander M. Cowan-
Richard & Panthea Burwell 19 Nov 1799; b- John Wright con- Lewis Burwell, father min- John Cameron-
Robert & Parthena Hendrick 2 Jan 1826; b- Thomas Hendrick, father con- Thomas Torian, guardian for Robert min- Pleasant Gold- (Baptist)- 5Jan1826
Robert & Sarah Anderson Jones 20 Apr 1789; b- Major Butler con- Alexander Boyd, father con- Tignal Jones, father min- Thomas Scott-
Robert & Tabitha Walker 11 May 1803; d of Henry Walker and Martha Bolling Walker b- John Dortch min- John Cameron-
William (Jr) & Lucy G E Carter 13 Sep 1817; b- Alexander Boyd con- John Nelson, guardian of Lucy min- John S. Ravenscroft- (Episcopal)- 9Oct1817
William H & Susan S Davis 1 Feb 1848; b- A G Boyd con- John Davis Sr, father min- William A. Smith- 16Feb1848

Boyland
Alexander M & Priscilla P Hall 15 Oct 1828; b- James B Jones min- Allen D. Metcalf-

Boynton

Elijah & Elizabeth Neal 31 Dec 1808; b- James Mealer

Bracey

Hugh D & Frances O'Brian 27 Nov 1851; con- Mrs. P. Bracey, mother, who test. Hugh under 21 and gives consent min- P.F. August-

Paschall & Mary Nancy Poynor 13 Aug 1827; b- William B Cleaton con- Diggs Poynor, guardian of Mary, daughter of John Poynor, dec.

Paschall & Angelina E Simmons 4 Oct 1835; d of William B Simmons, dec. b- James Holmes con- Robert Moore, guardian of Angelina min- James McAden-

Bradley

Henry & Jane Bennett 28 Dec 1834; b- Martin Lambert

John & Mary Riggans 27 Sep 1814; b- William L Taylor

John & Mary Taylor 16 Nov 1772; b- Lewis Speed

Joseph & Rebecca Patillo 17 Feb 1794; b- Solomon Patillo min- John Loyd- 27Feb1794

Bradshaw

William & Ann Mills 21 Aug 1826; b- Thomas Hailey con- Mrs. Unity Bradshaw, mother of William who is under 21 min- Pleasant Gold- (Baptist)- 24Aug1826

Bragg

David & Susanna Goodwin 9 Jan 1797; b- Bennett Goodwin min- John Loyd- 22Jan1797

Joel P & Mary A Crenshaw 19 Jun 1841; b- James C Bridgeforth con- Elizabeth Crenshaw, mother

Robert W & Emily F Taylor 21 May 1839; b- Thomas R Moss con- Martha Taylor, mother min- James McAden-

William L & Frances M D Crenshaw 24 Oct 1831; b- John Crenshaw con- Elizabeth Crenshaw, mother min- David Wood- 10Dec1831

Brame

David W & Lucy Ann Puryear 18 Feb 1850; b- Giles R Puryear

David & Barbara Hester 28 Nov 1807; b- James Hester min- William Richards- 3Dec1807

Dickey & Anna Hutcheson 29 Jan 1795; b- Archibald Phillips con- Richard Hutcheson, Sr., father min- Charles Ogburn- (Methodist)- 5Feb1795

Francis & Eliza Brame 19 Dec 1831; b- W. Brame

George W & Dianna Clark 9 Apr 1804; b- Lewis Roffe min- James Meacham- 17Apr1804

Henry & Sarah H Wootton 18 Nov 1816; b- Samuel Wootton min- William Richards- 20Nov1816

James C & Elizabeth B Daly 9 Sep 1806; b- William Daly min- James Meacham- 11Sep1806

James D & Susanna Brame 23 Oct 1810; b- Warner L Brame min- James Meacham- 1Nov1810

James & Martha W Baptist 18 Jan 1847; b- David G Smith con- Richard H Baptist, father

James & Mary Ann Turner 16 Feb 1835; b- William S Pully con- Judith J Turner, mother min- M.P. Parks- 18Feb1835

John D & Eliza D Smith 1 Dec 1831; b- John Smith con- Nancy Smith, mother min- John B. Smith-

John & Lilly Hester 9 Dec 1805; b- William W V Clausel min- William Richards- 19Dec1805

John & Mary Norman 18 Mar 1768; b- John Norment

John & Elizabeth Smith 17 Apr 1829; min- Allen D. Metcalf-

Joseph & Jane Hester 10 Mar 1806; b- William V Clausel min- William Richards- 20Mar1806

Joseph & Hannah Puryear 6 Jun 1815; b- John Brame

Melchizedeck & Sarah Bailey 1 Feb 1797; b- William Rowlett min- Samuel D. Brame- 2Feb1797

Melchizedeck & Susan Clausel 21 Mar 1822; min- John S. Ravenscroft- (Episcopal)-

Samuel & Elizabeth Roffe 21 Sep 1802; b- Ingram Roffe con- James Brame, father

Thomas (Jr) & Barbara Brame 5 Apr 1824; b- Joseph Brame

Thomas R & Louisa T Puryear 14 Dec 1843; b- James H Gregory con- Thomas B Puryear, father

Thomas & Martha Johnson 29 May 1814; b- Richins Brame con- Caleb Johnson, father

Walter & Lucy S. Hutcheson 13 Dec 1823; b- Melchizedec Brame con- John Hutcheson, father min- John Thompson- 18Dec1823

William (Jr) & Elizabeth Wright 11 Apr 1834; b- John Brame Jr

William & Hannah H Clausel 12 Dec 1808; b- Alexander B Puryear min- William Richards- 22Dec1808

Branch

James & Catharine D Carter 13 Jun 1835; b- Robert Carter

Julius C & Martha M Hinton 11 Apr 1834; 'Dr' Julius C Branch b- Presly Hinton con- John Hinton of Petersburg, gdn for Martha min- William Steel- (Episcopal)- 23Apr1834

Brandon

Archer & Martha Jane Thomas 11 Feb 1839; b- James M Chavous con- Robert Thomas, father

Edward & Elizabeth Chavous 10 Mar 1806; b- Frederick Irby

Peter & Agatha Cole 27 Dec 1825; b- Beverly Averett min- William Richards- 28Dec1825

Bressie

Francis & Sarah Royster 13 Apr 1778; b- Joseph Royster d of Joseph Royster s of Francis Bressie and Elizabeth Bressie

Brewer

Ambrose & Ann J Atkinson 20 Aug 1840; b- Solomon Atkinson min- Charles F. Burnley-

John Wyatt & Ruth H Atkinson 25 Dec 1838; b- Solomon Atkinson con- J Edward Brewer, father of John con- Solomon Atkinson, father min- John B. Smith-

Bridgewater

William & Barbara Hester 13 Jul 1792; b- William Hundley d of Abraham Hester, dec. min- James Read- (Baptist)

Briggs

James & Polly Arnold 10 Feb 1794; b- John Arnold d of James Arnold and Mary Arnold min- Charles Ogburn- (Methodist)- 27Feb1794

James & Rebecca Johnson 16 Nov 1818; b- Charles Ogburn min- Charles Ogburn- (Methodist) 19Dec1818

Brightwell

Jason & Jane Poindexter 21 Apr 1817; b- George C Poindexter

Brodie

Edmond G & Ann N Haskins 4 Dec 1802; 'Dr.' Edmond G Brodie b- John S Jeffries con- Christopher Haskins, father

Brogdon

William & Caty Carter 31 Aug 1786; b- Benjamin Ferrell

Brooking

Robert Edward & Lucy Delony 9 May 1779; b- Henry Delony Jr. con- Henry Delony, Sr., father con- Vivian Brooking, father Robert from Amelia County

Brooks

John W & Mary A Crowder 20 Feb 1832; b- William Brummell min- John B. Smith-

Robert Rose & Mary Parham 20 Nov 1780; b- Daniel Baugh con- Robert Brooks, father (Robert Rose under 21)

Wade & Tabitha Jones 7 Jan 1796; b- John Webb min- John Loyd- 9Jan1796

Willis & Martha Allgood 13 Jul 1831; b- Edward Allgood con- Dicey Allgood, mother min- William Steel- (Episcopal)- 14Jul1831

Browder

Isham & Talitha Cox 3 Feb 1767; b- John Cox Isham from Halifax County con- Mary Cox, mother & guardian of Talitha con- John Cox, bro of Talitha

Jesse & Susan Owen 31 Dec 1830; b- Joseph Owen min- Pleasant Gold- (Baptist)- 4Jan1831

Jonathon & Nancy Ligon 25 Mar 1825; b- Jesse Browder con- Frances Ligon, mother minister's name missing- ceremony dated 29Mar1825

Thomas & Elizabeth Bing 26 Mar 1852; con- John Bing, father min- James McAden- 26Mar1852

Thomas & Betsy Bland 21 Jul 1796; b- Jesse Bugg min- William Creath- 22Jul1796

Brown

Henry & Elvira F Walker 29 Sep 1853; con- David A Walker, father min- James McAden- 29Sep1853

James P & Mary Burnett 21 Nov 1814; b- Richard Burnett min- Milton Robertson- (Warren County, N.C.) 24Nov1814

James & Sarah Hutson 29 Dec 1789; b- James Cox min- Thomas Scott-

Jeremiah & Elizabeth Douglas 28 Aug 1770; b- William Douglas

Jesse & Ann N Hutcheson 17 Sep 1838; b- Charles S Hutcheson con- Elizabeth G Hutcheson, mother

Jesse & Ann Bolling Murray 16 Sep 1786; b- Samuel Goode con- Susanna Murray, mother Ann daughter of John Murray

Jesse & Patsy Vaughan 28 May 1798; b- Thomas Vaughan

John Jordan & Susan Ann Hundley 11 Dec 1834; b- William H Hundley

Richard & Martha Hutcheson 19 Sep 1814; b- John Hutcheson min- Charles Ogburn- (Methodist) 22Sep1814

Warner & Martha Spain 30 Mar 1846; b- Robert W Spain con- Royal Spain, father min- John B. Smith- 1Mar1846

William & Sally Hutcheson 14 Dec 1789; b- Richard Hutcheson min- Thomas Scott-

Wilson & Rebecca N Hutcheson 7 Oct 1833; b- T E Brown con- Joseph Hutcheson min- Joshua Leigh- 15Oct1833

Wilson & Manerva J Manning 13 Sep 1830; b- James M Manning min- James Smith- 15Sep1830

Brummell

Pleasant & Eliza Harris 18 Dec 1816; b- Alex Gillespie

Robert & Mary Ann Burnett 4 Nov 1811; b- Jonathon Bennett

William & Elizabeth H Moody 18 Nov 1824; b- William Moody min- William Richards-

Brydie

Charles & Susan E Boswell 19 Mar 1844; b- Christopher Wood con- Joseph Boswell Sr, father min- William V. Wilson-

Buckner

James & Martha Taylor 1 May 1817; b- William Drumwright con- Goodwin Taylor, father

Buford

John & Sophia M Knox 17 Nov 1817; b- John W Lewis con- Ann M Knox, mother min- John S. Ravenscroft- (Episcopal)-

Bugg

Benjamin & Mary Allen 12 Mar 1834; b- Henry Moody con- Lucy S Allen, mother

Benjamin & Anne Andrews 3 Sep 1785; b- Ephraim Andrews, Jr. con- Ephraim Andrews, Sr., father

Edmond & Sarah Jeffries 10 Dec 1792; b- Swepson Jeffries min- John Loyd- 13Dec1792

Jacob L & Georgetta Virginia Nolley - --- 18--; b- George W Nolley, father min- William A. Smith-

Jacob & Sarah Davis 27 Jul 1791; b- Sherwood Bugg con- John Davis, father

Jacob & Rebecca Farrar 12 Mar 1811; b- James Noel con- Samuel Farrar, father min- James Meacham- 14Mar1811

Jacob & Mary Thweate Tucker 11 Sep 1798; b- Benjamin Tucker, Jr.

James S & Mary Ann Hudgins 27 Dec 1847; b- William O Manning con- Emanuel H Hudgins, father con- Richard D Bugg, gdn for James min- Thomas Adams- (Lunenburg Co.)- 29Dec1847

Jesse & Martha Andrews 27 Jan 1811; b- Varney Andrews

Jesse & Jane Cole 10 Jan 1822; b- Bartlett Cole min- James Smith- 21Jan1822

John C & Elizabeth Nolley 17 Jul 1837; b- Richard B Baptist

John J & Ann C Warren 2 Jul 1819; b- George B Hamner con- Samuel Holmes, grandfather and gdn of Ann min- James Smith- 14Jul1819

John & Rebeccah Mitchell 17 Dec 1788; b- James Sandifer, Jr.

Richard D & Amanda Sarah Watson 5 Nov 1845; b- John T Crute con- Littleberry Watson, father

Robert H & Virginia Andrews 11 Dec 1851; min- William V. Wilson-

Samuel (Jr) & Elizabeth Bilbo 25 Mar 1794; b- Bennett Sandifer

Samuel & Jane Holloway 15 Dec 1835; b- J G Bugg con- Mary Holloway, mother

Sherwood & Sarah Speed 31 Dec 1787; b- Joseph Speed min- Thomas Scott-

William H & Martha Talley 24 Mar 1822; b- James Crook min- Alexander M. Cowan-

William & Lucy Hix 7 Nov 1773; b- Amos Hix

Zachariah & Mary J Goode - --- 1832; min- James McAden-

Bullington

John & Bicy Reader 20 Mar 1797; 'Dicy?' b- John Cox con- Grace Reader, mother min- William Richards- 23Mar1797

Bullock

Richard & Unity A Wright 13 Jun 1843; b- Arthur H Davis con- John M Wright, gdn of Unity min- Joseph Goodman-

William H & Panthea C Birchett 16 Dec 1822; b- John Bullock con- William B Birchett, father min- John S. Ravenscroft- (Episcopal)- 19Dec1822

William & Elizabeth Lewis 20 Aug 1766; b- Edmund Taylor Elizabeth widow of James Lewis, nee Elizabeth Taylor, sis of Edmund Taylor

Burger

Henry B & Nancy Holloway 7 Aug 1820; b- Austin Wright Sr

Burnett

Edmund & Rebecca Crowder 31 Oct 1797; b- Isaac Arnold con- John Crowder, father min- Charles Ogburn- (Methodist)- 20Nov1797

Henry & Milly Crowder 21 Oct 1789; b- John Crowder

Phillip & Martha W Andrews 10 Jul 1799; b- Isaac Arnold con- George Andrews, father min- Charles Ogburn- (Methodist)

Phillip & Martha W Andrews 10 Jul 1799; b- Isaac Arnold con- George Andrews, father

Robert & Nancy Whoberry 23 Oct 1798; b- William Whoberry con- Jacob Whoberry, father

Thomas (Jr) & Lillia Crowder 15 Apr 1811; b- Joseph Lett min- William Richards- 16Apr1811

Thomas & Elizabeth Jeffries 4 Aug 1785; b- George H Baskervill con- Swepson Jeffries, father

William & Martha Jeffries 1 Oct 1794; b- Swepson Jeffries, Jr con- Swepson Jeffries, Sr., father min- Charles Ogburn- (Methodist)- 2Oct1794

William & Nancy Williams 13 Feb 1799; b- Lewis Williams min- Ebenezer McGowan- 14Feb1799

Willis & Mildred Smith 15 Apr 1821; b- John Smith min- Charles Ogburn- (Methodist)

Burney

James & Henrietta M Russell 2 Sep 1835; con- William Hendrick, gdn of Henrietta con- John Burney of New Bern, NC

Burns

Richard & Mary Robertson 12 Dec 1825; b- Robert Burns con- John Robertson, father min- George Petty- 13Dec1825

Burt

William & Susanna Sims 3 Nov 1812; b- Henry Sims con- Joseph Sims, gdn for his sister

Burton

Allen & Rebeccah Hamblen 22 Mar 1786; b- Isaac Pully s of Robert Burton

Benjamin & Monica Humphries 19 Jun 1775; b- John Humphries

Charles & Elizabeth Johnston 9 Sep 1793; b- Thomas Wilson

Edmund & Catharine Griffin 13 Feb 1813; d of John b- Jonas Burton

Hillary G & Mary Puryear 26 Nov 1836; b- Alexander Gillespie con- John Puryear, father

Ithy G & Nancy W Evans 11 Apr 1832; b- Ishmael Thomason

James & Cuzzy Lambert 8 Dec 1792; b- Mark Lambert Jackson min- John Loyd- 13Dec1792

John & Clary Vaughan 20 Feb 1787; b- Ambrose Vaughan of Brunswick County

Jones & Mildred Lambert 15 Dec 1818; b- Zachariah Garrett

Micajah & Susanna Puryear 3 Jul 1791; b- Robert Burton min- James Read- (Baptist)- 18Jul1791

Owen & Mary Hester 8 Jan 1798; b- Robert Marshall min- William Richards- 10Jan1798

Robert & Jane Burton 17 Aug 1846; b- William P Drumwright con- Temperance Burton, mother of Jane, who test husband deceased min- James J. Sledge-

Robert & Margaret A Jeffress 18 Oct 1847; b- James H Jeffress min- S.G. Mason- 19Oct1847

Thomas Hailey & Martha Humphries 30 Sep 1783; b- John Humphries

William & Molly Brooks 22 Jan 1774; b- William Brooks

Burwell

Armistead & Lucy Crawley 14 Nov 1791; b- Robert Crawley

George W & Elizabeth F Gayle 30 Aug 1849; b- William A Burwell con- Thomas Gayle, father

Pleasant & Elizabeth Harris 21 Dec 1815; min- Richard Richards

Butler

George W & Mary F Talley 28 Jul 1847; b- Deverly Williamson con- Peyton R Talley, father

George & Mary Ann Daniel 15 May 1841; b- William Cutts con- Martin Daniel, father

James & Ann Eliza Moore 26 Oct 1850; con- Marshall A Moore, father min- Robert Burton- 30Oct1850

John W & Evelina Hutcherson 10 Dec 1838; b- Alexander H Hutcherson con- Joseph Hutcherson, father min- Benjamin R. Duval-

Joseph W & Martha D Walker 20 Dec 1847; b- Robert W Land

Joseph & Frances Oliver 9 Jun 1783; b- John Oliver

Major & Elizabeth Oliver 29 Dec 1790; b- John Farrar min- Edward Almand- 30Dec1790

Theophilus W & Elizabeth Toone 16 Mar 1835; b- Asa Garner

Butterworth

Telemachus & Elizabeth Agnes McAden 20 Sep 1842; b- William Turner con- James McAden, father

Byasee

William & Martha E Harris 26 Jan 1836; b- Thomas D Crutchfield con- John Harris, father min- James McAden-

Byers

Anderson & Sally Dortch 14 Dec 1813; b- John D Hank

Cabiness

Asa B & Rebecca S Bowen 17 Nov 1823; b- Sanford Bowen min- James Smith- 26Nov1823

Charles & Lucy Worsham Ingram 5 Jan 1795; b- William Burton con- Pines Ingram, father min- Charles Ogburn- (Methodist)- 8Jan1795

George & Jinny Elliott 30 Nov 1799; b- Thomas Finch con- Martin Elliott, father min- William Richards- 2Dec1799

Callis

Daniel G & Charlotte Elam 22 Sep 1813; b- Joel Elam con- Jane Elam, mother con- William Callis, father min- William Richards- 30Sep1813

Elijah & Nancy Winn 6 Jan 1820; b- Nathaniel Fowlker con- Sally Winn, mother min- William Richards-

Henry & Sally Graves 18 Nov 1816; b- William Graves min- William Richards- 19Nov1816

Henry & Sally Green 21 Dec 1821; b- Daniel Graves min- William Richards-

James R & Ann E Singleton 8 Jan 1853; con- Mary W Singleton, mother min- James McAden-

James & Prudence McCutcheon 13 Mar 1833; b- Richard Hastin con- Charles McCutcheon, father min- John B Smith

Thomas H & Mariah F Walker 28 Aug 1841; b- Richard W Turner con- Edward Walker

William & Frances Gregory 13 Dec 1790; b- Andrew Gregory min- John Williams- 22Dec1790

Calloway

Achilles & Elizabeth Hudson 9 Feb 1795; b- Richard Hudson Achilles from Pittsylvania County min- William Creath-

Calltharp

John & Mary Crowder 10 Feb 1784; b- Samuel Edmundson

Camp

George & Mary G Norment 1 Feb 1811; b- James Norment min- William Richards- 7Feb1811

George & Mary Palmer 30 Jul 1772; n- Nicholas Maynard

John & Mary Smith 12 May 1783; widow of Drury Smith b- George Tarry

Joshua & Nancy Gregory 10 Jan 1814; b- George Camp con- John Gregory, father min- William Richards- 16Jan1814

Campbell

Collin & Fanny Epperson 30 Nov 1785; b- John Campbell

Cannon

Archibald & Rebecca J Kidd 23 Dec 1844; b- Roderick Temple min- James McAden-

Thomas & Jane Wade 29 Oct 1847; b- Martin F Lambert

Cardin

Reuben & Stacy Bowen 8 Jan 1793; b- Zachariah Bowen con- John Cardin, father con- James Bowen, father min- William Creath- 10Jan1793

Robert & Lockey Hunt 4 Jan 1787; b- Joel Moore con- John Cardin, father con- William Hunt, father

Cardwell

James H & Patience Lockett 20 Dec 1819; b- Royal Lockett, who also gives consent to his daughter min- William Richards- 25Nov1819

John & Lucy Henry 15 Jan 1844; b- Henry Wood

William S & Maria Foster 17 Dec 1831; b- Creed Haskins min- John B Smith

Carleton

Gabriel & Elizabeth Edwards 14 Jan 1788; b- John Edwards Gabriel son of Thomas Carleton min- Thomas Scott-

Carpenter

Samuel & Nancy Stone 7 Nov 1816; b- John Stone con- Elijah Stone, father min- James Meacham-

William W & Rebecca P Bland 21 Jan 1817; b- Samuel Bland con- Samuel Carpenter min- James Meacham- 22Jan1817

Carrier

John & Elizabeth Parsons 13 Jun 1785; b- Francis Barnes con- Thomas Parsons, father

Carroll

Isaac & Polly Douglas 18 Sep 1811; d of Senior Douglas b- William Burton

Isaac & Amey Mackecy 18 Dec 1821; b- James Mackecy con- Elizabeth Mackecy, mother, who test that Amey is under 21

James & Sally Greffies 12 Dec 1786; b- Mark Lambert Jackson

James & Delila Lambert 16 Apr 1823; min- Thomas Jones (married in Warren Co., NC

John S & Lilly Ann Skipwith Parrish 8 Oct 1818; b- William Parrish min- William Robertson-

John & Amey Crowder 28 Nov 1793; b- Daniel Tucker

John & Anne Crowder 23 Dec 1793; b- Richard Fox min- John Loyd- 24Dec1793

John & Caty Humphries 22 Apr 1797; b- William Carroll min- Charles Ogburn- (Methodist)

Thomas & Mary A V Daly 5 Feb 1850; b- John W Baskerville Thomas Carroll from Warren Co., NC min- William A Smith- 14Feb1850

William & Mary Crowder 3 Jan 1788; b- Bailey Turner

Carter

Charles T & Judith Gregory 19 Jul 1813; b- Barnet Gregory con- Charles T Carter, gdn

David N & Kerenhappuck Brame 1 Jan 1824; b- Melchizedec Brame min- William Richards- 13Jan1824

Granderson L & Sally N Gordon 14 Jul 1824; b- William Stone min- James Smith- 20Jul1824

James & Polly Matthews 30 Mar 1825; b- William H Wilson con- Elizabeth Matthews, mother min- James McAden-

John T & Sarah A Crews 1 Jan 1844; b- William G Kimbrough

John T & Jane Gregory 19 Jun 1820; b- Charles T Carter min- Pleasant Gold- (Baptist)- 22Jun1820

John & Polly Stevens 12 Dec 1788; b- Thomas Stevens

Littleberry & Nancy Moore 7 Mar 1815; b- A G Keen con- George Moore, father min- Reuben Pickett- 10Apr1815

Littleberry & Juliet Ann Puryear 21 Dec 1835; b- William N Puryear

Richard & Mary Haile 14 Jan 1793; b- Ellyson Crew

Robert A & Fathia J McDaniel 9 Jun 1852; con- Daniel W McDaniel, father min- Robert Burton- 16Jun1852

William Henry & Martha Murray 18 Sep 1843; b- Robert Carter con- bride herself, who test she is 21

William J & Maria A Atkinson 24 Dec 1850; con- Solomon Atkinson, father min- William A. Smith- 24Dec1850

William M & Elizabeth Jones 12 Dec 1832; b- Thomas Jones con- Samuel Jones, father min- John B Smith-

Cary

William & Prudence Winn 21 Jan 1822; b- Joseph B Clausel min- William Richards- 31Jan1822

Cater

William J & Elizabeth H Green 16 Aug 1851; min- Hartwell Arnold- 16Aug1851

Caveniss

Edward & Mary A Johnson 31 May 1838; b- James Yancey

Caviness

William & Elizabeth Culbreath 8 Feb 1796; 'Cabiness?' b- Henry Hester

Cazy

William & Polly Evans 23 Dec 1786; b- Kinchen Chavous

Certain

Asa & Susanna Holmes 5 Jan 1814; d of William Holmes b- Richard Crowder, Jr min- Milton Robertson- (Warren County, N.C.) 5Jan1814

Chambers

James & Elizabeth Holloway 14 Dec 1814; b- David Holloway

John & Eliza Lightfoot 21 Jan 1834; b- George C Daniel min- John B Smith-

Nathaniel & Mary Small 6 Sep 1790; b- James Chambers

Chambliss

James & Mary Stigall 10 Nov 1785; b- Mial Wall

John & Martha Caroline Morris 20 Aug 1835; b- Daniel Morris

John & Susan Vaughan 24 Dec 1835; b- Turner Saunders con- William Vaughan, father

Robert B & Nannie P Northington 31 Dec 1825; b- Samuel Northington con- John Northington, father min- Edward L Tabb-

William & Polly Saunders 15 Oct 1819; b- John Chambliss con- John Saunders, Sr, father

Chandler

Chappell & Mary Carter 16 Dec 1817; b- Benjamin Carter, father

Daniel & Julia Harria 10 Mar 1818; b- Thomas B Puryear con- Susan Harriss, mother min- William Richards- 26Mar1818

David & Susanna Hamblin 19 Nov 1821; b- Stark Daniel

Joel & Silvany Glasscock 13 Nov 1845; b- Andrew J Chandler con- Zachariah Glasscock, father min- Alfred Apple-

Joel & Agness Light 12 Apr 1772; b- Nathaniel Hix

Joel & Lucy Moore 29 Mar 1852; min- S.A. Creath- 4Apr1852

John & Adelia Irby 27 Oct 1824; b- John W Irby con- Peter Irby min- Pleasant Gold- (Baptist)-

Robert & Lucretia Graves 28 Feb 1797; b- John P Finch con- Elijah Graves and Lucretia Graves, parents min- William Creath-

Samuel & Lina Stewart 23 Dec 1793; b- William Chandler min- William Creath- 28Dec1793

William & Elizabeth Hendrick 26 Jan 1827; b- Thomas Hendrick min- Pleasant Gold- (Baptist)- 11Feb1827

Chappell

Robert B & Julia W Harrison 19 Dec 1842; b- George Jefferson

Charlton

Blunt & Mary Morris 13 Mar 1850; b- George Guy

Chatman

William & Mary Ann Ligon 9 Apr 1832; b- Obadiah Ligon con- Francis Ligon, father

Chavous

Allen & Sally Clanch 7 Sep 1804; 'Claunch?' b- Drury Johnsob

Anthony & Rebecca Stewart 10 Sep 1792; b- Henry Royster min- James Read- (Baptist)

Banister & Milly Walden 29 Dec 1819; b- John Stewart min- Alexander M. Cowan-

Bolling & Sukey Thomason 25 Jan 1798; b- Banister Thomason con- Amy Thomason, mother of Susanna min- Charles Ogburn- (Methodist) 7Feb1798

Earby & Fanny McLin 9 Mar 1797; b- Thomas McLin min- John Loyd- 10Mar1797

Edward & Biddy Jones 20 Dec 1817; b- Robert L Jones

Gilliam P & Mary Evans 21 Jul 1829; b- Admiral Dunston min- Charles Ogburn- (Methodist)

Jacob S & Martha J Chavous 5 Nov 1831; b- Randolph Chavous min- Charles Ogburn- (Methodist) 10Nov1831

Jacob & Pheby Scott 8 Dec 1800; b- Thomas A Jones con- James Mayne min- Edward Almand- 24Dec1800

James & Luvinia Nash 24 Feb 1829; b- Edward Brandon min- William Steel- (Episcopal)-

James & Nancy Stewart 15 Dec 1835; b- Edward Brandon min- William Steel- (Episcopal)-

John J & Frances Stewart 17 Dec 1832; b- Randolph Chavous

John & Sally Blair 27 Jul 1801; b- Thomas Cypress

Kinchen & Milly Chavous 22 Dec 1788; b- William Thomerson

Pleasant & Dicey Singleton 28 Dec 1821; b- Henry Stewart min- Alexander M. Cowan-

William & Precilla Drew 29 Dec 1806; b- Benjamin Lewis min- William Richards- 30Dec1806

William & Elizabeth Ivy 6 Mar 1819; b- Edward Brandon min- Alexander M. Cowan-

Cheatham

Bartlett & Jane Walker 4 Feb 1812; b- William Davis Sr Jane daughter of Daniel Walker

Daniel & Rebecca Cooper 21 Jun 1790; b- William Drumwright con- Elisha Arnold, guardian of Rebecca Rebecca daughter of Francis Cooper, dec.

James & Caty Johnson 11 Jan 1794; b- Wyatt Harper min- John Neblett- 15Jan1794

James & Ann Wilson 9 Feb 1784; b- John Wilson

John & Nancy Vaughan 23 Feb 1808; b- Ambrose Vaughan

Madison & Martha F Gregory - Nov 1836; b- Peter Averett con- Thomas S Gregory, father min- John B Smith-

Obadiah & Lucy Jones 21 Dec 1787; b- William Drumwright con- Balaam Jones, father

Samuel & Nancy Davis 22 Dec 1803; b- William Davis

Samuel & Elizabeth Keeton 12 May 1800; b- Warner Keeton min- Matthew Dance- 15May1800

Childress

Augustus W & Ann Eliza Lydick 21 Dec 1841; b- Stith G Yancey

William F & Rebecca P Totty 22 Jul 1842; b- Hugh M T Rogers con- Thomas E Totty, father min- Charles F. Burnley-

William R & Mary Childress 17 Mar 1828; b- William Childress min- John B Smith-

Childrey

Jesse & Lucy Jackson 18 May 1814; b- William Childrey

Christian

Jesse & Rebecca Johnson - Feb 1841; b- Samuel Vaughan

John & Martha C Morris 22 Jan 1838; b- John J Morris con- Daniel Morris min- James McAden-

Christmas

Obadiah & Mary Ann Wilkins 19 Jul 1853; con- James Wilkins, father min- John E. Montague- 19Jul1853

Christopher

Jacobus P & Rebecca Blanks 4 Sep 1815; b- John Blanks con- Ann Blanks, mother min- Reuben Pickett- 14Sep1815

Jacobus & Lurita Dennis - --- 178-; b- Moses Overton

Church

Robert & Elizabeth Jones 9 Dec 1799; b- Richard Jones

Cirkes

Jesse & Ellender Ornsby 11 May 1786; b- William Singleton

Clack

Frederick W & Martha Lewis 12 Jan 1818; b- William Townes con- John Lewis Sr, father

John S & Ann E Walker 13 Sep 1790; b- Henry Walker d of Henry and Martha Bolling Walker

Claiborne

George W & Rebecca King 23 Dec 1833; b- Baxter Smith

Leonard & Mary M Stokes 13 May 1799; b- John Powell

Clardy

James & Luritta Daniel 18 Jun 1810; b- William Daniel

Clark

Archibald & Sarah Northington 24 Jun 1807; b- Scarborough Penticost con- Nathan Northington, father

Edward & Mary Greenwood 1 Jan 1812; b- Hepburn Wiles

Edward & Polly Yancey 15 Jun 1816; b- John Culbreath

Elisha & Nancy Waller 2 Jan 1810; b- John Waller

Henry & Elizabeth Wilson 6 Jan 1801; b- Henry Wilson

James & Martha Jones 23 Oct 1799; b- James Jones min- William Creath-

James & Lucy Yancey 11 Oct 1838; b- Charles H Yancey con- John Yancey, father

John & Harriet Ann Averett 9 Oct 1851; con- Bowen Averett, father min- John E Montague

John & Elizabeth Hill 21 Aug 1815; b- Daniel Elam

John & Ann A Johnson 20 Dec 1813; b- Thomas Atkins con- Caleb Johnson, father

Joseph & Sally Mullins 9 Feb 1795; b- James Hudson min- William Richards- 24Feb1795

Richard & Caty Wall 20 Jan 1800; b- Richard Overby

William & Jinny Insco 3 Sep 1785; b- James Insco con- John Clark, father

William & Nancy Yancey 15 Jan 1827; b- John Yancey min- Pleasant Gold- (Baptist)- 23Jan1827

Clarke

Carter & Martha Farrar 9 Nov 1778; b- Edward Finch con- John Farrar who test that bride over 21

Joseph & Sarah Toone 14 Dec 1795; b- Bolling Clarke

Claunch

Dennis & Nancy Beasley 8 Nov 1803; b- William Justice

Jeremiah & Prudence Jackson 21 Mar 1799; b- Samuel Allgood

Matthew & Elizabeth Allgood 29 Aug 1799; b- Samuel Allgood

William & Betsy Alvis 5 Aug 1793; b- William Blacketter con- Jeremiah Claunch, father con- David Alvis, father

Clausel

Joseph B & Susannah Brame 23 Feb 1799; b- John Puryear Jr min- William Richards- 28Feb1799

Richard W & Anne D Harwell 20 Dec 1819; b- Clausel Williams con- James Harwell, father

William W & Elizabeth Brame 19 Jul 1803; b- John Puryear Jr min- William Richards- 21Jul1803

Clay

Eleazar & Elizabeth Whitehead 7 Jan 1789; b- Richard Whitehead Eleazar from Chesterfield County

John & Sally Coleman 11 Feb 1805; b- James Coleman min- William Richards- 16Feb1805

Tolbert & Nancy Harris 7 Apr 1805; b- John E Harris

Clayton

John & Harriet S Creath 9 Mar 1822; b- William P Creath min- Thomas M. Jeffries- (Lunenburg County)- 29Mar1822

Cleaton

Charles & Frances Walker 2 Dec 1816; b- Thomas W Walker con- Wilson Walker, father min- Charles Ogburn- (Methodist) 4Dec1816

Edward S & Margaret J Rainey 2 Feb 1845; b- John J Rainey con- Williamson Rainey, Jr, who test. that Margaret is 21 min- James McAden-

George W & Elizabeth C Morris - Dec 1846; b- Thomas Drumwright min- James McAden-

Isham & Lucy Taylor 8 Mar 1809; b- William Cleaton

John & Martha Taylor 10 Nov 1787; b- David Taylor

Thomas (Sr) & Lucy Malone 3 Mar 1808; b- Thomas Nance min- James Meacham-

Thomas & Nancy Webb 27 Nov 1787; b- Abel Dortch

William (Jr) & Polly Bailey 18 Mar 1835; b- Richard H L Bailey min- James McAden-

William B & Polly Poynor 30 May 1822; b- William H Walker con- Diggs Poynor, gdn of Polly min- Stephen Jones- (Lynchburg, Va.)- 6Jun1822

William & Elizabeth Walker 13 Dec 1817; b- Thomas Wartman min- Charles Ogburn- (Methodist) 18Dec1817

Woodley & Sally Harris 2 Jan 1805; b- John Harris

Clements

Alexander & Jane Taylor 18 Jan 1820; 'Capt' Alexander Clements b- George T Taylor con- William Taylor, gdn of Jane

Austin & Mary M Mayne 11 Feb 1805; b- Henry W Overby con- James Mayne, father Austin from Charlotte County min- Edward Almand- 14Feb1805

William R B & Sally A Green 5 Nov 1814; b- Henry Wilson con- Howell P Harper, gdn of Sally min- Charles Ogburn- (Methodist) 7Nov1814

William & Sarah Bignal 5 Jun 1789; b- Joseph Speed min- Thomas Scott-

Clemmonds

Edmund & Sarah L Wright 12 Nov 1805; b- Richard Moss

Matthew & Elizabeth Allgood 3 Mar 1789; b- John Allgood

Cliborne

James & Emily Puryear 23 Dec 1835; b- Giles Puryear

John & Elizabeth Vaughan 17 Dec 1849; b- David Shelton con- Peter G Vaughan, father

Cobb

John & Elizabeth W Haskins 13 Feb 1816; b- Charles L Jeffries con- Christopher Haskins, Sr., father

Cobbs

Thomas & Elizabeth H Phillips 23 Oct 1806; b- John Dortch min- Charles Ogburn- (Methodist) 24Oct1806

Cocke

James & Nancy Davis 16 Dec 1816; b- Stephen Power

James & Mary Ann Harris 27 Jul 1824; b- John C Carroll con- Mary King, mother of Mary Ann Harris (nee Mary Ann King)

James & Elizabeth Moss 26 Jul 1800; b- Lewis Moss

Cogbill

Benjamin D & Harriett R Dodson 31 Oct 1853; min- J.W. Chesley- 1Nov1853

Cole

Bartlett & Polly Puryear 26 Dec 1826; b- William Kersey min- William Richards- 28Dec1826

Bartlett & Levina Tisdale 27 Oct 1789; b- Edward Tisdale min- Thomas Scott-

Charles B & Roxanna A Hudson 14 Dec 1850; min- James McAden-

Edward T & Ann Eliza Neal 17 Dec 1823; b- John M Yates min- Charles Ogburn- (Methodist)

Edward & Jane Wall 27 Nov 1817; b- Thomas B Wall con- John Wall

James W & Elizabeth Hazelwood 17 Dec 1850

James & Micah Bevill 13 Mar 1797; b- Francis M Neal min- William Creath-

John T & Martha Cheatham 20 Oct 1823; b- Joseph Keeton min- Matthew Dance- (Lunenburg County)- 24Oct1823

John T & Rebecca Lambert 11 Apr 1845; b- Isaac Holmes

John & Selina Skipwith 25 Apr 1822; b- John S Ravenscroft min- John S. Ravenscroft- (Episcopal)- (married Thursday evening, 25Apr1822, at Prestwould)

Robert   &   Mary Stewart   31 Dec 1802;   b- Martin Cousins   min- William
   Creath- 2Jan1803
Robert   &   Mary A Thomas   20 Nov 1848;   b- James M Chavous   con-
   Robert Thomas, father
Thomas   &   Anne Kirkland   21 Dec 1792;   b- James Cole   min- William
   Creath- 24Dec1792

Coleman
Benjamin W   &   Mary C Coleman   19 Jan 1814;   b- Thomas Neal   con-
   William Pettus, gdn of Mary   min- Charles Ogburn- (Methodist) 22Jan1814
Burwell   &   Martha Daws   28 Jan 1794;   b- Isaac Daws   min- William
   Creath- 1Feb1794
Cain   &   Betsy Grigg   11 Apr 1791;   b- Jesse Grigg
Cain   &   Sally Inge   5 Jan 1803;   b- Richard Taylor
Cain   &   Anne Reamey   9 Jan 1804;   b- Richard Carter
Cain   &   Jemima Spain   30 Jan 1816;   b- James Spain   min- William
   Richards- 30Jan1816
Charles B   &   Sarah A Eaton   13 Feb 1836;   min- William Steel- (Episcopal)-
Cicero A   &   Jane M Haskins   8 Apr 1852;   min- Robert Burton- 15Apr1852
Daniel   &   Elizabeth Haskins   14 Nov 1791;   b- Henry Towns   con- Thomas
   Haskins, father   Henry Twons from Halifax County   Daniel Coleman from
   Pittsylvania County
Daniel   &   Susanna Overton   14 Sep 1801;   b- John Overton   min- William
   Creath-
Henry E   &   Ella M Alexander   11 May 1852;   con- Nathaniel Alexander,
   father   min- F.H. McGuire-
James B   &   Sally Williams   9 Nov 1819;   b- Phillip Johnson
James   &   Sarah Whitehead   14 Nov 1785;   b- Richard Swepson   James son
   of Cluverius Coleman
John J   &   Ann R Burwell   4 Dec 1839;   b- William T Z Finch   min- F.H.
   McGuire-
John   &   Eliza Clarke   28 Jul 1835;   min- William Steel- (Episcopal)-
John   &   Martha Pettus   11 Dec 1799;   b- William Stone   John son of
   Cluverius Coleman   min- William Creath-
Peter W   &   Sarah A Barner   18 Aug 1845;   b- John F Barner   min- James
   McAden-
Richard H   &   Julia G Simmons   2 Nov 1829;   b- James Holmes   min-
   James Smith- 4Nov1829
Richard R   &   Happy Stone   30 Apr 1824;   b- James Royer   con- Elizabeth
   Stone, mother
Roderick   &   Lucy Daws   18 Dec 1794;   b- Isaac Daws   con- James Daws,
   father   min- Charles Ogburn- (Methodist) 25Dec1794
Thomas G   &   Laplata J S Brydie   10 Dec 1851;   con- Charles Brydie, father
   min- William V. Wilson- 10Dec1851
Thomas   &   Sally Rowlett   5 Jan 1799;   b- William Brown   con- William
   Rowlett, father   Thomas son of Cluverius Coleman   min- William Creath-
   10Jan1799
Wesley W   &   Lucy B Coleman   15 Feb 1830;   b- Richard H Coleman   con-
   Burwell B Coleman, father   min- James Smith- 24Feb1830
William B   &   Matilda Baptist   2 Jun 1803;   b- Joseph N Meredith   con-
   William Glanville Baptist, father   William B from Spotsylvania County
   min- William Richards-
William T   &   Elizabeth Prichett   28 Dec 1824;   b- Harwood Prichett   con-
   Thomas Prichett, father   min- C.L. Jeffries-

Coles

Tucker & Helen Skipwith 21 May 1810; b- John S Ravenscroft con- Jean Skipwith, mother   Tucker from Albemarle County   min- George Micklejohn-

Coley

Albert & Elizabeth Morgan 16 Apr 1832; b- Robert Talley

David & Elizabeth Matthews 12 Mar 1787; b- William Wills Green

Isham & Frances Weekes 9 Apr 1787; b- George Tucker

Richard & Caroline B Keeton 19 Dec 1826; b- Leonard Keeton

Thomas & Catherine Tucker 24 Feb 1800; b- Leonard Keeton

Colley

Charles P & Ann B Almand 18 Jan 1841; b- Sterling T Smithson con- Rebecca W Almand, mother   min- John B. Smith-

Samuel & Obedience Williams 24 Mar 1785; b- Thomas Clark

Sherwood G & Lucy L Walker 18 Nov 1816; b- Nicholas E Walker min- Richard Dabbs- (Lunenburg County)- 22Nov1816

Collier

Benjamin & Martha Graves 24 Dec 1850; con- Phebe Graves, mother min- Robert Burton- 24Dec1850

Dabney & Phoebe Elam 3 Jun 1824; min- William Steel- (Episcopal)- 3Jun1824

Frederick & Ann Lark 4 Sep 1781; b- Edward Pennington

Howell & Hannah Creedle 16 Nov 1793; b- Lewis Collier

Howell & Polly Small 27 Sep 1816; b- Ranson Stroud con- George Small, father min- James Meacham- 28Sep1816

John M & Elizabeth J Flinn 22 Dec 1848; b- Jeremiah Johnson min- Robert Burton-

Thomas & Catharine Nelson 14 Feb 1825; b- George N Kennon con- N Nelson, father min- William Steel- (Episcopal)-

William T & Agnes Collier 20 May 1833; b- Dabney Collier min- William Steel- (Episcopal)- 25May1833

Wylie W & Nancy S Toone 15 Feb 1825; b- Richard Russell

Collins

James & Martha A Graves 12 Nov 1849; b- William Flinn con- Thomas J Graves James Collins from Charlotte Co., VA   min- S. G. Mason- 29Nov1849

William & Tabitha Whitlow 28 Nov 1825; b- William Loafman min- William Richards- 29Nov1825

Conley

Munford & Bedia Chavous 7 Aug 1834; b- John Chavous con- Charles Chavous, father min- George Petty- 14Aug1834

Connaway

James & Rebecca W Royster 24 Dec 1816; widow of Dennis Royster, dec. b- Randolph Westbrook

John & Susanna Royster 19 Nov 1810; b- Alexander B Puryear min- William Richards- 24Nov1810

Connell

Benjamin & Martha Hatch 27 Aug 1788; b- William Taylor con- Freeman Short, guardian and father-in-law of Martha   Benjamin son of Daniel Connell

George & Ursley Taylor 31 Oct 1812; b- Robert Westmoreland

James & Jane Pennington 6 Aug 1785; b- John Adams

William & Jane Powers 22 Dec 1836; b- Allen Powers con- William Powers, father min- James McAden-

Conner

William & Martha Carroll 18 Sep 1804; b- Dennis Roberts

Cook
>Herbert & Penelope Taylor 20 Dec 1802; b- John Taylor
>Herbert & Sally Walker 6 Nov 1805; b- Tilman Elder
>John & Sally W Pennington 22 Dec 1812; d of William Pennington, dec.
>b- Benjamin Pennington con- Charles Smithson, gdn of Sally
>Kirby & Lizzy Adams 2 Jan 1788; b- Thomas Adams daughter of Thomas
>and Lucy Adams
>Samuel H & Ann J Ezell 3 Apr 1836; b- William E Ezell con- Elizabeth
>Exell, mother min- James McAden-
>William P & Mary L Smith 20 Dec 1845; b- Albert J Smith con- Sterling
>Smith
>William & Fanny Rainey 5 May 1803; b- Buckner Rainey

Cooper
>Francis & Betty Arnold 25 Apr 1769; b- James Arnold Francis from
>Amelia County Betty daughter of James Arnold Sr and Martha Arnold
>Goodwin & Rebecca Ann Pettiford 7 Aug 1844; b- William Kelly con-
>Parkey Pettifoed, mother min- James McAden-

Copley
>Anderson & Martha Whittemore 23 Mar 1846; b- James W Whittemore
>con- D Middagh, gdn of Martha min- James McAden-

Corpier
>Wilson & Elizabeth Moss 16 Apr 1827; b- Christopher W Baird con-
>Martha Moss, mother min- Stephen Turner- 19Apr1827
>Wilson & Mary G Poynor 2 Mar 1820; b- Charles W Baird min- James
>Smith-

Couch
>John S & Sophia W Scott 27 Jan 1829; min- John B. Smith- 27Jan1829
>John & Susanna Smith 25 Oct 1799; b- Archer Smith Susanna daughter
>of Johnand Martha Smith
>Thomas & Sarah Gregory 26 Nov 1801; b- Archibald Smith min- William
>Richards-

Cousins
>Austin & Elizabeth Brandon - --- 1802; b- Robert Cole (date portion
>of bond illegible)
>Martin & Jincy Cole 31 Dec 1802; b- Robert Cole min- William Creath-

Couzens
>Peter & Phibby A Marshall 15 Dec 1800; b- Francis Marshall min-
>William Richards- 24Dec1800

Cowan
>Alford & Martha Puryear 4 Aug 1828; b- John Puryear con- Morgan
>Puryear, father min- Pleasant Gold- (Baptist)- 7Aug1828

Cox
>Alanson M & Martha R Weatherford 6 Feb 1841; b- Henry E
>Weatherford min- John B. Smith-
>Alexander & Avy Sizemore 16 Nov 1835; b- Daniel Sizemore min- John
>B. Smith-
>Archer & Polly Lewis Hatsel 8 Feb 1802; b- John Talley
>Banister & Rebecca Burrus 26 Oct 1803; b- John Pritchett min- William
>Creath-
>Bartlett & Jane Hudson 24 Oct 1820; b- Stephen Hudson min- William
>Richards-
>Bartley & Lucy Allgood 18 Sep 1786; b- Allen Burton min- John
>Marshall- (Baptist) 20Sep1786
>Bartley & Susanna Carleton 12 Nov 1781; b- Asa Oliver d of Thomas
>Carleton
>Charles & Sarah Royster 3 Nov 1845; b- Huel Stone

Edward & Sally Brown 3 Jan 1795; b- Joseph Hamilton

Edward & Dianna Holloway 31 Dec 1767; b- Henry Delony

Edwin & Sally E Tucker 16 May 1825; b- Daniel Tucker min- Charles Ogburn- (Methodist) 17May1825

John (Jr) & Faithy Coleman 12 May 1825; b- Eli Cox min- William Richards- 13May1825

John (Jr) & Martha B Hall 11 Jul 1803; b- William Marshall min- William Richards- 14Jul1803

John H & Lucinda M Avery 5 Apr 1841; b- George W R Avery con- Bowen Avery, father

Kennon & Pricilla Smith 14 Mar 1803; b- John Morgan min- William Creath-

Miles & Mary Phillips 13 Jan 1829; b- John Phillips con- Allen Phillips, father min- Pleasant Gold- (Baptist)- 15Jan1829

Samuel & Sally Hutt 16 Jul 1806; b- Archer Cox min- John Meacham- 17Jul1806

Thomas & Mary Draper 7 Mar 1796; b- Thomas Pritchett min- William Creath- 8Mar1796

Thomas & Margary Hudson 17 Mar 1794; b- David Hudson min- William Creath- 18Mar1794

Thomas & Joanna Stone 11 May 1813; b- Archer Cox con- Elijah Stone, father con- James Cox, father min- James Meacham- 18May1813

William & Nancy Johnson 28 Jun 1834; b- Samuel Bugg con- Phillip Johnson, father min- C.L. Jeffries- 29Jun1834

Craddock

David & Nancy Neal 25 Oct 1800; b- G H Baskervill

Edward A & Jane E Phillips 2 Aug 1830; b- James Oliver con- Joseph Hutcheson, gdn of Jane min- Charles Ogburn- (Methodist) 12Aug1830

Felix & Martha M Boswell 18 Nov 1839; b- E A Craddock con- Joseph Boswell, father

Griffin & Elizabeth Norment 6 Dec 1811; b- William B Stokes min- William Richards- 10Dec1811

Jesse & Mary E Estes 27 Apr 1841; b- Harwood B Tucker con- Charles Estes, father

Crafton

Giles T & Mary Frances Gregory 16 Apr 1845; b- Robert T Gregory con- Robert S Gregory, father min- John B. Smith-

Craig

James & Mary Tarry 19 Feb 1766; 'Rev' James Craig b- Edmund Taylor James Craig from Lunenburg County Mary daughter of Samuel Tarry

Creath

Samuel & Mary Waller 19 Jan 1818; b- Thomas Abernathy con- John Waller, father

William & Lucy Brame 11 Jun 1792; b- Reuben Vaughan con- Elizabeth Brame, mother & widow of Thomas Brame, dec. min- John Williams- 14Jun1792

Creedle

Briant & Martha H Drumwright 24 Feb 1834; b- Wesley F Edmundson con- Ephraim Drumwright, father

Drury & Patsy Mason 22 Sep 1798; b- Jeremiah Adams min- Charles Ogburn- (Methodist) 25Sep1798

Drury & Clarimore Thompson 14 Dec 1829; b- John L Hightower min- Charles Ogburn- (Methodist) 17Dec1829

Edmond & Mary Ann Talley 11 Feb 1791; b- Drury Creedle

Crenshaw

John & Elizabeth Walker 14 Dec 1801; b- Thomas A Jones

Moses & Polly Hunt 7 Jan 1812; daughter of William Hunt, dec. b- John Thompson

Crew

Charles & Nancy Hutt 11 Jan 1808; b- Samuel Cox

Ellyson & Sally Carter 4 Jun 1790; b- Winkfield Hayes min- James Read- (Baptist)

Crews

Alexander & Mary Royster 19 Dec 1825; b- Matthew C Gill

John & Sarah Nash 25 Jul 1782; b- Nathaniel Moss

John & Mary E Winn 20 Nov 1834; b- William Webb con- William Winn, father min- William Steel- (Episcopal)-

Josiah & Nancy C Brame 16 Nov 1812; b- Nathaniel Maclin

Josiah & Susan Hester 18 Jan 1819; b- John Clark min- James Meacham- 21Jan1819

Robert B & Fanny Keeton 18 May 1824; b- Leonard Keeton min- James Smith-

Robert B & Harriett M Royster 13 Dec 1834; b- James Brame con- Francis Royster, father

Crook

Beverly & Catherine Chavous 31 Jan 1839; b- Pleasant Chavous

William & Martha Edwards 11 Apr 1791; b- John Edwards Jr min- Edward Almand- 13Apr1791

Crow

Alexander & Eliza Wells 15 Oct 1831; b- Baker Wells min- Charles Ogburn- (Methodist) 20Oct1831

Benjamin & Eliza Roberts 10 Dec 1853; con- Mary Roberts, mother min- George W. Andrews- 19Dec1853

John & Martha Easter 28 Dec 1802; b- Jeremiah Adams

John & Nancy Hutcheson 23 Jun 1814; b- Thomas Hutcheson con- Amey Hutcheson, mother min- Charles Ogburn- (Methodist)

Samuel G & Nancy G McDaniel 7 Aug 1827; b- John L Hightower min- Charles Ogburn- (Methodist) 8Aug1827

William & Nancy Thompson 3 Dec 1799; b- Charles Thompson con- John Crow, father min- Charles Ogburn- (Methodist)

Crowder

Abraham & Eliza King 6 Jun 1815; b- Charles King con- Lewis King, father

Abraham & Martha Loyd 7 Dec 1805; b- Elijah Crowder

Anderson & Polly Brummell 20 Jan 1796; b- Abram Crowder Jr min- William Richards- 28Jan1796

Beverly & Jane Bing 21 Apr 1845; b- Zachariah Curtis con- Elizabeth Bing, mother min- James McAden-

Charles W & Frances L Temple 23 Jul 1849; b- James F Temple con- Roderick Temple, father

David Harrison & Nancy Evans 7 Dec 1841; b- Claiborne Evans min- David Petty-

David & Easter Jones 30 Apr 1795; b- Charles Kelly

Elijah & Rebekah Lloyd 9 Aug 1803; b- Richard Crowder Sr

Ezekiel & Mary P Johnson 9 Dec 1812; b- John Cook Jr con- James Johnson, father

Frederick I & Milly Bowen 4 Dec 1797; b- James Bowen min- Charles Ogburn- (Methodist)

Gardiner & Amy Tucker 4 Dec 1788; b- David Crowder

George & Nancy Bailey 26 Jan 1798; b- Richard Crowder min- William Creath-

George & Sally Wright 28 Oct 1803; b- Elijah Crowder

Green W & Lucy G Crenshaw 10 Jan 1831; b- John R Crenshaw con- Elizabeth Crenshaw, mother min- John Wesley Childs- 12Jan1831

Howell C & Martha E Lambert 18 Dec 1850; con- Mary Lambert, mother con- Bartlett Crowder, father min- Hartwell Arnold-

James & Martha Brooks 24 Jan 1818; b- William Blanton

James & Betsy Minor 28 Dec 1795; b- George Minor min- William Creath- 31Dec1795

James & Elizabeth Tucker 12 Dec 1810; b- Daniel Tucker Sr

John & Sally Johnson 16 Aug 1813; b- Thomas Jones con- John Johnson, father

Larkin & Lucy Rottenberry 29 Sep 1789; b- Samuel Rottenberry

Miles T & Susanna B Jeffries 27 Oct 1806; b- Achilles Jeffries min- James Meacham- 5Nov1806

Nathaniel & Martha Rainey 25 Nov 1805; b- Buckner Rainey

Richard & Lucy Clausel 13 Feb 1797; b- Richard Hutcheson min- William Creath-

Robert A & Phoebe Moody 18 Dec 1815; b- Marshall Moody con- Arthur Moody, father

Robert & Lively Hasten 2 Sep 1788; b- Absolem Hasten min- Edward Almand-

Sterling & Martha Lambert 20 Dec 1826; b- John Lambert con- Julius Lambert, father

Theophilus & Mary Williams 20 Jul 1843

Thomas & Nancy Mills 4 Jan 1825; b- B H Bailey min- James Smith- 5Jan1825

Thomas & Elizabeth Puryear 14 Feb 1786; b- Solomon Draper min- John Marshall- (Baptist)

Thomas & Fanny Rhodes 29 Mar 1785; b- John Rhodes

Thomas & Patsy Russell 18 Dec 1787; b- Thomas Jones con- Ann Russell, mother min- Edward Almand- 14Jan1788

Wiley W & Nancy D Wood 17 Oct 1839; b- Richard Wood

William & Milly Byers 22 Jan 1819; b- Jeremiah Russell min- Charles Ogburn- (Methodist) 25Jan1819

Crutcher

John & Amanda C Hardy 14 Jan 1823; b- Jesse Craddock con- Miles Hardy, father

Crutchfield

Adams & Nancy House 3 Jan 1810; b- Bartley Cheatham

James M & Mary L Cabaniss 29 Dec 1842; b- William Hightower con- William Cabaniss, father

Lafayette & Martha B Ezell 19 Dec 1850; con- Rebecca A Tucker, mother of Martha min- James McAden-

Lewis G & Mary E Vaughan 21 Dec 1829; b- Livingston H. Vaughan min- James McAden-

Michael E & Martha C Taylor 16 Dec 1837; b- Isaac B Watson min- James McAden-

Peter & Betsy C McDaniel 17 Jan 1822; b- Crafford McDaniel min- Charles Ogburn- (Methodist) 22Jan1822

Samuel & Patsy Ellis 25 Dec 1804; b- Jesse Perkinson

Thomas & Martha Harris 5 Mar 1831; b- William Crutchfield con- Sally Harris, mother min- Charles Ogburn- (Methodist) 6Mar1831

William C & Sarah E H Harwell 24 May 1852; min- Hartwell Arnold-

Crute

Willis R V & Nancy T Dortch 20 Mar 1843; 'Dr.' Willis R V Crute and 'Mrs.' Nancy T Dortch b- Christopher Gayle min- Joseph A Brown-

Crymes

Leonard & Susan M V Moore 19 Jan 1847; b- Phillip W Moore min- S.G. Mason- 2Feb1847

Culbreath

James & Polly Monroe 12 Dec 1803; b- Ellyson Crew

John & Mary Clark 13 Dec 1790; b- Elijah Graves

John & Rosetta Overby 21 Nov 1821; b- Eggleston Overby con- Peter Z Overby, father

Thomas & Polly Culbreath 8 May 1809; b- Hughes Matthews

Thomas & Sarah Gregory 12 Jan 1822; b- Charles T Carter min- Pleasant Gold- (Baptist)- 24Jan1822

William & Temperance Gregory 15 Jul 1819; b- Garrett Avery

William & Tempe Wiles 13 Mar 1804; b- Isaac Pinson

Cumbia

George & Permelia A B Wells 12 Apr 1834; b- John Gwaltney con- Henry Wells, father

Thomas & Martha C Tucker 7 Oct 1839; b- Alexander Prichett min- Benjamin R. Duval-

Cunningham

George W & Mary P King 3 Mar 1834; b- Isaac B Jones

James & Alice Marshall 10 Jul 1809; b- Robert Marshall min- William Richards- 22Jul1809

Robert M & Eliza F Boyd 22 Sep 1829; b- Alexander Boyd min- Allen D. Metcalf-

William & Mary Burwell 22 Oct 1831; b- James Cunningham min- William Steel- (Episcopal)- 3Nov1831

William & Sally Marshall 10 Dec 1798; b- Robert Marshall min- William Richards- 20Dec1798

Curtis

Chesley & Faithy H Lett 13 Mar 1833; b- Peter B Lett con- Hardaway Lett, father

Churchwell & Rebecca Johnson 17 Jun 1801; b- Jesse Curtis

Churchwell & Sarah J Palmer 19 Nov 1838; b- William Palmer min- Benjamin R. Duval-

Claiborne & Martha L Kirks 9 Nov 1833; b- John B Tunstall con- James Kirks, father

Claiborne & Anne Smith 23 Nov 1812; daughter of Buckner Smith b- Edward Smith min- James Meacham-

Elemeleck & Polly Nunnelly 2 Jan 1798; b- Micajah Gwaltney min- Charles Ogburn- (Methodist)

Elias & Nancy Drummond 28 Jan 1794; b- Thomas Drummond con- Jane Drummond, mother min- Charles Ogburn- (Methodist) 31Jan1794

Green & Parmelia G Lett 27 Jan 1837; b- Joseph A Lett con- Joseph Lett, father min- James McAden-

Jesse & Mary Moore 27 Feb 1792; b- James Moore

John & Betsy Johnson 19 Dec 1806; b- Crafford McDaniel min- Charles Ogburn- (Methodist) 21Dec1806

John & Rebecca Whitt 9 Mar 1834; b- Alexander M Watts

William W & Rebecca A Simmons 18 Jan 1830; b- William N Smith con- Samuel Simmons min- Charles Ogburn- (Methodist) 20Jan1830

Zachariah & Sally Powers 16 Feb 1795; b- Drury Creedle min- Charles Ogburn- (Methodist)

Zachariah & Harriet C Rainey 11 Dec 1840; b- John Baisey con- Williamson Rainey, father min- James McAden-

Cutts

Uriah & Nancy J Vaughan 13 Dec 1847; b- William H Cutts con- Peter G Vaughan, father

William & Mary Mullins 22 Nov 1791; b- John Ragsdale min- John Williams- 25Dec1791

Cypress

William & Polly Thomas 8 Feb 1816; b- Christopher Guy

Dabbs

George J & Pamela Susan Blanks 13 Oct 1833; b- E A Williams con- Allen Blanks, gdn of Pamela min- John B. Smith-

Dacus

Alexander & Jane Duprey 17 Nov 1789; b- Drury Duprey Alexander Dacus from Lunenburg County

Daley

Ambrose & Sarah Taylor 30 Jan 1809; b- James Taylor

Daniel & Elizabeth Bugg 1 Jul 1794; b- Abel Dortch min- John Loyd- 3Jul1794

Vines & Rebecca Adams 14 Oct 1795; b- William Adams min- John Loyd- 15Oct1795

Daly

Ambrose & Betsy Ann Tanner 19 Feb 1816; b- Ludwell Tanner con- Ludwell Tanner, father

Daniel & Elizabeth Holmes 22 Dec 1788; b- Sherwood Smith

John & Mary T Northington 18 Sep 1815; b- Edward L Tabb con- Jabez Northington, father min- Thomas Adams- (Lunenburg Co.)- 10Oct1815

John & Mary Russell 11 Mar 1782; b- Samuel Goode

Josiah (Jr) & Mary Moody 14 Nov 1800; b- John Daly Jr

Josiah & Jinny McKinney 21 Oct 1795; s of John Daly b- Bennett Goodwin min- John Loyd-

Samuel & Louisa Caroline Edwards - Sep 1821; b- James Crook min- James Smith- 6Sep1821

William & Lucy Abernathy 10 Mar 1807; min- Charles Ogburn- (Methodist) 12Mar1807 b- Tignal Abernathy Jr con- Burwell Abernathy, father

Dance

Stephen E & S A Coleman 17 Oct 1848; b- James C Gregory min- Matthew Dance- (Lunenburg County)- 25Oct1848

Stephen & Elizabeth Briggs 11 May 1805; b- Charles Ogburn

Daniel

John W & Rebecca F Barnes 21 Dec 1852; con- Henry Barnes, father

John & Jane Wall 11 Feb 1820; b- James Clardy min- Abner W. Clopton-

Martin & Polly Daniel 9 Jun 1800; b- Thomas Daniel

Martin & Avey Yancey 2 Jun 1817; b- Charles T Carter con- Zachariah Yancey, father min- Reuben Pickett- 5Jun1817

Samuel & Elizabeth Holloway 8 Nov 1820; b- John Jones con- Gray Holloway, father min- Pleasant Gold- (Baptist)-

Samuel & Martha Short 13 Nov 1809; b- Henry Wall min- James Meacham- 16Nov1809

Stark & Lucy Yancey 19 Oct 1818; b- James Feild

Starky & Frances Royster 4 Jan 1803; b- Robert Shanks min- Balaam Ezell- 5Jan1803

Wade W & Dolly Scott 4 Feb 1818; b- Drury Scott

Walter & Jane Puryear 2 May 1804; b- Benjamin Bugg con- Peter Bailey

William & Elizabeth Short 29 Jun 1807; b- Wyatt Short

William & Elizabeth Wootton 9 Jan 1806; b- John Winckler

Daves

Adam O & Martha E Hughes 13 Jun 1848; b- R A Puryear con-Susannah C Hughes, mother

Edmond O & Elizabeth F Butler 13 Oct 1845; b- John W Butler con-Frances C Butler, mother min- Jacob Manning- 15Oct1845

John J & Frances S Butler 24 Aug 1844; b- Henry C Moss con- Frances C Butler, mother

Peter & Henriette M W Winn 4 Oct 1814; min- Charles Ogburn- (Methodist) 4Oct1814

Davis

Arthur H & Louisa C Jackson 29 Nov 1845; b- Robert B Chappell con-Waddy I Jackson, father

Bartlett & Frances Griffin 19 Feb 1816; b- Franklin Moore con- Careen Griffin

Benjamin & Emily W Nance 20 Dec 1824; b- Benjamin Evans con- John Nance, father

Charles L & Margaret Saunders - Dec 1824; b- Robert Jones con- John Saunders, father

Charles & Elizabeth Hopkins 11 Dec 1784; b- John Hopkins

Edward | & Martha S Royster 5 Mar 1825; b- Edward Royster con-Clark Royster, father

Hardaway & Elizabeth Davis 12 Aug 1771; b- Capt. William Davis

Henry & Tabitha Nance 5 Apr 1819; b- John Nance

James & Lucy Cleaton 11 Jun 1821; b- Reuben Booth

James & Sarah Holmes 9 Mar 1767; b- John Ballard Jr Sarah daughter of Isaac Holmes

James & Mary Vaughan 8 Jun 1824; b- Edwin Owen con- Drusella Vaughan, mother min- Pleasant Gold- (Baptist)- 11Jun1824

John (Jr) & Rebecca Ballard 10 Dec 1804; b- John Holmes Jr

John (Jr) & Susanna Swepson 28 Mar 1786; b- Richard Swepson min-John Cameron-

John J & Lucy Roffe 2 Dec 1822; b- Bennett Goode min- James Smith-23Dec1822

John & Polly Chandler 18 Aug 1817; b- William Davis con- David Chandler, father

John & Pheby Floyd 12 Nov 1787; b- Charles Floyd

John & Mary Ann Pennington 11 Sep 1822; b- E S McCraw min- James Smith- 3Oct1822

John & Rebecca Watson 11 Nov 1778; b- Michael Watson

Joshua & Nancy Wright 3 Jan 1805; b- William Wright

Matthew H & Polly Lett 22 Dec 1801; b- Hardaway Lett con- Joseph Lett Sr, father

Meredith W & Elizabeth L Smith 26 Nov 1822; b- John Robinson con-Mabel Smith, mother min- William Richards-

Stephen & Rebecca Wells 20 Apr 1829; b- Jesse Parrish min- Charles Ogburn- (Methodist) 23Apr1829

Thomas & Martha Hix 15 Nov 1814; min- James Meacham-

William (Jr) & Martha W Rogers 20 Oct 1822; b- Diggs Poynor min-James Smith- 26Oct1822

William L & Caroline I Pennington 13 Jun 1840; b- Phillip Pennington con- Ralph Hubbard, gdn of Caroline

William & Mary Cheatham 10 Oct 1804; b- Daniel Cheatham min-William Creath-

William & Martha Thompson 17 Sep 1765; William from Brunswick County b- Wells Thompson

Daws

James & Elizabeth T Ferrell 11 Jun 1798; b- Hubbard Ferrell min- William Creath- 19Jul1798

Thomas & Martha Hicks 17 Oct 1814; b- Thomas A Jones min- James Meacham- 15Nov1814

William & Rebecca Ezell 19 Dec 1814; b- Edward L Tabb con- William Ezell, father

Day

James & Jane Baker 3 Apr 1822; min- Charles Ogburn- (Methodist)

John & Elizabeth Keeton 21 Oct 1815; d of Joseph Keeton b- James Days min- Milton Robertson- (Warren County, N.C.) 26Oct1815

John & Mary Keeton 6 Aug 1819; b- Abel B Dunnavant min- Silas Shelburne- (Lunenburg County)- 16Sep1819

DeGraffenreid

Francis & Ermin Boswell 12 Nov 1781; b- Asa Oliver con- Joseph Boswell, father

DeGraffenreidt

Tscharner & Susan B Crowder 2 Mar 1822; b- William B Stokes con- Godfrey Crowder, father min- William Richards- 5Mar1822

Decker

Henry & Patsy Talley 30 Dec 1791; b- William Decker

Dedman

Henry H & Amanda A Wiles 20 Jan 1832; b- John F Yancey con- Ruth Wile, mother

Henry & Jincy White 11 May 1795; b- William White min- William Richards- 18May1795

James W & Jane Hudson 15 Feb 1830; b- Robert Redd min- John B. Smith- 25Feb1830

John & Susanna Harris 20 Oct 1834; b- Allen Gillespie min- William Steel- (Episcopal)- 23Oct1834

John & Elizabeth White 11 Feb 1799; b- Henry H Dedman min- William Richards- 12Feb1799

Samuel & Ursley Hudson 19 Feb 1822; b- John Dedman min- William Richards- 28Feb1822

W James & Ann E Brummell - Jul 1846; b- John R Taylor min- John B. Smith-

William W & Elizabeth Haile 23 Dec 1819; min- William Richards-

Dennis

Matthew & Nancy Griffin 8 May 1797; b- Jacobus Christopher

Dew

David & Polly Cole - Aug 1822; b- John Dew min- Alexander M. Cowan-

John & Susan Mayo 16 Aug 1822; b- Daniel Dew min- Alexander M. Cowan-

Dewes

Thomas & Elizabeth Mallett 3 Sep 1849; b- William H Homes min- William A. Smith-

Dickerson

William T & Martha J Coley 29 Nov 1847; b- Richard Coley min- Robert Burton-

Dickins

Samuel & Jane Vaughan 25 May 1801; b- John Wilson

Dixon

Benjamin & Elizabeth Wagstaff 20 Nov 1800; b- John Wagstaff min- William Richards- 9Dec1800

Dodson

Benjamin F & Delia B Boyd 19 Nov 1851; min- George W. Andrews-

Bird L & Nancy Gregory 22 Feb 1826; daughter of James Gregory, dec.
b- Benjamin Doggett min- George Petty-

Edward & Mary Green 7 Jun 1814; b- John T Keen min- James
Meacham- 14Jun1814

James H & Sarah J Rowlett 6 Dec 1844; b- William G Coleman min-
John B. Smith-

John S & Harriet R Boyd 29 Jul 1844; b- Amasa P Wright con- Matilda
Boyd, mother

John T & Sally Ann Rowlett 14 Jan 1834; b- Peter D Hudson

Stephen & Margaret Wiles 26 May 1823; b- Thomas Rowlett

Dortch

Abel & Mary Holmes 29 Oct 1793; b- David Dortch min- John Loyd-
31Oct1793

Abel & Sally Taylor 24 May 1785; b- Goodwyn Taylor

Alexander & Mary J Holmes 8 Dec 1824; b- L H Jones con- Samuel
Holmes, father min- James Smith-

David & Betsy Taylor 30 May 1798; b- Abel Dortch min- Ebenezer
McGowan- 31May1798

James L & Ann I Dortch 15 Nov 1824; b- L H Jones con- Betsy Dortch,
mother min- James Smith- 9Dec1824

James P & Martha J Harriss 14 Dec 1853; con- John R Harriss, father
min- James McAden-

Jesse & Ora Saunders 24 Jan 1792; b- Jacob Bugg con- Mary Saunders,
mother min- John Loyd- 26Jan1792

Lewis & Mary Speed 2 Jan 1796; b- James Speed min- John Loyd-
9Jan1796

Newman & Sarah Speed 29 Mar 1800; b- John Dortch min- Ebenezer
McGowan- 30Mar1800

Noah & Ann Lucas 25 Apr 1780; b- William Baskervill

Samuel & Ann E Jeffress 16 May 1842; b- John M Gregory con- Richard
Phillips, stepfather of Ann min- John B. Smith-

William & Susanna Burton 29 Sep 1786; b- Robert Pennington

William & Elizabeth P Eubank 21 Oct 1848; William from Missouri b-
Christopher Gayle min- Thomas Adams- (Lunenburg Co.)- 22Oct1848

Douglas

Bryant & Rhoda D Johnson 28 May 1821; b- Tarisa Johnson

David & Martha Jones 6 Nov 1777; b- Francis Lightfoot

James & Nancy Johnson 21 Oct 1808; b- Terasha Johnson

Samuel A & Mary A Baskervill 21 Mar 1814; b- Joel Watkins con-
Elizabeth Baskervill, mother

Samuel & Susan R Yates 18 Nov 1811; b- Charles Baskervill con- John
M Yates, gdn of Susan min- Matthew Dance- (Lunenburg County)-
28Nov1811

Doyle

John & Lucy Mealler 17 Dec 1821; b- John Cook

John & Lucy Walker 17 Jan 1823; min- Stephen Jones- (Lynchburg, Va.)-

Draper

Stephen & Rebecca Tisdale 26 Aug 1815; b- William Tucker min- Milton
Robertson- (Warren County, N.C.)

Drew

Benjamin C & Emily A Rogers 6 Nov 1850; con- George Rogers, father
min- William A. Smith-

George W & Betsy Mayo 2 Aug 1850; min- George W. Andrews-

Hardaway & Polly Guy 17 Feb 1813; b- Thomas Kersey

James & Polly Stewart 24 Nov 1817; b- Benjamin R Pulliam min- William
Richards- 27Nov1817

Drummond

David & Nancy Johnson 27 Nov 1787; b- Howell Johnson con- James Johnson

Drumwright

Claiborne & Caroline T Ezell 30 Jan 1837; b- Benjamin H Rogers con- Rebecca A Ezell, mother con- William Drumwright, father min- James McAden-

Ephraim A & Martha J Hightower 6 Apr 1840; b- John Hightower

Ephraim & Elizabeth Pennington 3 — 1808; b- Wyatt Harper

Gee & Minerva J Bailey 30 Aug 1836; b- Richard A L Bailey con- Richard A L Bailey, father min- James M. Jeter- (Lunenburg County)-

Gee & Emily Benford 13 Dec 1828; b- Jones Drumwright con- Thomas Benford, father

Gee & Sarah H Reekes 13 Dec 1842; b- Irby Creath

James M & Lucy A Nance 28 Dec 1830; b- Samuel S Saunders con- Benjamin W Davis, gdn of Lucy min- James McAden-

James & Lydia Crowder 9 Oct 1794; b- William Drumwright con- Richard Crowder, father min- John Loyd- 23Oct1794

Richard H & Elizabeth H Rainey 6 Nov 1821; b- James Rainey con- Buckner Rainey, father min- Stephen Jones- (Lynchburg, Va.)- 8Nov1821

Thomas F & Margaret E Ezell 19 Oct 1840; b- Claiborne Drumwright con- Rebecca A Ezell, mother con- William Drumwright, father, who test. William under 21

Thomas F & Araminta N Sands - Jan 1853; min- James McAden-

Thomas & Oslin Williams 18 Jan 1804; b- Lewis Williams Sarah daughter of Lewis Williams Sr

William (Jr) & Libelar Crowder 14 Jul 1797; b- William Drumwright min- Charles Ogburn- (Methodist) 21Jul1797

William (Jr) & Lucy Gee 28 Feb 1803; b- Thomas Drumwright con- Jones Gee, father

William (Sr) & Sally Gilliam Bradley 24 Sep 1811; b- Goodwin Taylor

Duffee

Allen & Sarah Averett 2 Feb 1829; b- Henry E Weatherford con- Thomas Averett, father min- John B. Smith- 15Feb1829

Patrick & Michiel Scott 22 Dec 1828; b- Edmund Young min- James Smith- 25Dec1828

Dugger

Allison C & Sarah M Rogers 7 Sep 1830; b- Thomas C Dugger con- George Rogers, father min- James Smith- 9Sep1830

Thomas C & Mary Clark 10 Oct 1832; b- James Clark con- Sarah Clark, mother

William & Jean Stainback 23 Oct 1804; b- James Stainback William from Brunswick County min- William Creath-

Dunn

David & Susan Overby 16 Dec 1823; b- Alexander Overby min- Pleasant Gold- (Baptist)-

James H & Betsy A W Bowers 21 Feb 1825; b- Sanford Bowers min- James McAden-

Dunnavant

Abel B & Sarah Marriott Mitchell 29 Jul 1811; b- Isaac Holmes con- Elizabeth Mitchell, mother

Marvill W & Eliza Stiner 29 Mar 1825; b- John V Cawthorn con- Ann Stiner, mother

Peter & Mary Marriott Mitchell 27 Jul 1818; b- Thomas Warren con- Elizabeth Mitchell, mother

Dunnington
> Reuben & Polly Wright 11 Jul 1798; b- William Wright con- Reuben Wright, father

Dunston
> Miles & Nancy Stewart 18 Feb 1802; b- Thomas Spence

Dupree
> John & Nancy Short 11 Dec 1787; b- Thomas Buford con- Jacob and Mary Short, parents John Dupree from Brunswick County
> Warren & Sally B Sydnor 13 Feb 1838; b- Thomas H Laird con- Ruby Sydnor, mother min- William B. Rowzee-

Duprey
> Drury & Ann Atkinson 8 Mar 1784; b- John Crews con- Median Atkinson, mother and widow of Lewis Duprey, dec.
> Lewis & Median Atkinson 11 Oct 1784; b- Drury Duprey min- Henry Lester- (Baptist)

Durham
> Benjamin & Nancy Thomas 2 Dec 1831; b- Luke Burks min- John Wesley Childs- 15Dec1831

Duty
> Benjamin & Mary Wagstaff 20 Nov 1804; b- Bazzell Wagstaff con- John Wagstaff, father min- William Richards-

Earles
> Presley & Elizabeth Pointer 13 May 1807; b- Roberts Nanney

Easley
> William B & Maria A Boyd 1 Oct 1827; b- Daniel T Hicks min- Allen D. Metcalf- 3Oct1827
> William B & Nannie W Morton 25 Aug 1841; b- Frank W Boyd con- Anderson C Morton, father

Eaton
> William A & Jean B Burwell 19 Dec 1843; b- Allen A Burwell

Edmonds
> James W H & Elizabeth Parrish 7 Jan 1852; con- Peter Parrish, father min- P.F. August- 8Jan1852
> John & Martha S Crow 18 Mar 1844; b- Thomas Edmonds min- Thomas E. Locke- (Lunenburg County)- 1Apr1844

Edmondson
> John & Judith Clay 6 Oct 1792; b- Coleman Edmondson
> Robert Spilsby & Nancy Singleton 29 Jan 1803; b- Thomas Crow con- Patsy Singleton, mother
> Thomas & Milly Arnold 8 Aug 1796; b- Jeremiah Arnold Milly daughter of James Arnold and Mary Arnold min- Charles Ogburn- (Methodist) 11Aug1796

Edmonson
> Charles R & Ann E Arnold 9 Dec 1839; b- Hartwell Arnold min- Benjamin R. Duval-
> Edwin P & Mary Emma Jones 16 Dec 1852; con- R D Jones, father
> Richard H & Angelina C Ogburn 15 Jan 1816; b- Charles Ogburn con- Charles Ogburn, father min- James Meacham- 16Jan1816

Edmunds
> Abel & Dolly Hudgins 24 Feb 1800; b- James Hudgins
> James & Mary Garrott 9 Nov 1825; b- James W Taylor con- Zachariah Garrott, father min- James McAden-
> Joseph N & Elizabeth B Hodge 4 Jul 1828; Joseph from Halifax Co., VA b- S V Morton con- A E Henderson, gdn for Elizabeth
> Littleton & Indiana G Powell 27 Aug 1844; b- R D Powell

Edmundson

Banister & Janey Davis 16 Dec 1793; b- George B Hamner con- John Davis, father min- William Creath- 19Dec1793

Benjamin & Keziah Hood 17 Oct 1785; b- Charles Hood

Richard Coleman & Elizabeth Featherston 18 May 1812; b- Drury Creedle min- Charles Ogburn- (Methodist)

Wesley F & Elizabeth S Simmons 7 Jan 1837; b- Samuel Simmons min- James McAden-

Edwards

George R & Catherine Simmons 12 Jan 1797; b- Joseph Simmons

John & Sarah Hyde 8 Nov 1784; b- Burwell Russell

Thomas & Agness Hobsin 6 Nov 1798; b- Charles Patterson min- William Creath- 7Nov1798

Thomas & Caty Wall 10 Mar 1800; b- Thomas Daniel

William & Sarah Kirkland 13 Feb 1798; b- Jeffrey Mustian min- Charles Ogburn- (Methodist)

Elam

Alexander & Jane Norment 14 Mar 1785; b- Thomas Norment min- John Williams- 17Mar1795

Andrew G & Matilda H Puryear 17 Dec 1827; b- Littleberry Stone con- Thomas B Puryear, father min- John B. Smith- 20Dec1827

Daniel & Nancy Graves 12 Apr 1826; b- James Callis con- Frances Graves, mother min- William Richards- 13Apr1826

David & Sally Jeffries 11 Jan 1845; both of Sally's parents deceased bond and consent by Creed T Haskins for his adopted daughter Sally

Edward & Martha Smith 13 Nov 1786; b- Edward Finch con- John Smith, father

James E & Polly Hurt 19 Oct 1812; b- Wagstaff Hurt min- William Richards- 28Oct1812

Joel & Susanna Elam 17 Feb 1812; b- John Elam min- William Richards- 20Feb1812

John G & Mary J Overby 13 Nov 1829; b- Henry H Newton con- Milly W Overby, mother min- Alfred Apple- 14Nov1849

John & Elizabeth Elam 13 Oct 1806; b- James Hurt min- William Richards- 23Oct1806

John & Polly W Garner 23 Oct 1797; b- Archibald Clark con- James Garner, father min- William Richards- 26Oct1797

John & Susan M Hall 23 Sep 1829; b- Miles Hall min- John B. Smith-

John & Martha Yancey 5 Dec 1835; b- Thomas W Owen con- Charles Yancey, father min- John B. Smith-

Peter & Susanna Gregory 8 Aug 1791; b- Andrew Gregory min- John Loyd- 18Aug1791

Peter & Polly Vaughan 3 Aug 1811; daughter of Willie Vaughan b- John J Norment min- William Richards- 7Aug1811

Reps J & Elizabeth B Stokes 29 Dec 1819; b- Thomas Gregory min- Silas Shelburne- (Lunenburg County)- 6Jan1820

Richard T & Harriet J Newton 24 Sep 1842; b- James W Newton con- James H Newton, father min- John B. Smith-

Samuel & Martha Garner 13 Oct 1800; b- John Elam con- James Garner, father min- Edward Almand- 6Nov1800

William & Patience Hurt 19 Nov 1810; b- William Hurt min- William Richards- 12Dec1810

Elder

Tilman & Elizabeth Walker 17 Dec 1798; b- John Holloway min- John Neblett- 24Dec1798

Elibeck
John D & Elizabeth Hutcheson 18 Jul 1808; b- John Hutcheson
Ellington
David & Letitia Cox 2 Dec 1793; b- Thomas Green min- John Williams-
19Dec1793
John & Catharine V Arnold 20 Feb 1842; b- Hartwell Arnold
Pleasant & Elizabeth E Harper 4 Dec 1840; b- William P Drumwright
con- John P Harper, father min- James McAden-
William & Leannah Johnson 17 Dec 1807; b- John Johnson
Elliott
Greenville & Elizabeth Griffin 12 Apr 1825; b- Stark Daniel min-
Pleasant Gold- (Baptist)- 13Apr1825
William & Rebecca Boothe 20 Dec 1809; b- Reuben Boothe
Elvin
William & Mary R Nance 16 Oct 1843; b- Isaac Watson min- James
McAdam-
Epperson
Bentley & Jane M Harrison 25 Feb 1823; b- Horace T Royster
Joseph & Polly Hundley 10 Oct 1803; b- William Hundley
Thomas & Martha Gregory 24 Sep 1829; min- Pleasant Gold- (Baptist)-
Eppes
Victor M & Martha M Jones 12 Nov 1844; Victor from Sussex Co., VA
b- William H Jones con- Tignal Jones, father
Estes
Phillip C & Jane Keeton 17 Dec 1821; b- Edward Neal min- William
Richards- 19Dec1821
Thomas H & Lucy Griffin 15 Sep 1828; b- Elijah Griffin min- Pleasant
Gold- (Baptist)-
Eubank
James & Susanna Dailey 1 Dec 1801; b- John Ferguson
James & Cary Hudson 27 Jun 1814; d of Thomas Hudson b- William
Brown, son of James Brown min- James Meacham- 30Jun1814
James & Eliza Puryear 3 Jul 1830; b- David G Hutcherson con- Hezekiah
Puryear, father min- William Steel- (Episcopal)-
William H & Elmira A Barnes 15 Jan 1844; b- Charles H Robertson
con- Joania Barnes, mother
William L & Mary A E Roffe 19 Dec 1837; b- R J Eubank con- Samuel
D Roffe, father min- James McAden-
William & Mary A Holmes 15 Jan 1800; b- Pennington Holmes min-
Charles Ogburn- (Methodist) 16Jan1800
Evans
Allen B & Martha W Glover 13 Jan 1830; Martha terst. that she is 22
years old b- David Oslin min- James McAden-
Anthony & Martha E Walker - Jul 1846; b- David R Walker con-
Elizabeth Walker, mother min- James McAden-
Benjamin & ----- Lambert 16 Jun 1828; bride's given name missing on
bond b- Baxter Lambert
Benjamin & Sally Walker 5 Jun 1811; b- Wilson Walker
Charles & Martha Jeffries 17 Aug 1796; b- Kenchen Chavous min- John
Loyd- 18Aug1796
Donaldson P & Elvira Evans 21 Jan 1838; b- Hartwell Johnson
Evan & Polly Lunsford 24 Dec 1807; b- John Wright
Isaac & Dicey Stewart 24 Dec 1792; b- William Baskervill min- William
Creath- 25Dec1792
James & Eliza Ann Johnson 11 Dec 1837; b- William G Davis
John (Jr) & Nancy W Singleton 19 Oct 1835; b- Thomas Jones

John & Temperance Clay 5 Nov 1792; b- John F Reazon

John & Betsy Massey 11 Sep 1800; b- Stephen Evans

Ludwell & Jane B Hardy 19 Nov 1810; b- John S Jeffries min- William Richards- 20Dec1810

Ludwell & Mary Hogan 25 Feb 1783; b- Edward Finch con- Edward Hogan, father

Ludwell & Aggatha W Thomason 13 Aug 1816; b- Salathiel Bowen con- Anna Thomason, mother

Matthew & Becky Barnett 5 Oct 1804; b- John Barnett

Osborne & Elizabeth Tucker 22 May 1838; b- Burwell Brown

Peter & Mary Lewis 16 Jul 1831; b- Randolph Chavous min- Charles Ogburn- (Methodist) 19Jul1831

Peter & Elizabeth Ornsby 1 Sep 1792; b- Jeremiah Singleton min- John Loyd- 4Sep1792

Robert & Sarah Prichett 15 Jun 1835; b- William Evans con- Sarah Prichett, mother

Robert & Nancy Roberts 15 Jan 1847; b- William Evans

Robin & Amy Stewart 13 Feb 1809; b- James Chavous min- William Richards- 17Feb1809

Starling & Letty Thompson 12 Oct 1801; b- Bernard Thompson min- William Richards- 15Oct1801

Stephen & Milly Mason 22 Nov 1797; b- Ananias Grainger min- Charles Ogburn- (Methodist) 23Nov1797

Sterling & Rebecca Burks 33 Aug 1844; b- Edward A Rawlins con- Lucy Burks, mother

Thomas & Mary Crowder 18 Jul 1821; b- Theophilus Crowder con- Martha Crowder, mother

Thomas & Margaret Mitchell 16 Oct 1849; b- Norman Smith min- James McAden-

Walker & Eliza A Evans - Sep 1845; b- John P Smith con- Benjamin Evans, father

William R & Mary E G Floyd 7 Feb 1848; b- James W Whittemore con- Zachariah Floyd and Amey Floyd, parents min- James McAden-

William & Ede Hogan 10 Apr 1775; b- Edward Hogan

William & Polly Johnson 23 Dec 1830; b- Edward Cox con- Phillip Johnson, father min- Charles Ogburn- (Methodist) 25Dec1830

William & Julia A Walker 22 Jun 1840; b- William E Walker con- Thomas H Walker, father min- James McAden-

William & Polly Walker 8 Dec 1802; b- Wilson Walker min- James Meacham- 9Dec1802

Ezell

Balaam (Jr) & Sally Childers 14 Nov 1808; b- Balaam Ezell Sr con- Thomas Hamblin, gdn, who test that Sally under age

Balaam & Elizabeth Mayes 27 Dec 1803; b- Thomas Owen min- William Richards- 28Dec1803

Benjamin & Elizabeth Walker 15 Dec 1814; b- Robertson Ezell

Berryman & Phebe Hamblin 8 Aug 1803; b- Peter Hamblin con- Thomas Hamblin, father

John H & Martha E J Turner 29 Nov 1841; b- James W Brame con- Judith J Turner, mother

John W & Mary T Walker 21 Sep 1853; con- Elizabeth Walker, mother min- James McAden-

Robertson & Rebecca Northington 20 Mar 1815; b- William Evans con- John Northington, father

William & Elizabeth Daly 22 Apr 1811; b- Charles Baskervill

Fagins

Paschall & Martha Smith 27 Dec 1853; min- James McAden-

Fargeson

Joseph & Elizabeth Holloway 6 Feb 1789; b- Benjamin Ferrell

Peter T & Elizabeth Jackson 5 Jul 1809; b- Cavil Jackson

Farley

Henry F & Nancy H White 21 Nov 1814; b- Henry H Dedman min- William Richards- 22Nov1814

James & Martha Evans 26 Jul 1786; James from Amelia County b- Henry Farley con- James Farley Sr., father con- Stephen Evans, father

Farmer

Thomas & Susanna Stone 9 Dec 1804; b- Jordan Stone

Farrar

Abel & Sarah Clark 22 Aug 1788; b- Matthew Lancaster Easter min- Edward Almand- 20Aug1788

Alexander & Martha W Goods 13 Oct 1834; min- William Steel- (Episcopal)- 16Oct1834

Dabney & Nancy Bugg 9 Jun 1812; b- James Phillips con- John Bugg, father min- James Meacham- 10Jun1812

Dabney & Elizabeth Puryear 16 Dec 1816; b- Samuel Puryear min- William Richards- 24Dec1816

George & Elizabeth Boyd 22 Aug 1783; b- Richard Swepson Jr

George & Ann Hester 30 Oct 1828; daughter of Samuel Hester b- John Culbreath min- Pleasant Gold- (Baptist)- 6Nov1828

John & Ann Baskervill 24 Dec 1794; b- Robert Baskervill

John & Nancy Hunt 13 Jun 1808; b- John P Finch

Joseph C & Georgianna C Middagh 5 Feb 1834; b- D Middagh min- James McAden-

Pettus & Angelina W Harwell 18 Jun 1849; b- C R Edmonson min- Thomas Adams- (Lunenburg Co.)- 27Jun1849

Pettus & Martha G Read 20 Nov 1826; b- James O White con- Clement Read, father min- John B. Smith- 22Nov1826

Richardson & Susanna Baskervill 12 Jun 1810; b- Newman Dortch

Samuel (Jr) & Mary Ann Daly 1 Dec 1817; b- David C Hutcheson con- Josiah Daly, father min- Charles Ogburn- (Methodist) 4Dec1817

Samuel & Rebecca W Eubank 8 Aug 1848; b- Christopher Gayle min- James McAden- 9Aug1848

Samuel & Lucy Ann Hudson 3 Apr 1826; b- Peter Hudson con- Charles Hudson, father min- James Smith- 5Apr1826

Samuel & Elizabeth Phillips 10 Nov 1786; b- Hardy Jones

Thomas & Sarah Farrar 13 Dec 1790; b- James Faucet

Thomas & Hannah Walker 22 Nov 1819; b- Zachariah H Jones con- Wilson Walker, father min- James Smith- 24Nov1819

William H & Rebecca B Wright 1 Aug 1825; b- B H Bailey con- Austin Wright, Sr., father

William & Hannah Farrar 22 Dec 1824; b- John Farrar min- James Smith-

William & Lucy Medley 24 Jul 1780; b- John Farrar

Farris

Henry C W & Jane E Farrar 4 Jun 1832; b- Dabney Farrar min- William Steel- (Episcopal)-

Faulkner

Johnson & Mary Griffin 8 Apr 1799; b- Stephen P'Pool con- William Griffin, father

Fausett
  Jackson & Martha Gillespie 7 Dec 1837; b- William Thomason con-
  Nancy Gillespie, mother
Feagins
  John & Patty Lanier 5 Jan 1786; b- John Saunders min- John King-
  7Jan1786
  Richardson & Martha Apperson 3 Feb 1779; b- Thomas Pinson con-
  David Apperson, father
Featherston
  Thomas & Sally Griffin 13 Apr 1821; b- Elijah Griffin
Feggin
  Thomas & Polly Maclin 22 Jan 1818; b- William Cypress con- Thomas
  Maclin, father
Feild
  Alexander & Nancy T Feild 22 Dec 1832; b- Robert S Feild con- Eliza
  B Feild, mother min- William Steel- (Episcopal)- 24Dec1832
  Alexander & Mary A Jones 23 Jun 1817; b- John W Jones min- James
  Meacham- 24Jun1817
  Charles G & Catharine Thomas Read 11 Mar 1842; b- John S Feild
  con- William B Green, gdn of Catharine min- F.H. McGuire-
  Drury S & Eliza Feild 23 Mar 1814; b- Edmund Taylor
  Drury & Amelia E Steel 30 May 1832; 'Dr' Drury Feild b- Alexander
  Feild con- William Steel, father min- William Steel- (Episcopal)-
  31May1832
  Edmund & Mary Tanner 14 Sep 1807; b- G H Baskervill min- James
  Meacham- 19Sep1807
  James Wister & Ellen Augusta Goode 7 Dec 1848; b- John M Hayes
  con- McKarness Goode, father
  James & Henryetta Maria Anderson 17 Feb 1789; daughter of Thomas
  Anderson Sr b- Thomas Anderson Jr
  James & Sally Taylor 19 Apr 1814; b- Joel Watkins con- William Taylor,
  gdn of Sally, who is orphan of Anderson Taylor, dec. 'Dr' James Feild
  John S & Martha C Feild 19 Jun 1832; b- Robert Redd min- William
  Steel- (Episcopal)-
  John Shaw & Jane Walker 9 Jun 1788; b- Henry Walker daughter of
  Henry Walker min- Thomas Scott-
  Thomas A & Susan Green 10 Jun 1814; b- Abraham G Keen min- James
  Meacham- 30Jun1814
  Thomas & Mary White 11 Jan 1782; b- James Anderson
Fennell
  Benjamin & Eliza H Creath 11 Jun 1831; b- J W D Creath min- John
  B. Smith-
  William W & Angelina Peete 13 Nov 1824; b- Charles H Ogburn con-
  E H Peete, father 'Dr' William W Fennell
Ferguson
  Berryman & Nancy Collier 8 Jan 1811; b- Jesse Russell
  Peter T & Elizabeth Ogburn 2 Dec 1818; b- Thomas Ogburn con-
  Martha Ogburn, mother min- James Smith- 3Dec1818
  Thomas H & Susanna Daly 10 Jul 1816; b- Josiah Daly min- James
  Meacham- 11Jul1816
Ferrell
  Benjamin P & Sarah M Hutcherson 9 Jan 1832; b- Joseph W Hutcherson
  con- Sarah Hutcherson, mother min- David Wood- 14Jan1832
  Benjamin & Mary Burton 12 Mar 1770; b- James Ferrell
  Benjamin & Sarah Collier 13 Dec 1773; b- Howell Collier
  Benjamin & Ann Dortch 11 Feb 1784; b- William Baskervill

Drury A & Mary B Keeton 19 Jan 1835; b- Leonard Keeton min- John B. Smith-

Hutchens B & Ann C Hutcherson 20 Aug 1832; b- Alex W Hutcherson con- Sarah Hutcherson, mother min- James McAden-

William & Dolly Bailey 9 Apr 1795; b- James Ferrell William from Halifax County

William & Dolly Bailey 9 Apr 1795; b- James Ferrell William from Halifax County min- William Creath-

William & Nancy C Keeton 13 Apr 1846; b- Leonard Keeton min- John B. Smith-

Field

Charles G & Agnes M Steel 28 Oct 1828; min- William Steel- (Episcopal)-

George & Sarah Jones 10 Nov 1829; b- Robert S Feild con- John Jones, father

John T & Martha W Redd 20 Nov 1821; b- William M Swepson min- William Richards- 22Nov1821

Robert & Frances A Jones 13 Jul 1821; b- John Jones min- Alexander M. Cowan-

Finch

Adam & Lucy S Goode 20 Dec 1824; b- Richard H Moss

Edward & Martha Cunningham 12 Feb 1845; b- William E Dodson con- James Cunningham, father

Edward & Jane Puryear 13 Mar 1775; b- John Puryear

George & Amy Arnold 22 Sep 1803; b- Jeremiah Arnold

George & Janey Short 7 Dec 1796; b- Freeman Short min- John Loyd- 21Dec1796

Henry & Martha Steagall 2 Jun 1794; b- Robert Pennington

John P & Nancy Graves 14 Sep 1795; b- Elijah Graves min- William Creath-

John R & Frances Cunningham 2 May 1845; b- William E Dodson con- James Cunningham, father

John & Elizabeth Farrar 18 Apr 1787; b- Peter Farrar con- John Farrar, father

John & Frances Smith 14 Dec 1814; b- Edward Haskins con- Robert Smith min- William Richards- 15Dec1814

Langston B & Maria Cunningham 17 Dec 1832; b- Robert M Cunningham min- William Steel- (Episcopal)- 20Dec1832

Langston B & Lucy Pentecost 16 Dec 1816; b- David Shelton min- William Richards- 19Dec1816

Langston E & Martha Boyd 4 Sep 1851; con- Richard Boyd, father min- J.D. Blackwell- 10Seo1851

William T Z & Martha L Pettus 1 Oct 1835; b- Benjamin W Coleman

William & Elizabeth Christopher 31 Jan 1780; b- William Christopher daughter of David Christopher

William & Rebecca Clay 14 Aug 1775; b- Edward Finch con- Henry Clay

Fisher

Jonathon & Susannah Booth 5 May 1801; b- Reuben Booth min- James Meacham-

Fitts

Henry G & Lucy E M Davis 20 Mar 1837; con- Anne Davis, mother b- Horace Palmer

James M & Ann M Davis 9 Jun 1841; b- Henry G Fitts con- Anne Davis, mother

John & Jane Jones 3 Dec 1822; b- Charles Yancey min- Pleasant Gold- (Baptist)- 5Dec1822

Samuel & Almiranda J Wilkinson 30 Dec 1852

William & Mary J Tutor 18 Sep 1843; b- John J Tutor con- John G
Tutor, father min- William H. Maddox- 7Oct1843

Fitzackerly
John & Betsy J Holmes 19 Dec 1817; b- Pennington Holmes min-
Charles Ogburn- (Methodist) 24Dec1817

Fleming
John & Mary Ann Brame 16 Dec 1833; b- Francis Brame min- John B.
Smith-

Flinn
James M & Peggy Graves 21 Dec 1846; b- Jeremiah M Johnson con-
James Graves, father min- Robert Burton-

Flood
William & Molly Harris Brogdon 12 Nov 1785; b- Thomas Macklin con-
William Brogdon, who test bride 21

Floyd
Drury & Betsy Lanier 25 Oct 1791; b- Josiah Floyd con- Lemuel Lanier,
father min- John Loyd- 27Oct1791
Josiah & Rebecca Bugg 28 Mar 1810; b- Jesse Bugg
Stephen (Jr) & Julia A Gregory 28 Oct 1844; b- Thomas A Sale con-
Robert S Gregory, father con- D A Paschall, gdn of Stephen min- John
B. Smith-

Flynn
John & Nancy Graves 9 Dec 1816; b- Thomas Graves min- William
Richards- 12Dec1816

Flynne
John & Sarah Green 11 Apr 1791; b- David Green min- Henry Ogburn-

Fontaine
Joseph & Mary Goode 8 Feb 1773; b- Edward Goode

Foote
John L & Sarah A Thomas 17 Mar 1846; b- David W Thomas

Fore
Edward W & Adeline G McCargo 24 Sep 1850; con- Susannah J McCargo,
mother min- William V. Wilson-
John A & Eliza A Crute 12 Aug 1850; b- Joseph Crute

Forlines
Hiram & Sally O Puryear 27 Jul 1852; con- Thomas B Puryear, father
min- Robert Burton- 29Jul1852
Josiah & Judith G Wade 3 Nov 1838; Josiah from Halifax Co, VA b-
Henderson Overby con- L G Wade, father

Forman
John & Martha Ann Smithson 4 Dec 1839; b- William R Mason con-
Sterling T Smithson, father

Foster
Booker & Mariah Jeffries 26 Oct 1816; b- Andrew Y Elam con- Richard
Russell, gdn of Mariah min- William Richards- 29Oct1816
Patrick H & Eleanor Boyd 15 Sep 1819; 'Dr' Patrick H Foster b- Thomas
Howerton con- Elizabeth Boyd, mother

Fowler
Starling & Sarah Ellis 4 Dec 1802; b- Jesse Perkinson min- James
Meacham- 8Dec1802

Fowlkes
Nathaniel & Lucy Winn 1 Jul 1816; b- James Winn con- Richard Winn,
father min- George Petty- 4Jul1816

Fox
Benjamin & Martha Nowell 29 May 1792; b- Young Nowell min- William
Creath- 9Jun1792

Richard & Mary Rainey 22 Mar 1775; b- William Davis
Richard & Nancy Wright 4 Oct 1792; b- Solomon Patillo
Robert & Polly Warren 26 Nov 1801; b- John Warren

Francis
John & Elizabeth Epperson 8 Sep 1794; b- Joseph Townes min- William
    Richards- 1Nov1794

Frasar
John & Lucy Adams 4 Jan 1780; b- William Crutchfield John Frasar
    from Prince Edward County Lucy daughter of Thomas and Lucy Adams

Fraser
Daniel & Martha Fargeson 14 Feb 1805; b- John Fraser

Frazer
Howell & Nancy Hester 13 Oct 1817; b- Chisholm Hester con- Henry
    Hester and Mary Hester, parents
James & Happy Brame 3 Jun 1778; b- John Brame daughter of Richins
    Brame
Walter & Nancy Brame 21 Jan 1811; b- William Brown min- William
    Richards- 31Jan11811

Frazier
Daniel & Martha Dodson 18 Feb 1822; b- Richard C Williams min-
    Charles Ogburn- (Methodist) 21Feb1822

Freeman
Benjamin & Mary Roberts 26 May 1803; b- Stephen Roberts min-
    William Creath-
George & Mary Penn 13 Jul 1839; b- Thomas Penn Jr con- Thomas
    Penn, father min- Benjamin R. Duval-
Gideon & Mary Elam 10 Jan 1803; b- Philemon Hurt min- William
    Richards- 19Jan1803
John & Polly Allen 13 Dec 1796; b- Thomas Allen min- William
    Richards- 22Dec1796
John & Polly Allen 13 Dec 1796; b- Thomas Allen
John & Lucy Hudson 9 Oct 1798; b- Stephen Hudson con- George
    Freeman, father min- William Richards- 11Oct1798
John & Mary Thompson 22 Mar 1842; b- Edward R Chambers con-
    John Freeman
John & Agatha Walker 22 Jul 1806; b- John Johnson

French
William L & Susan A Harper 21 Apr 1851

Fuller
Mersa D & Martha W Cook 19 May 1852

Gabard
John & Betsey Curtis 25 Feb 1792; b- Ely Curtis min- John Loyd-
    28Feb1792

Gafford
William H & Mary E Johnson 21 Dec 1842; b- William A Homes con-
    William Johnson, father

Gaines
David & Alice Wilson 27 Dec 1831; b- Ezekiel Gaines con- Drury
    Wilson, father min- William Steel- (Episcopal)-

Gardner
Lyman B & Selina Yancey 15 Oct 1838; b- Richard Yancey min- John
    B. Smith-

Garey
William G & Martha F Stone 12 Feb 1839; b- Elijah Griffin con-
    Margaret Stone, mother

Garland

Landon C & Mary Cole Burwell 27 Oct 1831; b- Hugh A Garland con- Armistead Burwell, father min- William Steel- (Episcopal)-

Thomas & Polly Lowry 8 Jul 1783; 'Capt' Thomas Garland from Lunenburg County b- John Speed con- John Ragsdale, gdn of Polly

Garner

Conrad & Cisily Ann Johnson 20 Dec 1847; min- S. G. Mason- 21Dec1847 b- Thomas Johnson

James & Lucy Eddins 11 Jan 1790; b- Thomas Dance min- Edward Almand-

James & Mary Smith 10 Nov 1806; b- Hume R Feild min- William Richards- 20Nov1806

Lewis & Barbara Holloway 4 Jun 1827; b- William B Holloway con- Gray Holloway, father

Samuel P & Ophelia P Garner 13 Feb 1847; b- Samuel Vincent Garner min- Robert Burton- 15Feb1847

Vinson & Nancy Jeffries 9 Nov 1807; b- Richard Jeffries min- William Richards- 12Nov1807

William D & Susan M Smith 20 Nov 1844; b- Asa Garner min- John B. Smith-

William & Lucinda Doggett 21 Sep 1825; b- Edward Toone min- William Richards- 22Sep1825

William & Roanna Garner 17 Dec 1840; min- Charles F. Burnley-

Garrett

Jacob & Hannah Pettyford 4 Nov 1802; b- Drury Pettyford min- William Richards- 6Nov1802

Jacob & Hannah Pettyford 4 Nov 1802; b- Drury Pettyford

James & Mary B Henry 9 Nov 1842; b- Thomas S Jones min- Charles F. Burnley-

James & Mary Hudgins 1 Nov 1825; b- John Hundley con- Judith A Hudgins, mother min- James McAden-

James & Elizabeth Towler 17 Mar 1819; b- John Winckler min- James Meacham- 29Mar1819

Thomas & Elizabeth Garrett 27 Jun 1816; b- William Peebles min- James Meacham- 4Jul1816

William & Martha Simmons 15 Dec 1828; widow b- Sanford Bowers min- James Smith- 25Dec1828

Garrott

William & Mary Roberts 9 Nov 1795; b- Thomas Massey min- William Creath-

Gayle

Christopher & Mary J Dortch 19 Dec 1825; b- Zachariah H Jones min- James Smith- 22Dec1825

Christopher & Nancy H Jones 7 Oct 1846; b- Dabney Farrar min- James McAden-

John & Nancy Whitehead 23 Mar 1793; b- William Whitehead John Gayle from Halifax County min- William Creath- 26Mar1793

Matthew & Martha Allen 7 Jan 1822; b- Richard Allen min- Alexander M. Cowan-

Thomas & Elizabeth Coleman 8 Dec 1819; b- James Coleman

Gee

Alfred & Nancy C Edmonson 15 Oct 1821; min- Charles Ogburn- (Methodist)

Benjamin & Frances W Harper 21 Dec 1812; b- Hundley Hudgins con- John Harper, father

George W & Martha J Mason 24 Dec 1839; b- William R Toone con-
Jordan Mason, father min- James Delk-

Henry & Milly T Harper 15 Jun 1818; b- Howell P Harper min- Charles
Ogburn- (Methodist) 25Jun1818

Henry & Anna Wilson 10 Nov 1817; b- Henry Wilson

James Street & Nancy Gee 10 Nov 1798; b- Jones Gee min- William
Creath- 14Nov1798

James & Lucy Bugg 6 Feb 1797; James from Lunenburg County b- John
Bugg con- Nevil Gee, father min- John Loyd- 16Feb1797

Jeremiah & Betsey Andrews 19 Nov 1804; Elizabeth 'Betsey' daughter of
Varney Andrews Sr b- Varney Andrews

Jesse & Mary Susan Smith 21 Dec 1846; b- W P Haskins con- John
Smith, father min- Daniel Petty- 25Dec1846

Jones & Martha Bing 5 Dec 1831; b- Daniel Tucker min- Charles
Ogburn- (Methodist)

Nathan & Sally W Mason 26 Mar 1851; con- Jordan Mason, father min-
S.A. Creath- 26Mar1851

Nevil & Elizabeth Andrews 19 Jul 1797; b- Varney Andrews con- Nevil
Gee Sr, father con- George Andrews, father min- Charles Ogburn-
(Methodist) 20Jul1797

Peter R & Elizabeth H Daly 18 Jan 1808; b- Tignal Abernathy

Peter & Mary A Moore 16 Dec 1833; b- Robert Moore min- James
McAden-

William & Catherine Jones 12 Dec 1787; William from Lunenburg County
b- Varney Andrews

William & Nancy Ragsdale 19 Nov 1827; b- William G Coleman min-
Charles Ogburn- (Methodist) 6Dec1827

George

Beverly & Fanny Wingfield 2 Dec 1853

Jeremiah & Mary Lambert 6 Jun 1797; b- Thomas Lambert

Giles

Edward & Martha Ezell 31 Jan 1801; b- Thomas Nancy

Edward & Angelica Mabry 3 Jan 1810; b- Walter Pennington con-
Stephen Mabry, father

Edward & Angelica Mabry 3 Jan 1810; b- Walter Pennington con-
Stephen Mabry, father

Edward & Fanny M Nance 12 Feb 1818; b- Thomas Cleaton

William & Lucy Standley 17 Dec 1804; b- James Standley

Gill

Metcalf & Sukey Cola 14 Jun 1799; b- John Allgood

Metcalf & Sukey Cole 4 Jun 1799; b- John Allgood

Phillip & Mary Ballard 20 Jan 1817; b- James Jones min- Charles
Ogburn- (Methodist) 4Feb1817

Phillip & Nancy W Simmons 15 Mar 1830; b- Samuel Jones min- James
Smith- 20Mar1830

William & Judith Maynard 8 Dec 1783; b- Nicholas Maynard

Gillespie

Abdias & Nancy Vaden 20 Jul 1818; b- Richard Apperson

Alexander & Martha Harris 29 Jan 1816; b- Robert Harris con- Robert
Harris, father min- William Richards- 18Feb1816

Harper & Mary Harris 29 Nov 1819; b- James Harris con- Robert Harris,
father min- William Richards- 1Dec1819

Hugh W & Jane Harris 4 Jan 1817; b- Thomas Puryear min- William
Richards- 13Feb1817

Martin & Elizabeth Elam 10 Feb 1806; b- Henry H Dedman min-
William Richards- 20Feb1806

Richard O & Mary E Moody 26 Feb 1844; b- William T White

William M & Lucinda G Weatherford 2 Dec 1844; b- George W Gillespie con- James W Dedman, gdn of Lucinda

Glasgow

Richard & Amey Chappell 28 Dec 1785; b- Philip Reekes

William & Lockey Avery 1 Feb 1800; b- Richard Glasgow

William & Lockey Avery 1 Feb 1800; b- Richard Glasgow

Glasscock

James & Elizabeth Ware 11 Sep 1841; b- Richard Glasscock con- Zachariah Glasscock, father con- Bartlett Tillotson, relation not mentioned min- Solomon Apple-

Richard & Elizabeth Vaughan 19 Sep 1840; b- Joseph Yancey

Robert & Nancy Ligon 19 Jan 1835; b- John Newton

Thomas & Elizabeth Worsham 19 Nov 1821; b- Eggleston Overby min- John S. Ravenscroft- (Episcopal)- 28Nov1821

William & Elizabeth Griffin 18 Oct 1820; b- Bartlett Davis con- Keron Griffin, mother min- Pleasant Gold- (Baptist)- 19Oct1820

Zachariah & Mary Worsham 3 Dec 1850; min- Alfred Apple-

Glidewell

John & Anne Whitlow 20 Aug 1785; b- Thomas Whitlow min- John Williams- 30Sep1785

Glover

Daniel & Mary Westmoreland 8 Nov 1806; b- Robert Westmoreland

Godsey

Henry & Minerva Ann Freeman 20 Dec 1830; b- James Y Jones con- Benjamin Freeman, father

Goen

Anderson & Sarah Stewart 24 Dec 1838; b- Osborne Mayo

Frederick & Mary Brandon 29 Dec 1800; 'Gowen?' b- Ephraim Drew min- William Richards- 1Jan1801

Frederick & Susey Chavous 9 Mar 1789; b- Frederick Ivey con- Henry Chavous Sr, father min- Phillip Cox-

Goff

William O & Anne Clarke 3 Dec 1835; b- James W Stanfield con- Elizabeth Clarke, mother, who test. that Anne is under 21 min- William B. Rowzee- 6Dec1835

Gold

Alexander & Sarah Owen 19 Dec 1828; b- Moore Gold con- Thomas Owen, father min- Pleasant Gold- (Baptist)- 25Dec1828

Charles T & Dolly Daniel 28 Nov 1853; con- Avye R Daniel, mother min- John E. Montague- (Granville County, N.C.)- 1Dec1853

Ephraim & Jane Hailey 8 Jul 1799; b- Elijah Griffin con- Thomas Hailey, father

Ephraim & Jane Hailey 8 Jul 1799; b- Elijah Griffin con- Thomas Hailey, father min- William Creath-

Joseph & Martha Averett 3 Jun 1816; b- Charles M Royster

Moore & Elizabeth Owen 12 Oct 1825; b- Parham Owen con- Thomas Owen, father min- Pleasant Gold- (Baptist)- 20Oct1825

Gooch

Joseph & Anne Lockett 27 Jun 1794; widow of Abner Lockett Joseph Gooch from Granville County NC b- William Marshall

Goode

Bennett & Sally L Roffe 13 Jan 1818; b- Thomas Burnett con- Samuel Simmons, gdn of Sally con- Edward Deloney, gdn of Bennett min- Milton Robertson- (Warren County, N.C.) 14Jan1818

Edward & Joice Holmes 13 Dec 1798; daughter of Samuel Holmes b- Richard Cox min- Charles Ogburn- (Methodist) 18Dec1798

George M & Sally G Keen 23 Sep 1822; b- John P Keen

Hillary L M & Sally Boyd 21 Jan 1839; b- Richard Russell con- Richard Boyd, Jr., father

John B & Permelia B Hendrick 2 Jul 1804; b- Amasa Palmer min- James Meacham- 4Jul1804

John & Mary Jones 8 May 1809; b- William G Goode min- William Richards- 11May1809

John & Martha Moore 19 Apr 1790; b- John Wilson Jr

John & Rebecca J Pully 18 Jul 1796; b- John Dortch

John & Rebecca J Pully 18 Jul 1796; b- John Dortch

Joseph & Martha Birtchett 31 Aug 1790; b- Philip Morgan

Mackarness & Mary Eliza Hayes 18 Mar 1822; b- John T Hayes

Richard & Nancy Charlotte Poindexter 8 Oct 1781; b- Phil Poindexter Jr con- Philip Poindexter Sr, father

Samuel H & Mary S Farrar 18 Apr 1846; b- Charles Baskervill con- Robert Farrar, father

Samuel H & Martha S Jones 10 Mar 1840; b- George Rogers con- Robert H Jones, father min- F.H. McGuire- 18Mar1840

Samuel & Mary Armistead Burwell 28 Sep 1786; b- Nicholas Bilbo con- Lewis Burwell, father

Thomas (Jr) & Nancy Boyd - Dec 1812; b- Joel Watkins

Thomas & Mary Anne Knox 15 Jan 1816; 'Dr' Thomas Goode b- John Tabb con- Ann M Knox, mother

William G & Mary Tabb 2 Sep 1798; b- G H Baskervill min- Alexander Hay- (Antrim Glebe, Antrim Parish, Halifax County) 4Sep1798

Goodwin

Beal & Elizabeth Frazer 10 Dec 1798; b- James Brame con- Henry Frazer, father min- William Richards- 29Jan1799

Samuel & Lucy Smith 22 Mar 1793; b- Thomas Hord con- Mary Hord, mother and widow of Drury Smith dec.

Gordon

Obediah & Mary A Lacy 29 Apr 1825; b- Shadrach Lacy min- William Richards- 30Apr1825

William S & Nancy Y Elam 30 Oct 1851; con- Daniel Elam, father min- John E. Montague- (Granville County, N.C.)-

Graham

Samuel L & Judith C Watkins 22 Apr 1836; b- Charles L Read con- James Daniel, father min- P. Calhoun- 26Apr1836

Granger

Moses & Polly Hunt 9 Jan 1812; min- Charles Ogburn- (Methodist)

Grasty

John S & Ella G Pettus 15 Nov 1851; 'Rev' John S Grasty con- Thomas H Pettus, gdn of Ella

Graves

Daniel & Mary Spain 27 Mar 1820; b- Noel Spain con- Jemima Coleman, mother of Mary min- William Richards-

Frederick & Nancy Brandon 29 Dec 1800; b- Ephraim Drew

Howell & Elizabeth Hunt 13 Apr 1801; b- James Hunt

James & Phebe Elam 23 Dec 1818; b- Nathan Graves min- William Richards- 29Dec1818

John T & Mahala B Jeffries - — 18–; b- Luther R Jeffries min- John B. Smith-

John Y & Mary Ann Graves 21 Dec 1840; b- William T White con- James Graves, father of Mary Ann

Nathan & Sally Hudson 23 Dec 1816; b- James Winn min- William Richards- 24Dec1816

Ralph & Elizabeth Graves 9 Feb 1789; b- Henry Walker

Richard Harris & Mary Ellen Allgood 26 Dec 1853; Richard 23, son of Thomas and Mary Graves Mary Ellen 22, daughter of George and Dicey Allgood min- A.F. Davidson-

Thomas & Henrietta Greenwood 4 Mar 1828; b- William Brame min- John B. Smith- 6Mar1828

Thomas & Mary Harris 26 Dec 1808; b- John Stembridge min- William Richards- 27Dec1808

William & Frances Elam 14 Oct 1795; b- Thomas Graves min- William Richards- 20Oct1795

William & Anne Neal - --- ----; min- James Read- (Baptist)

Gray

Thomas A & Louisa L Pool 28 Nov 1837; b- William Hogan

Green

Abraham & Ann Coleman 2 Mar 1799; b- James W Oliver min- William Creath- 14Mar1799

Abraham & Ann Coleman 2 Mar 1799; b- James W Oliver

Anderson & Sarah Stewart 29 Dec 1838; b- Osborne Mayo min- Charles F. Burnley-

Anderson & Sally Stone 15 Nov 1819; b- Charles Yancey con- Frances Stone, mother min- Pleasant Gold- (Baptist)-

Archibald & Judith Taylor 11 Oct 1802; b- Thomas Rowlett min- F S Stewart- 9Nov1802

Francis O D & Elizabeth H Small 20 Sep 1842; b- William S Pully

Grief & Anne M Knox 23 Dec 1817; b- Joel Watkins min- Charles Ogburn- (Methodist) 25Dec1817

Henry & Molly Vaughan 2 Aug 1799; b- Stephen P'Pool

Henry & Molly Vaughan 12 Aug 1799; b- Stephen Pettypool

James & Nancy Yancey 9 Jan 1792; b- William Hendrick min- James Read- (Baptist) 11Jan1792

Lewis & Elizabeth Crawley 8 Sep 1788; b- John Baskervill min- Thomas Scott-

Nathaniel T & Catharine Somerville 17 Nov 1831; b- George T Taylor min- William Steel- (Episcopal)- 24Nov1831

Thomas & Francinia Cox 22 Mar 1792; Thomas from Lunenburg County b- John Cox Jr min- John Williams- 5Apr1792

William W & Mary Poindexter 3 Jan 1803; Mary (Hinton) widow of Phillip Poindexter Jr b- G H Baskervill min- Matthew Dance- 11Jan1803

William & Nancy B Clark 19 Sep 1814; b- Edward H Vaughan

William & Mary Anne Ripley 10 Feb 1821; b- Edward Dodson min- Edward Almand- (Lunenburg County)- 1Mar1821

William & Nancy Stone 2 Dec 1833; b- Eli Stone min- John B. Smith-

Greenwood

Abraham & Phebe Royster 24 Nov 1825; b- William L Willis con- Dabney Collier- relation not cited min- William Richards- 29Nov1825

James & Henrietta Hester 9 Jun 1794; daughter of Abraham Hester, dec. con- James Hester, uncle of Henrietta min- William Richards- 11Junm1794 b- Henry H Dedman

James & Mary Ann Nash 20 Mar 1827; b- Burwell B Moss con- Lily Ann Nash, mother min- Allen D. Metcalf- 24Mar1827

James & Jane Saunders 10 May 1779; b- James Hall

Thomas (Jr) & Martha Williams 8 Oct 1792; b- James T Hayes min- William Creath- 25Oct1792

William M & Jane Catharine Greenwood 29 May 1833; b- E A Holloway con- Robert Greenwood, father of Jane Catharine

Gregory

Abel & Nancy Owen 21 Aug 1815; b- Barnett Gregory con- Thomas Owen, father

Andrew B & Martha Jane Smith 23 Oct 1843; b- William R Doggett con- J B Smith, father min- John B. Smith-

Anthony & Nancy Childress 6 Jan 1814; b- William Childress min- Reuben Pickett- 8Jan1814

Banister & Susanna Griffin 29 Aug 1808; b- Elijah Griffin con- John Gregory

Barnett & Susannah Owen 20 Mar 1815; b- Thomas Owen

Elijah & Nancy Moody 8 Jun 1801; b- Robert Smith min- William Richards- 10Jun1801

Francis R & Nancy Alexander 15 May 1832; 'Dr' Francis R Gregory b- John Young min- James McAden-

James C & Harriett F Coleman 30 Oct 1841; b- Benjamin W Coleman

James C & Elizabeth A Walker 15 Jan 1851; con- Elizabeth A Walker min- George W. Andrews-

James H & Letty C Puryear 14 Dec 1832; b- Andrew G Elam con-' Thomas B Puryear, father min- John B. Smith-

James & Sarah Doggett 14 Sep 1801; b- John Swansbow min- William Richards- 1Oct1801

John C & Julia A Williamson 13 Jul 1837; b- John Clark con- James Williamon, father

John E & Ann E McCargo 21 Oct 1839; b- James McCargo min- John B. Smith-

John S & Frances Coleman Gregory 6 Jan 1836; b- John G Coleman min- John B. Smith-

John W & Eliza C Northington 13 Oct 1834; b- John N Wright

John & Polly Apperson 19 Dec 1786; b- John Apperson con- David Apperson, father min- Henry Lester- (Baptist) 23Dec1786

John & Susannah M Creath 10 Nov 1812; b- James Creath con- William Creath, father min- Richard Dabbs- (Lunenburg County)-

Latteny M & Susan S Jeffries 16 Dec 1839; b- William R Jeffries con- Richard Jeffries, father min- John B. Smith-

Nathaniel & Mary Ann Beckley - Jan 1787; b- Edward L Tabb

Richard C (Sr) & Eliza T Bailey 12 Dec 1830; b- Joseph S Gregory min- James Smith-

Robert S & Letty Couch 14 Aug 1809; b- John Couch min- William Richards- 26Aug1809

Robert S & Letty Couch 14 Aug 1809; b- John Couch

Robert T & Elloisa R Jeffress 13 Jun 1853; con- James H Jeffress, father min- Robert Burton- 15Jun1853

Roger (Jr) & Elizabeth Speed 21 Oct 1791; b- Sherwood Bugg

Thomas S & Rebecca S Doggett 19 Dec 1827; b- Francis Barnes min- William Richards- 28Dec1827

West & Fanny Gregory 28 Aug 1811; b- Francis Gregory min- Charles Ogburn- (Methodist) 29Aug1811

William D & Lucy S Haskins 8 Jul 1852; con- C T Haskins, father min- Robert Burton-

William O & Mary B Alexander 6 Oct 1826; b- W O Goode con- Nathaniel Alexander, gdn of Mary min- John B. Smith- 12Oct1826

Gresham

Gregory & Susanna Smith 23 Jul 1806; b- Thomas Smith con- William Smith, father con- Asa Gresham Sr, father

Griffin

Byrd & Ann Northington 2 Oct 1820; b- John S Northington con- Nathan Northington, father min- Pleasant Gold- (Baptist)- 4Oct1820

Craddock & Elizabeth Norment 10 Dec 1811; min- William Richards-

Elias & Eliza Gold 19 Dec 1839; b- Robert Rowlett con- E Kennon, gdn of Eliza min- Charles F. Burnley-

Elisha & Sally Stone 6 Dec 1830; b- Jordan Stone min- John B. Smith-

George F & Mary D Watson 10 Nov 1840; b- Boswell T Crute con- Littleberry Watson, father

Gold & Mary Puryear 17 Nov 1823; b- Thomas B Puryear min- William Richards- 27Nov1823

James & Polly Tindal 14 Dec 1807; b- Overton Wiles

John & Tabitha Farrar 22 Dec 1815; b- John Winckler min- James Meacham- 25Dec1815

John & Elizabeth Yancey 11 Aug 1794; b- Robert Williamson

Lewis & Nancy Yancey 25 May 1817; b- John B Yancey min- Reuben Pickett- 5Jun1817

Robert & Rebecca Jones 17 Sep 1821; b- Benjamin Jones min- Pleasant Gold- (Baptist)- 20Sep1821

William & Edna Blanks 26 Sep 1803; b- Joseph Blanks

William & Ann O Farrar 16 Oct 1820; b- John J Farrar con- John Farrar Sr, father

Zachariah & Mary Tucker 13 Aug 1849; b- W H Somervill con- William Tucker, father

Zephanier & Nancy Overby 15 Feb 1830; b- Alexander Overby min- Pleasant Gold- (Baptist)- 18Feb1830

Griffith

John & Rainey Rottenbury 14 Dec 1790; b- John Lambert con- John Griffith Sr, father min- John King- 16Dec1790

Grigg

Arthur A & Susan E Morton 18 Oct 1843; b- Joseph Morton con- William H Morton, father

Burwell & Labia Elam 8 Oct 1787; b- Alexander Elam min- John Williams-

Drury & Anna Chavous 13 Apr 1807; b- Saunders Harris

Jesse & Martha Elam 11 Dec 1786; b- James Elam

Lewis & Patsy Malone 30 Mar 1808; b- Thomas Cleaton

Randolph & Elizabeth Jordan 13 Dec 1805; b- Samuel Jordan con- Mary Jordan, mother

William & Mary M Jordan 8 Dec 1800; b- John Matthews min- James Meacham- 11Dec1800

Grimes

James & Ann Willis 3 Jul 1832; b- Alexander Gillespie

Grymes

Benjamin & Ann Nicholas 22 Dec 1778; b- John Nicholas

Guy

Daniel & Nancy Erby 26 Feb 1806; b- William Chandler

George & Nancy Drew 11 Dec 1799; b- William Chandler min- Ebenezer McGowan- 12Dec1799

George & Nancy Drew 11 Dec 1799; b- William Chandler

Spencer & Sally Barnard 26 Nov 1815; b- Thomas Barnard con- Thomas Barnard, father

Willis & Sarah Garner 20 Jul 1840; b- Edward Mayo

Willis & Lucinda Guy 21 Dec 1815; b- Spencer Guy con- John Guy, father

Gwaltney

John & Lucy Bowen 12 Feb 1798; b- Micajah Gwaltney min- Charles Ogburn- (Methodist)

John & Mary A Sullivan 19 Oct 1840; b- John B Sullivan

John & Wilhelmina Underwood 4 Dec 1806; b- William Gwaltney min- Matthew Dance- 5Dec1806

Peterson & Sarah G Tucker 28 Jul 1846; b- Robert D Sullivan

William T & Sarah N Sullivan 13 Dec 1841; b- Robert D Sullivan

William & Agness Colley 23 May 1801; b- James Brown

Hagerman

Alex S & Mariah V Burnett 17 Dec 1838; b- George J Dabbs

Hagood

John & Jane E Crowder 22 Dec 1841; b- William W Parks con- W T Crowder, father min- John B. Smith-

Haile

Dudley & Patsy Carter 12 Jan 1795; b- William Willis

Dudley & Susanna Smith 10 Feb 1794; b- Harrison Winn

Dudley & Mary Willis - Dec 1781; b- Thomas Haile

Leman & Elizabeth Avory 19 Jun 1802; 'Avery?' b- Elijah Avory min- William Creath-

Thomas & Nancy Blacketter 25 Sep 1805; b- Harwood Rudd

Thomas & Sally Rudd 17 Dec 1804; b- Harwood Rudd min- William Richards- 19Dec1804

Hailey

David & Lucy Crow 3 Dec 1804; b- Jachonias Towler

Isaac & Mary Wallace 27 Nov 1829; b- Hugh Wallace, father

Meredith & Dorothy L Andrews 8 Mar 1820; b- William Hodges con- Varney Andrews, father

Phillip & Sarah A R Moore 18 May 1833; b- John Elliott con- George W Moore, gdn of Sarah min- John B. Smith-

Richard & Nancy Wilson 26 Jan 1805; b- John E Harris min- William Creath-

Thomas & Martha Tinsley 22 Oct 1823; b- Joseph Watkins min- Pleasant Gold- (Baptist)-

Hailstock

James & Susan Cowen 15 Sep 1851

Haley

David & Elizabeth Brooks 8 Dec 1783; b- Elijah Graves

John & Dycey Blanks 8 Jul 1799; b- Elijah Griffin con- Joseph Blanks, father

Thomas & Elizabeth Gold 9 Jun 1794; b- Daniel Gold Jr Elizabeth widow of Daniel Gold Sr min- James Read- (Baptist) 12Jun1794

Hall

Amos & Margaret Collier 21 Sep 1818; b- Berryman Ferguson, gdn of Margaret, who also gives consent

Benjamin B & Alice Morris 3 Apr 1829; b- William J Morris

Miles T & Mary F Wilkerson 30 Apr 1839; b- Thomas W Owen con- Washington Wilkerson, father min- John B. Smith-

Miles & Nancy Cox 8 Sep 1806; b- John Cox min- William Richards- 18Sep1806

Miles & Susanna Marshall 4 May 1781; b- Richard Winn con- James Hall, father con- Dancy McGraw, guardian of Susanna

Richard Carter & Elizabeth Mayes 11 Aug 1794; b- John Hall con- John Mayes, father

Richard F & Frances C Gregory 15 Dec 1853; con- Mary S Gregory, mother min- F.N. Whaley-

William & Elizabeth Bradley 6 Dec 1802; b- John Bradley

Zachariah & Sophia Malone 4 Dec 1792; b- Thomas Roberts min- John Loyd- 5Dec1792

Hamblin

John & Milly Daniel 13 Jul 1807; b- Stephen Stone con- Martin Daniel, father

Thomas & Jean Childress 10 Nov 1806; b- Balaam Ezell

Hamilton

Andrew & Elizabeth Skinner 14 Feb 1782; b- Josiah Daly Andrew from Prince George County

Baxter & Prissey Bailey 10 Jan 1798; b- Robert Roberts min- William Creath-

Charles E & Jane C Coleman 16 Jul 1840; b- E A Coleman con- E A Coleman, gdn for his sister min- F.H. McGuire- 21Jul1840

Charles E & Sally A Watkins 25 Feb 1853; min- J.W. Chesley- 2Mar1853

John B & Frances Hatchell - --- 1843; b- James L Hatchell (bond damaged)

John & Polly Hatsell 12 Jan 1795; b- Stephen Hatsell

Joseph & Sarah Cox 16 May 1791; b- Edward Hatsell

Patrick & Mary Eston Baskervill 24 Dec 1812; b- Joel Watkins min- Charles Ogburn- (Methodist)

Robert A & Sarah C Alexander 10 Dec 1844; b- George Tarry con- Nathaniel Alexander, father

Walter & Elizabeth Hatsell 24 Aug 1785; b- Mary Hatsell

William & Nancy Christopher 14 Jan 1799; b- William Christopher

Hamlett

William & Mary Brooke 27 Oct 1789; b- Gabriel Carleton William from Halifax County

Hamlin

Charles & Susanna Owen 24 Apr 1785; min- Henry Lester- (Baptist)

William B & Christian Burwell 18 Dec 1794; b- Daniel Mayes con- Mary Hamlin, mother con- Lewis Burwell, father Daniel Mayes from Dinwiddie County

Hamme

Frederick & Elizabeth D Butler 12 Mar 1804; b- John White min- Matthew Dance- 22Mar1804

Hammond

Frederick & Polly Stewart 14 Aug 1807; b- Frederick Dyson min- William Richards- 4Sep1807

Hamner

George B (Jr) & Eliza Redd 1 Sep 1828; b- Samuel Young min- Allen D. Metcalf- 5Sep1828

George B & Anne Edmundson 16 Dec 1793; b- Banister Edmundson con- Samuel Edmundson, father min- William Creath- 19Dec1793

John & Mary Whoberry 22 Dec 1790; b- John Whoberry

Hanbury

William C & Harriet N Stanley 10 Apr 1843; b- R B Noblin

Hancock

David M & Gabriella W Crute 15 Oct 1849; b- Stephen C Lockett min- William Hamersley- 24Oct1849

Hanserd

Archer W & Elizabeth H Ryland 21 Oct 1828; b- Thomas Ryland min- James Smith-

Richard (Jr) & Lilly Johnson 24 Dec 1811; b- William G Pettus

Richard & Sarah Ferguson 18 Jun 1801; b- John Dortch min- James Meacham-

Richard & Sarah Speed 12 Dec 1774; b- Robert Ballard
Hardie
 Cephas & Elizabeth Jane Brame 17 Dec 1832; b- John R Buford con-
   Thomas Brame Sr, father
 John H & Mary R Moss 14 May 1816; b- William Moss con- William
   Moss, gdn of Mary, who was daughter of Roy Moss, dec. min- James
   Meacham- 17May1816
Hardin
 Jeremiah & Lucy Ann Royster 19 Dec 1844; b- Giles H Crowder con-
   Clark Royster, father
Hardy
 James W & Harriett G Jones 25 Jun 1838; b- James R Thomas
 James & Mary Wilson 12 Jan 1801; b- John Boswell
 Miles & Elizabeth E W Holmes 7 Dec 1846; b- William T M Holmes
   con- Isaac Holmes, father min- James McAden- 12Dec1846
 William T & Ann Hester 6 Dec 1820; b- William S Willis con- Nathaniel
   Hester, father min- William Richards- 7Dec1820
Hargrove
 Burnett & Biddy Lambert 23 Jan 1788; b- Matthew Smith
 Hartwell W & Jane W Sims 10 Nov 1837; b- Robert Chapman con-
   Stephen and Mary Hendrick, grandparents of Jane
 James & Polly Wyatt Jackson 6 Sep 1813; b- Mark L Jackson minister's
   name missing- 8Sep1813
 James & Nancy Thomas 14 Dec 1797; b- John Thomas
Harper
 Benjamin J & Elizabeth E Harper 11 Jun 1821; b- John P Harper con-
   Martha Harper, mother min- Thomas Adams- (Lunenburg Co.)-
   13Jun1821
 Charles O & Susan Ann Pettus 19 Jul 1841; b- Richard C Puryear
 Howell P & Lucy H Ogburn 16 Jan 1813; b- Charles Ogburn, father
 John P & Elizabeth R Tanner 10 Nov 1832; b- Robert Tanner min-
   James McAden-
 John Peterson & Elizabeth Ann Jeffries 21 Sep 1821; con- Isaac Waller
 John & Martha Pennington 7 Dec 1785; b- John George Pennington
   con- John Harper Sr, father
 Thomas & Lucy Gillam Booth 22 Jan 1791; b- Thomas Booth Thomas
   Harper from Dinwiddie County min- Henry Ogburn- 10Feb1791
 Wyatt & Mary M Pennington 29 Jul 1799; b- William Pennington min-
   John Neblett- 30Jul1799
Harris
 Allen & Susanna Harris 1 Mar 1800; b- James Reamy con- Reuben
   Harris, father min- William Richards- 4Mar1800
 Benjamin H & Martha V Hudson 24 Nov 1835; b- Dabney A Hudson
   con- Robert W Hudson, father
 Drury & Patsy Butler 10 Oct 1803; b- Charles Carter con- John Butler
   Sr, father
 George A & Ann Eliza R Moore 28 Aug 1850; con- Thomas Moore,
   father min- William V. Wilson-
 Henry & Polly Roper 20 Oct 1809; b- Wilson Harris
 Henry & Elizabeth Stewart 30 Jul 1849; b- John Wilson min- John
   Bayley-
 Ivey & Judith Allgood - Dec 1809; b- John Allgood
 James R & Rebecca Crowder 25 Nov 1831; b- Henry Simmons min-
   Charles Ogburn- (Methodist) 15Dec1831
 James & Eliza Brummell 29 Nov 1819; b- Harper Gillespie min- William
   Richards- 9Dec1819

James & Virginia Ann Dedman 10 Nov 1851; con- James W Dedman, father

James & Alice E Goode 31 Aug 1826; b- Samuel H Goode, who also test that Alice will be 21 next February (Note: James Harris from Nottowat Co) con- Mary A Goode, mother min- John B. Smith- 14Sep1826

James & Rebecca Nolley 20 Dec 1806; b- Nevison Nolley

Jeremiah & Lydia Chavous 13 Nov 1797; b- James Chavous min- Matthew L. Easter- 27Nov1797

John R & Nancy Crutchfield 12 Oct 1835; b- Benjamin H Harris

John & Sarah Berry 25 Dec 1786; b- George Hudson

John & Martha Crutchfield 19 Dec 1803; b- William Crutchfield

John & Rittah Stewart 27 Dec 1802; b- Jeremiah Harris

John & Polly B Wilson 17 Apr 1837; b- Benjamin H Harris min- James McAden-

Mastin & Patsy Reamey 14 Dec 1807; b- William Harris min- William Richards- 18Dec1807

Reuben T & Sally Crutchfield 21 Sep 1835; b- Peter Crutchfield

Reuben & Prudence Harris 15 Nov 1830; b- James Harris min- John B. Smith-

Reuben & Sarah Matthews 20 Dec 1808; b- John Cook

Richard W & Harriet Jane Pettus 5 Sep 1825; Richard W Harris from Halifax Co, Va b- Richard E Walker con- John Pettus, father min- James Smith- 6Sep1825

Robert B & Martha Reekes 1 Jan 1836; daughter of Capt. Thomas Reekes b- Richard C Puryear min- John B. Smith-

Robert & Mary White 10 Jan 1791; b- William White min- James Read- (Baptist)

Samuel T & Rebecca A Toone 11 Dec 1849; b- John R Toone con- Lewis Toone, father

Sherwood & Joannah Ragsdale 25 Oct 1800; b- Robert Ragsdale min- William Richards- 1Nov1800

Silas H & Elizabeth Kennon 16 Jan 1832; 'Dr' Silas H Harris b- James B Maclin con- E Kennon, father min- William Steel- (Episcopal)- 17Jan1832

Thomas & Elizabeth Graves 28 Dec 1795; b- Peter Elam min- Edward Almand- 3Jan1796

Thomas & Elizabeth Graves 18 Dec 1841; b- Asa Garner con- Thomas Graves, father min- Charles F. Burnley-

Thomas & Elizabeth Jane Stewart 28 Jan 1841; b- Pettus Stewart

Washington & Mary Mills 23 Jun 1847; b- Henry Walden

William (Jr) & Ellen Cousen 5 Dec 1844; b- William Harris Sr con- Henry Cousen, grandfather

William A & Martha E A Crenshaw 3 Dec 1838; b- John P Crenshaw min- Benjamin R. Duval-

William L & Maria Speed 9 Dec 1843; b- Benjamin W Leigh

William W & Clary Hudson 14 Jun 1802; b- William Hudson min- William Richards-

William & Mary I Elam 27 Sep 1799; b- Daniel Wilson con- Barklet Elam, father

William & Anna Reamy 12 Nov 1804; b- Abraham Reamy con- James Reamy, father min- Edward Almand- 20Dec1804

Wilson & Lucy H Harper 3 Jan 1845; b- Charles H Ogburn min- James McAden-

Harrison

Greenwood & Susannah Mullins 11 Feb 1799; b- Edward Holloway min- William Richards- 14Mar1799

James & Tabitha Webb 5 Dec 1801; b- Abdias P Webb con- E Webb, father min- James Meacham- 8Dec1801

John & Betsy Lelilah Parham 22 Mar 1797; b- William Kirks John Harrison from Northampton County NC min- Edward Dromgoole- 27Mar1792

Robert & Martha Baugh 19 Jan 1787; b- William Baugh Martha daughter of James and Agnes Baugh

Thomas & Elizabeth Neal 9 Sep 1811; b- Ichabod Neal

William & Margaret Wade 16 Nov 1790; b- Absolom Hasting

Harwell

James M & Sarah C Tanner 3 Jan 1820; b- John B Harwell con- Martha Tanner

Richard H & Elvira A Arnold 19 Dec 1831; b- William T Ezell min- James McAden-

Richard H & Angelina W Harper 2 Apr 1834; b- Benjamin J Walker con- Charles Ogburn, gdn of Angelina min- James McAden-

Samuel & Marina Cook 18 Jan 1825; b- Thomas B Creath con- Sarah Cook, mother

Samuel & Martha Harwell 18 Dec 1804; b- William Harwell con- James Harwell

Harwood

John W & Kitty R Jeffries 23 Nov 1820; min- William Richards-

Haskins

Christopher (Jr) & Nancy N Young 28 Nov 1815; b- John H Hardie con- M Jones, gdn of Nancy min- James Meacham- 12Dec1815

Creed T & Prudence Sandys 31 Jul 1828; min- William Richards-

Edward & Martha M Norment 12 Sep 1825; b- C H Pettus min- William Richards- 19Sep1825

George M & Jane George 23 Nov 1845; b- Beverly George

James E & Minerva Overby 9 Nov 1846; b- E A Williams con- Robert Y Overby, father

William Z & Lucy Ann Bugg 27 Feb 1843; b- E A Williams con- Rebecca P Bugg, mother

William & Sally S Smith 29 May 1817; b- Richard Russell con- Daniel Smith, father min- William Richards- 4Jun1817

Hastin

Absolom & Patsy Wade 12 Jan 1789; b- John Wagstaff min- Edward Almand- 22Jan1789

Harrison & Martha Elam 8 Nov 1815; b- Charles Taylor con- Eli Elam, father

Henry & Fanny W Graves 19 Jun 1799; b- Thomas Graves min- William Richards- 20Jun1799

John & Nancy Elam 8 Oct 1787; b- Absolom Hastin

Richard H & Harriett B McCutcheon 21 Jun 1830; b- John Y Richards min- John B. Smith-

Hastings

Clayton & Martha Gwaltney 17 Dec 1825; b- John Gwaltney min- Charles Ogburn- (Methodist) 20Dec1825

Hatchell

Benjamin & Betsy Thomason 17 Jul 1815; b- Thomas Taylor

James & Mary Martin 1 Jun 1819; b- Archer Cox con- Betsy Martin, mother min- James Meacham- 10Jun1819

Obey & Nancy Carpenter 3 Feb 1818; widow b- Archibald Cox min-
James Meacham- 4Feb1818

Stephen & Nancy Roberts 12 Nov 1792; b- William Nanney min- John
Loyd- 15Nov1792

Hatcher

Benjamin D & Martha G Goode 15 Dec 1852; min- John A. Dell-

Benjamin D & Mary J Morton 20 Mar 1843; b- Reuben A Puryear con-
Anderson C Morton, father min- Charles F. Burnley- 22Mar1843

Benjamin David & Martha T Norment 6 Dec 1836; b- C H Pettus con-
Edward Haskins, gdn of Martha min- Joseph S. Baker- 8Dec1836

Daniel B & Lucy R Blanks 10 Feb 1841; b- Thomas L Jones con- Allen
Blanks, gdn of Lucy min- Charles F. Burnley-

Hatsel

Stephen & Nancy J Patrick 22 Sep 1817; b- Hughberry Nanney

Hatsell

Edward & Sarah Cox 16 Mar 1804; b- Stephen Hatsell

John & Prudence Halton 17 Feb 1786; b- William Baskervill

John & Aggy Smith 5 Apr 1786; b- John Lollis

Hawkins

Claiborne & Margaret Barry 2 May 1789; b- Frederick Andrews min-
Thomas Scott-

Green & Mounring Carroll 27 Dec 1802; b- Mark L Jackson

James & Elizabeth J Johnson 13 Jan 1834; b- David B Johnson con-
Thomas Johnson, father

John D & Jane A Boyd 11 Apr 1803; b- Richard Boyd min- John
Cameron-

John & Elizabeth Goode 19 Dec 1785; b- Robert Goode con- Edward
Goode, father

Jonathon & Lucy King 7 Aug 1811; b- John Ingram

Joseph & Mary F Boyd 3 Apr 1811; Joseph from Warren Co., NC b-
James Boyd

Lewis & Missouri Ann Ivey 26 Apr 1849; b- William Mitchell min-
William A. Smith-

Phil & Lucy Davis 22 Aug 1775; daughter of William Davis Phil from
Bute County NC b- William Davis

Thomas P & Mary Boyd 3 Nov 1834; b- Alfred Boyd min- William Steel-
(Episcopal)- 4Nov1834

Uriah & Lucy Green Jones 7 Mar 1798; b- William Jones min- Ebenezer
McGowan-

William & Nancy Boyd 12 Dec 1803; b- Richard Boyd min- John
Cameron-

Hawks

Joseph & Phoebe Westbrook 13 May 1799; b- Thomas Westbrook min-
Charles Ogburn- (Methodist)

Hawthorne

John & Eliza A Harper 7 Jan 1833; b- Henry W Harper

Hayes

Archer & Hannah F Dortch 19 Sep 1842; b- Isaac H Jones con- Alex
Dortch, father

Durmont & Lucy Ann Coleman 19 Sep 1845; b- William J Carter con-
William T Coleman, father

George F & Catharine Roffe 28 Nov 1850; con- Jesse Roffe, father

Henry C & Ann E Walker 16 May 1838; b- Archer Hayes con- Eliza
Walker, mother min- Charles F. Burnley- 18May1838

Hyram & Phebe Hill 8 Aug 1791; n- Nicholas Jeter min- John Williams-

James T & Lucy Crowder 31 Oct 1821; b- John T Hayes min- John S. Ravenscroft- (Episcopal)- 1Nov1821

James T & Jane Johnson 21 Feb 1814; b- Caleb Johnson, father, who also gives consent

James T & Susanna Walker 15 Jul 1816; b- Lewis Green

James Toy & Mary Puryear 23 Dec 1791; b- Reuben Puryear min- William Creath- 29Dec1791

James & Patsy Green 22 Mar 1806; b- James T Hayes con- William Wills Green, father min- James Meacham- 25Mar1806

John (Jr) & Catey Decker 19 Aug 1794; b- William Decker

John T & Elizabeth Brame 23 Jan 1822; b- Melchizedeck Brame min- William Richards- 24Jan1822

Richard H & Susan E Coleman 4 Apr 1849; b- William T Coleman

Hayles

John & Mary Sullivant 26 May 1783; b- William Baskervill

Haynes

George & Sarah Gregory 9 Feb 1795; b- Joseph Gregory George from Charlotte County

Hazelwood

Daniel C & Caroline L Jones 4 Jan 1832; b- James Oslin min- James McAden-

Daniel & Susanna Gresham 15 Jan 1821; b- Daniel Daly min- Charles Ogburn- (Methodist) 17Jan1821

Green & Mary Chavous 21 Jul 1829; b- Randolph Chavous min- James Smith-

Hazlewood

Daniel & Lucy Waller 2 Aug 1803; b- John Waller min- William Creath-

Hearn

John & Elizabeth Hill Whitby 18 Dec 1793; b- Nathaniel Chambers con- Mary Crowder, mother of Elizabeth min- John Loyd- 19Dec1793

Hedderly

Thomas M & Ann M Huddleston 19 Nov 1832; b- John J Ewing

Heggie

John & Mary Ann Hunt 29 Aug 1807; b- Absolom Hunt con- James Hunt, father

Helm

William & Roanna Evans 22 Jul 1830; b- Benjamin Evans min- James Smith-

Hendrick

Archibald & Susan J Moss 11 May 1847; b- Thomas R Moss

John & Edith King 25 Oct 1800; b- Henry King

Murray (Jr) & Mary Jane Carter 15 Dec 1851; con- Robert A Carter, father min- James A. Duncan- 24Dec1851

Thomas & Sally Wall 12 Dec 1803; b- Charles Hamblin

William T & Augusta E Hendrick 27 Jul 1853; con- Murray Hendrick, father min- James S. Kennedy- 27Jul1853

William & Susannah Crews 8 Mar 1772; b- John Atkinson

William & Mary Ann Leckie 19 Oct 1836; b- Samuel T Jones min- William Compton-

William & Nancy Russell 24 Nov 1817; min- James Meacham-

William & Eleanor D Taylor 4 Dec 1830; b- Samuel Hester con- George Taylor, father min- John B. Smith-

William & Rebecca Wall 11 Feb 1805; b- Howell Graves

Hepbourne

Alexander M & Charity A Swepson 6 Sep 1844; b- John S Feild

Hepburn

William & Mary Watte McHarg 12 Sep 1785; b- George Tarry

Hester

Abner & Sarah Royster 16 Apr 1816; b- James Hester min- William Richards- 18Apr1816

Francis B & Mary E Gordon 12 Dec 1853; con- Allen Gordon, father min- John E. Montague- (Granville County, N.C.)- 24Dec1853

Francis & Ann Greenwood 13 Dec 1779; b- James Hester con- Thomas Greenwood, father

Harrison & Martha Elam 8 Nov 1815; min- Ezekiel Blanch-

Henry & Mary Blanks 26 Nov 1827; b- John Blanks con- James Blanks, father min- Pleasant Gold- (Baptist)- 29Nov1827

Henry & Amelia Hester 30 Nov 1826; b- William Townes min- Allen D. Metcalf- 3Dec1826

James & Elizabeth Hix 3 Sep 1767; b- Amos Hix

James & Polly Keeton 20 Jul 1818; b- Richard C Williams

Nathan & Mary McCutcheon 7 Nov 1821; b- Charles McCutcheon min- William Richards- 15Nov1821

Nathan & Nancy Overton 14 Dec 1812; b- Christopher Overton con- J B Clausel, gdn of Nancy, who test she is under 21 min- Edward Almand- (Lunenburg County)- 17Dec1812

Robert & Mary Crowder 29 Jul 1795; b- Robert Hester Sr min- William Richards- 1Aug1795

Robert & Lucy Culbreath 12 Jan 1807; b- John Farrar

Robert & Susannah Garner 11 Jan 1802; b- Richard Swepson

Robert & Nancy Lockett 13 Feb 1792; b- John Wilson min- James Read- (Baptist) 28Feb1792

Samuel & Eliza S Greenwood 12 Nov 1821; b- W A Maddox con- Robert Greenwood, father

Samuel & Elizabeth Greenwood 8 Nov 1784; b- Caleb Johnston con- Thomas Greenwood, father

Hethcock

Whittemore & Henrietta Ladd 26 Nov 1808; b- James Drumwright

Hewes

John H & Margarett Daniel 17 Dec 1849; b- Thomas Daniel con- A R Daniel, father

Hicks

Benjamin & Lucy Brooking 15 Jun 1786; b- William Lucas Benjamin from Chesterfield County SC

Charles P & Margarett Joyce 4 Dec 1840; b- R B Baptist min- James McAden-

Daniel & Frances Delony 18 Sep 1788; b- William Delony daughter of Henry Delony

David & Nancy Thompson 23 Jan 1795; b- George Thompson min- John Loyd- 31Jan1795

Hastin & Martha Crenshaw 1 Jun 1813; b- Wylie Crowder

Isaac & Frances Lucas 10 Mar 1807; b- John R Lucas

Isaac & Lucy T Mason 28 Oct 1815; b- Christopher Haskins Jr

Jacob & Jincy Gordon 31 Oct 1794; b- Arthur F Winfield min- John Loyd- 6Nov1794

John & Gracey Coleman 22 Jun 1789; b- Pettus Phillips Grace daughter of Cluverius Coleman min- Thomas Scott-

Joseph M & Mary E Yancey 22 Feb 1851; con- James Yancey min- William V. Wilson- 27Feb1851

William A & Mary E Coleman 11 Sep 1834; b- William G Coleman con- William G Coleman, gdn of Mary, daughter of Thomas Coleman, dec.

Hightower

Benjamin B & Mary E Roffe 21 Nov 1842; b- Ephraim A Drumwright con- Jesse Roffe, father min- James McAden-

Devereaux & Susanna Hutcheson 18 Aug 1800; b- Joseph Hutcheson con- Charles Hutcheson, father min- William Creath-

John S & Susan Thompson 8 Dec 1815; b- William R B Clements con- Charles Thompson, father min- Charles Ogburn- (Methodist)

Stephen & Tabitha Baugh 16 Jul 1808; b- Richard Baugh daughter of James and Agnes Baugh

William H & Elizabeth J Crutchfield 29 Dec 1842; b- James M Crutchfield con- Samuel Crutchfield, father min- James McAden-

Hill

Dabney P & Isabella Burnett 18 Jan 1828; b- Mark A Burnett min- James Smith- 24Jan1828

Edward & Jemima Blankenship 28 Jul 1802; b- John Webb

John & Elizabeth Marshall 20 Feb 1799; b- John Dortch con- Robert Marshall, father min- William Richards- 27Feb1799

Richard & Sally Burnett 17 Jul 1806; b- Jesse Burnett min- Thomas Hardie- 11Aug1806

Richard & Nancy Phillips 29 Jan 1800; b- William Brown con- Dabney Phillips Sr, father

Robert & Sally Valentine 15 Jan 1821; b- Randolph Chavous min- Matthew Dance- (Lunenburg County)- 30Jan1821

Thomas & Fanny R Baptist 31 Oct 1811; b- Edward Baptist con- John G Baptist, gdn of Fanny min- William Richards- 7Nov1811

William W & Mary E Nelson 23 Jan 1851; con- Edward A Nelson, father min- Alfred Apple-

William & Ann Freeman Wagstaff 8 Jun 1789; b- Britain Wagstaff min- John Williams- 17Jun1789

Hilton

William & Jincy Hutt 10 Feb 1800; b- Thomas Hutt min- William Creath-

Hines

Henry W & Mary V Hubbard 24 Nov 1840; b- Walter P Hite con- Ralph Hubbard, father min- James McAden-

Hinton

Benjamin I & Elvira Greenwood 9 Dec 1826; b- Henry Hester con- Robert Greenwood, father min- Allen D. Metcalf- 11Dec1826

Erasmus G & Martha Ann Hester 24 Aug 1830; b- Benjamin J Hinton con- Robert Hester, father min- William Steel- (Episcopal)-

Presley L & Minerva J Davis 27 Jun 1836; b- Arthur K Davis con- Ann Davis, gdn of Minerva min- William B. Rowzee-

Presley & Elizabeth Worsham 10 Jan 1801; b- William Blanton min- James Meacham- 14Jan1801

Hite

Bedford & Amanda Chandler 26 Nov 1838; b- John Talley con- Daniel C Chandler, father

Edmund M & Ann E Moore 28 Aug 1840; b- William P Drumwright con- E I Moore, mother min- James McAden-

James L & Martha H Moore 30 Mar 1844; b- William B McAden con- E P Moore, father min- James McAden-

John & Wincy Davis 10 Jan 1853; con- John O Davis, father

Thomas & Elizabeth Davis 2 Oct 1843; b- Edward Davis con- John O Davis, father min- Thomas King- (Halifax County)-

Vincent & Nancy Wilborn 14 Dec 1807; b- Thomas Wilborn con- John Wilborn, father

Walter W & Lucy A Simmons 2 Dec 1843; b- William P Drumwright con- Paschall Bracey, gdn of Lucy min- James McAden-

William L & Eliza H Gayle 15 Nov 1847; b- Christopher Gayle

Hix

Daniel & Susannah Jeffries 12 Apr 1784; b- John Jeffries

Jesse & Sarah Bugg 26 Nov 1774; daughter of Samuel Bugg Sr and Martha Bugg b- Samuel Bugg

Nathaniel & Frances Burton 9 Oct 1783; Nathaniel from Georgia daughter of Samuel Bugg Sr and Martha Bugg v- Sherwood Bugg

Sherwood & Ann Gordon 18 Jan 1782; b- Walter Leigh

Thomas & Elizabeth Bevill 13 Dec 1796; b- Francis Neal min- William Creath-

Hodge

John & Jane Thornton 24 Oct 1787; b- Hugh B Nanney

Hogan

William G & Rebecca T Jackson 19 Dec 1825; b- Waddy J Jackson min- James Smith- 29Dec1825

William & Mary T Poole 5 Jan 1824; b- Isaac Watson min- Stephen Jones- (Lynchburg, Va.)- 12Feb1824

Holcomb

Allen H & Eliza J Royster 28 Apr 1831; b- Edward B Davis con- Clark Royster, faqther

Philemon & Lucy Anderson 13 Dec 1784; daughter of Thomas & Sarah Anderson Philemon from Prince Edward County b- Charles Lewis

Holloway

Anderson & Susanna Gillespie 1 Jul 1799; b- John Dortch min- William Richards- 2Jul1799

David & Mary Wright 21 Dec 1799; b- John Holmes min- Ebenezer McGowan- 24Dec1799

Edward & Nancy Farrar 8 Nov 1806; b- Francis Ballard min- James Meacham- 11Nov1806

Edward & Mary Jeter 3 May 1811; b- Charles Baskervill min- James Meacham-

George & Anne Hall 24 Oct 1774; b- William Holloway con- James Hall, father

Gray & Maryanna Baker 24 Jan 1801; b- William Holloway

John & Frances Crowder 12 Jan 1795; b- Godfrey Crowder min- William Richards- 22Jan1795

John & Ann Sterling 17 Dec 1793; b- Richard Hanserd con- William Starling, father

Samuel H & Frances Holloway 25 Oct 1844; b- William Holloway min- Alfred Apple-

Samuel Henry & Martha A Walker 7 Dec 1853; con- Edward Walker, father min- James McAden-

William & Mary A C Baird 5 Feb 1836; b- Archer W Hanserd con- Charles W Baird, father

William & Lettice H Dodson 9 Aug 1825; b- Christopher W Baird con- Edward Dodson, father min- James Smith- 11Aug1825

William & Elizabeth C Jeffries 20 Jan 1840; b- James M Crowder min- John B. Smith-

Holmes

Benjamin H & Elizabeth Dortch 24 Dec 1827; b- J H Jones con- Zachariah H Jones, gdn of Elizabeth, daughter of David Dortch, dec. min- James Smith- 27Dec1827

David & Elizabeth Clark 15 Jan 1790; b- Samuel Holmes Jr David son of Isaac & Lucy Holmes

David & Creasy Seward 1 Jan 1810; b- Lemuel Vaughan

Edward & Elizabeth Allen 17 Jun 1797; b- James Jones min- Charles Ogburn- (Methodist) 20Jun1797

George & Sally Burnett Smith 7 Dec 1818; b- Augustine Smith min- Charles Ogburn- (Methodist) 10Dec1818

Isaac P & Susan F Phillips 23 Dec 1829; b- James Holmes con- Joseph Hutcheson, gdn min- James Smith-

James & Eliza R Ryland 17 Oct 1853; con- Eliza R Ryland, mother min- Adam Finch- 8Nov1853

James & Mary Williams Walker 8 Dec 1835; b- William L Eubank con- Allen Walker, father min- William B. Rowzee- 16Dec1835

John & Mary Taylor 20 Dec 1779; b- Jones Taylor John son of Isaac & Lucy Holmes

John & Milly Turner 31 Aug 1797; b- Matthew Turner Jr con- John Turner, father

Pennington & Rebecca Daws 29 Jun 1798; b- John Daws min- Charles Ogburn- (Methodist) 4Jul1798

Samuel (Jr) & Hannah Fox 13 Dec 1796; b- Edward Holmes con- William Holmes Sr, father

Samuel S & Martha C Dortch 1 Nov 1830; b- Arthur G Holmes con- Rebecca J Dortch, mother. con- Alexander Dortch, gdn of Martha min- James Smith- 4Nov1830

Samuel & Prudence Courtney 23 Oct 1775; b- William Turnbull Prudence widow of Clack Courtney

Thomas E & Lucinda J Davis 24 Oct 1848; b- William A Holmes con- George Holmes, father

William & Betsy Crowder 25 Feb 1783; b- Charles Davis

William & Ann S Walton 15 Dec 1831; 'Rev' William Holmes b- John Clark

Holt

Thomas B & Jane Field 25 May 1802; b- John Dortch

Thomas & Lucy Charlotte Blackbourn 12 Oct 1780; Thomas from Chesterfield County Lucy daughter of Thomas Blackbourn b- John Brown

Holtsford

Eli J & Lucinda Rainey 13 Dec 1828; b- Thomas L Wright con- Smith Rainey, father min- James Smith- 17Dec1828

Homes

William A & Ann M Towler 12 Nov 1844; b- Henry A Towler con- William Towler, father

Hood

Charles & Sarah Durham 28 Jun 1786; b- James Willis min- John Marshall- (Baptist) 15Jul1786

John & Sally Rudd 8 Oct 1804; b- William Birtchett min- James Meacham- 16Oct1804

Starling & Martha Vaughan 11 Jul 1785; b- George Barnes Starling son of Robert Hood

Hooper

John & Mary Turner 7 Jul 1806; b- Benjamin Reekes min- Charles Ogburn- (Methodist) 10Jul1806

Hopkins

Edmund & Martha Cary Jones 25 Jul 1796; b- John Dortch con- Tignal Jones, father min- William Creath- 27Jul1796

Samuel (Jr) & Betty Bugg 18 Jan 1783; daughter of Jacob Bugg Sr b- George Nicholas

Hord

James & Martha Puryear 14 Nov 1803; b- Thomas Thompson James son of Thomas Hord min- William Richards- 24Nov1803

Jesse & Mary C Erskine 12 Feb 1798; son of Thomas Hord b- William Christopher min- Edward Almand- 15Mar1798

Thomas & Mary Camp 26 Dec 1785; b- John Holmes Mary widow of John Camp

House

Andrew J & Mary C Murrill 22 Dec 1853; min- James McAden-

James & Lucy T Mason 1 Feb 1847; b- John T Wootton con- Jordan Mason, father min- William A. Smith- 23Feb1847

John & Sally Evans 9 Apr 1808; b- Labon Short con- Elizabeth Evans, mother

John & Polly Rainey 30 Aug 1837; b- Reaman R Smith

Marriott & Polly Short 23 Aug 1790; Marriott from Brunswick County b- Miles House con- Jacob Short, father

Miles & Sally Short 23 Jan 1788; Miles from Brunswick County b- John Stegall con- Jacob & Mary Short, parents

Howard

John & Susanna Overby 29 Jul 1822; b- David Overby John Howard from Granville Co., NC min- Pleasant Gold- (Baptist)- 1Aug1822

Howerton

Thomas & Elizabeth Graves 18 Jul 1814; b- Abraham Hester, who test Elizabeth is 20 years old

Hubbard

Duncan C & Eliza G Chambers 21 Jan 1846; b- Edward R Chambers

Ralph & Peggy Pennington 19 Mar 1814; b- Thomas Smith con- Drury Pennington, gdn of Peggy

Hudgins

Emanuel Hundley & Anne Harper 23 Jan 1811; b- John Thomason

Hudson

Benjamin William & Sally Vaughan 21 Mar 1797; b- Thomas Chappell Singleton con- Richard Vaughan, father min- John Loyd- 23Mar1797

Charles Owen & Polly Ragsdale 15 Dec 1812; b- Young Hudson, who test Polly daughter of Drury Ragsdale, dec., and is 21 years old

Charles & Nancy Goode 18 Dec 1790; b- Chiles Hutcheson con- Joseph Goode, father

Dabney A & Mary Cook 1 Mar 1841; b- William P Drumwright con- John Cook, father min- James McAden-

David & Sarah Draper 3 Dec 1789; b- John Hudson min- Edward Almand- 5Dec1789

Edwin & Elizabeth Watkins 3 Jul 1830; widow b- Caphas Hudson min- William Steel- (Episcopal)-

George & Molly Berry 11 Dec 1786; b- William Harris con- Thomas Berry, father

George & Penelope Nanney 15 Oct 1818; b- James Webb

Hall & Dicy Allgood 9 Nov 1801; b- John Hudson

Jacob & Sarah Wade 8 Sep 1788; b- William Lancaster min- John Williams-

James & Elizabeth Mullins 1 Feb 1786; b- Cox Whitlow min- Henry Lester- (Baptist) 21Feb1786

John P & Elvira J Walker 21 Jul 1853; con- Elizabeth Walker, mother min- James McAden-

John & Fanny Bland 30 Apr 1801; b- Swepson Jeffries Jr con- Samuel Bland, father min- William Creath- 1May1801

John & Rebecca Ezell 26 Mar 1794; b- Thomas Calvery min- John Loyd- 28Mar1794

John & Lucy Tucker 10 Dec 1804; b- Richard Walden

John & Sally Williams 14 Jul 1800; b- Christopher Robertson min- William Creath-

Joseph Y & Lucretia J Seward 23 Dec 1817; min- James Meacham-

Paschall & Susan Hull 11 Oct 1819; b- Jesse Peebles min- Alexander M. Cowan-

Peter D & Louisa E Dodson 19 Feb 1828; b- Edmund Hester con- Edward Dodson, uncle of Louisa min- James Smith- 20Feb1828

Peter & Cinthey Keeton 16 Apr 1838; b- Thomas Keeton min- Albert Anderson- 2May1838

Peter & Eliza Ann Keeton 16 Apr 1824; b- Joseph Keeton

Richard & Elizabeth Dodson 30 Jul 1810; b- Edward Dodson min- James Meacham- 31Jul1810

Richard & Patsy Holloway 14 Jan 1805; b- Jordan Mason min- William Richards- 17Jan1805

Samuel & Nancy White 8 Feb 1790; b- William White min- Edward Almand- 11Feb1790

Stephen & Martha Ragsdale 16 Dec 1816; b- Drury Ragsdale min- William Richards- 24Dec1816

Theoderick & Mary A Hudson 18 Dec 1843; b- Cephas Hudson

William & Elizabeth Keeton 8 Oct 1804; b- Richard Hudson

William & Taffanus Moore 2 Mar 1787; b- John Wagstaff min- John Williams-

William & Jane Puryear - Nov 1803; b- Peter Puryear min- William Creath-

Young & Fanny Hutcheson 9 Jul 1804; b- John Pritchett min- James Meacham- 16Jul1804

Hughes

Barrett & Patsy H Wootton 16 Dec 1816; b- Samuel Wootton min- James Meacham- 26Dec1816

Frederick E & Mary E Venable 28 Aug 1851; 'Dr' Frederick E Hughes con- P C Venable, father

James & Frances Norment 13 Mar 1769; b- William Norment

Richard & Sally Christopher 17 Aug 1786; b- David Stokes Jr Sally daughter of David Christopher dec.

William C & Elizabeth R Ferguson 8 Nov 1838; b- Adam O Daves con- Celia F Ferguson, mother min- Benjamin R. Duval-

Woodson & Sally Page Nelson 18 Nov 1839; b- Wood Bouldin con- William Nelson, father min- John T. Clark- 27Nov1839

Humphries

Benjamin & Mary Keeton 25 Nov 1788; b- Joseph Keeton

Hundley

Byer & Ann Holmes 26 Jul 1791; daughter of Samuel Holmes b- Isaac Holmes

Willis & Joice Lark Taylor 23 Sep 1809; b- Jones Taylor min- George Micklejohn-

Hunt

Allen & Caroline C Crenshaw 6 Dec 1819; b- John Crenshaw min- Silas Shelburne- (Lunenburg County)- 23Dec1819

James & Prudence Loafman 26 Sep 1801; b- William Graves min- Edward Almand- 20Oct1801

Jesse & Polly Wagstaff 8 May 1799; b- William Hunt min- Edward Almand- 30May1799

Samuel Goodwin & Martha Drumwright 20 Dec 1802; b- William Drumwright, father

William (Sr) & Sarah Allgood 28 Jul 1788; bride gives own consent and test. that she is 30 years old b- William Johnson

William H & Jane Shackleford 7 Oct 1828; b- Jacob W Stone con Zachariah Shackleford, father min- Charles Ogburn- (Methodist) 8Oct1828

William & Matilda Wagstaff 2 Dec 1814; b- John Tabb con- Britain Wagstaff, father min- William Richards- 15Dec1814

Hunter

Fox & Rebecca Lambert 12 Oct 1819; b- Daniel Hopwood con- Taylor Lambert, father

Hurst

Jeremiah & Susannah Coleman 30 Jun 1829; b- James B Maclin con- Roderick Coleman, father min- James Smith- 1Jul1829

Hurt

James & Ermer Vaughan 11 Sep 1809; b- William Burton min- William Richards-

John G & Susan Hudson 8 Jan 1836; b- Cephas Hudson min- William Steel- (Episcopal)-

Moza & Sally Overton 10 Nov 1808; b- John Doggett min- William Richards- 27Nov1808

Phiemon & Mary Hudson 15 Jun 1818; b- William S Willis min- William Richards-

William & Betty Hudson 22 Jul 1790; b- John Hudson min- John Williams- 27Jul1790

Hutcherson

Alexander W & Martha James Phillips 10 Dec 1838; b- John W Butler con- Martin Phillips, father min- Edward Wadsworth- 13Dec1838

Charles & Elizabeth Brummell 19 Feb 1824; b- James Harris min- William Richards-

Charles & Jane Lett 13 Nov 1821; b- Drury Lett min- Charles Ogburn- (Methodist) 15Nov1821

Charles & Nancy J Wootton 28 Feb 1818; b- John P Wootton con- Samuel Wootton Sr, father min- William Richards- 19Mar1818

David G & Sarah Butler 28 Jan 1828; b- Major Butler con- Joseph Butler, Sr, father min- N.T. Barham- 10Mar1828

David G & Mary P Lett 17 Feb 1840; b- James W Simmons con- Pennington Lett, father

Elijah & Mary A Neathery 29 Jul 1839; b- William D Justice

John & Mary Clay 19 Feb 1840; b- Paschall H Bowers

Joseph W & Lucy S Phillips 3 Jul 1832; b- Benjamin P Ferrell con- Joseph Hutcheson, gdn of Lucy min- James McAden-

Robert M & Indiana Virginia C Hutcherson 20 Nov 1843; b- James W Simmons

William & Elizabeth Bridgforth 4 Dec 1818; b- Edward B Brown con- Elizabeth Bridgforth, mother min- Charles Ogburn- (Methodist) 9Dec1818

Hutcheson

Charles S & Mary M Hutcheson 6 Nov 1823; b- Charles C Phillips con- Joseph Hutcheson, father of Mary con- John Hutcheson, father of Charles min- James Smith- 12Nov1823

Chiles & Fanny Moss 23 Dec 1791; b- William Coleman con- Ray Moss, father min- William Creath- 29Dec1791

David C & Elizabeth Ogburn 12 Jun 1817; b- Joseph G Hudson con-Charles Ogburn, father con- John Hutcheson, father min- Charles Ogburn- (Methodist)

John & Sarah Baugh 23 Dec 1793; daughter of James Baugh b- James Baugh min- John Loyd- 2Jan1794

John & Sarah Hutcheson 22 Nov 1786; b- Peter Hutcheson con- Charles Hutcheson, father

John & Nancy Stone 9 Dec 1793; daughter of William Stone b- William Stone min- William Creath- 24Dec1793

John & Molly Suggett 31 Aug 1801; b- Samuel Hutcheson min- William Creath- 1Sep1801

Joseph & Mary C Valentine 17 Nov 1835; b- Melchizedeck Roffe min-Charles Ogburn- (Methodist)

Peter W & Eliza F Carlton 14 Mar 1818; b- James Crook min- James Meacham- 19Mar1818

Peter & Lilly Wagstaff 11 Dec 1797; b- John Wagstaff min- William Richards- 21Dec1797

Richard (Jr) & Wilmouth Turner 11 Oct 1804; b- Jacob Shelor Richard son of John Hutcheson min- William Creath-

Richard & Sally Turner 24 Nov 1798; b- Matthew Turner min- William Creath- 29Nov1798

Samuel & Hannah C Brame 18 Oct 1796; b- William Phillips con- James Brame, guardian min- Charles Ogburn- (Methodist) 27Oct1796

William & Amy W Brown 13 Dec 1790; b- Thomas Brown

Hutton

Jabe Clark & Maria Moore Keeton 29 Dec 1853; con- Joseph Keeton, father J C Hutton born Washington Co., VA, aged 18, s of James and Nancy Hutton Maria M Keeton born Mecklenburg Co., VA, age 18, daughter of Joseph and Elizabeth Keeton min- A.F. Davidson-

Hyde

John (Jr) & Anne Walton 16 Nov 1786; b- Edward Walton John son of John Hyde Sr min- Henry Lester- (Baptist) 21Dec1786

Hynt

James (Jr) & Susan Johnson 22 Sep 1822; b- Jrtisha Johnson

Inge

Richard & Sarah Johnson 7 Nov 1785; b- William Davis min- Devereaux Jarrott- 9Nov1785

Ingram

John & Sarah Collier 7 Jun 1773; b- Charles Hutcheson

Samuel & Martha Vaughan 25 Sep 1792; b- William Green min- William Creath- 4Oct1792

Insco

Daniel & Elizabeth Creedle 13 Mar 1822; min- Charles Ogburn- (Methodist)

James S & Martha James Insco 29 Sep 1852; min- George W. Andrews- 30Sep1852

Peter & Polly Brasley 5 Nov 1827; b- Alfred Vaughan min- James Smith- 6Nov1827

Thomas & Martha Creedle 24 Dec 1833; b- Bryant Creedle con- Martha Creedle, mother

William & Lucy Hawkins 31 Dec 1827; b- Pennington Lett min- Charles Ogburn- (Methodist) 1Jan1828

Isham

Frederick & Frances Avory 10 Nov 1794; b- Harwood Rudd min- William Creath- 22Nov1794

Ivey

Frederick & Prissey Stewart 14 Dec 1795; b- William Willis min- William Creath- 29Dec1795

Jackson

Abraham & Cornelia S Rowlett 19 Dec 1850; min- H.G. Leigh-

Archer & Everlina F Holmes 6 Oct 1834; b- James Holmes con- Rebecca Holmes, mother min- James McAden-

Beckley & Martha Brown 12 Jun 1809; b- William Hutcheson

Bins & Polly Turner 23 Apr 1803; b- Drury Turner min- William Creath-

Burwell & Nancy Thompson 19 Nov 1803; b- Drury Turner

Corbin & Martha Watkins 4 Nov 1816; b- Joseph Watkins

Fleming & Patty Power 9 Oct 1792; b- Sampson Power

Francis & Elizabeth Curtis 2 May 1807; b- Samuel Simmons min- Charles Ogburn- (Methodist) 16May1807

Jaral & Mary Garrott 13 Nov 1798; b- Cavel Jackson con- Thomas Garrott, father min- William Creath- 22Nov1798

Mark L & Leannah Basey Webb 3 Jul 1797; b- John Webb

Mark Lambert & Drucilla Rainey 8 Nov 1784; b- Francis Rainey

Matthew W & Amanda C Crutcher 26 May 1826; b- Robert C Hardy con- Miles Hardy, father

Nathaniel & Nancy Turner 24 Nov 1804; b- William Baskervill min- William Creath-

Reuben & Annis Ligon 10 Mar 1800; b- John Walker min- William Richards-

Salle & Celey Epperson 2 Oct 1802; b- Henry Jackson min- Balaam Ezell- 7Oct1802

Waddy J & Martha G Crook 15 Jan 1821; b- William B Crook con- Martha Crook, mother min- James Smith- 5Feb1821

William B & Flavala A Rowlett 27 Feb 1838; b- Stephen Rowlett min- James McAden-

William & Nancy Bugg 11 Sep 1807; b- John Bugg

James

George W & Nancy L Chandler 23 Dec 1845; b- Joel Chandler

Thomas W & Sally Chavous 17 Nov 1836; b- Jacob Cahvous min- William Steel- (Episcopal)-

Jarrott

Zachariah & Peggy M Burton 12 Apr 1806; b- Jones Burton

Jefferson

George & Louisa C Hamme 26 Nov 1835; b- Richard H Hamme con- Frederick Hamme, father

Jeffress

Charles L & Jane T Carpenter 7 May 1824; b- Thomas Farrar min- Stephen Jones- (Lynchburg, Va.)- 13May1824

Hillary T & Susan F Scott 24 Oct 1849; b- Robert C Scott, father, who also consents min- S. G. Mason-

John E & Lucy Haskins 20 Sep 1819; b- Creed Haskins con- Emma Haskins, mother

Jeffreys

Albert G & Sarah E F Puryear 20 Feb 1843; b- Richard C Puryear

Jeffries

Achilles & Elizabeth Smith 14 Sep 1772; b- Drury Smith con- Eli Smith, father

Achillis S & Sally K Boyd 27 May 1831; b- Howell L Jeffries min- William Steel- (Episcopal)- 8Jun1831

Benjamin W & Nancy Evans 11 Dec 1809; b- Matthew Baptist min- William Richards- 14Dec1809

Charles L & Lucy Berry 7 Apr 1815; b- Thomas Burnett con- John B Goode, gdn of Lucy min- James Meacham- 15Apr1815

Howell L & Martha B Boyd 8 Aug 1820; b- John W Lewis min- John S. Ravenscroft- (Episcopal)- 9Aug1820 (married at the home of Mrs. Tabitha Boyd)

Howell L & Anna Matilda Nelson 6 May 1840; b- William O Goode con- William Nelson, father

James & Ann Hogan 11 May 1789; b- Lewis Toone min- John Williams- 2Jun1789

Jennings M & Jane Pettus 28 Oct 1841; b- E A Williams min- John B. Smith-

John L & Rebecca Richards 8 Sep 1806; b- William Richards

Paul C & Mary B Evans 1 Dec 1817; b- Booker Foster con- William and Mary Richards, parents min- William Richards- 4Dec1817

Richard J & Elizabeth Sandys 14 Nov 1835; b- Joseph C Brame con- A S Jeffries

Richard & Sarah Hamner 4 Oct 1824; 'Dr' Richard Jeffries b- Epps S McCraw con- George B Hamner, father min- William Steel- (Episcopal)- 7Oct1824

Richard & Prudence Russell 19 Jun 1797; b- Thomas Burnett min- William Richards- 22Jun1797

Richard & Jane Whitehead 1 Jul 1783; b- Robert Smith

Swepson (Jr) & Elizabeth Coleman 6 Mar 1788; b- William Baskervill con- Swepson Jeffries Sr, father Elizabeth daughter of Cluverius Coleman min- Thomas Scott-

Swepson (Jr) & Sarah Minor 10 Mar 1800; b- George Minor

Swepson (Sr) & Isabell Goode 8 Feb 1789; b- Benjamin Pennington

Thomas & Mary Richeson 26 Feb 1798; b- James Harrison min- Edward Almand- 28Feb1798

William B & Elizabeth Jeffries 5 Oct 1801; b- Richard Jeffries min- Edward Almand-

Jenkins

John & Frances Wilson 3 Jun 1816; b- William Drumwright con- Ann Wilson, mother min- Charles Ogburn- (Methodist) 6Jun1816

W Robert & Nancy Hurt 26 Dec 1816; b- Andrew G Elam con- William Hurt, father min- William Richards-

Jerman

Thomas P & Lucy B Sydnor 27 Apr 1850; 'Dr' Thomas P Jerman con- B Sydnor, father

Jeter

Charles P & Mary Phillips 22 Dec 1802; b- Williamson Patillo con- Dabney Phillips Sr, father

William & Lucy Speed 11 Dec 1780; b- Dabney Phillips

Jewell

John & Martha A Edwards 18 Jan 1833; b- John Wortham

Jiggetts

David E & Susan Davis 13 Feb 1816; b- William Hendrick min- James Meacham- 15Feb1816

Johns

Samuel G & Elizabeth Colley 6 Feb 1831; min- Charles Ogburn- (Methodist)

Johnson

Alexander & Sally F Curtis 4 Feb 1825; b- Peter T Ferguson con- Zachariah Curtis, father min- James Smith- 10Feb1825

Allen & Polly Hutcheson 12 Nov 1792; b- Chiles Hutcheson min- Aaron Brown- (Methodist) 13Nov1792

Archer & Nancy Durham 14 May 1804; b- James Williams min- William Richards- 25May1804

David B & Elizabeth A Holmes 11 Sep 1840; b- Henry F Gill con- George Holmes, father

Henry R & Catherine H Wood 22 Aug 1848; b- James A Wimbish con- Henry Wood, gdn of Henry

Isaac & Rebecca Bowen 30 Jan 1802; b- Littleberry Bowen

Jacob & Linchey Crowder 5 Feb 1795; b- Edmund Burnett con- John Crowder, father min- Charles Ogburn- (Methodist) 7Feb1795

James & Rittah Burns 20 Aug 1811; min- Richard Dabbs- (Lunenburg County)-

James & Sarah Pettus 10 Nov 1794; b- Thomas Pettus

James & Patsy Reader 14 Jan 1799; b- Thomas Reader min- William Richards- 31Jan1799

James & Elizabeth Russell 30 Oct 1780; b- Jeremiah Crowder

James & Sally Russell 28 Feb 1786; b- John Tisdale

Jeremiah & Ann Flinn 16 Mar 1846; b- William T White

John W G & Susannah Byassee 20 May 1827; b- Cargill Thompson con- William Crowder, stepfather of Susannah con- Mildrige Crowder, mother of Susannah min- Charles Ogburn- (Methodist)

John W & Mary F Maclin 12 Aug 1839; min- Stephen Turner-

John W & Julia C Wright 6 Nov 1843; b- John Tarpley min- Joseph Goodman- 10Nov1843

John & Elizabeth Harrison 11 Jan 1802; b- Greenwood Harrison min- William Richards- 21Jan1802

John & Betsy Green Marshall 22 Dec 1802; b- Jordan McKinney con- Richard Marshall, father

John & Mary F Marshall 21 Jan 1839; b- John Read

John & Parmelia Mayne 10 Dec 1804; b- Samuel Weatherford con- James Mayne, father min- Edward Almand- 11Dec1804

John & Martha Toone 27 Jan 1810; b- Thomas Johnson

John & Martha Toone 27 Jan 1810; b- Thomas Johnson

Michael & Sally Carter 10 Dec 1781; b- John Johnson

Patrick & Elizabeth Ann Thomas 14 Jun 1830; b- Robert A Crowder con- William Thomas, father min- Pleasant Gold- (Baptist)- 18Jun1830

Phillip (Jr) & Mary B N Prichett 23 May 1839; b- B B Goode min- Benjamin R. Duval-

Phillip R & Martha Farrar 26 Jan 1812; b- Woodson V Johnson con- George Farrar, father min- Charles Ogburn- (Methodist) 29Jan1812

Phillip & Polly Stainback 24 Jan 1794; b- Daniel Wilson con- Laura Stainback, mother con- William Johnson, father

Samuel G & Elizabeth Colley 1 Dec 1831; b- Charles P Colley con- Charles Colley, father

Thomas D & Adaline H Daniel 12 Apr 1845; Thomas from Caswell Co., NC b- A C Finley

Thomas & Lucy S Boyd 15 Aug 1832; b- James F Maclin con- Alexander Boyd, father

Thomas & Henrietta Burns 5 Aug 1811; b- Robert Burns min- Richard Dabbs- (Lunenburg County)- 20Aug1811

Thomas & Agnes Keeton 9 Jun 1812; b- Joseph Keeton con- Joseph Keeton, father

Tilman (Jr) & Priscilla D Holloway 16 Jul 1842; b- H Holloway con- Gray Holloway, father min- Alfred Apple-

Warner K & Sophia Garner 21 Dec 1846; b- William G Coleman

William A & Mildred J Morris 17 Nov 1845; b- Daniel Morris min- James McAden-

William G & Elizabeth C Carrington 4 Sep 1846; b- William D Haskins con- T Carrington, father

William W & Martha A Penn 12 Aug 1839; b- Alexander Prichett min- Benjamin R. Duval-

William Whitehead (Jr) & Minor Parsons Scott 29 Jul 1793; b- Samuel Scott con- William Johnson, father min- William Creath- 27Aug1793

William & Rebeccah Bowen 3 Mar 1813; b- Lowry Bowen con- Berry Bowen, grandfather of Rebeccah

William & Nancy Burns 11 Aug 1815; b- Champion Burns

Woodson V & Elizabeth T Whittemore 22 Feb 1812; b- John Whittemore con- Buckner Whittemore, father min- Charles Ogburn- (Methodist) 24Feb1812

Johnston

Burwell & Martha McCarter 3 Sep 1828; b- Richard C Bibb con- James McCarter, grandfather of Martha min- William Steel- (Episcopal)- 5Sep1828

James & Sarah Cox 12 Sep 1796; L James Johnson

William R & Rebecca A Tucker 16 Aug 1835; b- Robert A Crowder con- S G Tucker, father min- William Steel- (Episcopal)- 13Aug1835

Jones

Abner & Martha Ann Wilkinson 10 Jan 1853; con- Edward Wilkinson, father

Benjamin & Jane S Coleman 12 Dec 1808; b- William Coleman daughter Swepson daughter of James Coleman dec.

Benjamin & Jane W Jeffries 3 Apr 1811; b- Richard C Russell con- Nathaniel S Jeffries, father min- William Richards- 4Apr1811

Benjamin & Linne Pierce 10 Jun 1803; b- Richard Jones con- Lucy Pierce, mother

Charles S & Martha E P Harwell 18 Dec 1848; b- James M Harwell Jr con- James M Harwell, Sr., father min- Thomas Adams- (Lunenburg Co.)- 20Dec1848

Cleaton (Jr) & Jane Mallett 10 Jul 1841; b- Bennett B Goode

Cleaton & Parthena Crew 13 Jul 1807; b- Ruel Allen min- William Richards- 17Jul1807

Cleaton & Eliza M Roberts 18 Apr 1839; b- Bennett B Goode min- Edward Wadsworth-

Daniel H & Jane Russell 18 May 1824; b- William J Hightower con- Theophilus Russell, father

Daniel & Martha Hamlin 31 Mar 1792; daughter of Thomas Hamlin son of Capt. Thomas Jones b- Thomas Vaughan

Daniel & Eliza W Hutcheson 20 Dec 1819; b- Peter W Hutcheson con- Peter Hutcheson, Sr, father

Darling & Keziah Blacketter 21 Mar 1798; b- William Jones

Edmond & Susanna Stone 21 Dec 1822; b- Jordan Stone min- Pleasant Gold- (Baptist)- 24Dec1822

Edward & Sarah Butler 9 Jul 1792; b- Elijah Graves min- James Read- (Baptist) 19Jul1792

Francis & Nancy Booth 18 Sep 179?; b- Harper Booth con- Thomas Booth, father

Frederick & Nelly Brooks 16 Oct 17??; b- Jurdain Brooks con- Robert Brooks, father

Frederick & Rebecca Jones 4 Jan 1832; b- James Oslin min- James McAden-

George W & Mary Cousins Roffe 20 Oct 1853; min- Adam Finch- 27Oct1853

Isaac H & Mary Daves 14 Dec 1836; b- Adam O Daves con- Ann Daves, mother min- James McAden-

Isaac & Maria Dortch 16 Dec 1822; b- Edward Walker min- James Smith- 19Dec1822

James A & Maria S Bowen 7 Dec 1846; b- Alfred Bowen min- Alfred Apple- 9Dec1846

James B & Jane J Davis 3 Aug 1810; b- G H Baskervill

James T & Elizabeth E Overby 27 Nov 1850; con- Milly W Overby, mother min- Alfred Apple-

James T & Louisa Ann Yancey 1 Sep 1836; b- James Yancey con- Richard Yancey min- Joseph S. Baker- 8Sep1836

James & Nancy Hite 25 Jan 1816; min- Reuben Pickett-

James & Elizabeth Holmes 20 Dec 1790; b- Pennington Holmes

James & Ann Hurt 13 Mar 1804; min- William Richards- b- Philemon Hurt Jr

James & Nancy Robertson 13 Oct 1794; b- James Hudson min- William Creath- 19Oct1794

James & Susan Townes 21 Jan 1826; b- William Townes

John & Judith Booth 22 Jan 1807; b- Harper Booth min- James Meacham-

John & Judith Elam 23 Dec 1818; b- William Jones

John & Philadelphia Tillotson 18 Dec 1822; b- John Tillotson

Joseph H & Louisa Taylor 10 Dec 1840; b- John H Taylor con- Martha Taylor, mother min- James McAden-

Joseph & Ann B Rogers 7 Dec 1807; b- James Whitlow Jr

Littleton & Jane Gregory 18 Nov 1834; b- John C Gregory con- John and Nancy Newton, parents of Jane

Ludwell E & Lucy D Hicks 24 Nov 1819; b- Edward Deloney min- James Smith- 25Nov1819

Major Harwood & Rachel Crenshaw 20 Oct 1809; b- G H Baskervill con- Thomas A Jones, guardian of Rachel min- William Richards- 24Oct1809

Martin & Sally Clark 19 Jan 1813; b- Milton Robertson min- Milton Robertson- (Warren County, N.C.)

Peter & Sarah Jackson 11 Dec 1797; b- Jeremiah Clanch

Pleasant & Sally Willis 10 Oct 1848; b- Bennett B Goode con- Ann Willis, mother

Richard D & Martha Colley 16 Dec 1831; b- William E Wilson con- Charles Colley, father min- Charles Ogburn- (Methodist) 23Dec1831

Richard & Martha Fowler 8 Oct 1813; con- Briggs Fowler, father b- William Jones minister not cited- 14Oct1813

Richard & Nancy Hamblin 23 Feb 1799; b- Daniel Jones con- Thomas Hamblin, father

Robert E & Ann E Barnes 4 Oct 1848; b- Bennett B Goode con- Jane Barnes, mother

Robert H & Elizabeth Baskervill 9 Apr 1807; b- Robert Park min- Charles Ogburn- (Methodist)

Robert & Elizabeth Guy 8 Aug 1809; b- Daniel Guy con- Lucy Guy, mother

Robert & Betsy Ann Jackson 8 Dec 1810; b- Mark L Jackson

Robert & Mary Morgan 14 Dec 1795; b- Samuel Puryear min- William Creath- 23Dec1795

Samuel H & Ann R Eubank 5 Jan 1827; b- Green Jackson min- John B. Smith- 9Jan1827

Samuel & Dosha Hailey 9 Mar 1789; b- Daniel Jones daughter of Thomas Hailey

Samuel & Milly Thompson 19 Oct 1824; b- Edward Tillotson min- Pleasant Gold- (Baptist)- 25Oct1824

Stephen & Nancy Griffin 17 Jul 1826; b- Elijah Griffin min- Pleasant Gold- (Baptist)- 25Jul1826

Thomas A & Mary Crenshaw 18 Dec 1799; b- James Jones

Thomas D & Martha Malone 16 Dec 1844; b- Hampton Malone

Thomas F & Fanny A Pennington 9 Jul 1834; b- Edwin Benford con- Benjamin P Pennington, father

Thomas L & Mary Puryear 16 Feb 1852; con- Peter Puryear, father min- Adam Finch- 17Feb1852

Thomas S & Mary A White 5 Nov 1844; b- William T White con- Jane A White, mother

Thomas Williamson & Mary Armistead Goode 27 Jan 1814; b- Alexander Boyd Jr con- Samuel Goode, father

Thomas & Susannah Jones 2 Oct 1815; b- Daniel Jones min- John Terry- 17Nov1815

Thomas & Sally Reekes 21 Sep 1815; b- Thomas Taylor min- Charles Ogburn- (Methodist) 5Oct1815

Thomas & Cecilia Stone 20 Jan 1823; b- Jordan Stone min- Pleasant Gold- (Baptist)- 25Jan1823

Thomas & Nancy Winfield 26 Nov 1787; b- Joshua Winfield

Tignal (Sr) & Sarah Anderson 16 Nov 1767; daughter of Thomas Anderson b- Tignal Jones Jr

William A & Frances A Lockett 13 May 1833; b- Samuel L Lockett min- William Steel- (Episcopal)- 22May1833

William A & Rebecca S E Tanner 17 Dec 1850; daughter of Mary Tanner con- J B Northington, gdn of Rebecca min- Nathaniel Thomas-

William B & Araminta P Northington 27 Nov 1833; b- Daniel C Hazelwood con- John Northington, father min- James McAden-

William D & Mary Speed 27 Oct 1813; b- William G Jones

William T & Mary Ann Gary 28 Apr 1842; b- William P Gary

William & Eliza Carter 24 Dec 1840; b- William H Carter con- James Jones, father

William & Susanna Clark 26 Dec 1792; b- John Hudson min- William Creath- 27Dec1792

William & Lucy A H Elliott 24 Jan 1848; b- Elias Griffin con- Elizabeth Elliott, mother

William & Charity Jackson 22 Oct 1794; b- John M Carter min- William Creath- 24Oct1794

William & Mary Jackson 9 Dec 1843; b- Richard B Baptist min- James McAden-

William & Lucy Lockett 14 Dec 1801; daughter of Abner Lockett b- James Wilson min- William Richards- 15Dec1801

William & Metealy Phillips 3 Jan 1822; b- William Leneve con- Elizabeth Moore

William & Patsy B Rogers 8 Dec 1810; b- Joseph Jones

Willis & Polly Stone 4 Nov 1803; daughter of William & Tabitha Stone b- William Stone min- William Creath-

Wylie & Martha W Johnson 14 Dec 1818; b- Ezekiel Crowder con- James Johnson, father

Jordan

Miles & Harriett Pettus 12 Nov 1804; b- John Pettus con- William Pettus, brother & guardian of Harriett min- John Cameron-

Samuel & Nancy Taylor 1 Dec 1811; b- Samuel Holmes min- James Meacham- 3Dec1811

Justice
>William D & Catherine D Branch 4 Oct 1838; b- William J Carter min-
>Benjamin R. Duval-

Keeling
>Joseph H & Martha Wootton 8 Dec 1845; b- John W Wootton
>Joseph H & Susan P Wootton 15 Nov 1841; b- John Wootton min-
>James Delk-

Keen
>Abraham Green & Martha M Birchett 11 Oct 1816; b- William Birchett
>Abraham & Margaret Tabb 29 Dec 1790; b- Edward L Tabb
>Milton & Permelia Yancey 10 Jul 1837; b- James M Yancey con
>Hezekiah Yancey, father

Keeton
>Edward & Martha Puryear 15 Nov 1813; b- William N Puryear min-
>John Allen-
>James S N & Ann E Barlow 18 Mar 1847; b- Robert P Keeton con-
>Eliza H Barlow, mother con- Warner C Keeton, father min- James
>McAden- 19Mar1847
>John & Nancy Allgood 5 May 1792; son of Joseph Keeton b- William
>Westbrook con- Moses Allgood, father
>Joseph A & Lucy M Royster 25 Apr 1848; b- John F Royster con-
>Francis Royster
>Joseph & Frances Browder 20 Nov 1851; con- W T Fourqurean, gdn of
>Frances min- Drury Seat-
>Joseph & Sarah Cheatham 8 Aug 1803; b- Warner Keeton min- Matthew
>Dance- 31Aug1803
>Joseph & Betsy Moore 13 Oct 1806; b- James Johnson
>Leonard & Polly C Hicks 4 Apr 1834; min- John B. Smith-
>Leonard & Mary Tucker 9 Mar 1801; b- Thomas Coley min- William
>Creath-
>Leonard & Polly Tucker 10 Nov 1794; b- Daniel Tucker min- William
>Creath- 22Nov1794
>Thomas & Nancy Bing 13 Nov 1805; b- James Keeton
>Warner C & Mary J Barner 19 Jul 1847; b- John R Barner con- John
>F Barner, father min- James McAden-
>Warner & Lucy Mason 13 Feb 1804; b- William Stone min- William
>Creath-
>William A & Susan W Eubank 17 May 1841; b- Samuel A Jones
>William & Elizabeth Bing 12 Nov 1798; b- Thomas Dance con- George
>Bing, father min- William Creath- 20Nov1798

Kelley
>Francis & Delilah Crowder 25 May 1785; b- William Baskervill con-
>George Crowder, father
>Henry & Mary Roberts 13 Mar 1793; Henry from Brunswick County b-
>William Nanney min- John Loyd- 14Mar1793

Kelly
>Abner & Molly Lanier 23 Feb 1798; b- John Feagins con- Leonard
>Lanier, father min- Charles Ogburn- (Methodist) 1Mar1798
>John & Frances Crowder 6 Dec 1804; b- Charles Kelly
>William & Mary Pettiford 23 Dec 1844; b- David Pettiford con- Parkey
>Pettiford, mother min- James McAden-

Kendrick
>James & Elizabeth Wright 12 Dec 1797; b- John Wright

Kennedy
>David B & Margarett F Walker 10 Dec 1839; b- William M Bennett
>con- Freeman Walker, father min- James McAden-

Kennon

Clement R & Nancy Nelson Kennon 27 Jul 1835; b- George C Scott con- Erasmus Kennon, father of Nancy

Erasmus & Anne Carter Nelson 14 Nov 1808; b- George Craighead min- George Micklejohn-

George N & Maria Ridley 12 Jan 1836; 'Dr' George N Kennon b- Robert Park min- William Steel- (Episcopal)-

Richard & Elizabeth Beverley Munford 16 May 1780; Richard from Chesterfield County b- William Randolph con- Robert Munford, father

Kersey

Thomas & Sally Kersey 22 Dec 1813; b- Hardiway Drew both are 21 or over min- James Meacham-

William & Margaret Ivy 5 Dec 1822; b- John Nash min- John S. Ravenscroft- (Episcopal)-

Keys

James H & Jane B Butler 8 Apr 1817; b- Howell L Jeffries min- James Meacham-

Kidd

James & Frances Robertson 8 Aug 1795; b- Mark Robertson

John & Betsy M Rainey 16 Feb 1818; b- William Rainey con- Williamson Rainey Sr., father

William & Judy Carter 8 Aug 1781; b- Leman Williams

William & Jane C Puryear 15 Oct 1838; b- John G Puryear min- John B. Smith-

Kimbrough

William G & Lucy Rollins Maclin 28 Jun 1841; b- Thomas H Laird con- Nathaniel Maclin, father

King

Averett & Peggy Haskins Bennett 23 Dec 1816; b- William Bennett con- Jordan Bennett, father min- Charles Ogburn- (Methodist) 24Dec1816

Charles & Martha A Butler 24 Jul 1828; b- David G Hutcherson con- Frances C Butler, mother min- James Smith-

Charles & Mary Davis 25 Oct 1819; b- John Daws min- James Smith- 28Oct1819

Charles & Elizabeth C Hutcheson 16 Dec 1809; b- John Poyner

Charles & Elizabeth C Hutcheson 16 Dec 1809; b- John Poynor

George G & Margaret J Hunter 18 Dec 1848; b- Charles S Jones min- Thomas Adams- (Lunenburg Co.)- 21Dec1848

Henry & Sarah Taylor 18 Jul 1804; Henry from Brunswick County b- James Minge Thompson

James & Sarah Morgan 27 Mar 1779; b- Reuben Morgan, father

John & Anne Short 25 May 1811; b- Austin Wright Jr

Miles & Frances Powell Burwell 15 Jul 1799; 'Capt.' Miles King from Norfolk b- William Baskervill con- Ann Burwell, mother min- John Cameron-

Richard & Rebecca Bass 26 Dec 1831; b- John M Perkinson

Spancer & Elizabeth Y Taylor 26 Jan 1829; b- David Poythress min- James Smith- 29Jan1829

William & Elizabeth Rainey 6 Sep 1815; b- Smith Rainey

Wright & Caroline A Harwell 3 Oct 1830; b- Richard H Harwell con- James Harwell, father min- James Smith- 7Oct1830

Kinker

Henry & Lucy G B Nance 16 Sep 1852; con- Mary R Elvin, mother

Kirk

Anderson & Susan Brandon 26 Jan 1830; b- John Stewart con- Jane Kirk, mother min- William Steel- (Episcopal)-

John & Martha S Westmoreland 4 Feb 1828; b- Marriott Kirk con-Robert Westmoreland, father

Littleton & Judith Singleton 11 Mar 1813; b- Robert Singleton, father

Marriott & Priscilla Taylor 27 Jan 1831; b- Thomas Kirk

Thomas & Angelina Bowen 22 Sep 1821; b- William Thomason min-Stephen Jones- (Lynchburg, Va.)- 24Sep1821

Kirkland

George & Martha Johnson Stainback 29 Jun 1809; b- Phillip Johnson min- James Meacham- 12Jul1809

Howard & Polly Poole 25 Feb 1813; b- Burwell Coleman Polly daughter of Mitchell Poole min- James Meacham- 17Apr1813

Thomas & Betsy Carroll 6 Mar 1816; b- Burwell Coleman min- Milton Robertson- (Warren County, N.C.)

Kirks

Charles & Mary Persize 10 Nov 1787; b- Joseph Moon min- Edward Almand- 13Nov1787

William & Jane Arnold 26 Jan 1790; b- James McCann con- Samuel Kirks, father

William & Ann Parham 8 Jul 1788; b- Lewis Parham

Kittrell

Eaton H & Rosa P Hunt 16 Feb 1820; b- Spencer McClenahan con-Mary Ann Hunt, mother con- Robert Jones of Granville Co., NC, gdn of Eaton

Knight

William & Elizabeth Oliver 16 Oct 1799; b- Richard Oliver min- William Creath-

Knott

William & Elizabeth J Moody 19 Nov 1812; b- Josiah Daly Jr con-Francis Moody, father min- John Allen-

Knowell

Jones & Ann Lewis 6 Sep 1819; b- John Stewart con- Emanuel Lewis, father min- James A. Riddick-

Ladd

Amos & Elizabeth Crowder 15 Oct 1792; b- John Ladd Jr min- John Loyd- 16Oct1792

Jesse & Mary Newton 3 Mar 1832; b- John Newton con- William Newton, father

John (Jr) & Jincy Cleaton 12 Dec 1798; b- Joseph Ladd min- Ebenezer McGowan-

Noble & Mary Rottenberry 29 Dec 1792; b- John Ladd min- John Loyd-3Jan1793

Noble & Jane E Walker 8 Apr 1844; b- Samuel J Vaughan min- James McAden-

Thomas (Jr) & Mary Crowder 6 Aug 1788; b- Josiah Floyd

Thomas & Elizabeth Woodall 16 Dec 1844; b- Jacob Woodall min- Jacob Manning-

Thomas & Parthena Wortham 24 Oct 1836; b- James Wortham min-John B. Smith-

William & Martha Gilliam 8 Feb 1787; b- Jacob Ladd

William & Faitha Pennington 29 Dec 1800; b- John T Pennington con-Henry Pennington, father

Laffoon

Nathaniel & Mary Chambliss 17 Nov 1808; b- George Small

Nathaniel & Polly Merryman 18 Dec 1804; b- John Nash

Laine

Benjamin & Patsy M Mayne 10 Nov 1800; b- Owen Lowry con- James Mayne, father min- Edward Almand- 20Nov1800

Laird

Alexander T & Sarah Virginia Chambers 20 Dec 1853; con- Edward R Chambers, father min- William A. Smith-

Thomas H & Martha E Chambers 16 Jan 1849; 'Dr' Thomas H Laird b- Edward R Chambers min- William A. Smith- 17Jan1849

Lamay

Richard & Elizabeth Cook 18 Jan 1804; b- Herbert Cook

Lambert

Ezekiel & Biddy Roberts - Feb 1804; b- Robert Roberts

John E & Mary A F Shaw 15 Oct 1833; b- Richard H L Bailey con- Mary Shaw, mother min- James McAden-

John & Elizabeth Gregory 11 Dec 1809; b- William Vaughan con- Richard Gregory, father

John & Jemima Jackson 2 Aug 1785; b- Joseph Lambert

John & Rebecca Thomason 20 Apr 1826; b- Benjamin Evans min- John B. Smith-

Julius & Jincy Brooks 13 Dec 1796; b- John McKinney min- John Loyd- 14Dec1796

Samuel & Mary Burton 27 Jul 1819; b- James Lambert con- Milly Burton, mother

Thomas & Frances Watson 18 Apr 1797; b- Richard Stone

William & Sarah Bottom 31 May 1800; b- James Burton min- Ebenezer McGowan- 1May1800

Lamkin

Cleophas & Mary Doggett 19 Dec 1785; b- James Garner con- John and Mary Doggett, parents min- John Marshall- (Baptist) 23Dec1785

Land

Phillip L & Nancy Cheatham 9 Jul 1824; b- Livingston H Vaughan min- James McAden-

Robert C & Elizabeth B Hutcheson 5 Apr 1824; b- John Hutcheson

Langhorne

Creed T & Lucy H Jeter 4 May 1840; b- Alexander Langhorne min- Charles F. Burnley-

Langley

John & Mary J Read 18 May 1833; 'Capt' John Langley b- Lewis G Meacham con- Clement Read, father

John & Lucy Young 6 Dec 1798; b- Allen Young

Leonard & Sarah M N Palmer 7 Sep 1829; b- Abner P Wright min- James Smith- 10Sep1829

Thomas & Joyce Bugg 24 Apr 1773; b- Samuel Hopkins

Walter C & Judith B Young 5 Nov 1803; b- Jesse Dortch con- Allen Young, father

Lanier

Allen & Polly Davis 21 Nov 1791; b- Josiah Floyd con- Charles & Martha Floyd, parents min- John King-

C V & Harriet Speed 16 Nov 1841; b- Henry F Speed

James & Martha T Green 8 Jun 1814; b- Joel Watkins con- Grief Green, father, who test Martha under 21 min- James Meacham- 9Jun1814

Nicholas & Sarah Bugg 23 Mar 1796; b- John Nance min- James Tolleson- 2Apr1796

William & Mary Garland Ballard 4 Sep 1794; b- James Bullock con- John Ballard, father

Lawrence

　William & Savory Mise 12 Apr 1827; b- P L Long min- James Smith-

Lawson

　Benjamin T & Louisa I Spain 2 Sep 1846; b- John Flinn con- Royal
　　Spain, father min- John B. Smith-

　William & Martha Graves 25 Dec 1817; b- Nathan Graves con- Thomas
　　Graves, father min- William Richards-

Lawton

　William H & Ann Bolling Green 4 Nov 1843; b- Thomas H Laird

Leach

　James (Jr) & Patsy Gregory 18 Jan 1802; b- Francis Gregory con- Roger
　　Gregory, Sr, father

Leaker

　William & Mary A Craddock 7 Jun 1832; b- Charles Hudson Jr

Lear

　Samuel & Harriett Gary 10 Aug 1843; b- William A Holmes

Lee

　Amos & Elizabeth Thompson 13 Nov 1809; b- Margarian Thompson
　　min- William Richards- 28Dec1809

　Jesse & Elizabeth Northington 3 Dec 1803; b- Samuel Butler

　John & Martha Hardy 15 Jan 1833; b- William S Wilson con- Miles
　　Hardy, father

Leftwich

　William W & Martha L Pettus 6 Oct 1851; con- C H Pettus, father min-
　　Adam Finch- 5Nov1851

Leigh

　Anselm & Sally Greenwood 20 Jan 1790; b- Walter Leigh con- Thomas
　　Greenwood, father

　John R & Mary C Carrington 21 Apr 1852; 'Dr' John R Leigh con-
　　Tucker Carrington, father min- F.N. Whaley-

　Solomon & Sophia Aigner 12 Aug 1837; b- John O Wingfield

　Walter & Patty Holmes 1 Dec 1784; daughter of Samuel Holmes b-
　　Samuel Holmes

Leneve

　Ewell & Rebecca T Apperson 19 Feb 1833; b- Samuel Watkins con-
　　Mary Apperson, mother min- John B. Smith-

　John (Jr) & Milly Newton 25 Jan 1830; b- Robert Newton con- James
　　Newton, father min- Pleasant Gold- (Baptist)- 28Jan1830

　Samuel & Mary Malone 6 Jun 1825; b- Alex Blankenship con- Nancy
　　Malone, mother min- Pleasant Gold- (Baptist)- 9Jun1825

　William & Elizabeth Yancey 1 Dec 1828; b- Stith G Yancey con-
　　Zachariah Yancey, father min- Pleasant Gold- (Baptist)- 24Dec1828

Lester

　A W & Elvira N Moore 23 Oct 1848; b- Thomas E Moore

　Leroy H & Mary Ann Moore 22 Feb 1846; b- Thomas E Moore min-
　　E. Chambers- 27Feb1846

Lett

　Drury & Mary Simmons 6 Jan 1827; b- Isaac H Jones con- Samuel
　　Simmons, father min- John B. Smith- 9Jan1827

　Edward & Eliza Crook 10 Jun 1814; b- Osborne Crook min- Charles
　　Ogburn- (Methodist) 12Jun1814

　Francis & Elizabeth Thompson 21 Sep 1797; b- James Lett

　Hardaway & Mary Burton 1 Sep 1806; b- Pennington Lett

　Joseph (Jr) & Polly Jeffries Burnett 28 Jan 1804; b- Matthew H Davis
　　con- Thomas Burnett, father

Joseph A & Jane C Lett 20 Feb 1837; b- William Bowers min- James McAden-

Joseph H & Virginia N Roffe 4 Nov 1844; b- James Connelly con- Samuel D Roffe, father

Pennington & Frances Pennington 14 Feb 1810; b- John T Pennington con- Josiah Floyd, guardian of Frances

Robert & Suckey Burrus Lett 17 Apr 1794; b- William Parrish min- John Loyd- 18Apr1794

Lewis

Abraham & Louisa Averett 11 Feb 1805; b- C Granderson Feiuld min- William Richards- 21Feb1805

Abraham & Elizabeth Clark 8 Oct 1804; b- James Parham

Abraham & Avarella Sadler 27 Nov 1811; b- George W Holloway

Berry & Delilah Drew 22 Aug 1839; b- George Stoneham con- James and Polly Drew, parents min- Edward Wadsworth-

Charles & Mary Anderson 8 Nov 1779; b- Howell Taylor con- Thomas Anderson Sr, father

Emanuel & Frances Stewart 21 Jun 1819; b- Randolph Chavous min- Milton Robertson- (Warren County, N.C.) 24Jun1819

Francis & Elizabeth Hester 30 Apr 1786; b- Henry Sandifer Elizabeth daughter of Abraham Hester dec. min- Henry Lester- (Baptist) 30Apr1786

James & Susannah Anderson 25 Jun 1774; b- Thomas Anderson daughter of Thomas Anderson Sr

John F & Mary G Davis 31 Mar 1819; b- Alexander Goode con- Gray F Dunn, gdn of Mary

John R & Delia Ann Dunston 11 Jul 1839; b- Thomas Stewart min- Benjamin R. Duval-

John W & Caroline Matilda Nelson 19 Jun 1821; b- Berry Lewis con- George Nelson, father

John & Naomi Robinson 24 Mar 1818; b- Woodson Palmore con- John Robinson, father con- Benjamin Lewis, father

Robert & Ann Bugg 10 Nov 1788; min- John Cameron-

Robert & Charlotte Butler 8 Jan 1810; b- Jones Allen

Robert & Elizabeth Jones 25 Feb 1794; b- Asa Thomas con- Tignal Jones, father

Robert & Nancy Willis 22 Aug 1799; b- Edward Willis con- Edward Lewis, father William Willis, father

Thomas & Elizabeth Birtchett 22 Mar 1806; b- John Dortch min- Thomas Hardie-

William D & Elizabeth Dunston 5 Aug 1845; b- Henderson Dunston

William H & Christian B Boyd 29 Jun 1836; b- John McNeal con- Matilda Boyd, mother min- William Steel- (Episcopal)-

Lifford

John & Lettice Jones 3 Dec 1796; b- Buckner Whittemore

Ligon

David & Mary E Wilkinson 21 Aug 1848; b- Darrell Miles con- Edward Wilkinson, father

Henry & Leatha Garner 27 Apr 1831; min- John B. Smith-

Henry & Frances J Wilkinson 16 Dec 1844; b- Stephen Williamson con- Edmond Wilkinson, father

Irby & Evelina Dunston 29 Oct 1833; b- Richard Dunston con- Sophia Ligon, mother min- William Steel- (Episcopal)- 30Oct1833

James & Hannah Christopher 11 Oct 1796; b- John Ligon min- William Richards- 24Nov1796

James & Anne Gregory 14 Nov 1798; b- James Reamy min- William Richards- 22Nov1798

William D & Sally S Kennon 1 Mar 1841; b- E A Williams Sally daughter of Erasmus Kennon, dec. min- F.H. McGuire- 4Mar1841

William & Nancy Phillips 7 Oct 1840; b- Thomas Glasscock min- John B. Smith-

Lisk

William & Dicy Eastham 21 Dec 1803; b- Richard Crowder

Loafman

William & Sally R Harris 29 Nov 1823; b- Robert Harris min- William Richards- 4Dec1823

Lockett

Abner A & Elizabeth Osborne 12 Nov 1824; b- L B Barnes con- Thomas Goode, gdn of Elizabeth min- William Richards- 16Nov1824

Francis & Martha Goode Marshall 8 Mar 1802; b- Valentine McCutcheon con- William Marshall, father

Napoleon & Mary C Lockett 26 Jun 1834; b- Samuel L Lockett min- William Steel- (Episcopal)-

Royall & Prudence Clay 20 Aug 1789; b- James Elam con- Charles & Phebe Clay, parents

Loftis

Archibald & Polly Watkins 17 Oct 1814; b- Joseph Watkins con- Joseph Watkins, father

Thomas & Sarah Carter 3 Dec 1841; b- Richard H Jones con- William H Carter, father

Lollis

John & Aggy (Jr) Spurlock 5 Apr 1786; b- John Hatsell

Lomax

Lucien H & Mary Elizabeth Duncan 21 Jul 1845; b- David Duncan min- William B. Rowzee- 26Jul1845

Lonnon

Henry & Mary Elam 13 Dec 1803; b- Phillip Ryan min- Edward Almand- 15Dec1803

Love

Allen C & Ann A F Hutcheson 11 Feb 1846; b- Charles L Hutcheson

Charles T & Lucretia J Creath 24 Feb 1841; b- M L Creath con- Lucretia Creath, mother min- Joseph W.D. Creath- (Nottoway County)-

James W & Pamelia B Goode 23 Aug 1819; b- Christopher Haskins Jr min- James Meacham- 24Aug1819

Thomas J & Lucy F Boswell 31 May 1853; con- Joseph Boswell Sr, father min- William Doswell- (Lunenburg County)-

William H & Jane W Gregory 7 Apr 1852; con- John W Gregory, father

William & Susanna Brame 6 May 1803; b- Ingram Roffe con- James Brame, guardian of Susanna daughter of George Baskervill

Lowery

Waddill & Rebecca Glasscock 16 Dec 1850; con- Elizabeth Glasscock, mother min- Thomas King- (Halifax County)-

William A & Samantha Jane Robertson 29 Sep 1853; con- N T Robertson, father min- P.F. August-

Loyd

Joel M & Rebecca Thomas 16 Aug 1819; b- Riddick Wilson

Lucas

Frederick & Martha Baskervill 27 Oct 1779; b- William Baskervill daughter of George Baskervill

George & Patty Arnold 21 Mar 1770; b- James Arnold daughter of James Arnold Sr and Martha Arnold

John R & Hannah H Brown 26 Apr 1806; 'Dr.' John R Lucas b- John Dortch con- R Watson, guardian of Hannah min- James Meacham-

Littleton C & Martha B Nash 7 Dec 1811; b- James Nash, father
Lukes
James C & Rebecca Yancey 4 Dec 1843; b- Leander O Yancey con-
Hezekiah Yancey, father min- Alfred Apple- 7Dec1843
Lumpkin
Anthony & Polly Yancey 14 Nov 1808; b- Charles Yancey
Lumsdon
John & Elizabeth Eastland 8 Feb 1788; b- Robert White min- Edward
Almand- 9Feb1788
Lunsford
Moses & Mary Fox 28 Jan 1796; daughter of Richard Fox b- John
McKenny min- John Loyd-
Samuel & Martha Dunnavon 13 Feb 1822; min- Pleasant Gold- (Baptist)-
Lyle
Alexander B & Martha P McCutcheon 20 Dec 1839; b- John E
McCutcheon con- Charles McCutcheon, father min- John B. Smith-
Lynch
Daniel & Frances Baird 21 Dec 1829; b- Charles W Baird min- James
Smith-
Mabry
Joshua & Mary Ann Short 2 Jan 1818; b- William Bilbo min- James
Meacham- 7Jan1818
Stephen & Tabitha Nance 19 Apr 1775; b- John Cook con- Isham Nance,
brother
MacGowan
Ebenezer & Frances Baugh 29 Jul 1797; daughter of James and Agnes
Baugh b- James Baugh
Mackecy
John & Jane Garrett 13 Feb 1823; b- Richard Coleman min- Thomas
R. Brame-
Maclin
Mark & Mary Theny Feggins 23 Dec 1851; con- Thomas Maclin,
grandfather of Mark
William B & Emily Peete 20 Jul 1829; b- James F Maclin con- Edwin
H Peete, father min- James McAden- 21Jul1829
William & Mary A Burks 3 Jan 1850; b- Sterling Evans min- James
McAden- 4Jan1850
William & Elizabeth Moon 1 May 1848; b- Wyatt W Brandon min-
James McAden- 2May1848
Major
Drury J & Mary R Crowder 18 Sep 1843; b- Creed T Haskins
Mallett
George W & Mary A R Smith 22 Sep 1846; b- Redmon R Smith con-
Nancy Mallett, mother
Howell & Martha E Collier 10 Jun 1814; b- William Mallett min- James
Meacham- 17Jan1815
Howell & Emma Roberts 18 Jul 1848; b- E A Williams con- Panby
Reese, gdn of Emma
Thomas & Betsy H Allgood - Feb 1804; b- George Allgood min- William
Creath-
William (Jr) & Elizabeth Freeman 18 Mar 1833; b- Samuel Bugg con-
Liddy Walker, grandmother of Elizabeth
William & Sally A Collier 12 May 1812; b- Absolem Roberts con-
Absolem Roberts, gdn of Sallie, who is daughter of Lewis Collier, dec.
min- James Meacham- 11Jun1812

William & Mary Ann Neathery 6 Mar 1850; b- Robert F Neathery min-Thomas Crowder-

Mallory

Roger & Elizabeth S Keen 19 Jan 1814; b- John T Keen con- Abraham Keen, gdn of Elizabeth min- Charles Ogburn- (Methodist) 21Jan1814

Malone

Anderson & Susanna Malone 16 Dec 1816; b- Benjamin Reekes min-Lewis Grigg- 26Dec1816

Drury & Penelope Taylor 14 Jun 1774; b- Lewis Parham

Frederick & Susannah Bilbo 24 May 1774; b- John Bilbo

Frederick & Judith Puckett 19 May 1779; b- John Puckett

George & Sarah Fowlkes 23 Oct 1804; b- Gabriel Fowlkes min- William Richards- 25Oct1804

Hampton & Susanna Green 17 Jun 1822; b- James Stone min- Pleasant Gold- (Baptist)- 20Jun1822

Isaac & Ann C Courtney 22 Sep 1790; b- Josiah Floyd min- John King- 23Sep1790

Isaac & Lucy Saulsberry 24 May 1795; b- Joseph Walker min- John Loyd-

Jesse C & Mary R Blackwell 28 Aug 1831; b- Sterling Smith min- James McAden-

Nathaniel & Elizabeth Evans 31 May 1777; b- Stephen Mabry con- Stephen Evans, father

William & Martha E Bracy 12 Feb 1850; b- George Speaks min- James McAden- 18Feb1850

William & Eliza LeNeve 12 Feb 1844; b- Robert A Phillips con- John LeNeve, father

Manley

John & Harriett Stone 1 Jul 1822; b- Elijah Stone

Richard (Jr) & Ann Edmonson 16 Aug 1824; b- Samuel Simmons Sr min- Charles Ogburn- (Methodist) 30Aug1824

Mann

Daniel & Ann B Holmes 12 Nov 1821; b- Isaac Holmes, father min-James Smith- 13Nov1821

Manning

Benjamin & Fanny Guy 5 May 1796; b- Earbe Chavous min- John Loyd-8May1796

James & Elizabeth Farrar 19 Mar 1827; b- John Farrar, gdn, who also gives consent min- John B. Smith- 20Mar1827

John C & Elizabeth E Robertson 18 Feb 1836; b- James B Dugger con-Hannah C Robertson, mother min- M.P. Parker-

Thomas D & Elvira A S B Crowder 19 Dec 1830; b- John L Meacham min- James McAden-

Marable

Edward T & Elizabeth D Butler 29 Sep 1829; b- Charles G Butler min-James Smith- 8Oct1829

John & Lucy R Billups 12 Dec 1791; b- John Billups min- John Williams-13Dec1791

William & Frances Christopher 1 Dec 1801; b- Jesse Hord min- William Richards- 5Dec1801

Markam

Francis O & Susan Somervill 19 Jun 1834; b- George C Scott con-Eleanor H Somervill, mother

Marshall

Burnett & Lucy Wilson 13 Oct 1803; b- Frederick Watkins con- James Wilson, guardian of Lucy

Dennis & Frances Harper 27 Aug 1792; b- John Harper Dennis son of Samuel & Cassandra Marshall

Francis & Jane Hester 7 Nov 1803; b- Daniel Johnson con- Samuel Hester, father min- William Creath-

Isaac & Sally Finn 23 May 1795; b- David Pennington min- John Loyd- 26May1795

Josiah & Elizabeth Winn 17 Feb 1802; b- Banister Winn min- William Richards- 3Mar1802

Thomas & Elizabeth L Baptist 1 Mar 1802; b- John G Baptist con- William Glanvil Baptist, father min- William Creath-

William & Nancy Butler 28 Dec 1816; b- Joseph Butler min- James Meacham- 9Jan1817

William & Rebeccah Evans 17 Dec 1803; b- Matthew Evans

Martin

James & Margaret Allen 12 Mar 1800; b- John Puryear Jr min- William Creath-

John & Elizabeth Coppedge 3 Apr 1799; b- Charles Coppedge min- Ebenezer McGowan-

John & Cary Crowder 30 May 1797; b- Philemon Hurt, Jr min- William Richards- 1Jun1797

Oliver & Elizabeth Mallett 13 Mar 1799; b- Richard M Allen min- William Creath- 21Mar1799

Warner & Martha Bailey 6 Oct 1783; b- Benjamin Ferrell con- William Bailey, father

Mason

Albert G & Mary H Davis 16 Sep 1824; b- Daniel T Hicks con- William Davis, father

Allen S & Mary E Tunstall 17 Oct 1853; con- John B Tunstall, father min- George W. Andrews- 28Oct1853

James S & Camilla N Walker 19 Nov 1849; b- Henry C Hayes con- Eliza Walker, mother min- Robert Burton- 28Nov1849

Jordan & Agnes Walker 10 Oct 1808; b- Allen Walker daughter of Richard & Lucy Walker

Robert H & Ann B Marshall 22 Dec 1845; b- Major Butler

Robert & Martha Johnson 31 Mar 1797; b- John Edwards con- Jincy Hawkins, mother of Patsy (Martha) min- Charles Ogburn- (Methodist) 3Apr1797

William J & Mary Ann Ezell 7 Oct 1833; b- James Connell con- Robertson Ezell, father

William W & Nancy Crenshaw 9 Sep 1805; b- G H Baskervill min- Matthew Dance- 13Sep1805

William & Susanna Campbell 14 Jan 1795; b- Benjamin Fargeson Jr min- John Loyd- 22Jan1795

William & Elizabeth G Smithson 15 Dec 1831; b- Silas D Wright con- Sterling T Smithson, father min- Abner W. Clopton- 20Dec1831

Massey

Peter & Hannah Wells 11 Mar 1802; b- William Garrott min- William Creath-

Thomas & Peggy Barry 24 Apr 1799; b- James Johnson

Matthews

Enos & Liddy Overby 17 Sep 1788; b- Richard Thompson min- Thomas Scott-

John & Martha Wingfield Jordan 18 Dec 1799; b- Wilkins Ogburn con- Mary Jordan, mother min- James Meacham- 24Dec1799

Thomas & Betsy Wilkerson 22 Mar 1809; b- John Rainey

May

Charles & Nancy S Smith 16 May 1837; b- William H Smith con- John Smith, father

John & Martha Jane Coleman 7 Sep 1837; b- Jeremiah Hirst con- Lucy Coleman, mother

Mayes

Bozeman & Mary Neal 10 Nov 1783; b- William Hundley con- William Neal, father

John & Elizabeth Hamblin 7 Jan 1789; b- John Wynne

Stephen & Susannah Jones 16 Sep 1811; b- Marshall Moody con- Edward Jones

William & Lucretia Cox 26 Dec 1806; b- Miles Hall min- William Richards- 29Dec1806

Mayfield

William E & Winifred I Palmer 9 Dec 1829; b- Jeremiah Hilliard min- James Smith- 16Dec1829

Maynard

Wagstaff & Fanny Hord 10 Dec 1792; b- James Hord daughter of Thomas Hord

Mayne

James & Sarah Tibbs 8 Mar 1779; b- William Tibbs

Mayo

Cuffey & Celey Stewart 2 Apr 1802; b- Daniel Mayo

Harris & Delany Fagins 15 Dec 1842; b- William H Boyd con- Polly Fagins, mother, who test Delany 21

Hutchins & Sally Stewart 10 Feb 1806; b- Daniel Mayo Betsy mother of Sally

Jacob & Sally Evans 15 Feb 1841; b- James Mayo

James & Mary Brandon 18 Dec 1838; b- Osborne Mayo

Osborne & Elizabeth Smith 18 Dec 1838; b- James Mayo min- John B. Smith-

Pompy & Nancy Marks 17 Dec 1801; b- Minge Mayo

Robert & Mary Brandon 31 Dec 1811; b- Edward Mayo

Samuel & Sally Parker 27 Dec 1853; min- F.N. Whaley-

William Henry & Mary Frances Hayes 14 Mar 1844; b- Frederick Nowell con- Matilda Hayes, mother

McAden

James & Ann Simmons 21 Feb 1821; b- William B Simmons min- James Smith-

William B & Susan A M Davis 20 May 1850; b- J W McAden con- Benjamin W Davis, father min- D.J.C. Slaughter- 28May1850

McCarter

James & Sarah Avery 21 Mar 1814; b- James J Avery con- Nancy Avery, mother min- William Richards- 31Mar1814

James & Liza Bowen 3 Dec 1804; b- James Bowen

Thomas & Caty Bowen 23 Jun 1803; b- James Bowen min- William Creath-

McCraw

Miller W & Mary A Crute 21 Sep 1835; b- Willis R V Crute min- William B. Rowzee- 6Oct1835

McCutcheon

Charles & Prudence Evans 11 Dec 1797; b- Richard Jeffries min- Edward Almand- 14Dec1797

Valentine & Anna Hester 10 Mar 1800; b- Richard Brown min- William Richards- 18Mar1800

McDaniel

Crawford & Elva Estes 15 Jan 1819; min- Charles Ogburn- (Methodist) 19Jan1819

Daniel W & Dianna Farrar 10 Nov 1831; b- Jesse H Clarke min- Charles Ogburn- (Methodist)

Daniel W & Dolly Lett 5 Feb 1818; min- Charles Ogburn- (Methodist)

John & Leatha Ann Johnson 8 Aug 1826; b- Gregory Johnson con- John Johnson, father min- Charles Ogburn- (Methodist)

John & Lucy R Tucker 10 Aug 1844; b- Isaac R Watson min- James McAden-

Thomas L & Rebecca E Carter 13 Nov 1850; con- Robert Carter, father min- Robert Burton-

William & Rody Mason 11 Aug 1795; b- Ezekiel Redding min- Charles Ogburn- (Methodist) 13Aug1795

William & Sally Russell 4 Nov 1816; b- John Curtis con- John Russell, father min- Milton Robertson- (Warren County, N.C.) 6Nov1816

McDearman

Thomas R & Margaret W Sandys 21 Jan 1840; b- James M Crowder min- John B. Smith-

McDowell

Samuel & Jane Elam 25 May 1833; b- Andrew G Elam con- Daniel Elam, father min- George Petty- 28May1833

McGowan

John & Sarah Ann Holmes 10 Dec 1811; b- Isaac Holmes min- Charles Ogburn- (Methodist) 13Dec1811

McKinney

John & Elizabeth Douglas 24 Dec 1792; b- David Thomas con- S Douglas, father min- John Loyd- 27Dec1792

John & Sally Jackson 26 Dec 1817; b- Jesse Childress

Munford & Patsy Morgan 10 Dec 1789; b- John Morgan min- John Phaup- 17Dec1789

Willis & Nancy Glover 25 Feb 1801; b- William Blanton min- Ebenezer McGowan- 26Feb1801

McLin

Thomas & Delilah Evans 23 Dec 1794; b- John Guy min- John Loyd- 24Dec1794

William & Anne Venable - Apr 1801; William from Greensville County b- James McLin

McNeal

John & Martha Rainey 22 Sep 1836; b- Phillip Rainey min- William B. Rowzee-

Robert A & Martha B Green 17 May 1838; b- Daniel T Hicks con- G P Green, father min- Edward Wadsworth-

McQuie

William & Sarah Brook 11 Jan 1785; b- Burwell Russell

McRilon

Harrison & Mary T Insco 27 May 1811; min- Charles Ogburn- (Methodist)

Meacham

John S & Mary B Norvell 20 Mar 1828; b- Lewis G Meacham min- James Smith- 2Apr1828

Lewis G & Sarah L Wright 18 May 1833; b- John Langley con- Mary Wright, mother

Mealer

Nicholas & Tabitha Ragsdale 12 Jul 1802; b- James Wilson min- William Richards- 5Aug1802

Phillip & Patty Jones 14 May 1781; b- Jesse Saunders con- Thomas
  Jones, father
William & Nancy Humphries 11 Sep 1775; b- John Humphries
William & Elizabeth P Puryear 9 Nov 1807; b- Thomas Lewis
Mealey
Edmund B & Rebecca B Farrar 10 Jan 1843; b- Francis T Weaver
Medley
Bartholomew & Sally Holloway 23 Dec 1797; b- Benjamin Fargeson
Isaac & Sally A Cabiness 23 Sep 1845; b- Joseph T Ladd con- William
  Cabiness, father min- James McAden-
Isaac & Sally L Drumwright 17 Apr 1843; b- William P Drumwright
  con- Sally O Drumwright, mother min- Joseph A Brown- 20Apr1843
Joseph & Elanner White 10 Jan 1807; b- John Dortch min- William
  Richards- 1Jan1807
Meldrum
Reuben & Mary A Stewart 16 Dec 1843; b- William Stewart con- Nancy
  Stewart, mother
Meredith
Joseph N & Mary Baptist 12 May 1800; b- G H Baskervill min- William
  Creath-
Merritt
Thomas & Elizabeth Suggett 14 Dec 1785; b- Pennington Holmes con-
  Edgecomb Suggett, father
William H E & Eliza W Goode 2 Apr 1827; b- Bevil G Wyche con-
  William Hendrick, gdn of Eliza min- John B. Smith- 4Apr1827
Merryman
Benjamin & Julia A Singleton 11 Apr 1848; b- Joseph C Singleton min-
  James McAden- 12Apr1848
Epps & Amey Kirks 26 Jan 1790; b- James McCann
Epps & Elizabeth Thomerson 5 Jan 1803; b- William Thomerson
Isham & Lucretia Turner 4 Apr 1787; b- Abram Merryman
Watkins L & Lucy Thomason 17 Dec 1850; con- Elizabeth Thomason,
  mother min- James McAden-
Middagh
Daniel & Elizabeth Gregory 5 Jul 1813; b- Charles William Baird
Miller
Alfred B & Louise Moore 17 Dec 1847; b- William T Hodges con-
  Elizabeth Moon, grandmother of Louise
Henry & Elizabeth Smith 17 Jun 1800; b- Zachariah Curtis
Mills
Charles & Jincy Baker 9 Dec 1799; b- George Baker min- Matthew
  Dance- 19Dec1799
Charles & Rebecca Ann Curtis 31 Oct 1845; b- Grief Green min- James
  J. Sledge-
George & Emily Morgan 23 Dec 1843; b- Albert Coley
John & Lucy Dunnavant 13 Feb 1850; b- Bennett B Goode
John & Susanna Pool 22 Nov 1808; b- Robert Greenwood
William & Sally Johnson 6 Sep 1843; b- Charles Mills
Mimms
John & Wilmouth Jones - Jan 1788; min- William Creath-
Thomas & Elizabeth Noel 5 May 1802; b- George Meanly
Thomas & Elizabeth Noel 5 May 1802; b- George Meanly
Mims
Robert E F & Martha E Daws 19 Jul 1853; min- George W. Andrews-
  20Jul1853

Minor

Henry & Martha Averett 10 Dec 1839; b- George W Averett min- John
    B. Smith-

Mise

John & Frances Hudson 2 Feb 1829; b- Robert B Chambliss

Mitchell

Benjamin & Catharine Ivey 7 Nov 1836; min- William Steel- (Episcopal)-

Benjamin & Mary Stone 14 Dec 1795; b- William Stone

Clement & Betsy C Northington 27 Jul 1825; b- B Northington con-
    John Northington, father min- James McAden- 10Aug1825

Gideon & Sally Wagstaff 7 Feb 1804; b- Allen Wagstaff min- William
    Richards- 8Feb1804

Ishmael & Elizabeth Nance 6 Jan 1808; b- Isham Nance Jr

Reuben & Ann Pennington 2 Apr 1783; b- Edward Pennington

Robert & Sally Allen 27 Jan 1818; b- Thomas Warren con- Thomas T
    Allen, father min- James Meacham- 5Feb1818

Thomas & ----- Malone 3 Aug 1785; bond torn b- John Burton

Thomas & Fanny Pully 31 Oct 1810; b- William Daly

Thomas & Susan C Tucker 18 Apr 1851

William & Frances W Dunnavant 19 Aug 1816; b- Abel B Dunnavant
    con- Joel Dunnavant, father min- James Meacham- 21Aug1816

William & Catharine Ivey 7 Nov 1836; b- George Ivey min- William
    Steel- (Episcopal)-

William & Elizabeth Warren 22 Jul 1786; b- Richard Stone con- Thomas
    Marriott Sr, guardian of Elizabeth

Mize

Henry & Elizabeth Yeargen 12 Jan 1807; b- John Mize Henry from
    Brunswick County

John & Lemenda Lambert 24 Mar 1795; b- Thomas Lambert min- John
    Loyd- 25Mar1795

John & Nancy Yeargen 30 Dec 1805; b- Jerry Mize

Randolph & Martha Matthews 28 Apr 1798; b- Hudson Nipper min-
    Ebenezer McGowan- 3May1798

Monday

Jesse & Judith Naish 13 Nov 1792; b- Moore Comer of Halifax County

Monroe

John & Margaret Culbreath 10 Mar 1789; b- Thomas Culbreath

Montague

Mickelborough & Nancy Vaughan 30 Jul 1798; b- Reuben Vaughan min-
    William Creath- 2Aug1798

Montgomery

Richard P & Sarah Hudson 30 Jan 1804; b- Richard Hudson min-
    Matthew Dance- 2Feb1804

Moody

Arthur & Mary Hester 13 Dec 1796; b- James Palmer con- James Hester,
    father min- William Richards- 15Dec1796

Benjamin & Dolly Yancey 15 Nov 1813; b- William Moody con- Mary
    Yancey, mother min- William Richards- 16Nov1813

Francis A & Susan E Puryear 18 Nov 1833; b- Thomas B Puryear min-
    William Steel- (Episcopal)- 26Nov1833

Francis & Anna Hester 26 Dec 1805; b- Harwood Jones con- James
    Hester, father min- Thomas Hardie-

Francis & Patsy Vaughan 14 Sep 1789; b- William Moody con- Henry
    Moody, father con- Reuben Vaughan, father min- Thomas Scott-

Henry & Susan Hester 22 Dec 1827; b- David C Wootton min- Allen
    D. Metcalf- 25Dec1827

Henry & Polly Moody 20 Jun 1793; b- Robert Hester con- Arthur Moody, father min- William Creath- 29Jun1793

Marshall & Nancy Phillips 18 Mar 1811; b- John C Phillips min- William Richards- 21Mar1811

Marshall & Elizabeth Speed 17 Mar 1823; b- David Shelton min- William Richards- 19Mar1823

Richard H & Eliza J White 20 Nov 1843; b- William White con- Jan A White, mother min- Charles F. Burnley- 22Nov1843

William & Mary Brummell 5 Aug 1819; b- John Brummell min- William Richards- 12Aug1819

William & Phebe Gregory 22 Feb 1825; b- Silas M Gregory min- William Richards- 1Mar1825

Moon

Joseph & Jane Johnson 24 Jan 1787; b- Isaac Johnson

Moore

Asa & Eliza Ann Gregory 12 Mar 1835; b- Elijah Gregory min- John B. Smith-

David & Larrisa Worsham 20 Dec 1830; b- William Vaughan con- S V Worsham, father min- Pleasant Gold- (Baptist)- 23Dec1830

Feild & Sarah Lidderdal 26 Nov 1774; b- Thomas Moore con- Thomas Anderson, guardian of Sarah

Franklin & Lucy Keeton - Nov 1835; b- William Boyd con- Joseph Keeton, father min- John B. Smith-

George M & Louiseanna Overby 9 Dec 1824; b- John Culbreath min- Pleasant Gold- (Baptist)-

George & Elizabeth Moody 14 Jul 1788; b- Thomas Moore min- John Williams- 24Jul1788

Henderson & Margaret Owen 17 Aug 1829; b- Joseph Owen min- Pleasant Gold- (Baptist)- 20Aug1829

James & Eliza Glasscock 19 Jan 1829; b- Granderson Glasscock con- Zachariah Glasscock, father min- Pleasant Gold- (Baptist)- 22Jan1829

John J & Martha R Brown 2 Oct 1823; b- William Hutcheson min- James Smith- 9Oct1823

John & Hannah Hutcheson 11 Aug 1801; b- Charles Hutcheson min- William Creath-

Littleberry & Mary Baker Yancey 21 Dec 1824; b- Richard Yancey min- Pleasant Gold- (Baptist)-

Marcus & Betsy Roberts 3 Mar 1813; daughter of William Roberts b- Nicholas Roberts

Marshall & Frances Gregory 2 Jan 1826; b- Elijah Gregory min- William Steel- (Episcopal)- 12Jan1826

Philip B & Phebe Elam - Dec 1789; b- Peter Elam min- John Williams- 24Dec1789

Robert & Nancy Harrison 21 Jul 1796; b- John Ogburn min- Charles Ogburn- (Methodist)

Robert & Betsy James Simmons 5 Sep 1821; b- John Simmons min- James M. Allen-

Starling & Huldy Ladd 27 Dec 1791; b- William Drumwright min- John Loyd- 29Dec1791

Warner & Betsy Edwards Northington 6 May 1805; b- Robert Moore con- Jabez Northington, mother

William (Jr) & Jane Williams 8 Nov 1787; b- William Moore Sr con- Edward Williams, mother

William H & Caroline Belcher 23 Apr 1832; b- Burwell B Belcher

William & Dorothy Hailey 20 Aug 1821; b- Meredith Hailey min- Pleasant Gold- (Baptist)- 23Aug1821

Morgan

Archelus & Martha Hicks Bowen 24 May 1814; b- William Bowen con-
William Bowen

Benjamin & Mary Bilbo 19 Dec 1785; b- Frederick Rainey con- James
Bilbo, father min- John King- 22Dec1785

Benjamin & Lucy W Ladd 8 Dec 1820; b- William Cleaton

Jesse & Elizabeth H Mills 10 Feb 1834; b- Albert Coley

John (Jr) & Nancy Cole 14 Mar 1789; b- Philip Morgan Sr

John & Agnes Bilbo 24 Aug 1779; b- Joseph Bilbo con- James Bilbo,
father

John & Sarah Chamberlain - --- 1803; b- Nathaniel Moss min- William
Creath- Apr1803

John & Sally Coleman 26 Dec 1818; b- Robert Talley con- Burwell
Coleman, father min- James Meacham- 29Dec1818

John & Ann W Norment 28 Feb 1820; b- John J Norment con- James
Norment, father min- William Richards-

John & Mary Pool 17 Feb 1790; b- Phil Morgan

John & Lucy Royster 9 Mar 1801; b- John Pritchett min- William
Richards- 26Mar1801

Philip & Patty Puckett 13 Oct 1784; b- Frederick Rainey

Robert & Tabitha Griffin 12 May 1821; b- John Watkins min- Pleasant
Gold- (Baptist)- 18May1821

Starling & Celia Loyd 7 Aug 1797; b- John Loyd min- Charles Ogburn-
(Methodist) 10Aug1797

William E & Sally Ann Puryear 10 Jun 1852; con- R A Puryear, father
min- Adam Finch- 16Jun1852

Morris

Archibald & Mary Guy 2 Feb 1841; b- Lethe Guy

Daniel J & Martha Wrenn 31 May 1843; b- William A Homes

Daniel & Nancy Saunders 15 Dec 1807; b- John Feagins con- John
Saunders Sr, father

Edward & Prudence Finn 8 Feb 1799; b- Nicholas Lanier min- William
Creath- 11Feb1799

Harrison R & Martha A Cheatham 4 Dec 1853; b- William G Cheatham
con- Nancy Tandy, mother of Martha

Henry & Lucy Drumwright 15 Dec 1807; b- William Drumwright

Jesse & Sally Williams Drumwright 26 Jan 1804; b- William Drumwright
con- William Drumwright, father min- William Creath-

John E & Mary Ann Chambers 7 Aug 1843; b- Randolph B Noblin con-
George D Chambers, father min- Thomas S. Campbell- 10Aug1843

Lucas & Rebecca W Drumwright 15 Dec 1840; b- E A Drumwright con-
Ephraim Drumwright, father min- James McAden-

Lunsford J & Frances P Saunders - Dec 1832; min- John B. Smith-

William J & Nancy Drumwright 24 Jan 1831; b- Lucas Drumwright con-
William Drumwright, father min- James McAden-

Morton

Samuel V & Rebecca Tarry 19 Aug 1850; con- Edward Tarry, father

Tazewell S & Mary C Scott 14 Jul 1832; b- George C Scott

Thomas L & Harriet A Jones 30 Jan 1842; b- William H Jones min-
F.H. McGuire-

William & Margaret E Watkins 5 Jan 1853; con- Ann V Watkins, mother
min- F.N. Whaley-

Moseley

Harrison & Mary Evans 16 May 1825; b- William Evans

James E & Mary H Richards 4 Nov 1852; con- John G Richards, father
min- Robert Burton- 17Nov1852

Lemuel & Susanna Richards 17 Jul 1815; b- John Tabb con- William Richards, father

Thomas B & Ann E Griffin 25 May 1841; b- William T White con- Spencer C Griffin, father min- John B. Smith-

Moss

Burwell & Lucy Roffe 19 Oct 1812; b- William Brown, son of James Brown con- William Brown, gdn of Lucy min- James Meacham- 10Nov1812

Henry A & Bettie P Farrar 25 Nov 1852; con- Henry C Moss, father con- Samuel Farrar, father min- George W. Andrews-

Henry C & Lucy A Burton 8 Sep 1823; b- Boswell B Moss

James A & Sophronia M Johnson 11 Dec 1851; con- John W Johnson, father min- George W. Andrews-

James O & Mary A Bowers 13 Aug 1838; b- Oswald M Moss con- Sanford Bowers, father min- James McAden-

John & Rebecca Cox 11 Dec 1809; b- Charles Cox min- James Meacham- 21Dec1809

Lewis & Nancy Franklin 15 May 1815; b- Thomas Moss

Meredith & Nancy Osling 21 May 1792; b- Samuel Oslin con- Jesse Osling, father Meredith from Brunswick County min- John Loyd- 31May1792

Nathaniel & Helina Dortch 8 Oct 1777; b- Labon Wright

Nathaniel & Martha Speed 19 Apr 1794; b- Lewis Dortch min- John Loyd- 25Apr1794

Oswald M & Margaret J Tanner 15 Nov 1841; b- Matthew Williams min- James McAden-

Ray & Jane Coleman 16 Mar 1782; b- William Coleman con- Richard Coleman

Robert H & Laura A Clack 16 Dec 1846; b- R F Moss con- Robert R Clack, father

Starling & Martha Howard - Oct 1802; b- Stephen Roberts

Thomas & Amey Blanks 11 May 1814; b- John Blanks min- John Ligon- 15May1814

William R & Amanda H Puryear 22 Dec 1845; b- William W Winckler con- Hezekiah Puryear, father min- E. Chambers-

William & Mary Robinson 12 Oct 1809; b- Henry Royall min- James Meacham- 13Oct1809

William & Sarah Stainback 9 Dec 1805; b- James Stainback con- Susie Stainback, mother

Mountcastle

William R & Elizabeth M A Manning 3 Sep 1839; b- John C Manning min- James A. Riddick-

Mullins

James & Frances Reamey 18 Jan 1827; b- James Reamey min- William Richards- 25Jan1827

Matthew & Elizabeth Crowder 14 Sep 1795; b- James Hudson min- William Richards- 22Dec1795

Pleasant & Polly Reamey 20 Dec 1852; con- Abraham Reamey, father min- Robert Burton- 23Dec1852

Spencer & Martha Hutcherson 19 Sep 1848; b- Pleasant Mullins

Valentine & Patsy Grigg 10 Nov 1794; b- James Hudson min- William Richards- 13Nov1794

Murphey

William & Elizabeth Eppes 8 May 1779; b- Isham Eppes

Murray

John & Elizabeth Malone 20 May 1811; daughter of Robert Malone b-
William Hendrick Jr

John & Martha Ann Wade - Oct 1839; b- Richard Wood min- John B.
Smith-

Richard & Eliza Gregory 18 Dec 1830; b- Barnett Gregory min- Pleasant
Gold- (Baptist)- 23Dec1830

Robert & Sarena Jones 3 Dec 1842; b- Allen Jones min- Alfred Apple-

Thomas & Mary H Atkinson 16 Aug 1841; b- Creed T Haskins con-
Solomon and Elizabeth Atkinson, parents min- Charles F. Burnley-

Thomas & Ruther Wood 26 Dec 1832; b- William Johnson con- Richard
Wood, father min- William Steel- (Episcopal)-

William & Quincey Francis Ligon 11 Dec 1846; b- David L Ligon con-
Phebe Ligon, mother min- Alfred Apple- 17Dec1846

William & Ann Malone 21 Aug 1827; b- James Newton con- Ann
Malone, mother min- Pleasant Gold- (Baptist)- 22Aug1827

Murrell

William & Celia Pennington 6 Feb 1811; b- William Drumwright

Mustian

Jeffrey & Elizabeth Stegall 5 Feb 1787; b- James Chambliss

Nance

Daniel & Sarah Russell 13 Mar 1780; b- James Standley

Isaac & Polly Standley 26 Nov 1818; b- Edward Giles con- William
Standley, father con- John Nance, father

Isham (Jr) & Nancy Rainey 8 Aug 1803; b- Thomas Nance min- Matthew
Dance- 11Aug1803

Isham & Susan Vaughan 17 Aug 1835; b- Ambrose Vaughan con-
Livingston H Vaughan, father

John (Jr) & Mary R Roberts 19 Dec 1831; b- William Pool con- John
Nance Sr, father

John & Frances Bugg 10 Apr 1786; b- Robert Nance con- John Bugg,
father

John & Frances Winn 17 Mar 1795; b- John Thomas min- John Loyd-
19Mar1795

Robert & Fatha Pennington 14 Jan 1790; b- William Drumwright con-
James Pennington, father

Thomas & Elizabeth Cleaton 20 Dec 1791; b- Thomas Cleaton min-
John Loyd- 22Dec1791

Thomas & Elizabeth Giles 4 Oct 1795; b- John Cleaton min- John Loyd-
28Oct1795

Thomas & Sally Malone 10 Jan 1810; b- Thomas Cleaton

William & Patsy Williams 4 Feb 1800; b- Lewis Williams min- Ebenezer
McGowan- 6Feb1800

Wyatt & Polly Cook 9 Jan 1794; b- John Cook

Nanney

Bennett & Eliza Davis 26 Feb 1848; b- Dabney A Hudson con- Henry
Davis, father

Charles & Brambly R Roberts 1 Aug 1846; b- William B King

Hewberry & Patsy Roberts 12 Jan 1792; b- John Fowler con- William
Roberts, father min- John Loyd- 13Jan1792

Hugh Berry & Tabitha Roberts 31 Jan 1817; b- William Bennett

Isaac H & Mary A Harris 23 Jun 1852; min- James McAden-

Isaac & Nancy Watson 18 Apr 1821; b- James B Watson con- Isaac
Watson, father min- James Smith- 19Apr1821

John & Mary Roberts 4 Nov 1822; b- James W Drumwright min-
Stephen Jones- (Lynchburg, Va.)- 6Nov1822

John & Tency Roberts 5 Oct 1835; b- Lewis G Wright con- Stephen Roberts, father

Marshall & Frances B Waller 19 Jan 1849; b- Charles Nanney con- John Waller, father min- James McAden- 20Jan1849

Roberts & Sarah Morgan 30 Jul 1804; b- Starling Morgan con- Benjamin Morgan, father

William & Frances King 5 May 1806; b- Hughberry Nanney con- Lewis King, father

Willis A & Henrietta Riggin 14 May 1850; b- William F White con- James Riggin, father min- Robert Burton- 15May1850

Nash

Abraham & Polly Carter 14 Nov 1796; b- William Naish min- William Creath-

Banister & Tempy Dunston 10 Mar 1835; b- James Chavous min- William Steel- (Episcopal)-

David H & Mary W Bracey 15 Oct 1849; b- Robert Malone min- Thomas Adams- (Lunenburg Co.)- 16Oct1849

Francis & Mary Ann Hardie 1 Jul 1822; b- Thomas A Gillespie min- William Richards- 22Jul1822

Hugh William & Martha Jane Mullins 22 May 1842; b- William J Carter

Hugh Wyley & Jane Crowder 16 May 1853; con- Theophilus Crowder, father min- George W. Andrews- 18May1853

Irby & Ann Eliza Dunston 15 Nov 1830; b- Richard M Dunn min- William Steel- (Episcopal)-

James & Sukey Pennington 23 Dec 1786; b- John George Pennington

John & Betsy Chambers 16 Dec 1795; b- Williamson Patillo min- John Loyd- 17Dec1795

John & Olive Ivey 11 Dec 1823; b- James Drew min- William Richards- 18Dec1823

Wiley & Anne Pennington 5 Jan 1807; b- John Harper

William & Mary Cox 17 Nov 1828; b- Wilson Cox con- Archer Cox, father min- James Smith- 18Nov1828

William & Leliah Hutt 12 Oct 1801; b- Thomas Hutt min- William Creath-

Wylie & Nancy Nash 14 Feb 1820; b- Shelton Powell con- Abram Nash, father of Nancy con- Thomas Nash, father of Wylie min- William Richards-

Neal

James & Emily Lunsford 4 Jan 1842; b- Volin Lunsford min- Charles F. Burnley-

John & Clarissa Poindexter 9 Jan 1775; b- Moses Overton Clarissa daughter of Phillip Poindexter Sr

Leonard & Jane Griffin 22 Jan 1816; b- DavidNeal min- Reuben Pickett- 1Feb1816

Leonard & Nancy Tillotson 22 May 1827; b- James Newton con- Thomas Tillotson, father min- Pleasant Gold- (Baptist)- 31May1827

Obadiah & Mary Griffin 10 May 1821; b- James H Newton min- Pleasant Gold- (Baptist)- 17May1821

Reaves & Elizabeth Worsham 8 Oct 1792; b- William Neal min- James Read- (Baptist)

Thomas & Elizabeth Brown 1 Jan 1787; b- Thomas Brown Thomas son of William Neal Sr

Thomas & Elizabeth C Coleman 8 Oct 1804; b- William Coleman s of Francis Moore Neal daughter of James Coleman dec. min- James Meacham- 23Oct1804

William & Harriett Apperson 10 Dec 1827; b- Alexander Blankenship
min- Pleasant Gold- (Baptist)-
William & Elizabeth S Roffe 28 Feb 1814; b- Jesse Roffe min- James
Meacham- 2Mar1814
Neathery
Buckner S & Sarah A Mallett 4 Apr 1846; b- William Mallett
Daniel & Sally Smith 14 Feb 1816; b- Edward Smith
Richard & Martha Baker 8 Oct 1830; b- WilliamBaker min- John B.
Smith-
Robert T & Emily J L Smith 20 Dec 1841; b- William C Neathery con-
Martha Smith, mother
Neathry
John & Nancy Westbrook 26 Dec 1815; b- Jesse Westbrook
Neblett
Sterling & Ann Daly 4 Oct 1798; b- Charles Ogburn con- Josiah Daly,
father min- Charles Ogburn- (Methodist) 8Oct1798
Neely
Thomas & Nancy Edwards 9 Feb 1813; b- James Meacham min- James
Meacham- 11Feb1813
Nelson
Edward & Margaret Williamson 19 Jul 1830; b- James Williamson min-
Pleasant Gold- (Baptist)- 22Jul1830
Nathaniel B & Mary Speed 23 Oct 1833; b- Edward Speed con- John J
Speed, father min- Benjamin Kidd- 31Oct1833
Norborne T & Lucy Nelson 8 Apr 1805; b- Henry Young min- Alexander
Hay- (Antrim Glebe, Antrim Parish, Halifax County) 15Apr1805
Robert C & Mary Scott Watkins 20 Dec 1847; b- T W Venable con-
Samuel V Watkins, father 'Dr' Robert C Nelson
William & Martha P Walker 16 Dec 1816; b- Thomas Blackburne con-
Richard H Walker, father min- Charles Ogburn- (Methodist) 23Dec1816
Nethery
Thomas & Ann Baker 27 Jan 1789; b- George Baker min- Thomas Scott-
Newman
John & Frederica C Claiborne 30 Jan 1825; b- William Brown con-
Henry Claiborne, father
John & Nancy Malone 12 Jan 1830; b- Michael Tarwater min- Pleasant
Gold- (Baptist)- 16Jan1830
Newsom
Robert & Martha Ruffin 2 Oct 1772; b- Francis Ruffin con- John Ruffin,
father
Newton
Henry Ezell & Martha R Elam 13 Nov 1849; b- John G Elam con-
Daniel Elam, father min- Alfred Apple- 30Nov1849
Henry & Patsy Ezell 23 Dec 1811; b- Thomas Stovall con- Balaam Ezell,
father
James W & Sally M Elam 21 Nov 1842; b- Richard T Elam con- Daniel
Elam, father
James & Elizabeth Newton 14 Mar 1803; b- Robert Newton
James & Mary Newton 3 Dec 1817; b- Joseph Newton con- Mary
Newton, mother
John J & Eliza T Averett 16 Oct 1848; b- Richard H Averett con-
Rebecca Averett, mother
John & Eliza F Brame 1 Dec 1849; b- David W Brame min- J.D.
Blackwell-
John & Eliza J Cox 22 Jan 1827; b- James H Newton con- John Cox,
father min- Pleasant Gold- (Baptist)- 24Jan1827

John & Nancy Gregory 16 Sep 1830; b- Samuel Puryear min- Pleasant Gold- (Baptist)-

Joseph & Mary Kimball 24 Dec 1817; b- James Newton con- William and Elizabeth Kimball, parents

Robert J & Phebe Cox 18 Aug 1828; b- James H Newton min- Pleasant Gold- (Baptist)- 22Aug1828

Robert & Margaret Malone 23 Sep 1833; b- James Newton con- Nancy Malone, mother min- Pleasant Gold- (Baptist)- 25Sep1833

Robert & Mary Read 8 Sep 1788; b- Elijah Graves

Robert & Louisa Vaughan 24 Jan 1844; b- Harman Newton con- Peter Vaughan, father min- Alfred Apple-

William P & Ann E Wright 21 Oct 1842; b- Daniel Yancey con- Nancy Wright, mother min- Alfred Apple-

William & Jane Farrar 25 Dec 1823; b- Abel Farrar min- Pleasant Gold- (Baptist)-

William & Mary Newton 20 Dec 1830; b- James Newton min- Pleasant Gold- (Baptist)- 23Dec1830

Nicholson

Albert G & Araminta S Jones 17 Jun 1847; b- William H Northington min- John C Blackwell- (Lunenburg County)- 22Jun1847

John W & Jane E T Denton 12 Jun 1853; con- Elizabeth G Denton, mother min- Willis N. Pence-

Richard & Frances Toone 16 Nov 1840; b- George W Freeman

Starling & Elizabeth Moore 5 Jul 1802; b- Lewis Nicholson

William & Martha Hardy 19 Nov 1786; widow b- Richard Swepson Sr

Nipper

Hutson & Frances Vaughan 16 Nov 1792; b- Ambrose Vaughan min- John Loyd- 22Nov1792

Pace & Rody Vaughan 23 Oct 1792; b- Hudson Nipper min- John Loyd- 24Oct1793

Noblin

Thomas & Philadelphia Williamson 18 Oct 1813; b- Edward Tillotson con- Robert Williamson, father

Noel

Fielding & Frances Wall 10 Dec 1823; b- Henry Wall min- James Smith-

Foster & Mary Jones 12 May 1812; b- West Gregory min- Milton Robertson- (Warren County, N.C.) 22May1812

William & Eliza S Roffe 2 Mar 1814; b- Jesse Roffe min- James Meacham-

Nolley

Alexander & Joyce B Langley 22 Mar 1823; b- John C Bugg min- Stephen Jones- (Lynchburg, Va.)- 25Mar1823

Francis A & Susan Delk 19 Feb 1842; b- William H Gee

James & Elizabeth E Moore 1 Aug 1817; b- John Bugg min- Charles Ogburn- (Methodist) 5Aug1817

John N & Elizabeth M Bugg 16 Jul 1827; b- Alexander Nolley min- James Smith- 25Jul1827

William & Sally G Smith 11 Feb 1833; b- Jesse Perkinson con- Thomas Smith, father

Norman

John & Martha Ann Smithson 24 Dec 1839; min- John B. Smith-

Norment

James & Jane Jeffries 28 Jun 1793; b- Richard Jeffries min- John Williams- 30Jun1793

Thomas (Jr) & Martha M Pettus 23 Jul 1818; b- Andrew Gregory con- William Pettus Sr, father min- William Richards- 24Jul1818

Thomas & Ann Jeffries 14 Feb 1785; b- John Jeffries min- John Marshall- (Baptist) 23Mar1785

Northcross

William Renn & Frances Hatsell 4 Mar 1786; b- John McCarter

Northington

David & Martha Crowder 13 Aug 1804; b- Peter Crowder min- James Watkins- 6Sep1804

Jonathon B & Elizabeth Wartmen 16 Dec 1822; b- Thomas W Walker con- Elizabeth Wartman, mother min- Stephen Jones- (Lynchburg, Va.)- 20Dec1822

William H & Mary A Northington 17 Oct 1849; b- J B Northington min- Thomas Adams- (Lunenburg Co.)-

Norvell

George W & Martha Ann Young 8 Aug 1840; b- Edmond Young

James & Elizabeth W Bland 22 Dec 1817; b- William H Bugg con- Samuel Bland, father min- James Meacham- 25Dec1817

Thomas A & Charlotte Ann Tucker 15 Dec 1834; b- Pettus Farrar min- M.P. Parks- 18Dec1834

William H & Martha E Goode - Nov 1840; b- Thomas A Norvell

William & Sally Booth 17 Feb 1817; b- Reuben Booth min- James Meacham- 27Feb1817

Norwood

Joseph A & Mary Y Gregory 28 May 1840; b- William Moody min- John B. Smith-

N M & Elizabeth C Holloway 8 Apr 1850; b- C T Haskins min- Robert Burton- 25Apr1850

Nowell

Allen & Elizabeth Stewart 14 Jul 1800; b- Frederick Nowell

John & Elizabeth Chamberlain 22 Mar 1785; b- John Hamner con- Thomas Chamberlain, father

Thomas & Sally Fox 12 Oct 1790; b- Thomas Roberts min- John King- 14Oct1790

Nunn

James T & Elizabeth Jones 7 Oct 1844; b- Allen Jones

William & Jane Bowen 17 Aug 1830; b- Allen Bowen min- Pleasant Gold- (Baptist)-

O'Briant

John & Patsy Moss 14 Dec 1795; b- William Moore

Ogburn

Matthew & Sarah Daly 15 Feb 1792; b- Charles Ogburn min- John Loyd- 16 Feb1792 con- Josiah Daly, father

Oliver

Alexander G & Ann F Tatum 1 Jul 1834; b- Benjamin W Coleman con- Benjamin Tatum, gdn of Ann

Asa & Sarah Wray 1 Dec 1772; b- John Oliver

George W (Jr) & Jane Burnett 6 Apr 1812; b- Richard Burnett min- James Meacham- 16Apr1812

James W & Elizabeth Green 2 Mar 1799; b- Abraham Green son of Asa and Sarah Oliver min- William Creath- 16Mar1799

James & Signiora Green 20 Nov 1830; b- Daniel T Hicks con- Grief Green, father min- William Steel- (Episcopal)- 1Dec1830

John & Elizabeth Bailey 8 Dec 1794; b- William Durham min- Charles Ogburn- (Methodist) 24Dec1794

Richard & Elizabeth Jeffries 12 Dec 1803; b- William Bilbo

Robert & Martha Moss - Dec 1805; b- Henry Coleman min- James Meacham- 18Dec1805

William & Lucy Hyde 18 Nov 1816; b- Irwin Hyde con- William Knight, gdn of William min- James Meacham- 22Nov1816

Organ

Thomas & Sarah Lucas 11 Nov 1805; b- John Dortch

Osborn

Jones & Nancy Fowlkes 12 Jun 1797; b- Edward Elam

Osborne

Samuel G & Elizabeth Callis 19 Nov 1821; b- William Callis min- William Richards- 25Nov1821

Thomas & Rebecca Johnson 4 Jul 1816; b- Miles Hall min- George Petty-

Oslin

David & Mary E J Barnes 16 Nov 1852; min- James McAden-

Isaac & Ann Pennington 1 Mar 1800; b- David Pennington

James & Susan Jones 8 Dec 1817; b- William S Oslin con- Wood Jones, father min- Thomas Adams- (Lunenburg Co.)-

Jesse & Clara Jane Green 22 Jan 1845; b- Richard B Baptist

Jesse & Elizabeth Pennington 26 Oct 1829; b- David Oslin min- James McAden-

John & Judith D Powers 28 Aug 1849; b- Samuel N Oslin min- James McAden- 29Aug1849

Lucas & Mary A Arnold 10 Dec 1826; b- Thomas C Batte min- James McAden- 12Dec1826

Samuel & Martha Bugg 7 Mar 1789; b- John Bugg

William S & Frances Nolley 26 Jan 1813; widow b- John Wright

Outland

Richard W & Susan A Richardson 10 Aug 1839; b- William A Richardson

Overby

Adam W & Elizabeth King 23 Dec 1813; b- Green Blanton con- John King, father

Anderson & Sally Newton 21 Jul 1828; b- James H Newton min- Pleasant Gold- (Baptist)-

David & Nancy Chandler 31 Dec 1821; b- Littleberry Chandler con- David Chandler, father min- Pleasant Gold- (Baptist)- 18Jan1822

David & Mary A C Holloway 16 Aug 1849; b- J G Moss

Edmund P & Dulcema Vaughan 17 Jul 1819; b- John F Carter con- Peter Z Overby, father con- S W Vaughan, father

Eggleston & Sally Williamson 17 Nov 1817; b- Thomas Noblin con- Robert Williamson, father

Eleazar & Sarah White 25 May 1824; b- David Dunn min- Pleasant Gold- (Baptist)- 3Jun1824

Goodwin S & Pauline W Smith 18 Oct 1836; b- James J Grimshaw con- John H Smith, gdn of Pauline

Henry & Silvana Overby 25 Dec 1824; min- Pleasant Gold- (Baptist)-

Henry & Martha Owen 21 Oct 1834; b- Thomas W Owen, father, who also gives consent

Hezekiah & Elizabeth Pool 7 Nov 1823; b- James Williamson con- H P Pool, father con- Peter Z Overby, father min- Pleasant Gold- (Baptist)- 22Nov1823

Isaac & Ann E Jones 29 Oct 1831; b- Royall Lockett Jr con- J M Jeffreys (Charlotte Co.), gdn of Ann min- John B. Smith-

James M & Matilda M Marshall 19 May 1832; b- Robert D Marshall

James & Elizabeth Overby 24 Feb 1817; b- John Vaughan

Jechonias & Jane Greenwood 11 Jan 1796; b- Hume R Feild min- William Creath-

John & Elizabeth Childress 11 Jun 1804; b- William Overby con- Jincey Childress, mother

Littleberry & Elizabeth J Overby 12 May 1843; b- James E Haskins

Obadiah & Edith Wilbourn 22 Dec 1817; b- William Wilbourn

Peter R & Emily Newton 30 Oct 1829; b- Reuben H Newton con- James H Newton, father min- Pleasant Gold- (Baptist)- 4Nov1829

Peter W & Elizabeth W Overby 29 Jun 1843; b- L B Overby

Peter & Cynthia H Worsham 7 Feb 1827; b- James Keen con- S V Worsham, father min- Pleasant Gold- (Baptist)- 1May1827

Robert Y & Mary Pettypool 28 Oct 1820; b- Phillip Rainey min- Pleasant Gold- (Baptist)- 27Nov1820

William & Edith Overby 23 Feb 1818; b- William Vaughan

William & Susannah Yancey 11 Jun 1804; b- Howell Graves

Overton

Edward & Mary C Wilkerson 22 Jun 1846; b- John T Wootton min- John B. Smith-

John & Martha Elizabeth Ballard 10 Nov 1806; b- Francis Ballard min- Charles Ogburn- (Methodist) 12Nov1806

John & Susannah Christopher 10 Jan 1772; daughter of David Christopher b- William Christopher

Thomas & Martha Toone 13 Apr 1795; b- Edward Hogan min- Edward Almand- 16Apr1795

William S & Mary Baskervill 10 Dec 1799; b- E Baskervill min- William Creath-

Owen

Edward E & Jane Jackson 19 Jul 1853; min- John E. Montague- (Granville County, N.C.)-

Evan & Eliza Neal 24 Jul 1838; b- William Owen con- Obadiah Neal, father

Joseph & Mary Ann Talley 18 Nov 1833; b- Abraham Talley min- John B. Smith-

Parham & Harriet Gold 31 Aug 1824; b- Thomas Owen con- Pleasant Gold, father min- Pleasant Gold- (Baptist)-

Sherwood & Sally Harris 7 Nov 1796; daughter of James Harris Sherwood from Halifax County b- James Harris min- Edward Almand- 8Nov1796

Stephen & Harriet Owen 9 Nov 1843; b- John Owen con- William Owen, father min- Alfred Apple-

Thomas W & Polly Newton 27 Sep 1834; b- John Wright con- James H Newton, father min- John B. Smith-

Thomas & Polly Griffin 28 Jan 1843; b- Elias Griffin min- Thomas King- (Halifax County)- 26Feb1843

Thomas & Frances S Ligon 7 Jan 1833; b- Obadiah Ligon con- Frances Ligon, mother min- John B. Smith-

William & Nancy Carter 27 May 1815; b- Charles T Carter, father, who also consents min- Reuben Pickett- 10Jun1815

William & Nancy Stone 20 Dec 1819; b- Hardy Stone con- Joseph Owen, father min- Pleasant Gold- (Baptist)-

William & Nancy Vaughan 1 Oct 1847; b- Henry H Newton con- C Vaughan, father min- Alfred Apple- 2Nov1847

Pace

J Alexander & Mary C Spain 19 Oct 1853; J Alexander Pace from Petersburg, VA con- Henry M Spain, father min- S.T. Moorman-

Paine

William L & Rebecca A Davis 19 Jul 1824; b- T A Boyd con- Thomas Power, gdn of Rebecca

Palmer
Amasa & Sally Davis 2 Mar 1774; b- William Davis
Amasa & Judith Hendrick 13 Dec 1800; b- Christopher Haskins
Horace & Susan T Russell 30 Jun 1827; b- Samuel Young con- William
Hendrick, gdn of Susan min- James Smith- 5Jul1827
James & Martha Hester 9 May 1791; b- William Durham Watkins
Paul M & Sally S Langley 17 Mar 1828; b- Samuel Tarry con- Jane T
Langley, mother min- James Smith- 26Mar1828
William & Elizabeth Lewis 12 Oct 1772; b- Edward Lewis
Parham
Lewis & Betsy Baird 22 May 1769; b- John Tabb
Robert & Nancy W Evans 31 Oct 1845; b- John Hunley min- James
McAden-
William & Frances Smith 2 Jun 1851; min- J.D. Blackwell-
Paris
John & Maria C Yancey 17 Dec 1849; b- C F Harris min- C.F. Harris-
Parish
Jesse C & Alethea Colley 29 Jun 1846; b- Whitehead M Coleman min-
E. Chambers-
Parker
John & Martha Ann Allgood 7 Jan 1840; b- Richard H Allgood con-
George Allgood, father
Parrish
Jesse & Elizabeth Hutcheson 27 Jun 1810; b- John Ingram
William & Frances Lett 30 Dec 1786; b- Isaac Adams
William & Martha Rudd 19 Nov 1807; b- Augustine Smith min- Richard
Dabbs- 21Nov1807
William & Camilla Tudor 9 Dec 1801; b- William Roberts
Parrott
William & Jean Elizabeth Johnson 15 Apr 1819; min- Charles Ogburn-
(Methodist)
Patillo
Charles M & Caroline B Barlow 17 Dec 1850; con- Eliza Barlow, mother
min- S.A. Creath-
Edward M & Mary J Neal 30 Aug 1845; b- W M Coleman min- John
B. Smith-
James H & Susan H Land 16 Dec 1845; b- Robert W Land
John P & Pamelia R Brame 4 Feb 1834; b- William A Clausel min-
John B. Smith-
Robert A & Helen M Land 21 Nov 1849; b- James H Patillo con-
Elizabeth B Land
Samuel H & Sally E Phillips 15 Dec 1808; b- John C Phillips con- Pettus
Phillips min- James Meacham-
William J & Martha Jones 20 Jan 1812; b- Joel Watkins min- James
Meacham-
Williamson & Jane Phillips 13 Jul 1808; b- Martin Phillips min- James
Meacham-
Patrick
John & Sarah Kendrick 29 Sep 1779; b- John Kendrick
Patterson
Hardy & Betsy C McKinney 20 Mar 1815; b- William King Betsy
daughter of Munford McKinney
Samuel & Sicily Poindexter 11 Jan 1773; daughter of Phillip Poindexter
Sr b- Phil Poindexter
Paul
D'Arcy W & Mary J Rainey 29 Apr 1845; b- Phillip Rainey

Paulette

Jesse M & Martha J Feilder 30 Jan 1850; b- W O Manning con- Dennis R Feilder, father

Paull

James & Elizabeth Brook 12 Feb 1776; b- Dudley Brook

Paylor

Byrd D & Marstelle A Williamson 20 Apr 1850; b- Beverly Williamson con James Williamson, father

Payne

Charles L & Mary Ann Lewis 26 Mar 1834; b- Frederick Lewis con- John Lewis Sr, father min- A.D. Montgomery- 'Dr' Charles L Payne

Pearcy

John R & Rebecca Hall 15 Feb 1815; daughter of John Hall b- John Hall

Pearson

John J D & Rhoda R A Thomas 25 Nov 1846; b- R W Thomas con- Tinsy Thomas, mother min- James McAden-

John & Mary Ann Rainey 30 Sep 1811; b- Smith Rainey

Littleberry & Nanny Thomas 1 Dec 1786; b- Peter Thomas

Littleberry & Sally Thomas 13 Sep 1819; b- Riddick Pearson

Thomas (Jr) & Mary Delony 19 Sep 1768; daughter of Henry Delony b- Henry Delony

Peebles

Robert & Maria Roberts 24 Dec 1821; b- Edmond Roberts

Thomas E & Susanna P Lucas 20 Mar 1804; b- William Parham

William R & Susan Hutcherson 13 Oct 1817; b- Giles Puryear min- James Meacham- 14Oct1817

Peek

William & Martha Ann Griffin 2 Sep 1833; b- Elias Griffin

Peete

Edwin H & Nancy Speed 8 Jan 1807; b- Charles Ogburn con- James Wilson, guardian of Nancy min- James Meacham- 13Jan1807

Pennington

Drury & Nancy Conner 24 Oct 1823; b- John H Hardie

Drury & Mary L Oslin 20 Nov 1833; b- Richard B Baptist min- James McAden-

Drury & Polly Quarles 6 Dec 1809; b- John Wright

John T & Elizabeth Hall 22 Feb 1813; b- John Hall, father, who consents and test. Elizabeth 21 yrs old

Philip & Mary Burton 31 May 1798; b- John Hubbard min- Ebenezer McGowan- 14Jun1798

Philip & Patty Floyd 29 Jan 1787; b- John Saunders

Philip & Martha A Hubbard 9 Dec 1839; b- David Oslin con- Ralph Hubbard, father min- James McAden-

Robert & Frances Finch 26 Jan 1787; b- Sherwood Smith

Walter & Polly Mabry 22 Dec 1802; b- Isham Nance Jr

Penticost

Scarborough & Phebe Lockett 8 Feb 1790; b- Daniel D Watkins min- John Williams- 18Feb1790

Peoples

Nathaniel M & Lucy R Eubank 5 Oct 1836; b- Thomas G Boyd con- Benjamin Coleman, gdn of Lucy min- William B. Rowzee-

Thomas & Lucy Hutt 25 Feb 1828; b- William Brummell min- William Steel- (Episcopal)- 26Feb1828

Perkins

David & Matilda Moore 19 Aug 1811; b- Franklin Moore con- George
Moore, father

Perkinson

Jesse & Mary Ann Tucker 15 Oct 1833; b- William Smelley con- George
Tucker, father min- James McAden-

John & Mary Ann Thomas 12 Dec 1825; b- Leonard Thomas

Rowlett & Susanna Pettus 19 Jan 1798; b- Matthew Pettus min- William
Creath-

Travis & Mary E Quincey 12 Aug 1839; b- William N Smith con- William
A Quincey, brother of Mary

William & Mary Pettus 8 Feb 1790; b- Thomas Pettus

Wyatt T & Susan Keeton 3 Nov 1849; b- Joseph A Keeton

Perry

James G & Eleanor F Tucker 25 Feb 1841; min- Charles F. Burnley-

Pescud

P F & Mary J Wilson 27 Apr 1843; b- Wesley Whitaker Jr min- John
B. Smith-

Pettiford

Collin S & Aggy Brandon 26 Jan 1830; b- John Stewart min- William
Steel- (Episcopal)- 28Jan1830

Pettipool

Wiltshire Gromarin & Martha Ingram 21 Dec 1792; b- William Green
con- Pines Ingram, father

Pettus

David & Jane F Puryear 27 Jan 1827; b- John Smith

Horatio & Mary S Poindexter 9 Dec 1799; daughter of Phillip and Sarah
Poindexter b- William Pettus min- Edward Almand- 17Dec1799

John E & Eliza W McCutcheon 29 Dec 1841; b- John E McCutcheon
con- Charles McCutcheon, father min- Charles F. Burnley- 5Jan1842

John H & Martha W Taylor 15 Nov 1830; b- William W Oliver con-
Martha Taylor, mother min- James Smith- 24Nov1830

John & Mary F Norment 19 Feb 1821; b- John Binford con- Thomas
Norment, father min- William Richards- 24Feb1821

John & Elizabeth Walker Pettus 12 Aug 1782; daughter of Thomas Pettus
b- Thomas Pettus Jr

Musgrove L & Susan D Smith 25 Feb 1833; b- Giles R Smith min-
William Richards- 27Feb1833

Thomas P & Elizabeth R Jones 1 May 1811; daughter of Edward Jones,
dec. b- Charles Baskervill con- Richard R and Elizabeth Jones, gdns of
Elizabeth min- William Richards- 16May1811

William & Betsy Ann Poindexter 9 Mar 1789; daughter of Phillip and
Sarah Poindexter b- Samuel Hopkins Jr

Pettway

John & Nartha Alexander 11 Aug 1792; b- John Alexander

Petty

Mathias & Elizabeth Fowlkes 24 Dec 1814; n- Nathaniel Fowlkes con-
Thompson Fowlkes, father min- William Richards- 27Dec1814

Pettypool

Allen & Sally Pettypool 15 Mar 1813; b- Stephen Pettypool

Edward P & Sally Gregory 18 Apr 1836; b- John Clark con- James
Williamson, gdn of Sally, daughter of Atha Gregory, dec. min- John B.
Smith-

Edward & Mary LeNeve 9 Oct 1838; b- Robert A Phillips con- John
LeNeve, father

Edward & Tarissa Ann Talley 7 Nov 1843; b- Burwell Barron con- Peyton R and Jane Talley, parents min- John B. Smith-

George W & Emily H Yancey 30 Oct 1837; b- James Yancey con- Richard Yancey, father

John E & Frances Blanks 18 Jul 1814; b- John Blanks con- Ann Blanks, mother

Peterson & Elizabeth A Cheatham 13 Oct 1835; b- Woodson V Johnson

Spencer & Elizabeth Talley 6 Feb 1844; b- William L Yancey con- Payton R Talley, father

William & Sarah Bugg 19 Jul 1830; b- William Turner min- James McAden-

William & Frances Owen 2 Oct 1837; b- Edmond F Pettypool con- Thomas Owen, father

William & Mary Martha Ragsdale 10 Mar 1828; b- Hutchins F Tanner Washington Maddox test that Mary is under 21 min- James McAden- 13Mar1828

William & Jane Talley 15 Aug 1814; b- Stephen Pettypool con- Stephen Pettypool, gdn of Jane min- Reuben Pickett- 30Aug1814

Phillips

Archibald & Mary Hanserd 26 Nov 1795; b- Richard Hanserd

Charles C & Mary C Hutcheson 4 Apr 1825; b- William Stone con- Joseph Hutcheson, father

Dabney (Jr) & Martha Hutcheson 6 Jan 1801; b- William Brown con- Dabney Phillips Sr, father con- Charles Hutcheson, father min- William Creath-

Dyer & Patience Clay 18 Dec 1786; b- Thomas Dawson con- Charles Clay, father

James D & Sylvania Elliott 27 Nov 1851; con- Sylvania Elliott, mother min- John E. Montague- (Granville County, N.C.)-

James H & Permelia M Roffe 3 Nov 1846; b- Joseph H Lett con- Samuel D Roffe, father min- T.W. Sydnor- 10Nov1846

John B & Mary H Gee 12 Oct 1840; b- H W Harper con- Milly T Gee, mother min- James McAden-

John C & Sally Simmons 5 Jun 1816; b- James Phillips Joseph Simmons, father min- James Meacham- 6Jun1816

John & Susanna Cox 2 Dec 1829; min- Pleasant Gold- (Baptist)-

John & Lilly Hansard 18 Dec 1816; b- Charles H Baird min- Charles Ogburn- (Methodist)-

John & Fanny Walker 10 Sep 1798; John from Prince George County b- Theophilus Feild min- Alexander Hay- (Antrim Glebe, Antrim Parish, Halifax County) 16Sep1798

Jonathon & Martha Abernathy 20 Dec 1809; b- Liles Abernathy

Jonathon & Susan Curtis 19 Feb 1827; b- James D Brame con- Susan Curtis, mother min- Allen D. Metcalf-

Martin & Lucy Suggett 5 Nov 1808; b- John Hutcheson

Pettus C & Susan J Hughes 20 Dec 1847; b- James C Hughes con- Susannah C Hughes, mother

Pettus & Rebeccah Coleman 6 Mar 1788; daughter of Cluverius Coleman b- Lewis Parham min- Thomas Scott-

Pettus & Dorcas Pettus 31 May 1814; b- Edward M Patillo con- Samuel Pettus, father min- James Meacham-

Richard & Elizabeth Green 20 Nov 1815; b- Stephen Stone

Richard & Lucinda Poindexter 4 Jan 1825; b- George Poindexter

Robert A & Caroline LeNeve 21 Dec 1840; b- John LeNeve Sr

Robert & Emily C Hurt 10 Apr 1845; b- James W Crenshaw min- William J. Norfleet- 16Apr1845

Robert & Minerva J Johnson 1 Aug 1853; min- James McAden-

Thomas D & Elizabeth G Hudson 7 Dec 1846; b- O J Phillips con- Charles Hudson, father

William P & Elizabeth G Smith 9 Nov 1841; b- Thomas D Phillips con- James Smith, father min- James McAden-

William & Rachel Edmundson 14 Oct 1793; b- George B Hamner con- Samuel Edmundson, father

William & Betsy Turner 20 Dec 1799; b- Matthew Turner Jr con- John Turner, father min- William Creath-

Piller

Edward Alexander & Narcissa A B Rainey 5 Sep 1843; b- John W Piller con- Buckner M D Rainey, father min- Daniel Petty-

Pinson

Gilbert & Nancy Bowen 29 Sep 1824; b- Benjamin Bowen min- Pleasant Gold- (Baptist)- 5Oct1824

Joseph & Mary Jones 12 May 1794; b- Arthur Atkinson con- Richard Jones, father min- James Read- (Baptist)

Thomas & Lucy Johnston 12 Feb 1810; b- Caleb Johnston

Plummer

Alfred & Frances J Love 13 Jun 1835; b- John J Davis con- Horace Palmer, gdn of Frances

Poarch

Independence & Patsy Ellis 2 Feb 1807; b- Morris Green Burton

Independence & Lucy Hudson 8 Aug 1801; b- Thomas Webb min- James Meacham- 13Aug1801

Isham & Nancy Matthews 2 Jan 1802; b- Benjamin W Hudson min- James Meacham- 6Jan1802

Poindexter

George & Nancy Hinton 24 Dec 1791; son of Phillip and Sarah Poindexter b- Randolph Westbrook min- John Williams- 27Dec1791

Philip (Jr) & Jane Goode 13 Jun 1768; b- Richard Witton, Jr. con- Edward Goode, father

Philip (Jr) & Mary Hinton 12 Aug 1799; b- Thomas Dance

William H & Sarah W Langhorne 6 Jun 1837; b- A Langhorne min- Charles F. Burnley-

Pool

Alexander & Angelina Crowder 11 Oct 1790; b- Thomas Norment

Poole

Mitchell & Nancy Christopher 16 Aug 1797; b- Turner Sharp

William (Jr) & Rebecca Tanner 17 Jan 1797; b- Thomas Tanner min- John Loyd- 18Jan1797

Pope

Richard C & Maria Cunningham 29 Nov 1852; con- James Cunningham, father min- J.W. Chesley- 30Nov1852

Portwood

Robert H & Rebecca A Vaughan 10 Jan 1845; b- Adonis M Evans con- Balaam Vaughan, father

Potter

Abraham & Sarah Hawkins 6 Feb 1771; b- John Potter

Donaldson & Jane Wright 3 Sep 1804; b- Edmund Clements min- James Meacham- 6Sep1804

Potts

Hamlin & Mause Adaline Wall 16 May 1838; b- Benjamin T Willard con- Ann D Wall, mother

John W & Lucy Nelson Boyd 3 Nov 1834; b- Alfred Boyd min- William Steel- (Episcopal)- 4Nov1834

Powell

Shelton & Nancy Haile 8 Jan 1818; b- Thomas Gillespie min- William Richards-

William & Lucinda Rainey 21 Feb 1810; b- William Cook

Powers

Allen & Selah W Nash 13 Dec 1838; b- George C Nash min- James McAden-

Henry & Mary Ann Abernathy 19 Dec 1831; b- John P Smith min- Charles Ogburn- (Methodist) 22Dec1831

Thomas & Rebecca Wright 19 Mar 1827; b- Christopher Haskins Jr

Poynor

Diggs & Janet Walker 14 Sep 1814; b- Phillip Rainey con- Henry Walker, father

John & Mary G Holloway 27 Jan 1814; b- John Davis min- James Meacham-

Poythress

David & Mary Speed Dortch 17 Dec 1827; b- Isaac Taylor con- Ann Dortch, mother

Edward & Mahaley Nance 2 Nov 1828; b- William Drumwright min- James Smith- 10Dec1828

Lewis Y & Mary C Ferguson 20 Jul 1846; b- William A Dortch

Lewis & Elizabeth Giles 26 Dec 1792; b- Meredith Poythress min- John Loyd- 27Dec1792

Lewis & Rebecca B Taylor 9 Apr 1802; b- Thomas Watson min- James Meacham-

Lewis & Martha E Walker - Jul 1846; min- James McAden-

Meredith & Edith Cleaton 14 Jul 1781; b- William Cleaton

William & Ann Bently 10 Nov 1802; b- Thomas Rogers

Prather

William H & Mary C Johnson 16 May 1843; b- Irby Creath

Preston

Joshua & Lisha Feagins 18 Dec 1792; b- John Saunders Joshua from Brunswick County min- John Loyd- 20Dec1792

Price

Henry & Nancy Daves 18 Oct 1821; b- William B Easley min- Alexander M. Cowan-

Pugh Williamson & Elizabeth Williamson 4 Jul 1794; groom from Prince Edward County b- Josiah Price con- Robert Williamson, father min- William Richards- 5Jul1794

William B & Jane B Bailey 20 Jan 1820; b- Richard C Bibb con- P Bailey, father min- Richard Dabbs- (Lunenburg County)-

Prichett

Alexander & Louisa Jane Johnson 21 Dec 1829; b- William T Coleman con- Phillip Johnson, father min- Charles Ogburn- (Methodist) 29Dec1829

Pride

William & Mary H Harwell 30 Aug 1827; b- William Harwell con- James Harwell, father min- James Smith- 5Sep1827

William & Elizabeth C Hutcheson 11 Jan 1843; b- Charles S Hutcheson con- Joseph Hutcheson, father

Pritchett

James & Catherine Cumbia 19 Aug 1839; b- Thomas Cumbia min- Benjamin R. Duval-

John & Susanna Cox 14 Dec 1795; b- William Hudson min- William Creath- 23Dec1795

Thomas (Jr) & Sally Hunt Hatsell 7 Aug 1798; b- Edward Hatsell min- Matthew L. Easter- 10Aug1798

Thomas & Susan C Tucker 18 Apr 1851; min- J.D. Blackwell-
Thomas & Mary Weatherford 3 Jun 1835; b- Alexander Pritchett
Pryor
Richard & Virginia Boyd 24 Dec 1821; b- William B Easley min- John S. Ravenscroft- (Episcopal)-
Puckett
Banister & Betsy Page 7 Jan 1801; b- Isaac Bowen
John & Jane Hopkins 28 Feb 1792; b- John Farrar
Pugh
Richard C & Lucy Ann Higgerson 4 May 1853; con- Charles Higgerson, father
Pulliam
Benjamin & Ann Hester 8 Mar 1784; b- Stephen Mabry
Byrd & Susanna Phillips 8 Apr 1791; b- James Pulliam min- James Read- (Baptist)- no date given
John & Elizabeth Wilson 11 Sep 1775; b- Benjamin Pulliam
Richard & Martha Mealer 1 Oct 1791; b- Elijah Graves min- James Read- (Baptist) -6Oct1791
Pullian
Drury & Eliza Griffin 20 Dec 1843; b- Ranson Elliott Drury from Halifax Co., VA min- Alfred Apple-
Pully
Hutchins & Rebecca Jones 21 Dec 1821; b- Archer Phillips con- Berryman Jones, father min- James Smith-
James & Lucy Moss 21 Dec 1805; b- David Moss
William D & Rhoann R Drumwright 18 Dec 1850; con- George Drumwright, father min- James McAden-
William & Margaret Lawrence 26 Nov 1784; b- Hubbard Ferrell
Puryear
Achillis & Virginia Lewis Jeffries 23 Oct 1850; con- Rebecca Jeffries, mother
Achillis & Sarah B Lockett 15 Apr 1831; b- Royall Locket Jr con- Royal Lockett Sr, father min- William Richards- 19Apr1831
Alexander B & Polly F Edwards 30 Jun 1815; b- Philip Rainey con- Thomas Neal, gdn of Polly, who is daughter of Peter Edwards, dec.
Alexander & Sarah Jones 10 Dec 1847; b- Anderson Puryear con- Richard Jones, father
Elijah & Elizabeth Overton 2 Dec 1802; b- John Overton Jr min- Edward Almand- 9Dec1802
Giles R & Lucy A Roffe 22 Apr 1850; b- John B Roffe con- Jesse Roffe, father
Giles & Martha Hutcherson 21 Apr 1819; b- Wright King min- James Meacham- 22Apr1819
Grandison F & Ann Puryear 31 Aug 1840; b- Applin Puryear min- Solomon Apple- 8Sep1840
Hezekiah & Kitty Hayes 10 Jan 1803; b- Thomas Puryear min- Matthew Dance- 17Feb1803
Hezekiah & Mary Hudson 16 Sep 1811; b- William M Sewpson con- John Hudson, father min- Charles Ogburn- (Methodist) 18Sep1811
Hezekiah & Rebecca Jones 24 Dec 1821; b- Andrew J Elam con- Drury A Bacon, gdn of Rebecca Jones min- William Richards- 26Dec1821
Hezekiah & Eliza I Oliver 1 Nov 1826; b- James T Moss con- Robert Oliver, father min- John B. Smith-
James H & Ann Talley 15 Nov 1841; b- Burwell Barron con- William Talley, father min- John B. Smith-
James & Milly Moseley 12 Dec 1808; b- John Puryear

John (Jr) & Johannah ----- 20 Jun 178-; b- Samuel Puryear bond torn
John (Jr) & Sally S Clausel 24 Oct 1799; b- Hezekiah Puryear min- William Creath-
John & Polly Hudson 12 Dec 1808; b- Samuel Hudson min- William Richards-
John & Betsy Thompson 19 Aug 1822; b- Charles T Carter min- Pleasant Gold- (Baptist)- 27Aug1822
Littleberry S & Dolly Carter 16 Dec 1837; b- William Carter
Parsons G & Maria L Gillespie 13 Nov 1850; con- Martha Gillespie, mother min- William V. Wilson-
Peter & Ann F Barnes 7 Nov 1840; b- William E Roffe con- Henry Barnes, father min- Edward Wadsworth- 12Nov1840
Peter & Phebe Burton 10 Dec 1792; b- Thomas Crowder
Randolph & Susanna Hunt 3 Dec 1813; b- Solomon Hunt
Reuben & Martha Clausel 23 Dec 1791; b- James T Hayes min- William Creath- 27Dec1791
Reuben & Ann E Hamner 29 Oct 1826; b- B H Bailey con- George B Hamner, father min- John B. Smith- 1Nov1826
Richard C & Mary A Pettus 22 Jul 1834; b- Benjamin W Coleman
Richardson & Lucy Smith 16 Dec 1833; b- Giles R Smith min- William Richards- 18Dec1833
Samuel & Frances Clausel 17 Jan 1786; b- Richard Clausel
Samuel & Mary R Edwards 17 Dec 1822; b- R C Puryear con- Martha R Edwards, widow, mother min- John S. Ravenscroft- (Episcopal)-
Samuel & Mary R Lindley 31 Oct 1815; b- Giles Puryear minister not listed, but ceremony date 2Nov1815
Samuel & Martha Newton 21 Dec 1829; b- William Newton min- Pleasant Gold- (Baptist)- 24Dec1829
Samuel & Sally Stith Puryear 20 Sep 1810; b- Mackintosh Puryear con- Sarah Puryear, mother of Sally
Samuel & Susannah Stone 28 Feb 1842; b- Alexander Puryear con- Hardy Stone, father min- Alfred Apple-
Semour & Sarah Royster 10 Apr 1775; b- John Puryear
Seymour & Fanny Vaughan 11 Mar 1807; b- Wiley Burrus con- Nancy Foster, aunt of Fanny
Thomas & Patsy Harris 25 Mar 1801; b- Allen Harris con- Reuben Harris, father min- William Richards- 2Apr1801
Thomas & Elizabeth Marshall 13 May 1805; b- Francis Lockett min- William Richards- 23May1805
William M & Sally Keeton 8 Nov 1815; Sally daughter of John Keeton b- Giles Puryear
William M & Louisa J Tarwater 1 Dec 1832; b- Edward A Tarwater con- Michael Tarwater, father min- William Steel- (Episcopal)- 4Dec1832
William N & Dorothy A Crutchfield 18 Jun 1849; b- William C Crutchfield con- Peter Crutchfield, father min- James McAden- 21Jun1849
William & Rebecca Carleton 22 Sep 1785; b- John Farrar con- Thomas Carleton, father

Quarles
Williamson & Polly Benford 14 Jan 1806; b- Thomas Benford
Quinchett
Alexander & Margaret Susanna Stewart 29 Mar 1845; b- G W Mallett
Richard & Martha Parker 5 Jul 1839; b- Berry Lewis Susan Parker, sister of Martha, test that Martha over 21 min- James Delk-

Rachael

Alexander & Polly Renn 2 Jan 1819; b- Burwell Coleman con- Phillip Johnson, to whom Alexander was apprenticed min- Milton Robertson- (Warren County, N.C.) 14Jan1819

Ragland

Abner & Nancy Fox 3 Mar 1799; b- Richard Fox min- Ebenezer McGowan- 5Mar1799

Ragsdale

Anthony & Anne Wells 1 Oct 1793; b- William Westbrook con- David Wells, father min- William Creath- 3Oct1793

Cornelius & Frances Mealer 5 Oct 1795; b- William Hundley min- William Richards- 15Oct1795

Drury & Susanna Mealer 22 Dec 1785; b- Thomas Wilbourn

Edward & Obedience Hudson 3 Dec 1817; b- Stephen Hudson min- William Richards-

Richard & Barsheba Bishop 8 Feb 1802; b- Littleberry Carter min- William Creath-

Richard & Judith Hudson 23 May 1799; b- Richeson Farrar

Robert & Ann J Taylor 16 Aug 1828; min- John B. Smith-

Robert & Nancy I Taylor 31 Dec 1825; b- Sherwood Harris

Smith Y & Elizabeth Stone 4 Feb 1843; b- William G Gary con- Margaret Stone, mother min- John B. Smith-

William J & Emily Tillotson 6 Oct 1834; b- James Yancey con- William Tillotson, gdn of Emily

Rainey

Allen & Hannah Harwell 20 Oct 1817; b- James L Nance con- Annie Harwell, mother, who test Hannah is 21 min- James Meacham- 22Oct1817

Buckner & Rebecca Holmes 12 Jun 1780; b- Samuel Lark

Buckner & Mary H Nance 21 Nov 1828; b- Paschall Bracey con- John Nance, father min- James Smith- 22Nov1828

Edmond & Polly H Morgan 21 Oct 1807; b- Starling Morgan

Edwin & Elizabeth Harris 15 Jul 1811; min- David McCargo- (Charlotte County, Va.)

Francis & Judith Lambert 7 Jan 1797; b- Mark Lambert Jackson

Frederick & Molly Morgan 10 May 1775; b- John Tabb

Herbert B & Martha A O Hutcheson 20 Mar 1853; min- Robert Burton-

Isham & Betsy Morgan 20 Jan 1789; b- Frederick Rainey min- Phillip Cox- 21Jan1789

Leroy & Eliza Cook 14 Jun 1841; b- William P Cook con- John Cook, father min- James McAden-

Peter H & Sarah S Drumwright - Jan 1853; min- James McAden-

Phillip & Ann Lewis Boyd 3 Jun 1824; b- William B Easley con- Alexander Boyd, father

Reuben & Catherine Cleaton 22 Aug 1811; daughter of Thomas Cleaton, Sr, who serves as bondsman

Robert & Levisy Crowder 27 Mar 1805; b- Nathaniel Crowder

Smith & Ann Standley 31 Dec 1796; b- James Standley min- John Loyd- 4Jan1797

Thomas H & Eliza P Baird 17 Oct 1836; b- Charles W Baird min- James McAden-

William & Betsy W Rainey 17 Jun 1822; b- William Rainey Jr con- Smith Rainey, father of Mary min- Stephen Jones- (Lynchburg, Va.)- 19Jun1822

William & Lucy Williams 27 Nov 1817; b- Wright King con- Lewis Williams, father min- Thomas Moore- 4Dec1817

Williamson & Martha Cook 22 Dec 1810; b- Charles D Cleaton con-
John Cook Sr, father
Williamson & Martha Cook 22 Dec 1810; b- Charles D Cleaton con-
John Cook, Sr., father
Williamson & Edith Morgan 23 Nov 1779; b- Francis Rainey con- Reuben
Morgan

Ramsey

Thomas & Judith Ann Wilkinson 5 Aug 1841; b- Spencer C Wilkinson
min- John B. Smith-

Ransom

James & Mary Hayes 9 Jul 1787; b- James T Hayes James from Amelia
County

Ravenscroft

John Stark & Anne Spottswood Burwell 13 Aug 1792; d of Lewis b-
William Hepburn

Read

Charles & Jane A Boyd 18 Oct 1816; 'Dr' Charles Read b- Alexander
Boyd Jr con- William Boyd, father
Horace L & Elizabeth J Boyd 12 Apr 1819; b- Alexander Boyd con-
William Boyd, father
Isaac & Panthea Burwell 21 Oct 1816; b- Armistead Burwell
M C & Jane C Burwell 3 Oct 1842; b- Edward Keen con- J R Burwell,
father, who test Jane 21yrs old

Reader

Jehu & Phebe Robards 13 Jul 1801; b- James Wilson min- William
Richards- 21Jul1801
Jephthah & Winny Harrison 10 Jan 1803; b- Greenwood Harrison min-
William Richards- 19Jan1803
Robert & Mary Mullins 25 Dec 1792; b- James Hudson min- John
Williams- -27Dec1792
Thomas & Lucy Mullins 10 Dec 1798; b- Richard Hughes min- William
Richards- 13Dec1798

Reagan

John F & Catharine Evans 5 Oct 1791; b- William Taylor min- Edward
Almand- 23Oct1791

Reamey

Abraham & Harriet Royster 15 Aug 1814; b- Thomas A Gillespie min-
William Richards- 6Oct1814
Daniel & Malvina Wall 2 Sep 1817; b- Mastin Harris con- Martha Wall,
mother min- James Meacham- 3Sep1817
Edwin & Elizabeth Harris 15 Jul 1811; b- William Harris min- David
McCargo- (Charlotte County, Va.)
Gholson T & Amanda W Mullins 16 Jun 1853; con- James Mullins, father
min- Robert Burton-
Humbleston & Martha T Mullins 22 Dec 1848; b- James Mullins min-
Robert Burton-
Leander & Eleanor Gillespie 29 Nov 1848; b- Humbleston Reamey con-
Mary Gillespie, mother min- Robert Burton- 7Dec1848

Reams

Jeremiah & Dolly Fowler 15 Dec 1800; b- Starling Fowler
John T & Maria B Goode 26 Oct 1830; min- William Steel- (Episcopal)-

Reamy

Abraham & Susanna Hudson 13 Mar 1809; b- William Harris min-
William Richards- 16Mar1809
Thomas A & Phebe Burton 13 Jan 1800; b- James Wilson min- William
Richards- 16Jan1800

Redd
> George & Elizabeth Young 17 Sep 1812; b- James Meacham min- James Meacham-
> Martin & Catherine Malone 19 Aug 1822; b- James Stone con- Nancy Malone, mother min- Pleasant Gold- (Baptist)- 20Aug1822
> Robert & Mary E Feild 14 Apr 1834; b- John S Feild min- William Steel- (Episcopal)- 22Apr1834
> William S & Frances T Daws 2 Nov 1844; b- William Daws

Redding
> Ezekiel & Rebecca Mason 18 Apr 1791; b- Thomas Marriott

Redford
> Henry M & Virginia Clark 15 Jun 1840; b- George J Dabbs con- Eliza Clark, mother min- D.B. Nicholson- 9Jul1840

Reekes
> Benjamin & Lucy Ingram 12 Aug 1801; b- Richard Crowder min- William Creath-
> Hartwell & Jane B Edmonson 24 Nov 1834; b- Samuel G Patillo
> James & Sally Holmes 13 Dec 1796; d of Samuel Holmes b- John Walton min- John Neblett- 15Dec1796
> Thomas C & Sarah W Walker 30 Nov 1847; b- William E Dodson con- Charles P Walker, father
> Thomas E & Araminta H Walker 19 Dec 1846; b- George Speaks con- David A Walker, father min- James McAden-

Reese
> John & Lucy Ann Cox 13 Apr 1853; min- P.F. August-
> John & Nancy Hatchell 31 Dec 1842; b- Samuel Carpenter
> Joseph A & Mary E Hatchell 8 Oct 1842; b- Benjamin Hatchell
> Joseph T & Cornelia F Yancey 23 Jun 1842; b- James B Dupuy con- Eliza Yancey, mother

Renn
> Edward K & Sarah J Tucker 18 Aug 1846; b- Robert M Hutcherson

Reynolds
> Robert & Martha Burnett 20 Dec 1830; b- John Winckler min- James Smith- 23Dec1830
> William H C & Ann E Joyce 12 May 1846; b- Robert Joyce

Rice
> Basil W & Nancy Towler 21 May 1821; b- John Winckler
> Nathaniel & Milly Johnston 16 Aug 1832; b- Patrick Johnson min- William Steel- (Episcopal)-
> William & Margaret J W Williams 9 Aug 1815; b- Edward Travis min- Cary Syme-

Richards
> William & Mary Evans 14 Dec 1801; b- Richard Jeffries min- William Creath-

Richardson
> James G & Martha A Hayes 30 Oct 1834; b- James Hayes min- William Steel- (Episcopal)- 23Oct1834
> Robert & Caroline Jones 9 Jan 1827; b- Langston Bacon
> William A & Patience C Reamey 29 Jul 1839; b- James Mullins

Ridout
> Gordon & Sally Grigg 6 Feb 1802; b- William Ezell con- Lewis Grigg, father min- James Meacham- 10Feb1802

Riggins
> D R & Elvira I Carlin 19 Jun 1848; b- William A Nash
> Edmund H & Ann J Patillo 6 Dec 1845; b- Tatnai Ellis min- James McAden-

James B & Mary Greenwood 22 Feb 1830; b- John J Ewing Mary herself
test. she is 24 yrs old min- William Steel- (Episcopal)-
John & Mary Hutt 14 May 1798; b- William Hilton min- Edward
Almand- 17May1798

Rives

William & Mary Turner 1 Jan 1788; b- Nicholas Bilbo con- Thomas
Rives, father con- Stephen Turner, father

Roach

Cuthbert W & Sarah S Jones 19 Nov 1821; b- Drury A Bacon

Robards

Edward & Nancy Russell 28 Dec 1824; b- James Russell min- Charles
Ogburn- (Methodist)
George W & Selina Ann Lockett 17 Jan 1838; George from Granville
Co., NC b- Beverly Sydnor con- Samuel L Lockett, father, who test
Selina under 21
John & Harriet Childress - Oct 1841; min- John B. Smith-

Roberts

Absolom & Susannah B Collier 3 Sep 1807; b- Phillip Roberts
Alexander & Susan Wells 20 Oct 1822; b- John Garrett con- Henry
Wells, father
Allen & Nancy Cunningham 26 Apr 1813; b- Benjamin Freeman
Amos & Sarah Benford 6 Feb 1835; b- John J Morris
Anselm & Nancy Bottom 22 Jul 1806; b- Hughberry Nanney min- James
Meacham- 23Jul1806
Dennis & Lucy Roberts 21 Dec 1798; b- William Roberts min- William
Creath- 25Dec1798
Dennis & Amey Watson 6 Mar 1821; b- John Watson min- James Smith-
E F & Matilda Boyd 12 Dec 1849; b- Phillip Rainey min- William A.
Smith- 31Dec1849
George & Polly Stembridge 15 Oct 1810; b- James Stembridge
James & Elizabeth C Reekes 30 Nov 1835; b- Thomas C Reekes, father,
who also gives consent min- William B. Rowzee- 24Dec1835
John A & Ann Jones Osborne 3 Jul 1828; min- William Richards-
John T & Mary F Reamey 24 Nov 1840; b- John A Walker
John & Leanna Allen 21 May 1799; b- William Allen
John & Harriett Childry 30 Oct 1844; b- William A Hester, Jr con-
William Childry, father
John & Mary Evans 15 Dec 1828; b- Samuel S Simmons con- Robert
Evans, father
Lewis & Priscilla May 17 Oct 1797; b- Henry Roberts
Phillip & Judith Benford 17 Jun 1818; b- Dennis Roberts
Phillip & Tabitha Watson 29 Dec 1802; b- Thomas Shelton
Richard J & Sally R Byasee 14 Jan 1833; b- Jesse Russell con- Mildridge
Crowder, mother of Sally
Richard & Sally Moss 17 Jan 1820; b- Alexander Dortch con- Martha
Moss, who test. Sally 21 yrs old min- James Smith- 20Jan1820
Robert & Elizabeth Rook 20 Feb 1799; b- Starling Morgan
Stephen & Martha Gregory 20 Aug 1810; b- Nathaniel Fowlkes min-
David McCargo- (Charlotte County, Va.) 30Aug1810
Theodrick M & Ann E Burwell 1 Dec 1848; b- John S R Burwell
William (Jr) & Frances Roberts 21 Aug 1802; b- Phillip Roberts min-
William Creath-
Williamson P & Sally Sandys 12 Mar 1827; b- Phillip L Sandys

Robertson

Allen & Amasa Burrus 4 Sep 1801; b- Henry Royall min- William
Creath-

David & Jane Puryear 14 Aug 1844; b- William H Ligon

Drury & Mary Winfield 4 Feb 1786; b- Matthew Turner

John Moody & Mary E Lamb 1 Mar 1792; b- Pines Ingram con- Joseph Boswell, gdn for Mary

Lemuel & Nancy J Smith 23 Apr 1821; b- Augustine Smith min- Charles Ogburn- (Methodist) 25Apr1821

Leoderick & Nancy Thomas 11 Mar 1806; b- John Allgood min- Thomas Hardie-

Major & Sarah Gregory 21 Dec 1818; b- Elijah Gregory min- William Richards- 29Dec1818

Milton & Elizabeth K Clark 16 Sep 1811; b- Carter Clark min- Charles Ogburn- (Methodist)

Nathaniel & Nancy Crews 9 Dec 1799; b- Richard H Walker

Taylor D & Margarett S Floyd 25 Oct 1849; min- James McAden-

Thomas & Elizabeth Roberts 16 Jun 1787; b- Thomas Roberts

Robinson

Clack & Elanor Young 11 Oct 1809; b- Walter Langley min- James Meacham-

James & Martha Winfield 2 Nov 1803; b- William Thomas con- Joshua Winfield, father min- James Meacham- 9Nov1803

Roffe

Edward E & Elizabeth Ann Dortch 10 Nov 1845; b- Benjamin D Hightower con- Nancy T Crute, mother of Elizabeth min- James J. Sledge-

Edward & Miney Burton 16 Jul 1787; b- William Johnson con- Robert Burton, father

Edward & Margaret Puryear 28 Nov 1816; b- Peter Puryear min- James Meacham-

Ingram & Agnes Love 17 Feb 1803; b- William Love con- Charles Love, father

Jesse & Edney Cleaton 21 Dec 1818; b- Bennett Goode

John B & Elizabeth B Farrar 17 Jan 1825; b- William H Farrar con- John Farrar Jr, father min- Charles Ogburn- (Methodist) 20Jan1825

John B & Ann F Puryear 20 Nov 1848; b- Giles R Puryear

John & Martha Simmons 1 Jan 1794; b- Samuel Simmons min- William Creath- 2Jan1794

Melchizedeck & Ann Dodson 12 Dec 1800; b- William Dodson

Samuel & Susan N Stone 5 Jun 1815; b- Melchizedeck Roffe

William E & Ann Eliza Moss 15 Dec 1841; b- Thomas R Moss

William & Sarah Knight 9 Oct 1794; b- Ingram Vaughan min- William Creath- 19Oct1794

Rogers

George P & Elizabeth A Cleaton 16 Feb 1849; b- James H Cleaton con- William Barner Cleaton, father min- Nathaniel Thomas- 23Feb1849

Hugh & Agnes D Totty 14 May 1840; b- Michael H Tarwater con- Thomas E Totty, father min- D.B. Nicholson-

John & Selena K Winckler 6 Feb 1835; b- Richard D Bugg con- John Winckler, father

Robert R & Cornelia Cunningham 17 Oct 1826; b- R N Cunningham min- John B. Smith-

Rose

Anderson & Polly Puryear 9 Jul 1804; b- Valentine McCutcheon

Thomas & Martha Bennett 21 Dec 1822; b- Joseph Bennett con- Jordan Bennett, father min- Stephen Jones- (Lynchburg, Va.)- 25Dec1822

Ross
> Robert & Lucy Arnold 14 Nov 1792; b- Elisha Arnold min- John Neblett- 22Nov1792

Rottenberry
> Charles & Sally Glover 4 Dec 1798; b- James Burton min- Ebenezer McGowan- 24Dec1798
> McDaniel & Nancy Bowen 3 Mar 1797; b- John Thomerson min- John Loyd- 8Mar1797
> Winn & Elizabeth F Hudgins 26 Nov 1801; b- Abel Edmunds con- James Hudgins, father

Rowland
> Richard & Rachel Ragsdale 10 Dec 1781; b- Henry Robertson
> Robert & Susanna Gold 19 Feb 1829; b- Alexander Gold con- Pleasant Gold, father min- Pleasant Gold- (Baptist)- 24Feb1829

Rowlett
> Thompson & Polly Dodson 9 Nov 1805; min- James Meacham- 18Nov1805

Royal
> Henry & Letty Hutt 18 Jul 1805; b- Peter Puryear
> Joseph & Elizabeth Thomas 11 Aug 1794; b- Matthew Clements min- William Creath- 14Sep1794
> William & Sally Robertson 10 Jun 1799; b- Allen Robertson

Royer
> James & Harriett Spurlock 18 Mar 1823; b- Richard Coleman min- James Smith- 27Mar1823

Royster
> Alfred & Elizabeth J Cox 20 Jul 1838; b- Eli Cox
> Benjamin & Nancy Elam 19 Nov 1838; b- Silas M Gregory min- John B. Smith-
> Benjamin & Mary Gregory 31 May 1847; min- Robert Burton-
> Charles & Elizabeth Burrows ' 14 Nov 1803; b- Jordan Mason con- William T Burrows, father
> Charles & Marilla Sizemore 19 Aug 1839; b- Alexander Puryear con- Daniel Sizemore, father con- George Royster, father
> Clark & Lucy Apperson 11 Oct 1802; b- Archibald Clarke min- Balaam Ezell- 12Oct1802
> Dennis & Rebecca Royster 17 Jan 1807; b- Stark Daniel min- William Richards-
> Francis & Ann Roberts 13 Dec 1802; b- Valentine McCutcheon min- William Creath-
> George & Susanna Hall 7 Aug 1790; b- William Marshall
> Henry & Frances Draper 8 Nov 1790; b- Joseph Royster
> J R & Mary R Jeter 7 Apr 1853; con- William Jeter, father
> James H & Panthea F Averett 12 Jul 1845; b- G W R Averett con- Bryan Averett, father
> John F & Elizabeth R Taylor 27 Aug 1853
> John F & Mary M Toone 10 Jul 1848; b- A Jackson Toone con- Louis and Mildred Toone, parents
> Joseph & Elizabeth Draper 12 Dec 1791; b- Holeman Rice min- James Read- (Baptist) 27Dec1791
> Wilkins & Mary Robertson 13 Feb 1797; b- Samuel Hester Jr min- William Richards- 18Feb1797
> William H & Nancy Culbreath 16 Aug 1813; b- Gray Holloway Nancy daughter of John Culbreath
> William J & Ella Ann Tandy 23 Nov 1838; b- Samuel Watkins min- John B. Smith-
> Willis & Milly Griffin 23 Aug 1821; min- Pleasant Gold- (Baptist)-

Willis & Susanna Willis 8 May 1811; b- Robert Shanks

Rudd

John & Elizabeth Edmundson 15 Oct 1810; b- Brown Avory min- William Richards- 25Oct1810

Reuben A & Mary C Love 17 May 1847; b- Alan C Love con- Martha Love, mother

Rudder

Alexander & Elizabeth McLaughlin 21 Dec 1791; b- Edward Brodnax of Lunenburg County min- James Read- (Baptist) 22Dec1791

Ruffin

Theoderick Bland & Susanna Murray 14 Jan 1788; b- Jesse Brown con- William Yates, gdn of Susanna min- Thomas Scott-

Russell

Benjamin H & Sarah Ann Eliza Haskins 3 Feb 1834; b- John Knox con- Charles Haskins, father

Burwell & Prudence Hogan 11 Jan 1785; b- William McQuie

James & Parthena W Curtis 25 Jun 1832; b- John F Curtis con- John Curtis, father

Jeremiah & Jilley Atkins 26 Aug 1795; Jeremiah from Brunswick County b- James Atkins min- John Loyd- 27Aug1795

Jeremiah & Sarah Thompson 21 Dec 1809; b- Theophilus Russell

Jeremiah & Sarah Thompson 21 Dec 1809; b- Theophilus Russell

Jesse & Rebekah Harris 11 Dec 1798; b- Stephen Evans min- Charles Ogburn- (Methodist) 20Dec1798

Jesse & Nancy Mitchell 13 Dec 1832; b- William H Byasee

Jesse & Rebecca Robards 11 Dec 1839; b- William Robards min- Benjamin R. Duval-

John & Catherine Stone 30 Mar 1801; b- Benjamin Mitchell min- John Neblett- 2Apr1801

Mark & Mary Puckett 3 Dec 1785; b- John Daly

Ryan

Elijah J & Martha Atkinson 19 Sep 1840; b- Asa Garner min- Charles F. Burnley-

Ryland

Harrison M & Mary Howlett Insco 25 May 1811; b- William Insco

Hundley & Catharine Saunders 10 Mar 1830; b- Jesse Parrish min- James Smith- 18Mar1830

Hundley & Nancy Walker 11 Jan 1802; b- John Brown

Iverson & Lucy Dortch 23 Feb 1784; n- Nathaniel Moss

John & ---- ---- 11 Jan 1786; b- Thomas Adams (bride's name not written on bond)

Joseph H & Caroline F Tucker 20 Dec 1841; b- John Tucker min- John B. Smith-

Thomas & Martha Coleman 16 Dec 1803; b- John Ryland

William P & Janette N Coleman 4 Dec 1829; b- Samuel A Tarry con- Cluverius R Coleman, father min- James Smith- 15Dec1829

Sadler

William & Avarilla Greenwood 12 Nov 1798; b- John Greenwood con- Thomas Greenwood, father

Salley

James & Audrey Keeton 9 Dec 1793; b- Reuben Cardin min- William Creath- 19Dec1793

Sammons

James H & Harriett N Keeton 21 May 1832; b- James Hester

Samuel

Andrew & Delina Tanner 11 May 1786; b- Thomas Tanner

Sandifer
Henry & Martha Taylor 14 Dec 1785; b- Samuel Durham
Sandys
William C & Prudence Jeffries 24 Jun 1816; b- Andrew G Elam min- William Richards- 2Jul1816
Saunders
Benjamin & Mary Anne Moore 19 Feb 1791; b- Philip B Moore
George & Hally Emery 3 Dec 1804; b- Thomas Saunders
Samuel S & Pamela J Morris 15 Oct 1830; b- William J Morris min- John B. Smith-
Thomas & Polly Morris 19 Dec 1803; b- Edward Morris con- John Saunders, father con- Jesse Morris, Sr., father min- William Creath-
Turner & Lucy Vaughan 20 Dec 1820; b- George Saunders con- W Vaughan, father
William & Polly Emery 30 Sep 1812; b- Daniel Morris min- Richard Dabbs- (Lunenburg County)- 1Oct1812
Savage
George & Ann E Gregory 1 Jun 1825; b- Joseph S Gregory min- James McAden-
John & Mary Taylor 1 May 1787; b- James Day
Scott
Avory & Elizabeth Chavous 9 Jan 1809; b- Frederick Ivey con- Elizabeth Chavous, mother min- William Richards- 21Jan1809
George C & Sally A Morton 7 Aug 1850; con- A C Morton, father min- William V. Wilson-
John B & Mary E Redd 3 Aug 1841; b- John S Feild min- F.H. McGuire-
John L & Louisa Royster 14 Mar 1833; b- Ruel Allen min- William Steel- (Episcopal)- 15Mar1833
Robert & Elizabeth Pettus 8 Sep 1806; b- William Pettus Elizabeth daughter of Samuel con- Samuel Pettus, Sr.
Samuel & Martha Henly 5 Jan 1792; Samuel from Dinwiddie County b- William Johnson min- William Creath- 11Jan1792
Scruggs
C T & Nancy Craddock 19 Sep 1842; b- E A Craddock
Sculthorp
Alexander & Henrietta Winn 30 Mar 1835; b- William C Hudson con- William Winn, father min- John B. Smith-
Selden
Joseph & Mary Burwell 11 Apr 1785; b- Samuel Goode
Seward
George & Elizabeth W Valentine 17 Oct 1825; b- Isham Valentine
Isaac & Lucy Valentine 25 Oct 1803; b- Isham Valentine
James & Martha Gregory 11 May 1813; b- John Gregory min- James Meacham- 19May1813
John (Jr) & Sarah Hanserd 6 Dec 1799; b- Richard Hanserd min- James Meacham- 11Dec1799
John & Betsy Malone 2 Jun 1771; b- Drury Malone
Randall & Sally Hailstock Kiser 19 May 1817; b- James Nolley
Shackleford
Zachariah & Susannah Allgood Salley 9 Oct 1797; b- John Ilgood min- William Creath-
Shanks
Robert & Tabitha T Ezell 17 Feb 1841; b- John H Ezell min- James McAden-

Sharp

Turner & Elizabeth Jones 11 May 1807; b- Martin Gillespie d of Richard Jones, dec. con- Charles Jones, gdn of Elizabeth min- William Richards-14May1807

Turner & Martha Jones 24 Jan 1797; b- James Elam con- Richard Jones, father min- William Creath- 26Jan1797

Shaw

John & Susanna Carter 4 Aug 1790; b- Drury Creedle

John & Patsy Crowder 10 Nov 1800; b- Thomas Marriott min- William Creath-

Shearer

James & Nancy Allen 13 Nov 1797; b- John Cox min- William Richards-30Nov1797

Shell

Freeman & Becky Tisdale 18 Mar 1806; b- Bartlett Cox min- Charles Ogburn- (Methodist)- 21Mar1806

Herman & Martha Eppes 9 Oct 1790; Herman from Brunswick County b- John Eppes min- William Heath- (Methodist)- 19Oct1790

John & Lizzy Malone 28 May 1786; b- Hardy Jones

Shelton

David & Ann Baker 9 Nov 1820; b- John Bullock min- William Richards-16Nov1820

Edward & Phebe Walker 22 Dec 1803; b- Bartlett Cheatham

James & Nancy Marshall 12 Feb 1810; b- Phillip Lockett min- William Richards- 14Feb1810

James & Nancy Marshall 12 Feb 1810; b- Phillip Lockett

James & Adaline Overby 2 Oct 1848; 'Dr' James Shelton b- J Harper Shelton con- Robert Y Overby, father

Thomas & Martha Watson 29 Dec 1799; b- Jordan Bennett min-Ebenezer McGowan- 31Dec1799

Short

Batte & Patsy Lett 30 May 1791; b- James Bing

Batte & Seller Murdock 2 Nov 1798; b- John Carroll min- Charles Ogburn- (Methodist) 9Nov1798

Edmund & Susanna Bilbo 6 Aug 1787; b- John Bilbo

Freeman & Elizabeth Evans 1 Sep 1808; b- George Finch

Isaac & Susanna Toone 12 Jan 1795; b- John Stegall

Jacob & Phebe Finch 23 Oct 1794; b- William Finch min- John Loyd-

John & Rebecca Goode 28 Jan 1807; b- Edward Holloway min- James Meacham-

William & Rebecca Connell 23 Oct 1812; daughter of William Connell, dec. b- John T Pennington

Wyatt & Mary Adams 11 Dec 1809; b- Richard M Allen min- James Meacham- 28Dec1809

Simmons

Edmund & Elizabeth Collier 30 Jul 1822; b- Amos Hall min- James McAden- 10Aug1822

Edward & Permelia Edmonson 18 Mar 1814; b- Richard H Edmonson

Henry & Betsy Harris 30 Dec 1830; b- Thomas D Crutchfield con- John Harris, father min- Charles Ogburn- (Methodist)

James L & Alice Crowder 18 Jan 1837; b- James R Harriss

James W & Martha E Hutcheson 19 Aug 1840; b- Joseph G Hutcheson con- Elizabeth G Hutcheson, mother

James & Martha Bowers 20 Feb 1815; daughter of Sanford Bowers b- Richard H Edmonson min- Charles Ogburn- (Methodist) 25Feb1815

James & Mourning Lark 3 Jan 1805; b- James Noel

John James & Caroline B Lucas 13 Dec 1824; b- William Lucas con-
John R Lucas, father min- James McAden-

John & Elizabeth Baugh 23 Sep 1790; b- James Baugh, father Elizabeth
daughter of James and Agnes Baugh min- John Easter- 30Sep1790

John & Elizabeth Daws 27 Oct 1826; b- Isaac Holmes min- John B.
Smith-

Joseph P & Martha Mallett 30 Jan 1840; b- Pleasant Burnett

Joseph & Elizabeth Harrison 8 May 1797; b- Samuel Simmons con-
Johnand Sarah Ogburn, guardians of Elizabeth min- Charles Ogburn-
(Methodist) 11May1797

Joseph & Martha Phillips 4 May 1816; widow b- Edmund Noel min-
Charles Ogburn- (Methodist) 6May1816

Joseph & Elizabeth Simmons 18 Oct 1820; min- James Smith-

Robert S & Ann F Hughes 24 Dec 1832; b- Richard F Hughes con-
Crawford Hughes, father min- James McAden-

Samuel S & Sally Creedle 20 Jun 1825; b- Francis C Edmundson

Samuel & Elizabeth Booker 6 Apr 1822; b- Samuel S Simmons min-
Charles Ogburn- (Methodist) 9Apr1822

Samuel & Elizabeth Coleman 7 Aug 1795; b- Thomas Coleman min-
Charles Ogburn- (Methodist) 15Aug1795

Samuel & Emily Moore 1 Sep 1852; min- John A. Doll-

Samuel & Mary Moore 28 Sep 1814; b- John Daws

Samuel & Nancy Roffe 16 Feb 1824; b- Richard H Edmonson

William B & Nancy Watkins Ogburn 14 Oct 1811; b- Charles Ogburn

William & Jane Davis 15 Jan 1830; b- Thomas Vaughan con- William
Davis, father

Wilshire & Angelina Edmonson 1 Mar 1830; b- Samuel Simmons min-
James Smith- 2Mar1830

Simpson
Edwin & Mahala Stewart 12 Dec 1808; b- Saunders Harris

Sims
Leonard & Sarah Swepson 12 Mar 1770; b- Richard Swepson

Saunders & Lucy Hutcheson 21 Jan 1794; b- Charles Hutcheson min-
William Creath- 28Jan1794

Singleton
Howell & Sarah Morris 23 Sep 1831; b- William Morris min- Daniel
Petty-

John & Rebeccah Crook 8 Oct 1801; b- James Nash

John & Ann Daly 4 Sep 1793; b- Daniel Daly min- John Loyd- 5Sep1793

John & Frances Johnson 19 Dec 1810; b- John Curtis marriage ceremony
20Dec1810 (no minister's name included)

Joseph C & Eliza J Floyd 14 Aug 1848; b- B H Merryman con-
Zachariah Floyd, father

Robert & Polly Thomason 30 Dec 1795; d of John and Mary Thomason
b- William Barrett min- John Loyd- 31Dec1795

William & Susanna Gwaltney 13 Jan 1798; b- Richard Stone con- William
Gawltney, father

Sizemore
Ledford & Martha J Wilkinson 15 Mar 1845; b- Alexander Puryear con-
Washington Wilkinson, father

Leroy & Nancy Jones 19 Dec 1836; b- Richard Jones

Slate
Robert & Elizabeth Vaughan 12 Nov 1802; Robert from Brunswick county
b- John Saunders min- William Creath-

Slaughter
Robert A & Frances Brooks 15 May 1852; min- Adam Finch-

Spancer & Susan Wallace 30 Nov 1830; b- Isaac T Hailey

Small

George & Edith Overby 30 Mar 1799; b- Charles Hudson

George & Edith Overby 30 Mar 1799; b- Charles Hudson

George & Sarah Pully 25 Sep 1816; b- James Pully min- James Meacham- 26Sep1816

Smelley

William T & Mary Araminta Barnett 20 Dec 1847; b- James L Thomason min- James McAden- 25Dec1847

Willis R & Eliza Puryear 23 Dec 1844; b- William N Puryear min- James McAden-

Smith

Alexander & Elizabeth Gregory 13 Dec 1835; b- John S Couch con- Robert S Gregory, father min- John B. Smith-

Alexander & Sarah P Ryland 11 Jan 1849; b- Thomas E Ryland con- Thomas Ryland, father min- John Bagby- 17Feb1849

Anderson & Elizabeth Maryann Avary 9 Jun 1783; b- John Avary, father

Augustine (Jr) & Nancy Rudd 8 Feb 1790; b- William Insco

Benjamin & Caty Page 2 Apr 1803; b- Thomas Smith

Buckner & Susan Toone 15 Jan 1821; b- William Johnson con- Archibald Toone, father

Daniel & Patsy Poindexter 10 Dec 1792; s of Johnand Martha Smith d of Phillip Poindexter Sr min- Edward Almand- b- Robert Smith

Daniel & Nancy Watkins 21 Dec 1821; b- James Watkins con- Joseph Watkins, father

David G & Lucy Boyd 17 Oct 1831; b- William W Oliver con- William Boyd, father min- John B. Smith-

Edwin P & Martha C Moore 24 Mar 1824; b- John J Moore min- Charles Ogburn- (Methodist)

George & Sarah H Pully 16 Sep 1850; con- Mary B Pully, mother min- Hartwell Arnold-

Giles R & Ann Maria Langhorne 21 Aug 1837; b- A Langhorne min- Charles F. Burnley- 29Aug1837

Green & Malvina Mayo 3 Oct 1830; b- Osborne Mayo

Ichabod & Lucy Pennington 31 Oct 1795; s of Johnand Paulina Smith b- Henry Pennington min- William Creath- 15Nov1795

James (Jr) & Ann W DeGraffenreid 15 Sep 1815; b- John J Wells con- Tscharner DeGraffenreid, gdn of Ann, daughter of William DeGraffenreid, dec.

James A & Martha E Baptist 15 Sep 1839; b- William Baptist con- William Baptist, father min- John B. Smith-

James F & Rebecca A C Andrews 9 Jun 1834; b- Allen T Andrews con- Wilson Harriss, gdn of Rebecca

James & Matilda Graves 28 Apr 1845; b- John F Royster

James & Elinor Hyde 12 Dec 1791; s of John and Martha Smith b- Robert Hyde

James & Jane Stembridge 28 Oct 1839; b- Burwell Barron min- John B. Smith-

James & Jane Williamson 14 Feb 1843; b- Robert A Phillips con- Ritta Williamson, mother

Jesse J & Lucy S Drumwright 12 Jun 1852; con- Gee Drumwright, father min- James McAden-

John A & Sarenah S Arnold 21 Dec 1849; b- William Stone con- John J Arnold, father

John B & Nancy Smith 29 Nov 1817; b- John F Finch con- Robert Smith, father of Nancy min- William Richards- 2Dec1817

John P & Roannah Halm 22 Jul 1833; b- Thomas Rogers con- Benjamin Evans, father

John P & Martha A Jones 3 Oct 1825; b- Joseph Bennett Jr con- Ann B Jones, mother

John P & Polly Oslin 30 Oct 1801; b- Isaac Oslin

John Prior & Susanna Smith 7 Oct 1776; d of Drury Smith b- Achilles Jeffreis

John & Sally Ellis 29 Jan 1796; b- John Loyd min- John Loyd- 30Jan1796

John & Elizabeth Hudson 28 Nov 1821; b- Stephen Hudson min- William Richards- 29Nov1821

John & Nancy Smith 29 Mar 1791; b- Augustine Smith

Joseph & Elizabeth Burnett 11 Sep 1792; b- Silvanus Ingram min- Rice Haggard- 20Sep1792

Joshua & Olive Brown 6 Jan 1801; b- William Hutcheson

Mabry & Susan Pully 1 Nov 1821; b- Frederick Wall min- James Smith-

Madison D & Elmira S Moody 29 Oct 1850; 'Major' Madison D. Smith con- L A Paschall, gdn of Elmira min- W.W. Jordan- (Oxford, NC)-

Matthew & Sibbie Lambert 24 Nov 1787; b- Joseph Lambert

Obadiah & Tabitha Wilson 22 May 1798; s of Peartree Smith b- James Wilson con- Tabitha Wilson, mother and guardian min- Alexander Hay- (Antrim Glebe, Antrim Parish, Halifax County) 24May1798

Orlando Marcellus & Lavenia Field 4 Feb 1841; b- Henry F Jones con- Anthony M Smith, father of Orlando, who is under 21

Redmond R & Judith J Farrar 18 Feb 1824; b- Lemuel Robertson con- Farrar, gdn of Judith min- Charles Ogburn- (Methodist)

Robert & Nancy Norment 8 Jan 1787; s of John and Martha Smith b- Thomas Norment

Samuel Hancock & Jane Wright Russell 24 Jul 1806; b- Thomas A Jones min- William Richards- 26Jul1806

Sherwood & Faithy Holmes 21 Dec 1786; d of Isaac Holmes, dec. b- William Starling

Thomas & Patsy Hubbard 15 Mar 1806; b- John Hubbard

Thomas & Elizabeth Wartman 25 Nov 1818; b- John Wartman

Thomas & Elizabeth Wilson 14 Jul 1821; b- John W Binford con- Henry Wilson, father min- Stephen Jones- (Lynchburg, Va.)- 19Jul1821

Thomas & Mary Wilson 28 Sep 1795; b- James Day min- Charles Ogburn- (Methodist) 1Oct1795

William H & Emily E Phillips 20 Dec 1847; b- John C Phillips

William H & Martha Rudder 19 Sep 1842; b- Thomas I Penn

William H & Mary Walker 12 Feb 1808; d of Aurelius and Nancy Walker b- Matthew Walker

William J & Elizabeth W Browder 15 Dec 1845; b- Oswin J Phillips con- William Browder, father min- E. Chambers-

William N & Amanda N Bailey 19 May 1835; b- Allen T Andrews min- James McAden-

William & Orpah Garner 3 Feb 1812; b- William Garner min- William Richards- 5Fev1812

William & Anne Pitts 13 Oct 1787; b- William Nowell

Smithson

Bartley C & Charlotte M Lester 5 Oct 1845; b- Edward Overton con- Bryan Lester, father min- Daniel Petty-

Bartley & Sarah Weatherford 30 Nov 1799; b- Freeman Weatherford con- William Weatherford, father min- Matthew Dance- 4Dec1799

Briant & Dolly Burton 13 Jun 1796; b- Peter Puryear min- William Creath- 16Jun1796

Charles C & Joyce H McCargo 19 Nov 1842; b- John G Oliver con-
James McCargo, father
Charles & Betsy Cheatham 8 Dec 1800; b- Samuel Cheatham
Francis & Susan Brame 30 Sep 1843; b- Abner Maxey

Snead
Joseph H & Jane C Crenshaw 16 Jan 1834; b- John R Crenshaw min-
Daniel Petty-

Somervill
William H & Tabitha W Whitlow 26 Sep 1849; b- Champion Whitlow

Sommervill
George & Elenor H Birtchett 23 Mar 1811; b- Henry Hicks min- George
Micklejohn-

Soward
Anderson & Mary Mayo 19 Apr 1842; b- Joseph Thompson con-
Elizabeth Mayo, mother
Jesse & Harriett Soward 13 Jun 1838; b- Cary J Valentine

Spain
Abraham & Elizabeth Allen 6 May 1795; b- Henderson Wade min-
William Richards- 7May1795
Daniel & Judith Allen 18 Nov 1802; b- Abraham Spain min- William
Richards- 19Nov1802
Henry M & Elizabeth S Stith 10 Apr 1833; b- Francis C Spain
James N & Kitty Harris 29 Aug 1838; b- Royall Spain
James R & Martha Overby 5 May 1819; b- Edward Travis con- James
Overby, father
James & Polly Moss 15 Jun 1812; b- William Elam min- William
Richards- 18Jun1812
John & Martha Coleman 15 Dec 1817; b- Matthew L Baptist min-
William Richards- 18Dec1817
John & Martha Smith 1 May 1845; b- James Smith min- John B. Smith-
Joshua & Lucy C Spain 16 Dec 1835; b- Royall Spain min- John B.
Smith-
Royall & Tabitha Harris 19 Sep 1812; b- James Spain min- William
Richards- 30Sep1812
Royall & Harriet W Wootton 17 Dec 1838; b- John P Wootton min-
John B. Smith-
Stephen & Julia Graves 17 Jul 1849; b- William D Stembridge con-
Phebe Graves, mother
Thomas & Elizabeth Haskins 6 Jan 1797; b- William Lucas min- Edward
Almand- 7Jan1797
Thomas & Susan Hudson 1 Dec 1824; b- John Marshall min- William
Richards-
Thomas & Nancy Stewart 14 Aug 1801; b- Frederick Ivey
Wiley & Jane Graves 25 Apr 1821; b- Thomas Graves min- William
Richards- 26Apr1821
William & Judith Harris 13 Dec 1802; b- James Clack min- William
Richards- 27Dec1802

Sparks
William & Judith Thompson 9 Jan 1804; b- Bernard Thompson min-
William Richards- 19Jan1804

Speaks
George & Martha Matthews 8 Nov 1809; b- John Matthews

Speed
Henry G & Maria Speed 19 Nov 1838; b- John J Speed con- John J
Speed, father min- Edward Wadsworth- 20Nov1838

John J & Ann S Jones 19 Sep 1825; b- Daniel T Hicks min- William Steel- (Episcopal)-

John James & Mary T Nicholson 27 Feb 1811; b- John H Speed min- Charles Ogburn- (Methodist) 28Feb1811

John James & Lucy Swepson 26 Jan 1801; b- G H Baskervill min- William Richards- 29Jan1801

John & Polly Wade 3 Jul 1798; b- Joseph Speed Jr con- Joseph Townes, guardian of Polly

Joseph F & Elizabeth Shelton 4 Mar 1812; b- John H Speed min- William Richards- 11Mar1812

Robert & Polly A Coleman 15 Jan 1809; d of James Coleman, dec. b- William Coleman

Spence

Thomas & Nancy Stewart 14 Sep 1801; b- Francis Ivey min- William Creath-

Spencer

Abraham & Martha B Bilbo 13 Mar 1816: b- John H Hardie

John (Jr) & Emily J Barnes 8 Dec 1842; b- John G Barnes

John J R & Nancy A M Bacon 27 Jul 1846; b- Joseph G Sneed con- Lydall Bacon, father, who test Nancy will be 27 on 29Oct1846 min- E. Chambers-

John J R & Eliza Speed - Sep 1841; b- H G Speed

John W & Fanny J Spencer 15 Apr 1850; b- Wiley N Moring con- John J R Spencer, father of Fanny

Spraggins

Stith B & Eliza A Green 30 Dec 1824; b- John G Baptist con- G Green, father min- William Steel- (Episcopal)-

Spurlock

William & Tempy Nanney 9 Dec 1798; b- William Roberts min- William Creath- 27Dec1798

Zachariah & Elizabeth Mealer 13 Oct 1792; b- John Farrar min- John Loyd-

Stainback

James & Mary E Hodges 9 Oct 1849; b- Allen T Andrews min- James McAden- 10Oct1849

Peter & Ann Eliza Moore 17 Oct 1836: b- Turner Abernathy

Robert & Polly Andrews 13 Dec 1804; Robert from Brunswick County b- Isaac Arnold

Stalcup

Tobias & Lucy Pearce 9 Jan 1809; b- Baalam Ezell

Stamps

William L & Elizabeth T B Jiggetts 11 May 1840; b- William Baskervill Jr con- D E Jiggetts, father

Standley

Benjamin & Rebecca L Poythress 22 Jan 1832; b- David Poyhtress con- Lewis Poythress, father min- James McAden-

Stanfield

Drew & Honora Heathcock 13 Dec 1803; b- George Guy

Drew & Honora Heathcock 13 Dec 1803; b- George Guy

Stanley

Isham John & Bramley M Lambert 13 Oct 1834; b- Martin F Lambert

Stegall

Alexander & Mary Tatum 17 Nov 1845; b- Henry Coley con- Lucy L Stegall, mother con- Mary E Tatum, mother

George & Mary F Short 23 Jan 1799; b- Henry Finch min- John Neblett-

Jesse & Betsy B Webb 19 Nov 1817; b- Bushrod Webb, father, who also consents

John & Susanna Beddingfield 12 Dec 1786; b- William Finch

Peter & Lucy Bennett 28 Dec 1813; b- William Bennett

Stembridge

James & Elizabeth Gregory 31 Dec 1801; b- John Stembridge min- William Richards- 7Jan1802

John & Sally Graves 24 Dec 1803; b- Obadiah Belcher min- Edward Almand- 28Dec1803

John & Ann W Royster 18 Dec 1837; b- Benjamin R Royster min- John B. Smith-

Stevens

John Nowell & Thene Maclin 3 May 1819; b- Thomas Feggins con- Thomas Maclin, father

Stewart

Archer & Elizabeth Brandon 18 Dec 1818; b- Ned Brandon min- William Richards- 22Dec1818

Archer & Jincy Chavous 14 Aug 1809; b- Edward Brandon min- James Meacham- 25Aug1809

Asa & Amanda J Harrison 5 Oct 1848; b- Archer P Stewart min- John Bayley- 12Oct1848

Balaam & Elizabeth Wilson 11 Mar 1839; b- John Drew

Bartlett & Elizabeth Drew 21 Oct 1807; b- George Guy

Charles & Sarah Elam 14 Nov 1808; b- Frederick Ivey min- William Richards- 7Apr1809

Christopher & Ann Evans 12 Jan 1841; b- Richard Mayo min- Edward Wadsworth-

George & Jean Chandler 27 Dec 1797; b- Moses Stewart

James (Jr) & Ryte Chavous 11 Feb 1788; b- James Stewart Sr

John E & Barbara Ann Kersey 20 Dec 1841; b- James M Chavous

John Ginnet & Polly Manning 9 Dec 1794; b- Irby Chavous con- Susanna Chavous, mother of Polly

John & Sucky Brown 10 Jun 1820; b- Banister Chavous min- Alexander M. Cowan- 11Jun1820

Matthew & Eliza Stewart 8 Feb 1802; b- Miles Dunston

Matthew & Priscilla Walden 25 Feb 1799; b- William Chandler min- Ebenezer McGowan- 26Feb1799

Thomas & Sarah Cattiler 15 Jul 1800; b- Richeson Farrar

Thomas & Olive Cousins 24 Oct 1838; b- William Mitchell

Stith

Obadiah & Mary B Bugg 14 Nov 1843; Obadiah from Brunswick County b- Joseph S Gregory min- James McAden-

Stokes

Richard H & Eliza T Goode 21 Jan 1822; b- Hugh Nelson

William B & Nancy A Shelton 19 Jul 1813; b- Thomas Burnett min- William Richards- 24Jul1813

Stone

Asher & Frances Cox 13 Nov 1797; s of William Stone Sr and Tabitha Stone b- John Cox min- William Richards- 30Nov1797

Daniel & Rebecca Overton 16 Sep 1817; b- Thomas Overton min- Matthew Dance- (Lunenburg County)-

Daniel & Phoebe Stewart 15 Aug 1825; b- Robert Thomas

Drury & Nancy Hundley 12 Nov 1798; b- William Hundley

Elijah & Rebecca Roberts 13 Aug 1792; b- Thomas Roberts min- William Creath- 15Aug1792

Ewell & Halcarna D Hall 12 Dec 1836; b- William H Green con- Miles Hall, father min- John B. Smith-

Jacob W & Elizabeth Shackelford 19 Dec 1825; b- Benjamin W Coleman con- Zachariah Shackelford, father min- Charles Ogburn- (Methodist) 20Dec1825

James & Elizabeth Griffin 12 Mar 1810; b- Elijah Griffin

James & Johanna Jones 10 Jan 1791; d of Capt. Thomas Jones & sis of Daniel Jones, bondsman b- Daniel Jones min- James Read- (Baptist)

John & Sally Carpenter 21 Feb 1816; b- David Moss con- Samuel Carpenter, father min- James Meacham- 22Feb1816

John & Elizabeth Hutcheson 11 Dec 1797; b- William Stone

Jordan & Margaret Griffin 17 Dec 1803; b- Elijah Griffin

Marvell G & Elizabeth Thompson 7 Jan 1846; b- John W Wootton min- John B. Smith-

Meredith & Elizabeth Ann Garrett 6 Mar 1826; b- Edmund Taylor con- Mary Ann Garrett, mother

Samuel & Philadelphia Bridgforth 24 May 1822; b- William Hutcheson con- Elizabeth Bridgforth, mother min- Silas Shelburne- (Lunenburg County)- 30May1822

William (Jr) & Susanna Hutcheson 21 Nov 1795; b- Jesse Carsley con- William Stone Sr, gdn of Susanna min- Charles Ogburn- (Methodist) 26Nov1795

William & Frances C Hutcherson 6 Nov 1823; daughter of Joseph and Rebecca Hutcheson b- Charles C Phillips min- James Smith- 13Nov1823

Stovall

William & Mary Stone 21 May 1832; b- Jordan Stone min- John B. Smith-

Strange

Henry Hall & Julia Johnson 8 Feb 1836; b- James B Dupuy min- P. Calhoun-

James & Olivia Ann Johnson 24 Nov 1838; b- William Johnson

James & Sarah J Moore - May 1849; b- W O Manning con- Thomas E Moore, father

Owen G & Emily F Ezell 16 Dec 1844; b- Joseph M Drumwright con- Claiborne Drumwright, gdn of Emily min- James McAden-

Straub

Jacob & Sarah Wilkerson 4 Mar 1852; min- Thomas King- (Halifax County)-

Stroud

John & Sarah Bennett 23 Dec 1817; b- William Bennett

Ranson & Diana W Baisey 20 Dec 1826; b- Edward Giles

Willis & Elizabeth Blanton 11 Sep 1792; b- George Small min- John Loyd-

Strum

James & Henrietta Hester 16 Dec 1847; b- Richard H Averett con- Robert Hester, father

Stuart

James & Prescilla Stuart 14 Nov 1791; b- John Walden

John W & Virginia E Toone 13 Jun 1853; con- Edward F Toone, father min- James S. Kennedy- 22Jun1853

Moses & Polly Walden 20 Dec 1788; b- Eaton Walden con- JohnCharles Walden, father

William & Keziah Corn 21 --- ----; bond torn b- Robert Corn

Sturdivant

Armistead B & Elizabeth D Puryear 15 Oct 1849; b- Samuel H Goode

Charles & Lucy Armistead Burwell 30 May 1825; b- Richard Taylor con- Lucy Burwell, mother

Randal & Dicy Rainey 27 May 1776; b- Francis Rainey

Randolph & Mourning Lambert 5 Jan 1797; b- David Thomas con- Joseph Lambert, father min- John Loyd-

Sullivan

James H & Julia A F Ryland 21 Dec 1829; b- Churchwell Curtis min- James Smith- 24Dec1829

William D & Lucy J Keeton 19 Dec 1836; b- Warner C Keeton

Swepson

Richard & Mary Tabb 12 Apr 1779; widow of John Tabb b- Achilles Jeffries

William M & Elizabeth I Speed 27 Mar 1805; b- John James Speed

William W & Nancy E Redd 12 Jun 1816; b- John Tabb con- George Redd, father min- James Meacham-

Sydnor

Samuel H & Mary C Reekes 1 Feb 1825; b- Drury Lett con- Benjamin Reekes, father min- Charles Ogburn- (Methodist)

Tabb

Edward L & Elizabeth Blair Burwell 31 Jan 1791; s of John and Mary Tabb b- G H Baskervill con- Lewis Burwell, father

John & Lucy Smith Crenshaw 13 Nov 1816; b- John T Keen min- William Richards-

Talley

Abraham & Elizabeth Chandler 15 Jan 1816; b- Joel Chandler min- Reuben Pickett- 1Feb1816

George & Lucy McDaniel 12 Dec 1787; b- James Moore con- John and Mary McDaniel, parents

George & Martha Wilson 18 Oct 1813; b- John E Pettypool

Grief & Lucy Curtis 16 Sep 1799; b- Drury Creedle min- Charles Ogburn- (Methodist)

Larkin & Polly Blacketter 27 Sep 1805; b- Samuel Bugg

Levy & Elvira D Palmer 2 Jan 1837; b- Horace Palmer

Obadiah & Lucy C Brame 9 Dec 1850; con- William Brame, father

Page & Elizabeth Perkinson 23 Dec 1830; b- John C Perkinson con- Guilford Talley, gdn of Page Page from Warren Co., NC min- James McAden-

Peyron R & Jane Yancey 30 Nov 1819; b- John B Yancey con- Zachariah Yancey, father min- Reuben Pickett- 16Dec1819

Robert & Nancy Brame 18 Dec 1816; b- Charles W Baird min- Charles Ogburn- (Methodist) 19Dec1816

Russell & Elizabeth Creedle 14 Jul 1791; b- Bryant Creedle

Thomas E & Frances Stone 19 Feb 1821; b- Charles L Jeffries

Tanner

Benjamin & Elizabeth Cleaton 19 Dec 1815; b- Thomas Tanner con- Thomas Cleaton, father

David & Martha Ferrell 6 May 1802; b- Hutchins Ferrell

Evans & Rebecca Collier 21 Dec 1818; b- Joseph Bennett con- Howell Collier, father

Evans & Rebecca H Tanner 23 Apr 1834; b- Robert Tanner min- William B. Rowzee-

Hutchins F & Mary B Northington 17 Dec 1832; b- William B Jones con- John Northington, father min- James McAden-

Jonathon & Mary Young 5 Jun 1798; b- Allen Young

Ludwell & Lucy Holmes 2 Dec 1781; d of Isaac Holmes b- John Baskervill

Mortimer D & Elizabeth H Walker 21 Dec 1846; b- David D Walker con- Edward Walker, father

Richard & Nancy Andrews 15 Oct 1808; d of Varney Andrews Sr b- Varney Andrews

Robert E & Araminta M Tanner 14 Nov 1845; b- Robert Tanner min- James McAden-

Robert & Nancy Walker 19 Jan 1835; b- Wilson Walker min- James McAden-

Samuel Y & Martha Phillips 28 Apr 1818; b- Samuel A D Young con- Martha Phillips, mother con- Clack Robinson, gdn of Samuel min- Charles Ogburn- (Methodist) 30Apr1818

William M & Mary M H Tanner 21 Dec 1853; con- J B Northington, gdn of Mary min- Nathaniel Thomas-

Tarry

Berryman G & Elvira E Reekes 5 Apr 1839; b- Thomas C Reekes min- Benjamin R. Duval-

George & Sarah Taylor 7 Dec 1790; b- Anderson Taylor

James P & Martha A Bridgforth 11 Nov 1840; b- Robert F Bridgforth min- James McAden-

Robert & Nancy Smith 10 Jun 1793; Robert from Halifax County d of Peartree Smith b- Joseph Townes

Samuel A & Mary Brame 17 Dec 1827; b- Joseph Brame min- James Smith- 19Dec1827

Samuel T & Sarah C Marshall 27 Oct 1845; b- Alex W Hutcherson con- Henry C Moss, gdn of Sarah

Samuel & Mary Brown 14 Mar 1808; b- George Craighead min- James Meacham- 16Mar1808

Samuel & Amey Pettus 8 Jul 1799; b- William Coleman

Tarwater

Edward A & Eleanor Royster 14 Jun 1834; b- E A Holloway min- John B. Smith-

Joseph A & Sarah Ann Geoghegan 20 Sep 1847; b- E A Williams con- Charles Geoghegan, father

Taylor

Absolom & Martha C Barnett 29 Dec 1809; b- John Hudgins

Benjamin & Elizabeth House 17 Nov 1845; b- Phillip Pennington

Binford & Martha Binford 23 Dec 1829; b- David A Walker min- James McAden-

Charles H K & Martha A Feild 11 Mar 1839; b- Henry E Lockett

Charles & Elizabeth Wilson 23 Jul 1817; b- Lewis G Thomas Elizabeth daughter of Edward Wilson

Clark & Elizabeth Whitehead 13 Feb 1786; b- Richard Swepson

David D & Martha Small 17 Dec 1825; b- Isaac Taylor min- Sterling M. Fowler- 19Dec1825

David & Catharine Bowen 25 Mar 1829; b- William Matthews

David & Rebecca Dortch 9 May 1778; d of David Dortch b- William Taylor

Edmond & Mahala Crowder 9 Dec 1811; daughter of Richard Crowder Sr b- Richard Crowder

George R & Delphia Cleaton 12 Dec 1831; b- Woodly Cleaton min- Charles Ogburn- (Methodist) 21Dec1831

George T & Mary Goodloe Somervill 25 Apr 1825; b- William Taylor con- John Somervill, father

Goodwyn & Elizabeth Davis 5 May 1802; b- David Dortch

Goodwyn & Nancy Drumwright 10 Jan 1794; b- William Drumwright min- John Loyd- 21Jan1794

Howell A & Susan A Hayes 6 Oct 1843; b- James Hayes
Howell M & Phoebe Edmonds 31 Mar 1823; b- David Taylor
Howell & Susanna Young 30 Dec 1778; b- Samuel Young
Isaac & Julia Ann Floyd 21 Oct 1844; b- Ashley Daniel con- Zachary
    and Christany Floyd, parents
James (Jr) & Priscilla Fox 9 Dec 1801; b- Josiah Floyd min- James
    Meacham- 10Dec1801
James A & Louisa Thomas 29 Dec 1845; b- R W Thomas con- Robert
    Thomas, father min- James McAden-
Jesse & Phebe Moody 27 Jun 1789; b- Francis Moody con- Henry
    Moody, father min- Thomas Scott-
John A & Ann M Young 26 Apr 1852; con- Dianitia M Young, mother
John R & Elizabeth Puryear 10 Oct 1839; b- William T White con-
    Thomas Puryear, father min- Charles F. Burnley-
John Y & Mary B Somervill 26 Jan 1829; b- George T Taylor con- John
    Somervill, gdn
John & Happy Cook 5 Jan 1802; (Kerrenhappuck Cook) b- Abel Dortch
Jones M & Martha Cook 20 Dec 1845; b- Allen J Smith con- John
    Cook, father min- James McAden-
Jones & Joice Lark 11 Apr 1780; b- John Holmes
Jones & Ann J Vaughan 2 Feb 1813; b- Caleb Manning no minister cited,
    but ceremony performed 3Feb1813
Joseph & Elizabeth Willis Goode 29 Feb 1796; b- Francis Jones con-
    Swepson Jeffries, gdn of Elizabeth min- William Creath- 1Mar1796
Richard (Jr) & Anne S Burwell 21 Nov 1814; b- Alexander Boyd Jr
Richard B & Mary C Gregory 4 Dec 1798; b- Richard Gregory
Robertson D & Margaret Susan Floyd 24 Oct 1849; b- James W
    Whittemore con- Christany Floyd, mother
Robertson D & Nancy Kirks 5 Dec 1836; b- Goodwin L Overby
Samuel Allen & Frances B Maclin 27 Aug 1817; b- John G Baptist
Stephen & Elizabeth Moss 19 Jan 1824; b- R Brame
Thomas & Sally Benford 28 Sep 1792; b- William Drumwright min- John
    Loyd- 14Oct1792
Thomas & Lucy Crutchfield 24 Jan 1797; b- William Drumwright min-
    John Loyd- 31Jan1797
Thomas & Martha Cocke Hamblin 18 Oct 1800; b- Reuben Vaughan
    con- Agnes Hamblin, mother & gdn of Martha min- John Cameron-
Thomas & Sally Lark 26 Dec 1797; b- Samuel Lark
Thomas & Martha Leach 5 Aug 1808; b- Francis Gregory
William B & Rebecca J Dupree 20 Jul 1839; b- Obadiah Hatchell
    Rebecca herself test. that she is 23 min- Benjamin R. Duval-
William H & Mary Ann Drumwright 14 Aug 1839; b- E A Drumwright
    con- Ephraim Drumwright, father min- Benjamin R. Duval-
William H & Emma Walker 13 Dec 1830; b- James Holmes con- Wilson
    Walker, father min- James Smith- 16Dec1830
William Ladd & Mary Ambrose 2 Dec 1785; b- William Drumwright
    min- John King-
William & Molly Gober 4 Jul 1798; b- John Gober
William & Elizabeth Holloway 26 Apr 1785; b- Samuel Durham

Temple

Riddick & Elizabeth Ann Kidd 20 Jul 1825; b- John B Kidd con- John
    L Kidd, father
Samuel & Susanna Coppedge 11 Nov 1793; b- Charles Coppedge min-
    John Loyd- 14Nov1793

Terrell
> Jonathon & Sally Watkins 9 Dec 1830; b- James Watkins, father min- Pleasant Gold- (Baptist)- 23Dec1830

Terry
> Rowland & Mary Watkins 12 Oct 1707; b- Overton Wiles

Thacker
> David & Elizabeth Smith 7 Oct 1844; b- John W Pillar con- David Smith, father min- John C Blackwell- (Lunenburg County)-

Tharp
> Lewis & Sally O Hayes 15 Dec 1852; con- James Hayes Sr, father min- John A. Doll-

Thomas
> Bennett & Patsy Jones 24 Mar 1810; b- William Jones
> Billy & Lucy Stuart 10 Apr 1786; b- Francis Stuart min- John Williams- 20Apr1786
> Charles & Margarett Cleaton 18 Nov 1850; b- Christopher T Thomas min- Hartwell Arnold-
> Christopher & Elizabeth Basey 19 Dec 1829; b- Wynn Thomas
> Daniel F & Martha Greenwood 28 May 1833; b- George Lumpkin con- Robert Greenwood, father
> David W & Mary W Arnold 9 Sep 1844; b- Charles R Edmundson min- James McAden-
> David W & Rebecca A Thomas 16 Oct 1826; b- Riddick Wilson
> David & Sally Crowder 18 Jan 1825; b- John J Singleton
> Green J & Susan Dortch 31 Oct 1836; b- William B King con- Rebecca T Dortch, mother con- Alexander Dortch, gdn of susan
> Henry R & Emily R Rainey 20 Dec 1847; b- John J Rainey con- Williamson Rainey Jr, father min- Thomas Adams- (Lunenburg Co.)- 23Dec1847
> James J & Caroline B Williamson 17 Aug 1846; b- William B Greenwood con- James Williamson, father
> James & Delila Evans 27 Dec 1819; b- John Stewart con- Elizabeth Evans, mother
> John F & Martha W Evans 16 Nov 1829; b- William Evans min- James Smith- 18Nov1829
> John J & Martha L Thomas 5 Dec 1836; b- Martin F Lambert con- William B Thomas, father
> Leonard & Tinsey Winn Thomas 3 Nov 1824; b- Lewis Poythress
> Paschall & Mary Ann Rainey 17 Jul 1815; b- Allen Rainey con- Williamson Rainey, father
> Phillip H & Mary W Evans 18 Nov 1839; b- Anthony Evans con- Benjamin Evans, father min- James McAden-
> Robertson & Sally Rainey 22 Dec 1823; b- Williamson Rainey Jr con- Williamson Rainey Sr, father min- Stephen Jones- (Lynchburg, Va.)- 24Dec1823
> William & Frances H Carless 20 Dec 1790; b- Peter Thomas Jr min- John King- 24Dec1790
> William & Jane Hunt 7 May 1840; b- John Wilmouth con- Elizabeth Hunt, mother min- Charles F. Burnley-
> William & Mary Hunt 9 Nov 1840; b- John W Thomas
> William & Susan Ann Perkinson 19 Dec 1831; b- John C Perkinson
> Winn (Jr) & Parasade Cleaton 21 Jan 1828; b- William Thomas

Thomason
> Banister & Mary Singleton 25 Jul 1795; d of John and Mary Thomason b- William Thomason min- John Loyd- 30Jul1795

Cargill & Gincy Beasley 30 Mar 1825; b- William Insco con- Martha N Vaughan, mother con- Theoderick Vaughan, step-father of Gincy min- Charles Ogburn- (Methodist) 7Apr1825

George & Patsy Wall 2 Jan 1812; .b- Thomas Benford

James & Molly Thompson 4 Dec 1804; s of John and Mary Thomason b- David Hicks

Josiah & Polly Williams 17 Sep 1817; b- John Thompson James Taylor test that Polly the daughter of his sister Elizabeth Williams, and that Polly 21

L James & Mary Ann Smelley 20 Aug 1841; b- Willis Smelley min- James McAden-

Mial & Judith Merryman 24 Dec 1812; b- William Thomason

Thomas & Delia Ann Akin 6 Sep 1836; b- Edward Allgood con- Nancy Akin, mother min- William Steel- (Episcopal)-

Thomas & Elizabeth Crowder 20 Dec 1830; b- Charles W Baird con- Abraham Crowder, father min- James McAden-

William (Jr) & Patsy Laffoon 7 Feb 1805; b- William Thomason Sr

William T & Oney Taylor 16 Dec 1822; b- Ludwell Evans con- Thomas I Taylor, father min- Stephen Jones- (Lynchburg, Va.)-

Thompson

Bernard & Milly Yates 10 Dec 1804; b- John Walton

Charles B & Lucy A Rainey 25 Nov 1848; b- Charles G Turner con- William Rainey, father

Ervin A & Anna V H Piemont 16 Jun 1851; min- J.D. Blackwell- 17Jun1851

Fendall & Lucy A Russell 12 Oct 1853; con- Jesse Russell, father min- James McAden-

Henderson & Mary A Tucker 30 Sep 1816; b- Thomas Burnett con- Daniel Tucker, father con- John Thompson Jr, father

Henry R & Amey Evans Thompson 17 Dec 1840; b- William Evans con- Lucy Evans, mother

James Mims & Nancy Jackson 3 Jan 1789; b- John Allen con- John Thompson, for James con- Fleming and Elizabeth Jackson, parents

James & Susanna Nunnery 27 Aug 1806; b- Daniel Tucker Sr min- Charles Ogburn- (Methodist) 30Aug1806

James & Mary B Rudd 16 Jun 1817; b- Matthew Walker min- Charles Ogburn- (Methodist) 3Jul1817

John W & Jane Graves 20 Mar 1844; b- Samuel Dedman

John & Nancy Burnett 13 Apr 1801; b- Richard Burnett min- William Creath-

John & Mary Sally 12 Oct 1807; b- Stephen Pettypool

John & Sarah Thompson 8 May 1775; b- Asa Oliver

John & Phebe Tisdale 12 Jan 1795; b- William Thompson min- William Creath-

Lewis & Mary B Vaughan 18 Mar 1825; b- David C Vaughan

Peter & Martha Seward 18 Jul 1842; b- Joe Thompson con- Sally Deward, mother

Richard & Parthena Hudson 24 Dec 1832; b- John Hudson

Richard & Frances Anne Watts 14 Jun 1802; b- Henry Ashton con- Anna Watts, mother min- Matthew Dance- 29Jul1802

Samuel & Amelia Blanks 7 Oct 1817; b- John Blanks

Stith & Elizabeth Parker 24 Jul 1785; min- Henry Lester- (Baptist)

Stith & Elizabeth Parker 24 Jul 1785; min- Henry Y. Lester

Thomas C & Mary E Rainey 15 Sep 1853; con- Williamson Rainey, father min- Willis N. Pence-

William D & Rebecca Talley 18 Nov 1847; b- Robert Talley

William & Nancy Butler 27 Dec 1802; b- James Thompson
William & Mary Hailestock 19 Feb 1808; b- Abel Stewart
William & Julia Stegall 20 Dec 1819; b- Drury Pennington con- George Stegall, father
William & Thrudy Stewart 11 Nov 1805; b- Neely Stewart

Thomson
Archer & Elizabeth Cox 16 Mar 1812; b- William Mayes min- William Richards- 19Mar1812
Edward & Frances Booker 10 May 1822; b- Henderson Thompson con- John Booker, father min- Charles Ogburn- (Methodist) 23May1822
Joseph & Mary Williams 18 Sep 1817; min- Charles Ogburn- (Methodist)

Thornton
Francis A & Lucy N Potts 3 Nov 1838; b- George D Baskervill min- Edward Wadsworth-

Threadgill
Thomas & Tabitha Ingram 9 Sep 1782; b- Reuben Vaughan

Throgmorton
James D & Mary F Whitlow 18 Dec 1849; .b- German D Dedman con- Champion Whitlow, father con- F Throgmorton, father

Thrower
William & Ann C Taylor 20 Oct 1817; b- Zachariah Bugg min- Thomas Moore- 27Oct1817

Tillotson
Bartlett & Amelia Daniel 16 Jul 1823; b- James Tillotson min- Pleasant Gold- (Baptist)-
Edward & Milly Gold 2 Feb 1808; d of Daniel Gold, dec. b- John Hailey con- William Tillotson, father con- Thomas Hailey, stepfather of Milly
James & Frances White 27 Nov 1823; b- Elam S Wall min- Pleasant Gold- (Baptist)- 2Dec1823
John & Nancy Tillotson 19 May 1828; b- John Jones con- John Tillotson Sr, father min- Pleasant Gold- (Baptist)-
John & Delphia Yancey 16 Jan 1801; b- Richard Murray
Thomas & Sarah Overby 5 Mar 1835; b- James Griffin con- Alexander and Sarah Parker Overby, parents min- John B. Smith-
William H & Mary Griffin 10 Jan 1843; b- James Griffin min- Alfred Apple- 12Jan1843
William & Julianna Gregory 19 Feb 1835; b- James Tillotson con- Barnett Gregory, father min- John B. Smith-
William & Mary Gregory 25 Jun 1832; b- James Yancey

Tisdale
John D & Ann B Bennett 16 Apr 1849; b- Thomas Rose min- James McAden- 17Apr1849
John D & Elizabeth A Crenshaw 20 Feb 1832; b- John R Crenshaw con- Elizabeth Crenshaw, mother min- Daniel Petty-
John & Nancy Clark 13 Mar 1787; b- Thomas Clark
William R & Mary Colley 30 Nov 1829; b- Charles Colley min- James Smith- 9Dec1829

Tompkins
Harry & Susan Ann Arnold 28 Apr 1828; b- James M Whittle con- Joseph A Arnold, father min- James McAden-

Toone
Argelon & Mary Freeman 13 Oct 1783; b- James Hix
Edward H & Jane F Wilson 11 Jul 1832; b- John S Feild min- William Steel- (Episcopal)- 12Jul1832
George & Joanna Toone 10 Oct 1814; b- Thomas Abernathy min- Milton Robertson- (Warren County, N.C.) 31Oct1814

James & Milly Daniel 9 Apr 1770; b- William Taylor con- William Daniel, father

Lewis L & Elizabeth E Wootton 14 Oct 1844; b- William R Toone min- John B. Smith-

Lewis & Rebeccah Moore 15 Aug 1787; b- Francis Lewis

Lewis & Millicent Richards 11 Feb 1805; b- Abraham Keen con- W W Richards, father min- James Shelburne- 4Mar1805

Tavener & Ann Marshall 20 May 1809; b- George Bilbo

Tavner & Rebecca Waller 16 Nov 1818; b- Isaac H Waller con- Daniel Waller, father min- Milton Robertson- (Warren County, N.C.) 19Nov1818

Thomas & Winny Garner 11 Aug 1800; b- Richard Brown con- James Garner, father min- Edward Almand- 21Aug1800

William R & Mary Ann Mason 19 Dec 1836; b- William R Mason

William & Elizabeth Hamblin 22 Mar 1786; b- Isaac Pully

Townes

Alfred & Ann M Maclin 31 Mar 1836; b- J B Maclin

David & Polly Marshall 23 Dec 1812; daughter of Richard Marshall b- Theophilus Marshall

Edward & Ellen F Townes 21 Dec 1844; b- William Townes

Henry & Polly Davis 31 Dec 1784; con- Barton Davis, father

Joseph & Isabella Wade 28 Jun 1784; Henry from Halifax County b- Henry Townes

William & Lucy R Maclin 27 Nov 1817; min- John S. Ravenscroft- (Episcopal)-

Townsend

Peter & Lucy Hundley 11 Jul 1808; b- Willis Hundley

Travis

Edward & Peggy Blanton 15 Jul 1816; b- Diggs Poynor

Traylor

Cary & Elizabeth Thompson 7 Nov 1786; b- John Johnson

Trice

Thomas & Mary Green 11 Aug 1777; widow of Thomas Green b- Edmund Taylor

Tucker

Alexander S & Elizabeth Bing 16 Sep 1816; b- John Bing min- Milton Robertson- (Warren County, N.C.)

Daniel (Jr) & Mary Parrish 8 Feb 1808; b- William Parrish

Daniel & Jincy Cardin 17 Jul 1787; b- George Stainback con- John Cardin, father

George & Rebecca A Ezell 4 Apr 1842; b- Edward R Chambers min- James McAden-

George & Eddy Short 23 Apr 1800; b- Daniel Tucker min- Charles Ogburn- (Methodist)

George & Polly Smith 29 Oct 1814; b- John Davis

Harwood B & Nancy Mason 9 Jan 1809; b- William Stone

Henry & Selina S Burwell 13 Jul 1851; min- Adam Finch-

Isham N & Mary Ryland 10 Sep 1817; widow b- William Insco, father of Mary min- Milton Robertson- (Warren County, N.C.)

Isham & Sarah Booker 11 May 1803; b- William Renn min- William Creath-

Isham & Rose Eaton 2 Feb 1786; b- James Bing

James M & Lucy R Dortch 20 Oct 1824; b- Newman Dortch min- James Smith-

James P & Catherine Tucker 14 Dec 1772; b- Robert Williams

James & Ruth Puckett 17 May 1810; b- G B Hudson

James & Jane Tucker 6 Sep 1809; b- William Insco

Jesse   &   Nancy Carroll   7 Nov 1793;   b- John Carroll

John   &   Sally Nunnery   22 Jan 1793;   b- Charnal Deardin   min- Charles
   Ogburn- (Methodist) 25Jan1793

John   &   Martha Jane Poythress   16 Oct 1848;   b- J S Moss   con- David
   Poythress, father   min- Thomas Adams- (Lunenburg Co.)- 18Oct1848

John   &   Frances Tucker   10 Dec 1798;   b- Leonard Keeton   min- William
   Creath- 28Dec1798

Littleberry   &   Elizabeth Kelly   22 Dec 1797;   b- John Tucker   min- Charles
   Ogburn- (Methodist) 29Dec1797

Merritt   &   Martha Tucker   6 Dec 1833;   b- Usham N Tucker

Robert   &   Sarah Smith   12 Nov 1787;   b- Edward Elam

Tapla   &   Nancy Kelly   9 Dec 1799;   b- Daniel Tucker   min- William Creath-

Thomas J   &   Susannah Short   4 Jan 1814;   b- William Marshall   min- James
   Meacham- 6Jan1814

Thomas   &   Mary Neathery   20 Nov 1824;   b- George Neathery

Wiley   &   Susannah Keeton   16 Jan 1815;   daughter of Joseph Keeton, Sr
   b- John Hutcheson

William   &   Ruth Hendrick   22 Jan 1824;   b- John LeNeve   con- Rebecca
   Tucker, mother

William   &   Nancy Stone   18 Aug 1828;   b- Samuel D Roffe   min- James
   Smith- 19Aug1828

Worsham   &   Mary Gordon   5 Dec 1804;   b- John Gosee   min- Matthew
   Dance- 6Dec1804

Tudor

John G   &   Lucy T Freeman   12 Feb 1824;   b- John Toone   con- Benjamin
   T Freeman, father   min- James Smith-

John   &   Milly Spurlock   16 Jul 1787;   b- Zachariah Spurlock

Tunstall

John B   &   Tabitha Griffin   6 Feb 1823;   b- James T Jones   min- James
   Smith-

John B   &   Sarah C Hutcheson   19 Feb 1852;   con- Mary C Hutcheson, gdn
   of Sarah   min- George W. Andrews-

William H   &   Martha E Apperson   6 Jan 1840;   b- William Townes   min-
   F.H. McGuire- 7Jan1840

Turnbull

Robert D   &   Lavinia Stith   20 Dec 1838;   b- James B Dupuy   min- Thomas
   T. Castleman- (Lunenburg County)-

Turner

Bailey   &   Susanna Easter   1 Dec 1792;   b- John Oliver   min- Edward
   Almand- 20Dec1792

Benjamin U   &   Nancy J Davis   17 Dec 1849;   b- John C Davis   con- Willis
   S Davis,, father   min- Richard E.G. Adams- (Lunenburg County)-
   20Dec1849

Charles G   &   Sarah W Rainey   13 Dec 1838;   b- Thomas J Rainey   con-
   Williamson Rainey, Jr, father   min- Benjamin R. Duval-

Drury   &   Tallathacuma Jackson   11 Dec 1802;   b- Matthew Jackson

John J   &   Judith J Farrar   16 May 1815;   b- William R Bilbo   con- John
   Farrar, father   min- James Meacham- 20May1815

John   &   Mary Hutcheson   13 Oct 1800;   b- Aurelius Walker

John   &   Rebeccah Taylor   8 Dec 1800;   b- James Taylor, Jr   min- James
   Meacham- 11Dec1800

Stephen   &   Susan A T Read   12 May 1832;   Stephen from Warren Co. NC
   b- Lewis G Meacham   con- Clement Read, father   min- Stephen Turner-
   18Jun1832

Stephen   &   Martha Wright   11 Mar 1801;   b- Austen Wright

Terisha & Joanah Reaves 19 Dec 1785; b- John Burton con- Stephen Turner con- Thomas Rives min- John King- 22Dec1785

Thomas & Nancy Baskervill 16 Jan 1817; b- George D Baskervill min- Charles Ogburn- (Methodist) 21Jan1817

William H & Elizabeth A Hubbard 11 Feb 1848; b- J W McAden con- Ralph Hubbard, father min- James McAden-

William & Susan Ferguson 19 Aug 1817; b- John Winckler

Tutor

Henry & Jane Pully 20 Dec 1824; b- Hutchins F Pully min- James Smith- 23Dec1824

John G & Elizabeth A Meacham 20 Apr 1833; b- Lewis G Meacham con- Mary Meacham, mother

John J & Sarah E Thomas 9 Dec 1850; con- T W Thomas, father min- Hartwell Arnold-

Valentine

Beverly & Martha Feagons 21 Dec 1840; b- John Stewart con- Thomas Feagos, father min- James McAden-

Buckner & Sine Chavous 21 Dec 1802; b- Bolling Chavous

Charles & Nancy Chavous 28 Nov 1785; b- Thomas Macklin

Isaac & Permelia Evans 28 May 1838; b- John Stewart con- Mary Chavous, mother of Permelia min- Benjamin R. Duval- 19Jun1838

John & Mary McLin 4 Jan 1797; b- Earby Chavous min- John Loyd- 5Jan1797

Thomas & Sally Stewart 18 May 1818; b- Randolph Chavous min- Milton Robertson- (Warren County, N.C.) 21May1818

William & Eliza J Stewart 17 Aug 1846; b- Charles Stewart

Vaughan

Alfred & Nancy Whittemore 9 Sep 1833; b- Churchwell Curtis

Ambrose (Sr) & Martha Land 3 Mar 1813; b- John Cheatham

Ambrose & Elizabeth C Dortch 16 Dec 1835; b- Jones M Taylor min- Stephen Turner- 17Dec1835

Asa & Sarah Newton 6 Jan 1846; b- Haman Newton con- James Newton, father min- Alfred Apple-

Baalam & Polly Burnes 11 Dec 1809; b- Robert Burnes min- Richard Dabbs- 12Dec1809

Binns & Martha L Arnold 20 Jun 1798; b- Thomas Edmundson min- Charles Ogburn- (Methodist) 21Jun1798

Coleman & Elizabeth Childress 18 Dec 1833; b- William Childress min- William Steel- (Episcopal)- 24Dec1833

David & Philadelphia Griffin 14 Dec 1807; b- Hezekiah Yancey con- James Griffin, father

David & Patty Kirks 3 Aug 1803; b- John Hudgins

Edmund H & Sally H Walker 5 Jun 1809; b- Francis E Walker min- George Micklejohn-

Grandison & Mary Wortham 28 Dec 1827; b- James Vaughan min- Pleasant Gold- (Baptist)-

Henry G & Nancy O Wade 3 Jan 1803; b- William Wade min- William Richards- 5Jan1803

Henry & Sally H Craddock 21 Oct 1829; b- David Almand con- Jesse Craddock, brother of Sally

Henry & Mary Ann Cutts 16 Dec 1837; b- John F Yancey con- Robert Yancey, father-in-law of Mary Ann(?)

Henry & Amanda E J Wells 4 Mar 1834; b- Ligon Wells con- Baker Wells, father min- John Wesley Childs- 5Mar1834

Ingram & Ann Lewis 20 Aug 1785; b- William Baskervill con- Edward Lewis, brother & gdn of Ann

Ishmael & Caty Roberts 24 Oct 1797; b- William Roberts

Jairus & Hannah Vaughan 11 Jul 1796; b- Craddock Vaughan daughter of Reuben and Elizabeth Vaughan con- Richard Vaughan, father of Jairus min- Charles Ogburn- (Methodist) 3Aug1796

James E & Susan G Puryear 12 Dec 1842; b- Willis Smelley con- Mary Puryear, mother min- James McAden-

James & Mary Crow 26 Dec 1808; b- William Crow

James & Susannah Harris 11 Jun 1803; b- Richard Jeffries con- William Harris, father min- William Richards- 30Jun1803

James & Judy Spain 11 Dec 1797; b- Sterling Spain con- Thomas Spain, father min- William Richards- 19Dec1797

John J & Elizabeth A Richardson 19 May 1848; b- John Forman con- Robert Richardson, father

John & Nancy Hayes 13 Dec 1802; b- Starkey Hayes min- Balaam Ezell-

John & Louisa Spain 23 Dec 1823; b- Royall Spain min- William Richards- 25Dec1823

John & Nancy Wortham 29 Apr 1823; b- Pleasant Gold min- Pleasant Gold- (Baptist)- 1May1823

Ledford & Elizabeth Vaughan 20 Dec 1830; b- William Vaughan con- Priscilla Vaughan, mother of Elizabeth min- Pleasant Gold- (Baptist)- 22Dec1830

Peter & Patsy Chandler 12 Jan 1829; b- William Vaughan min- Pleasant Gold- (Baptist)- 15Jan1829

Peter & Nancy Glasscock 10 Jan 1842; b- William Glasscock min- Alfred Apple-

Peter & Jane Vaughan 24 Feb 1821; b- Atha Gregory con- S C Vaughan, father min- Pleasant Gold- (Baptist)- 10Apr1821

Richard B & Anna Hall 11 Oct 1815; daughter of John Hall Sr b- John Hall Jr

Richard S & Elizabeth A Rook 1 Jan 1850; b- B B Vaughan con- William G Rook, father min- Hartwell Arnold-

Richard & Mary Thompson 21 Jan 1826; b- William Stone min- Charles Ogburn- (Methodist) 29Jan1826

Robert A & Rebecca M Davis 4 Jan 1806; b- Bushrod Webb con- Ambrose Vaughan, father con- Randolph Davis, father

Samuel J & Martha Walker 1 Dec 1836; b- William Cleaton

Samuel & Mildred Thomas 1 Jan 1811; b- John Cheatham

Samuel & Rebecca Wilson 30 May 1816; b- Charles Taylor con- E T Wilson, father

Spencer C & Elizabeth Murray 16 Dec 1811; b- Garrett Avery

Spencer C & Rebecca Talley 27 Dec 1844; b- Edward Davis con- Abraham Talley, father min- Thomas King- (Halifax County)- 29Jun1844

Theoderick & Martha Beasley 16 Jan 1813; widow b- Harrison W Ryland con- William Insco, Sr, father of Martha min- Milton Robertson- (Warren County, N.C.)

Thomas & Mary Alford Blackbourn 11 Mar 1799; d of Thomas b- John Wilson

Thomas & Elizabeth Davis 4 Feb 1828; b- Lewis G Crutchfield con- William Davis, father, who test Elizabeth 21

Thomas & Martha Lewis 8 Oct 1781; b- Edward Lewis

Thomas & Ann Smith 12 Oct 1772; b- Swepson Jeffries

William & Anne C Gregory 6 Apr 1795; b- Richard Gregory min- Charles Ogburn- (Methodist) 9Apr1795

William & Elizabeth Saunders 3 Mar 1794; b- Ambrose Vaughan of Brunswick County con- Richard Vaughan, father con- John Saunders, father min- John Loyd- 6Mar1794

William & Mary Smith 4 Jan 1811; b- John Lambert

William & Nancy Tucker 20 Dec 1821; min- Charles Ogburn- (Methodist)

William & Elizabeth Wall 15 Dec 1818; b- Thomas Hendrick min-Reuben Pickett-

Woody & Sarah Farrar 11 Dec 1804; b- Sanford Bowers con- George Farrar, father

Venable

Francis W & Nancy C Nelson 24 Dec 1833; min- William Steel-(Episcopal)-

Samuel & Ann Anderson 5 Mar 1782; d of Thomas and Sarah Anderson Samuel from Prince Edward County b- Thomas Anderson, father?

William G & Sally T Venable 26 Nov 1845; b- William M Womack con-P C Venable, father

Vercer

Francis & Paulina Poindexter 8 Apr 1830; b- W McNeely con- George E Poindexter, father

Vowell

William H & Martha Malone 1 Nov 1841; b- Anderson Malone

Wade

Augustus D & Elizabeth Moore 19 Aug 1816; b- Franklin Moore

George D & Harriet B Holloway 21 Feb 1837; b- James Holloway

Grandison G & Sarah R Perkins 11 Nov 1842; b- George W Perkins min- Alfred Apple- 15Nov1842

Henderson & Elizabeth Wilburn 6 Jan 1795; b- William Harrison min-William Richards- 11Jan1795

William & Martha Russell 9 Nov 1767; b- William Robertson

William & Polly Mealer Vaughan 12 Aug 1799; b- Willis Vaughan min-Edward Almand- 15Aug1799

Wagstaff

Allen & Susannah Overton 12 Dec 1803; b- Philemon Hurt, Jr min-William Richards- 25Dec1803

Bazzell & Elizabeth Camp 5 Mar 1806; b- Allen Wagstaff min- William Richards- 6Mar1806

Britain & Anne Freeman 7 Feb 1778; d of Allen Freeman b- Allen Freeman

Cuthbert & Mary Burrows 30 May 1822; b- Francis McCraw con-Elizabeth Burton, mother of Mary min- William Richards-

Edward & Hannah Hunt 16 Jan 1815; b- Wagstaff Hunt con- William Hunt, father min- William Richards- 25Jan1815

Walden

Eaton & Nanny Evans 20 Dec 1788; b- Moses Stuart con- Charles Evans, father

Jarrel & Mourning Jackson 16 Sep 1801; b- John Harris

Jesse & Milly Stewart 8 Apr 1805; b- Frederick Ivey min- William Creath-

John A & Susan Cardwell 27 Jul 1840; b- John J Roberts con- James H Cardwell, father

John & Betsy Stewart 21 Apr 1804; b- Kinchen Chavous

William L & Mary Cardwell 12 Feb 1842; b- John A Walden con- James H Cardwell, father min- Charles F. Burnley-

Walker

Aurelius & Nancy Turner 23 Nov 1784; d of Matthew Turner b- William Allen son of Sylvanus Walker

Benjamin J & Emily J Brown 2 Sep 1834; b- Henry Turpin con- J Brown, father min- James M. Jeter- (Lunenburg County)-

Benjamin J & Martha E F Wartman 15 Dec 1845; b- William N Walker min- James McAden-

Charles P & Judith C Wilson 30 Dec 1839; b- Thomas C Reekes min- John B. Smith-

Daniel & Mary Brown 5 Aug 1793; b- Thomas Brown Daniel from Nottoway County

Daniel & Martha E Johnson 9 Sep 1816; b- Jacob Johnson min- Charles Ogburn- (Methodist) 11Sep1816

David D & Emma W Cleaton 10 Dec 1839; b- Samuel Dortch con- Charles Cleaton, father min- James McAden-

David D & Sarah A Hudson 3 Jul 1847; b- William T Owen min- James McAden- 5Jul1847

Edward & Harriet Dortch 6 Jan 1817; b- William Evans con- David Dortch, father min- Charles Ogburn- (Methodist) 8Jan1817

Evans & Elvira A Evans - — 1845; min- James McAden-

Freeman & Elizabeth Bennett 28 Oct 1833; b- Joseph Bennett min- James McAden-

Freeman & Polly Toone 12 Jul 1789; b- Lewis Toone min- John Williams- 14Jul1789

George & Phebe Cheatham 14 Dec 1789; George son of Sylvanus and Susannah Walker b- Obadiah cheatham con- Daniel Cheatham, father, who test. daughter under age

Henry A & Mary E Moss 18 Jan 1841; b- James W Brame con- David Moss, father min- James McAden-

Henry W & Ermin E Smith 20 Dec 1841; b- Benjamin J Walker min- James McAden-

Henry & Frances Hutcheson 7 Dec 1818; b- John Hutcheson min- Charles Ogburn- (Methodist) 10Dec1818

James S & Mary E Smith 20 Nov 1843; b- Phillip H Thomas min- James McAden-

James W & Lucy M Evans 29 Jun 1847; b- Phillip H Thomas con- Ben S Evans, father min- James McAden- 1Jul1847

John A & Maria E Arnold 7 Nov 1852; con- John J Arnold, father min- George W. Andrews-

John H & Mary Jane Rainey 17 Nov 1845; b- Buckner M Rainey min- James McAden-

John H & Mary M Wartman 21 Feb 1846; b- Isaac Watson con- Thomas Wartman, father min- James J. Sledge-

John O & Amanda C Walker 25 Oct 1852; con- Emma F Walker, mother min- James McAden-

John R & Helen Cunningham 2 Feb 1853; con- James Cunningham, father min- J.W. Chesley- 8Feb1853

John & Lucy Creedle 8 Mar 1843; b- William H Creedle min- James McAden-

John & Anna Gregory 12 Nov 1798; b- Thomas Reamy min- William Richards- 15Nov1798

Joseph R & Dolly Winfield 6 Dec 1796; b- William Abernathy con- Joshua Winfield, father

Joshua E & Mary A Cleaton 20 Dec 1845; b- David D Walker con- William B Cleaton, father min- James McAden-

Jugurtha & Catharine Baisey 18 Sep 1834; b- John Baisey min- William B. Rowzee-

Matthew & Rebecca Powers 21 Dec 1805; b- John Turner Jr

Matthew & Sally Stone 4 Oct 1809; d of William and Tabitha Stone s of Aurelius and Nancy Walker b- William Stone min- Richard Dabbs- 19Oct1809

Renison & Mary A Coleman 20 Dec 1852; min- Adam Finch- 29Dec1852

Richard E & Martha H Phillips 11 Dec 1826; b- Robert C Hardy min- James D. Tompkins- 21Dec1826

Richard H (Jr) & Eugenia F Davis 27 May 1850; b- John Nelson con- Martha S Davis, mother

Richard H & Nancy Vaughan 10 Jul 1798; b- Thomas Vaughan Richard son of Henry and Martha Walker

Richardson & Mary Finney 14 Aug 1823; b- John Haskins con- William Haskins, gdn of Mary min- Pleasant Gold- (Baptist)-

Robert A & Rebecca Hutcheson 18 Dec 1820; b- Edwin C Tarry min- Charles Ogburn- (Methodist) 20Dec1820

Robert & Rebecca Johnson 9 Dec 1816; b- Henry Davis min- Charles Ogburn- (Methodist) 11Dec1816

Samuel E & Ann D Walker 20 Jan 1845; b- Robert W Ezell con- E Walker, father min- James McAden-

Samuel H & Elizabeth Ezell 18 Dec 1815; b- Diggs Poynor con- William Ezell, father

Sylvanus & Elizabeth Hutcheson 17 Mar 1820; b- Henry Walker min- James Smith-

Thomas D & Mary V Hines 5 Nov 1847; b- William H Turner con- Ralph Hubbard for Mary V Hines, alias Mary V Hubbard min- James McAden- 6Nov1847

Thomas W & Ann Wartman 18 Dec 1820; b- Diggs Poynor

William E & Nancy W Evans 20 Jan 1845; b- David R Walker con- Benjamin Evans, father min- James McAden-

William & Mary Bugg 7 Aug 1779; b- Henry Pennington con- John and Lucy Bugg, parents

Wall

Benjamin & Mary S Bugg 2 Apr 1800; b- Frederick Wall con- Molly Bugg, mother

Braxton & Sally Neal 16 Apr 1827; b- William Neal min- Pleasant Gold- (Baptist)- 1May1827

Burwell & Mary Burks 30 Sep 1794; b- Miles House Mary gives own consent and states that she is 25 years old

Charles F & Ann Neal 20 Oct 1828; b- William Neal min- Pleasant Gold- (Baptist)- 18Nov1828

Daniel & Nancy Berry 3 Apr 1811; b- Polly W Berry

David S & Rebecca J Short 3 Jul 1805; b- George Stegall

Drury & Tabitha Browder 16 Aug 1824; b- Thompson Browder min- Pleasant Gold- (Baptist)- 25Aug1824

Elam S & Lucy Tillotson 27 Nov 1823; b- James Tillotson con- John Tillotson, father min- Pleasant Gold- (Baptist)- 11Dec1823

Frederick & Patsy Wooton Daniel 13 Jun 1803; b- William Daniel

Henry & Sally Daniel 17 Dec 1810; b- Frederick Wall

John & Amey Hall 10 Dec 1787; John from Halifax County b- James Hall

John & Meloda Overby 22 Feb 1808; John from Halifax County b- Peter Overby Jr

Major & Mary James 10 Jan 1803; b- Frederick Poarch

Miles S & Ann Jones 29 Nov 1821; b- John Jones min- John S. Ravenscroft- (Episcopal)- 13Dec1821

Thomas & Jane Edmundson 13 Jan 1800; b- John Whobry min- William Creath-

Thomas & Elizabeth H Short 30 Sep 1797; b- Freeman Short

Wallace
David & Nancy M Wills 22 Mar 1798; b- Larkin Crowder min- Charles Ogburn- (Methodist) 24Mar1798
Waller
Daniel & Frances Holmes 29 Apr 1788; b- John Waller min- Thomas Scott-
James & Susanna Wilson 16 Mar 1792; b- James Wilson min- John Loyd-
John W & Louisa E Smith 6 Aug 1853; con- John Smith, father min- James McAden-
John & Ann Holmes 5 Mar 1782; b- John Ballard
John & Catharine Morris 19 Dec 1825; b- William Morris con- Jesse Morris, father min- James McAden-
Starling & Rebecca Drumwright 1 Sep 1796; b- William Drumwright
Walthall
John & Amelia M P Leverman 8 Nov 1834; b- J A Gregory
Walton
Henry C & Nancy J Clark 16 Sep 1825; b- Edward Royster con- Archibald Clark, father
John & Dolly Ricks 14 Oct 1798; b- Richard Brown
Ware
William W & Silvanah Wall 10 Jan 1843; b- James Glasscock min- Alfred Apple-
Warren
John L & Mary E Wootton 7 Dec 1838; b- Samuel Wootton Jr min- John B. Smith-
John & Betsy Holmes 5 Dec 1792; d of Samuel Holmes b- Walter Leigh
Marriott & Mary Holmes 17 Dec 1794; Marriott from Richmond County, Georgia b- Benjamin Suggett con- Samuel Holmes, Sr, father min- John Neblett-
Samuel H & Elizabeth Rebecca Delony 12 Dec 1820; b- Ludwell E Jones min- James Smith- 14Dec1820
Thomas M & Caroline Gee 10 Dec 1823; b- David G Moore con- Jeremiah Gee, gdn for Caroline con- Elizabeth Warren, gdn for Thomas min- James McAden-
William & Lucinda Holmes 17 Apr 1798; b- Samuel Holmes min- Charles Ogburn- (Methodist) 18Apr1798
Wartman
Henry & Sarah Nance 8 Sep 1835; b- Isham Nance con- John Nance, father of Sarah, who test she is 21
John Henry & Tabitha Epps 24 Nov 1787; b- Isham Epps
John & Martha N Giles 14 Nov 1831; b- Edward Giles con- John Nance gdn of Martha min- John Wesley Childs-
Thomas & Lucy F Walker 1 Feb 1821; b- William B Cleaton con- Henry Walker, father min- James Smith- 8Feb1821
Watkins
George T & Susan A Lynch 20 Nov 1850; con- B W Lynch, father min- William V. Wilson-
James & Ann Nuckols 9 Sep 1789; b- Philip Morgan
James & Mary Tansley 22 May 1822; min- Pleasant Gold- (Baptist)-
Joel T & Sally Tarry 9 Mar 1842; b- Samuel D Booker con- Edward Tarry, father
Joel & Judith C Daniel 19 Feb 1818; b- Howell L Jeffries
John & Elizabeth Davis 28 Apr 1824; b- Stephen Davis con- Matthew Davis, gdn of Elizabeth min- Charles Ogburn- (Methodist)

John & Elizabeth Jackson 20 Oct 1819; b- Vincent Jackson con- Judith Jackson, mother con- Joseph Watkins, father min- Pleasant Gold- (Baptist)-

Richard W & Mary Ann Baskervill 12 May 1837; b- John Coleman min- William Steel- (Episcopal)-

Samuel & Ann V Daniel 7 Mar 1826; b- James B Daniel con- James Daniel, father

Samuel & Jane Tandy 18 Jan 1826; b- Thomas Hailey con- James Watkins, gdn of Jane, daughter of John Tandy, dec., of New Kent County min- Pleasant Gold- (Baptist)-

Thomas & Ellinor Farrar 8 Nov 1790; b- Thomas Farrar min- James Read- (Baptist)

Thomas & Mary Northington 10 Aug 1819; b- James Hunt con- Nathan Northington, father

William Durham & Jane Bailey 9 Dec 1793; b- Henry Bailey min- William Creath- 25Dec1793

William & Eveline Culbreath 28 Nov 1840; b- William Culbreath

Watson

Benjamin B & Amanda M J F Norment 15 May 1835; b- John H Pettus

Benjamin G & Elizabeth R Barnes 4 Nov 1845; b- Dabney Farrar

Isaac B & Sarah G Taylor 21 Mar 1825; b- William Hogan

Isaac D & Nancy G Hunt 6 May 1837; b- Claiborne Drumwright min- James McAden-

James T & Elizabeth Lark 6 Oct 1803; b- Samuel Lark Sr

James & Agatha Roberts 30 Dec 1813; b- John Nance

James & Polly Jones Taylor 27 Jan 1796; b- Abel Dortch min- John Loyd- 28Jan1796

Littleberry & Sarah Tunstall 9 Dec 1843; b- Richard D Bugg con- John B Tunstall, father

Samuel & Serzener M Harper 26 Mar 1844; b- Edwin Binford con- John Harper, father min- James McAden-

Thomas & Susanna Taylor 27 Dec 1791; b- William Poole con- Abel Dortch

William T & Jane T Norment 14 Oct 1828; min- William Richards-

William & Rebecca J Taylor 29 Apr 1841; b- John Wartman

Watts

Alexander & Sally Freeman 29 Jun 1833; b- George Gordan

Richard & Lucy Collier 10 Mar 1806; b- William Lipford

Weatherford

Freeman & Polly Smith 8 Dec 1800; b- Richard Thompson con- Buckner Smith, father min- William Creath-

William S & Elizabeth J Hall 19 Feb 1828; b- Miles Hall min- John B. Smith- 20Feb1828

William & Catherine C Claiborne 16 Jun 1827; b- Henry C Ward

Weaver

John & Susan Crowder 17 Feb 1844; b- Charles W Crowder con- Abraham Crowder, father min- James McAden-

Thomas & Betty Merryman 1 Nov 1786; b- Isham Merryman con- James Turner, father

Webb

Abdias & Patty Fain 15 Dec 1790; b- Frederick Rainey

Bushrod & Catherine Lovingston 7 Jan 1800; b- Mark L Jackson min- Ebenezer McGowan- 8Jan1800

Isaac & Polly R Thomas 28 Dec 1813; b- Bushrod Webb

John & Sine Blankenship 16 Dec 1802; b- Mark L Jackson

Thomas & Sarah Chambliss 12 Oct 1835; b- Robert D Chambliss con- John Chambliss, father min- George A. Bain-

William & Emma Inge 19 Jan 1835; b- William Winn min- John B. Smith-

Webster

Samuel & Charlotte Winkler 1 Aug 1788; b- Richardson Davis

Wells

Baker & Levinia Underwood 10 Sep 1798; b- Zaccheus Ezell min- Matthew Dance- 15Sep1798

Benjamin A & Minerva C Harris 4 Dec 1843; b- Thomas A Crutchfield Minerva is 23

David & Nancy Garrott 11 Oct 1799; b- Elijah Wells con- Thomas Garrott, father min- William Creath-

Elijah & Sarah Ferrell 14 Sep 1795; b- John Hudson

Elisha & Mary Wilmoth 16 Nov 1840; b- Jesse Wilmoth

George H & Eliza C Vaughan 21 Nov 1842; 'Elvira C.' according to minister return b- Pleasant Vaughan min- Daniel Petty- 28Nov1842

Howard & Nancy W Estes 18 Dec 1818; min- Charles Ogburn- (Methodist)

James & Elizabeth S Stone 26 Dec 1850; min- S.A. Creath-

John D & Martha A Harris 8 Oct 1839; b- D A Hudson min- Benjamin R. Duval-

Robert & Frances E Stone 10 Jun 1846; b- James Wells con- Jacob W Stone, father min- Daniel Petty-

Silas & Martha Johnson 11 Feb 1845; b- James Wells min- Daniel Petty-

Wesson

Harrison & Elizabeth L Thomas 13 Dec 1825; b- Edward Poythress con- Winn Thomas, father

Roderick & Tabitha Thomas 3 Jun 1814; min- James Meacham- 7Jun1814

Westbrook

Jesse & Amy Weatherford 9 Dec 1805; b- James Baker

Randolph & Kerenhappuck Sally 10 Dec 1798; b- John Allgood min- William Creath- 26Dec1798

Thomas & Sally Burrus 9 Dec 1805; b- Jesse Westbrook min- Edward Almand- 24Dec1805

William & Sarah Cliborne 5 Aug 1822; b- William Cliborne min- Pleasant Gold- (Baptist)- 10Aug1822

Westmoreland

Robert & Polly Pennington 5 Dec 1804; b- George Tucker

White

Henry & Rebecca Overby 21 Dec 1805; Bond says 'Rebecca Davis' while consent says 'Rebecca Overby' b- Robert Davis con- Edward Delony gives consent for Henry to marry 'Rebecca Overby'

James & Mary Greenwood 28 Feb 1786; b- William Willis con- Thomas Greenwood, gdn of Mary min- John Marshall- (Baptist) 12Mar1786

James & Phoebe Gregory 15 May 1837; b- James H Gregory con- Elijah Gregory, father min- John B. Smith-

John & Nancy Baker 12 Mar 1787; d of Zachariah and Jane Baker b- Thomas Feild

John & Nancy Holloway 12 Dec 1797; b- Edward Holloway min- Edward Almand- 14Dec1797

Larkin & Nelly Dedman 9 Dec 1793; b- Henry Dedman

Robert S & Martha F Oliver 17 Dec 1849; b- James W Oliver con- Alexander G Oliver

Robert & Jane Winn 5 Dec 1807; b- John Dedman min- William Richards- 10Dec1807

Samuel & Nancy Hester 7 Apr 1812; b- William G Pettus con- F G Hester, father

William & Frances Greenwood 21 Jun 1791; b- John Greenwood con- Thomas Greenwood, gdn of Frances min- James Read- (Baptist) 20Jul1791

Whitlow

Champion & Pamelia Hasting 1 Aug 1820; min- William Richards-

James (Sr) & Penelope Hogwood 18 May 1803; b- John Bilbo

Jesse & Prudence Hasting 24 May 1819; b- Thomas J Norment con- Frances Hasting, mother min- William Richards- 25May1819

Phillip & Leatha Bailey 19 Dec 1825; b- Horace Palmer con- Henry Bailey, father

William (Jr) & Mary Saunders 12 Oct 1795; b- Charles Burton min- William Richards- 17Oct1795

Whitt

Littleberry & Rebecca Draper 13 Oct 1826; b- James Jones min- John B. Smith-

Whittemore

James & Jane Hundley 10 Oct 1822; b- John Hundley min- James McAden-

John & Elizabeth Farrar 17 Dec 1816; b- Phillip R Johnson con- George Farrar, father min- Charles Ogburn- (Methodist) 18Dec1816

Wyatt B & Nancy Ryland 12 Nov 1811; b- Harrison M Ryland con- John Ryland, father min- Charles Ogburn- (Methodist) 14Nov1811

Whittle

Conway D & Gilberta M Sinclair 20 Oct 1845; 'Dr' Conway D Whittle b- S D Whittle

Whitworth

Samuel & Mary Hubbard Walden 9 Mar 1778; b- Peter Burton, who test. that Mary is over 21

Whoberry

John M & Margarett B Royal 30 Nov 1826; b- Hugh L Norvell con- Margarett Norvell, mother of Margarett B min- Charles Ogburn- (Methodist) 21Dec1826

Whobry

John & Sarah Bugg 6 Mar 1794; b- John Bugg min- William Creath- 9Mar1794

Wiggins

John W & Catharine R Bennett 11 Aug 1848; b- William M Bennett min- James McAden- 12Aug1848

Wilbourne

Robert & Nancy Malone 9 Oct 1837; b- John Malone

Wilburn

Julius & Lucy Puryear 15 Mar 1798; b- William Powell con- Thomas Puryear, father min- William Creath-

Thomas & Phebe Moore 11 Jul 1806; b- William Jones con- George Moore, father

William & Patty Avery 28 Feb 1782; b- James Harrison

William & Elizabeth Hudson 28 Jan 1793; b- William Hudson min- Edward Almand- 30Jan1793

Wiles

David W & Sally Gold 21 Dec 1837; b- Elijah Gregory con- Erasmus Kennon, gdn of Sally

Hepburn & Ruth Johnson 1 Jan 1812; b- Edward Clark

Leroy B & Elizabeth F Puryear 13 Dec 1838; b- John Puryear con- Peter Puryear, father

Luke & Sarah Moss 27 Dec 1811; b- Banister Gregory

Mastin & Claresy Epperson 13 Sep 1802; b- Joseph Epperson min-Balaam Ezell- 16Oct1802

Wiley

Jones & Martha W Johnson 14 Dec 1818; b- Ezekiel Crowder con- James Johnson, father

Wilkerson

Edmund & Martha Jones 19 Dec 1814; b- Thomas H Mayes con- Susan Jones, father

George W & Elizabeth J Wilkerson 2 Jan 1843; b- William Wilkerson con- Edward Wilkerson, father of Elizabeth con- Charles Wilkerson, father of George

Howell & Mary Wootton 15 Dec 1834; b- John Wootton min- John B. Smith-

James & Susan H Ligon 10 Dec 1838; b- William James con- Francis Ligon, father

James & Joyce Tillotson 6 Oct 1834; b- James Yancey con- William Tillotson, gdn of Joyce min- William Steel- (Episcopal)- 9Oct1834

John H & Avis Jones 17 Sep 1836; b- Alexander Puryear con- Samuel Jones, father

John & Barbara B Chandler 4 Jan 1847; b- Pleasant Gold con- Joel and Hannah Chandler, parents

Mark & Mary Arrington 23 Aug 1822; b- Wiley Daniel min- Pleasant Gold- (Baptist)-

Richard & Martha A Wootton 19 May 1835; b- John Wootton

Spencer C & Tabitha Daniel 19 Sep 1826; b- Stark Daniel min- Pleasant Gold- (Baptist)- 26Sep1826

Washington & Cecily Daniel 1 Aug 1820; b- Stark Daniel

William L & Dosha H Wilkerson 21 Dec 1842; b- Ranson Elliott min-John B. Smith-

William P & Pamela Roberts 29 Oct 1853; con- E F Pettypool, gdn of Pamela min- John E. Montague- (Granville County, N.C.)- 2Nov1853

Wilkes

Benjamin F & Elizabeth C Lacy 24 Jan 1826; b- Shadrach Lacy

Wilkins

Charles & Elizabeth Puryear 22 Jun 1795; Charles from Rutherford County, NC b- John Farrar min- William Creath-

Wilkinson

Alexander & Lucy T Gordon 24 Nov 1852; con- Allen Gordon, father

James M & Cornelia Hayes 18 Dec 1849; b- William J Carter con- Lily Hayes, mother min- Robert Burton- 19Dec1849

Thomas R & Julia Ann Jones 28 Oct 1844; b- Richard Yancey con-James Jones, father

Willard

Benjamin T & Barbara J Towler 24 Dec 1827; b- John A Willard con-John Winckler, gdn of Barbara con- Humphrey Willard, father min-James Smith- 26Dec1827

Williams

Allen & Amelia E Thompson 19 Oct 1830; b- John Puryear con- Samuel Jones, gdn of Amelia min- Pleasant Gold- (Baptist)- 21Oct1830

David & Milly Newton 11 Jun 1804; b- John Williams

Edward & Ann Bing 19 Jun 1820; b- James Bing con- Martha Bing, mother

Edwin A & Lucy P Kennon 24 Feb 1841; b- Richard B Baptist min-F.H. McGuire-

Fielding L & Frances P Boyd 31 Jan 1827; b- B H Bailey con- William Boyd, father min- Allen D. Metcalf- 14Feb1827

George & Rebecca D Poynor 9 Sep 1833; b- Matthew Williams con-Diggs Poynor, gdn of Rebecca (Note: Diggs Poynor from Lawrenceville, Brunswick Co)

James & Mary Furham 8 May 1797; b- Eusebius Stone min- William Richards- 17May1797

Jeremiah & Dolly Carter 27 Nov 1802; b- Joseph N Meredith min-Edward Almand- 1Dec1802

John B & Martha A Moody 7 Sep 1845; b- William Moody min- A.M. Poindexter- 10Sep1845

John R & Mary C Jones 19 Jan 1824; b- Robert Jones

John R & Nancy Meldrum 20 Aug 1849; b- William Wilmoth con- Mary Meldrum, mother min- Thomas Adams- (Lunenburg Co.)- 22Aug1849

John T A & Mary E Farrar 6 Dec 1852; con- John B Roffe, gdn of Mary min- George W. Andrews- 8Dec1852

John & Judith P Clark 16 Aug 1844; b- Alexander J Watson con- Isham Clark, father

John & Martha T Jones 21 Oct 1816; b- Robert Jones min- Thomas Adams- (Lunenburg Co.)-

John & Mary Pettus 30 Nov 1813; b- Joseph Boswell con- Samuel O Pettus, father min- Matthew Dance- (Lunenburg County)- 2Dec1813

John & Elizabeth Taylor 26 Oct 1791; b- Samuel Holmes Jr min- John Loyd- 27Oct1791

John & Mary Ann Tucker 15 Jan 1838; b- John Doyle min- James McAden-

Jonathon & Jane Bing 13 Dec 1823; b- Edward Williams con- Martha Bing, mother min- Charles Ogburn- (Methodist)

Leroy & Amey Mills 24 Dec 1794; b- George Baker con- Susanna Stubbs, mother of Amey min- Charles Ogburn- (Methodist) 27Dec1794

Lewis & Sally Neal 13 Oct 1819; b- Thomas Neal

Matthew & Rebecca M Daves 13 Dec 1841; b- Adam O Daves min-James McAden-

Thomas L & Pamela Burton 2 Dec 1824; b- Edward Royster min-William Steel- (Episcopal)-

Thomas & Sally Alderson 27 Jul 1808; b- Robert Garrott

Thomas & Mary J Williams 22 Dec 1823; b- Matthew Williams con-Lewis Williams, Sr., father min- Stephen Jones- (Lynchburg, Va.)-24Dec1823

William B & Eliza J Lockett 27 Jan 1831; b- Thomas C Dugger con- B Lockett, father min- William Steel- (Episcopal)-

William J & Polly E Bennett 6 Dec 1824; b- Matthew Williams con-William Bennett, father min- James McAden-

William & Judith Baker 8 Jan 1796; b- George Baker min- William Creath- 11Feb1796

Zachariah & Martha Holloway 8 Feb 1830; b- Thomas Farrar con- D H Abernathy, gdn of Martha

Williamson

George & Lucy Ann Wiles 17 Dec 1833; b- Henry H Dedman con- Ruth Wiles, mother min- John B. Smith-

James & Agnes Goode 26 Oct 1837; b- Edward R Chambers con- W O Goode, brother of Agnes min- William Steel- (Episcopal)-

James & Sally Pettypool 19 Nov 1821; b- Eggleston Overby con- J W Pettypool, father con- Robert Williamson, father min- John S. Ravenscroft- (Episcopal)- 30Nov1821

John & Susanna Yancey 3 Sep 1802; b- Richard Murray con- Robert Yancey, father min- Balaam Ezell- 4Sep1802

Merryman & Sally Thomason 29 Jul 1803; b- Archibald Merryman

Robert & Lina Overby 17 Jun 1822; b- Thomas Noblin min- Pleasant Gold- (Baptist)- 20Jun1822

Robert & Mary Yancey 25 Jan 1793; b- William Baskervill min- James Read- (Baptist) 31Jan1793

Samuel & Nancy M Yancey 30 Nov 1852; min- F.N. Whaley-

Thomas & Eliza Overby 17 Jan 1825; b- Eggleston Overby min- Pleasant Gold- (Baptist)- 27Jan1825

William & Martha Y Harwood 3 Oct 1816; b- Melchizedeck Roffe min- William Richards- 9Oct1816

Willis

Edward & Polly Moore 21 Dec 1801; b- James Browder

James A & Nancy Hudson 22 Nov 1825; b- Samuel Dedman con- Samuel Hudson, father min- William Richards- 1Dec1825

James & Lucy Nash 14 Nov 1783; b- John Crews

John & Sally Pulliam 10 Dec 1792; b- Richard Carter min- James Read- (Baptist) 15Dec1792

William L & Rebecca Hudson 23 Dec 1814; b- Ruell Allen con- John Willis, father min- William Richards- 24Dec1814

William S & Sally W Puryear 15 Dec 1823; b- Peter Puryear

William & Lucy Moore 16 Apr 1782; b- James Willis

Wills

Robert & Jane Colley 13 Oct 1788; b- Edward Colley

Wilmoth

John W & Nancy Thomas 31 Jan 1835; b- Allen G Barnes con- William Thomas, father

John & Susan Ann Roberts 16 Nov 1848; b- Paschall H Bowers con- Mary Roberts, mother

Wilson

Archibald & Martha Bevill 26 Oct 1785; b- Hutchins Burton

Caleb & Elizabeth Ballard 5 Jan 1803; Caleb from Orange County, NC b- Francis Ballard

Cephas L & Emily B Brown 19 Aug 1835; b- Charles S Hutcheson min- William B. Rowzee- 1Sep1835

Daniel & Elizabeth Cheatham 28 Aug 1778; b- William Waddill con- Leonard Cheatham, father

Edward A & Susanna Burton 6 Apr 1852; con- Peter Burton, father min- John A. Doll-

Henry & Susanna Hickman 24 Nov 1837; b- William C Wade min- James McAden-

Henry & Caty Waller 25 Jun 1790; b- Daniel Waller

James W & Frances B Waller 15 Jan 1827; b- Samuel H Warren con- Daniel Waller, father min- James McAden-

John (Jr) & Elizabeth Smith 12 Sep 1791; b- Thomas Burnett con- Joseph Townes, gdn of Elizabeth

John & Nancy Goodwin 2 Jan 1793; b- Robert Baskervill

Matthew A & Elizabeth Fox 17 Jan 1825; b- E H Peete con- Mary Fox, mother min- James Smith- 19Jan1825

Miles & Margaret Feild 13 Feb 1809; b- Erasmus Kennon con- Jane Feild, mother min- George Micklejohn-

Robert & Eleanor Dedman 9 Jun 1794; b- Larkin White min- John Williams- 13Jun1794

Robert & Hannah Stone 9 May 1808; d of William and Tabitha Stone b- William Stone min- Richard Dabbs- 18May1808

Roderick & Tabitha Thomas 3 Jun 1814; b- Winn Thomas, father

Thomas & Elizabeth Vaughan 10 Nov 1789; b- Robert Birtchett min- Thomas Scott-

Wiley & Sarah Mayes 20 Nov 1811; b- Charles Hamblin con- Charles Hamblin, gdn of Sarah

William E & Martha A Love 6 Feb 1843; b- Allen C Love con- chappell Love, father

William & Rebecca Brown 9 Sep 1782; b- Thomas Brown

William & Martha Quinchett 24 Jan 1845; b- Thomas Harris min- John B. Smith-

Wiltse

Edward & Mary Eliza Davis 21 Jun 1847; b- James B Dupuy co- Martha S Davis, mother min- William V. Wilson- 23Jun1847

Wimbish

John & Lucy Ann Townes 16 Oct 1839; b- William Townes min- A.M. Poindexter-

Lewis W & Mary J Townes 15 Apr 1842; b- Alfred Boyd con- William Townes, father min- A.M. Poindexter-

Winckler

John H & Lucy G Puryear 27 Jan 1848; b- Peter Puryear min- John Bayley-

John & Judith M Turner 15 Apr 1816; b- Charles L Turner min- James Meacham- 17Apr1816

William W & Martha F Pennington 20 Nov 1848; b- David Oslin min- Thomas Adams- (Lunenburg Co.)- 28Nov1848

Winfield

Arthur Freeman & Susannah Courtney 2 Jun 1786; d of Clack and Prudence Courtney b- Samuel Holmes

Joel & Polly Booth 3 Mar 1801; b- Joshua Winfield min- James Meacham- 4Mar1801

Winfree

Isaac & Martha Ann Jones 23 Jun 1826; b- Edward B Lipscomb

John James & Mary A Oliver 21 Jan 1850; b- Burwell B Barron min- Thomas Crowder-

Richard E & Mary R Moss 28 Dec 1851; con- Thomas R Moss, father min- P.F. August- 6Jan1852

Wingfield

Benjamin & Ann Maria Curtis 13 Sep 1840; b- Solomon Lea min- Edward Wadsworth-

George & Roberts B Kennon 3 Sep 1849; b- John S Feild, Jr con- E A Williams, gdn of Roberts

Henderson & Susan Evans 20 May 1833; b- Thomas Evans min- William Steel- (Episcopal)- 21May1833

Winn

Banister & Nancy Naish 11 Dec 1809; b- Benjamin Blake min- William Richards- 12Dec1809

Harrison & Frances Haile 11 Jul 1785; b- Thomas Haile

Littleberry & Mary Maynard 29 Dec 1783; b- William Maynard

Richard & Sarah Hall 14 Aug 1775; b- James Hall

Thomas & Catherine Haile 1 Apr 1822; b- William W Dedman min- William Richards- 9Apr1822

William & Ann H Greenwood 18 Nov 1816; b- Joseph B Clausel min- William Richards- 21Nov1816

William & Eleanor Robards 18 Dec 1848; b- Howard Mallett co - E A Williams, gdn of Eleanor

Winstead

Bushrod & Susan Cox 10 Apr 1811; b- Eli Cox con- John Cox, father min- William Richards- 11Apr1811

Wood

James N & Cecily Garner 15 Dec 1845; b- Richard H Wood min- John B. Smith-

Richard T & Elizabeth Dedman 21 Feb 1853; con- Amanda A Dedman, mother (Note: Richard gdn of Elizabeth Dedman) min- James S. Kennedy-

Samuel B & Mary C Tarry 18 Aug 1824; b- Thomas Ryland con- Samuel Tarry, father min- James Smith-

Woodruff

George & Eliza Chambliss 3 Jun 1835; b- Richard P Montgomery con- G D Chambliss, father, who test she is under 21

Jesse & Susan Ladd 15 Jan 1812; b- Thomas Ladd con- Thomas Ladd, father

Woodson

Miller (Jr) & Sophia W Hendrick 8 Aug 1803; b- Amasa Palmer

Tacharner & Lucy Michaux 8 Sep 1788; b- William Hendrick con- Joseph Michaux, gdn

Woody

James & Virginia K Pully 21 Apr 1851; con- Mary B Pully, mother min- Hartwell Arnold-

Ruffin & Elizabeth B Pully 16 Jun 1853; con- Mary B Pully, mother min- John E. Montague- (Granville County, N.C.)-

Wootton

David C & Fanny Brame 20 Feb 1815; b- Richins Brame, father

James T & Martha Brame 15 Oct 1838; min- Benjamin R. Duval-

John W & Eliza A Carter 25 Jun 1845; b- John T Carter con- David N Carter, father min- Jacob Manning-

John & Mary Christopher 18 Mar 1785; d of David Christopher, dec. b- William Daniel

John & Elizabeth Overton 21 Nov 1814; b- Thomas Overton

John & Elizabeth Simmons 4 Dec 1841; b- James Crawford Hughes min- James McAden-

Joseph L & Sally A Daws 27 Dec 1843; b- Howell Wilkerson con- John Wootton, father

Powell & Susanna Overton 28 Oct 1820; b- Thomas Overton min- William Richards- 6Nov1820

Richard & Mary Overton 18 Dec 1820; b- Samuel Wootton con- Thomas Overton, father min- William Richards- 21Dec1820

Samuel & Martha Hyde 10 Nov 1788; d of John Hyde Sr b- John Hyde min- Thomas Scott- 27Nov1788

Worsham

James & Martha A Owen 5 Dec 1842; b- Henry H Newton min- John B. Smith-

John & Nancy Apperson 24 Dec 1833; b- John Blanks min- William Steel- (Episcopal)- 25Dec1833

John & Lucy Hamblin 12 Nov 1804; b- Stephen Pettypool

Stephen & Nancy Blanks 14 Sep 1807; b- Daniel Jones

Stephen & Mary Green - Mar 1843; b- John Vaughan

Wortham

James & Jincy McQuie 11 Nov 1799; b- Thomas A Jones

James & Frances E Vaughan 14 May 1850; b- Henry Newton

John & Martha Vaughan 30 Aug 1821; b- William E Wortham con- Wyatt and Maggie Vaughan, parents min- Pleasant Gold- (Baptist)- 12Sep1821

Thomas P & Eliza H Davis 17 Dec 1823; b- Horace Palmer con- William Hendrick, gdn of Eliza

Thomas & Jane Griffin 17 Jul 1826; b- Elijah Griffin min- Pleasant Gold- (Baptist)- 25Jul1826

William E & Mary Ann Wilkerson 24 Dec 1833; b- Cole Vaughan con- Amy Wilkerson, mother min- William Steel- (Episcopal)-

Wright

Abner P & Julia C Wright 16 May 1836; b- Horace Palmer con- John M Wright, gdn of Julia

Anderson & Elizabeth Langford 6 Dec 1794; b- James Watson min- John Loyd- 30May1794

Anderson & Phebe Malone Watson 27 May 1793; b- William Poole Jr min- John Loyd- 30May1793

Austin (Jr) & Mary Nicholson 28 Jun 1811; b- Tavner Toone

Austin (Sr) & Lucy Holloway 1 Mar 1806; b- Francis Ballard

Bolling & Milly Saunders 30 Jul 1787; b- John Feagins con- John Saunders, father

Claiborne & Patsy Nanney 27 Dec 1792; b- Hughberry Nanney min- John Loyd- 29Dec1792

David & Nancy Wright 28 Dec 1797; David from Lunenburg County b- Roderick Wright

George & Elizabeth Hester 16 Jun 1823; b- Robert Hester

George & Nancy Wiles 12 Sep 1812; b- Mastin Wiles

Henry & Leatha W Whitlow 12 Feb 1831; widow of Phillip Whitlow b- Lewis G Meacham min- Stephen Turner- 17Feb1831

James A & Ireanna Garner 27 Oct 1851; con- Lewis Garner, father

James & Sarah Easter 23 Dec 1784; b- Leonard Smith

James & Elizabeth Newton 15 Dec 1840; b- James Newton min- John B. Smith-

Job & Polly Thompson 15 Jul 1811; b- Samuel Thompson min- David McCargo- (Charlotte County, Va.) 16Jul1811

John E & Mary G Wright 14 Dec 1836; b- Thomas Johnson min- Stephen Turner-

John M & Jane Davis 10 Mar 1838; b- James T Russell con- John Davis, father min- William B. Rowzee-

John R & Susan A Richardson 12 Nov 1838; b- William Walden

John & Peggy Boswell 14 Feb 1822; b- John T Sizemore min- Pleasant Gold- (Baptist)-

John & Sarah Fox 3 Oct 1797; b- William Taylor con- Richard Fox, father

John & Sally Holmes 13 May 1801; b- John Holmes min- Ebenezer McGowan- 21May1801

John & Nancy Matthews 9 May 1820; b- George Jackson min- Pleasant Gold- (Baptist)- 10May1820

John & Rebecca Oslin 19 Jun 1802; b- Isaac Oslin

Lewis G & Ann J Roberts 24 Nov 1828; b- Isaac Watson

Newton & Sally Farmer 30 Nov 1819; b- John B Yancey con- James Farmer, father min- Pleasant Gold- (Baptist)-

Reuben & Unity C Davis 18 Apr 1814; b- Green Blanton

Reuben & Catharine Wingfield 20 Feb 1812; b- William Bilbo

Robert & Nancy Wright 16 Nov 1792; b- Austin Wright Robert from Brunswick County

Roderick & Martha Cleaton 19 Sep 1795; b- Thomas Cleaton Jr min- John Loyd- 24Sep1795

Silas D & Susan Palmer 20 Feb 1843; b- John E P Wright min- James D. Conkling-

Sterling & Silviah Davis 4 Jul 1788; b- Josiah Floyd

Thomas & Judith Patrick 9 Jan 1821; b- Hughberry Nanney con- E D
Middagh, gdn of Judith

William N & Rebecca W Roberts 19 Jul 1824; b- William Davis con-
Tabitha Nanney, mother of Rebecca

William & Nancy Palmer 12 Dec 1804; b- Thomas Wright

Wyatt

Walter & Elizabeth Brame 16 Dec 1792; b- James Brame

William & Martha Smith 14 Dec 1848; b- Joseph Evans Martha test.
she is 21

Yancey

Alex & Mary Elam 22 Oct 1839; b- Daniel Elam min- John B. Smith-

Charles H & Anne Wade 27 Feb 1841; b- Marshall P Yancey con-
Lanstat G Wade, father min- Solomon Apple-

Charles & Polly Jones 19 Oct 1812; b- Gordon Stone

Charles & Parmelia Yancey 25 Feb 1828; b- Richard Yancey min-
Pleasant Gold- (Baptist)- 26Feb1828

Daniel & Elizabeth Jane Newton 16 Oct 1843; b- William P Newton
con- James H Newton, father

Hezekiah & Sally Worsham 10 Oct 1808; b- John Williamson

James M & Temperance Yancey 13 Oct 1837; b- James Yancey min-
John B. Smith- 18Oct1837

James & Eliza Cunningham 22 Apr 1815; b- Abraham G Keen

James & Penelope Griffin 4 Mar 1828; b- Francis Griffin min- Pleasant
Gold- (Baptist)- 6Mar1828

James & Ann Tillotson 19 Nov 1825; b- Edward Tillotson min- Pleasant
Gold- (Baptist)- 23Nov1825

Jechonias & Rebecca L Royster 15 Dec 1788; b- George Royster

John B & Polly Williamson 16 Aug 1813; b- Hepburn Wiles con- Robert
Williamson, father

John R & Virginia J White 14 Sep 1851; con- Jane A White, mother
min- Alfred Apple-

John & Mary Hamblin 14 Oct 1799; b- Daniel Jones con- Thomas
Hamblin, father min- William Creath-

Joseph & Martha Dunnavant 18 Oct 1839; b- Richard Glasscock min-
John B. Smith-

Joseph & Susanna Wilkins 21 Dec 1823; b- William Wilkins min- Pleasant
Gold- (Baptist)-

Lewis N & Letha Worsham 4 Jan 1827; b- John Worsham

Lewis T & Sally Tillotson 14 Jun 1837; b- John Tillotson

Minge & Frances Knott 9 May 1888; b- Samuel C Brame

Reazin P & Susan Elam 12 Oct 1840; b- Daniel Elam

Richard E & Elizabeth Jane Overby 18 Sep 1848; b- John J Newton
con- Anderson Overby, father min- Alfred Apple- 20Sep1848

Richard H & Mary E Jones 15 Sep 1845; b- Burwell B Barron

Richard H & Nancy LeNeve 21 Dec 1835; b- William Malone con- John
LeNeve, father min- John B. Smith-

Richard & Harriett Pendleton Yancey 27 Feb 1832; b- John F Yancey
con- Robert Yancey, Sr, father of Harriett

Robert & Agnes Wilkerson 11 Oct 1796; b- Francis Griffin

Robert & Parthena Yancey 15 Aug 1833; b- James M Yancey con-
Hezekiah Yancey, father of Parthena min- John B. Smith-

Stith G & Malvina D Lydick 8 Nov 1834; b- J A Gregory

Thomas & Martha Daniel 26 Oct 1825; b- James Williamson con- Stark
Daniel, father min- Pleasant Gold- (Baptist)- 2Nov1825

William H & Elizabeth Perkins 13 Dec 1835; b- Charles H Yancey con-
David Perkins, father

William L & Nancy Jones 22 Dec 1824; b- Peyton R Talley con- Daniel
  Jones, father   con- Zachariah Yancey, father   min- Pleasant Gold-
  (Baptist)-

Yates

Edward Randolph & Elizabeth Murray 20 Sep 1783; d of John Murray
  b- Asa Oliver con- William Yates, gdn of Edward

Young

Allen & Sarah Davis 22 May 1779; d of William Davis b- Samuel Young
Coleman & Mary Standley 18 Dec 1788; b- James Standley
Henry & Margaret R Harrison 11 Nov 1822; b- Howell L Read
John & Dianitia M Pennington 28 Nov 1825; b- Wesley W Young con-
  Ann Davis, mother of Dianitis   min- Charles Ogburn- (Methodist)
  29Nov1825
John & Jane Swepson 24 Jan 1784; b- Enos Easter
Samuel & Judith M T Palmer 6 Jan 1823; b- Richard Coleman con-
  Christopher Haskins, gdn of Judith min- James Smith- 9Jan1823
William H & Elizabeth Perkins 13 Dec 1835; min- William Steel-
  (Episcopal)-

—— & John Ryland 11 Jan 1786; b- Thomas Adams (bride's name not written on bond)

Johannah & John (Jr) Puryear 20 Jun 178-; b- Samuel Puryear bond torn

Abernathy

Lucy & William Daly 10 Mar 1807; min- Charles Ogburn- (Methodist) 12Mar1807 b- Tignal Abernathy Jr con- Burwell Abernathy, father

Martha & Jonathon Phillips 20 Dec 1809; b- Liles Abernathy

Mary Ann & Henry Powers 19 Dec 1831; b- John P Smith min- Charles Ogburn- (Methodist) 22Dec1831

Adams

Lizzy & Kirby Cook 2 Jan 1788; b- Thomas Adams daughter of Thomas and Lucy Adams

Lucy Ann & Joseph P Allen 18 Dec 1832; b- Richard Adams

Lucy & Thomas Allen 13 Dec 1796; b- John Freeman min- William Richards- 22Dec1796

Lucy & John Frasar 4 Jan 1780; b- William Crutchfield John Frasar from Prince Edward County Lucy daughter of Thomas and Lucy Adams

Mary & Wyatt Short 11 Dec 1809; b- Richard M Allen min- James Meacham- 28Dec1809

Rebecca & Vines Daley 14 Oct 1795; b- William Adams min- John Loyd- 15Oct1795

Aigner

Sophia & Solomon Leigh 12 Aug 1837; b- John O Wingfield

Akin

Delia Ann & Thomas Thomason 6 Sep 1836; b- Edward Allgood con- Nancy Akin, mother min- William Steel- (Episcopal)-

Eliza & Edward Allgood 24 Nov 1828; b- Thomas Atkins con- Nancy Akin, mother min- John B. Smith- 27Nov1828

Alderson

Sally & Thomas Williams 27 Jul 1808; b- Robert Garrott

Alexander

Ella M & Henry E Coleman 11 May 1852; con- Nathaniel Alexander, father min- F.H. McGuire-

Lucy Jane & Lawson Henderson Alexander 2 Oct 1823; b- Nathaniel Alexander con- Mark Alexander min- James Smith

Mary B & William O Gregory 6 Oct 1826; b- W O Goode con- Nathaniel Alexander, gdn of Mary min- John B. Smith- 12Oct1826

Nancy & Francis R Gregory 15 May 1832; 'Dr' Francis R Gregory b- John Young min- James McAden-

Nartha & John Pettway 11 Aug 1792; b- John Alexander

Sarah C & Robert A Hamilton 10 Dec 1844; b- George Tarry con- Nathaniel Alexander, father

Allen

Anne & John Bailey 2 Mar 1791; b- Elisha Arnold min- Henry Ogburn- 5Mar1791

Elizabeth & Edward Holmes 17 Jun 1797; b- James Jones min- Charles Ogburn- (Methodist) 20Jun1797

Elizabeth & Abraham Spain 6 May 1795; b- Henderson Wade min- William Richards- 7May1795

Jane & James Adams 8 Jan 1835; b- Benjamin Bugg con- Lucy Allen, mother

Judith & Daniel Spain 18 Nov 1802; b- Abraham Spain min- William Richards- 19Nov1802

Leanna & John Roberts 21 May 1799; b- William Allen

Margaret & James Martin 12 Mar 1800; b- John Puryear Jr min- William Creath-

Martha & Matthew Gayle 7 Jan 1822; b- Richard Allen min- Alexander M. Cowan-

Mary & Benjamin Bugg 12 Mar 1834; b- Henry Moody con- Lucy S Allen, mother

Nancy & James Shearer 13 Nov 1797; b- John Cox min- William Richards- 30Nov1797

Polly & John Freeman 13 Dec 1796; b- Thomas Allen min- William Richards- 22Dec1796

Polly & John Freeman 13 Dec 1796; b- Thomas Allen

Rebecca & Thomas Averett 13 Jul 1807; b- Joel Averett min- William Richards- 23Jul1807

Sally & Richard Adams 28 Oct 1808; b- Fielding Noel min- John Meacham- 17Nov1808

Sally & Robert Mitchell 27 Jan 1818; b- Thomas Warren con- Thomas T Allen, father min- James Meacham- 5Feb1818

Virginia Anne & Leroy P Allen 8 Feb 1845; b- John T Wootton con- Martha C Allen, mother

Allgood

Betsy H & Thomas Mallett - Feb 1804; b- George Allgood min- William Creath-

Dicy & Hall Hudson 9 Nov 1801; b- John Hudson

Elizabeth & William Blacketter 24 Dec 1793; b- Bartlett Cox

Elizabeth & Matthew Claunch 29 Aug 1799; b- Samuel Allgood

Elizabeth & Matthew Clemmonds 3 Mar 1789; b- John Allgood

Judith & Ivey Harris - Dec 1809; b- John Allgood

Lucy & Bartley Cox 18 Sep 1786; b- Allen Burton min- John Marshall- (Baptist) 20Sep1786

Martha Ann & John Parker 7 Jan 1840; b- Richard H Allgood con- George Allgood, father

Martha & Willis Brooks 13 Jul 1831; b- Edward Allgood con- Dicey Allgood, mother min- William Steel- (Episcopal)- 14Jul1831

Mary Ellen & Richard Harris Graves 26 Dec 1853; Richard 23, son of Thomas and Mary Graves Mary Ellen 22, daughter of George and Dicey Allgood min- A.F. Davidson-

Nancy & John Keeton 5 May 1792; son of Joseph Keeton b- William Westbrook con- Moses Allgood, father

Sarah & William (Sr) Hunt 28 Jul 1788; bride gives own consent and test. that she is 30 years old b- William Johnson

Almand

Ann B & Charles P Colley 18 Jan 1841; b- Sterling T Smithson con- Rebecca W Almand, mother min- John B. Smith-

Alvis

Betsy & William Claunch 5 Aug 1793; b- William Blacketter con- Jeremiah Claunch, father con- David Alvis, father

Ambrose

Mary & William Ladd Taylor 2 Dec 1785; b- William Drumwright min- John King-

Anderson

Ann & Samuel Venable 5 Mar 1782; d of Thomas and Sarah Anderson Samuel from Prince Edward County b- Thomas Anderson, father?

Henryetta Maria & James Feild 17 Feb 1789; daughter of Thomas Anderson Sr b- Thomas Anderson Jr

Lucy & Philemon Holcomb 13 Dec 1784; daughter of Thomas & Sarah Anderson Philemon from Prince Edward County b- Charles Lewis

Mary & Charles Lewis 8 Nov 1779; b- Howell Taylor con- Thomas Anderson Sr, father

Sarah & Tignal (Sr) Jones 16 Nov 1767; daughter of Thomas Anderson b- Tignal Jones Jr

Susannah & James Lewis 25 Jun 1774; b- Thomas Anderson daughter of Thomas Anderson Sr

Andrews

Anne & Isaac Arnold 16 May 1795; b- George Hightower Walker con- George Andrews con- John Arnold min- Charles Ogburn- (Methodist)- 21May1795

Anne & Benjamin Bugg 3 Sep 1785; b- Ephraim Andrews, Jr. con- Ephraim Andrews, Sr., father

Betsey & Jeremiah Gee 19 Nov 1804; Elizabeth 'Betsey' daughter of Varney Andrews Sr b- Varney Andrews

Dorothy L & Meredith Hailey 8 Mar 1820; b- William Hodges con- Varney Andrews, father

Elizabeth & Nevil Gee 19 Jul 1797; b- Varney Andrews con- Nevil Gee Sr, father con- George Andrews, father min- Charles Ogburn- (Methodist) 20Jul1797

Martha W & Phillip Burnett 10 Jul 1799; b- Isaac Arnold con- George Andrews, father min- Charles Ogburn- (Methodist)

Martha W & Phillip Burnett 10 Jul 1799; b- Isaac Arnold con- George Andrews, father

Martha & Jesse Bugg 27 Jan 1811; b- Varney Andrews

Nancy & Richard Tanner 15 Oct 1808; d of Varney Andrews Sr b- Varney Andrews

Polly & Robert Stainback 13 Dec 1804; Robert from Brunswick County b- Isaac Arnold

Rebecca A C & James F Smith 9 Jun 1834; b- Allen T Andrews con- Wilson Harriss, gdn of Rebecca

Virginia & Robert H Bugg 11 Dec 1851; min- William V. Wilson-

Apperson

Harriett & William Neal 10 Dec 1827; b- Alexander Blankenship min- Pleasant Gold- (Baptist)-

Lucy & Clark Royster 11 Oct 1802; b- Archibald Clarke min- Balaam Ezell- 12Oct1802

Martha E & William H Tunstall 6 Jan 1840; b- William Townes min- F.H. McGuire- 7Jan1840

Martha & Alexander Blankenship 15 Jan 1821; b- George Williams con- W S Apperson, father min- Pleasant Gold- (Baptist)- 25Jan1821

Martha & Richardson Feagins 3 Feb 1779; b- Thomas Pinson con- David Apperson, father

Nancy & John Worsham 24 Dec 1833; b- John Blanks min- William Steel- (Episcopal)- 25Dec1833

Polly & John Gregory 19 Dec 1786; b- John Apperson con- David Apperson, father min- Henry Lester- (Baptist) 23Dec1786

Rebecca T & Ewell Leneve 19 Feb 1833; b- Samuel Watkins con- Mary Apperson, mother min- John B. Smith-

Arnold

Amy & George Finch 22 Sep 1803; b- Jeremiah Arnold

Ann E & Charles R Edmonson 9 Dec 1839; b- Hartwell Arnold min- Benjamin R. Duval-

Betty & Francis Cooper 25 Apr 1769; b- James Arnold Francis from Amelia County Betty daughter of James Arnold Sr and Martha Arnold

Catharine V & John Ellington 20 Feb 1842; b- Hartwell Arnold

Elvira A & Richard H Harwell 19 Dec 1831; b- William T Ezell min-
James McAden-

Jane & William Kirks 26 Jan 1790; b- James McCann con- Samuel Kirks,
father

Lucy & Robert Ross 14 Nov 1792; b- Elisha Arnold min- John Neblett-
22Nov1792

Maria E & John A Walker 7 Nov 1852; con- John J Arnold, father min-
George W. Andrews-

Martha L & Binns Vaughan 20 Jun 1798; b- Thomas Edmundson min-
Charles Ogburn- (Methodist) 21Jun1798

Mary A & Lucas Oslin 10 Dec 1826; b- Thomas C Batte min- James
McAden- 12Dec1826

Mary W & David W Thomas 9 Sep 1844; b- Charles R Edmundson
min- James McAden-

Milly & Thomas Edmondson 8 Aug 1796; b- Jeremiah Arnold Milly
daughter of James Arnold and Mary Arnold min- Charles Ogburn-
(Methodist) 11Aug1796

Nancy G & William A Andrews 7 Sep 1827; b- Joseph A Arnold min-
James McAden-

Patty & George Lucas 21 Mar 1770; b- James Arnold daughter of James
Arnold Sr and Martha Arnold

Polly & James Briggs 10 Feb 1794; b- John Arnold d of James Arnold
and Mary Arnold min- Charles Ogburn- (Methodist)- 27Feb1794

Sarenah S & John A Smith 21 Dec 1849; b- William Stone con- John
J Arnold, father

Susan Ann & Harry Tompkins 28 Apr 1828; b- James M Whittle con-
Joseph A Arnold, father min- James McAden-

Arrington

Mary & Mark Wilkerson 23 Aug 1822; b- Wiley Daniel min- Pleasant
Gold- (Baptist)-

Atkins

Jilley & Jeremiah Russell 26 Aug 1795; Jeremiah from Brunswick County
b- James Atkins min- John Loyd- 27Aug1795

Atkinson

Ann J & Ambrose Brewer 20 Aug 1840; b- Solomon Atkinson min-
Charles F. Burnley-

Ann & Drury Duprey 8 Mar 1784; b- John Crews con- Median Atkinson,
mother and widow of Lewis Duprey, dec.

Maria A & William J Carter 24 Dec 1850; con- Solomon Atkinson, father
min- William A. Smith- 24Dec1850

Martha & Elijah J Ryan 19 Sep 1840; b- Asa Garner min- Charles F.
Burnley-

Mary H & Thomas Murray 16 Aug 1841; b- Creed T Haskins con-
Solomon and Elizabeth Atkinson, parents min- Charles F. Burnley-

Median & Lewis Duprey 11 Oct 1784; b- Drury Duprey min- Henry
Lester- (Baptist)

Ruth H & John Wyatt Brewer 25 Dec 1838; b- Solomon Atkinson con-
J Edward Brewer, father of John con- Solomon Atkinson, father min-
John B. Smith-

Avary

Elizabeth Maryann & Anderson Smith 9 Jun 1783; b- John Avary. father

Averett

Eliza T & John J Newton 16 Oct 1848; b- Richard H Averett con-
Rebecca Averett, mother

Harriet Ann & John Clark 9 Oct 1851; con- Bowen Averett, father min-
John E Montague

Louisa & Abraham Lewis 11 Feb 1805; b- C Granderson Feiuld min-
William Richards- 21Feb1805

Martha & Joseph Gold 3 Jun 1816; b- Charles M Royster

Martha & Henry Minor 10 Dec 1839; b- George W Averett min- John
B. Smith-

Panthea F & James H Royster 12 Jul 1845; b- G W R Averett con-
Bryan Averett, father

Sarah & Allen Duffee 2 Feb 1829; b- Henry E Weatherford con- Thomas
Averett, father min- John B. Smith- 15Feb1829

Avery

Lockey & William Glasgow 1 Feb 1800; b- Richard Glasgow

Lockey & William Glasgow 1 Feb 1800; b- Richard Glasgow

Lucinda M & John H Cox 5 Apr 1841; b- George W R Avery con-
Bowen Avery, father

Mary & Wingfield Averett 15 Nov 1813; b- Matthew Averett con-
Langston Avery

Mary & Wingfield Avery 1 Dec 1813; min- William Richards-

Missouri & Henry W Avery 21 Nov 1835; con- John Nelson, gdn of
Missouri min- John B. Smith-

Patty & William Wilburn 28 Feb 1782; b- James Harrison

Sarah & James McCarter 21 Mar 1814; b- James J Avery con- Nancy
Avery, mother min- William Richards- 31Mar1814

Avory

Elizabeth & Leman Haile 19 Jun 1802; 'Avery?' b- Elijah Avory min-
William Creath-

Frances & Frederick Isham 10 Nov 1794; b- Harwood Rudd min- William
Creath- 22Nov1794

Bacon

Nancy A M & John J R Spencer 27 Jul 1846; b- Joseph G Sneed con-
Lydall Bacon, father, who test Nancy will be 27 on 29Oct1846 min- E.
Chambers-

Bailey

Amanda N & William N Smith 19 May 1835; b- Allen T Andrews min-
James McAden-

Dolly & William Ferrell 9 Apr 1795; b- James Ferrell William from
Halifax County

Dolly & William Ferrell 9 Apr 1795; b- James Ferrell William from
Halifax County min- William Creath-

Eliza T & Richard C (Sr) Gregory 12 Dec 1830; b- Joseph S Gregory
min- James Smith-

Elizabeth & John Oliver 8 Dec 1794; b- William Durham min- Charles
Ogburn- (Methodist) 24Dec1794

Jane B & William B Price 20 Jan 1820; b- Richard C Bibb con- P Bailey,
father min- Richard Dabbs- (Lunenburg County)-

Jane & William Durham Watkins 9 Dec 1793; b- Henry Bailey min-
William Creath- 25Dec1793

Leatha & Phillip Whitlow 19 Dec 1825; b- Horace Palmer con- Henry
Bailey, father

Martha & Warner Martin 6 Oct 1783; b- Benjamin Ferrell con- William
Bailey, father

Minerva J & Gee Drumwright 30 Aug 1836; b- Richard A L Bailey con-
Richard A L Bailey, father min- James M. Jeter- (Lunenburg County)-

Nancy & George Crowder 26 Jan 1798; b- Richard Crowder min- William
Creath-

Polly & William (Jr) Cleaton 18 Mar 1835; b- Richard H L Bailey min-
James McAden-

Prissey & Baxter Hamilton 10 Jan 1798; b- Robert Roberts min- William Creath-

Sarah & Melchizedeck Brame 1 Feb 1797; b- William Rowlett min- Samuel D. Brame- 2Feb1797

Baird

Betsy & Lewis Parham 22 May 1769; b- John Tabb

Eliza P & Thomas H Rainey 17 Oct 1836; b- Charles W Baird min- James McAden-

Frances & Daniel Lynch 21 Dec 1829; b- Charles W Baird min- James Smith-

Mary A C & William Holloway 5 Feb 1836; b- Archer W Hanserd con- Charles W Baird, father

Baisey

Catharine & Jugurtha Walker 18 Sep 1834; b- John Baisey min- William B. Rowzee-

Diana W & Ranson Stroud 20 Dec 1826; b- Edward Giles

Baker

Ann & Thomas Nethery 27 Jan 1789; b- George Baker min- Thomas Scott-

Ann & David Shelton 9 Nov 1820; b- John Bullock min- William Richards- 16Nov1820

Jane & James Day 3 Apr 1822; min- Charles Ogburn- (Methodist)

Jincy & Charles Mills 9 Dec 1799; b- George Baker min- Matthew Dance- 19Dec1799

Judith & William Williams 8 Jan 1796; b- George Baker min- William Creath- 11Feb1796

Martha & Richard Neathery 8 Oct 1830; b- WilliamBaker min- John B. Smith-

Maryanna & Gray Holloway 24 Jan 1801; b- William Holloway

Nancy & John White 12 Mar 1787; d of Zachariah and Jane Baker b- Thomas Feild

Sarah & Peter Bailey 27 Aug 1792; b- Thomas Jeffries Sarah daughter of Zachariah Baker and Jane Baker

Ballard

Elizabeth & Caleb Wilson 5 Jan 1803; Caleb from Orange County, NC b- Francis Ballard

Martha Elizabeth & John Overton 10 Nov 1806; b- Francis Ballard min- Charles Ogburn- (Methodist) 12Nov1806

Mary Garland & William Lanier 4 Sep 1794; b- James Bullock con- John Ballard, father

Mary & Phillip Gill 20 Jan 1817; b- James Jones min- Charles Ogburn- (Methodist) 4Feb1817

Rebecca & John (Jr) Davis 10 Dec 1804; b- John Holmes Jr

Baptist

Elizabeth L & Thomas Marshall 1 Mar 1802; b- John G Baptist con- William Glanvil Baptist, father min- William Creath-

Fanny R & Thomas Hill 31 Oct 1811; b- Edward Baptist con- John G Baptist, gdn of Fanny min- William Richards- 7Nov1811

Martha E & James A Smith 15 Sep 1839; b- William Baptist con- William Baptist, father min- John B. Smith-

Martha W & James Brame 18 Jan 1847; b- David G Smith con- Richard H Baptist, father

Mary & Joseph N Meredith 12 May 1800; b- G H Baskervill min- William Creath-

Matilda & William B Coleman 2 Jun 1803; b- Joseph N Meredith con-
William Glanville Baptist, father William B from Spotsylvania County
min- William Richards-

Barlow

Ann E & James S N Keeton 18 Mar 1847; b- Robert P Keeton con-
Eliza H Barlow, mother con- Warner C Keeton, father min- James
McAden- 19Mar1847

Caroline B & Charles M Patillo 17 Dec 1850; con- Eliza Barlow, mother
min- S.A. Creath-

Barnard

Sally & Spencer Guy 26 Nov 1815; b- Thomas Barnard con- Thomas
Barnard, father

Barner

Mary J & Warner C Keeton 19 Jul 1847; b- John R Barner con- John
F Barner, father min- James McAden-

Sarah A & Peter W Coleman 18 Aug 1845; b- John F Barner min-
James McAden-

Barnes

Ann E & Robert E Jones 4 Oct 1848; b- Bennett B Goode con- Jane
Barnes, mother

Ann F & Peter Puryear 7 Nov 1840; b- William E Roffe con- Henry
Barnes, father min- Edward Wadsworth- 12Nov1840

Elizabeth R & Benjamin G Watson 4 Nov 1845; b- Dabney Farrar

Elmira A & William H Eubank 15 Jan 1844; b- Charles H Robertson
con- Joania Barnes, mother

Emily J & John (Jr) Spencer 8 Dec 1842; b- John G Barnes

Mary E J & David Oslin 16 Nov 1852; min- James McAden-

Rebecca F & John W Daniel 21 Dec 1852; con- Henry Barnes, father

Barnett

Becky & Matthew Evans 5 Oct 1804; b- John Barnett

Lucy & Lowry Bowen 19 Nov 1818; b- Salathiel Bowen con- William
Barnett, father

Martha C & Absolom Taylor 29 Dec 1809; b- John Hudgins

Mary Araminta & William T Smelley 20 Dec 1847; b- James L Thomason
min- James McAden- 25Dec1847

Pamela Ann & Josiah Beckwith 18 Dec 1843; b- Joseph Connell con- P
Barnett, father

Barry

Margaret & Claiborne Hawkins 2 May 1789; b- Frederick Andrews min-
Thomas Scott-

Peggy & Thomas Massey 24 Apr 1799; b- James Johnson

Basey

Elizabeth & Christopher Thomas 19 Dec 1829; b- Wynn Thomas

Baskervill

Ann & John Farrar 24 Dec 1794; b- Robert Baskervill

Elizabeth & Robert H Jones 9 Apr 1807; b- Robert Park min- Charles
Ogburn- (Methodist)

Martha & Frederick Lucas 27 Oct 1779; b- William Baskervill daughter
of George Baskervill

Mary A & Samuel A Douglas 21 Mar 1814; b- Joel Watkins con-
Elizabeth Baskervill, mother

Mary Ann & Richard W Watkins 12 May 1837; b- John Coleman min-
William Steel- (Episcopal)-

Mary Eston & Patrick Hamilton 24 Dec 1812; b- Joel Watkins min-
Charles Ogburn- (Methodist)

Mary & William S Overton 10 Dec 1799; b- E Baskervill min- William Creath-

Nancy & Thomas Turner 16 Jan 1817; b- George D Baskervill min- Charles Ogburn- (Methodist) 21Jan1817

Susanna & Richardson Farrar 12 Jun 1810; b- Newman Dortch

Bass

Rebecca & Richard King 26 Dec 1831; b- John M Perkinson

Sylvia & William Baird 29 Nov 1802; b- Independence Poarch min- John Meacham- 1Dec1802

Baugh

Agnes & John Aldridge 20 Jan 1800; b- E Macgowan min- Ebenezer McGowan- 22Jan1800 widow of James Baugh

Elizabeth & John Simmons 23 Sep 1790; b- James Baugh, father Elizabeth daughter of James and Agnes Baugh min- John Easter- 30Sep1790

Frances & Ebenezer MacGowan 29 Jul 1797; daughter of James and Agnes Baugh b- James Baugh

Martha & Robert Harrison 19 Jan 1787; b- William Baugh Martha daughter of James and Agnes Baugh

Sarah & John Hutcheson 23 Dec 1793; daughter of James Baugh b- James Baugh min- John Loyd- 2Jan1794

Tabitha & Stephen Hightower 16 Jul 1808; b- Richard Baugh daughter of James and Agnes Baugh

Beasley

Gincy & Cargill Thomason 30 Mar 1825; b- William Insco con- Martha N Vaughan, mother con- Theoderick Vaughan, step-father of Gincy min- Charles Ogburn- (Methodist) 7Apr1825

Martha & Theoderick Vaughan 16 Jan 1813; widow b- Harrison W Ryland con- William Insco, Sr, father of Martha min- Milton Robertson- (Warren County, N.C.)

Nancy & Dennis Claunch 8 Nov 1803; b- William Justice

Beckley

Mary Ann & Nathaniel Gregory - Jan 1787; b- Edward L Tabb

Beddingfield

Susanna & John Stegall 12 Dec 1786; b- William Finch

Belcher

Caroline & William H Moore 23 Apr 1832; b- Burwell B Belcher

Benford

Emily & Gee Drumwright 13 Dec 1828; b- Jones Drumwright con- Thomas Benford, father

Judith & Phillip Roberts 17 Jun 1818; b- Dennis Roberts

Polly & Williamson Quarles 14 Jan 1806; b- Thomas Benford

Sally & Thomas Taylor 28 Sep 1792; b- William Drumwright min- John Loyd- 14Oct1792

Sarah & Amos Roberts 6 Feb 1835; b- John J Morris

Bennett

Ann B & John D Tisdale 16 Apr 1849; b- Thomas Rose min- James McAden- 17Apr1849

Catharine R & John W Wiggins 11 Aug 1848; b- William M Bennett min- James McAden- 12Aug1848

Elizabeth & Freeman Walker 28 Oct 1833; b- Joseph Bennett min- James McAden-

Jane & Henry Bradley 28 Dec 1834; b- Martin Lambert

Lucy & Peter Stegall 28 Dec 1813; b- William Bennett

Martha & Thomas Rose 21 Dec 1822; b- Joseph Bennett con- Jordan Bennett, father min- Stephen Jones- (Lynchburg, Va.)- 25Dec1822

Mary & Joseph Arnold 2 Nov 1837; b- Joseph Bennett Jr min- James McAden-

Peggy Haskins & Averett King 23 Dec 1816; b- William Bennett con- Jordan Bennett, father min- Charles Ogburn- (Methodist) 24Dec1816

Polly E & William J Williams 6 Dec 1824; b- Matthew Williams con- William Bennett, father min- James McAden-

Sarah & John Stroud 23 Dec 1817; b- William Bennett

Bently

Ann & William Poythress 10 Nov 1802; b- Thomas Rogers

Berry

Lucy & Charles L Jeffries 7 Apr 1815; b- Thomas Burnett con- John B Goode, gdn of Lucy min- James Meacham- 15Apr1815

Molly & George Hudson 11 Dec 1786; b- William Harris con- Thomas Berry, father

Nancy & Daniel Wall 3 Apr 1811; b- Polly W Berry

Sarah & John Harris 25 Dec 1786; b- George Hudson

Bevil

Mary Ann & Benjamin L Allgood 15 Oct 1851; min- George W. Andrews- 16Oct1851

Bevill

Elizabeth & Thomas Hix 13 Dec 1796; b- Francis Neal min- William Creath-

Martha & Archibald Wilson 26 Oct 1785; b- Hutchins Burton

Micah & James Cole 13 Mar 1797; b- Francis M Neal min- William Creath-

Bigger

Elizabeth B & John Boswell 13 Feb 1840; b- J W Yates, Jr con- John Bigger, father

Bignal

Sarah & William Clements 5 Jun 1789; b- Joseph Speed min- Thomas Scott-

Bilbo

Agnes & John Morgan 24 Aug 1779; b- Joseph Bilbo con- James Bilbo, father

Elizabeth & Samuel (Jr) Bugg 25 Mar 1794; b- Bennett Sandifer

Martha B & Abraham Spencer 13 Mar 1816; b- John H Hardie

Martha Minge & William B Baugh 15 Nov 1804; s of James Baugh, dec. b- William Baskervill con- John Aldridge and Agnes Aldridge

Mary & Benjamin Morgan 19 Dec 1785; b- Frederick Rainey con- James Bilbo, father min- John King- 22Dec1785

Susanna & Edmund Short 6 Aug 1787; b- John Bilbo

Susannah & Frederick Malone 24 May 1774; b- John Bilbo

Billups

Lucy R & John Marable 12 Dec 1791; b- John Billups min- John Williams- 13Dec1791

Binford

Martha & Binford Taylor 23 Dec 1829; b- David A Walker min- James McAden-

Bing

Ann & Edward Williams 19 Jun 1820; b- James Bing con- Martha Bing, mother

Elizabeth & Thomas Browder 26 Mar 1852; con- John Bing, father min- James McAden- 26Mar1852

Elizabeth & William Keeton 12 Nov 1798; b- Thomas Dance con- George Bing, father min- William Creath- 20Nov1798

Elizabeth & Alexander S Tucker 16 Sep 1816; b- John Bing min- Milton
Robertson- (Warren County, N.C.)

Jane & Beverly Crowder 21 Apr 1845; b- Zachariah Curtis con- Elizabeth
Bing, mother min- James McAden-

Jane & Jonathon Williams 13 Dec 1823; b- Edward Williams con- Martha
Bing, mother min- Charles Ogburn- (Methodist)

Martha & Jones Gee 5 Dec 1831; b- Daniel Tucker   min- Charles
Ogburn- (Methodist)

Nancy & Thomas Keeton 13 Nov 1805; b- James Keeton

Tabitha & Briant Bowen 27 Jul 1839; b- Zachariah Curtis con- John
Bing, father min- Benjamin R. Duval-

Birchett

Martha M & Abraham Green Keen 11 Oct 1816; b- William Birchett

Panthea C & William H Bullock 16 Dec 1822; b- John Bullock con-
William B Birchett, father min- John S. Ravenscroft- (Episcopal)-
19Dec1822

Birtchett

Elenor H & George Sommervill 23 Mar 1811; b- Henry Hicks min-
George Micklejohn-

Elizabeth & Thomas Lewis 22 Mar 1806; b- John Dortch min- Thomas
Hardie-

Martha & Joseph Goode 31 Aug 1790; b- Philip Morgan

Polly R & John Barnes 1 Apr 1822; widow b- Enoch Jones

Bishop

Barsheba & Richard Ragsdale 8 Feb 1802; b- Littleberry Carter min-
William Creath-

Blackbourn

Lucy Charlotte & Thomas Holt 12 Oct 1780; Thomas from Chesterfield
County Lucy daughter of Thomas Blackbourn b- John Brown

Mary Alford & Thomas Vaughan 11 Mar 1799; d of Thomas b- John
Wilson

Blacketter

Elizabeth B & Richard Allen 6 Nov 1809; b- David Blacketter

Keziah & Darling Jones 21 Mar 1798; b- William Jones

Nancy & Thomas Haile 25 Sep 1805; b- Harwood Rudd

Polly & Larkin Talley 27 Sep 1805; b- Samuel Bugg

Blackwell

Mary R & Jesse C Malone 28 Aug 1831; b- Sterling Smith min- James
McAden-

Blair

Sally & John Chavous 27 Jul 1801; b- Thomas Cypress

Blake

Jinsey & John Allgood 31 Dec 1798; b- Edward Goodrich min- William
Creath- 3Jan1799

Bland

Betsy & Thomas Browder 21 Jul 1796; b- Jesse Bugg min- William
Creath- 22Jul1796

Elizabeth W & James Norvell 22 Dec 1817; b- William H Bugg con-
Samuel Bland, father min- James Meacham- 25Dec1817

Fanny & John Hudson 30 Apr 1801; b- Swepson Jeffries Jr con- Samuel
Bland, father min- William Creath- 1May1801

Rebecca P & William W Carpenter 21 Jan 1817; b- Samuel Bland con-
Samuel Carpenter min- James Meacham- 22Jan1817

Blankenship

Jemima & Edward Hill 28 Jul 1802; b- John Webb

Sine & John Webb 16 Dec 1802; b- Mark L Jackson

Blanks

Amelia & Samuel Thompson 7 Oct 1817; b- John Blanks

Amey & Thomas Moss 11 May 1814; b- John Blanks min- John Ligon- 15May1814

Dycey & John Haley 8 Jul 1799; b- Elijah Griffin con- Joseph Blanks, father

Edna & William Griffin 26 Sep 1803; b- Joseph Blanks

Elizabeth Jane & William F Blanks 10 Dec 1853; con- John A Blanks, father min- John E. Montague- (Granville County, N.C.)- 15Dec1853

Frances & John E Pettypool 18 Jul 1814; b- John Blanks con- Ann Blanks, mother

Lucy R & Daniel B Hatcher 10 Feb 1841; b- Thomas L Jones con- Allen Blanks, gdn of Lucy min- Charles F. Burnley-

Mary & Henry Hester 26 Nov 1827; b- John Blanks con- James Blanks, father min- Pleasant Gold- (Baptist)- 29Nov1827

Nancy & Stephen Worsham 14 Sep 1807; b- Daniel Jones

Pamela Susan & George J Dabbs 13 Oct 1833; b- E A Williams con- Allen Blanks, gdn of Pamela min- John B. Smith-

Rebecca & Jacobus P Christopher 4 Sep 1815; b- John Blanks con- Ann Blanks, mother min- Reuben Pickett- 14Sep1815

Blanton

Elizabeth & Willis Stroud 11 Sep 1792; b- George Small min- John Loyd-

Peggy & Edward Travis 15 Jul 1816; b- Diggs Poynor

Booker

Elizabeth & Samuel Simmons 6 Apr 1822; b- Samuel S Simmons min- Charles Ogburn- (Methodist) 9Apr1822

Frances & Edward Thomson 10 May 1822; b- Henderson Thompson con- John Booker, father min- Charles Ogburn- (Methodist) 23May1822

Sarah & Isham Tucker 11 May 1803; b- William Renn min- William Creath-

Booth

Judith & John Jones 22 Jan 1807; b- Harper Booth min- James Meacham-

Lucy Gillam & Thomas Harper 22 Jan 1791; b- Thomas Booth Thomas Harper from Dinwiddie County min- Henry Ogburn- 10Feb1791

Nancy & Francis Jones 18 Sep 1799; b- Harper Booth con- Thomas Booth, father

Polly & Joel Winfield 3 Mar 1801; b- Joshua Winfield min- James Meacham- 4Mar1801

Sally & William Norvell 17 Feb 1817; b- Reuben Booth min- James Meacham- 27Feb1817

Susannah & Jonathon Fisher 5 May 1801; b- Reuben Booth min- James Meacham-

Boothe

Rebecca & William Elliott 20 Dec 1809; b- Reuben Boothe

Boswell

Ermin & Francis DeGraffenreid 12 Nov 1781; b- Asa Oliver con- Joseph Boswell, father

Lucy F & Thomas J Love 31 May 1853; con- Joseph Boswell Sr, father min- William Doswell- (Lunenburg County)-

Martha M & Felix Craddock 18 Nov 1839; b- E A Craddock con- Joseph Boswell, father

Peggy & John Wright 14 Feb 1822; b- John T Sizemore min- Pleasant Gold- (Baptist)-

Susan E & Charles Brydie 19 Mar 1844; b- Christopher Wood con- Joseph Boswell Sr, father min- William V. Wilson-

Bottom

Nancy & Anselm Roberts 22 Jul 1806; b- Hughberry Nanney min- James Meacham- 23Jul1806

Sarah & William Lambert 31 May 1800; b- James Burton min- Ebenezer McGowan- 1May1800

Bowen

Angelina & Thomas Kirk 22 Sep 1821; b- William Thomason min-Stephen Jones- (Lynchburg, Va.)- 24Sep1821

Catharine G & William Bowen 17 Dec 1849; b- John W Nicholson

Catharine & David Taylor 25 Mar 1829; b- William Matthews

Caty & Thomas McCarter 23 Jun 1803; b- James Bowen min- William Creath-

Charlotte & Asa Bowen 6 Dec 1796; b- Charles Bowen Asa son of Charles Bowen and Amey Bowen min- John Loyd- 13Dec1796

Jane & William Nunn 17 Aug 1830; b- Allen Bowen min- Pleasant Gold- (Baptist)-

Judy & Reuben Booker 19 Jun 1801; b- Daniel Tucker Jr.

Lively & Salathiel Bowen 18 May 1811; b- Littleberry B Kirks

Liza & James McCarter 3 Dec 1804; b- James Bowen

Lucy & John Gwaltney 12 Feb 1798; b- Micajah Gwaltney min- Charles Ogburn- (Methodist)

Maria S & James A Jones 7 Dec 1846; b- Alfred Bowen min- Alfred Apple- 9Dec1846

Martha Hicks & Archelus Morgan 24 May 1814; b- William Bowen con- William Bowen

Milly & Frederick I Crowder 4 Dec 1797; b- James Bowen min- Charles Ogburn- (Methodist)

Nancy A & David Bowen 24 Dec 1838; b- Grandison Glasscock

Nancy & Gilbert Pinson 29 Sep 1824; b- Benjamin Bowen min- Pleasant Gold- (Baptist)- 5Oct1824

Nancy & McDaniel Rottenberry 3 Mar 1797; b- John Thomerson min-John Loyd- 8Mar1797

Omea & Charnel Bowen 15 Oct 1805; b- Berry Bowen

Rebecca S & Asa B Cabiness 17 Nov 1823; b- Sanford Bowen min-James Smith- 26Nov1823

Rebecca & Isaac Johnson 30 Jan 1802; b- Littleberry Bowen

Rebeccah & William Johnson 3 Mar 1813; b- Lowry Bowen con- Berry Bowen, grandfather of Rebeccah

Stacy & Reuben Cardin 8 Jan 1793; b- Zachariah Bowen con- John Cardin, father con- James Bowen, father min- William Creath- 10Jan1793

Bowers

Betsy A W & James H Dunn 21 Feb 1825; b- Sanford Bowers min-James McAden-

Martha & James Simmons 20 Feb 1815; daughter of Sanford Bowers b-Richard H Edmonson min- Charles Ogburn- (Methodist) 25Feb1815

Mary A & James O Moss 13 Aug 1838; b- Oswald M Moss con- Sanford Bowers, father min- James McAden-

Boyd

Ann Lewis & Phillip Rainey 3 Jun 1824; b- William B Easley con-Alexander Boyd, father

Christian B & William H Lewis 29 Jun 1836; b- John McNeal con-Matilda Boyd, mother min- William Steel- (Episcopal)-

Delia B & Benjamin F Dodson 19 Nov 1851; min- George W. Andrews-

Eleanor & Patrick H Foster 15 Sep 1819; 'Dr' Patrick H Foster b-Thomas Howerton con- Elizabeth Boyd, mother

Eliza F & Robert M Cunningham 22 Sep 1829; b- Alexander Boyd min-
Allen D. Metcalf-

Elizabeth J & Horace L Read 12 Apr 1819; b- Alexander Boyd con-
William Boyd, father

Elizabeth & George Farrar 22 Aug 1783; b- Richard Swepson Jr

Frances P & Fielding L Williams 31 Jan 1827; b- B H Bailey con-
William Boyd, father min- Allen D. Metcalf- 14Feb1827

Harriet R & John S Dodson 29 Jul 1844; b- Amasa P Wright con-
Matilda Boyd, mother

Jane A & John D Hawkins 11 Apr 1803; b- Richard Boyd min- John
Cameron-

Jane A & Charles Read 18 Oct 1816; 'Dr' Charles Read b- Alexander
Boyd Jr con- William Boyd, father

Lucy Nelson & John W Potts 3 Nov 1834; b- Alfred Boyd min- William
Steel- (Episcopal)- 4Nov1834

Lucy S & Thomas Johnson 15 Aug 1832; b- James F Maclin con-
Alexander Boyd, father

Lucy & David G Smith 17 Oct 1831; b- William W Oliver con- William
Boyd, father min- John B. Smith-

Maria A & William B Easley 1 Oct 1827; b- Daniel T Hicks min- Allen
D. Metcalf- 3Oct1827

Martha B & Howell L Jeffries 8 Aug 1820; b- John W Lewis min- John
S. Ravenscroft- (Episcopal)- 9Aug1820 (married at the home of Mrs.
Tabitha Boyd)

Martha & Langston E Finch 4 Sep 1851; con- Richard Boyd, father min-
J.D. Blackwell- 10Seo1851

Mary A & John Bennett 30 Nov 1829; b- Alexander Boyd min- William
Steel- (Episcopal)-

Mary F & Joseph Hawkins 3 Apr 1811; Joseph from Warren Co., NC
b- James Boyd

Mary & Thomas P Hawkins 3 Nov 1834; b- Alfred Boyd min- William
Steel- (Episcopal)- 4Nov1834

Matilda & E F Roberts 12 Dec 1849; b- Phillip Rainey min- William A.
Smith- 31Dec1849

Nancy & Thomas (Jr) Goode - Dec 1812; b- Joel Watkins

Nancy & William Hawkins 12 Dec 1803; b- Richard Boyd min- John
Cameron-

Sally K & Achillis S Jeffries 27 May 1831; b- Howell L Jeffries min-
William Steel- (Episcopal)- 8Jun1831

Sally & Hillary L M Goode 21 Jan 1839; b- Richard Russell con- Richard
Boyd, Jr., father

Virginia & Richard Pryor 24 Dec 1821; b- William B Easley min- John
S. Ravenscroft- (Episcopal)-

Bozwell

Martha & William Booker 14 Jan 1799; b- Benjamin Bozwell min-
William Creath- 17Jan1799

Bracey

Mary W & David H Nash 15 Oct 1849; b- Robert Malone min- Thomas
Adams- (Lunenburg Co.)- 16Oct1849

Bracy

Martha E & William Malone 12 Feb 1850; b- George Speaks min- James
McAden- 18Feb1850

Bradley

Elizabeth & William Hall 6 Dec 1802; b- John Bradley

Sally Gilliam & William (Sr) Drumwright 24 Sep 1811; b- Goodwin Taylor

Brame

Barbara & Thomas (Jr) Brame 5 Apr 1824; b- Joseph Brame

Eliza F & John Newton 1 Dec 1849; b- David W Brame min- J.D. Blackwell-

Eliza & Francis Brame 19 Dec 1831; b- W. Brame

Elizabeth Jane & Cephas Hardie 17 Dec 1832; b- John R Buford con- Thomas Brame Sr, father

Elizabeth & William W Clausel 19 Jul 1803; b- John Puryear Jr min- William Richards- 21Jul1803

Elizabeth & John T Hayes 23 Jan 1822; b- Melchizedeck Brame min- William Richards- 24Jan1822

Elizabeth & Walter Wyatt 16 Dec 1792; b- James Brame

Fanny & David C Wootton 20 Feb 1815; b- Richins Brame, father

Hannah C & Samuel Hutcheson 18 Oct 1796; b- William Phillips con- James Brame, guardian min- Charles Ogburn- (Methodist) 27Oct1796

Happy & James Frazer 3 Jun 1778; b- John Brame daughter of Richins Brame

Kerenhappuck & David N Carter 1 Jan 1824; b- Melchizedec Brame min- William Richards- 13Jan1824

Lucy C & Obadiah Talley 9 Dec 1850; con- William Brame, father

Lucy & William Creath 11 Jun 1792; b- Reuben Vaughan con- Elizabeth Brame, mother & widow of Thomas Brame, dec. min- John Williams- 14Jun1792

Martha & James T Wootton 15 Oct 1838; min- Benjamin R. Duval-

Mary Ann & John Fleming 16 Dec 1833; b- Francis Brame min- John B. Smith-

Mary & ---- --- 11 Apr 1796; son of John and Martha Smith b- James Norment min- William Richards- 21Apr1796

Mary & Samuel A Tarry 17 Dec 1827; b- Joseph Brame min- James Smith- 19Dec1827

Nancy C & Josiah Crews 16 Nov 1812; b- Nathaniel Maclin

Nancy & Walter Frazer 21 Jan 1811; b- William Brown min- William Richards- 31Jan11811

Nancy & Robert Talley 18 Dec 1816; b- Charles W Baird min- Charles Ogburn- (Methodist) 19Dec1816

Pamelia R & John P Patillo 4 Feb 1834; b- William A Clausel min- John B. Smith-

Susan & Francis Smithson 30 Sep 1843; b- Abner Maxey

Susanna & James D Brame 23 Oct 1810; b- Warner L Brame min- James Meacham- 1Nov1810

Susanna & William Love 6 May 1803; b- Ingram Roffe con- James Brame, guardian of Susanna daughter of George Baskervill

Susannah & Joseph B Clausel 23 Feb 1799; b- John Puryear Jr min- William Richards- 28Feb1799

Branch

Catherine D & William D Justice 4 Oct 1838; b- William J Carter min- Benjamin R. Duval-

Brandon

Aggy & Collin S Pettiford 26 Jan 1830; b- John Stewart min- William Steel- (Episcopal)- 28Jan1830

Eliza & Royal Bolling 23 Aug 1832; b- John Stewart min- William Steel- (Episcopal)- 25Aug1832

Elizabeth & Austin Cousins - --- 1802; b- Robert Cole (date portion of bond illegible)

Elizabeth & Archer Stewart 18 Dec 1818; b- Ned Brandon min- William Richards- 22Dec1818

Mary & Frederick Goen 29 Dec 1800; 'Gowen?' b- Ephraim Drew min-
William Richards- 1Jan1801

Mary & James Mayo 18 Dec 1838; b- Osborne Mayo

Mary & Robert Mayo 31 Dec 1811; b- Edward Mayo

Nancy & Frederick Graves 29 Dec 1800; b- Ephraim Drew

Susan & Anderson Kirk 26 Jan 1830; b- John Stewart con- Jane Kirk,
mother min- William Steel- (Episcopal)-

Brasley

Polly & Peter Insco 5 Nov 1827; b- Alfred Vaughan min- James Smith-
6Nov1827

Brawner

Mary & Matthew Allen 8 May 1797; b- James Thompson

Bridgforth

Elizabeth & William Hutcherson 4 Dec 1818; b- Edward B Brown con-
Elizabeth Bridgforth, mother min- Charles Ogburn- (Methodist) 9Dec1818

Martha A & James P Tarry 11 Nov 1840; b- Robert F Bridgforth min-
James McAden-

Philadelphia & Samuel Stone 24 May 1822; b- William Hutcheson con-
Elizabeth Bridgforth, mother min- Silas Shelburne- (Lunenburg County)-
30May1822

Briggs

Elizabeth & Stephen Dance 11 May 1805; b- Charles Ogburn

Broadfoot

Margaret & Thomas Andrews 29 Mar 1791; b- Frederick Andrews

Brogdon

Molly Harris & William Flood 12 Nov 1785; b- Thomas Macklin con-
William Brogdon, who test bride 21

Brook

Elizabeth & James Paull 12 Feb 1776; b- Dudley Brook

Sarah & William McQuie 11 Jan 1785; b- Burwell Russell

Brooke

Mary & William Hamlett 27 Oct 1789; b- Gabriel Carleton William from
Halifax County

Brooking

Lucy & Benjamin Hicks 15 Jun 1786; b- William Lucas Benjamin from
Chesterfield County SC

Brooks

Elizabeth & David Haley 8 Dec 1783; b- Elijah Graves

Frances & Robert A Slaughter 15 May 1852; min- Adam Finch-

Jincy & Julius Lambert 13 Dec 1796; b- John McKinney min- John Loyd-
14Dec1796

Lucy & Daniel Baugh 10 Oct 1780; b- John Eppes

Martha & James Crowder 24 Jan 1818; b- William Blanton

Molly & William Burton 22 Jan 1774; b- William Brooks

Nelly & Frederick Jones 16 Oct 1787; b- Jurdain Brooks con- Robert
Brooks, father

Browder

Elizabeth W & William J Smith 15 Dec 1845; b- Oswin J Phillips con-
William Browder, father min- E. Chambers-

Frances & Joseph Keeton 20 Nov 1851; con- W T Fourqurean, gdn of
Frances min- Drury Seat-

Tabitha & Drury Wall 16 Aug 1824; b- Thompson Browder min- Pleasant
Gold- (Baptist)- 25Aug1824

Brown

Amy W & William Hutcheson 13 Dec 1790; b- Thomas Brown

Anne & Richard Bailey 12 Jan 1795; b- William Brown

Catherine & Samuel Bagwell 12 Nov 1788; Samuel from Brunswick County b- Richard Edmondson

Elizabeth & Thomas Neal 1 Jan 1787; b- Thomas Brown Thomas son of William Neal Sr

Emily B & Cephas L Wilson 19 Aug 1835; b- Charles S Hutcheson min- William B. Rowzee- 1Sep1835

Emily J & Benjamin J Walker 2 Sep 1834; b- Henry Turpin con- J Brown, father min- James M. Jeter- (Lunenburg County)-

Hannah H & John R Lucas 26 Apr 1806; 'Dr.' John R Lucas b- John Dortch con- R Watson, guardian of Hannah min- James Meacham-

Martha R & John J Moore 2 Oct 1823; b- William Hutcheson min- James Smith- 9Oct1823

Martha & Beckley Jackson 12 Jun 1809; b- William Hutcheson

Mary & Samuel Tarry 14 Mar 1808; b- George Craighead min- James Meacham- 16Mar1808

Mary & Daniel Walker 5 Aug 1793; b- Thomas Brown Daniel from Nottoway County

Olive & Joshua Smith 6 Jan 1801; b- William Hutcheson

Rebecca & William Wilson 9 Sep 1782; b- Thomas Brown

Sally & Edward Cox 3 Jan 1795; b- Joseph Hamilton

Sucky & John Stewart 10 Jun 1820; b- Banister Chavous min- Alexander M. Cowan- 11Jun1820

Brummell

Ann E & W James Dedman - Jul 1846; b- John R Taylor min- John B. Smith-

Eliza & James Harris 29 Nov 1819; b- Harper Gillespie min- William Richards- 9Dec1819

Elizabeth & Charles Hutcherson 19 Feb 1824; b- James Harris min- William Richards-

Mary & William Moody 5 Aug 1819; b- John Brummell min- William Richards- 12Aug1819

Polly & Anderson Crowder 20 Jan 1796; b- Abram Crowder Jr min- William Richards- 28Jan1796

Brydie

Laplata J S & Thomas G Coleman 10 Dec 1851; con- Charles Brydie, father min- William V. Wilson- 10Dec1851

Bugg

Ann & Robert Lewis 10 Nov 1788; min- John Cameron-

Betty & Samuel (Jr) Hopkins 18 Jan 1783; daughter of Jacob Bugg Sr b- George Nicholas

Elizabeth M & John N Nolley 16 Jul 1827; b- Alexander Nolley min- James Smith- 25Jul1827

Elizabeth & John Allen 3 Oct 1791; b- Thomas Langley John Allen from Buckingham County min- Edward Almand- 6Oct1791

Elizabeth & Daniel Daley 1 Jul 1794; b- Abel Dortch min- John Loyd- 3Jul1794

Frances & John Nance 10 Apr 1786; b- Robert Nance con- John Bugg, father

Joyce & Thomas Langley 24 Apr 1773; b- Samuel Hopkins

Lucy Ann & William Z Haskins 27 Feb 1843; b- E A Williams con- Rebecca P Bugg, mother

Lucy & James Gee 6 Feb 1797; James from Lunenburg County b- John Bugg con- Nevil Gee, father min- John Loyd- 16Feb1797

Martha & Samuel Oslin 7 Mar 1789; b- John Bugg

Mary B & Obadiah Stith 14 Nov 1843; Obadiah from Brunswick County b- Joseph S Gregory min- James McAden-

Mary S & Benjamin Wall 2 Apr 1800; b- Frederick Wall con- Molly Bugg, mother

Mary & William Walker 7 Aug 1779; b- Henry Pennington con- John and Lucy Bugg, parents

Nancy & Dabney Farrar 9 Jun 1812; b- James Phillips con- John Bugg, father min- James Meacham- 10Jun1812

Nancy & William Jackson 11 Sep 1807; b- John Bugg

Rebecca & Josiah Floyd 28 Mar 1810; b- Jesse Bugg

Sarah & Jesse Hix 26 Nov 1774; daughter of Samuel Bugg Sr and Martha Bugg b- Samuel Bugg

Sarah & Nicholas Lanier 23 Mar 1796; b- John Nance min- James Tolleson- 2Apr1796

Sarah & William Pettypool 19 Jul 1830; b- William Turner min- James McAden-

Sarah & John Whobry 6 Mar 1794; b- John Bugg min- William Creath- 9Mar1794

Burks

Mary A & William Maclin 3 Jan 1850; b- Sterling Evans min- James McAden- 4Jan1850

Mary & Burwell Wall 30 Sep 1794; b- Miles House Mary gives own consent and states that she is 25 years old

Rebecca & Sterling Evans 33 Aug 1844; b- Edward A Rawlins con- Lucy Burks, mother

Burnes

Polly & Baalam Vaughan 11 Dec 1809; b- Robert Burnes min- Richard Dabbs- 12Dec1809

Burnett

Elizabeth & George T Barnes 1 Mar 1821; b- Lewis Winn

Elizabeth & Joseph Smith 11 Sep 1792; b- Silvanus Ingram min- Rice Haggard- 20Sep1792

Isabella & Dabney P Hill 18 Jan 1828; b- Mark A Burnett min- James Smith- 24Jan1828

Jane & George W (Jr) Oliver 6 Apr 1812; b- Richard Burnett min- James Meacham- 16Apr1812

Mariah V & Alex S Hagerman 17 Dec 1838; b- George J Dabbs

Martha & Robert Reynolds 20 Dec 1830; b- John Winckler min- James Smith- 23Dec1830

Mary Ann & Robert Brummell 4 Nov 1811; b- Jonathon Bennett

Mary & James P Brown 21 Nov 1814; b- Richard Burnett min- Milton Robertson- (Warren County, N.C.) 24Nov1814

Nancy & John Thompson 13 Apr 1801; b- Richard Burnett min- William Creath-

Polly Jeffries & Joseph (Jr) Lett 28 Jan 1804; b- Matthew H Davis con- Thomas Burnett, father

Sally & John Bland 22 Apr 1794; b- Anselm Bugg con- Elizabeth Burnett, mother min- Charles Ogburn- (Methodist)- 26Apr1794

Sally & Richard Hill 17 Jul 1806; b- Jesse Burnett min- Thomas Hardie- 11Aug1806

Burns

Henrietta & Thomas Johnson 5 Aug 1811; b- Robert Burns min- Richard Dabbs- (Lunenburg County)- 20Aug1811

Nancy & William Johnson 11 Aug 1815; b- Champion Burns

Rittah & James Johnson 20 Aug 1811; min- Richard Dabbs- (Lunenburg County)-

Burrows

Elizabeth & Charles Royster 14 Nov 1803; b- Jordan Mason con- William T Burrows, father

Mary & Cuthbert Wagstaff 30 May 1822; b- Francis McCraw con- Elizabeth Burton, mother of Mary min- William Richards-

Burrus

Amasa & Allen Robertson 4 Sep 1801; b- Henry Royall min- William Creath-

Elizabeth & Joseph Bennett 9 Apr 1787; b- Anthony Bennett

Rebecca & Banister Cox 26 Oct 1803; b- John Pritchett min- William Creath-

Sally & Thomas Westbrook 9 Dec 1805; b- Jesse Westbrook min- Edward Almand- 24Dec1805

Burton

Dolly & Briant Smithson 13 Jun 1796; b- Peter Puryear min- William Creath- 16Jun1796

Frances & Nathaniel Hix 9 Oct 1783; Nathaniel from Georgia daughter of Samuel Bugg Sr and Martha Bugg v- Sherwood Bugg

Jane & Robert Burton 17 Aug 1846; b- William P Drumwright con- Temperance Burton, mother of Jane, who test husband deceased min- James J. Sledge-

Lucy A & Henry C Moss 8 Sep 1823; b- Boswell B Moss

Martha & John Baskervill 30 Jul 1765; s of George Baskervill b- Samuel Young

Mary & Benjamin Ferrell 12 Mar 1770; b- James Ferrell

Mary & Samuel Lambert 27 Jul 1819; b- James Lambert con- Milly Burton, mother

Mary & Hardaway Lett 1 Sep 1806; b- Pennington Lett

Mary & Philip Pennington 31 May 1798; b- John Hubbard min- Ebenezer McGowan- 14Jun1798

Miney & Edward Roffe 16 Jul 1787; b- William Johnson con- Robert Burton, father

Pamela & Thomas L Williams 2 Dec 1824; b- Edward Royster min- William Steel- (Episcopal)-

Peggy M & Zachariah Jarrott 12 Apr 1806; b- Jones Burton

Phebe & Peter Puryear 10 Dec 1792; b- Thomas Crowder

Phebe & Thomas A Reamy 13 Jan 1800; b- James Wilson min- William Richards- 16Jan1800

Susanna & William Dortch 29 Sep 1786; b- Robert Pennington

Susanna & Edward A Wilson 6 Apr 1852; con- Peter Burton, father min- John A. Doll-

Burwell

Ann E & Theodrick M Roberts 1 Dec 1848; b- John S R Burwell

Ann R & John J Coleman 4 Dec 1839; b- William T Z Finch min- F.H. McGuire-

Anne S & Richard (Jr) Taylor 21 Nov 1814; b- Alexander Boyd Jr

Anne Spottswood & John Stark Ravenscroft 13 Aug 1792; d of Lewis b- William Hepburn

Christian & William B Hamlin 18 Dec 1794; b- Daniel Mayes con- Mary Hamlin, mother con- Lewis Burwell, father Daniel Mayes from Dinwiddie County

Elizabeth Blair & Edward L Tabb 31 Jan 1791; s of John and Mary Tabb b- G H Baskervill con- Lewis Burwell, father

Frances Powell & Miles King 15 Jul 1799; 'Capt.' Miles King from Norfolk b- William Baskervill con- Ann Burwell, mother min- John Cameron-

Jane C & M C Read 3 Oct 1842; b- Edward Keen con- J R Burwell, father, who test Jane 21yrs old

Jean B & William A Eaton 19 Dec 1843; b- Allen A Burwell

Lucy Armistead & Charles Sturdivant 30 May 1825; b- Richard Taylor con- Lucy Burwell, mother

Mary A & William C Boswell 31 Jul 1851; con- P R Burwell, father min- Adam Finch- 20Aug1851

Mary Armistead & Samuel Goode 28 Sep 1786; b- Nicholas Bilbo con- Lewis Burwell, father

Mary Cole & Landon C Garland 27 Oct 1831; b- Hugh A Garland con- Armistead Burwell, father min- William Steel- (Episcopal)-

Mary & William Cunningham 22 Oct 1831; b- James Cunningham min- William Steel- (Episcopal)- 3Nov1831

Mary & Joseph Selden 11 Apr 1785; b-. Samuel Goode

Matilda & Alexander Boyd 10 Oct 1803; b- John Dortch Matilda daughter of Lewis Burwell, dec. con- Armistead Burwell, guardian for sister min- John Cameron-

Panthea & Richard Boyd 19 Nov 1799; b- John Wright con- Lewis Burwell, father min- John Cameron-

Panthea & Isaac Read 21 Oct 1816; b- Armistead Burwell

Selina S & Henry Tucker 13 Jul 1851; min- Adam Finch-

Butler

Charlotte & Robert Lewis 8 Jan 1810; b- Jones Allen

Elizabeth D & Frederick Hamme 12 Mar 1804; b- John White min- Matthew Dance- 22Mar1804

Elizabeth D & Edward T Marable 29 Sep 1829; b- Charles G Butler min- James Smith- 8Oct1829

Elizabeth F & Edmond O Daves 13 Oct 1845; b- John W Butler con- Frances C Butler, mother min- Jacob Manning- 15Oct1845

Frances S & John J Daves 24 Aug 1844; b- Henry C Moss con- Frances C Butler, mother

Jane B & James H Keys 8 Apr 1817; b- Howell L Jeffries min- James Meacham-

Martha A & Charles King 24 Jul 1828; b- David G Hutcherson con- Frances C Butler, mother min- James Smith-

Mary & John Bell 12 Jan 1785; b- William Lucas

Nancy & William Marshall 28 Dec 1816; b- Joseph Butler min- James Meacham- 9Jan1817

Nancy & William Thompson 27 Dec 1802; b- James Thompson

Patsy & Drury Harris 10 Oct 1803; b- Charles Carter con- John Butler Sr, father

Sarah & David G Hutcherson 28 Jan 1828; b- Major Butler con- Joseph Butler, Sr, father min- N.T. Barham- 10Mar1828

Sarah & Edward Jones 9 Jul 1792; b- Elijah Graves min- James Read- (Baptist) 19Jul1792

Byasee

Sally R & Richard J Roberts 14 Jan 1833; b- Jesse Russell con- Mildridge Crowder, mother of Sally

Byassee

Susannah & John W G Johnson 20 May 1827; b- Cargill Thompson con- William Crowder, stepfather of Susannah con- Mildrige Crowder, mother of Susannah min- Charles Ogburn- (Methodist)

Byers

Milly & William Crowder 22 Jan 1819; b- Jeremiah Russell min- Charles Ogburn- (Methodist) 25Jan1819

Cabaniss

Mary L & James M Crutchfield 29 Dec 1842; b- William Hightower con-William Cabaniss, father

Cabiness

Sally A & Isaac Medley 23 Sep 1845; b- Joseph T Ladd con- William Cabiness, father min- James McAden-

Callis

Elizabeth & Samuel G Osborne 19 Nov 1821; b- William Callis min-William Richards- 25Nov1821

Camp

Elizabeth & Bazzell Wagstaff 5 Mar 1806; b- Allen Wagstaff min- William Richards- 6Mar1806

Mary & Thomas Hord 26 Dec 1785; b- John Holmes Mary widow of John Camp

Campbell

Susanna & William Mason 14 Jan 1795; b- Benjamin Fargeson Jr min-John Loyd- 22Jan1795

Cardin

Jincy & Daniel Tucker 17 Jul 1787; b- George Stainback con- John Cardin, father

Cardwell

Mary & William L Walden 12 Feb 1842; b- John A Walden con- James H Cardwell, father min- Charles F. Burnley-

Susan & John A Walden 27 Jul 1840; b- John J Roberts con- James H Cardwell, father

Carless

Frances H & William Thomas 20 Dec 1790; b- Peter Thomas Jr min-John King- 24Dec1790

Carleton

Rebecca & William Puryear 22 Sep 1785; b- John Farrar con- Thomas Carleton, father

Susanna & Bartley Cox 12 Nov 1781; b- Asa Oliver d of Thomas Carleton

Carlin

Elvira I & D R Riggins 19 Jun 1848; b- William A Nash

Carlton

Eliza F & Peter W Hutcheson 14 Mar 1818; b- James Crook min- James Meacham- 19Mar1818

Carpenter

Jane T & Charles L Jeffress 7 May 1824; b- Thomas Farrar min- Stephen Jones- (Lynchburg, Va.)- 13May1824

Nancy & Obey Hatchell 3 Feb 1818; widow b- Archibald Cox min-James Meacham- 4Feb1818

Sally & John Stone 21 Feb 1816; b- David Moss con- Samuel Carpenter, father min- James Meacham- 22Feb1816

Carrington

Elizabeth C & William G Johnson 4 Sep 1846; b- William D Haskins con- T Carrington, father

Mary C & John R Leigh 21 Apr 1852; 'Dr' John R Leigh con- Tucker Carrington, father min- F.N. Whaley-

Carroll

Betsy & Thomas Kirkland 6 Mar 1816; b- Burwell Coleman min- Milton Robertson- (Warren County, N.C.)

Judith & Isaac Adams 30 Dec 1786; b- William Parish

Martha & William Conner 18 Sep 1804; b- Dennis Roberts

Mounring & Green Hawkins 27 Dec 1802; b- Mark L Jackson

Nancy & Jesse Tucker 7 Nov 1793; b- John Carroll

Carter

Catharine D & James Branch 13 Jun 1835; b- Robert Carter

Caty & William Brogdon 31 Aug 1786; b- Benjamin Ferrell

Dolly & Littleberry S Puryear 16 Dec 1837; b- William Carter

Dolly & Jeremiah Williams 27 Nov 1802; b- Joseph N Meredith min- Edward Almand- 1Dec1802

Eliza A & John W Wootton 25 Jun 1845; b- John T Carter con- David N Carter, father min- Jacob Manning-

Eliza & William Jones 24 Dec 1840; b- William H Carter con- James Jones, father

Judy & William Kidd 8 Aug 1781; b- Leman Williams

Lucy G E & William (Jr) Boyd 13 Sep 1817; b- Alexander Boyd con- John Nelson, guardian of Lucy min- John S. Ravenscroft- (Episcopal)- 9Oct1817

Mary Jane & Murray (Jr) Hendrick 15 Dec 1851; con- Robert A Carter, father min- James A. Duncan- 24Dec1851

Mary & Chappell Chandler 16 Dec 1817; b- Benjamin Carter, father

Nancy & William Owen 27 May 1815; b- Charles T Carter, father, who also consents min- Reuben Pickett- 10Jun1815

Patsy & Dudley Haile 12 Jan 1795; b- William Willis

Polly & Abraham Nash 14 Nov 1796; b- William Naish min- William Creath-

Prudence & Edwin Arnold 16 Aug 1830; min- William Steel- (Episcopal)-

Prudence & Edwin Averett 26 Aug 1830; b- Robert Carter con- James M Averett, father

Rebecca E & Thomas L McDaniel 13 Nov 1850; con- Robert Carter, father min- Robert Burton-

Sally & Ellyson Crew 4 Jun 1790; b- Winkfield Hayes min- James Read- (Baptist)

Sally & Michael Johnson 10 Dec 1781; b- John Johnson

Sarah & Thomas Loftis 3 Dec 1841; b- Richard H Jones con- William H Carter, father

Susanna & John Shaw 4 Aug 1790; b- Drury Creedle

Cattiler

Sarah & Thomas Stewart 15 Jul 1800; b- Richeson Farrar

Chamberlain

Elizabeth & John Nowell 22 Mar 1785; b- John Hamner con- Thomas Chamberlain, father

Sarah & John Morgan - --- 1803; b- Nathaniel Moss min- William Creath- Apr1803

Chambers

Betsy & John Nash 16 Dec 1795; b- Williamson Patillo min- John Loyd- 17Dec1795

Eliza G & Duncan C Hubbard 21 Jan 1846; b- Edward R Chambers

Martha E & Thomas H Laird 16 Jan 1849; 'Dr' Thomas H Laird b- Edward R Chambers min- William A. Smith- 17Jan1849

Mary Ann & John E Morris 7 Aug 1843; b- Randolph B Noblin con- George D Chambers, father min- Thomas S. Campbell- 10Aug1843

Sarah Virginia & Alexander T Laird 20 Dec 1853; con- Edward R Chambers, father min- William A. Smith-

Chambliss

Eliza & George Woodruff 3 Jun 1835; b- Richard P Montgomery con- G D Chambliss, father, who test she is under 21

Elizabeth L & John F Barner 3 Jul 1821; b- John Chambliss

Mary G & Wyatt Adams 2 Dec 1823; b- John T Barner con- John
  Chambliss, father
Mary & Nathaniel Laffoon 17 Nov 1808; b- George Small
Sarah & Thomas Webb 12 Oct 1835; b- Robert D Chambliss con- John
  Chambliss, father min- George A. Bain-

Chandler
Amanda & Bedford Hite 26 Nov 1838; b- John Talley con- Daniel C
  Chandler, father
Barbara B & John Wilkerson 4 Jan 1847; b- Pleasant Gold con- Joel
  and Hannah Chandler, parents
Elizabeth & Abraham Talley 15 Jan 1816; b- Joel Chandler min- Reuben
  Pickett- 1Feb1816
Jean & George Stewart 27 Dec 1797; b- Moses Stewart
Nancy L & George W James 23 Dec 1845; b- Joel Chandler
Nancy & David Overby 31 Dec 1821; b- Littleberry Chandler con- David
  Chandler, father min- Pleasant Gold- (Baptist)- 18Jan1822
Patsy & Peter Vaughan 12 Jan 1829; b- William Vaughan min- Pleasant
  Gold- (Baptist)- 15Jan1829
Polly & John Davis 18 Aug 1817; b- William Davis con- David Chandler,
  father

Chappell
Amey & Richard Glasgow 28 Dec 1785; b- Philip Reekes

Chavous
Anna & Drury Grigg 13 Apr 1807; b- Saunders Harris
Bedia & Munford Conley 7 Aug 1834; b- John Chavous con- Charles
  Chavous, father min- George Petty- 14Aug1834
Catharine & David Allen 17 Nov 1836; b- Jacob Chavous min- William
  Steel- (Episcopal)-
Catherine & Beverly Crook 31 Jan 1839; b- Pleasant Chavous
Elizabeth & Edward Brandon 10 Mar 1806; b- Frederick Irby
Elizabeth & Avory Scott 9 Jan 1809; b- Frederick Ivey con- Elizabeth
  Chavous, mother min- William Richards- 21Jan1809
Jincy & Archer Stewart 14 Aug 1809; b- Edward Brandon min- James
  Meacham- 25Aug1809
Lydia & Jeremiah Harris 13 Nov 1797; b- James Chavous min- Matthew
  L. Easter- 27Nov1797
Martha J & Jacob S Chavous 5 Nov 1831; b- Randolph Chavous min-
  Charles Ogburn- (Methodist) 10Nov1831
Mary & Green Hazelwood 21 Jul 1829; b- Randolph Chavous min- James
  Smith-
Milly & Kinchen Chavous 22 Dec 1788; b- William Thomerson
Nancy & Charles Valentine 28 Nov 1785; b- Thomas Macklin
Ryte & James (Jr) Stewart 11 Feb 1788; b- James Stewart Sr
Sally & Thomas W James 17 Nov 1836; b- Jacob Cahvous min- William
  Steel- (Episcopal)-
Sine & Buckner Valentine 21 Dec 1802; b- Bolling Chavous
Susey & Frederick Goen 9 Mar 1789; b- Frederick Ivey con- Henry
  Chavous Sr, father min- Phillip Cox-

Cheatham
Betsy & Charles Smithson 8 Dec 1800; b- Samuel Cheatham
Elizabeth A & Peterson Pettypool 13 Oct 1835; b- Woodson V Johnson
Elizabeth & Daniel Wilson 28 Aug 1778; b- William Waddill con-
  Leonard Cheatham, father
Martha A & Harrison R Morris 4 Dec 1853; b- William G Cheatham
  con- Nancy Tandy, mother of Martha

Martha & John T Cole 20 Oct 1823; b- Joseph Keeton min- Matthew Dance- (Lunenburg County)- 24Oct1823

Mary & William Davis 10 Oct 1804; b- Daniel Cheatham min- William Creath-

Nancy & Phillip L Land 9 Jul 1824; b- Livingston H Vaughan min- James McAden-

Phebe & George Walker 14 Dec 1789; George son of Sylvanus and Susannah Walker b- Obadiah cheatham con- Daniel Cheatham, father, who test. daughter under age

Sarah & Joseph Keeton 8 Aug 1803; b- Warner Keeton min- Matthew Dance- 31Aug1803

Childers

Sally & Balaam (Jr) Ezell 14 Nov 1808; b- Balaam Ezell Sr con- Thomas Hamblin, gdn. who test that Sally under age

Childress

Elizabeth & John Overby 11 Jun 1804; b- William Overby con- Jincey Childress, mother

Elizabeth & Coleman Vaughan 18 Dec 1833; b- William Childress min- William Steel- (Episcopal)- 24Dec1833

Harriet & John Robards - Oct 1841; min- John B. Smith-

Jean & Thomas Hamblin 10 Nov 1806; b- Balaam Ezell

Mary & William R Childress 17 Mar 1828; b- William Childress min- John B Smith-

Nancy & Anthony Gregory 6 Jan 1814; b- William Childress min- Reuben Pickett- 8Jan1814

Childry

Harriett & John Roberts 30 Oct 1844; b- William A Hester, Jr con- William Childry, father

Christopher

Elizabeth & William Finch 31 Jan 1780; b- William Christopher daughter of David Christopher

Frances & William Marable 1 Dec 1801; b- Jesse Hord min- William Richards- 5Dec1801

Hannah & James Ligon 11 Oct 1796; b- John Ligon min- William Richards- 24Nov1796

Mary & John Wootton 18 Mar 1785; d of David Christopher, dec. b- William Daniel

Nancy & William Hamilton 14 Jan 1799; b- William Christopher

Nancy & Mitchell Poole 16 Aug 1797; b- Turner Sharp

Sally & Richard Hughes 17 Aug 1786; b- David Stokes Jr Sally daughter of David Christopher dec.

Susannah & John Overton 10 Jan 1772; daughter of David Christopher b- William Christopher

Clack

Laura A & Robert H Moss 16 Dec 1846; b- R F Moss con- Robert R Clack, father

Claiborne

Catherine C & William Weatherford 16 Jun 1827; b- Henry C Ward

Frederica C & John Newman 30 Jan 1825; b- William Brown con- Henry Claiborne, father

Clanch

Sally & Allen Chavous 7 Sep 1804; 'Claunch?' b- Drury Johnsob

Clark

Dianna & George W Brame 9 Apr 1804; b- Lewis Roffe min- James Meacham- 17Apr1804

Elizabeth K & Milton Robertson 16 Sep 1811; b- Carter Clark min-
Charles Ogburn- (Methodist)

Elizabeth & David Holmes 15 Jan 1790; b- Samuel Holmes Jr David
son of Isaac & Lucy Holmes

Elizabeth & Abraham Lewis 8 Oct 1804; b- James Parham

Judith P & John Williams 16 Aug 1844; b- Alexander J Watson con-
Isham Clark, father

Mary & John Culbreath 13 Dec 1790; b- Elijah Graves

Mary & Thomas C Dugger 10 Oct 1832; b- James Clark con- Sarah
Clark, mother

Nancy B & William Green 19 Sep 1814; b- Edward H Vaughan

Nancy J & Henry C Walton 16 Sep 1825; b- Edward Royster con-
Archibald Clark, father

Nancy & John Tisdale 13 Mar 1787; b- Thomas Clark

Sally & Martin Jones 19 Jan 1813; b- Milton Robertson min- Milton
Robertson- (Warren County, N.C.)

Sarah & Abel Farrar 22 Aug 1788; b- Matthew Lancaster Easter min-
Edward Almand- 20Aug1788

Susanna & William Jones 26 Dec 1792; b- John Hudson min- William
Creath- 27Dec1792

Virginia & Henry M Bedford 9 Jul 1840; min- D.B. Nicholson-

Virginia & Henry M Redford 15 Jun 1840; b- George J Dabbs con-
Eliza Clark, mother min- D.B. Nicholson- 9Jul1840

Clarke

Anne & William O Goff 3 Dec 1835; b- James W Stanfield con-
Elizabeth Clarke, mother, who test. that Anne is under 21 min- William
B. Rowzee- 6Dec1835

Eliza & John Coleman 28 Jul 1835; min- William Steel- (Episcopal)-

Polly & Arva Allen 1 Aug 1786; b- Bolling Clarke min- John Marshall-
(Baptist)- 19Aug1786

Claunch

Jinny & Samuel Allgood 29 Dec 1804; b- Matthew Claunch

Clausel

Aphia W & Matthew Baptist 11 Dec 1809; b- Benjamin W Jeffries min-
George Micklejohn-

Frances & Samuel Puryear 17 Jan 1786; b- Richard Clausel

Hannah H & William Brame 12 Dec 1808; b- Alexander B Puryear min-
William Richards- 22Dec1808

Lucy & Richard Crowder 13 Feb 1797; b- Richard Hutcheson min-
William Creath-

Martha & Reuben Puryear 23 Dec 1791; b- James T Hayes min- William
Creath- 27Dec1791

Sally S & John (Jr) Puryear 24 Oct 1799; b- Hezekiah Puryear min-
William Creath-

Susan & Melchizedeck Brame 21 Mar 1822; min- John S. Ravenscroft-
(Episcopal)-

Clay

Judith & John Edmondson 6 Oct 1792; b- Coleman Edmondson

Mary & John Hutcherson 19 Feb 1840; b- Paschall H Bowers

Patience & Dyer Phillips 18 Dec 1786; b- Thomas Dawson con- Charles
Clay, father

Prudence & Royall Lockett 20 Aug 1789; b- James Elam con- Charles
& Phebe Clay, parents

Rebecca & William Finch 14 Aug 1775; b- Edward Finch con- Henry
Clay

Temperance & Stephen Black 8 Jan 1793; b- Britain Clay min- John Williams- 10Jan1793 Stephen from Campbell County

Temperance & John Evans 5 Nov 1792; b- John F Reazon

Cleaton

Amanda C & Benjamin W Barker 13 Nov 1853; con- Margaret Cleaton, mother min- James McAden-

Catherine & Reuben Rainey 22 Aug 1811; daughter of Thomas Cleaton, Sr, who serves as bondsman

Delphia & George R Taylor 12 Dec 1831; b- Woodly Cleaton min- Charles Ogburn- (Methodist) 21Dec1831

Edith & Meredith Poythress 14 Jul 1781; b- William Cleaton

Edney & Jesse Roffe 21 Dec 1818; b- Bennett Goode

Elizabeth A & George P Rogers 16 Feb 1849; b- James H Cleaton con- William Barner Cleaton, father min- Nathaniel Thomas- 23Feb1849

Elizabeth & Thomas Nance 20 Dec 1791; b- Thomas Cleaton min- John Loyd- 22Dec1791

Elizabeth & Benjamin Tanner 19 Dec 1815; b- Thomas Tanner con- Thomas Cleaton, father

Emma W & David D Walker 10 Dec 1839; b- Samuel Dortch con- Charles Cleaton, father min- James McAden-

Jincy & John (Jr) Ladd 12 Dec 1798; b- Joseph Ladd min- Ebenezer McGowan-

Lucy & James Davis 11 Jun 1821; b- Reuben Booth

Margarett & Charles Thomas 18 Nov 1850; b- Christopher T Thomas min- Hartwell Arnold-

Martha & Roderick Wright 19 Sep 1795; b- Thomas Cleaton Jr min- John Loyd- 24Sep1795

Mary A & Joshua E Walker 20 Dec 1845; b- David D Walker con- William B Cleaton, father min- James McAden-

Parasade & Winn (Jr) Thomas 21 Jan 1828; b- William Thomas

Clemonds

Mary & John Bilbo 28 Sep 1786; b- Nicholas Bilbo

Cliborne

Sarah & William Westbrook 5 Aug 1822; b- William Cliborne min- Pleasant Gold- (Baptist)- 10Aug1822

Cola

Sukey & Metcalf Gill 14 Jun 1799; b- John Allgood

Cole

Agatha & Peter Brandon 27 Dec 1825; b- Beverly Averett min- William Richards- 28Dec1825

Ann & Isaac Basey 27 Sep 1832; b- R Temple con- Isaac Cole, father

Jane & Jesse Bugg 10 Jan 1822; b- Bartlett Cole min- James Smith- 21Jan1822

Jincy & Martin Cousins 31 Dec 1802; b- Robert Cole min- William Creath-

Nancy & John (Jr) Morgan 14 Mar 1789; b- Philip Morgan Sr

Polly & David Dew - Aug 1822; b- John Dew min- Alexander M. Cowan-

Sukey & Metcalf Gill 4 Jun 1799; b- John Allgood

Coleman

Ann & Abraham Green 2 Mar 1799; b- James W Oliver min- William Creath- 14Mar1799

Ann & Abraham Green 2 Mar 1799; b- James W Oliver

Elizabeth C & Thomas Neal 8 Oct 1804; b- William Coleman s of Francis Moore Neal daughter of James Coleman dec. min- James Meacham- 23Oct1804

Elizabeth & Thomas Gayle 8 Dec 1819; b- James Coleman

Elizabeth & Swepson (Jr) Jeffries 6 Mar 1788; b- William Baskervill con- Swepson Jeffries Sr, father Elizabeth daughter of Cluverius Coleman min- Thomas Scott-

Elizabeth & Samuel Simmons 7 Aug 1795; b- Thomas Coleman min- Charles Ogburn- (Methodist) 15Aug1795

Faithy & John (Jr) Cox 12 May 1825; b- Eli Cox min- William Richards- 13May1825

Gracey & John Hicks 22 Jun 1789; b- Pettus Phillips Grace daughter of Cluverius Coleman min- Thomas Scott-

Harriett F & James C Gregory 30 Oct 1841; b- Benjamin W Coleman

Jane C & Charles E Hamilton 16 Jul 1840; b- E A Coleman con- E A Coleman, gdn for his sister min- F.H. McGuire- 21Jul1840

Jane S & Benjamin Jones 12 Dec 1808; b- William Coleman daughter Swepson daughter of James Coleman dec.

Jane & Ray Moss 16 Mar 1782; b- William Coleman con- Richard Coleman

Janette N & William P Ryland 4 Dec 1829; b- Samuel A Tarry con- Cluverius R Coleman, father min- James Smith- 15Dec1829

Lucy Ann & Durmont Hayes 19 Sep 1845; b- William J Carter con- William T Coleman, father

Lucy B & Wesley W Coleman 15 Feb 1830; b- Richard H Coleman con- Burwell B Coleman, father min- James Smith- 24Feb1830

Martha Jane & John May 7 Sep 1837; b- Jeremiah Hirst con- Lucy Coleman, mother

Martha & Thomas Ryland 16 Dec 1803; b- John Ryland

Martha & John Spain 15 Dec 1817; b- Matthew L Baptist min- William Richards- 18Dec1817

Mary A & Renison Walker 20 Dec 1852; min- Adam Finch- 29Dec1852

Mary C & Benjamin W Coleman 19 Jan 1814; b- Thomas Neal con- William Pettus, gdn of Mary min- Charles Ogburn- (Methodist) 22Jan1814

Mary E & William A Hicks 11 Sep 1834; b- William G Coleman con- William G Coleman, gdn of Mary, daughter of Thomas Coleman, dec.

Mary & John Boswell 16 Feb 1784; b- James Coleman con- Cluverius Coleman, father John son of Joseph Boswell

Polly A & Robert Speed 15 Jan 1809; d of James Coleman, dec. b- William Coleman

Rebeccah & Pettus Phillips 6 Mar 1788; daughter of Cluverius Coleman b- Lewis Parham min- Thomas Scott-

S A & Stephen E Dance 17 Oct 1848; b- James C Gregory min- Matthew Dance- (Lunenburg County)- 25Oct1848

Sally & John Clay 11 Feb 1805; b- James Coleman min- William Richards- 16Feb1805

Sally & John Morgan 26 Dec 1818; b- Robert Talley con- Burwell Coleman, father min- James Meacham- 29Dec1818

Susan E & Richard H Hayes 4 Apr 1849; b- William T Coleman

Susannah & Jeremiah Hurst 30 Jun 1829; b- James B Maclin con- Roderick Coleman, father min- James Smith- 1Jul1829

Coley

Martha J & William T Dickerson 29 Nov 1847; b- Richard Coley min- Robert Burton-

Colley

Agness & William Gwaltney 23 May 1801; b- James Brown

Alethea & Jesse C Parish 29 Jun 1846; b- Whitehead M Coleman min- E. Chambers-

Elizabeth & Jeremiah Bishop 8 Feb 1802; b- Charles Colley min- William Creath-

Elizabeth & Samuel G Johns 6 Feb 1831; min- Charles Ogburn- (Methodist)

Elizabeth & Samuel G Johnson 1 Dec 1831; b- Charles P Colley con- Charles Colley, father

Jane & Robert Wills 13 Oct 1788; b- Edward Colley

Martha & John Allen 12 Nov 1798; b- William Brown min- Charles Ogburn- (Methodist)- 22Dec1798

Martha & Richard D Jones 16 Dec 1831; b- William E Wilson con- Charles Colley, father min- Charles Ogburn- (Methodist) 23Dec1831

Mary & William R Tisdale 30 Nov 1829; b- Charles Colley min- James Smith- 9Dec1829

Collier

Agnes & William T Collier 20 May 1833; b- Dabney Collier min- William Steel- (Episcopal)- 25May1833

Elizabeth & Edmund Simmons 30 Jul 1822; b- Amos Hall min- James McAden- 10Aug1822

Lucy & Richard Watts 10 Mar 1806; b- William Lipford

Margaret & Amos Hall 21 Sep 1818; b- Berryman Ferguson, gdn of Margaret, who also gives consent

Martha E & Howell Mallett 10 Jun 1814; b- William Mallett min- James Meacham- 17Jan1815

Nancy & Berryman Ferguson 8 Jan 1811; b- Jesse Russell

Rebecca & Evans Tanner 21 Dec 1818; b- Joseph Bennett con- Howell Collier, father

Sally A & William Mallett 12 May 1812; b- Absolem Roberts con- Absolem Roberts, gdn of Sallie, who is daughter of Lewis Collier, dec. min- James Meacham- 11Jun1812

Sarah & Benjamin Ferrell 13 Dec 1773; b- Howell Collier

Sarah & John Ingram 7 Jun 1773; b- Charles Hutcheson

Susannah B & Absolom Roberts 3 Sep 1807; b- Phillip Roberts

Comer

Frances & James Allen 13 Apr 1795; b- Burwell Russell min- William Richards- 15 Apr1795

Connell

Rebecca & William Short 23 Oct 1812; daughter of William Connell, dec. b- John T Pennington

Conner

Nancy & Drury Pennington 24 Oct 1823; b- John H Hardie

Cook

Eliza & Leroy Rainey 14 Jun 1841; b- William P Cook con- John Cook, father min- James McAden-

Elizabeth & Richard Lamay 18 Jan 1804; b- Herbert Cook

Happy & John Taylor 5 Jan 1802; (Kerrenhappuck Cook) b- Abel Dortch

Marina & Samuel Harwell 18 Jan 1825; b- Thomas B Creath con- Sarah Cook, mother

Martha W & Mersa D Fuller 19 May 1852

Martha & Williamson Rainey 22 Dec 1810; b- Charles D Cleaton con- John Cook Sr, father

Martha & Williamson Rainey 22 Dec 1810; b- Charles D Cleaton con- John Cook, Sr., father

Martha & Jones M Taylor 20 Dec 1845; b- Allen J Smith con- John Cook, father min- James McAden-

Mary & Dabney A Hudson 1 Mar 1841; b- William P Drumwright con- John Cook, father min- James McAden-

Polly & Wyatt Nance 9 Jan 1794; b- John Cook

Cooper

Nancy & Meredith Allen 9 Aug 1788; b- John Bailey con- William Allen, father

Rebecca & Daniel Cheatham 21 Jun 1790; b- William Drumwright con- Elisha Arnold, guardian of Rebecca Rebecca daughter of Francis Cooper, dec.

Coppedge

Elizabeth & John Martin 3 Apr 1799; b- Charles Coppedge min- Ebenezer McGowan-

Susanna & Samuel Temple 11 Nov 1793; b- Charles Coppedge min- John Loyd- 14Nov1793

Corn

Keziah & William Stuart 21 --- ---; bond torn b- Robert Corn

Couch

Letty & Robert S Gregory 14 Aug 1809; b- John Couch min- William Richards- 26Aug1809

Letty & Robert S Gregory 14 Aug 1809; b- John Couch

Courtney

Ann C & Isaac Malone 22 Sep 1790; b- Josiah Floyd min- John King- 23Sep1790

Prudence & Samuel Holmes 23 Oct 1775; b- William Turnbull Prudence widow of Clack Courtney

Susannah & Arthur Freeman Winfield 2 Jun 1786; d of Clack and Prudence Courtney b- Samuel Holmes

Cousen

Ellen & William (Jr) Harris 5 Dec 1844; b- William Harris Sr con- Henry Cousen, grandfather

Cousins

Olive & Thomas Stewart 24 Oct 1838; b- William Mitchell

Covington

Eliza K & William T Allgood 15 Feb 1836; b- Edmund Young

Cowen

Susan & James Hailstock 15 Sep 1851

Cox

Eliza J & John Newton 22 Jan 1827; b- James H Newton con- John Cox, father min- Pleasant Gold- (Baptist)- 24Jan1827

Elizabeth J & Alfred Royster 20 Jul 1838; b- Eli Cox

Elizabeth & Archer Thomson 16 Mar 1812; b- William Mayes min- William Richards- 19Mar1812

Frances & Asher Stone 13 Nov 1797; s of William Stone Sr and Tabitha Stone b- John Cox min- William Richards- 30Nov1797

Francinia & Thomas Green 22 Mar 1792; Thomas from Lunenburg County b- John Cox Jr min- John Williams- 5Apr1792

Letitia & David Ellington 2 Dec 1793; b- Thomas Green min- John Williams- 19Dec1793

Lucretia & William Mayes 26 Dec 1806; b- Miles Hall min- William Richards- 29Dec1806

Lucy Ann & John Reese 13 Apr 1853; min- P.F. August-

Mary F & David Blacketter 13 Dec 1796; b- Edward Cox

Mary & William Nash 17 Nov 1828; b- Wilson Cox con- Archer Cox, father min- James Smith- 18Nov1828

Nancy & Miles Hall 8 Sep 1806; b- John Cox min- William Richards- 18Sep1806

Patsey & John Allen 14 Jan 1793; b- Thomas Cox min- William Creath- 22Jan1793

Phebe & Lowry Booker 11 Dec 1780; b- John Clay con- John Cox, Sr. (relation not cited)

Phebe & Robert J Newton 18 Aug 1828; b- James H Newton min- Pleasant Gold- (Baptist)- 22Aug1828

Rebecca & John Moss 11 Dec 1809; b- Charles Cox min- James Meacham- 21Dec1809

Sarah & Joseph Hamilton 16 May 1791; b- Edward Hatsell

Sarah & Edward Hatsell 16 Mar 1804; b- Stephen Hatsell

Sarah & James Johnston 12 Sep 1796; b- James Johnson

Susan & Bushrod Winstead 10 Apr 1811; b- Eli Cox con- John Cox, father min- William Richards- 11Apr1811

Susanna & John Phillips 2 Dec 1829; min- Pleasant Gold- (Baptist)-

Susanna & John Pritchett 14 Dec 1795; b- William Hudson min- William Creath- 23Dec1795

Talitha & Isham Browder 3 Feb 1767; b- John Cox Isham from Halifax County con- Mary Cox, mother & guardian of Talitha con- John Cox, bro of Talitha

Craddock

Mary A & William Leaker 7 Jun 1832; b- Charles Hudson Jr

Nancy & C T Scruggs 19 Sep 1842; b- E A Craddock

Sally H & Henry Vaughan 21 Oct 1829; b- David Almand con- Jesse Craddock, brother of Sally

Crawley

Elizabeth & Lewis Green 8 Sep 1788; b- John Baskervill min- Thomas Scott-

Lucy & Armistead Burwell 14 Nov 1791; b- Robert Crawley

Creath

Eliza H & Benjamin Fennell 11 Jun 1831; b- J W D Creath min- John B. Smith-

Harriet S & John Clayton 9 Mar 1822; b- William P Creath min- Thomas M. Jeffries- (Lunenburg County)- 29Mar1822

Lucretia J & Charles T Love 24 Feb 1841; b- M L Creath con- Lucretia Creath, mother min- Joseph W.D. Creath- (Nottoway County)-

Susannah M & John Gregory 10 Nov 1812; b- James Creath con- William Creath, father min- Richard Dabbs- (Lunenburg County)-

Creedle

Elizabeth & Daniel Insco 13 Mar 1822; min- Charles Ogburn- (Methodist)

Elizabeth & Russell Talley 14 Jul 1791; b- Bryant Creedle

Hannah & Howell Collier 16 Nov 1793; b- Lewis Collier

Lucy & John Walker 8 Mar 1843; b- William H Creedle min- James McAden-

Martha & Thomas Insco 24 Dec 1833; b- Bryant Creedle con- Martha Creedle, mother

Sally & Samuel S Simmons 20 Jun 1825; b- Francis C Edmundson

Crenshaw

Caroline C & Allen Hunt 6 Dec 1819; b- John Crenshaw min- Silas Shelburne- (Lunenburg County)- 23Dec1819

Elizabeth A & John D Tisdale 20 Feb 1832; b- John R Crenshaw con- Elizabeth Crenshaw, mother min- Daniel Petty-

Frances M D & William L Bragg 24 Oct 1831; b- John Crenshaw con- Elizabeth Crenshaw, mother min- David Wood- 10Dec1831

Jane C & Joseph H Snead 16 Jan 1834; b- John R Crenshaw min- Daniel Petty-

Lucy G & Green W Crowder 10 Jan 1831; b- John R Crenshaw con- Elizabeth Crenshaw, mother min- John Wesley Childs- 12Jan1831

Lucy Smith & John Tabb 13 Nov 1816; b- John T Keen min- William Richards-

Martha E A & William A Harris 3 Dec 1838; b- John P Crenshaw min- Benjamin R. Duval-

Martha & Hastin Hicks 1 Jun 1813; b- Wylie Crowder

Mary A & Joel P Bragg 19 Jun 1841; b- James C Bridgeforth con- Elizabeth Crenshaw, mother

Mary & Thomas A Jones 18 Dec 1799; b- James Jones

Nancy & William W Mason 9 Sep 1805; b- G H Baskervill min- Matthew Dance- 13Sep1805

Rachel & Major Harwood Jones 20 Oct 1809; b- G H Baskervill con- Thomas A Jones, guardian of Rachel min- William Richards- 24Oct1809

Crew

Delia & Elijah Evans Avory 12 Jun 1809; b- Leeman Haile

Parthena & Cleaton Jones 13 Jul 1807; b- Ruel Allen min- William Richards- 17Jul1807

Crews

Nancy & Nathaniel Robertson 9 Dec 1799; b- Richard H Walker

Sarah A & John T Carter 1 Jan 1844; b- William G Kimbrough

Susannah & William Hendrick 8 Mar 1772; b- John Atkinson

Crook

Eliza & Edward Lett 10 Jun 1814; b- Osborne Crook min- Charles Ogburn- (Methodist) 12Jun1814

Martha G & Waddy J Jackson 15 Jan 1821; b- William B Crook con- Martha Crook, mother min- James Smith- 5Feb1821

Rebeccah & John Singleton 8 Oct 1801; b- James Nash

Crow

Lucy & David Hailey 3 Dec 1804; b- Jachonias Towler

Martha S & John Edmonds 18 Mar 1844; b- Thomas Edmonds min- Thomas E. Locke- (Lunenburg County)- 1Apr1844

Mary & James Vaughan 26 Dec 1808; b- William Crow

Crowder

Alice & James L Simmons 18 Jan 1837; b- James R Harriss

Amey & John Carroll 28 Nov 1793; b- Daniel Tucker

Angelina & Alexander Pool 11 Oct 1790; b- Thomas Norment

Anne & John Carroll 23 Dec 1793; b- Richard Fox min- John Loyd- 24Dec1793

Betsy & William Holmes 25 Feb 1783; b- Charles Davis

Cary & John Martin 30 May 1797; b- Philemon Hurt, Jr min- William Richards- 1Jun1797

Delilah & Francis Kelley 25 May 1785; b- William Baskervill con- George Crowder, father

Elizabeth & Amos Ladd 15 Oct 1792; b- John Ladd Jr min- John Loyd- 16Oct1792

Elizabeth & Matthew Mullins 14 Sep 1795; b- James Hudson min- William Richards- 22Dec1795

Elizabeth & Thomas Thomason 20 Dec 1830; b- Charles W Baird con- Abraham Crowder, father min- James McAden-

Elvira A S B & Thomas D Manning 19 Dec 1830; b- John L Meacham min- James McAden-

Frances & John Holloway 12 Jan 1795; b- Godfrey Crowder min- William Richards- 22Jan1795

Frances & John Kelly 6 Dec 1804; b- Charles Kelly

Jane E & John Hagood 22 Dec 1841; b- William W Parks con- W T Crowder, father min- John B. Smith-

Jane & Hugh Wyley Nash 16 May 1853; con- Theophilus Crowder, father min- George W. Andrews- 18May1853

Levisy & Robert Rainey 27 Mar 1805; b- Nathaniel Crowder

Libelar & William (Jr) Drumwright 14 Jul 1797; b- William Drumwright min- Charles Ogburn- (Methodist) 21Jul1797

Lillia & Thomas (Jr) Burnett 15 Apr 1811; b- Joseph Lett min- William Richards- 16Apr1811

Linchey & Jacob Johnson 5 Feb 1795; b- Edmund Burnett con- John Crowder, father min- Charles Ogburn- (Methodist) 7Feb1795

Lucy & James T Hayes 31 Oct 1821; b- John T Hayes min- John S. Ravenscroft- (Episcopal)- 1Nov1821

Lydia & James Drumwright 9 Oct 1794; b- William Drumwright con- Richard Crowder, father min- John Loyd- 23Oct1794

Mahala & Edmond Taylor 9 Dec 1811; daughter of Richard Crowder Sr b- Richard Crowder

Martha & David Northington 13 Aug 1804; b- Peter Crowder min- James Watkins- 6Sep1804

Mary A & John W Brooks 20 Feb 1832; b- William Brummell min- John B. Smith-

Mary R & Drury J Major 18 Sep 1843; b- Creed T Haskins

Mary & John Calltharp 10 Feb 1784; b- Samuel Edmundson

Mary & William Carroll 3 Jan 1788; b- Bailey Turner

Mary & Thomas Evans 18 Jul 1821; b- Theophilus Crowder con- Martha Crowder, mother

Mary & Robert Hester 29 Jul 1795; b- Robert Hester Sr min- William Richards- 1Aug1795

Mary & Thomas (Jr) Ladd 6 Aug 1788; b- Josiah Floyd

Milly & Henry Burnett 21 Oct 1789; b- John Crowder

Obedience & Matthew Avery 12 Sep 1803; b- John Wagstaff min- William Richards-

Patsy & John Shaw 10 Nov 1800; b- Thomas Marriott min- William Creath-

Rebecca & Edmund Burnett 31 Oct 1797; b- Isaac Arnold con- John Crowder, father min- Charles Ogburn- (Methodist)- 20Nov1797

Rebecca & James R Harris 25 Nov 1831; b- Henry Simmons min- Charles Ogburn- (Methodist) 15Dec1831

Sally & David Thomas 18 Jan 1825; b- John J Singleton

Susan B & Tscharner DeGraffenreidt 2 Mar 1822; b- William B Stokes con- Godfrey Crowder, father min- William Richards- 5Mar1822

Susan & John Weaver 17 Feb 1844; b- Charles W Crowder con- Abraham Crowder, father min- James McAden-

Crutcher

Amanda C & Matthew W Jackson 26 May 1826; b- Robert C Hardy con- Miles Hardy, father

Crutchfield

Dorothy A & William N Puryear 18 Jun 1849; b- William C Crutchfield con- Peter Crutchfield, father min- James McAden- 21Jun1849

Elizabeth J & William H Hightower 29 Dec 1842; b- James M Crutchfield con- Samuel Crutchfield, father min- James McAden-

Lucy & Thomas Taylor 24 Jan 1797; b- William Drumwright min- John Loyd- 31Jan1797

Martha & John Harris 19 Dec 1803; b- William Crutchfield

Nancy & John R Harris 12 Oct 1835; b- Benjamin H Harris

Sally & Reuben T Harris 21 Sep 1835; b- Peter Crutchfield

Crute

Eliza A & John A Fore 12 Aug 1850; b- Joseph Crute

Gabriella W & David M Hancock 15 Oct 1849; b- Stephen C Lockett min- William Hamersley- 24Oct1849

Mary A & Miller W McCraw 21 Sep 1835; b- Willis R V Crute min- William B. Rowzee- 6Oct1835

Culbreath

Elizabeth & William Caviness 8 Feb 1796; 'Cabiness?' b- Henry Hester

Eveline & William Watkins 28 Nov 1840; b- William Culbreath

Lucy & Robert Hester 12 Jan 1807; b- John Farrar

Margaret & John Monroe 10 Mar 1789; b- Thomas Culbreath

Nancy & William H Royster 16 Aug 1813; b- Gray Holloway Nancy daughter of John Culbreath

Polly & Thomas Culbreath 8 May 1809; b- Hughes Matthews

Cumbia

Catherine & James Pritchett 19 Aug 1839; b- Thomas Cumbia min- Benjamin R. Duval-

Cunningham

Cornelia & Robert R Rogers 17 Oct 1826; b- R N Cunningham min- John B. Smith-

Eliza & James Yancey 22 Apr 1815; b- Abraham G Keen

Frances & John R Finch 2 May 1845; b- William E Dodson con- James Cunningham, father

Helen & John R Walker 2 Feb 1853; con- James Cunningham, father min- J.W. Chesley- 8Feb1853

Maria & Langston B Finch 17 Dec 1832; b- Robert M Cunningham min- William Steel- (Episcopal)- 20Dec1832

Maria & Richard C Pope 29 Nov 1852; con- James Cunningham, father min- J.W. Chesley- 30Nov1852

Martha & Edward Finch 12 Feb 1845; b- William E Dodson con- James Cunningham, father

Nancy & Allen Roberts 26 Apr 1813; b- Benjamin Freeman

Sally & John Baird 3 May 1805; b- Jesse Johnson

Curtis

Ann Maria & Benjamin Wingfield 13 Sep 1840; b- Solomon Lea min- Edward Wadsworth-

Betsey & John Gabard 25 Feb 1792; b- Ely Curtis min- John Loyd- 28Feb1792

Elizabeth & Francis Jackson 2 May 1807; b- Samuel Simmons min- Charles Ogburn- (Methodist) 16May1807

Jessie & Henry Bailey 17 Feb 1802; b- Jesse Curtis

Lucy & Grief Talley 16 Sep 1799; b- Drury Creedle min- Charles Ogburn- (Methodist)

Mary A & George Bing 15 Sep 1827; b- David B Johnson con- Zachariah Curtis, father min- Charles Ogburn- (Methodist) 20Sep1827

Parthena W & James Russell 25 Jun 1832; b- John F Curtis con- John Curtis, father

Rebecca Ann & Charles Mills 31 Oct 1845; b- Grief Green min- James J. Sledge-

Sally F & Alexander Johnson 4 Feb 1825; b- Peter T Ferguson con- Zachariah Curtis, father min- James Smith- 10Feb1825

Susan & Jonathon Phillips 19 Feb 1827; b- James D Brame con- Susan Curtis, mother min- Allen D. Metcalf-

Cutts

Mary Ann & Henry Vaughan 16 Dec 1837; b- John F Yancey con- Robert Yancey, father-in-law of Mary Ann(?)

Dailey

Susanna & James Eubank 1 Dec 1801; b- John Ferguson

Daly

Ann & Abel W Allen 14 Oct 1835; b- Cuthbert Wagstaff

Ann & Sterling Neblett 4 Oct 1798; b- Charles Ogburn con- Josiah Daly, father min- Charles Ogburn- (Methodist) 8Oct1798

Ann & John Singleton 4 Sep 1793; b- Daniel Daly min- John Loyd- 5Sep1793

Betsy & Sackfield Adams 23 Jun 1795; b- William Dailey min- John Loyd- 4 August 1795

Elizabeth B & James C Brame 9 Sep 1806; b- William Daly min- James Meacham- 11Sep1806

Elizabeth H & Peter R Gee 18 Jan 1808; b- Tignal Abernathy

Elizabeth & William Ezell 22 Apr 1811; b- Charles Baskervill

Mary A V & Thomas Carroll 5 Feb 1850; b- John W Baskerville Thomas Carroll from Warren Co., NC min- William A Smith- 14Feb1850

Mary Ann & Samuel (Jr) Farrar 1 Dec 1817; b- David C Hutcheson con- Josiah Daly, father min- Charles Ogburn- (Methodist) 4Dec1817

Sarah & Matthew Ogburn 15 Feb 1792; b- Charles Ogburn min- John Loyd- 16 Feb1792 con- Josiah Daly, father

Susanna & Thomas H Ferguson 10 Jul 1816; b- Josiah Daly min- James Meacham- 11Jul1816

Daniel

Adaline H & Thomas D Johnson 12 Apr 1845; Thomas from Caswell Co., NC b- A C Finley

Amelia & Bartlett Tillotson 16 Jul 1823; b- James Tillotson min- Pleasant Gold- (Baptist)-

Ann V & Samuel Watkins 7 Mar 1826; b- James B Daniel con- James Daniel, father

Cecily & Washington Wilkerson 1 Aug 1820; b- Stark Daniel

Dolly & Charles T Gold 28 Nov 1853; con- Avye R Daniel, mother min- John E. Montague- (Granville County, N.C.)- 1Dec1853

Frances Y & William Barnett 12 Jan 1836; b- Charles H Yancey con- Stark Daniel, father William Barnett from Granville Co., N.C. min- John B. Smith-

Judith C & Joel Watkins 19 Feb 1818; b- Howell L Jeffries

Luritta & James Clardy 18 Jun 1810; b- William Daniel

Margarett & John H Hewes 17 Dec 1849; b- Thomas Daniel con- A R Daniel, father

Martha & Thomas Yancey 26 Oct 1825; b- James Williamson con- Stark Daniel, father min- Pleasant Gold- (Baptist)- 2Nov1825

Mary Ann & George Butler 15 May 1841; b- William Cutts con- Martin Daniel, father

Mary Jane & Samuel D Booker 6 Oct 1837; b- Henry M Spencer con- James Daniel, father

Milly & John Hamblin 13 Jul 1807; b- Stephen Stone con- Martin Daniel, father

Milly & James Toone 9 Apr 1770; b- William Taylor con- William Daniel, father

Patsy Wooton & Frederick Wall 13 Jun 1803; b- William Daniel

Polly & Martin Daniel 9 Jun 1800; b- Thomas Daniel

Sally & Henry Wall 17 Dec 1810; b- Frederick Wall

Tabitha & Spencer C Wilkerson 19 Sep 1826; b- Stark Daniel min- Pleasant Gold- (Baptist)- 26Sep1826

Daves

Mary & Isaac H Jones 14 Dec 1836; b- Adam O Daves con- Ann Daves, mother min- James McAden-

Nancy & Henry Price 18 Oct 1821; b- William B Easley min- Alexander M. Cowan-

Rebecca M & Matthew Williams 13 Dec 1841; b- Adam O Daves min- James McAden-

Davis

Ann M & James M Fitts 9 Jun 1841; b- Henry G Fitts con- Anne Davis, mother

Edney W & Edwin B Archer 9 Dec 1833; widow b- Amos Roberts con- John Nance, father of Edney

Eliza H & Thomas P Wortham 17 Dec 1823; b- Horace Palmer con- William Hendrick, gdn of Eliza

Eliza & Bennett Nanney 26 Feb 1848; b- Dabney A Hudson con- Henry Davis, father

Elizabeth & Hardaway Davis 12 Aug 1771; b- Capt. William Davis

Elizabeth & Thomas Hite 2 Oct 1843; b- Edward Davis con- John O Davis, father min- Thomas King- (Halifax County)-

Elizabeth & Goodwyn Taylor 5 May 1802; b- David Dortch

Elizabeth & Thomas Vaughan 4 Feb 1828; b- Lewis G Crutchfield con- William Davis, father, who test Elizabeth 21

Elizabeth & John Watkins 28 Apr 1824; b- Stephen Davis con- Matthew Davis, gdn of Elizabeth min- Charles Ogburn- (Methodist)

Eugenia F & Richard H (Jr) Walker 27 May 1850; b- John Nelson con- Martha S Davis, mother

Jane H & John Alston 14 Dec 1799; b- Thomas H Davis min- Ebenezer McGowan- 19Dec1799

Jane J & James B Jones 3 Aug 1810; b- G H Baskervill

Jane & William Simmons 15 Jan 1830; b- Thomas Vaughan con- William Davis, father

Jane & John M Wright 10 Mar 1838; b- James T Russell con- John Davis, father min- William B. Rowzee-

Jancy & Banister Edmundson 16 Dec 1793; b- George B Hamner con- John Davis, father min- William Creath- 19Dec1793

Lucinda J & Thomas E Holmes 24 Oct 1848; b- William A Holmes con- George Holmes, father

Lucretia J & John Booth 3 Jan 1814; b- Hugh Davis min- John Allen- 4Jan1814

Lucy E M & Henry G Fitts 20 Mar 1837; con- Anne Davis, mother b- Horace Palmer

Lucy & Phil Hawkins 22 Aug 1775; daughter of William Davis Phil from Bute County NC b- William Davis

Mary Eliza & Edward Wiltse 21 Jun 1847; b- James B Dupuy co- Martha S Davis, mother min- William V. Wilson- 23Jun1847

Mary G & John F Lewis 31 Mar 1819; b- Alexander Goode con- Gray F Dunn, gdn of Mary

Mary H & Albert G Mason 16 Sep 1824; b- Daniel T Hicks con- William Davis, father

Mary & Charles King 25 Oct 1819; b- John Daws min- James Smith- 28Oct1819

Minerva J & Presley L Hinton 27 Jun 1836; b- Arthur K Davis con- Ann Davis, gdn of Minerva min- William B. Rowzee-

Nancy J & Benjamin U Turner 17 Dec 1849; b- John C Davis con- Willis S Davis,, father min- Richard E.G. Adams- (Lunenburg County)- 20Dec1849

Nancy & Samuel Cheatham 22 Dec 1803; b- William Davis

Nancy & James Cocke 16 Dec 1816; b- Stephen Power

Polly & Allen Lanier 21 Nov 1791; b- Josiah Floyd con- Charles & Martha Floyd, parents min- John King-

Polly & Henry Townes 31 Dec 1784; con- Barton Davis, father

Rebecca A & William L Paine 19 Jul 1824; b- T A Boyd con- Thomas Power, gdn of Rebecca

Rebecca M & Robert A Vaughan 4 Jan 1806; b- Bushrod Webb con- Ambrose Vaughan, father con- Randolph Davis, father

Sally & Amasa Palmer 2 Mar 1774; b- William Davis

Sarah & Jacob Bugg 27 Jul 1791; b- Sherwood Bugg con- John Davis, father

Sarah & Allen Young 22 May 1779; d of William Davis b- Samuel Young

Silviah & Sterling Wright 4 Jul 1788; b- Josiah Floyd

Susan A M & William B McAden 20 May 1850; b- J W McAden con- Benjamin W Davis, father min- D.J.C. Slaughter- 28May1850

Susan S & William H Boyd 1 Feb 1848; b- A G Boyd con- John Davis Sr, father min- William A. Smith- 16Feb1848

Susan & David E Jiggetts 13 Feb 1816; b- William Hendrick min- James Meacham- 15Feb1816

Susanah & Richard Atkinson 4 May 1815; widow b- William Bilbo

Susanna & Anthony Bennett 13 Dec 1779; b- John Brown

Unity C & Reuben Wright 18 Apr 1814; b- Green Blanton

Wincy & John Hite 10 Jan 1853; con- John O Davis, father

Daws

Elizabeth & John Simmons 27 Oct 1826; b- Isaac Holmes min- John B. Smith-

Frances T & William S Redd 2 Nov 1844; b- William Daws

Lucy & Roderick Coleman 18 Dec 1794; b- Isaac Daws con- James Daws, father min- Charles Ogburn- (Methodist) 25Dec1794

Martha E & Robert E F Mims 19 Jul 1853; min- George W. Andrews- 20Jul1853

Martha & Burwell Coleman 28 Jan 1794; b- Isaac Daws min- William Creath- 1Feb1794

Rebecca & Pennington Holmes 29 Jun 1798; b- John Daws min- Charles Ogburn- (Methodist) 4Jul1798

Sally A & Joseph L Wootton 27 Dec 1843; b- Howell Wilkerson con- John Wootton, father

Day

Patsy & John Bing 9 Jan 1816; b- Edmund Bing min- Charles Ogburn- (Methodist) 11Jan1816

DeGraffenreid

Ann W & James (Jr) Smith 15 Sep 1815; b- John J Wells con- Tscharner DeGraffenreid, gdn of Ann, daughter of William DeGraffenreid, dec.

Decker

Catey & John (Jr) Hayes 19 Aug 1794; b- William Decker

Dedman

Eleanor & Robert Wilson 9 Jun 1794; b- Larkin White min- John Williams- 13Jun1794

Elizabeth & Richard T Wood 21 Feb 1853; con- Amanda A Dedman, mother (Note: Richard gdn of Elizabeth Dedman) min- James S. Kennedy-

Nelly & Larkin White 9 Dec 1793; b- Henry Dedman

Virginia Ann & James Harris 10 Nov 1851; con- James W Dedman, father

Delk

Susan & Francis A Nolley 19 Feb 1842; b- William H Gee

Delony

Elizabeth Rebecca & Samuel H Warren 12 Dec 1820; b- Ludwell E Jones min- James Smith- 14Dec1820

Frances & Daniel Hicks 18 Sep 1788; b- William Delony daughter of Henry Delony

Lucy & Robert Edward Brooking 9 May 1779; b- Henry Delony Jr. con- Henry Delony, Sr., father con- Vivian Brooking, father Robert from Amelia County

Mary & Thomas (Jr) Pearson 19 Sep 1768; daughter of Henry Delony b- Henry Delony

Dennis

Lurita & Jacobus Christopher - — 178-; b- Moses Overton

Denton

Jane E T & John W Nicholson 12 Jun 1853; con- Elizabeth G Denton, mother min- Willis N. Pence-

Dodson

Ann & Melchizedeck Roffe 12 Dec 1800; b- William Dodson

Elizabeth & Richard Hudson 30 Jul 1810; b- Edward Dodson min- James Meacham- 31Jul1810

Harriett R & Benjamin D Cogbill 31 Oct 1853; min- J.W. Chesley- 1Nov1853

Lettice H & William Holloway 9 Aug 1825; b- Christopher W Baird con- Edward Dodson, father min- James Smith- 11Aug1825

Louisa E & Peter D Hudson 19 Feb 1828; b- Edmund Hester con- Edward Dodson, uncle of Louisa min- James Smith- 20Feb1828

Martha & Daniel Frazier 18 Feb 1822; b- Richard C Williams min- Charles Ogburn- (Methodist) 21Feb1822

Polly & Thompson Rowlett 9 Nov 1805; min- James Meacham- 18Nov1805

Doggett

Lucinda & William Garner 21 Sep 1825; b- Edward Toone min- William Richards- 22Sep1825

Mary & Cleophas Lamkin 19 Dec 1785; b- James Garner con- John and Mary Doggett, parents min- John Marshall- (Baptist) 23Dec1785

Rebecca S & Thomas S Gregory 19 Dec 1827; b- Francis Barnes min- William Richards- 28Dec1827

Sarah & James Gregory 14 Sep 1801; b- John Swansbow min- William Richards- 1Oct1801

Dortch

Ann I & James L Dortch 15 Nov 1824; b- L H Jones con- Betsy Dortch, mother min- James Smith- 9Dec1824

Ann & Benjamin Ferrell 11 Feb 1784; b- William Baskervill

Elizabeth Ann & Edward E Roffe 10 Nov 1845; b- Benjamin D Hightower con- Nancy T Crute, mother of Elizabeth min- James J. Sledge-

Elizabeth C & Ambrose Vaughan 16 Dec 1835; b- Jones M Taylor min- Stephen Turner- 17Dec1835

Elizabeth & Benjamin H Holmes 24 Dec 1827; b- J H Jones con- Zachariah H Jones, gdn of Elizabeth, daughter of David Dortch, dec. min- James Smith- 27Dec1827

Hannah F & Archer Hayes 19 Sep 1842; b- Isaac H Jones con- Alex Dortch, father

Harriet & Edward Walker 6 Jan 1817; b- William Evans con- David Dortch, father min- Charles Ogburn- (Methodist) 8Jan1817

Helina & Nathaniel Moss 8 Oct 1777; b- Labon Wright

Lucy R & James M Tucker 20 Oct 1824; b- Newman Dortch min- James Smith-

Lucy & Iverson Ryland 23 Feb 1784; n- Nathaniel Moss

Maria & Isaac Jones 16 Dec 1822; b- Edward Walker min- James Smith- 19Dec1822

Martha C & Samuel S Holmes 1 Nov 1830; b- Arthur G Holmes con- Rebecca J Dortch, mother con- Alexander Dortch, gdn of Martha min- James Smith- 4Nov1830

Mary J & Christopher Gayle 19 Dec 1825; b- Zachariah H Jones min- James Smith- 22Dec1825

Mary Speed & David Poythress 17 Dec 1827; b- Isaac Taylor con- Ann Dortch, mother

Nancy T & Willis R V Crute 20 Mar 1843; 'Dr.' Willis R V Crute and 'Mrs.' Nancy T Dortch b- Christopher Gayle min- Joseph A Brown-

Rebecca & David Taylor 9 May 1778; d of David Dortch b- William Taylor

Sally & Anderson Byers 14 Dec 1813; b- John D Hank

Sarah T & William R Baskerville 16 Feb 1824; b- Charles Baskerville min- James Smith- 19Feb1824

Susan & Green J Thomas 31 Oct 1836; b- William B King con- Rebecca T Dortch, mother con- Alexander Dortch, gdn of susan

Douglas

Elizabeth & Jeremiah Brown 28 Aug 1770; b- William Douglas

Elizabeth & John McKinney 24 Dec 1792; b- David Thomas con- S Douglas, father min- John Loyd- 27Dec1792

Polly & Isaac Carroll 18 Sep 1811; d of Senior Douglas b- William Burton

Draper

Elizabeth & Joseph Royster 12 Dec 1791; b- Holeman Rice min- James Read- (Baptist) 27Dec1791

Frances & Henry Royster 8 Nov 1790; b- Joseph Royster

Mary & Thomas Cox 7 Mar 1796; b- Thomas Pritchett min- William Creath- 8Mar1796

Rebecca & Littleberry Whitt 13 Oct 1826; b- James Jones min- John B. Smith-

Sarah & David Hudson 3 Dec 1789; b- John Hudson min- Edward Almand- 5Dec1789

Drew

Delilah & Berry Lewis 22 Aug 1839; b- George Stoneham con- James and Polly Drew, parents min- Edward Wadsworth-

Elizabeth & Bartlett Stewart 21 Oct 1807; b- George Guy

Nancy & George Guy 11 Dec 1799; b- William Chandler min- Ebenezer McGowan- 12Dec1799

Nancy & George Guy 11 Dec 1799; b- William Chandler

Precilla & William Chavous 29 Dec 1806; b- Benjamin Lewis min- William Richards- 30Dec1806

Drummond

Mavel & Zachariah Bowen 2 Oct 1795; b- Thomas Drummond Zachariah son of James Bowen and Susannah Bowen min- Charles Ogburn- (Methodist) 8Oct1795

Nancy & Elias Curtis 28 Jan 1794; b- Thomas Drummond con- Jane Drummond, mother min- Charles Ogburn- (Methodist) 31Jan1794

Drumwright

Eliza & Asbury Benford 6 Aug 1838; b- Gee Drumwright con- William Drumwright, father min- James McAden-

Frances & Joseph Arnold 24 Sep 1800; b- William Drumwright

Lucy S & Jesse J Smith 12 Jun 1852; con- Gee Drumwright, father min- James McAden-

Lucy & Henry Morris 15 Dec 1807; b- William Drumwright

Martha H & Briant Creedle 24 Feb 1834; b- Wesley F Edmundson con-
Ephraim Drumwright, father

Martha & Samuel Goodwin Hunt 20 Dec 1802; b- William Drumwright,
father

Mary Ann & William H Taylor 14 Aug 1839; b- E A Drumwright con-
Ephraim Drumwright, father min- Benjamin R. Duval-

Mary & Elisha Arnold 19 Dec 1831; con- William Drumwright, father
min- James McAden-

Nancy & William J Morris 24 Jan 1831; b- Lucas Drumwright con-
William Drumwright, father min- James McAden-

Nancy & Goodwyn Taylor 10 Jan 1794; b- William Drumwright min-
John Loyd- 21Jan1794

Rebecca W & Lucas Morris 15 Dec 1840; b- E A Drumwright con-
Ephraim Drumwright, father min- James McAden-

Rebecca & Starling Waller 1 Sep 1796; b- William Drumwright

Rhoann R & William D Pully 18 Dec 1850; con- George Drumwright,
father min- James McAden-

Sally L & Isaac Medley 17 Apr 1843; b- William P Drumwright con-
Sally O Drumwright, mother min- Joseph A Brown- 20Apr1843

Sally Williams & Jesse Morris 26 Jan 1804; b- William Drumwright con-
William Drumwright, father min- William Creath-

Sarah S & Peter H Rainey - Jan 1853; min- James McAden-

Duncan

Mary Elizabeth & Lucien H Lomax 21 Jul 1845; b- David Duncan min-
William B. Rowzee- 26Jul1845

Dunnavant

Frances W & William Mitchell 19 Aug 1816; b- Abel B Dunnavant con-
Joel Dunnavant, father min- James Meacham- 21Aug1816

Lucy & John Mills 13 Feb 1850; b- Bennett B Goode

Martha & Joseph Yancey 18 Oct 1839; b- Richard Glasscock min- John
B. Smith-

Dunnavon

Martha & Samuel Lunsford 13 Feb 1822; min- Pleasant Gold- (Baptist)-

Dunston

Ann Eliza & Irby Nash 15 Nov 1830; b- Richard M Dunn min- William
Steel- (Episcopal)-

Delia Ann & John R Lewis 11 Jul 1839; b- Thomas Stewart min-
Benjamin R. Duval-

Elizabeth & William D Lewis 5 Aug 1845; b- Henderson Dunston

Evelina & Irby Ligon 29 Oct 1833; b- Richard Dunston con- Sophia
Ligon, mother min- William Steel- (Episcopal)- 30Oct1833

Tempy & Banister Nash 10 Mar 1835; b- James Chavous min- William
Steel- (Episcopal)-

Dupree

Rebecca J & William B Taylor 20 Jul 1839; b- Obadiah Hatchell Rebecca
herself test. that she is 23 min- Benjamin R. Duval-

Duprey

Jane & Alexander Dacus 17 Nov 1789; b- Drury Duprey Alexander
Dacus from Lunenburg County

Durham

Nancy & Archer Johnson 14 May 1804; b- James Williams min- William
Richards- 25May1804

Patsy & Benjamin Bailey 11 Jun 1798; b- Valentine McCutcheon min-
William Richards- 28Jun1798

Sarah & Charles Hood 28 Jun 1786; b- James Willis min- John Marshall-
(Baptist) 15Jul1786

Easter

Margaret & Jordan Anderson 6 Jun 1785; b- Lewis Rolfe Jordan from Prince Edward County

Martha & John Crow 28 Dec 1802; b- Jeremiah Adams

Sarah & James Wright 23 Dec 1784; b- Leonard Smith

Susanna & Bailey Turner 1 Dec 1792; b- John Oliver min- Edward Almand- 20Dec1792

Eastham

Dicy & William Lisk 21 Dec 1803; b- Richard Crowder

Eastland

Elizabeth & John Lumsdon 8 Feb 1788; b- Robert White min- Edward Almand- 9Feb1788

Mary & Joseph Akin 10 Oct 1774; b- William Eastland

Eaton

Nancy & Mark Alexander 18 Oct 1804; b- William Baskervill

Rose & Isham Tucker 2 Feb 1786; b- James Bing

Sarah A & Charles B Coleman 13 Feb 1836; min- William Steel- (Episcopal)-

Eddins

Lucy & James Garner 11 Jan 1790; b- Thomas Dance min- Edward Almand-

Edmonds

Phoebe & Howell M Taylor 31 Mar 1823; b- David Taylor

Edmondson

Martha & Joseph Anderson 12 Aug 1794; b- William Phillips min- William Creath-

Edmonson

Angelina & Wilshire Simmons 1 Mar 1830; b- Samuel Simmons min- James Smith- 2Mar1830

Ann & Richard (Jr) Manley 16 Aug 1824; b- Samuel Simmons Sr min- Charles Ogburn- (Methodist) 30Aug1824

Jane B & Hartwell Reekes 24 Nov 1834; b- Samuel G Patillo

Nancy C & Alfred Gee 15 Oct 1821; min- Charles Ogburn- (Methodist)

Permelia & Edward Simmons 18 Mar 1814; b- Richard H Edmonson

Edmundson

Anne & George B Hamner 16 Dec 1793; b- Banister Edmundson con- Samuel Edmundson, father min- William Creath- 19Dec1793

Elizabeth & John Rudd 15 Oct 1810; b- Brown Avory min- William Richards- 25Oct1810

Jane & Thomas Wall 13 Jan 1800; b- John Whobry min- William Creath-

Rachel & William Phillips 14 Oct 1793; b- George B Hamner con- Samuel Edmundson, father

Edwards

Elizabeth & Gabriel Carleton 14 Jan 1788; b- John Edwards Gabriel son of Thomas Carleton min- Thomas Scott-

Louisa Caroline & Samuel Daly - Sep 1821; b- James Crook min- James Smith- 6Sep1821

Martha A & John Jewell 18 Jan 1833; b- John Wortham

Martha & William Crook 11 Apr 1791; b- John Edwards Jr min- Edward Almand- 13Apr1791

Mary R & Samuel Puryear 17 Dec 1822; b- R C Puryear con- Martha R Edwards, widow, mother min- John S. Ravenscroft- (Episcopal)-

Nancy & Thomas Neely 9 Feb 1813; b- James Meacham min- James Meacham- 11Feb1813

Polly F & Alexander B Puryear 30 Jun 1815; b- Philip Rainey con- Thomas Neal, gdn of Polly, who is daughter of Peter Edwards, dec.

Polly & Henry Bailey 9 Dec 1793; b- Thomas Edwards con- John Edwards, father

Elam

Charlotte & Daniel G Callis 22 Sep 1813; b- Joel Elam con- Jane Elam, mother con- William Callis, father min- William Richards- 30Sep1813

Elizabeth & John Elam 13 Oct 1806; b- James Hurt min- William Richards- 23Oct1806

Elizabeth & Martin Gillespie 10 Feb 1806; b- Henry H Dedman min- William Richards- 20Feb1806

Frances & William Graves 14 Oct 1795; b- Thomas Graves min- William Richards- 20Oct1795

Jane & Samuel McDowell 25 May 1833; b- Andrew G Elam con- Daniel Elam, father min- George Petty- 28May1833

Judith & John Jones 23 Dec 1818; b- William Jones

Labia & Burwell Grigg 8 Oct 1787; b- Alexander Elam min- John Williams-

Martha R & Henry Ezell Newton 13 Nov 1849; b- John G Elam con- Daniel Elam, father min- Alfred Apple- 30Nov1849

Martha & Jesse Grigg 11 Dec 1786; b- James Elam

Martha & Harrison Hastin 8 Nov 1815; b- Charles Taylor con- Eli Elam, father

Martha & Harrison Hester 8 Nov 1815; min- Ezekiel Blanch-

Mary I & William Harris 27 Sep 1799; b- Daniel Wilson con- Barklet Elam, father

Mary & Gideon Freeman 10 Jan 1803; b- Philemon Hurt min- William Richards- 19Jan1803

Mary & Henry Lonnon 13 Dec 1803; b- Phillip Ryan min- Edward Almand- 15Dec1803

Mary & Alex Yancey 22 Oct 1839; b- Daniel Elam min- John B. Smith-

Nancy Y & William S Gordon 30 Oct 1851; con- Daniel Elam, father min- John E. Montague- (Granville County, N.C.)-

Nancy & John Hastin 8 Oct 1787; b- Absolom Hastin

Nancy & Benjamin Royster 19 Nov 1838; b- Silas M Gregory min- John B. Smith-

Phebe & James Graves 23 Dec 1818; b- Nathan Graves min- William Richards- 29Dec1818

Phebe & Philip B Moore - Dec 1789; b- Peter Elam min- John Williams- 24Dec1789

Phoebe & Dabney Collier 3 Jun 1824; min- William Steel- (Episcopal)- 3Jun1824

Sally M & James W Newton 21 Nov 1842; b- Richard T Elam con- Daniel Elam, father

Sarah & Charles Stewart 14 Nov 1808; b- Frederick Ivey min- William Richards- 7Apr1809

Susan & Reazin P Yancey 12 Oct 1840; b- Daniel Elam

Susanna & Joel Elam 17 Feb 1812; b- John Elam min- William Richards- 20Feb1812

Elliott

Jinny & George Cabiness 30 Nov 1799; b- Thomas Finch con- Martin Elliott, father min- William Richards- 2Dec1799

Lucy A H & William Jones 24 Jan 1848; b- Elias Griffin con- Elizabeth Elliott, mother

Sylvania & James D Phillips 27 Nov 1851; con- Sylvania Elliott, mother min- John E. Montague- (Granville County, N.C.)-

Ellis

Patsy & Samuel Crutchfield 25 Dec 1804; b- Jesse Perkinson

Patsy & Independence Poarch 2 Feb 1807; b- Morris Green Burton

Sally & John Smith 29 Jan 1796; b- John Loyd min- John Loyd- 30Jan1796

Sarah & Starling Fowler 4 Dec 1802; b- Jesse Perkinson min- James Meacham- 8Dec1802

Emery

Hally & George Saunders 3 Dec 1804; b- Thomas Saunders

Polly & William Saunders 30 Sep 1812; b- Daniel Morris min- Richard Dabbs- (Lunenburg County)- 1Oct1812

Epperson

Celey & Salle Jackson 2 Oct 1802; b- Henry Jackson min- Balaam Ezell- 7Oct1802

Claresy & Mastin Wiles 13 Sep 1802; b- Joseph Epperson min- Balaam Ezell- 16Oct1802

Elizabeth & John Francis 8 Sep 1794; b- Joseph Townes min- William Richards- 1Nov1794

Fanny & Collin Campbell 30 Nov 1785; b- John Campbell

Eppes

Elizabeth & William Murphey 8 May 1779; b- Isham Eppes

Martha & Herman Shell 9 Oct 1790; Herman from Brunswick County b- John Eppes min- William Heath- (Methodist)- 19Oct1790

Epps

Tabitha & John Henry Wartman 24 Nov 1787; b- Isham Epps

Erby

Nancy & Daniel Guy 26 Feb 1806; b- William Chandler

Erskine

Mary C & Jesse Hord 12 Feb 1798; son of Thomas Hord b- William Christopher min- Edward Almand- 15Mar1798

Estes

Elva & Crawford McDaniel 15 Jan 1819; min- Charles Ogburn- (Methodist) 19Jan1819

Mary E & Jesse Craddock 27 Apr 1841; b- Harwood B Tucker con- Charles Estes, father

Nancy W & Howard Wells 18 Dec 1818; min- Charles Ogburn- (Methodist)

Eubank

Ann R & Samuel H Jones 5 Jan 1827; b- Green Jackson min- John B. Smith- 9Jan1827

Elizabeth P & William Dortch 21 Oct 1848; William from Missouri b- Christopher Gayle min- Thomas Adams- (Lunenburg Co.)- 22Oct1848

Lucy R & Nathaniel M Peoples 5 Oct 1836; b- Thomas G Boyd con- Benjamin Coleman, gdn of Lucy min- William B. Rowzee-

Rebecca W & Samuel Farrar 8 Aug 1848; b- Christopher Gayle min- James McAden- 9Aug1848

Susan W & William A Keeton 17 May 1841; b- Samuel A Jones

Evans

Ann & Christopher Stewart 12 Jan 1841; b- Richard Mayo min- Edward Wadsworth-

Catharine & John F Reagan 5 Oct 1791; b- William Taylor min- Edward Almand- 23Oct1791

Delila & James Thomas 27 Dec 1819; b- John Stewart con- Elizabeth Evans, mother

Delilah & Thomas McLin 23 Dec 1794; b- John Guy min- John Loyd- 24Dec1794

Eliza A & Walker Evans - Sep 1845; b- John P Smith con- Benjamin Evans, father

Elizabeth & Nathaniel Malone 31 May 1777; b- Stephen Mabry con- Stephen Evans, father

Elizabeth & Freeman Short 1 Sep 1808; b- George Finch

Elvira A & Evans Walker - — 1845; min- James McAden-

Elvira & Donaldson P Evans 21 Jan 1838; b- Hartwell Johnson

Lucy M & James W Walker 29 Jun 1847; b- Phillip H Thomas con- Ben S Evans, father min- James McAden- 1Jul1847

Martha W & John F Thomas 16 Nov 1829; b- William Evans min- James Smith- 18Nov1829

Martha & James Farley 26 Jul 1786; James from Amelia County b- Henry Farley con- James Farley Sr., father con- Stephen Evans, father

Mary B & Paul C Jeffries 1 Dec 1817; b- Booker Foster con- William and Mary Richards, parents min- William Richards- 4Dec1817

Mary W & Phillip H Thomas 18 Nov 1839; b- Anthony Evans con- Benjamin Evans, father min- James McAden-

Mary & Gilliam P Chavous 21 Jul 1829; b- Admiral Dunston min- Charles Ogburn- (Methodist)

Mary & Harrison Moseley 16 May 1825; b- William Evans

Mary & William Richards 14 Dec 1801; b- Richard Jeffries min- William Creath-

Mary & John Roberts 15 Dec 1828; b- Samuel S Simmons con- Robert Evans, father

Nancy W & Ithy G Burton 11 Apr 1832; b- Ishmael Thomason

Nancy W & Robert Parham 31 Oct 1845; b- John Hunley min- James McAden-

Nancy W & William E Walker 20 Jan 1845; b- David R Walker con- Benjamin Evans, father min- James McAden-

Nancy & David Harrison Crowder 7 Dec 1841; b- Claiborne Evans min- David Petty-

Nancy & Benjamin W Jeffries 11 Dec 1809; b- Matthew Baptist min- William Richards- 14Dec1809

Nanny & Eaton Walden 20 Dec 1788; b- Moses Stuart con- Charles Evans, father

Permelia & Isaac Valentine 28 May 1838; b- John Stewart con- Mary Chavous, mother of Permelia min- Benjamin R. Duval- 19Jun1838

Polly & William Cazy 23 Dec 1786; b- Kinchen Chavous

Prudence & Charles McCutcheon 11 Dec 1797; b- Richard Jeffries min- Edward Almand- 14Dec1797

Rebeccah & William Marshall 17 Dec 1803; b- Matthew Evans

Roanna & William Helm 22 Jul 1830; b- Benjamin Evans min- James Smith-

Sally & John House 9 Apr 1808; b- Labon Short con- Elizabeth Evans, mother

Sally & Jacob Mayo 15 Feb 1841; b- James Mayo

Susan & Henderson Wingfield 20 May 1833; b- Thomas Evans min- William Steel- (Episcopal)- 21May1833

Ezell

Ann J & Samuel H Cook 3 Apr 1836; b- William E Ezell con- Elizabeth Exell, mother min- James McAden-

Caroline T & Claiborne Drumwright 30 Jan 1837; b- Benjamin H Rogers con- Rebecca A Ezell, mother con- William Drumwright, father min- James McAden-

Elizabeth & Samuel H Walker 18 Dec 1815; b- Diggs Poynor con- William Ezell, father

Emily F & Owen G Strange 16 Dec 1844; b- Joseph M Drumwright con- Claiborne Drumwright, gdn of Emily min- James McAden-

Margaret E & Thomas F Drumwright 19 Oct 1840; b- Claiborne Drumwright con- Rebecca A Ezell, mother con- William Drumwright, father, who test. William under 21

Martha B & Lafayette Crutchfield 19 Dec 1850; con- Rebecca A Tucker, mother of Martha min- James McAden-

Martha & Edward Giles 31 Jan 1801; b- Thomas Nancy

Mary Ann & William J Mason 7 Oct 1833; b- James Connell con- Robertson Ezell, father

Patsy & Henry Newton 23 Dec 1811; b- Thomas Stovall con- Balaam Ezell, father

Rebecca A & George Tucker 4 Apr 1842; b- Edward R Chambers min- James McAden-

Rebecca & William Daws 19 Dec 1814; b- Edward L Tabb con- William Ezell, father

Rebecca & John Hudson 26 Mar 1794; b- Thomas Calvery min- John Loyd- 28Mar1794

Tabitha T & Robert Shanks 17 Feb 1841: b- John H Ezell min- James McAden-

Fagins

Delany & Harris Mayo 15 Dec 1842; b- William H Boyd con- Polly Fagins, mother, who test Delany 21

Fain

Patty & Abdias Webb 15 Dec 1790; b- Frederick Rainey

Fargeson

Martha & Daniel Fraser 14 Feb 1805; b- John Fraser

Farmer

Sally & Newton Wright 30 Nov 1819; b- John B Yancey con- James Farmer, father min- Pleasant Gold- (Baptist)-

Farrar

Ann O & William Griffin 16 Oct 1820: b- John J Farrar con- John Farrar Sr, father

Bettie P & Henry A Moss 25 Nov 1852; con- Henry C Moss, father con- Samuel Farrar, father min- George W. Andrews-

Dianna & Daniel W McDaniel 10 Nov 1831; b- Jesse H Clarke min- Charles Ogburn- (Methodist)

Elizabeth B & John B Roffe 17 Jan 1825; b- William H Farrar con- John Farrar Jr, father min- Charles Ogburn- (Methodist) 20Jan1825

Elizabeth & John Finch 18 Apr 1787; b- Peter Farrar con- John Farrar, father

Elizabeth & James Manning 19 Mar 1827; b- John Farrar, gdn, who also gives consent min- John B. Smith- 20Mar1827

Elizabeth & John Whittemore 17 Dec 1816; b- Phillip R Johnson con- George Farrar, father min- Charles Ogburn- (Methodist) 18Dec1816

Ellinor & Thomas Watkins 8 Nov 1790; b- Thomas Farrar min- James Read- (Baptist)

Hannah & William Farrar 22 Dec 1824; b- John Farrar min- James Smith-

Jane E & Henry C W Farris 4 Jun 1832; b- Dabney Farrar min- William Steel- (Episcopal)-

Jane & William Newton 25 Dec 1823; b- Abel Farrar min- Pleasant Gold- (Baptist)-

Judith J & Redmond R Smith 18 Feb 1824; b- Lemuel Robertson con- Farrar, gdn of Judith min- Charles Ogburn- (Methodist)

Judith J & John J Turner 16 May 1815; b- William R Bilbo con- John Farrar, father min- James Meacham- 20May1815

Martha & Allen Moss Bilbo 15 Dec 1810; b- Benjamin Whitlow min-James Meacham- 20Dec1810

Martha & Carter Clarke 9 Nov 1778; b- Edward Finch con- John Farrar who test that bride over 21

Martha & Phillip R Johnson 26 Jan 1812; b- Woodson V Johnson con-George Farrar, father min- Charles Ogburn- (Methodist) 29Jan1812

Mary E & John T A Williams 6 Dec 1852; con- John B Roffe, gdn of Mary min- George W. Andrews- 8Dec1852

Mary S & Samuel H Goode 18 Apr 1846; b- Charles Baskervill con-Robert Farrar, father

Nancy & Edward Holloway 8 Nov 1806; b- Francis Ballard min- James Meacham- 11Nov1806

Rebecca B & Edmund B Mealey 10 Jan 1843; b- Francis T Weaver

Rebecca & Jacob Bugg 12 Mar 1811; b- James Noel con- Samuel Farrar, father min- James Meacham- 14Mar1811

Sarah & Thomas Farrar 13 Dec 1790; b- James Faucet

Sarah & Woody Vaughan 11 Dec 1804; b- Sanford Bowers con- George Farrar, father

Tabitha & John Griffin 22 Dec 1815; b- John Winckler min- James Meacham- 25Dec1815

Feagins

Lisha & Joshua Preston 18 Dec 1792; b- John Saunders Joshua from Brunswick County min- John Loyd- 20Dec1792

Feagons

Martha & Beverly Valentine 21 Dec 1840; b- John Stewart con- Thomas Feagos, father min- James McAden-

Featherston

Elizabeth & Richard Coleman Edmundson 18 May 1812; b- Drury Creedle min- Charles Ogburn- (Methodist)

Feggins

Mary Theny & Mark Maclin 23 Dec 1851; con- Thomas Maclin, grandfather of Mark

Feild

Eliza & Drury S Feild 23 Mar 1814; b- Edmund Taylor

Margaret & Miles Wilson 13 Feb 1809; b- Erasmus Kennon con- Jane Feild, mother min- George Micklejohn-

Martha A & Charles H K Taylor 11 Mar 1839; b- Henry E Lockett

Martha C & John S Feild 19 Jun 1832; b- Robert Redd min- William Steel- (Episcopal)-

Mary E & Robert Redd 14 Apr 1834; b- John S Feild min- William Steel- (Episcopal)- 22Apr1834

Nancy T & Alexander Feild 22 Dec 1832; b- Robert S Feild con- Eliza B Feild, mother min- William Steel- (Episcopal)- 24Dec1832

Feilder

Martha J & Jesse M Paulette 30 Jan 1850; b- W O Manning con- Dennis R Feilder, father

Ferguson

Elizabeth R & William C Hughes 8 Nov 1838; b- Adam O Daves con-Celia F Ferguson, mother min- Benjamin R. Duval-

Mary C & Lewis Y Poythress 20 Jul 1846; b- William A Dortch

Sarah & Richard Hanserd 18 Jun 1801; b- John Dortch min- James Meacham-

Susan & William Turner 19 Aug 1817; b- John Winckler

Ferrell

Elizabeth T & James Daws 11 Jun 1798; b- Hubbard Ferrell min-William Creath- 19Jul1798

Martha & David Tanner 6 May 1802; b- Hutchins Ferrell

Sarah & Elijah Wells 14 Sep 1795; b- John Hudson

Field

Jane & Thomas B Holt 25 May 1802; b- John Dortch

Lavenia & Orlando Marcellus Smith 4 Feb 1841; b- Henry F Jones con- Anthony M Smith, father of Orlando, who is under 21

Fielder

Sarah E & Edward Barbee 3 Dec 1846; b- Dennis R Fielder

Finch

Frances & Robert Pennington 26 Jan 1787; b- Sherwood Smith

Phebe & Jacob Short 23 Oct 1794; b- William Finch min- John Loyd-

Polly & William Booker 10 Nov 1802; b- John Puryear Jr min- William Richards-

Susanna & Thomas Binford 2 May 1795; b- William Finch min- John Loyd- 3May1795

Finn

Jincy & Hugh Bowen 30 Nov 1801; b- Littleberry Bowen

Prudence & Edward Morris 8 Feb 1799; b- Nicholas Lanier min- William Creath- 11Feb1799

Sally & Isaac Marshall 23 May 1795; b- David Pennington min- John Loyd- 26May1795

Finney

Mary & Richardson Walker 14 Aug 1823; b- John Haskins con- William Haskins, gdn of Mary min- Pleasant Gold- (Baptist)-

Flinn

Ann & Jeremiah Johnson 16 Mar 1846; b- William T White

Elizabeth J & John M Collier 22 Dec 1848; b- Jeremiah Johnson min- Robert Burton-

Floyd

Eliza J & Joseph C Singleton 14 Aug 1848; b- B H Merryman con- Zachariah Floyd, father

Julia Ann & Isaac Taylor 21 Oct 1844; b- Ashley Daniel con- Zachary and Christany Floyd, parents

Margaret Susan & Robertson D Taylor 24 Oct 1849; b- James W Whittemore con- Christany Floyd, mother

Margarett S & Taylor D Robertson 25 Oct 1849; min- James McAden-

Mary E G & William R Evans 7 Feb 1848; b- James W Whittemore con- Zachariah Floyd and Amey Floyd, parents min- James McAden-

Patty & Philip Pennington 29 Jan 1787; b- John Saunders

Pheby & John Davis 12 Nov 1787; b- Charles Floyd

Foster

Maria & William S Cardwell 17 Dec 1831; b- Creed Haskins min- John B Smith

Fowler

Dolly & Jeremiah Reams 15 Dec 1800; b- Starling Fowler

Martha & Richard Jones 8 Oct 1813; con- Briggs Fowler, father b- William Jones minister not cited- 14Oct1813

Fowlkes

Elizabeth & Mathias Petty 24 Dec 1814; n- Nathaniel Fowlkes con- Thompson Fowlkes, father min- William Richards- 27Dec1814

Nancy & Jones Osborn 12 Jun 1797; b- Edward Elam

Sarah & George Malone 23 Oct 1804; b- Gabriel Fowlkes min- William Richards- 25Oct1804

Fox

Elizabeth & Matthew A Wilson 17 Jan 1825; b- E H Peete con- Mary Fox, mother min- James Smith- 19Jan1825

Hannah & Samuel (Jr) Holmes 13 Dec 1796; b- Edward Holmes con- William Holmes Sr, father

Mary & Moses Lunsford 28 Jan 1796; daughter of Richard Fox b- John McKenny min- John Loyd-

Nancy & Abner Ragland 3 Mar 1799; b- Richard Fox min- Ebenezer McGowan- 5Mar1799

Priscilla & James (Jr) Taylor 9 Dec 1801; b- Josiah Floyd min- James Meacham- 10Dec1801

Sally & Thomas Nowell 12 Oct 1790; b- Thomas Roberts min- John King- 14Oct1790

Sarah & John Wright 3 Oct 1797; b- William Taylor con- Richard Fox, father

Franklin

Nancy & Lewis Moss 15 May 1815; b- Thomas Moss

Frazer

Elizabeth & Beal Goodwin 10 Dec 1798; b- James Brame con- Henry Frazer, father min- William Richards- 29Jan1799

Freeman

Anne & Britain Wagstaff 7 Feb 1778; d of Allen Freeman b- Allen Freeman

Elizabeth & William (Jr) Mallett 18 Mar 1833; b- Samuel Bugg con- Liddy Walker, grandmother of Elizabeth

Lucy T & John G Tudor 12 Feb 1824; b- John Toone con- Benjamin T Freeman, father min- James Smith-

Mary & Argelon Toone 13 Oct 1783; b- James Hix

Minerva Ann & Henry Godsey 20 Dec 1830; b- James Y Jones con- Benjamin Freeman, father

Sally & Alexander Watts 29 Jun 1833; b- George Gordan

Furham

Mary & James Williams 8 May 1797; b- Eusebius Stone min- William Richards- 17May1797

Garner

Cecily & James N Wood 15 Dec 1845; b- Richard H Wood min- John B. Smith-

Ireanna & James A Wright 27 Oct 1851; con- Lewis Garner, father

Leatha & Henry Ligon 27 Apr 1831; min- John B. Smith-

Martha & Samuel Elam 13 Oct 1800; b- John Elam con- James Garner, father min- Edward Almand- 6Nov1800

Ophelia P & Samuel P Garner 13 Feb 1847; b- Samuel Vincent Garner min- Robert Burton- 15Feb1847

Orpah & William Smith 3 Feb 1812; b- William Garner min- William Richards- 5Fev1812

Polly W & John Elam 23 Oct 1797; b- Archibald Clark con- James Garner, father min- William Richards- 26Oct1797

Roanna & William Garner 17 Dec 1840; min- Charles F. Burnley-

Sarah & Willis Guy 20 Jul 1840; b- Edward Mayo

Sophia & Warner K Johnson 21 Dec 1846; b- William G Coleman

Susannah & Robert Hester 11 Jan 1802; b- Richard Swepson

Winny & Thomas Toone 11 Aug 1800; b- Richard Brown con- James Garner, father min- Edward Almand- 21Aug1800

Garrett

Elizabeth Ann & Meredith Stone 6 Mar 1826; b- Edmund Taylor con- Mary Ann Garrett, mother

Elizabeth & Thomas Garrett 27 Jun 1816; b- William Peebles min- James Meacham- 4Jul1816

Jane & John Mackecy 13 Feb 1823; b- Richard Coleman min- Thomas R. Brame-

Garrott

Mary & James Edmunds 9 Nov 1825; b- James W Taylor con- Zachariah Garrott, father min- James McAden-

Mary & Jaral Jackson 13 Nov 1798; b- Cavel Jackson con- Thomas Garrott, father min- William Creath- 22Nov1798

Nancy & David Wells 11 Oct 1799; b- Elijah Wells con- Thomas Garrott, father min- William Creath-

Gary

Harriett & Samuel Lear 10 Aug 1843; b- William A Holmes

Mary Ann & William T Jones 28 Apr 1842; b- William P Gary

Gayle

Eliza H & William L Hite 15 Nov 1847; b- Christopher Gayle

Elizabeth F & George W Burwell 30 Aug 1849; b- William A Burwell con- Thomas Gayle, father

Gee

Caroline & Thomas M Warren 10 Dec 1823; b- David G Moore con- Jeremiah Gee, gdn for Caroline con- Elizabeth Warren, gdn for Thomas min- James McAden-

Clarissa & Pennington Barnett 5 Jan 1820; b- William C Creath con- James Gee, father

Lucy & William (Jr) Drumwright 28 Feb 1803; b- Thomas Drumwright con- Jones Gee, father

Mary H & John B Phillips 12 Oct 1840; b- H W Harper con- Milly T Gee, mother min- James McAden-

Nancy & James Street Gee 10 Nov 1798; b- Jones Gee min- William Creath- 14Nov1798

Sally & Anderson Andrews 28 Nov 1816; min- Charles Ogburn- (Methodist)- 28Nov1816

Geoghegan

Sarah Ann & Joseph A Tarwater 20 Sep 1847; b- E A Williams con- Charles Geoghegan, father

George

Jane & George M Haskins 23 Nov 1845; b- Beverly George

Giles

Elizabeth & Thomas Nance 4 Oct 1795; b- John Cleaton min- John Loyd- 28Oct1795

Elizabeth & Lewis Poythress 26 Dec 1792; b- Meredith Poythress min- John Loyd- 27Dec1792

Jane Perrin & Jesse Baisey 19 Dec 1791; b- Isham Eppes con- Henry Edward Giles, father min- John Loyd- 21Dec1791

Martha N & John Wartman 14 Nov 1831; b- Edward Giles con- John Nance gdn of Martha min- John Wesley Childs-

Gillespie

Eleanor & Leander Reamey 29 Nov 1848; b- Humbleston Reamey con- Mary Gillespie, mother min- Robert Burton- 7Dec1848

Maria L & Parsons G Puryear 13 Nov 1850; con- Martha Gillespie, mother min- William V. Wilson-

Martha & Jackson Fausett 7 Dec 1837; b- William Thomason con- Nancy Gillespie, mother

Susanna & Anderson Holloway 1 Jul 1799; b- John Dortch min- William Richards- 2Jul1799

Gilliam

Martha & William Ladd 8 Feb 1787; b- Jacob Ladd

Glasscock

Eliza & James Moore 19 Jan 1829; b- Granderson Glasscock con-Zachariah Glasscock, father min- Pleasant Gold- (Baptist)- 22Jan1829

Mary & William Bowen 7 Dec 1846; b- William Yancey con- Thomas Glasscock, father

Nancy & Peter Vaughan 10 Jan 1842; b- William Glasscock min- Alfred Apple-

Rebecca & Waddill Lowery 16 Dec 1850; con- Elizabeth Glasscock, mother min- Thomas King- (Halifax County)-

Silvany & Joel Chandler 13 Nov 1845; b- Andrew J Chandler con-Zachariah Glasscock, father min- Alfred Apple-

Glover

Martha W & Allen B Evans 13 Jan 1830; Martha terst. that she is 22 years old b- David Oslin min- James McAden-

Nancy & Willis McKinney 25 Feb 1801; b- William Blanton min- Ebenezer McGowan- 26Feb1801

Sally & Charles Rottenberry 4 Dec 1798; b- James Burton min- Ebenezer McGowan- 24Dec1798

Gober

Molly & William Taylor 4 Jul 1798; b- John Gober

Gold

Eliza & Elias Griffin 19 Dec 1839; b- Robert Rowlett con- E Kennon, gdn of Eliza min- Charles F. Burnley-

Elizabeth & Thomas Haley 9 Jun 1794; b- Daniel Gold Jr Elizabeth widow of Daniel Gold Sr min- James Read- (Baptist) 12Jun1794

Harriet & Parham Owen 31 Aug 1824; b- Thomas Owen con- Pleasant Gold, father min- Pleasant Gold- (Baptist)-

Milly & Edward Tillotson 2 Feb 1808; d of Daniel Gold, dec. b- John Hailey con- William Tillotson, father con- Thomas Hailey, stepfather of Milly

Sally & David W Wiles 21 Dec 1837; b- Elijah Gregory con- Erasmus Kennon, gdn of Sally

Susanna & Robert Rowland 19 Feb 1829; b- Alexander Gold con-Pleasant Gold, father min- Pleasant Gold- (Baptist)- 24Feb1829

Goode

Agnes & James Williamson 26 Oct 1837; b- Edward R Chambers con-W O Goode, brother of Agnes min- William Steel- (Episcopal)-

Alice E & James Harris 31 Aug 1826; b- Samuel H Goode, who also test that Alice will be 21 next February (Note: James Harris from Nottowat Co) con- Mary A Goode, mother min- John B. Smith- 14Sep1826

Eliza T & Richard H Stokes 21 Jan 1822; b- Hugh Nelson

Eliza W & William H E Merritt 2 Apr 1827; b- Bevil G Wyche con-William Hendrick, gdn of Eliza min- John B. Smith- 4Apr1827

Elizabeth O & Thomas J Bailey - — 1842; b- J T Williamson

Elizabeth Willis & Joseph Taylor 29 Feb 1796; b- Francis Jones con-Swepson Jeffries, gdn of Elizabeth min- William Creath- 1Mar1796

Elizabeth & John Hawkins 19 Dec 1785; b- Robert Goode con- Edward Goode, father

Ellen Augusta & James Wister Feild 7 Dec 1848; b- John M Hayes con-McKarness Goode, father

Isabell & Swepson (Sr) Jeffries 8 Feb 1789; b- Benjamin Pennington

Jane & Philip (Jr) Poindexter 13 Jun 1768; b- Richard Witton, Jr con-Edward Goode, father

Lucy Ann & Richard (Jr) Boyd 5 Dec 1821; b- Beverly Sydnor con-John C Goode, guardian of Lucy min- Alexander M. Cowan-

Lucy H & George T Baskervill 11 Dec 1849; b- William Baskervill Jr con- William O Goode

Lucy S & Adam Finch 20 Dec 1824; b- Richard H Moss

Lucy & Charles Baskervill 25 Jun 1823; b- Thomas Goode min- John S. Ravenscroft- (Episcopal)-

Maria B & John T Reams 26 Oct 1830; min- William Steel- (Episcopal)-

Martha E & William H Norvell - Nov 1840; b- Thomas A Norvell

Martha G & Benjamin D Hatcher 15 Dec 1852; min- John A. Dell-

Martha & James B Bouldin 5 Feb 1825; b- William Townes min- William Steel- (Episcopal)- 17Feb1825

Mary Armistead & Thomas Williamson Jones 27 Jan 1814; b- Alexander Boyd Jr con- Samuel Goode, father

Mary J & Zachariah Bugg - --- 1832; min- James McAden-

Mary & Joseph Fontaine 8 Feb 1773; b- Edward Goode

Nancy & Charles Hudson 18 Dec 1790; b- Chiles Hutcheson con- Joseph Goode, father

Pamelia B & James W Love 23 Aug 1819; b- Christopher Haskins Jr min- James Meacham- 24Aug1819

Rebecca & John Short 28 Jan 1807; b- Edward Holloway min- James Meacham-

Sally & Richard H Baptist 28 Feb 1818; d of Samuel Goode b- John W Lewis min- John S. Ravenscroft- (Episcopal)-

Goods

Martha W & Alexander Farrar 13 Oct 1834; min- William Steel- (Episcopal)- 16Oct1834

Goodwin

Nancy & John Wilson 2 Jan 1793; b- Robert Baskervill

Susanna & David Bragg 9 Jan 1797; b- Bennett Goodwin min- John Loyd- 22Jan1797

Gordon

Ann & Sherwood Hix 18 Jan 1782; b- Walter Leigh

Jincy & Jacob Hicks 31 Oct 1794; b- Arthur F Winfield min- John Loyd- 6Nov1794

Lucy T & Alexander Wilkinson 24 Nov 1852; con- Allen Gordon, father

Mary E & Francis B Hester 12 Dec 1853; con- Allen Gordon, father min- John E. Montague- (Granville County, N.C.)- 24Dec1853

Mary & Worsham Tucker 5 Dec 1804; b- John Gosee min- Matthew Dance- 6Dec1804

Sally N & Granderson L Carter 14 Jul 1824; b- William Stone min- James Smith- 20Jul1824

Graves

Elizabeth & Ralph Graves 9 Feb 1789; b- Henry Walker

Elizabeth & Thomas Harris 28 Dec 1795; b- Peter Elam min- Edward Almand- 3Jan1796

Elizabeth & Thomas Harris 18 Dec 1841; b- Asa Garner con- Thomas Graves, father min- Charles F. Burnley-

Elizabeth & Thomas Howerton 18 Jul 1814; b- Abraham Hester, who test Elizabeth is 20 years old

Fanny W & Henry Hastin 19 Jun 1799; b- Thomas Graves min- William Richards- 20Jun1799

Jane & Wiley Spain 25 Apr 1821; b- Thomas Graves min- William Richards- 26Apr1821

Jane & John W Thompson 20 Mar 1844; b- Samuel Dedman

Julia & Stephen Spain 17 Jul 1849; b- William D Stembridge con- Phebe Graves, mother

Lucretia & Robert Chandler 28 Feb 1797; b- John P Finch con- Elijah Graves and Lucretia Graves, parents min- William Creath-

Martha A & James Collins 12 Nov 1849; b- William Flinn con- Thomas J Graves James Collins from Charlotte Co., VA min- S. G. Mason- 29Nov1849

Martha & Benjamin Collier 24 Dec 1850; con- Phebe Graves, mother min- Robert Burton- 24Dec1850

Martha & William Lawson 25 Dec 1817; b- Nathan Graves con- Thomas Graves, father min- William Richards-

Mary Ann & John Y Graves 21 Dec 1840; b- William T White con- James Graves, father of Mary Ann

Mary Owen & James P Allgood 6 Jun 1853; con- Thomas Graves, father min- James S. Kennedy- 9Jun1853

Matilda & James Smith 28 Apr 1845; b- John F Royster

Nancy & Daniel Elam 12 Apr 1826; b- James Callis con- Frances Graves, mother min- William Richards- 13Apr1826

Nancy & John P Finch 14 Sep 1795; b- Elijah Graves min- William Creath-

Nancy & John Flynn 9 Dec 1816; b- Thomas Graves min- William Richards- 12Dec1816

Peggy & James M Flinn 21 Dec 1846; b- Jeremiah M Johnson con- James Graves, father min- Robert Burton-

Sally & Henry Callis 18 Nov 1816; b- William Graves min- William Richards- 19Nov1816

Sally & John Stembridge 24 Dec 1803; b- Obadiah Belcher min- Edward Almand- 28Dec1803

Green

Ann Bolling & William H Lawton 4 Nov 1843; b- Thomas H Laird

Clara Jane & Jesse Oslin 22 Jan 1845; b- Richard B Baptist

Eliza A & Stith B Spraggins 30 Dec 1824; b- John G Baptist con- G Green, father min- William Steel- (Episcopal)-

Elizabeth H & William J Cater 16 Aug 1851; min- Hartwell Arnold- 16Aug1851

Elizabeth & James W Oliver 2 Mar 1799; b- Abraham Green son of Asa and Sarah Oliver min- William Creath- 16Mar1799

Elizabeth & Richard Phillips 20 Nov 1815; b- Stephen Stone

Martha B & Robert A McNeal 17 May 1838; b- Daniel T Hicks con- G P Green, father min- Edward Wadsworth-

Martha T & James Lanier 8 Jun 1814; b- Joel Watkins con- Grief Green, father, who test Martha under 21 min- James Meacham- 9Jun1814

Mary Ann & William G Baptist 27 Dec 1831; b- Hilliard J Manning con- G B Green, father min- William Steel- (Episcopal)-

Mary & Edward Dodson 7 Jun 1814; b- John T Keen min- James Meacham- 14Jun1814

Mary & Thomas Trice 11 Aug 1777; widow of Thomas Green b- Edmund Taylor

Mary & Stephen Worsham - Mar 1843; b- John Vaughan

Patsy & James Hayes 22 Mar 1806; b- James T Hayes con- William Wills Green, father min- James Meacham- 25Mar1806

Rebecca W & David Almand 20 May 1824; b- Archibald Green min- James Smith-

Sally A & William R B Clements 5 Nov 1814; b- Henry Wilson con- Howell P Harper, gdn of Sally min- Charles Ogburn- (Methodist) 7Nov1814

Sally & Henry Callis 21 Dec 1821; b- Daniel Graves   min- William
Richards-

Sarah & John Flynne 11 Apr 1791; b- David Green min- Henry Ogburn-

Signiora & James Oliver 20 Nov 1830; b- Daniel T Hicks con- Grief
Green, father min- William Steel- (Episcopal)- 1Dec1830

Susan & Thomas A Feild 10 Jun 1814; b- Abraham G Keen min- James
Meacham- 30Jun1814

Susanna & Hampton Malone 17 Jun 1822; b- James Stone min- Pleasant
Gold- (Baptist)- 20Jun1822

Greenwood

Ann H & William Winn 18 Nov 1816; b- Joseph B Clausel min- William
Richards- 21Nov1816

Ann & Francis Hester 13 Dec 1779; b- James Hester con- Thomas
Greenwood, father

Avarilla & William Sadler 12 Nov 1798; b- John Greenwood con- Thomas
Greenwood, father

Eliza S & Samuel Hester 12 Nov 1821; b- W A Maddox con- Robert
Greenwood, father

Elizabeth & Samuel Hester 8 Nov 1784; b- Caleb Johnston con- Thomas
Greenwood, father

Elvira & Benjamin I Hinton 9 Dec 1826; b- Henry Hester con- Robert
Greenwood, father min- Allen D. Metcalf- 11Dec1826

Frances & William White 21 Jun 1791; b- John Greenwood con- Thomas
Greenwood, gdn of Frances min- James Read- (Baptist) 20Jul1791

Henrietta & Thomas Graves 4 Mar 1828; b- William Brame min- John
B. Smith- 6Mar1828

Jane Catharine & William M Greenwood 29 May 1833; b- E A Holloway
con- Robert Greenwood, father of Jane Catharine

Jane & Jechonias Overby 11 Jan 1796; b- Hume R Feild min- William
Creath-

Martha & Daniel F Thomas 28 May 1833; b- George Lumpkin con-
Robert Greenwood, father

Mary & Edward Clark 1 Jan 1812; b- Hepburn Wiles

Mary & James B Riggins 22 Feb 1830; b- John J Ewing Mary herself
test. she is 24 yrs old min- William Steel- (Episcopal)-

Mary & James White 28 Feb 1786; b- William Willis con- Thomas
Greenwood, gdn of Mary min- John Marshall- (Baptist) 12Mar1786

Sally & Anselm Leigh 20 Jan 1790; b- Walter Leigh con- Thomas
Greenwood, father

Greer

Jane & Joseph Bilbo 11 Sep 1780; b- Zachariah Bevers con- Joseph
Greer, father

Greffies

Sally & James Carroll 12 Dec 1786; b- Mark Lambert Jackson

Gregory

Ann E & George Savage 1 Jun 1825; b- Joseph S Gregory min- James
McAden-

Anna & John Walker 12 Nov 1798; b- Thomas Reamy min- William
Richards- 15Nov1798

Anne C & William Vaughan 6 Apr 1795; b- Richard Gregory min-
Charles Ogburn- (Methodist) 9Apr1795

Anne & James Ligon 14 Nov 1798; b- James Reamy min- William
Richards- 22Nov1798

Eliza Ann & Asa Moore 12 Mar 1835; b- Elijah Gregory min- John B.
Smith-

Eliza & Richard Murray 18 Dec 1830; b- Barnett Gregory min- Pleasant Gold- (Baptist)- 23Dec1830

Elizabeth & John Lambert 11 Dec 1809; b- William Vaughan con- Richard Gregory, father

Elizabeth & Daniel Middagh 5 Jul 1813; b- Charles William Baird

Elizabeth & Alexander Smith 13 Dec 1835; b- John S Couch con- Robert S Gregory, father min- John B. Smith-

Elizabeth & James Stembridge 31 Dec 1801; b- John Stembridge min- William Richards- 7Jan1802

Fanny D & Charles W Baird 6 Dec 1808; b- West Gregory con- Richard Gregory, father

Fanny & West Gregory 28 Aug 1811; b- Francis Gregory min- Charles Ogburn- (Methodist) 29Aug1811

Frances C & Richard F Hall 15 Dec 1853; con- Mary S Gregory, mother min- F.N. Whaley-

Frances Coleman & John S Gregory 6 Jan 1836; b- John G Coleman min- John B. Smith-

Frances & William Callis 13 Dec 1790; b- Andrew Gregory min- John Williams- 22Dec1790

Frances & Marshall Moore 2 Jan 1826; b- Elijah Gregory min- William Steel- (Episcopal)- 12Jan1826

Jane W & William H Love 7 Apr 1852; con- John W Gregory, father

Jane & John T Carter 19 Jun 1820; b- Charles T Carter min- Pleasant Gold- (Baptist)- 22Jun1820

Jane & Littleton Jones 18 Nov 1834; b- John C Gregory con- John and Nancy Newton, parents of Jane

Judith & Charles T Carter 19 Jul 1813; b- Barnet Gregory con- Charles T Carter, gdn

Julia A & Stephen (Jr) Floyd 28 Oct 1844; b- Thomas A Sale con- Robert S Gregory, father con- D A Paschall, gdn of Stephen min- John B. Smith-

Julianna & William Tillotson 19 Feb 1835; b- James Tillotson con- Barnett Gregory, father min- John B. Smith-

Martha F & Madison Cheatham - Nov 1836; b- Peter Averett con- Thomas S Gregory, father min- John B Smith-

Martha P & James E P Bacon 20 Jun 1825; b- William Hicks min- James McAden-

Martha & Thomas Apperson 21 Sep 1829; b- Alexander Blankenship con- Mary Gregory, mother

Martha & Thomas Epperson 24 Sep 1829; min- Pleasant Gold- (Baptist)-

Martha & Stephen Roberts 20 Aug 1810; b- Nathaniel Fowlkes min- David McCargo- (Charlotte County, Va.) 30Aug1810

Martha & James Seward 11 May 1813; b- John Gregory min- James Meacham- 19May1813

Mary C & Richard B Taylor 4 Dec 1798; b- Richard Gregory

Mary Frances & Giles T Crafton 16 Apr 1845; b- Robert T Gregory con- Robert S Gregory, father min- John B. Smith-

Mary Y & Joseph A Norwood 28 May 1840; b- William Moody min- John B. Smith-

Mary & Benjamin Royster 31 May 1847; min- Robert Burton-

Mary & William Tillotson 25 Jun 1832; b- James Yancey

Nancy & Joshua Camp 10 Jan 1814; b- George Camp con- John Gregory, father min- William Richards- 16Jan1814

Nancy & Bird L Dodson 22 Feb 1826; daughter of James Gregory, dec. b- Benjamin Doggett min- George Petty-

Nancy & John Newton 16 Sep 1830; b- Samuel Puryear min- Pleasant Gold- (Baptist)-

Patsy & James (Jr) Leach 18 Jan 1802; b- Francis Gregory con- Roger Gregory, Sr, father

Phebe & William Moody 22 Feb 1825; b- Silas M Gregory min- William Richards- 1Mar1825

Phoebe & James White 15 May 1837; b- James H Gregory con- Elijah Gregory, father min- John B. Smith-

Sally & Edward P Pettypool 18 Apr 1836; b- John Clark con- James Williamson, gdn of Sally, daughter of Atha Gregory, dec. min- John B. Smith-

Sarah & Thomas Couch 26 Nov 1801; b- Archibald Smith min- William Richards-

Sarah & Thomas Culbreath 12 Jan 1822; b- Charles T Carter min- Pleasant Gold- (Baptist)- 24Jan1822

Sarah & George Haynes 9 Feb 1795; b- Joseph Gregory George from Charlotte County

Sarah & Major Robertson 21 Dec 1818; b- Elijah Gregory min- William Richards- 29Dec1818

Susanna & Peter Elam 8 Aug 1791; b- Andrew Gregory min- John Loyd- 18Aug1791

Temperance & William Culbreath 15 Jul 1819; b- Garrett Avery

Gresham

Susanna & Daniel Hazelwood 15 Jan 1821; b- Daniel Daly min- Charles Ogburn- (Methodist) 17Jan1821

Griffin

Ann E & Thomas B Moseley 25 May 1841; b- William T White con- Spencer C Griffin, father min- John B. Smith-

Catharine & Edmund Burton 13 Feb 1813; d of John b- Jonas Burton

Eliza & Drury Pullian 20 Dec 1843; b- Ranson Elliott Drury from Halifax Co., VA min- Alfred Apple-

Elizabeth & Greenville Elliott 12 Apr 1825; b- Stark Daniel min- Pleasant Gold- (Baptist)- 13Apr1825

Elizabeth & William Glasscock 18 Oct 1820; b- Bartlett Davis con- Keron Griffin, mother min- Pleasant Gold- (Baptist)- 19Oct1820

Elizabeth & James Stone 12 Mar 1810; b- Elijah Griffin

Frances & Bartlett Davis 19 Feb 1816; b- Franklin Moore con- Careen Griffin

Jane & Leonard Neal 22 Jan 1816; b- DavidNeal min- Reuben Pickett- 1Feb1816

Jane & Thomas Wortham 17 Jul 1826; b- Elijah Griffin min- Pleasant Gold- (Baptist)- 25Jul1826

Lucy & Thomas H Estes 15 Sep 1828; b- Elijah Griffin min- Pleasant Gold- (Baptist)-

Margaret & Jordan Stone 17 Dec 1803; b- Elijah Griffin

Martha Ann & William Peek 2 Sep 1833; b- Elias Griffin

Mary & Johnson Faulkner 8 Apr 1799; b- Stephen P'Pool con- William Griffin, father

Mary & Obadiah Neal 10 May 1821; b- James H Newton min- Pleasant Gold- (Baptist)- 17May1821

Mary & William H Tillotson 10 Jan 1843; b- James Griffin min- Alfred Apple- 12Jan1843

Milly & Willis Royster 23 Aug 1821; min- Pleasant Gold- (Baptist)-

Nancy & Matthew Dennis 8 May 1797; b- Jacobus Christopher

Nancy & Stephen Jones 17 Jul 1826; b- Elijah Griffin min- Pleasant Gold- (Baptist)- 25Jul1826

Penelope & James Yancey 4 Mar 1828; b- Francis Griffin min- Pleasant Gold- (Baptist)- 6Mar1828

Philadelphia & David Vaughan 14 Dec 1807; b- Hezekiah Yancey con- James Griffin, father

Polly & Thomas Owen 28 Jan 1843; b- Elias Griffin min- Thomas King- (Halifax County)- 26Feb1843

Sally & Thomas Featherston 13 Apr 1821; b- Elijah Griffin

Susanna & Banister Gregory 29 Aug 1808; b- Elijah Griffin con- John Gregory

Tabitha & Robert Morgan 12 May 1821; b- John Watkins min- Pleasant Gold- (Baptist)- 18May1821

Tabitha & John B Tunstall 6 Feb 1823; b- James T Jones min- James Smith-

Grigg

Betsy & Cain Coleman 11 Apr 1791; b- Jesse Grigg

Patsy & Valentine Mullins 10 Nov 1794; b- James Hudson min- William Richards- 13Nov1794

Sally & Gordon Ridout 6 Feb 1802; b- William Ezell con- Lewis Grigg, father min- James Meacham- 10Feb1802

Guy

Elizabeth & Robert Jones 8 Aug 1809; b- Daniel Guy con- Lucy Guy, mother

Fanny & Benjamin Manning 5 May 1796; b- Earbe Chavous min- John Loyd- 8May1796

Lucinda & Willis Guy 21 Dec 1815; b- Spencer Guy con- John Guy, father

Mary & Archibald Morris 2 Feb 1841; b- Lethe Guy

Polly & Hardaway Drew 17 Feb 1813; b- Thomas Kersey

Gwaltney

Martha & Clayton Hastings 17 Dec 1825; b- John Gwaltney min- Charles Ogburn- (Methodist) 20Dec1825

Susanna & William Singleton 13 Jan 1798; b- Richard Stone con- William Gawltney, father

Haile

Catherine & Thomas Winn 1 Apr 1822; b- William W Dedman min- William Richards- 9Apr1822

Elizabeth & William W Dedman 23 Dec 1819; min- William Richards-

Frances & Harrison Winn 11 Jul 1785; b- Thomas Haile

Mary & Richard Carter 14 Jan 1793; b- Ellyson Crew

Nancy & Shelton Powell 8 Jan 1818; b- Thomas Gillespie min- William Richards-

Hailestock

Mary & William Thompson 19 Feb 1808; b- Abel Stewart

Hailey

Dorothy & William Moore 20 Aug 1821; b- Meredith Hailey min- Pleasant Gold- (Baptist)- 23Aug1821

Dosha & Samuel Jones 9 Mar 1789; b- Daniel Jones daughter of Thomas Hailey

Jane & Ephraim Gold 8 Jul 1799; b- Elijah Griffin con- Thomas Hailey, father

Jane & Ephraim Gold 8 Jul 1799; b- Elijah Griffin con- Thomas Hailey, father min- William Creath-

Joybe & Washington Averett 13 Nov 1817; b- Josiah Gold con- Thomas Hailey, father

Martha & Armistead Blankenship 11 Jun 1822; b- William H Jones con- John Hailey, father min- Pleasant Gold- (Baptist)- 14Jun1822

Hall

Amey & John Wall 10 Dec 1787; John from Halifax County b- James Hall

Anna & Richard B Vaughan 11 Oct 1815; daughter of John Hall Sr b- John Hall Jr

Anne & George Holloway 24 Oct 1774; b- William Holloway con- James Hall, father

Elizabeth J & William S Weatherford 19 Feb 1828; b- Miles Hall min- John B. Smith- 20Feb1828

Elizabeth & John T Pennington 22 Feb 1813; b- John Hall, father, who consents and test. Elizabeth 21 yrs old

Halcarna D & Ewell Stone 12 Dec 1836; b- William H Green con- Miles Hall, father min- John B. Smith-

Martha B & John (Jr) Cox 11 Jul 1803; b- William Marshall min- William Richards- 14Jul1803

Priscilla P & Alexander M Boyland 15 Oct 1828; b- James B Jones min- Allen D. Metcalf-

Rebecca & John R Pearcy 15 Feb 1815; daughter of John Hall b- John Hall

Sarah & Richard Winn 14 Aug 1775; b- James Hall

Susan M & John Elam 23 Sep 1829; b- Miles Hall min- John B. Smith-

Susanna & George Royster 7 Aug 1790; b- William Marshall

Halm

Roannah & John P Smith 22 Jul 1833; b- Thomas Rogers con- Benjamin Evans, father

Halton

Prudence & John Hatsell 17 Feb 1786; b- William Baskervill

Hamblen

Rebeccah & Allen Burton 22 Mar 1786; b- Isaac Pully s of Robert Burton

Hamblin

Elizabeth & John Mayes 7 Jan 1789; b- John Wynne

Elizabeth & William Toone 22 Mar 1786; b- Isaac Pully

Lucy & John Worsham 12 Nov 1804; b- Stephen Pettypool

Martha Cocke & Thomas Taylor 18 Oct 1800; b- Reuben Vaughan con- Agnes Hamblin, mother & gdn of Martha min- John Cameron-

Mary & John Yancey 14 Oct 1799; b- Daniel Jones con- Thomas Hamblin, father min- William Creath-

Nancy & Richard Jones 23 Feb 1799; b- Daniel Jones con- Thomas Hamblin, father

Phebe & Berryman Ezell 8 Aug 1803; b- Peter Hamblin con- Thomas Hamblin, father

Susanna & David Chandler 19 Nov 1821; b- Stark Daniel

Hamilton

Polly H & William Allgood 16 Aug 1813; b- Samuel Bugg con- Joseph Hamilton, father con- Edward Allgood, father min- James Meacham- 26Aug1813

Hamlin

Martha & Daniel Jones 31 Mar 1792; daughter of Thomas Hamlin son of Capt. Thomas Jones b- Thomas Vaughan

Hamme

Louisa C & George Jefferson 26 Nov 1835; b- Richard H Hamme con- Frederick Hamme, father

Hamner

Ann E & Reuben Puryear 29 Oct 1826; b- B H Bailey con- George B Hamner, father min- John B. Smith- 1Nov1826

Sarah & Richard Jeffries 4 Oct 1824; 'Dr' Richard Jeffries b- Epps S
McCraw con- George B Hamner, father min- William Steel- (Episcopal)-
7Oct1824

Hansard

Lilly & John Phillips 18 Dec 1816; b- Charles H Baird min- Charles
Ogburn- (Methodist)

Hanserd

Mary & Archibald Phillips 26 Nov 1795; b- Richard Hanserd
Sarah & John (Jr) Seward 6 Dec 1799; b- Richard Hanserd min- James
Meacham- 11Dec1799

Hardie

Mary Ann & Francis Nash 1 Jul 1822; b- Thomas A Gillespie min-
William Richards- 22Jul1822

Hardy

Amanda C & John Crutcher 14 Jan 1823; b- Jesse Craddock con- Miles
Hardy, father
Jane B & Ludwell Evans 19 Nov 1810; b- John S Jeffries min- William
Richards- 20Dec1810
Martha & John Lee 15 Jan 1833; b- William S Wilson con- Miles Hardy,
father
Martha & William Nicholson 19 Nov 1786; widow b- Richard Swepson
Sr

Harper

Angelina W & Richard H Harwell 2 Apr 1834; b- Benjamin J Walker
con- Charles Ogburn, gdn of Angelina min- James McAden-
Anne & Emanuel Hundley Hudgins 23 Jan 1811; b- John Thomason
Eliza A & John Hawthorne 7 Jan 1833; b- Henry W Harper
Elizabeth E & Pleasant Ellington 4 Dec 1840; b- William P Drumwright
con- John P Harper, father min- James McAden-
Elizabeth E & Benjamin J Harper 11 Jun 1821; b- John P Harper con-
Martha Harper, mother min- Thomas Adams- (Lunenburg Co.)- , ,
13Jun1821
Frances W & Benjamin Gee 21 Dec 1812; b- Hundley Hudgins con-
John Harper, father
Frances & Dennis Marshall 27 Aug 1792; b- John Harper Dennis son
of Samuel & Cassandra Marshall
Lucy H & Wilson Harris 3 Jan 1845; b- Charles H Ogburn min- James
McAden-
Martha & Joseph Arnold 18 Dec 1820; b- Thomas Farrar min- Thomas
Adams- (Lunenburg Co.)-
Martha & Bolling Bottom 14 Mar 1796; b- Wyatt Harper Bolling from
Brunswick County min- John Neblett- 16Mar1796
Mary M & Hartwell Arnold 20 Dec 1830; b- Roberty Moore min- James
McAden-
Milly T & Henry Gee 15 Jun 1818; b- Howell P Harper min- Charles
Ogburn- (Methodist) 25Jun1818
Serzener M & Samuel Watson 26 Mar 1844; b- Edwin Binford con- John
Harper, father min- James McAden-
Susan A & William L French 21 Apr 1851

Harria

Julia & Daniel Chandler 10 Mar 1818; b- Thomas B Puryear con- Susan
Harriss, mother min- William Richards- 26Mar1818

Harris

Betsy & Henry Simmons 30 Dec 1830; b- Thomas D Crutchfield con-
John Harris, father min- Charles Ogburn- (Methodist)

Dicey & Jeremiah Allgood 13 Dec 1802; b- James Harris d of James Harris

Eliza & Pleasant Brummell 18 Dec 1816; b- Alex Gillespie

Elizabeth & Pleasant Burwell 21 Dec 1815; min- Richard Richards

Elizabeth & Edwin Rainey 15 Jul 1811; min- David McCargo- (Charlotte County, Va.)

Elizabeth & Edwin Reamey 15 Jul 1811; b- William Harris min- David McCargo- (Charlotte County, Va.)

Jane & Hugh W Gillespie 4 Jan 1817; b- Thomas Puryear min- William Richards- 13Feb1817

Judith & William Spain 13 Dec 1802; b- James Clack min- William Richards- 27Dec1802

Kitty & James N Spain 29 Aug 1838; b- Royall Spain

Martha A & John D Wells 8 Oct 1839; b- D A Hudson min- Benjamin R. Duval-

Martha E & William Byasee 26 Jan 1836; b- Thomas D Crutchfield con- John Harris, father min- James McAden-

Martha & Thomas Crutchfield 5 Mar 1831; b- William Crutchfield con- Sally Harris, mother min- Charles Ogburn- (Methodist) 6Mar1831

Martha & Alexander Gillespie 29 Jan 1816; b- Robert Harris con- Robert Harris, father min- William Richards- 18Feb1816

Mary A & Isaac H Nanney 23 Jun 1852; min- James McAden-

Mary Ann & James Cocke 27 Jul 1824; b- John C Carroll con- Mary King, mother of Mary Ann Harris (nee Mary Ann King)

Mary & Harper Gillespie 29 Nov 1819; b- James Harris con- Robert Harris, father min- William Richards- 1Dec1819

Mary & Thomas Graves 26 Dec 1808; b- John Stembridge min- William Richards- 27Dec1808

Minerva C & Benjamin A Wells 4 Dec 1843; b- Thomas A Crutchfield Minerva is 23

Nancy & Tolbert Clay 7 Apr 1805; b- John E Harris

Patsy & Thomas Puryear 25 Mar 1801; b- Allen Harris con- Reuben Harris, father min- William Richards- 2Apr1801

Prudence & Reuben Harris 15 Nov 1830; b- James Harris min- John B. Smith-

Rebecca & William Bevill 3 Mar 1829; b- William Graves min- John B. Smith- 5Mar1829

Rebekah & Jesse Russell 11 Dec 1798; b- Stephen Evans min- Charles Ogburn- (Methodist) 20Dec1798

Sally R & William Loafman 29 Nov 1823; b- Robert Harris min- William Richards- 4Dec1823

Sally & Woodley Cleaton 2 Jan 1805; b- John Harris

Sally & Sherwood Owen 7 Nov 1796; daughter of James Harris Sherwood from Halifax County b- James Harris min- Edward Almand- 8Nov1796

Susanna & John Dedman 20 Oct 1834; b- Allen Gillespie min- William Steel- (Episcopal)- 23Oct1834

Susanna & Allen Harris 1 Mar 1800; b- James Reamy con- Reuben Harris, father min- William Richards- 4Mar1800

Susannah & James Vaughan 11 Jun 1803; b- Richard Jeffries con- William Harris, father min- William Richards- 30Jun1803

Tabitha & Royall Spain 19 Sep 1812; b- James Spain min- William Richards- 30Sep1812

Harrison

Amanda J & Asa Stewart 5 Oct 1848; b- Archer P Stewart min- John Bayley- 12Oct1848

Elizabeth & John Johnson 11 Jan 1802; b- Greenwood Harrison min-William Richards- 21Jan1802

Elizabeth & Joseph Simmons 8 May 1797; b- Samuel Simmons con-Johnand Sarah Ogburn, guardians of Elizabeth min- Charles Ogburn- (Methodist) 11May1797

Jane M & Bentley Epperson 25 Feb 1823; b- Horace T Royster

Julia W & Robert B Chappell 19 Dec 1842; b- George Jefferson

Margaret R & Henry Young 11 Nov 1822; b- Howell L Read

Nancy & Robert Moore 21 Jul 1796; b- John Ogburn min- Charles Ogburn- (Methodist)

Winny & Jephthah Reader 10 Jan 1803; b- Greenwood Harrison min-William Richards- 19Jan1803

Harriss

Martha J & James P Dortch 14 Dec 1853; con- John R Harriss, father min- James McAden-

Harwell

Angelina W & Pettus Farrar 18 Jun 1849; b- C R Edmonson min-Thomas Adams- (Lunenburg Co.)- 27Jun1849

Anne D & Richard W Clausel 20 Dec 1819; b- Clausel Williams con-James Harwell, father

Caroline A & Wright King 3 Oct 1830; b- Richard H Harwell con- James Harwell, father min- James Smith- 7Oct1830

Elizabeth P & Richard Baugh 28 May 1800; b- Edward Patrick Davis con- James Harwell, father min- Ebenezer McGowan-

Hannah & Allen Rainey 20 Oct 1817; b- James L Nance con- Annie Harwell, mother, who test Hannah is 21 min- James Meacham- 22Oct1817

Martha E P & Charles S Jones 18 Dec 1848; b- James M Harwell Jr con- James M Harwell, Sr., father min- Thomas Adams- (Lunenburg Co.)- 20Dec1848

Martha & Samuel Harwell 18 Dec 1804; b- William Harwell con- James Harwell

Mary H & William Pride 30 Aug 1827; b- William Harwell con- James Harwell, father min- James Smith- 5Sep1827

Sarah E H & William C Crutchfield 24 May 1852; min- Hartwell Arnold-

Harwood

Martha Y & William Williamson 3 Oct 1816; b- Melchizedeck Roffe min- William Richards- 9Oct1816

Haskins

Ann N & Edmond G Brodie 4 Dec 1802; 'Dr.' Edmond G Brodie b-John S Jeffries con- Christopher Haskins, father

Elizabeth W & John Cobb 13 Feb 1816; b- Charles L Jeffries con-Christopher Haskins, Sr., father

Elizabeth & Daniel Coleman 14 Nov 1791; b- Henry Towns con- Thomas Haskins, father Henry Twons from Halifax County Daniel Coleman from Pittsylvania County

Elizabeth & Thomas Spain 6 Jan 1797; b- William Lucas min- Edward Almand- 7Jan1797

Jane M & Cicero A Coleman 8 Apr 1852; min- Robert Burton- 15Apr1852

Lucy S & William D Gregory 8 Jul 1852; con- C T Haskins, father min-Robert Burton-

Lucy & John E Jeffress 20 Sep 1819; b- Creed Haskins con- Emma Haskins, mother

Sarah Ann Eliza & Benjamin H Russell 3 Feb 1834; b- John Knox con-Charles Haskins, father

Hasten

Lively & Robert Crowder 2 Sep 1788; b- Absolem Hasten min- Edward Almand-

Hasting

Pamelia & Champion Whitlow 1 Aug 1820; min- William Richards-
Prudence & Jesse Whitlow 24 May 1819; b- Thomas J Norment con- Frances Hasting, mother min- William Richards- 25May1819

Hatch

Martha & Benjamin Connell 27 Aug 1788; b- William Taylor con- Freeman Short, guardian and father-in-law of Martha Benjamin son of Daniel Connell

Hatchell

Frances & John B Hamilton - --- 1843; b- James L Hatchell (bond damaged)

Mary E & Joseph A Reese 8 Oct 1842; b- Benjamin Hatchell
Nancy & John Reese 31 Dec 1842; b- Samuel Carpenter
Sally & Anderson Bottom 30 May 1809; b- William H Bugg min- James Meacham- 31May1809

Hatsel

Polly Lewis & Archer Cox 8 Feb 1802; b- John Talley

Hatsell

Elizabeth & Walter Hamilton 24 Aug 1785; b- Mary Hatsell
Frances & William Renn Northcross 4 Mar 1786; b- John McCarter
Polly & John Hamilton 12 Jan 1795; b- Stephen Hatsell
Sally Hunt & Thomas (Jr) Pritchett 7 Aug 1798; b- Edward Hatsell min- Matthew L. Easter- 10Aug1798

Hawkins

Lucy & William Insco 31 Dec 1827; b- Pennington Lett min- Charles Ogburn- (Methodist) 1Jan1828
Sarah & Abraham Potter 6 Feb 1771; b- John Potter

Hayes

Cornelia & James M Wilkinson 18 Dec 1849; b- William J Carter con- Lily Hayes, mother min- Robert Burton- 19Dec1849
Kitty & Hezekiah Puryear 10 Jan 1803; b- Thomas Puryear min- Matthew Dance- 17Feb1803
Martha A & James G Richardson 30 Oct 1834; b- James Hayes min- William Steel- (Episcopal)- 23Oct1834
Mary Eliza & Mackarness Goode 18 Mar 1822; b- John T Hayes
Mary Frances & William Henry Mayo 14 Mar 1844; b- Frederick Nowell con- Matilda Hayes, mother
Mary & James Ransom 9 Jul 1787; b- James T Hayes James from Amelia County
Nancy & John Vaughan 13 Dec 1802; b- Starkey Hayes min- Balaam Ezell-
Panthea & David Allgood 28 Nov 1840; b- Joseph Averett
Sally O & Lewis Tharp 15 Dec 1852; con- James Hayes Sr, father min- John A. Doll-
Susan A & Howell A Taylor 6 Oct 1843; b- James Hayes

Hazelwood

Elizabeth & James W Cole 17 Dec 1850

Heathcock

Honora & Drew Stanfield 13 Dec 1803; b- George Guy
Honora & Drew Stanfield 13 Dec 1803; b- George Guy

Hendrick

Ann V & Armistead G Boyd 25 Apr 1848; b- N M Thornton con- William Hendrick, father

Augusta E & William T Hendrick 27 Jul 1853; con- Murray Hendrick, father min- James S. Kennedy- 27Jul1853

Elizabeth & William Chandler 26 Jan 1827; b- Thomas Hendrick min- Pleasant Gold- (Baptist)- 11Feb1827

Judith & Amasa Palmer 13 Dec 1800; b- Christopher Haskins

Leah & William Baker 12 May 1800; b- George Baker min- Matthew Dance- 17May1800

Parthena & Robert Boyd 2 Jan 1826; b- Thomas Hendrick, father con- Thomas Torian, guardian for Robert min- Pleasant Gold- (Baptist)- 5Jan1826

Permelia B & John B Goode 2 Jul 1804; b- Amasa Palmer min- James Meacham- 4Jul1804

Ruth & William Tucker 22 Jan 1824; b- John LeNeve con- Rebecca Tucker, mother

Sophia W & Miller (Jr) Woodson 8 Aug 1803; b- Amasa Palmer

Henly

Martha & Samuel Scott 5 Jan 1792; Samuel from Dinwiddie County b- William Johnson min- William Creath- 11Jan1792

Henry

Lucy & John Cardwell 15 Jan 1844; b- Henry Wood

Mary B & James Garrett 9 Nov 1842; b- Thomas S Jones min- Charles F. Burnley-

Hester

Amelia & Henry Hester 30 Nov 1826; b- William Townes min- Allen D. Metcalf- 3Dec1826

Ann & George Farrar 30 Oct 1828; daughter of Samuel Hester b- John Culbreath min- Pleasant Gold- (Baptist)- 6Nov1828

Ann & William T Hardy 6 Dec 1820; b- William S Willis con- Nathaniel Hester, father min- William Richards- 7Dec1820

Ann & Benjamin Pulliam 8 Mar 1784; b- Stephen Mabry

Anna & Valentine McCutcheon 10 Mar 1800; b- Richard Brown min- William Richards- 18Mar1800

Anna & Francis Moody 26 Dec 1805; b- Harwood Jones con- James Hester, father min- Thomas Hardie-

Barbara & David Brame 28 Nov 1807; b- James Hester min- William Richards- 3Dec1807

Barbara & William Bridgewater 13 Jul 1792; b- William Hundley d of Abraham Hester, dec. min- James Read- (Baptist)

Elizabeth & Francis Lewis 30 Apr 1786; b- Henry Sandifer Elizabeth daughter of Abraham Hester dec. min- Henry Lester- (Baptist) 30Apr1786

Elizabeth & George Wright 16 Jun 1823; b- Robert Hester

Henrietta & James Greenwood 9 Jun 1794; daughter of Abraham Hester, dec. con- James Hester, uncle of Henrietta min- William Richards- 11Junm1794 b- Henry H Dedman

Henrietta & James Strum 16 Dec 1847; b- Richard H Averett con- Robert Hester, father

Jane & Joseph Brame 10 Mar 1806; b- William V Clausel min- William Richards- 20Mar1806

Jane & Francis Marshall 7 Nov 1803; b- Daniel Johnson con- Samuel Hester, father min- William Creath-

Lilly & John Brame 9 Dec 1805; b- William W V Clausel min- William Richards- 19Dec1805

Martha Ann & Erasmus G Hinton 24 Aug 1830; b- Benjamin J Hinton con- Robert Hester, father min- William Steel- (Episcopal)-

Martha & James Palmer 9 May 1791; b- William Durham Watkins

Mary & Owen Burton 8 Jan 1798; b- Robert Marshall min- William Richards- 10Jan1798

Mary & Arthur Moody 13 Dec 1796; b- James Palmer con- James Hester, father min- William Richards- 15Dec1796

Nancy & Howell Frazer 13 Oct 1817; b- Chisholm Hester con- Henry Hester and Mary Hester, parents

Nancy & Samuel White 7 Apr 1812; b- William G Pettus con- F G Hester, father

Susan & Josiah Crews 18 Jan 1819; b- John Clark min- James Meacham- 21Jan1819

Susan & Henry Moody 22 Dec 1827; b- David C Wootton min- Allen D. Metcalf- 25Dec1827

Hickman

Susanna & Henry Wilson 24 Nov 1837; b- William C Wade min- James McAden-

Hicks

Duannar & George Bailey 21 Oct 1799; b- Bartholomew Medley min- William Creath-

Lucy D & Ludwell E Jones 24 Nov 1819; b- Edward Deloney min- James Smith- 25Nov1819

Martha & Thomas Daws 17 Oct 1814; b- Thomas A Jones min- James Meacham- 15Nov1814

Polly C & Leonard Keeton 4 Apr 1834; min- John B. Smith-

Higgerson

Fanny C & Shadrach Barbour 22 Aug 1851; con- Charles Higgerson, father min- S.G. Mason-

Lucy Ann & Richard C Pugh 4 May 1853; con- Charles Higgerson, father

Hightower

Martha J & Ephraim A Drumwright 6 Apr 1840; b- John Hightower

Sarah & Daniel Beauford 24 Mar 1787; b- Thomas Jones

Hill

Elizabeth & John Clark 21 Aug 1815; b- Daniel Elam

Evalina & Francis Baker Bailey 4 May 1819; b- John Clark min- Alexander M. Cowan-

Phebe & Hyram Hayes 8 Aug 1791; n- Nicholas Jeter min- John Williams-

Hines

Mary V & Thomas D Walker 5 Nov 1847; b- William H Turner con- Ralph Hubbard for Mary V Hines, alias Mary V Hubbard min- James McAden- 6Nov1847

Hinton

Martha M & Julius C Branch 11 Apr 1834; 'Dr' Julius C Branch b- Presly Hinton con- John Hinton of Petersburg, gdn for Martha min- William Steel- (Episcopal)- 23Apr1834

Mary & Philip (Jr) Poindexter 12 Aug 1799; b- Thomas Dance

Nancy & George Poindexter 24 Dec 1791; son of Phillip and Sarah Poindexter b- Randolph Westbrook min- John Williams- 27Dec1791

Hite

Nancy & James Jones 25 Jan 1816; min- Reuben Pickett-

Hix

Elizabeth & James Hester 3 Sep 1767; b- Amos Hix

Lucy & William Bugg 7 Nov 1773; b- Amos Hix

Martha & Thomas Davis 15 Nov 1814; min- James Meacham-

Hobsin

Agness & Thomas Edwards 6 Nov 1798; b- Charles Patterson min- William Creath- 7Nov1798

Hodge

Elizabeth B & Joseph N Edmunds 4 Jul 1828; Joseph from Halifax Co., VA. b- S V Morton con- A E Henderson, gdn for Elizabeth

Hodges

Mary E & James Stainback 9 Oct 1849; b- Allen T Andrews min- James McAden- 10Oct1849

Hogan

Ann & James Jeffries 11 May 1789; b- Lewis Toone min- John Williams- 2Jun1789

Ede & William Evans 10 Apr 1775; b- Edward Hogan

Mary & Ludwell Evans 25 Feb 1783; b- Edward Finch con- Edward Hogan, father

Prudence & Burwell Russell 11 Jan 1785; b- William McQuie

Hogwood

Penelope & James (Sr) Whitlow 18 May 1803; b- John Bilbo

Hollins

Caty & Robert Jones Allen 1 Dec 1786; b- Thomas Richardson

Holloway

Barbara & Lewis Garner 4 Jun 1827; b- William B Holloway con- Gray Holloway, father

Dianna & Edward Cox 31 Dec 1767; b- Henry Delony

Elizabeth C & N M Norwood 8 Apr 1850; b- C T Haskins min- Robert Burton- 25Apr1850

Elizabeth & James Chambers 14 Dec 1814; b- David Holloway

Elizabeth & Samuel Daniel 8 Nov 1820; b- John Jones con- Gray Holloway, father min- Pleasant Gold- (Baptist)-

Elizabeth & Joseph Fargeson 6 Feb 1789; b- Benjamin Ferrell

Elizabeth & William Taylor 26 Apr 1785; b- Samuel Durham

Frances & Samuel H Holloway 25 Oct 1844; b- William Holloway min- Alfred Apple-

Harriet B & George D Wade 21 Feb 1837; b- James Holloway

Jane & Samuel Bugg 15 Dec 1835; b- J G Bugg con- Mary Holloway, mother

Lucy & Austin (Sr) Wright 1 Mar 1806; b- Francis Ballard

Martha & William Bailey 21 Nov 1801; b- Henry Bailey

Martha & Zachariah Williams 8 Feb 1830; b- Thomas Farrar con- D H Abernathy, gdn of Martha

Mary A C & David Overby 16 Aug 1849; b- J G Moss

Mary G & John Poynor 27 Jan 1814; b- John Davis min- James Meacham-

Nancy & Henry B Burger 7 Aug 1820; b- Austin Wright Sr

Nancy & John White 12 Dec 1797; b- Edward Holloway min- Edward Almand- 14Dec1797

Patsy & Richard Hudson 14 Jan 1805; b- Jordan Mason min- William Richards- 17Jan1805

Priscilla D & Tilman (Jr) Johnson 16 Jul 1842; b- H Holloway con- Gray Holloway, father min- Alfred Apple-

Sally & Bartholomew Medley 23 Dec 1797; b- Benjamin Fargeson

Holmes

Ann B & Daniel Mann 12 Nov 1821; b- Isaac Holmes, father min- James Smith- 13Nov1821

Ann & Byer Hundley 26 Jul 1791; daughter of Samuel Holmes b- Isaac Holmes

Ann & John Waller 5 Mar 1782; b- John Ballard

Betsy J & John Fitzackerly 19 Dec 1817; b- Pennington Holmes min- Charles Ogburn- (Methodist) 24Dec1817

Betsy & John Warren 5 Dec 1792; d of Samuel Holmes b- Walter Leigh

Elizabeth A & David B Johnson 11 Sep 1840; b- Henry F Gill con- George Holmes, father

Elizabeth E W & Miles Hardy 7 Dec 1846; b- William T M Holmes con- Isaac Holmes, father min- James McAden- 12Dec1846

Elizabeth & Daniel Daly 22 Dec 1788; b- Sherwood Smith

Elizabeth & James Jones 20 Dec 1790; b- Pennington Holmes

Everlina F & Archer Jackson 6 Oct 1834; b- James Holmes con- Rebecca Holmes, mother min- James McAden-

Faithy & Sherwood Smith 21 Dec 1786; d of Isaac Holmes, dec. b- William Starling

Frances & Daniel Waller 29 Apr 1788; b- John Waller min- Thomas Scott-

Joice & Edward Goode 13 Dec 1798; daughter of Samuel Holmes b- Richard Cox min- Charles Ogburn- (Methodist) 18Dec1798

Lucinda & William Warren 17 Apr 1798; b- Samuel Holmes min- Charles Ogburn- (Methodist) 18Apr1798

Lucy & Ludwell Tanner 2 Dec 1781; d of Isaac Holmes b- John Baskervill

Martha & Tignal Abernathy 8 May 1796; b- John Holmes min- John Loyd- 12May1796

Mary A & William Eubank 15 Jan 1800; b- Pennington Holmes min- Charles Ogburn- (Methodist) 16Jan1800

Mary J & Alexander Dortch 8 Dec 1824; b- L H Jones con- Samuel Holmes, father min- James Smith-

Mary & Abel Dortch 29 Oct 1793; b- David Dortch min- John Loyd- 31Oct1793

Mary & Marriott Warren 17 Dec 1794; Marriott from Richmond County, Georgia b- Benjamin Suggett con- Samuel Holmes, Sr, father min- John Neblett-

Patty & Walter Leigh 1 Dec 1784; daughter of Samuel Holmes b- Samuel Holmes

Polly & James Baker 4 Oct 1804; b- Richard Crowder

Rebecca & Buckner Rainey 12 Jun 1780; b- Samuel Lark

Sally & James Reekes 13 Dec 1796; d of Samuel Holmes b- John Walton min- John Neblett- 15Dec1796

Sally & John Wright 13 May 1801; b- John Holmes min- Ebenezer McGowan- 21May1801

Sarah Ann & John McGowan 10 Dec 1811; b- Isaac Holmes min- Charles Ogburn- (Methodist) 13Dec1811

Sarah & James Davis 9 Mar 1767; b- John Ballard Jr Sarah daughter of Isaac Holmes

Susanna & Asa Certain 5 Jan 1814; d of William Holmes b- Richard Crowder, Jr min- Milton Robertson- (Warren County, N.C.) 5Jan1814

Susannah & Edward Baskervill 4 Mar 1800; daughter of Samuel b- John Dortch min- Ebenezer McGowan- 5Mar1800

Homes

Phybie H & Joseph James Averett - Sep 1848; b- George Holmes

Hood

Keziah & Benjamin Edmundson 17 Oct 1785; b- Charles Hood

Hopkins

Elizabeth & Charles Davis 11 Dec 1784; b- John Hopkins

Jane & John Puckett 28 Feb 1792; b- John Farrar

Hord

Fanny & Wagstaff Maynard 10 Dec 1792; b- James Hord daughter of Thomas Hord

House

Elizabeth & Benjamin Taylor 17 Nov 1845; b- Phillip Pennington

Mary & William G Blair 9 Nov 1843; b- Daniel J Morris

Nancy & Adams Crutchfield 3 Jan 1810; b- Bartley Cheatham

Howard

Martha & Starling Moss - Oct 1802; b- Stephen Roberts

Hubbard

Elizabeth A & William H Turner 11 Feb 1848; b- J W McAden con-
Ralph Hubbard, father min- James McAden-

Martha A & Philip Pennington 9 Dec 1839; b- David Oslin con- Ralph
Hubbard, father min- James McAden-

Mary V & Henry W Hines 24 Nov 1840; b- Walter P Hite con- Ralph
Hubbard, father min- James McAden-

Patsy & Thomas Smith 15 Mar 1806; b- John Hubbard

Huddleston

Ann M & Thomas M Hedderly 19 Nov 1832; b- John J Ewing

Hudgins

Dolly & Abel Edmunds 24 Feb 1800; b- James Hudgins

Elizabeth F & Winn Rottenberry 26 Nov 1801; b- Abel Edmunds con-
James Hudgins, father

Mary Ann & James S Bugg 27 Dec 1847; b- William O Manning con-
Emanuel H Hudgins, father con- Richard D Bugg, gdn for James min-
Thomas Adams- (Lunenburg Co.)- 29Dec1847

Mary & James Garrett 1 Nov 1825; b- John Hundley con- Judith A
Hudgins, mother min- James McAden-

Hudson

Betty & William Hurt 22 Jul 1790; b- John Hudson min- John Williams-
27Jul1790

Cary & James Eubank 27 Jun 1814; d of Thomas Hudson b- William
Brown, son of James Brown min- James Meacham- 30Jun1814

Clary & William W Harris 14 Jun 1802; b- William Hudson min- William
Richards-

Dicey & George Allgood 23 Jan 1806; b- Thomas Mallett min- William
Richards- 29Jan1806

Elizabeth G & Thomas D Phillips 7 Dec 1846; b- O J Phillips con-
Charles Hudson, father

Elizabeth & Edward Allgood 28 Nov 1788; b- Bartlett Cox

Elizabeth & Achilles Calloway 9 Feb 1795; b- Richard Hudson Achilles
from Pittsylvania County min- William Creath-

Elizabeth & John Smith 28 Nov 1821; b- Stephen Hudson min- William
Richards- 29Nov1821

Elizabeth & William Wilburn 28 Jan 1793; b- William Hudson min-
Edward Almand- 30Jan1793

Frances & John Mise 2 Feb 1829; b- Robert B Chambliss

Jane & Bartlett Cox 24 Oct 1820; b- Stephen Hudson min- William
Richards-

Jane & James W Dedman 15 Feb 1830; b- Robert Redd min- John B.
Smith- 25Feb1830

Judith & Richard Ragsdale 23 May 1799; b- Richeson Farrar

Lucy Ann & Samuel Farrar 3 Apr 1826; b- Peter Hudson con- Charles
Hudson, father min- James Smith- 5Apr1826

Lucy & John Freeman 9 Oct 1798; b- Stephen Hudson con- George
Freeman, father min- William Richards- 11Oct1798

Lucy & Independence Poarch 8 Aug 1801; b- Thomas Webb min- James
Meacham- 13Aug1801

Margary & Thomas Cox 17 Mar 1794; b- David Hudson min- William Creath- 18Mar1794

Martha V & Benjamin H Harris 24 Nov 1835; b- Dabney A Hudson con- Robert W Hudson, father

Mary A & Theoderick Hudson 18 Dec 1843; b- Cephas Hudson

Mary & Phiemon Hurt 15 Jun 1818; b- William S Willis min- William Richards-

Mary & Hezekiah Puryear 16 Sep 1811; b- William M Sewpson con- John Hudson, father min- Charles Ogburn- (Methodist) 18Sep1811

Nancy & James A Willis 22 Nov 1825; b- Samuel Dedman con- Samuel Hudson, father min- William Richards- 1Dec1825

Obedience & Edward Ragsdale 3 Dec 1817; b- Stephen Hudson min- William Richards-

Parthena & Richard Thompson 24 Dec 1832; b- John Hudson

Polly & John Puryear 12 Dec 1808; b- Samuel Hudson min- William Richards-

Rebecca & William L Willis 23 Dec 1814; b- Ruell Allen con- John Willis, father min- William Richards- 24Dec1814

Roxanna A & Charles B Cole 14 Dec 1850; min- James McAden-

Sally & Nathan Graves 23 Dec 1816; b- James Winn min- William Richards- 24Dec1816

Sarah A & David D Walker 3 Jul 1847; b- William T Owen min- James McAden- 5Jul1847

Sarah & Richard P Montgomery 30 Jan 1804; b- Richard Hudson min- Matthew Dance- 2Feb1804

Susan & John G Hurt 8 Jan 1836; b- Cephas Hudson min- William Steel- (Episcopal)-

Susan & Thomas Spain 1 Dec 1824; b- John Marshall min- William Richards-

Susanna & Abraham Reamy 13 Mar 1809; b- William Harris min- William Richards- 16Mar1809

Ursley & Samuel Dedman 19 Feb 1822; b- John Dedman min- William Richards- 28Feb1822

Hughes

Ann F & Robert S Simmons 24 Dec 1832; b- Richard F Hughes con- Crawford Hughes, father min- James McAden-

Martha E & Adam O Daves 13 Jun 1848; b- R A Puryear con- Susannah C Hughes, mother

Susan J & Pettus C Phillips 20 Dec 1847; b- James C Hughes con- Susannah C Hughes, mother

Hull

Susan & Paschall Hudson 11 Oct 1819; b- Jesse Peebles min- Alexander M. Cowan-

Humphress

Stacy & Ephraim (Jr) Andrews 15 Feb 1786; b- Thomas Humphress

Humphries

Caty & John Carroll 22 Apr 1797; b- William Carroll min- Charles Ogburn- (Methodist)

Martha & Thomas Hailey Burton 30 Sep 1783; b- John Humphries

Monica & Benjamin Burton 19 Jun 1775; b- John Humphries

Nancy & William Mealer 11 Sep 1775; b- John Humphries

Hundley

Jane & James Whittemore 10 Oct 1822; b- John Hundley min- James McAden-

Lucy & Peter Townsend 11 Jul 1808; b- Willis Hundley

Nancy & Drury Stone 12 Nov 1798; b- William Hundley

Polly & Joseph Epperson 10 Oct 1803; b- William Hundley

Susan Ann & John Jordan Brown 11 Dec 1834; b- William H Hundley

Hunt

Elizabeth & Howell Graves 13 Apr 1801; b- James Hunt

Hannah & Edward Wagstaff 16 Jan 1815; b- Wagstaff Hunt con- William Hunt, father min- William Richards- 25Jan1815

Jane & William Thomas 7 May 1840; b- John Wilmouth con- Elizabeth Hunt, mother min- Charles F. Burnley-

Lockey & Robert Cardin 4 Jan 1787; b- Joel Moore con- John Cardin, father con- William Hunt, father

Mary Ann & John Heggie 29 Aug 1807; b- Absolom Hunt con- James Hunt, father

Mary & William Thomas 9 Nov 1840; b- John W Thomas

Nancy G & Isaac D Watson 6 May 1837; b- Claiborne Drumwright min- James McAden-

Nancy & John Farrar 13 Jun 1808; b- John P Finch

Polly & Moses Crenshaw 7 Jan 1812; daughter of William Hunt, dec. b- John Thompson

Polly & Moses Granger 9 Jan 1812; min- Charles Ogburn- (Methodist)

Rosa P & Eaton H Kittrell 16 Feb 1820; b- Spencer McClenahan con- Mary Ann Hunt, mother con- Robert Jones of Granville Co., NC, gdn of Eaton

Susanna & Randolph Puryear 3 Dec 1813; b- Solomon Hunt

Hunter

Margaret J & George G King 18 Dec 1848; b- Charles S Jones min- Thomas Adams- (Lunenburg Co.)- 21Dec1848

Hurt

Ann & James Jones 13 Mar 1804; min- William Richards- b- Philemon Hurt Jr

Emily C & Robert Phillips 10 Apr 1845; b- James W Crenshaw min- William J. Norfleet- 16Apr1845

Nancy & W Robert Jenkins 26 Dec 1816; b- Andrew G Elam con- William Hurt, father min- William Richards-

Patience & William Elam 19 Nov 1810; b- William Hurt min- William Richards- 12Dec1810

Polly & James E Elam 19 Oct 1812; b- Wagstaff Hurt min- William Richards- 28Oct1812

Hutcherson

Ann C & Hutchens B Ferrell 20 Aug 1832; b- Alex W Hutcherson con- Sarah Hutcherson, mother min- James McAden-

Evelina & John W Butler 10 Dec 1838; b- Alexander H Hutcherson con- Joseph Hutcherson, father min- Benjamin R. Duval-

Frances C & William Stone 6 Nov 1823; daughter of Joseph and Rebecca Hutcheson b- Charles C Phillips min- James Smith- 13Nov1823

Indiana Virginia C & Robert M Hutcherson 20 Nov 1843; b- James W Simmons

Martha & Spencer Mullins 19 Sep 1848; b- Pleasant Mullins

Martha & Giles Puryear 21 Apr 1819; b- Wright King min- James Meacham- 22Apr1819

Sarah M & Benjamin P Ferrell 9 Jan 1832; b- Joseph W Hutcherson con- Sarah Hutcherson, mother min- David Wood- 14Jan1832

Susan & William R Peebles 13 Oct 1817; b- Giles Puryear min- James Meacham- 14Oct1817

Hutcheson

Ann A F & Allen C Love 11 Feb 1846; b- Charles L Hutcheson

Ann N & Jesse Brown 17 Sep 1838; b- Charles S Hutcheson con-
Elizabeth G Hutcheson, mother

Anna & Dickey Brame 29 Jan 1795; b- Archibald Phillips con- Richard
Hutcheson, Sr., father min- Charles Ogburn- (Methodist)- 5Feb1795

Eliza W & Daniel Jones 20 Dec 1819; b- Peter W Hutcheson con- Peter
Hutcheson, Sr, father

Elizabeth B & Robert C Land 5 Apr 1824; b- John Hutcheson

Elizabeth C & Charles King 16 Dec 1809; b- John Poyner

Elizabeth C & Charles King 16 Dec 1809; b- John Poynor

Elizabeth C & William Pride 11 Jan 1843; b- Charles S Hutcheson con-
Joseph Hutcheson, father

Elizabeth & William Beaver 28 Dec 1789; b- James Jones

Elizabeth & John D Elibeck 18 Jul 1808; b- John Hutcheson

Elizabeth & Jesse Parrish 27 Jun 1810; b- John Ingram

Elizabeth & John Stone 11 Dec 1797; b- William Stone

Elizabeth & Sylvanus Walker 17 Mar 1820; b- Henry Walker min- James
Smith-

Fanny & Young Hudson 9 Jul 1804; b- John Pritchett min- James
Meacham- 16Jul1804

Frances & Henry Walker 7 Dec 1818; b- John Hutcheson min- Charles
Ogburn- (Methodist) 10Dec1818

Hannah & John Moore 11 Aug 1801; b- Charles Hutcheson min- William
Creath-

Lucy S. & Walter Brame 13 Dec 1823; b- Melchizedec Brame con- John
Hutcheson, father min- John Thompson- 18Dec1823

Lucy & Saunders Sims 21 Jan 1794; b- Charles Hutcheson min- William
Creath- 28Jan1794

Martha A O & Herbert B Rainey 20 Mar 1853; min- Robert Burton-

Martha E & James W Simmons 19 Aug 1840; b- Joseph G Hutcheson
con- Elizabeth G Hutcheson, mother

Martha & Richard Brown 19 Sep 1814; b- John Hutcheson min- Charles
Ogburn- (Methodist) 22Sep1814

Martha & Dabney (Jr) Phillips 6 Jan 1801; b- William Brown con-
Dabney Phillips Sr, father con- Charles Hutcheson, father min- William
Creath-

Mary B & Reps Barnes 22 Dec 1812; b- John A Speed con- John
Hutcheson, father min- James Meacham- 24Dec1812

Mary C & Charles C Phillips 4 Apr 1825; b- William Stone con- Joseph
Hutcheson, father

Mary M & Charles S Hutcheson 6 Nov 1823; b- Charles C Phillips con-
Joseph Hutcheson, father of Mary con- John Hutcheson, father of Charles
min- James Smith- 12Nov1823

Mary & John Turner 13 Oct 1800; b- Aurelius Walker

Nancy & John Crow 23 Jun 1814; b- Thomas Hutcheson con- Amey
Hutcheson, mother min- Charles Ogburn- (Methodist)

Polly & Allen Johnson 12 Nov 1792; b- Chiles Hutcheson min- Aaron
Brown- (Methodist) 13Nov1792

Rebecca N & Wilson Brown 7 Oct 1833; b- T E Brown con- Joseph
Hutcheson min- Joshua Leigh- 15Oct1833

Rebecca & Robert A Walker 18 Dec 1820; b- Edwin C Tarry min-
Charles Ogburn- (Methodist) 20Dec1820

Sally & William Brown 14 Dec 1789; b- Richard Hutcheson min- Thomas
Scott-

Sarah C & John B Tunstall 19 Feb 1852; con- Mary C Hutcheson, gdn
of Sarah min- George W. Andrews-

Sarah & John Hutcheson 22 Nov 1786; b- Peter Hutcheson con- Charles
Hutcheson, father
Susanna & Devereaux Hightower 18 Aug 1800; b- Joseph Hutcheson
con- Charles Hutcheson, father min- William Creath-
Susanna & William (Jr) Stone 21 Nov 1795; b- Jesse Carsley con- William
Stone Sr, gdn of Susanna min- Charles Ogburn- (Methodist) 26Nov1795

Hutson

Sarah & James Brown 29 Dec 1789; b- James Cox min- Thomas Scott-

Hutt

Jincy & William Hilton 10 Feb 1800; b- Thomas Hutt min- William
Creath-
Leliah & William Nash 12 Oct 1801; b- Thomas Hutt min- William
Creath-
Letty & Henry Royal 18 Jul 1805; b- Peter Puryear
Lucy & Thomas Peoples 25 Feb 1828; b- William Brummell min- William
Steel- (Episcopal)- 26Feb1828
Mary & John Riggins 14 May 1798; b- William Hilton min- Edward
Almand- 17May1798
Nancy & Charles Crew 11 Jan 1808; b- Samuel Cox
Sally & Samuel Cox 16 Jul 1806; b- Archer Cox min- John Meacham-
17Jul1806

Hyde

Elinor & James Smith 12 Dec 1791; s of John and Martha Smith b-
Robert Hyde
Lucy & William Oliver 18 Nov 1816; b- Irwin Hyde con- William Knight,
gdn of William min- James Meacham- 22Nov1816
Martha & Samuel Wootton 10 Nov 1788; d of John Hyde Sr b- John
Hyde min- Thomas Scott- 27Nov1788
Sarah & John Edwards 8 Nov 1784; b- Burwell Russell

Inge

Emma & William Webb 19 Jan 1835; b- William Winn min- John B.
Smith-
Sally & Cain Coleman 5 Jan 1803; b- Richard Taylor

Ingram

Lucy Worsham & Charles Cabiness 5 Jan 1795; b- William Burton con-
Pines Ingram, father min- Charles Ogburn- (Methodist)- 8Jan1795
Lucy & Benjamin Reekes 12 Aug 1801; b- Richard Crowder min- William
Creath-
Martha & Wiltshire Gromarin Pettipool 21 Dec 1792; b- William Green
con- Pines Ingram, father
Tabitha & Thomas Threadgill 9 Sep 1782; b- Reuben Vaughan

Insco

Jinny & William Clark 3 Sep 1785; b- James Insco con- John Clark,
father
Martha James & James S Insco 29 Sep 1852; min- George W. Andrews-
30Sep1852
Martha N & John Beasley 15 Jun 1801; b- William Insco
Mary Howlett & Harrison M Ryland 25 May 1811; b- William Insco
Mary T & Harrison McRilon 27 May 1811; min- Charles Ogburn-
(Methodist)

Irby

Adelia & John Chandler 27 Oct 1824; b- John W Irby con- Peter Irby
min- Pleasant Gold- (Baptist)-
Sally A & Athelston Anderson 27 May 1825; b- John W Irby con- Peter
Irby, father min- Pleasant Gold- (Baptist)- 2Jun1825

Ivey

Catharine & Benjamin Mitchell 7 Nov 1836; min- William Steel- (Episcopal)-

Catharine & William Mitchell 7 Nov 1836; b- George Ivey min- William Steel- (Episcopal)-

Missouri Ann & Lewis Hawkins 26 Apr 1849; b- William Mitchell min- William A. Smith-

Olive & John Nash 11 Dec 1823; b- James Drew min- William Richards- 18Dec1823

Ivy

Elizabeth & William Chavous 6 Mar 1819; b- Edward Brandon min- Alexander M. Cowan-

Margaret & William Kersey 5 Dec 1822; b- John Nash min- John S. Ravenscroft- (Episcopal)-

Jackson

Betsy Ann & Robert Jones 8 Dec 1810; b- Mark L Jackson

Charity & William Jones 22 Oct 1794; b- John M Carter min- William Creath- 24Oct1794

Elizabeth & Peter T Fargeson 5 Jul 1809; b- Cavil Jackson

Elizabeth & John Watkins 20 Oct 1819; b- Vincent Jackson con- Judith Jackson, mother con- Joseph Watkins, father min- Pleasant Gold- (Baptist)-

Jane & Edward E Owen 19 Jul 1853; min- John E. Montague- (Granville County, N.C.)-

Jemima & John Lambert 2 Aug 1785; b- Joseph Lambert

Louisa C & Arthur H Davis 29 Nov 1845; b- Robert B Chappell con- Waddy I Jackson, father

Lucy & Jesse Childrey 18 May 1814; b- William Childrey

Mary & William Jones 9 Dec 1843; b- Richard B Baptist min- James McAden-

Mourning & Jarrel Walden 16 Sep 1801; b- John Harris

Nancy & James Mims Thompson 3 Jan 1789; b- John Allen con- John Thompson, for James con- Fleming and Elizabeth Jackson, parents

Polly Wyatt & James Hargrove 6 Sep 1813; b- Mark L Jackson minister's name missing- 8Sep1813

Prudence & Jeremiah Claunch 21 Mar 1799; b- Samuel Allgood

Rebecca T & William G Hogan 19 Dec 1825; b- Waddy J Jackson min- James Smith- 29Dec1825

Sally & Thomas Beasley 22 Dec 1800; b- Mark L Jackson min- Ebenezer McGowan- 26Dec1800

Sally & John McKinney 26 Dec 1817; b- Jesse Childress

Sarah & Peter Jones 11 Dec 1797; b- Jeremiah Clanch

Tallathacuma & Drury Turner 11 Dec 1802; b- Matthew Jackson

James

Mary & Major Wall 10 Jan 1803; b- Frederick Poarch

Jeffress

Ann E & Samuel Dortch 16 May 1842; b- John M Gregory con- Richard Phillips, stepfather of Ann min- John B. Smith-

Elloisa R & Robert T Gregory 13 Jun 1853; con- James H Jeffress, father min- Robert Burton- 15Jun1853

Margaret A & Robert Burton 18 Oct 1847; b- James H Jeffress min- S.G. Mason- 19Oct1847

Jeffries

Ann & Thomas Norment 14 Feb 1785; b- John Jeffries min- John Marshall- (Baptist) 23Mar1785

Elizabeth Ann & John Peterson Harper 21 Sep 1821; con- Isaac Waller

Elizabeth C & William Holloway 20 Jan 1840; b- James M Crowder min- John B. Smith-

Elizabeth & Thomas Burnett 4 Aug 1785; b- George II Baskervill con- Swepson Jeffries, father

Elizabeth & William B Jeffries 5 Oct 1801; b- Richard Jeffries min- Edward Almand-

Elizabeth & Richard Oliver 12 Dec 1803; b- William Bilbo

Jane W & Benjamin Jones 3 Apr 1811; b- Richard C Russell con- Nathaniel S Jeffries, father min- William Richards- 4Apr1811

Jane & Brackett Barnes 8 May 1797; b- Swepson Jeffries, Sr. min- William Richards- 11May1797

Jane & James Norment 28 Jun 1793; b- Richard Jeffries min- John Williams- 30Jun1793

Kitty R & John W Harwood 23 Nov 1820; min- William Richards-

Mahala B & John T Graves - --- 18--; b- Luther R Jeffries min- John B. Smith-

Mariah & Booker Foster 26 Oct 1816; b- Andrew Y Elam con- Richard Russell, gdn of Mariah min- William Richards- 29Oct1816

Martha & William Burnett 1 Oct 1794; b- Swepson Jeffries, Jr con- Swepson Jeffries, Sr., father min- Charles Ogburn- (Methodist)- 2Oct1794

Martha & Charles Evans 17 Aug 1796; b- Kenchen Chavous min- John Loyd- 18Aug1796

Nancy & Vinson Garner 9 Nov 1807; b- Richard Jeffries min- William Richards- 12Nov1807

Prudence & William C Sandys 24 Jun 1816; b- Andrew G Elam min- William Richards- 2Jul1816

Sally & David Elam 11 Jan 1845; both of Sally's parents deceased bond and consent by Creed T Haskins for his adopted daughter Sally

Sarah & Edmond Bugg 10 Dec 1792; b- Swepson Jeffries min- John Loyd- 13Dec1792

Susan S & Latteny M Gregory 16 Dec 1839; b- William R Jeffries con- Richard Jeffries, father min- John B. Smith-

Susanna B & Miles T Crowder 27 Oct 1806; b- Achilles Jeffries min- James Meacham- 5Nov1806

Susannah & Daniel Hix 12 Apr 1784; b- John Jeffries

Virginia Lewis & Achillis Puryear 23 Oct 1850; con- Rebecca Jeffries, mother

Jeter

Leah & Matthew Avery 15 Dec 1843; b- Thomas Hayes

Lucy H & Creed T Langhorne 4 May 1840; b- Alexander Langhorne min- Charles F. Burnley-

Mary R & J R Royster 7 Apr 1853; con- William Jeter, father

Mary & Edward Holloway 3 May 1811; b- Charles Baskervill min- James Meacham-

Jiggetts

Elizabeth T B & William L Stamps 11 May 1840; b- William Baskervill Jr con- D E Jiggetts, father

Susanna R & William Baskervill 13 Mar 1839; b- Daniel T Hicks con- D E Jiggetts, father min- F.H. McGuire-

Johnson

Ann A & John Clark 20 Dec 1813; b- Thomas Atkins con- Caleb Johnson, father

Betsy & John Curtis 19 Dec 1806; b- Crafford ... Daniel min- Charles Ogburn- (Methodist) 21Dec1806

Caty & James Cheatham 11 Jan 1794; b- Wyatt Harper min- John Neblett- 15Jan1794

Cisily Ann & Conrad Garner 20 Dec 1847; min- S. G. Mason- 21Dec1847 b- Thomas Johnson

Eliza Ann & James Evans 11 Dec 1837; b- William G Davis

Elizabeth J & James Hawkins 13 Jan 1834; b- David B Johnson con- Thomas Johnson, father

Elizabeth & Spencer Bing 16 Jun 1828; b- Philip R Johnson con- Phillip Johnson, father min- Charles Ogburn- (Methodist) 19Jun1828

Frances & John Singleton 19 Dec 1810; b- John Curtis marriage ceremony 20Dec1810 (no minister's name included)

Jane & James T Hayes 21 Feb 1814; b- Caleb Johnson, father, who also gives consent

Jane & Joseph Moon 24 Jan 1787; b- Isaac Johnson

Jean Elizabeth & William Parrott 15 Apr 1819; min- Charles Ogburn- (Methodist)

Julia & Henry Hall Strange 8 Feb 1836; b- James B Dupuy min- P. Calhoun-

Leannah & William Ellington 17 Dec 1807; b- John Johnson

Leatha Ann & John McDaniel 8 Aug 1826; b- Gregory Johnson con- John Johnson, father min- Charles Ogburn- (Methodist)

Lilly & Richard (Jr) Hanserd 24 Dec 1811; b- William G Pettus

Louisa Jane & Alexander Prichett 21 Dec 1829; b- William T Coleman con- Phillip Johnson, father min- Charles Ogburn- (Methodist) 29Dec1829

Lucy & Edmund Bing 5 Oct 1812; b- Daniel Tucker con- Phil. Johnson, father min- James Meacham- 8Oct1812

Martha E & Daniel Walker 9 Sep 1816; b- Jacob Johnson min- Charles Ogburn- (Methodist) 11Sep1816

Martha W & Wylie Jones 14 Dec 1818; b- Ezekiel Crowder con- James Johnson, father

Martha W & Jones Wiley 14 Dec 1818; b- Ezekiel Crowder con- James Johnson, father

Martha & Thomas Brame 29 May 1814; b- Richins Brame con- Caleb Johnson, father

Martha & Robert Mason 31 Mar 1797; b- John Edwards con- Jincy Hawkins, mother of Patsy (Martha) min- Charles Ogburn- (Methodist) 3Apr1797

Martha & Silas Wells 11 Feb 1845; b- James Wells min- Daniel Petty-

Mary A & Edward Caveniss 31 May 1838; b- James Yancey

Mary C & William H Prather 16 May 1843; b- Irby Creath

Mary E & William H Gafford 21 Dec 1842; b- William A Homes con- William Johnson, father

Mary P & Ezekiel Crowder 9 Dec 1812; b- John Cook Jr con- James Johnson, father

Mary & William H Bailey 27 Nov 1820; b- Thomas Atkins min- Alexander M. Cowan-

Minerva J & Robert Phillips 1 Aug 1853; min- James McAden-

Nancy & William Cox 28 Jun 1834; b- Samuel Bugg con- Phillip Johnson, father min- C.L. Jeffries- 29Jun1834

Nancy & James Douglas 21 Oct 1808; b- Terasha Johnson

Nancy & David Drummond 27 Nov 1787; b- Howell Johnson con- James Johnson

Olivia Ann & James Strange 24 Nov 1838; b- William Johnson

Permelia & John Adams 10 Feb 1840; b- Phillip Johnson con- Polly Johnson, mother

Polly & William Evans 23 Dec 1830; b- Edward Cox con- Phillip Johnson, father min- Charles Ogburn- (Methodist) 25Dec1830

Rebecca & James Briggs 16 Nov 1818; b- Charles Ogburn min- Charles Ogburn- (Methodist) 19Dec1818

Rebecca & Jesse Christian - Feb 1841; b- Samuel Vaughan

Rebecca & Churchwell Curtis 17 Jun 1801; b- Jesse Curtis

Rebecca & Thomas Osborne 4 Jul 1816; b- Miles Hall min- George Petty-

Rebecca & Robert Walker 9 Dec 1816; b- Henry Davis min- Charles Ogburn- (Methodist) 11Dec1816

Rhoda D & Bryant Douglas 28 May 1821; b- Tarisa Johnson

Ruth & Hepburn Wiles 1 Jan 1812; b- Edward Clark

Sally & John Crowder 16 Aug 1813; b- Thomas Jones con- John Johnson, father

Sally & William Mills 6 Sep 1843; b- Charles Mills

Sarah & Richard Inge 7 Nov 1785; b- William Davis min- Devereaux Jarrott- 9Nov1785

Sophronia M & James A Moss 11 Dec 1851; con- John W Johnson, father min- George W. Andrews-

Susan & James (Jr) Hynt 22 Sep 1822; b- Jrtisha Johnson

Johnston

Elizabeth & Charles Burton 9 Sep 1793; b- Thomas Wilson

Lucy & Thomas Pinson 12 Feb 1810; b- Caleb Johnston

Milly & Nathaniel Rice 16 Aug 1832; b- Patrick Johnson min- William Steel- (Episcopal)-

Sally & Thomas Atkins 8 Jan 1810; b- Caleb Johnston

Jones

Ann E & Isaac Overby 29 Oct 1831; b- Royall Lockett Jr con- J M Jeffreys (Charlotte Co.), gdn of Ann min- John B. Smith-

Ann S & John J Speed 19 Sep 1825; b- Daniel T Hicks min- William Steel- (Episcopal)-

Ann & Miles S Wall 29 Nov 1821; b- John Jones min- John S. Ravenscroft- (Episcopal)- 13Dec1821

Araminta S & Albert G Nicholson 17 Jun 1847; b- William H Northington min- John C Blackwell- (Lunenburg County)- 22Jun1847

Avis & John H Wilkerson 17 Sep 1836; b- Alexander Puryear con- Samuel Jones, father

Biddy & Edward Chavous 20 Dec 1817; b- Robert L Jones

Caroline L & Daniel C Hazelwood 4 Jan 1832; b- James Oslin min- James McAden-

Caroline & Robert Richardson 9 Jan 1827; b- Langston Bacon

Catherine & William Gee 12 Dec 1787; William from Lunenburg County b- Varney Andrews

Dolly & William Blanks 13 Dec 1830; b- William Yancey con- Daniel Jones, father min- Pleasant Gold- (Baptist)- 22Dec1830

Easter & David Crowder 30 Apr 1795; b- Charles Kelly

Elizabeth R & Thomas P Pettus 1 May 1811; daughter of Edward Jones, dec. b- Charles Baskervill con- Richard R and Elizabeth Jones, gdns of Elizabeth min- William Richards- 16May1811

Elizabeth & John Arrington 18 Aug 1825; b- Mark Wilkinson con- Richard Jones, father min- Pleasant Gold- (Baptist)- 24Aug1825

Elizabeth & Drury A Bacon 16 Aug 1817; b- Thomas P Pettus

Elizabeth & Benjamin E Blackwell 15 May 1820; b- William T Oslin con- Wood Jones, father min- Thomas Adams- (Lunenburg Co.)-

Elizabeth & William M Carter 12 Dec 1832; b- Thomas Jones con- Samuel Jones, father min- John B Smith-

Elizabeth & Robert Church 9 Dec 1799; b- Richard Jones

Elizabeth & Robert Lewis 25 Feb 1794; b- Asa Thomas con- Tignal Jones, father

Elizabeth & James T Nunn 7 Oct 1844; b- Allen Jones

Elizabeth & Turner Sharp 11 May 1807; b- Martin Gillespie d of Richard Jones, dec. con- Charles Jones, gdn of Elizabeth min- William Richards- 14May1807

Frances A & Robert Field 13 Jul 1821; b- John Jones min- Alexander M. Cowan-

Harriet A & Thomas L Morton 30 Jan 1842; b- William H Jones min- F.H. McGuire-

Harriett G & James W Hardy 25 Jun 1838; b- James R Thomas

Jane & John Fitts 3 Dec 1822; b- Charles Yancey min- Pleasant Gold- (Baptist)- 5Dec1822

Johanna & James Stone 10 Jan 1791; d of Capt. Thomas Jones & sis of Daniel Jones, bondsman b- Daniel Jones min- James Read- (Baptist)

Julia Ann & Thomas R Wilkinson 28 Oct 1844; b- Richard Yancey con- James Jones, father

Lettice & John Lifford 3 Dec 1796; b- Buckner Whittemore

Lucy Green & Uriah Hawkins 7 Mar 1798; b- William Jones min- Ebenezer McGowan-

Lucy & Obadiah Cheatham 21 Dec 1787; b- William Drumwright con- Balaam Jones, father

Martha A & John P Smith 3 Oct 1825; b- Joseph Bennett Jr con- Ann B Jones, mother

Martha Ann & Isaac Winfree 23 Jun 1826; b- Edward B Lipscomb

Martha Cary & Edmund Hopkins 25 Jul 1796; b- John Dortch con- Tignal Jones, father min- William Creath- 27Jul1796

Martha M & Victor M Eppes 12 Nov 1844; Victor from Sussex Co., VA b- William H Jones con- Tignal Jones, father

Martha S & Samuel H Goode 10 Mar 1840; b- George Rogers con- Robert H Jones, father min- F.H. McGuire- 18Mar1840

Martha T & John Williams 21 Oct 1816; b- Robert Jones min- Thomas Adams- (Lunenburg Co.)-

Martha & James Clark 23 Oct 1799; b- James Jones min- William Creath-

Martha & David Douglas 6 Nov 1777; b- Francis Lightfoot

Martha & William J Patillo 20 Jan 1812; b- Joel Watkins min- James Meacham-

Martha & Turner Sharp 24 Jan 1797; b- James Elam con- Richard Jones, father min- William Creath- 26Jan1797

Martha & Edmund Wilkerson 19 Dec 1814; b- Thomas H Mayes con- Susan Jones, father

Mary A & Alexander Feild 23 Jun 1817; b- John W Jones min- James Meacham- 24Jun1817

Mary C & John R Williams 19 Jan 1824; b- Robert Jones

Mary E & Richard H Yancey 15 Sep 1845; b- Burwell B Barron

Mary Emma & Edwin P Edmonson 16 Dec 1852; con- R D Jones, father

Mary & John Goode 8 May 1809; b- William G Goode min- William Richards- 11May1809

Mary & Foster Noel 12 May 1812; b- West Gregory min- Milton Robertson- (Warren County, N.C.) 22May1812

Mary & Joseph Pinson 12 May 1794; b- Arthur Atkinson con- Richard Jones, father min- James Read- (Baptist)

Nancy H & Christopher Gayle 7 Oct 1846; b- Dabney Farrar min- James McAden-

Nancy & Leroy Sizemore 19 Dec 1836; b- Richard Jones

Nancy & William L Yancey 22 Dec 1824; b- Peyton R Talley con- Daniel Jones, father   con- Zachariah Yancey, father   min- Pleasant Gold- (Baptist)-

Patsy & Bennett Thomas 24 Mar 1810; b- William Jones

Patty & Phillip Mealer 14 May 1781; b- Jesse Saunders con- Thomas Jones, father

Polly & Harrison Barner 17 May 1786; b- Theophilus Harrison

Polly & Charles Yancey 19 Oct 1812; b- Gordon Stone

Rebecca & James Beasley 10 Sep 1800; b- Uriah Hawkins min- Ebenezer McGowan-

Rebecca & Robert Griffin 17 Sep 1821; b- Benjamin Jones min- Pleasant Gold- (Baptist)- 20Sep1821

Rebecca & Frederick Jones 4 Jan 1832; b- James Oslin min- James McAden-

Rebecca & Hutchins Pully 21 Dec 1821; b- Archer Phillips con- Berryman Jones, father min- James Smith-

Rebecca & Hezekiah Puryear 24 Dec 1821; b- Andrew J Elam con- Drury A Bacon, gdn of Rebecca Jones min- William Richards- 26Dec1821

Sarah Anderson & Robert Boyd 20 Apr 1789; b- Major Butler con- Alexander Boyd, father con- Tignal Jones, father min- Thomas Scott-

Sarah S & Cuthbert W Roach 19 Nov 1821; b- Drury A Bacon

Sarah & George Field 10 Nov 1829; b- Robert S Feild con- John Jones, father

Sarah & Alexander Puryear 10 Dec 1847; b- Anderson Puryear con- Richard Jones, father

Sarena & Robert Murray 3 Dec 1842; b- Allen Jones min- Alfred Apple-

Susan & James Oslin 8 Dec 1817; b- William S Oslin con- Wood Jones, father min- Thomas Adams- (Lunenburg Co.)-

Susannah & Thomas Jones 2 Oct 1815; b- Daniel Jones min- John Terry- 17Nov1815

Susannah & Stephen Mayes 16 Sep 1811; b- Marshall Moody con- Edward Jones

Tabitha & Wade Brooks 7 Jan 1796; b- John Webb min- John Loyd- 9Jan1796

Wilmouth & John Mimms - Jan 1788; min- William Creath-

Jordan

Elizabeth & Randolph Grigg 13 Dec 1805; b- Samuel Jordan con- Mary Jordan, mother

Martha Wingfield & John Matthews 18 Dec 1799; b- Wilkins Ogburn con- Mary Jordan, mother min- James Meacham- 24Dec1799

Mary M & William Grigg 8 Dec 1800; b- John Matthews min- James Meacham- 11Dec1800

Joyce

Ann E & William H C Reynolds 12 May 1846; b- Robert Joyce

Margarett & Charles P Hicks 4 Dec 1840; b- R B Baptist min- James McAden-

Keen

Elizabeth S & Roger Mallory 19 Jan 1814; b- John T Keen con- Abraham Keen, gdn of Elizabeth min- Charles Ogburn- (Methodist) 21Jan1814

Sally G & George M Goode 23 Sep 1822; b- John P Keen

Keeton

Agnes & Thomas Johnson 9 Jun 1812; b- Joseph Keeton con- Joseph Keeton, father

Audrey & James Salley 9 Dec 1793; b- Reuben Cardin min- William Creath- 19Dec1793

Caroline B & Richard Coley 19 Dec 1826; b- Leonard Keeton

Cinthey & Peter Hudson 16 Apr 1838; b- Thomas Keeton min- Albert Anderson- 2May1838

Eliza Ann & Peter Hudson 16 Apr 1824; b- Joseph Keeton

Elizabeth & Samuel Cheatham 12 May 1800; b- Warner Keeton min- Matthew Dance- 15May1800

Elizabeth & John Day 21 Oct 1815; d of Joseph Keeton b- James Days min- Milton Robertson- (Warren County, N.C.) 26Oct1815

Elizabeth & William Hudson 8 Oct 1804; b- Richard Hudson

Fanny & Robert B Crews 18 May 1824; b- Leonard Keeton min- James Smith-

Harriett N & James H Sammons 21 May 1832; b- James Hester

Jane & Phillip C Estes 17 Dec 1821; b- Edward Neal min- William Richards- 19Dec1821

Lucy J & William D Sullivan 19 Dec 1836; b- Warner C Keeton

Lucy & Franklin Moore - Nov 1835; b- William Boyd con- Joseph Keeton, father min- John B. Smith-

Maria Moore & Jabe Clark Hutton 29 Dec 1853; con- Joseph Keeton, father J C Hutton born Washington Co., VA, aged 18, s of James and Nancy Hutton Maria M Keeton born Mecklenburg Co., VA, age 18, daughter of Joseph and Elizabeth Keeton min- A.F. Davidson-

Mary B & Drury A Ferrell 19 Jan 1835; b- Leonard Keeton min- John B. Smith.

Mary & John Day 6 Aug 1819; b- Abel B Dunnavant min- Silas Shelburne- (Lunenburg County)- 16Sep1819

Mary & Benjamin Humphries 25 Nov 1788; b- Joseph Keeton

Nancy C & William Ferrell 13 Apr 1846; b- Leonard Keeton min- John B. Smith-

Nancy & Thomas Bevill 24 Jan 1797; b- Hutchins Burton min- William Creath- 26Jan1797

Polly & James Hester 20 Jul 1818; b- Richard C Williams

Sally & William M Puryear 8 Nov 1815; Sally daughter of John Keeton b- Giles Puryear

Susan & Wyatt T Perkinson 3 Nov 1849; b- Joseph A Keeton

Susannah & Wiley Tucker 16 Jan 1815; daughter of Joseph Keeton, Sr b- John Hutcheson

Kelly

Elizabeth & Littleberry Tucker 22 Dec 1797; b- John Tucker min- Charles Ogburn- (Methodist) 29Dec1797

Nancy & Tapla Tucker 9 Dec 1799; b- Daniel Tucker min- William Creath-

Kendrick

Sarah & John Patrick 29 Sep 1779; b- John Kendrick

Kennon

Elizabeth & Silas H Harris 16 Jan 1832; 'Dr' Silas H Harris b- James B Maclin con- E Kennon, father min- William Steel- (Episcopal)- 17Jan1832

Lucy P & Edwin A Williams 24 Feb 1841; b- Richard B Baptist min- F.H. McGuire-

Nancy Nelson & Clement R Kennon 27 Jul 1835; b- George C Scott con- Erasmus Kennon, father of Nancy

Roberts B & George Wingfield 3 Sep 1849; b- John S Feild, Jr con- E A Williams, gdn of Roberts

Sally S & William D Ligon 1 Mar 1841; b- E A Williams Sally daughter of Erasmus Kennon, dec. min- F.H. McGuire- 4Mar1841

Kersey

Barbara Ann & John E Stewart 20 Dec 1841; b- James M Chavous

Sally & Thomas Kersey 22 Dec 1813; b- Hardiway Drew both are 21 or over min- James Meacham-

Kidd

Elizabeth Ann & Riddick Temple 20 Jul 1825; b- John B Kidd con- John L Kidd, father

Rebecca J & Archibald Cannon 23 Dec 1844; b- Roderick Temple min- James McAden-

Kimball

Mary & Joseph Newton 24 Dec 1817; b- James Newton con- William and Elizabeth Kimball, parents

King

Edith & John Hendrick 25 Oct 1800; b- Henry King

Eliza & Abraham Crowder 6 Jun 1815; b- Charles King con- Lewis King, father

Elizabeth & Adam W Overby 23 Dec 1813; b- Green Blanton con- John King, father

Frances & William Nanney 5 May 1806; b- Hughberry Nanney con- Lewis King, father

Lucy & Jonathon Hawkins 7 Aug 1811; b- John Ingram

Mary P & George W Cunningham 3 Mar 1834; b- Isaac B Jones

Polly & William Baber 19 Aug 1817; b- Diggs Poynor

Polly & William Barrow 21 Sep 1817; min- Charles Ogburn- (Methodist)

Rebecca & George W Claiborne 23 Dec 1833; b- Baxter Smith

Kirkland

Anne & Thomas Cole 21 Dec 1792; b- James Cole min- William Creath- 24Dec1792

Sarah & William Edwards 13 Feb 1798; b- Jeffrey Mustian min- Charles Ogburn- (Methodist)

Kirks

Amey & Epps Merryman 26 Jan 1790; b- James McCann

Betsy S & Richard Jones Bowen 22 Nov 1808; b- James Bowen

Elizabeth & Wesley W Bowen 22 Dec 1835; b- Anderson Overby

Martha L & Claiborne Curtis 9 Nov 1833; b- John B Tunstall con- James Kirks, father

Nancy & Robertson D Taylor 5 Dec 1836; b- Goodwin L Overby

Patty & David Vaughan 3 Aug 1803; b- John Hudgins

Kiser

Sally Hailstock & Randall Seward 19 May 1817; b- James Nolley

Knight

Sarah & William Roffe 9 Oct 1794; b- Ingram Vaughan min- William Creath- 19Oct1794

Knott

Frances & Minge Yancey 9 May 1888; b- Samuel C Brame

Knox

Anne M & Grief Green 23 Dec 1817; b- Joel Watkins min- Charles Ogburn- (Methodist) 25Dec1817

Mary Anne & Thomas Goode 15 Jan 1816; 'Dr' Thomas Goode b- John Tabb con- Ann M Knox, mother

Sophia M & John Buford 17 Nov 1817; b- John W Lewis con- Ann M Knox, mother min- John S. Ravenscroft- (Episcopal)-

Lacy

Elizabeth C & Benjamin F Wilkes 24 Jan 1826; b- Shadrach Lacy

Mary A & Obediah Gordon 29 Apr 1825; b- Shadrach Lacy min- William Richards- 30Apr1825

Ladd

Henrietta & Whittemore Hethcock 26 Nov 1808; b- James Drumwright

Huldy & Starling Moore 27 Dec 1791; b- William Drumwright min- John Loyd- 29Dec1791

Lucy W & Benjamin Morgan 8 Dec 1820; b- William Cleaton

Susan & Jesse Woodruff 15 Jan 1812; b- Thomas Ladd con- Thomas Ladd, father

Laffoon

Patsy & William (Jr) Thomason 7 Feb 1805; b- William Thomason Sr

Lamb

Mary E & John Moody Robertson 1 Mar 1792; b- Pines Ingram con- Joseph Boswell, gdn for Mary

Lambert

----- & Benjamin Evans 16 Jun 1828; bride's given name missing on bond b- Baxter Lambert

Biddy & Burnett Hargrove 23 Jan 1788; b- Matthew Smith

Bramley M & Isham John Stanley 13 Oct 1834; b- Martin F Lambert

Cuzzy & James Burton 8 Dec 1792; b- Mark Lambert Jackson min- John Loyd- 13Dec1792

Delila & James Carroll 16 Apr 1823; min- Thomas Jones (married in Warren Co., NC

Judith & Francis Rainey 7 Jan 1797; b- Mark Lambert Jackson

Lemenda & John Mize 24 Mar 1795; b- Thomas Lambert min- John Loyd- 25Mar1795

Martha E & Howell C Crowder 18 Dec 1850; con- Mary Lambert, mother con- Bartlett Crowder, father min- Hartwell Arnold-

Martha & Sterling Crowder 20 Dec 1826; b- John Lambert con- Julius Lambert, father

Mary & Jeremiah George 6 Jun 1797; b- Thomas Lambert

Mildred & Jones Burton 15 Dec 1818; b- Zachariah Garrett

Mourning & Randolph Sturdivant 5 Jan 1797; b- David Thomas con- Joseph Lambert, father min- John Loyd-

Rebecca & John T Cole 11 Apr 1845; b- Isaac Holmes

Rebecca & Fox Hunter 12 Oct 1819; b- Daniel Hopwood con- Taylor Lambert, father

Sibbie & Matthew Smith 24 Nov 1787; b- Joseph Lambert

Land

Helen M & Robert A Patillo 21 Nov 1849; b- James H Patillo con- Elizabeth B Land

Martha & Ambrose (Sr) Vaughan 3 Mar 1813; b- John Cheatham

Susan H & James H Patillo 16 Dec 1845; b- Robert W Land

Langford

Elizabeth & Anderson Wright 6 Dec 1794; b- James Watson min- John Loyd- 30May1794

Langhorne

Ann Maria & Giles R Smith 21 Aug 1837; b- A Langhorne min- Charles F. Burnley- 29Aug1837

Jane T & Henry B Berry 7 Feb 1840; b- Alexander Langhorne min- Edward Wadsworth-

Sarah W & William H Poindexter 6 Jun 1837; b- A Langhorne min- Charles F. Burnley-

Langley

Joyce B & Alexander Nolley 22 Mar 1823; b- John C Bugg min- Stephen Jones- (Lynchburg, Va.)- 25Mar1823

Sally S & Paul M Palmer 17 Mar 1828; b- Samuel Tarry con- Jane T Langley, mother min- James Smith- 26Mar1828

Lanier

Betsy & Drury Floyd 25 Oct 1791; b- Josiah Floyd con- Lemuel Lanier, father min- John Loyd- 27Oct1791

Molly & Abner Kelly 23 Feb 1798; b- John Feagins con- Leonard Lanier, father min- Charles Ogburn- (Methodist) 1Mar1798

Nancy & Joseph Bennett 24 May 1785; b- Ingram Vaughan

Patty & John Feagins 5 Jan 1786; b- John Saunders min- John King- 7Jan1786

Tabitha & William Bennett 1 Oct 1807; b- Philip Roberts

Lark

Ann & Frederick Collier 4 Sep 1781; b- Edward Pennington

Elizabeth & James T Watson 6 Oct 1803; b- Samuel Lark Sr

Joice & Jones Taylor 11 Apr 1780; b- John Holmes

Mourning & James Simmons 3 Jan 1805; b- James Noel

Sally & Thomas Taylor 26 Dec 1797; b- Samuel Lark

Lawrence

Margaret & William Pully 26 Nov 1784; b- Hubbard Ferrell

LeNeve

Caroline & Robert A Phillips 21 Dec 1840; b- John LeNeve Sr

Eliza & William Malone 12 Feb 1844; b- Robert A Phillips con- John LeNeve, father

Mary & Edward Pettypool 9 Oct 1838; b- Robert A Phillips con- John LeNeve, father

Nancy & Richard H Yancey 21 Dec 1835; b- William Malone con- John LeNeve, father min- John B. Smith-

Leach

Martha & Thomas Taylor 5 Aug 1808; b- Francis Gregory

Leckie

Mary Ann & William Hendrick 19 Oct 1836; b- Samuel T Jones min- William Compton-

Lester

Charlotte M & Bartley C Smithson 5 Oct 1845; b- Edward Overton con- Bryan Lester, father min- Daniel Petty-

Lett

Dolly & Daniel W McDaniel 5 Feb 1818; min- Charles Ogburn- (Methodist)

Elizabeth Ann & William Bowers 17 Jul 1826; b- Waddy J Jackson con- Joseph Lett, father min- John B. Smith- 19Jul1826

Faithy H & Chesley Curtis 13 Mar 1833; b- Peter B Lett con- Hardaway Lett, father

Frances & William Parrish 30 Dec 1786; b- Isaac Adams

Jane C & Joseph A Lett 20 Feb 1837; b- William Bowers min- James McAden-

Jane & Charles Hutcherson 13 Nov 1821; b- Drury Lett min- Charles Ogburn- (Methodist) 15Nov1821

Mary P & David G Hutcherson 17 Feb 1840; b- James W Simmons con- Pennington Lett, father

Parmelia G & Green Curtis 27 Jan 1837; b- Joseph A Lett con- Joseph Lett, father min- James McAden-

Patsy & Batte Short 30 May 1791; b- James Bing

Polly & Matthew H Davis 22 Dec 1801; b- Hardaway Lett con- Joseph Lett Sr, father

Suckey Burrus & Robert Lett 17 Apr 1794; b- William Parrish min- John Loyd- 18Apr1794

Leverman

Amelia M P & John Walthall 8 Nov 1834; b- J A Gregory

Lewis

Ann & Jones Knowell 6 Sep 1819; b- John Stewart con- Emanuel Lewis, father min- James A. Riddick-

Ann & Ingram Vaughan 20 Aug 1785; b- William Baskervill con- Edward Lewis, brother & gdn of Ann

Elizabeth B & William B Baugh 27 Aug 1815; b- William B Simmons con- Ann Lewis, mother

Elizabeth & William Bullock 20 Aug 1766; b- Edmund Taylor Elizabeth widow of James Lewis, nee Elizabeth Taylor, sis of Edmund Taylor

Elizabeth & William Palmer 12 Oct 1772; b- Edward Lewis

Martha & Frederick W Clack 12 Jan 1818; b- William Townes con- John Lewis Sr, father

Martha & Thomas Vaughan 8 Oct 1781; b- Edward Lewis

Mary Ann & Charles L Payne 26 Mar 1834; b- Frederick Lewis con- John Lewis Sr, father min- A.D. Montgomery- 'Dr' Charles L Payne

Mary & Clement Blackbourn 21 Oct 1784; b- Francis Lewis Clement son of Thomas Blackbourn

Mary & Peter Evans 16 Jul 1831; b- Randolph Chavous min- Charles Ogburn- (Methodist) 19Jul1831

Nancy & Jones Allen 8 Jan 1810; b- Robert Lewis

Nancy & Thomas S Arthur 6 Aug 1844; b- Robert C Nelson

Lidderdal

Sarah & Feild Moore 26 Nov 1774; b- Thomas Moore con- Thomas Anderson, guardian of Sarah

Light

Agness & Joel Chandler 12 Apr 1772; b- Nathaniel Hix

Lightfoot

Eliza & John Chambers 21 Jan 1834; b- George C Daniel min- John B Smith-

Ligon

Annis & Reuben Jackson 10 Mar 1800; b- John Walker min- William Richards-

Frances S & Thomas Owen 7 Jan 1833; b- Obadiah Ligon con- Frances Ligon, mother min- John B. Smith-

Mary Ann & William Chatman 9 Apr 1832; b- Obadiah Ligon con- Francis Ligon, father

Nancy & Jonathon Browder 25 Mar 1825; b- Jesse Browder con- Frances Ligon, mother minister's name missing- ceremony dated 29Mar1825

Nancy & Robert Glasscock 19 Jan 1835; b- John Newton

Quincey Francis & William Murray 11 Dec 1846; b- David L Ligon con- Phebe Ligon, mother min- Alfred Apple- 17Dec1846

Susan H & James Wilkerson 10 Dec 1838; b- William James con- Francis Ligon, father

Lindley

Mary R & Samuel Puryear 31 Oct 1815; b- Giles Puryear minister not listed, but ceremony date 2Nov1815

Lloyd

Rebekah & Elijah Crowder 9 Aug 1803; b- Richard Crowder Sr

Loafman

Prudence & James Hunt 26 Sep 1801; b- William Graves min- Edward Almand- 20Oct1801

Lockett

Anne & Joseph Gooch 27 Jun 1794; widow of Abner Lockett Joseph Gooch from Granville County NC b- William Marshall

Eliza J & William B Williams 27 Jan 1831; b- Thomas C Dugger con- B Lockett, father min- William Steel- (Episcopal)-

Elizabeth & Frederick Black 11 Jan 1790; b- Royal Lockett min- John
   Williams-   Frederick from Campbell County   marriage celebrated
   12Jan1790

Frances A & William A Jones 13 May 1833; b- Samuel L Lockett min-
   William Steel- (Episcopal)- 22May1833

Lucy & William Jones 14 Dec 1801; daughter of Abner Lockett b- James
   Wilson min- William Richards- 15Dec1801

Mary C & Napoleon Lockett 26 Jun 1834; b- Samuel L Lockett min-
   William Steel- (Episcopal)-

Nancy & Robert Hester 13 Feb 1792; b- John Wilson min- James Read-
   (Baptist) 28Feb1792

Patience & James H Cardwell 20 Dec 1819; b- Royal Lockett, who also
   gives consent to his daughter min- William Richards- 25Nov1819

Phebe & Scarborough Penticost 8 Feb 1790; b- Daniel D Watkins min-
   John Williams- 18Feb1790

Sarah B & Achillis Puryear 15 Apr 1831; b- Royall Locket Jr con- Royal
   Lockett Sr, father min- William Richards- 19Apr1831

Selina Ann & George W Robards 17 Jan 1838; George from Granville
   Co., NC b- Beverly Sydnor con- Samuel L Lockett, father, who test
   Selina under 21

Love

Agnes & Ingram Roffe 17 Feb 1803; b- William Love con- Charles Love,
   father

Frances J & Alfred Plummer 13 Jun 1835; b- John J Davis con- Horace
   Palmer, gdn of Frances

Martha A & William E Wilson 6 Feb 1843; b- Allen C Love con-
   chappell Love, father

Mary C & Reuben A Rudd 17 May 1847; b- Alan C Love con- Martha
   Love, mother

Lovingston

Catherine & Bushrod Webb 7 Jan 1800; b- Mark L Jackson min-
   Ebenezer McGowan- 8Jan1800

Lowry

Polly & Thomas Garland 8 Jul 1783; 'Capt' Thomas Garland from
   Lunenburg County b- John Speed con- John Ragsdale, gdn of Polly

Loyd

Celia & Starling Morgan 7 Aug 1797; b- John Loyd min- Charles
   Ogburn- (Methodist) 10Aug1797

Martha & Abraham Crowder 7 Dec 1805; b- Elijah Crowder

Lucas

Ann & Noah Dortch 25 Apr 1780; b- William Baskervill

Caroline B & John James Simmons 13 Dec 1824; b- William Lucas con-
   John R Lucas, father min- James McAden-

Frances & Isaac Hicks 10 Mar 1807; b- John R Lucas

Sarah & Thomas Organ 11 Nov 1805; b- John Dortch

Susanna P & Thomas E Peebles 20 Mar 1804; b- William Parham

Lunsford

Emily & James Neal 4 Jan 1842; b- Volin Lunsford min- Charles F.
   Burnley-

Polly & Evan Evans 24 Dec 1807; b- John Wright

Lydick

Ann Eliza & Augustus W Childress 21 Dec 1841; b- Stith G Yancey

Malvina D & Stith G Yancey 8 Nov 1834; b- J A Gregory

Lynch

Susan A & George T Watkins 20 Nov 1850; con- B W Lynch, father
   min- William V. Wilson-

Mabry

Angelica & Edward Giles 3 Jan 1810; b- Walter Pennington con- Stephen Mabry, father

Angelica & Edward Giles 3 Jan 1810; b- Walter Pennington con- Stephen Mabry, father

Elizabeth & John Booth 29 Dec 1810; b- Edward Giles

Polly & Walter Pennington 22 Dec 1802; b- Isham Nance Jr

MacCarter

Elizabeth & James Averett 21 Jun 1813; b- Wingfield Averett min- William Richards- 1Jul1813

Mackecy

Amey & Isaac Carroll 18 Dec 1821; b- James Mackecy con- Elizabeth Mackecy, mother, who test that Amey is under 21

Maclin

Ann M & Alfred Townes 31 Mar 1836; b- J B Maclin

Eliza T & John G Baptist 10 Sep 1813; b- Thomas Hill con- James Maclin

Frances B & Samuel Allen Taylor 27 Aug 1817; b- John G Baptist

Jane E & Richard Apperson 26 Sep 1821; b- William Townes con- James Maclin, father min- Alexander M. Cowan-

Lucy R & William Townes 27 Nov 1817; min- John S. Ravenscroft- (Episcopal)-

Lucy Rollins & William G Kimbrough 28 Jun 1841; b- Thomas H Laird con- Nathaniel Maclin, father

Mary F & John W Johnson 12 Aug 1839; min- Stephen Turner-

Polly & Thomas Feggin 22 Jan 1818; b- William Cypress con- Thomas Maclin, father

Thene & John Nowell Stevens 3 May 1819; b- Thomas Feggins con- Thomas Maclin, father

Mallett

Elizabeth & Thomas Dewes 3 Sep 1849; b- William H Homes min- William A. Smith-

Elizabeth & Oliver Martin 13 Mar 1799; b- Richard M Allen min- William Creath- 21Mar1799

Jane & Cleaton (Jr) Jones 10 Jul 1841; b- Bennett B Goode

Martha & Joseph P Simmons 30 Jan 1840; b- Pleasant Burnett

Mary & William Adams 11 Jul 1839; b- Pleasant Burnett min- Benjamin R. Duval-

Sarah A & Buckner S Neathery 4 Apr 1846; b- William Mallett

Malone

---- & Thomas Mitchell 3 Aug 1785; bond torn b- John Burton

Ann & William Murray 21 Aug 1827; b- James Newton con- Ann Malone, mother min- Pleasant Gold- (Baptist)- 22Aug1827

Betsy & John Seward 2 Jun 1771; b- Drury Malone

Catherine & Martin Redd 19 Aug 1822; b- James Stone con- Nancy Malone, mother min- Pleasant Gold- (Baptist)- 20Aug1822

Elizabeth & John Murray 20 May 1811; daughter of Robert Malone b- William Hendrick Jr

Lizzy & John Shell 28 May 1786; b- Hardy Jones

Lucy & Thomas (Sr) Cleaton 3 Mar 1808; b- Thomas Nance min- James Meacham-

Margaret & Robert Newton 23 Sep 1833; b- James Newton con- Nancy Malone, mother min- Pleasant Gold- (Baptist)- 25Sep1833

Martha & Thomas D Jones 16 Dec 1844; b- Hampton Malone

Martha & William H Vowell 1 Nov 1841; b- Anderson Malone

Mary & Samuel Leneve 6 Jun 1825; b- Alex Blankenship con- Nancy Malone, mother min- Pleasant Gold- (Baptist)- 9Jun1825

Nancy & John Newman 12 Jan 1830; b- Michael Tarwater min- Pleasant Gold- (Baptist)- 16Jan1830

Nancy & Robert Wilbourne 9 Oct 1837; b- John Malone

Patsy & Lewis Grigg 30 Mar 1808; b- Thomas Cleaton

Rebecca & Reuben Booth 21 Sep 1812; b- Charles D Cleaton

Sally & Thomas Nance 10 Jan 1810; b- Thomas Cleaton

Sophia & Zachariah Hall 4 Dec 1792; b- Thomas Roberts min- John Loyd- 5Dec1792

Susanna & Anderson Malone 16 Dec 1816; b- Benjamin Reekes min- Lewis Grigg- 26Dec1816

Manning

Elizabeth M A & William R Mountcastle 3 Sep 1839; b- John C Manning min- James A. Riddick-

Manerva J & Wilson Brown 13 Sep 1830; b- James M Manning min- James Smith- 15Sep1830

Polly & John Ginnet Stewart 9 Dec 1794; b- Irby Chavous con- Susanna Chavous, mother of Polly

Marks

Nancy & Pompy Mayo 17 Dec 1801; b- Minge Mayo

Marriott

Constant & John Allen 3 Mar 1806; b- Thomas Marriott

Marshall

Alice & James Cunningham 10 Jul 1809; b- Robert Marshall min- William Richards- 22Jul1809

Ann B & Robert H Mason 22 Dec 1845; b- Major Butler

Ann & Tavener Toone 20 May 1809; b- George Bilbo

Betsy Green & John Johnson 22 Dec 1802; b- Jordan McKinney con- Richard Marshall, father

Elizabeth & John Hill 20 Feb 1799; b- John Dortch con- Robert Marshall, father min- William Richards- 27Feb1799

Elizabeth & Thomas Puryear 13 May 1805; b- Francis Lockett min- William Richards- 23May1805

Ellenor G & John F Barnes 17 Apr 1826; b- William Marshall con- Thomas Marshall, father

Martha Goode & Francis Lockett 8 Mar 1802; b- Valentine McCutcheon con- William Marshall, father

Mary A B & Daniel R Barnes 17 Feb 1812; b- William G Pettus min- William Richards- 4Mar1812

Mary Ann & John Bedford 10 Sep 1787; John from Charlotte County son of Thomas Bedford, Sr. and Mary Bedford min- James Watkins-

Mary F & John Johnson 21 Jan 1839; b- John Read

Matilda M & James M Overby 19 May 1832; b- Robert D Marshall

Nancy & James Shelton 12 Feb 1810; b- Phillip Lockett min- William Richards- 14Feb1810

Nancy & James Shelton 12 Feb 1810; b- Phillip Lockett

Phebe & William Bagley 16 Mar 1812; b- Daniel Middagh con- Dancy McGraw min- William Richards- 26Mar1812

Phibby A & Peter Couzens 15 Dec 1800; b- Francis Marshall min- William Richards- 24Dec1800

Polly & David Townes 23 Dec 1812; daughter of Richard Marshall b- Theophilus Marshall

Sally Read & John Booth 9 Apr 1805; b- John Johnson con- Richard Marshall, father

Sally & William Cunningham 10 Dec 1798; b- Robert Marshall min- William Richards- 20Dec1798

Sarah C & Samuel T Tarry 27 Oct 1845; b- Alex W Hutcherson con- Henry C Moss, gdn of Sarah

Susanna & Miles Hall 4 May 1781; b- Richard Winn con- James Hall, father con- Dancy McGraw, guardian of Susanna

Susannah & William Barrow 2 Oct 1801; b- Dennis Marshall daughter of Samuel min- John Phaup- 22Oct1801

Martin

Mary & James Hatchell 1 Jun 1819; b- Archer Cox con- Betsy Martin, mother min- James Meacham- 10Jun1819

Mason

Lucy T & Isaac Hicks 28 Oct 1815; b- Christopher Haskins Jr

Lucy T & James House 1 Feb 1847; b- John T Wootton con- Jordan Mason, father min- William A. Smith- 23Feb1847

Lucy & Warner Keeton 13 Feb 1804; b- William Stone min- William Creath-

Martha J & George W Gee 24 Dec 1839; b- William R Toone con- Jordan Mason, father min- James Delk-

Mary Ann & William R Toone 19 Dec 1836; b- William R Mason

Milly & Stephen Evans 22 Nov 1797; b- Ananias Grainger min- Charles Ogburn- (Methodist) 23Nov1797

Nancy & Harwood B Tucker 9 Jan 1809; b- William Stone

Patsy & Drury Creedle 22 Sep 1798; b- Jeremiah Adams min- Charles Ogburn- (Methodist) 25Sep1798

Rebecca & Ezekiel Redding 18 Apr 1791; b- Thomas Marriott

Rody & William McDaniel 11 Aug 1795; b- Ezekiel Redding min- Charles Ogburn- (Methodist) 13Aug1795

Sally W & Nathan Gee 26 Mar 1851; con- Jordan Mason, father min- S.A. Creath- 26Mar1851

Massey

Betsy & John Evans 11 Sep 1800; b- Stephen Evans

Mary & Joseph Barry 30 Dec 1795; b- Drury Andrews con- Thomas Massey and Mary Massey, parents min- Matthew Dance- 31Dec1795

Matthews

Elizabeth & David Coley 12 Mar 1787; b- William Wills Green

Martha & Randolph Mize 28 Apr 1798; b- Hudson Nipper min- Ebenezer McGowan- 3May1798

Martha & George Speaks 8 Nov 1809; b- John Matthews

Nancy & Isham Poarch 2 Jan 1802; b- Benjamin W Hudson min- James Meacham- 6Jan1802

Nancy & John Wright 9 May 1820; b- George Jackson min- Pleasant Gold- (Baptist)- 10May1820

Polly & James Carter 30 Mar 1825; b- William H Wilson con- Elizabeth Matthews, mother min- James McAden-

Sarah & Reuben Harris 20 Dec 1808; b- John Cook

May

Priscilla & Lewis Roberts 17 Oct 1797; b- Henry Roberts

Mayes

Elizabeth & Balaam Ezell 27 Dec 1803; b- Thomas Owen min- William Richards- 28Dec1803

Elizabeth & Richard Carter Hall 11 Aug 1794; b- John Hall con- John Mayes, father

Sarah & Wiley Wilson 20 Nov 1811; b- Charles Hamblin con- Charles Hamblin, gdn of Sarah

Maynard

Frances & James Bedford 14 Nov 1786; b- William Maynard

Judith & William Gill 8 Dec 1783; b- Nicholas Maynard

Mary & Littleberry Winn 29 Dec 1783; b- William Maynard

Mayne

Mary M & Austin Clements 11 Feb 1805; b- Henry W Overby con- James Mayne, father Austin from Charlotte County min- Edward Almand- 14Feb1805

Parmelia & John Johnson 10 Dec 1804; b- Samuel Weatherford con- James Mayne, father min- Edward Almand- 11Dec1804

Patsy M & Benjamin Laine 10 Nov 1800; b- Owen Lowry con- James Mayne, father min- Edward Almand- 20Nov1800

Mayo

Betsy & George W Drew 2 Aug 1850; min- George W. Andrews-

Malvina & Green Smith 3 Oct 1830; b- Osborne Mayo

Mary & Anderson Soward 19 Apr 1842; b- Joseph Thompson con- Elizabeth Mayo, mother

Susan & John Dew 16 Aug 1822; b- Daniel Dew min- Alexander M. Cowan-

McAden

Elizabeth Agnes & Telemachus Butterworth 20 Sep 1842; b- William Turner con- James McAden, father

McCargo

Adeline G & Edward W Fore 24 Sep 1850; con- Susannah J McCargo, mother min- William V. Wilson-

Ann E & John E Gregory 21 Oct 1839; b- James McCargo min- John B. Smith-

Joyce H & Charles C Smithson 19 Nov 1842; b- John G Oliver con- James McCargo, father

McCarter

Martha & Burwell Johnston 3 Sep 1828; b- Richard C Bibb con- James McCarter, grandfather of Martha min- William Steel- (Episcopal)- 5Sep1828

McCutcheon

Eliza W & John E Pettus 29 Dec 1841; b- John E McCutcheon con- Charles McCutcheon, father min- Charles F. Burnley- 5Jan1842

Harriett B & Richard H Hastin 21 Jun 1830; b- John Y Richards min- John B. Smith-

Martha P & Alexander B Lyle 20 Dec 1839; b- John E McCutcheon con- Charles McCutcheon, father min- John B. Smith-

Mary & Nathan Hester 7 Nov 1821; b- Charles McCutcheon min- William Richards- 15Nov1821

Prudence & James Callis 13 Mar 1833; b- Richard Hastin con- Charles McCutcheon, father min- John B Smith

McDaniel

Betsy C & Peter Crutchfield 17 Jan 1822; b- Crafford McDaniel min- Charles Ogburn- (Methodist) 22Jan1822

Fathia J & Robert A Carter 9 Jun 1852; con- Daniel W McDaniel, father min- Robert Burton- 16Jun1852

Lucy & George Talley 12 Dec 1787; b- James Moore con- John and Mary McDaniel, parents

Nancy G & Samuel G Crow 7 Aug 1827; b- John L Hightower min- Charles Ogburn- (Methodist) 8Aug1827

McHarg

Elizabeth Q & Mark Alexander 19 Jan 1797; b- Robert Baskervill min- John Loyd- 26Jan1797

Mary Watte & William Hepburn 12 Sep 1785; b- George Tarry

McKinney

Betsy C & Hardy Patterson 20 Mar 1815; b- William King Betsy daughter of Munford McKinney

Jinny & Josiah Daly 21 Oct 1795; s of John Daly b- Bennett Goodwin min- John Loyd-

McLaughlin

Elizabeth & Alexander Rudder 21 Dec 1791; b- Edward Brodnax of Lunenburg County min- James Read- (Baptist) 22Dec1791

McLin

Fanny & Earby Chavous 9 Mar 1797; b- Thomas McLin min- John Loyd- 10Mar1797

Mary & John Valentine 4 Jan 1797; b- Earby Chavous min- John Loyd- 5Jan1797

McNeal

Peggy & Joel Bass 8 Dec 1828; b- Charles Mills

McQuie

Jincy & James Wortham 11 Nov 1799; b- Thomas A Jones

Meacham

Elizabeth A & John G Tutor 20 Apr 1833; b- Lewis G Meacham con- Mary Meacham, mother

Mealer

Elizabeth & Zachariah Spurlock 13 Oct 1792; b- John Farrar min- John Loyd-

Frances & Cornelius Ragsdale 5 Oct 1795; b- William Hundley min- William Richards- 15Oct1795

Martha & Richard Pulliam 1 Oct 1791; b- Elijah Graves min- James Read- (Baptist) -6Oct1791

Susanna & Drury Ragsdale 22 Dec 1785; b- Thomas Wilbourn

Mealler

Lucy & John Doyle 17 Dec 1821; b- John Cook

Medley

Lucy & William Farrar 24 Jul 1780; b- John Farrar

Meldrum

Martha L & Edwin H Bowen 27 Sep 1827; b- Robert Moore

Nancy & John R Williams 20 Aug 1849; b- William Wilmoth con- Mary Meldrum, mother min- Thomas Adams- (Lunenburg Co.)- 22Aug1849

Merryman

Betty & Thomas Weaver 1 Nov 1786; b- Isham Merryman con- James Turner, father

Judith & Mial Thomason 24 Dec 1812; b- William Thomason

Polly & Nathaniel Laffoon 18 Dec 1804; b- John Nash

Sally & John Barnett 7 Aug 1805; b- Richard Hailey

Michaux

Lucy & Tacharner Woodson 8 Sep 1788; b- William Hendrick con- Joseph Michaux, gdn

Middagh

Georgianna C & Joseph C Farrar 5 Feb 1834; b- D Middagh min- James McAden-

Mills

Amey & Leroy Williams 24 Dec 1794; b- George Baker con- Susanna Stubbs, mother of Amey min- Charles Ogburn- (Methodist) 27Dec1794

Ann & William Bradshaw 21 Aug 1826; b- Thomas Hailey con- Mrs. Unity Bradshaw, mother of William who is under 21 min- Pleasant Gold- (Baptist)- 24Aug1826

Elizabeth H & Jesse Morgan 10 Feb 1834; b- Albert Coley

Mary & Washington Harris 23 Jun 1847; b- Henry Walden
Nancy & Thomas Crowder 4 Jan 1825; b- B H Bailey min- James Smith-
5Jan1825

Minor

Betsy & James Crowder 28 Dec 1795; b- George Minor min- William
Creath- 31Dec1795
Sarah & Swepson (Jr) Jeffries 10 Mar 1800; b- George Minor

Mise

Savory & William Lawrence 12 Apr 1827; b- P L Long min- James
Smith-

Mitchell

Margaret & Thomas Evans 16 Oct 1849; b- Norman Smith min- James
McAden-
Mary Marriott & Peter Dunnavant 27 Jul 1818; b- Thomas Warren con-
Elizabeth Mitchell, mother
Nancy & Jesse Russell 13 Dec 1832; b- William H Byasee
Rebeccah & John Bugg 17 Dec 1788; b- James Sandifer, Jr.
Sarah Marriott & Abel B Dunnavant 29 Jul 1811; b- Isaac Holmes con-
Elizabeth Mitchell, mother

Monroe

Polly & James Culbreath 12 Dec 1803; b- Ellyson Crew

Moody

Elizabeth H & William Brummell 18 Nov 1824; b- William Moody min-
William Richards-
Elizabeth J & William Knott 19 Nov 1812; b- Josiah Daly Jr con- Francis
Moody, father min- John Allen-
Elizabeth & George Moore 14 Jul 1788; b- Thomas Moore min- John
Williams- 24Jul1788
Elmira S & Madison D Smith 29 Oct 1850; 'Major' Madison D. Smith
con- L A Paschall, gdn of Elmira min- W.W. Jordan- (Oxford, NC)-
Martha A & John B Williams 7 Sep 1845; b- William Moody min- A.M.
Poindexter- 10Sep1845
Mary A M & Jonathon H Bennett 11 Sep 1832; b- Henry Moody con-
Arthur Moody, father min- William Steel- (Episcopal)- 20Sep1832
Mary E & Richard O Gillespie 26 Feb 1844; b- William T White
Mary & Josiah (Jr) Daly 14 Nov 1800; b- John Daly Jr
Nancy & Elijah Gregory 8 Jun 1801; b- Robert Smith min- William
Richards- 10Jun1801
Phebe & Jesse Taylor 27 Jun 1789; b- Francis Moody con- Henry Moody.
father min- Thomas Scott-
Phoebe & Robert A Crowder 18 Dec 1815; b- Marshall Moody con-
Arthur Moody, father
Polly & Henry Moody 20 Jun 1793; b- Robert Hester con- Arthur
Moody, father min- William Creath- 29Jun1793

Moon

Elizabeth & William Maclin 1 May 1848; b- Wyatt W Brandon min-
James McAden- 2May1848

Moore

Ann E & Edmund M Hite 28 Aug 1840; b- William P Drumwright con-
E I Moore, mother min- James McAden-
Ann Eliza R & George A Harris 28 Aug 1850; con- Thomas Moore,
father min- William V. Wilson-
Ann Eliza & James Butler 26 Oct 1850; con- Marshall A Moore, father
min- Robert Burton- 30Oct1850
Ann Eliza & Peter Stainback 17 Oct 1836; b- Turner Abernathy
Betsy & Joseph Keeton 13 Oct 1806; b- James Johnson

Elizabeth E & James Nolley 1 Aug 1817; b- John Bugg min- Charles Ogburn- (Methodist) 5Aug1817

Elizabeth & Starling Nicholson 5 Jul 1802; b- Lewis Nicholson

Elizabeth & Augustus D Wade 19 Aug 1816; b- Franklin Moore

Elvira N & A W Lester 23 Oct 1848; b- Thomas E Moore

Emily & Samuel Simmons 1 Sep 1852; min- John A. Doll-

Louise & Alfred B Miller 17 Dec 1847; b- William T Hodges con- Elizabeth Moon, grandmother of Louise

Lucy & Joel Chandler 29 Mar 1852; min- S.A. Creath- 4Apr1852

Lucy & William Willis 16 Apr 1782; b- James Willis

Martha C & Edwin P Smith 24 Mar 1824; b- John J Moore min- Charles Ogburn- (Methodist)

Martha H & James L Hite 30 Mar 1844; b- William B McAden con- E P Moore, father min- James McAden-

Martha & Thomas Abernathy 29 Oct 1814; b- Richard H Edmonson con- John J Moore, gdn of Martha min- Charles Ogburn- (Methodist) 30Oct1814

Martha & John Goode 19 Apr 1790; b- John Wilson Jr

Mary A & Peter Gee 16 Dec 1833; b- Robert Moore min- James McAden-

Mary Ann & Leroy H Lester 22 Feb 1846; b- Thomas E Moore min- E. Chambers- 27Feb1846

Mary Anne & Benjamin Saunders 19 Feb 1791; b- Philip B Moore

Mary & Jesse Curtis 27 Feb 1792; b- James Moore

Mary & Samuel Simmons 28 Sep 1814; b- John Daws

Matilda & David Perkins 19 Aug 1811; b- Franklin Moore con- George Moore, father

Nancy & Littleberry Carter 7 Mar 1815; b- A G Keen con- George Moore, father min- Reuben Pickett- 10Apr1815

Phebe & Thomas Wilburn 11 Jul 1806; b- William Jones con- George Moore, father

Polly & Edward Willis 21 Dec 1801; b- James Browder

Rebeccah & Lewis Toone 15 Aug 1787; b- Francis Lewis

Sarah A R & Phillip Hailey 18 May 1833; b- John Elliott con- George W Moore, gdn of Sarah min- John B. Smith-

Sarah J & James Strange - May 1849; b- W O Manning con- Thomas E Moore, father

Susan M V & Leonard Crymes 19 Jan 1847; b- Phillip W Moore min- S.G. Mason- 2Feb1847

Taffanus & William Hudson 2 Mar 1787; b- John Wagstaff min- John Williams-

Morgain

Nancy & John Allen 15 Dec 1783; b- Frederick Rainey s of William Allen

Morgan

Betsy & Isham Rainey 20 Jan 1789; b- Frederick Rainey min- Phillip Cox- 21Jan1789

Edith & Williamson Rainey 23 Nov 1779; b- Francis Rainey con- Reuben Morgan

Elizabeth & Albert Coley 16 Apr 1832; b- Robert Talley

Emily & George Mills 23 Dec 1843; b- Albert Coley

Mary & Robert Jones 14 Dec 1795; b- Samuel Puryear min- William Creath- 23Dec1795

Molly & Frederick Rainey 10 May 1775; b- John Tabb

Patsy & Munford McKinney 10 Dec 1789; b- John Morgan min- John Phaup- 17Dec1789

Polly H & Edmond Rainey 21 Oct 1807; b- Starling Morgan
Sarah & James King 27 Mar 1779; b- Reuben Morgan, father
Sarah & Roberts Nanney 30 Jul 1804; b- Starling Morgan con- Benjamin
    Morgan, father

Morris
Alice & Benjamin B Hall 3 Apr 1829; b- William J Morris
Catharine & John Waller 19 Dec 1825; b- William Morris con- Jesse
    Morris, father min- James McAden-
Elizabeth C & George W Cleaton - Dec 1846; b- Thomas Drumwright
    min- James McAden-
Martha C & John Christian 22 Jan 1838; b- John J Morris con- Daniel
    Morris min- James McAden-
Martha Caroline & John Chambliss 20 Aug 1835; b- Daniel Morris
Mary & Blunt Charlton 13 Mar 1850; b- George Guy
Mildred J & William A Johnson 17 Nov 1845; b- Daniel Morris min-
    James McAden-
Pamela J & Samuel S Saunders 15 Oct 1830; b- William J Morris min-
    John B. Smith-
Polly & Thomas Saunders 19 Dec 1803; b- Edward Morris con- John
    Saunders, father con- Jesse Morris, Sr., father min- William Creath-
Sarah & Howell Singleton 23 Sep 1831; b- William Morris min- Daniel
    Petty-

Morton
Mary J & Benjamin D Hatcher 20 Mar 1843; b- Reuben A Puryear con-
    Anderson C Morton, father min- Charles F. Burnley- 22Mar1843
Nannie W & William B Easley 25 Aug 1841; b- Frank W Boyd con-
    Anderson C Morton, father
Sally A & George C Scott 7 Aug 1850; con- A C Morton, father min-
    William V. Wilson-
Susan E & Arthur A Grigg 18 Oct 1843; b- Joseph Morton con- William
    H Morton, father

Moseley
Milly & James Puryear 12 Dec 1808; b- John Puryear

Moss
Ann Eliza & William E Roffe 15 Dec 1841; b- Thomas R Moss
Elizabeth & James Cocke 26 Jul 1800; b- Lewis Moss
Elizabeth & Wilson Corpier 16 Apr 1827; b- Christopher W Baird con-
    Martha Moss, mother min- Stephen Turner- 19Apr1827
Elizabeth & Stephen Taylor 19 Jan 1824; b- R Brame
Fanny & Chiles Hutcheson 23 Dec 1791; b- William Coleman con- Ray
    Moss, father min- William Creath- 29Dec1791
Lucy & James Pully 21 Dec 1805; b- David Moss
Martha & Robert Oliver - Dec 1805; b- Henry Coleman min- James
    Meacham- 18Dec1805
Mary E & Henry A Walker 18 Jan 1841; b- James W Brame con- David
    Moss, father min- James McAden-
Mary R & John H Hardie 14 May 1816; b- William Moss con- William
    Moss, gdn of Mary, who was daughter of Roy Moss, dec. min- James
    Meacham- 17May1816
Mary R & Richard E Winfree 28 Dec 1851; con- Thomas R Moss, father
    min- P.F. August- 6Jan1852
Patsy & John O'Briant 14 Dec 1795; b- William Moore
Polly & James Spain 15 Jun 1812; b- William Elam min- William
    Richards- 18Jun1812
Sally & Richard Roberts 17 Jan 1820; b- Alexander Dortch con- Martha
    Moss, who test. Sally 21 yrs old min- James Smith- 20Jan1820

Sarah & Luke Wiles 27 Dec 1811; b- Banister Gregory

Susan J & Archibald Hendrick 11 May 1847; b- Thomas R Moss

Mullins

Amanda W & Gholson T Reamey 16 Jun 1853; con- James Mullins, father min- Robert Burton-

Elizabeth & James Hudson 1 Feb 1786; b- Cox Whitlow min- Henry Lester- (Baptist) 21Feb1786

Lucy & Thomas Reader 10 Dec 1798; b- Richard Hughes min- William Richards- 13Dec1798

Martha Jane & Hugh William Nash 22 May 1842; b- William J Carter

Martha T & Humbleston Reamey 22 Dec 1848; b- James Mullins min- Robert Burton-

Mary & William Cutts 22 Nov 1791; b- John Ragsdale min- John Williams- 25Dec1791

Mary & Robert Reader 25 Dec 1792; b- James Hudson min- John Williams- -27Dec1792

Sally & Joseph Clark 9 Feb 1795; b- James Hudson min- William Richards- 24Feb1795

Susannah & Greenwood Harrison 11 Feb 1799; b- Edward Holloway min- William Richards- 14Mar1799

Munford

Elizabeth Beverley & Richard Kennon 16 May 1780; Richard from Chesterfield County b- William Randolph con- Robert Munford, father

Murdock

Seller & Batte Short 2 Nov 1798; b- John Carroll min- Charles Ogburn- (Methodist) 9Nov1798

Murfey

Nancy & Jordan Bennett 15 Dec 1795; b- Thomas Tanner min- John Loyd- 17Dec1795

Murray

Amcy & Burwell Belcher 15 Dec 1835; b- William Malone

Ann Bolling & Jesse Brown 16 Sep 1786; b- Samuel Goode con- Susanna Murray, mother Ann daughter of John Murray

Elizabeth & Spencer C Vaughan 16 Dec 1811; b- Garrett Avery

Elizabeth & Edward Randolph Yates 20 Sep 1783; d of John Murray b- Asa Oliver con- William Yates, gdn of Edward

Martha & William Henry Carter 18 Sep 1843; b- Robert Carter con- bride herself, who test she is 21

Nancy & John Bowen 8 Jan 1816; b- Christopher Singleton

Sally & Henry Bowen 14 Jan 1818; b- Charles Carter con- Catharine Murray, mother

Susanna & Theoderick Bland Ruffin 14 Jan 1788; b- Jesse Brown con- William Yates, gdn of Susanna min- Thomas Scott-

Murrill

Mary C & Andrew J House 22 Dec 1853; min- James McAden-

Naish

Judith & Jesse Monday 13 Nov 1792; b- Moore Comer of Halifax County

Nancy & Banister Winn 11 Dec 1809; b- Benjamin Blake min- William Richards- 12Dec1809

Nance

Elizabeth & Ishmael Mitchell 6 Jan 1808; b- Isham Nance Jr

Emily W & Benjamin Davis 20 Dec 1824; b- Benjamin Evans con- John Nance, father

Fanny M & Edward Giles 12 Feb 1818; b- Thomas Cleaton

Judith & Darling Allen 19 May 1783; b- Robert Nance s of William

Lucy A & James M Drumwright 28 Dec 1830; b- Samuel S Saunders con- Benjamin W Davis, gdn of Lucy min- James McAden-

Lucy G B & Henry Kinker 16 Sep 1852; con- Mary R Elvin, mother

Mahaley & Edward Poythress 2 Nov 1828; b- William Drumwright min- James Smith- 10Dec1828

Mary H & Buckner Rainey 21 Nov 1828; b- Paschall Bracey con- John Nance, father min- James Smith- 22Nov1828

Mary R & William Elvin 16 Oct 1843; b- Isaac Watson min- James McAdam-

Molly & Gray Allen 16 Dec 1791; b- William Drumwright con- Robert Nance, father con- Darling Allen, brother of Gray Gray s of William Allen

Sarah & Henry Wartman 8 Sep 1835; b- Isham Nance con- John Nance. father of Sarah, who test she is 21

Tabitha & Henry Davis 5 Apr 1819; b- John Nance

Tabitha & Stephen Mabry 19 Apr 1775; b- John Cook con- Isham Nance, brother

Nanney

Patsy & Claiborne Wright 27 Dec 1792; b- Hughberry Nanney min- John Loyd- 29Dec1792

Penelope & George Hudson 15 Oct 1818; b- James Webb

Tempy & William Spurlock 9 Dec 1798; b- William Roberts min- William Creath- 27Dec1798

Nash

Lucy & James Willis 14 Nov 1783; b- John Crews

Luvinia & James Chavous 24 Feb 1829; b- Edward Brandon min- William Steel- (Episcopal)-

Martha B & Littleton C Lucas 7 Dec 1811; b- James Nash, father

Mary Ann & James Greenwood 20 Mar 1827; b- Burwell B Moss con- Lily Ann Nash, mother min- Allen D. Metcalf- 24Mar1827

Nancy & Wylie Nash 14 Feb 1820; b- Shelton Powell con- Abram Nash, father of Nancy con- Thomas Nash, father of Wylie min- William Richards-

Sarah & John Crews 25 Jul 1782; b- Nathaniel Moss

Selah W & Allen Powers 13 Dec 1838; b- George C Nash min- James McAden-

Neal

Ann Eliza & Edward T Cole 17 Dec 1823; b- John M Yates min- Charles Ogburn- (Methodist)

Ann & Charles F Wall 20 Oct 1828; b- William Neal min- Pleasant Gold- (Baptist)- 18Nov1828

Anne & William Graves - --- ----; min- James Read- (Baptist)

Eliza & Evan Owen 24 Jul 1838; b- William Owen con- Obadiah Neal, father

Elizabeth & Elijah Boynton 31 Dec 1808; b- James Mealer

Elizabeth & Thomas Harrison 9 Sep 1811; b- Ichabod Neal

Mary J & Edward M Patillo 30 Aug 1845; b- W M Coleman min- John B. Smith-

Mary & Bozeman Mayes 10 Nov 1783; b- William Hundley con- William Neal, father

Nancy & David Craddock 25 Oct 1800; b- G H Baskervill

Sally & Braxton Wall 16 Apr 1827; b- William Neal min- Pleasant Gold- (Baptist)- 1May1827

Sally & Lewis Williams 13 Oct 1819; b- Thomas Neal

Neathery

Mary A & Elijah Hutcherson 29 Jul 1839; b- William D Justice

Mary Ann & William Mallett 6 Mar 1850; b- Robert F Neathery min- Thomas Crowder-

Mary & Thomas Tucker 20 Nov 1824; b- George Neathery

Nelson

Anna Matilda & Howell L Jeffries 6 May 1840; b- William O Goode con- William Nelson, father

Anne Carter & Erasmus Kennon 14 Nov 1808; b- George Craighead min- George Micklejohn-

Caroline Matilda & John W Lewis 19 Jun 1821; b- Berry Lewis con- George Nelson, father

Catharine & Thomas Collier 14 Feb 1825; b- George N Kennon con- N Nelson, father min- William Steel- (Episcopal)-

Lucy & Norborne T Nelson 8 Apr 1805; b- Henry Young min- Alexander Hay- (Antrim Glebe, Antrim Parish, Halifax County) 15Apr1805

Martha Walker & Thomas T Boswell 7 Jul 1846; b- T E Burton con- William Nelson, father

Mary E & William W Hill 23 Jan 1851; con- Edward A Nelson, father min- Alfred Apple-

Mary & P A Bennett 12 Jan 1835; b- C R Kennon con- N Nelson, father

Nancy C & Francis W Venable 24 Dec 1833; min- William Steel- (Episcopal)-

Sally Page & Woodson Hughes 18 Nov 1839; b- Wood Bouldin con- William Nelson, father min- John T. Clark- 27Nov1839

Newton

Elizabeth Jane & Daniel Yancey 16 Oct 1843; b- William P Newton con- James H Newton, father

Elizabeth & James Newton 14 Mar 1803; b- Robert Newton

Elizabeth & James Wright 15 Dec 1840; b- James Newton min- John B. Smith-

Emily & Peter R Overby 30 Oct 1829; b- Reuben H Newton con- James H Newton, father min- Pleasant Gold- (Baptist)- 4Nov1829

Harriet J & Richard T Elam 24 Sep 1842; b- James W Newton con- James H Newton, father min- John B. Smith-

Martha & Samuel Puryear 21 Dec 1829; b- William Newton min- Pleasant Gold- (Baptist)- 24Dec1829

Mary & Jesse Ladd 3 Mar 1832; b- John Newton con- William Newton, father

Mary & James Newton 3 Dec 1817; b- Joseph Newton con- Mary Newton, mother

Mary & William Newton 20 Dec 1830; b- James Newton min- Pleasant Gold- (Baptist)- 23Dec1830

Milly & John (Jr) Leneve 25 Jan 1830; b- Robert Newton con- James Newton, father min- Pleasant Gold- (Baptist)- 28Jan1830

Milly & David Williams 11 Jun 1804; b- John Williams

Nancy & James Bowen 29 Nov 1831; b- David Vaughan con- Mary Newton, mother min- Pleasant Gold- (Baptist)-

Polly & Thomas W Owen 27 Sep 1834; b- John Wright con- James H Newton, father min- John B. Smith-

Sally & Anderson Overby 21 Jul 1828; b- James H Newton min- Pleasant Gold- (Baptist)-

Sarah & Asa Vaughan 6 Jan 1846; b- Haman Newton con- James Newton, father min- Alfred Apple-

Nicholas

Ann & Benjamin Grymes 22 Dec 1778; b- John Nicholas

Nicholson
    Mary T   &   John James Speed   27 Feb 1811;   b- John H Speed   min-
        Charles Ogburn- (Methodist) 28Feb1811
    Mary   &   John Bilbo   2 Apr 1807;   b- George H Baskervill
    Mary   &   Austin (Jr) Wright   28 Jun 1811;   b- Tavner Toone
Noel
    Elizabeth   &   Thomas Mimms   5 May 1802;   b- George Meanly
    Elizabeth   &   Thomas Mimms   5 May 1802;   b- George Meanly
    Lucy   &   William Avery   16 Jul 1817;   b- James Avery   min- William
        Richards- 17Jul1817
Nolley
    Elizabeth   &   John C Bugg   17 Jul 1837;   b- Richard B Baptist
    Frances   &   William S Oslin   26 Jan 1813;   widow b- John Wright
    Georgetta Virginia   &   Jacob L Bugg - --- 18--;   b- George W Nolley, father
        min- William A. Smith-
    Rebecca   &   James Harris   20 Dec 1806;   b- Nevison Nolley
Norman
    Mary   &   John Brame   18 Mar 1768;   b- John Norment
Norment
    Amanda M J F   &   Benjamin B Watson   15 May 1835;   b- John H Pettus
    Ann W   &   John Morgan   28 Feb 1820;   b- John J Norment   con- James
        Norment, father   min- William Richards-
    Elizabeth   &   Griffin Craddock   6 Dec 1811;   b- William B Stokes   min-
        William Richards- 10Dec1811
    Elizabeth   &   Craddock Griffin   10 Dec 1811;   min- William Richards-
    Frances   &   James Hughes   13 Mar 1769;   b- William Norment
    Jane T   &   William T Watson   14 Oct 1828;   min- William Richards-
    Jane   &   Alexander Elam   14 Mar 1785;   b- Thomas Norment   min- John
        Williams- 17Mar1795
    Martha M   &   Edward Haskins   12 Sep 1825;   b- C H Pettus   min- William
        Richards- 19Sep1825
    Martha T   &   Benjamin David Hatcher   6 Dec 1836;   b- C H Pettus   con-
        Edward Haskins, gdn of Martha   min- Joseph S. Baker- 8Dec1836
    Mary F   &   John Pettus   19 Feb 1821;   b- John Binford   con- Thomas
        Norment, father   min- William Richards- 24Feb1821
    Mary G   &   George Camp   1 Feb 1811;   b- James Norment   min- William
        Richards- 7Feb1811
    Nancy   &   Robert Smith   8 Jan 1787;   s of John and Martha Smith   b-
        Thomas Norment
Northington
    Ann   &   Byrd Griffin   2 Oct 1820;   b- John S Northington   con- Nathan
        Northington, father   min- Pleasant Gold- (Baptist)- 4Oct1820
    Araminta P   &   William B Jones   27 Nov 1833;   b- Daniel C Hazelwood
        con- John Northington, father   min- James McAden-
    Betsy C   &   Clement Mitchell   27 Jul 1825;   b- B Northington   con- John
        Northington, father   min- James McAden- 10Aug1825
    Betsy Edwards   &   Warner Moore   6 May 1805;   b- Robert Moore   con-
        Jabez Northington, mother
    Eliza C   &   John W Gregory   13 Oct 1834;   b- John N Wright
    Elizabeth   &   Jesse Lee   3 Dec 1803;   b- Samuel Butler
    Jane   &   Robert Blackwell   30 Sep 1822;   b- John W L Northington   con-
        Nathan Northington, father
    Mary A   &   William H Northington   17 Oct 1849;   b- J B Northington
        min- Thomas Adams- (Lunenburg Co.)-
    Mary B   &   Hutchins F Tanner   17 Dec 1832;   b- William B Jones   con-
        John Northington, father   min- James McAden-

Mary T & John Daly 18 Sep 1815; b- Edward L Tabb con- Jabez Northington, father min- Thomas Adams- (Lunenburg Co.)- 10Oct1815

Mary & Thomas Watkins 10 Aug 1819; b- James Hunt con- Nathan Northington, father

Nannie P & Robert B Chambliss 31 Dec 1825; b- Samuel Northington con- John Northington, father min- Edward L Tabb-

Rebecca & Robertson Ezell 20 Mar 1815; b- William Evans con- John Northington, father

Sarah & Archibald Clark 24 Jun 1807; b- Scarborough Penticost con- Nathan Northington, father

Norvell

Mary B & John S Meacham 20 Mar 1828; b- Lewis G Meacham min- James Smith- 2Apr1828

Nowell

Martha & Benjamin Fox 29 May 1792; b- Young Nowell min- William Creath- 9Jun1792

Nuckols

Ann & James Watkins 9 Sep 1789; b- Philip Morgan

Nunnelly

Polly & Elemeleck Curtis 2 Jan 1798; b- Micajah Gwaltney min- Charles Ogburn- (Methodist)

Nunnery

Sally & John Tucker 22 Jan 1793; b- Charnal Deardin min- Charles Ogburn- (Methodist) 25Jan1793

Susanna & James Thompson 27 Aug 1806; b- Daniel Tucker Sr min- Charles Ogburn- (Methodist) 30Aug1806

O'Brian

Frances & Hugh D Bracey 27 Nov 1851; con- Mrs. P. Bracey, mother, who test. Hugh under 21 and gives consent min- P.F. August-

Ogburn

Angelina C & Richard H Edmonson 15 Jan 1816; b- Charles Ogburn con- Charles Ogburn, father min- James Meacham- 16Jan1816

Elizabeth & Peter T Ferguson 2 Dec 1818; b- Thomas Ogburn con- Martha Ogburn, mother min- James Smith- 3Dec1818

Elizabeth & David C Hutcheson 12 Jun 1817; b- Joseph G Hudson con- Charles Ogburn, father con- John Hutcheson, father min- Charles Ogburn- (Methodist)

Lucy H & Howell P Harper 16 Jan 1813; b- Charles Ogburn, father

Nancy Watkins & William B Simmons 14 Oct 1811; b- Charles Ogburn

Oliver

Eliza I & Hezekiah Puryear 1 Nov 1826; b- James T Moss con- Robert Oliver, father min- John B. Smith-

Elizabeth & Major Butler 29 Dec 1790; b- John Farrar min- Edward Almand- 30Dec1790

Elizabeth & William Knight 16 Oct 1799; b- Richard Oliver min- William Creath-

Frances & Joseph Butler 9 Jun 1783; b- John Oliver

Martha F & Robert S White 17 Dec 1849; b- James W Oliver con- Alexander G Oliver

Mary A & John James Winfree 21 Jan 1850; b- Burwell B Barron min- Thomas Crowder-

Ornsby

Elizabeth & Peter Evans 1 Sep 1792; b- Jeremiah Singleton min- John Loyd- 4Sep1792

Ellender & Jesse Cirkes 11 May 1786; b- William Singleton

Osborne

Ann Jones & John A Roberts 3 Jul 1828; min- William Richards-

Elizabeth & Abner A Lockett 12 Nov 1824; b- L B Barnes con- Thomas Goode, gdn of Elizabeth min- William Richards- 16Nov1824

Margaret T & Ludwell B Barnes 16 Nov 1824; b- Abner A Lockett con- Thomas Goode, gdn (?), who gives consent min- William Richards-

Oslin

Elizabeth & Thomas Binford 25 Dec 1786; b- John Oslin con- Jesse Oslin, father

Martha J & Allen T Andrews 12 Oct 1835; b- James Oslin min- James McAden-

Mary L & Drury Pennington 20 Nov 1833; b- Richard B Baptist min- James McAden-

Polly & John P Smith 30 Oct 1801; b- Isaac Oslin

Rebecca & John Wright 19 Jun 1802; b- Isaac Oslin

Osling

Nancy & Meredith Moss 21 May 1792; b- Samuel Oslin con- Jesse Osling, father Meredith from Brunswick County min- John Loyd- 31May1792

Overbey

Martha & James E Bowen 21 Jun 1847; b- S P[etty]pool con- James Overbey, father

Overby

Adaline & James Shelton 2 Oct 1848; 'Dr' James Shelton b- J Harper Shelton con- Robert Y Overby, father

Edith & William Overby 23 Feb 1818; b- William Vaughan

Edith & George Small 30 Mar 1799; b- Charles Hudson

Edith & George Small 30 Mar 1799; b- Charles Hudson

Eliza & Thomas Williamson 17 Jan 1825; b- Eggleston Overby min- Pleasant Gold- (Baptist)- 27Jan1825

Elizabeth E & James T Jones 27 Nov 1850; con- Milly W Overby, mother min- Alfred Apple-

Elizabeth J & Littleberry Overby 12 May 1843; b- James E Haskins

Elizabeth Jane & Richard E Yancey 18 Sep 1848; b- John J Newton con- Anderson Overby, father min- Alfred Apple- 20Sep1848

Elizabeth W & Peter W Overby 29 Jun 1843; b- L B Overby

Elizabeth & James Overby 24 Feb 1817; b- John Vaughan

Liddy & Enos Matthews 17 Sep 1788; b- Richard Thompson min- Thomas Scott-

Lina & Robert Williamson 17 Jun 1822; b- Thomas Noblin min- Pleasant Gold- (Baptist)- 20Jun1822

Louiseanna & George M Moore 9 Dec 1824; b- John Culbreath min- Pleasant Gold- (Baptist)-

Martha & William Bowen 22 Dec 1817; b- Zachariah Glasscock

Martha & James R Spain 5 May 1819; b- Edward Travis con- James Overby, father

Mary J & John G Elam 13 Nov 1829; b- Henry H Newton con- Milly W Overby, mother min- Alfred Apple- 14Nov1849

Meloda & John Wall 22 Feb 1808; John from Halifax County b- Peter Overby Jr

Minerva & James E Haskins 9 Nov 1846; b- E A Williams con- Robert Y Overby, father

Nancy D & Green Blanton 15 Feb 1810; b- Adam Overby min- James Meacham- 22Feb1810

Nancy & Zephanier Griffin 15 Feb 1830; b- Alexander Overby min- Pleasant Gold- (Baptist)- 18Feb1830

Rebecca & Henry White 21 Dec 1805; Bond says 'Rebecca Davis' while consent says 'Rebecca Overby' b- Robert Davis con- Edward Delony gives consent for Henry to marry 'Rebecca Overby'

Rosetta & John Culbreath 21 Nov 1821; b- Eggleston Overby con- Peter Z Overby, father

Sarah & Thomas Tillotson 5 Mar 1835; b- James Griffin con- Alexander and Sarah Parker Overby, parents min- John B. Smith-

Silvana & Henry Overby 25 Dec 1824; min- Pleasant Gold- (Baptist)-

Susan & David Dunn 16 Dec 1823; b- Alexander Overby min- Pleasant Gold- (Baptist)-

Susanna & John Howard 29 Jul 1822; b- David Overby John Howard from Granville Co., NC min- Pleasant Gold- (Baptist)- 1Aug1822

Overton

Elizabeth & Elijah Puryear 2 Dec 1802; b- John Overton Jr min- Edward Almand- 9Dec1802

Elizabeth & John Wootton 21 Nov 1814; b- Thomas Overton

Mary & Richard Wootton 18 Dec 1820; b- Samuel Wootton con- Thomas Overton, father min- William Richards- 21Dec1820

Nancy & Nathan Hester 14 Dec 1812; b- Christopher Overton con- J B Clausel, gdn of Nancy, who test she is under 21 min- Edward Almand- (Lunenburg County)- 17Dec1812

Rebecca & Daniel Stone 16 Sep 1817; b- Thomas Overton min- Matthew Dance- (Lunenburg County)-

Sally & Moza Hurt 10 Nov 1808; b- John Doggett min- William Richards- 27Nov1808

Susanna & Daniel Coleman 14 Sep 1801; b- John Overton min- William Creath-

Susanna & Powell Wootton 28 Oct 1820; b- Thomas Overton min- William Richards- 6Nov1820

Susannah & Allen Wagstaff 12 Dec 1803; b- Philemon Hurt, Jr min- William Richards- 25Dec1803

Owen

Elizabeth & Ranson Bowen 16 Sep 1822; b- Joseph Owen min- Pleasant Gold- (Baptist)- 17Sep1822

Elizabeth & Moore Gold 12 Oct 1825; b- Parham Owen con- Thomas Owen, father min- Pleasant Gold- (Baptist)- 20Oct1825

Frances & William Pettypool 2 Oct 1837; b- Edmond F Pettypool con- Thomas Owen, father

Harriet & Stephen Owen 9 Nov 1843; b- John Owen con- William Owen, father min- Alfred Apple-

Margaret & James Blanks 21 Jun 1830; b- Evan Owen con- Thomas Owen, father min- Pleasant Gold- (Baptist)- 2Jul1830

Margaret & Henderson Moore 17 Aug 1829; b- Joseph Owen min- Pleasant Gold- (Baptist)- 20Aug1829

Martha A & James Worsham 5 Dec 1842; b- Henry H Newton min- John B. Smith-

Martha & Henry Avery - Dec 1839; min- John B. Smith- Dec1839

Martha & Henry Overby 21 Oct 1834; b- Thomas W Owen, father, who also gives consent

Nancy & Abel Gregory 21 Aug 1815; b- Barnett Gregory con- Thomas Owen, father

Sarah & Alexander Gold 19 Dec 1828; b- Moore Gold con- Thomas Owen, father min- Pleasant Gold- (Baptist)- 25Dec1828

Susan & Jesse Browder 31 Dec 1830; b- Joseph Owen min- Pleasant Gold- (Baptist)- 4Jan1831

Susanna & Charles Hamlin 24 Apr 1785; min- Henry Lester- (Baptist)

Susannah   &   Barnett Gregory   20 Mar 1815;   b- Thomas Owen
Page
    Betsy   &   Banister Puckett   7 Jan 1801;   b- Isaac Bowen
    Caty   &   Benjamin Smith   2 Apr 1803;   b- Thomas Smith
Palmer
    Elvira D   &   Levy Talley   2 Jan 1837;   b- Horace Palmer
    Judith M T   &   Samuel Young   6 Jan 1823;   b- Richard Coleman   con-
        Christopher Haskins, gdn of Judith   min- James Smith- 9Jan1823
    Mary   &   George Camp   30 Jul 1772;   n- Nicholas Maynard
    Nancy   &   William Wright   12 Dec 1804;   b- Thomas Wright
    Sarah J   &   Churchwell Curtis   19 Nov 1838;   b- William Palmer   min-
        Benjamin R. Duval-
    Sarah M N   &   Leonard Langley   7 Sep 1829;   b- Abner P Wright   min-
        James Smith- 10Sep1829
    Susan   &   Silas D Wright   20 Feb 1843;   b- John E P Wright   min- James
        D. Conkling-
    Winifred I   &   William E Mayfield   9 Dec 1829;   b- Jeremiah Hilliard min-
        James Smith- 16Dec1829
Parham
    Ann   &   William Kirks   8 Jul 1788;   b- Lewis Parham
    Betsy Lelilah   &   John Harrison   22 Mar 1797;   b- William Kirks   John
        Harrison from Northampton County NC   min- Edward Dromgoole-
        27Mar1792
    Mary   &   Robert Rose Brooks   20 Nov 1780;   b- Daniel Baugh   con- Robert
        Brooks, father (Robert Rose under 21)
Parker
    Elizabeth   &   Stith Thompson   24 Jul 1785;   min- Henry Lester- (Baptist)
    Elizabeth   &   Stith Thompson   24 Jul 1785;   min- Henry Y. Lester
    Martha   &   Richard Quinchett   5 Jul 1839;   b- Berry Lewis Susan Parker,
        sister of Martha, test that Martha over 21   min- James Delk-
    Sally   &   Samuel Mayo   27 Dec 1853;   min- F.N. Whaley-
Parrish
    Ava H   &   Robert W Allgood   6 Mar 1848;   b- Benjamin S Allgood   con-
        Peter Parrish, father
    Elizabeth   &   James W H Edmonds   7 Jan 1852;   con- Peter Parrish, father
        min- P.F. August- 8Jan1852
    Emily   &   Creed A Allgood   3 Aug 1843;   b- Alexander Pritchett
    Lilly Ann Skipwith   &   John S Carroll   8 Oct 1818;   b- William Parrish
        min- William Robertson-
    Mary   &   Daniel (Jr) Tucker   8 Feb 1808;   b- William Parrish
Parsons
    Elizabeth   &   John Carrier   13 Jun 1785;   b- Francis Barnes   con- Thomas
        Parsons, father
Paschall
    Betsy T   &   Thomas Bennett   6 Jan 1817;   b- Philip Rainey   con- Anderson
        Paschall, father
Patillo
    Ann J   &   Edmund H Riggins   6 Dec 1845;   b- Tatnai Ellis   min- James
        McAden-
    Rebecca   &   Joseph Bradley   17 Feb 1794;   b- Solomon Patillo   min- John
        Loyd- 27Feb1794
Patrick
    Judith   &   Thomas Wright   9 Jan 1821;   b- Hughberry Nanney   con- E D
        Middagh, gdn of Judith
    Nancy J   &   Stephen Hatsel   22 Sep 1817;   b- Hughberry Nanney

Pearce

Lucy & Tobias Stalcup 9 Jan 1809; b- Baalam Ezell

Pearcy

Nancy & Jordan Bowen 25 Mar 1804; b- John Hudgins

Peete

Angelina & William W Fennell 13 Nov 1824; b- Charles H Ogburn con- E H Peete, father 'Dr' William W Fennell

Emily & William B Maclin 20 Jul 1829; b- James F Maclin con- Edwin H Peete, father min- James McAden- 21Jul1829

Penn

Martha A & William W Johnson 12 Aug 1839; b- Alexander Prichett min- Benjamin R. Duval-

Mary & George Freeman 13 Jul 1839; b- Thomas Penn Jr con- Thomas Penn, father min- Benjamin R. Duval-

Pennington

Ann & Reuben Mitchell 2 Apr 1783; b- Edward Pennington

Ann & Isaac Oslin 1 Mar 1800; b- David Pennington

Anne & Wiley Nash 5 Jan 1807; b- John Harper

Caroline I & William L Davis 13 Jun 1840; b- Phillip Pennington con- Ralph Hubbard, gdn of Caroline

Celia & William Murrell 6 Feb 1811; b- William Drumwright

Dianitia M & John Young 28 Nov 1825; b- Wesley W Young con- Ann Davis, mother of Dianitis min- Charles Ogburn- (Methodist) 29Nov1825

Elizabeth & Ephraim Drumwright 3 --- 1808; b- Wyatt Harper

Elizabeth & Jesse Oslin 26 Oct 1829; b- David Oslin min- James McAden-

Faitha & William Ladd 29 Dec 1800; b- John T Pennington con- Henry Pennington, father

Fanny A & Thomas F Jones 9 Jul 1834; b- Edwin Benford con- Benjamin P Pennington. father

Fatha & Robert Nance 14 Jan 1790; b- William Drumwright con- James Pennington, father

Frances & Pennington Lett 14 Feb 1810; b- John T Pennington con- Josiah Floyd, guardian of Frances

Jane & James Connell 6 Aug 1785; b- John Adams

Lucy & Ichabod Smith 31 Oct 1795; s of Johnand Paulina Smith b- Henry Pennington min- William Creath- 15Nov1795

Martha A & Isaac Benford 28 May 1850; b- Robert Malone min- Richard E.G. Adams- (Lunenburg County)-

Martha F & William W Winckler 20 Nov 1848; b- David Oslin min- Thomas Adams- (Lunenburg Co.)- 28Nov1848

Martha & John Harper 7 Dec 1785; b- John George Pennington con- John Harper Sr, father

Mary Ann & John Davis 11 Sep 1822; b- E S McCraw min- James Smith- 3Oct1822

Mary M & Wyatt Harper 29 Jul 1799; b- William Pennington min- John Neblett- 30Jul1799

Peggy & Ralph Hubbard 19 Mar 1814; b- Thomas Smith con- Drury Pennington, gdn of Peggy

Polly & Robert Westmoreland 5 Dec 1804; b- George Tucker

Sally W & John Cook 22 Dec 1812; d of William Pennington, dec. b- Benjamin Pennington con- Charles Smithson, gdn of Sally

Sukey & James Nash 23 Dec 1786; b- John George Pennington

Pentecost

Lucy & Langston B Finch 16 Dec 1816; b- David Shelton min- William Richards- 19Dec1816

Perkins
Elizabeth & William H Yancey 13 Dec 1835; b- Charles H Yancey con-David Perkins, father
Elizabeth & William H Young 13 Dec 1835; min- William Steel-(Episcopal)-
Sarah R & Grandison G Wade 11 Nov 1842; b- George W Perkins min-Alfred Apple- 15Nov1842

Perkinson
Elizabeth & Page Talley 23 Dec 1830; b- John C Perkinson con- Guilford Talley, gdn of Page Page from Warren Co., NC min- James McAden-
Susan Ann & William Thomas 19 Dec 1831; b- John C Perkinson

Persize
Mary & Charles Kirks 10 Nov 1787; b- Joseph Moon min- Edward Almand- 13Nov1787

Pettiford
Mary & William Kelly 23 Dec 1844; b- David Pettiford con- Parkey Pettiford, mother min- James McAden-
Rebecca Ann & Goodwin Cooper 7 Aug 1844; b- William Kelly con-Parkey Pettifoed, mother min- James McAden-

Pettus
Amey & Samuel Tarry 8 Jul 1799; b- William Coleman
Dorcas & Pettus Phillips 31 May 1814; b- Edward M Patillo con- Samuel Pettus, father min- James Meacham-
Elizabeth Walker & John Pettus 12 Aug 1782; daughter of Thomas Pettus b- Thomas Pettus Jr
Elizabeth & Robert Scott 8 Sep 1806; b- William Pettus Elizabeth daughter of Samuel con- Samuel Pettus, Sr.
Ella G & John S Grasty 15 Nov 1851; 'Rev' John S Grasty con- Thomas H Pettus, gdn of Ella
Harriet Jane & Richard W Harris 5 Sep 1825; Richard W Harris from Halifax Co, Va b- Richard E Walker con- John Pettus, father min-James Smith- 6Sep1825
Harriett & Miles Jordan 12 Nov 1804; b- John Pettus con- William Pettus, brother & guardian of Harriett min- John Cameron-
Jane & Jennings M Jeffries 28 Oct 1841; b- E A Williams min- John B. Smith-
Martha L & William T Z Finch 1 Oct 1835; b- Benjamin W Coleman
Martha L & William W Leftwich 6 Oct 1851; con- C H Pettus, father min- Adam Finch- 5Nov1851
Martha M & Thomas (Jr) Norment 23 Jul 1818; b- Andrew Gregory con- William Pettus Sr, father min- William Richards- 24Jul1818
Martha & John Coleman 11 Dec 1799; b- William Stone John son of Cluverius Coleman min- William Creath-
Mary A & Richard C Puryear 22 Jul 1834; b- Benjamin W Coleman
Mary B & John J Barnes 19 Oct 1846; b- Samuel F Barnes con- C H Pettus, father min- S.G. Mason- 27Oct1846
Mary & William Perkinson 8 Feb 1790; b- Thomas Pettus
Mary & John Williams 30 Nov 1813; b- Joseph Boswell con- Samuel O Pettus, father min- Matthew Dance- (Lunenburg County)- 2Dec1813
Sarah & James Johnson 10 Nov 1794; b- Thomas Pettus
Susan Ann & Charles O Harper 19 Jul 1841; b- Richard C Puryear
Susanna & Joseph Boswell 9 Dec 1805; b- Samuel Pettus, Sr. s of Ransom Boswell and Martha Boswell min- Thomas Hardie- 24Dec1805
Susanna & Rowlett Perkinson 19 Jan 1798; b- Matthew Pettus min-William Creath-

Pettyford

Hannah & Jacob Garrett 4 Nov 1802; b- Drury Pettyford min- William Richards- 6Nov1802

Hannah & Jacob Garrett 4 Nov 1802; b- Drury Pettyford

Pettypool

Mary & Robert Y Overby 28 Oct 1820; b- Phillip Rainey min- Pleasant Gold- (Baptist)- 27Nov1820

Rebecca & Joseph Blanks 15 Jan 1827; b- Stephen Pettypool min- Pleasant Gold- (Baptist)- 18Feb1827

Sally & Allen Pettypool 15 Mar 1813; b- Stephen Pettypool

Sally & James Williamson 19 Nov 1821; b- Eggleston Overby con- J W Pettypool, father con- Robert Williamson, father min- John S. Ravenscroft- (Episcopal)- 30Nov1821

Phillips

Elizabeth H & Thomas Cobbs 23 Oct 1806; b- John Dortch min- Charles Ogburn- (Methodist) 24Oct1806

Elizabeth & Samuel Farrar 10 Nov 1786; b- Hardy Jones

Emily E & William H Smith 20 Dec 1847; b- John C Phillips

Jane E & Edward A Craddock 2 Aug 1830; b- James Oliver con- Joseph Hutcheson, gdn of Jane min- Charles Ogburn- (Methodist) 12Aug1830

Jane & Williamson Patillo 13 Jul 1808; b- Martin Phillips min- James Meacham-

Lucy S & Joseph W Hutcherson 3 Jul 1832; b- Benjamin P Ferrell con- Joseph Hutcheson, gdn of Lucy min- James McAden-

Martha H & Richard E Walker 11 Dec 1826; b- Robert C Hardy min- James D. Tompkins- 21Dec1826

Martha James & Alexander W Hutcherson 10 Dec 1838; b- John W Butler con- Martin Phillips, father min- Edward Wadsworth- 13Dec1838

Martha & Joseph Simmons 4 May 1816; widow b- Edmund Noel min- Charles Ogburn- (Methodist) 6May1816

Martha & Samuel Y Tanner 28 Apr 1818; b- Samuel A D Young con- Martha Phillips, mother con- Clack Robinson, gdn of Samuel min- Charles Ogburn- (Methodist) 30Apr1818

Mary A & Charles W Baird 23 Sep 1812; widow b- John Gregory min- James Meacham- 24Sep1812

Mary & Miles Cox 13 Jan 1829; b- John Phillips con- Allen Phillips, father min- Pleasant Gold- (Baptist)- 15Jan1829

Mary & Charles P Jeter 22 Dec 1802; b- Williamson Patillo con- Dabney Phillips Sr, father

Metcaly & William Jones 3 Jan 1822; b- William Leneve con- Elizabeth Moore

Nancy & Richard Hill 29 Jan 1800; b- William Brown con- Dabney Phillips Sr, father

Nancy & William Ligon 7 Oct 1840; b- Thomas Glasscock min- John B. Smith-

Nancy & Marshall Moody 18 Mar 1811; b- John C Phillips min- William Richards- 21Mar1811

Sally E & Samuel H Patillo 15 Dec 1808; b- John C Phillips con- Pettus Phillips min- James Meacham-

Susan F & Isaac P Holmes 23 Dec 1829; b- James Holmes con- Joseph Hutcheson, gdn min- James Smith-

Susanna & Byrd Pulliam 8 Apr 1791; b- James Pulliam min- James Read- (Baptist)- no date given

Piemont

Anna V H & Ervin A Thompson 16 Jun 1851; min- J.D. Blackwell- 17Jun1851

Pierce

Linne & Benjamin Jones 10 Jun 1803; b- Richard Jones con- Lucy Pierce, mother

Pinson

Elizabeth & Arthur C Atkinson 12 Sep 1791; b- Thomas Pinson min- James Read- (Baptist)- 29Sep1791

Pitts

Anne & William Smith 13 Oct 1787; b- William Nowell

Poindexter

Betsy Ann & William Pettus 9 Mar 1789; daughter of Phillip and Sarah Poindexter b- Samuel Hopkins Jr

Clarissa & John Neal 9 Jan 1775; b- Moses Overton Clarissa daughter of Phillip Poindexter Sr

Jane & Jason Brightwell 21 Apr 1817; b- George C Poindexter

Lucinda & Richard Phillips 4 Jan 1825; b- George Poindexter

Mary S & Horatio Pettus 9 Dec 1799; daughter of Phillip and Sarah Poindexter b- William Pettus min- Edward Almand- 17Dec1799

Mary & William W Green 3 Jan 1803; Mary (Hinton) widow of Phillip Poindexter Jr b- G H Baskervill min- Matthew Dance- 11Jan1803

Nancy Charlotte & Richard Goode 8 Oct 1781; b- Phil Poindexter Jr con- Philip Poindexter Sr, father

Patsy & Daniel Smith 10 Dec 1792; s of Johnand Martha Smith d of Phillip Poindexter Sr min- Edward Almand- b- Robert Smith

Paulina & Francis Vercer 8 Apr 1830; b- W McNeely con- George E Poindexter, father

Sicily & Samuel Patterson 11 Jan 1773; daughter of Phillip Poindexter Sr b- Phil Poindexter

Pointer

Elizabeth & Presley Earles 13 May 1807; b- Roberts Nanney

Pool

Elizabeth & Hezekiah Overby 7 Nov 1823; b- James Williamson con- H P Pool, father con- Peter Z Overby, father min- Pleasant Gold- (Baptist)- 22Nov1823

Louisa L & Thomas A Gray 28 Nov 1837; b- William Hogan

Mary & John Morgan 17 Feb 1790; b- Phil Morgan

Susanna & John Mills 22 Nov 1808; b- Robert Greenwood

Poole

Mary T & William Hogan 5 Jan 1824; b- Isaac Watson min- Stephen Jones- (Lynchburg, Va.)- 12Feb1824

Polly & Howard Kirkland 25 Feb 1813; b- Burwell Coleman Polly daughter of Mitchell Poole min- James Meacham- 17Apr1813

Sarah & Young Allen 27 Feb 1786; b- Darling Allen Young s of William Allen

Potts

Lucy N & Francis A Thornton 3 Nov 1838; b- George D Baskervill min- Edward Wadsworth-

Powell

Indiana G & Littleton Edmunds 27 Aug 1844; b- R D Powell

Power

Patty & Fleming Jackson 9 Oct 1792; b- Sampson Power

Powers

Jane & William Connell 22 Dec 1836; b- Allen Powers con- William Powers, father min- James McAden-

Judith D & John Oslin 28 Aug 1849; b- Samuel N Oslin min- James McAden- 29Aug1849

Rebecca & Matthew Walker 21 Dec 1805; b- John Turner Jr

Sally & Zachariah Curtis 16 Feb 1795; b- Drury Creedle min- Charles Ogburn- (Methodist)

Poynor

Mary G & Wilson Corpier 2 Mar 1820; b- Charles W Baird min- James Smith-

Mary Nancy & Paschall Bracey 13 Aug 1827; b- William B Cleaton con- Diggs Poynor, guardian of Mary, daughter of John Poynor, dec.

Polly & William B Cleaton 30 May 1822; b- William H Walker con- Diggs Poynor, gdn of Polly min- Stephen Jones- (Lynchburg, Va.)- 6Jun1822

Rebecca D & George Williams 9 Sep 1833; b- Matthew Williams con- Diggs Poynor, gdn of Rebecca (Note: Diggs Poynor from Lawrenceville, Brunswick Co)

Poythress

Martha Jane & John Tucker 16 Oct 1848; b- J S Moss con- David Poythress, father min- Thomas Adams- (Lunenburg Co.)- 18Oct1848

Rebecca L & Benjamin Standley 22 Jan 1832; b- David Poyhtress con- Lewis Poythress, father min- James McAden-

Prewitt

Nancy & William Bevill 22 Dec 1800; b- Thomas Johnson

Prichett

Elizabeth & William T Coleman 28 Dec 1824; b- Harwood Prichett con- Thomas Prichett, father min- C.L. Jeffries-

Mary B N & Phillip (Jr) Johnson 23 May 1839; b- B B Goode min- Benjamin R. Duval-

Sarah & Robert Evans 15 Jun 1835; b- William Evans con- Sarah Prichett, mother

Puckett

Judith & Frederick Malone 19 May 1779; b- John Puckett

Mary & Mark Russell 3 Dec 1785; b- John Daly

Patty & Philip Morgan 13 Oct 1784; b- Frederick Rainey

Ruth & James Tucker 17 May 1810; b- G B Hudson

Pulliam

Mary & Ruel Allen 13 Jan 1794; b- James Norment min- William Creath- 21Jan1794

Sally & John Willis 10 Dec 1792; b- Richard Carter min- James Read- (Baptist) 15Dec1792

Pully

Elizabeth B & Ruffin Woody 16 Jun 1853; con- Mary B Pully, mother min- John E. Montague- (Granville County, N.C.)-

Fanny & Thomas Mitchell 31 Oct 1810; b- William Daly

Jane & Henry Tutor 20 Dec 1824; b- Hutchins F Pully min- James Smith- 23Dec1824

Rebecca J & John Goode 18 Jul 1796; b- John Dortch

Rebecca J & John Goode 18 Jul 1796; b- John Dortch

Sarah H & George Smith 16 Sep 1850; con- Mary B Pully, mother min- Hartwell Arnold-

Sarah & George Small 25 Sep 1816; b- James Pully min- James Meacham- 26Sep1816

Susan & Mabry Smith 1 Nov 1821; b- Frederick Wall min- James Smith-

Virginia K & James Woody 21 Apr 1851; con- Mary B Pully, mother min- Hartwell Arnold-

Puryear

Amanda H & William R Moss 22 Dec 1845; b- William W Winckler con- Hezekiah Puryear, father min- E. Chambers-

Ann F & John B Roffe 20 Nov 1848; b- Giles R Puryear

Ann & Grandison F Puryear 31 Aug 1840; b- Applin Puryear min- Solomon Apple- 8Sep1840

Eliza & James Eubank 3 Jul 1830; b- David G Hutcherson con- Hezekiah Puryear, father min- William Steel- (Episcopal)-

Eliza & Willis R Smelley 23 Dec 1844; b- William N Puryear min- James McAden-

Elizabeth D & Armistead B Sturdivant 15 Oct 1849; b- Samuel H Goode

Elizabeth F & Leroy B Wiles 13 Dec 1838; b- John Puryear con- Peter Puryear, father

Elizabeth P & William Mealer 9 Nov 1807; b- Thomas Lewis

Elizabeth & Thomas Crowder 14 Feb 1786; b- Solomon Draper min- John Marshall- (Baptist)

Elizabeth & Dabney Farrar 16 Dec 1816; b- Samuel Puryear min- William Richards- 24Dec1816

Elizabeth & John R Taylor 10 Oct 1839; b- William T White con- Thomas Puryear, father min- Charles F. Burnley-

Elizabeth & Charles Wilkins 22 Jun 1795; Charles from Rutherford County, NC b- John Farrar min- William Creath-

Ellen & Burwell B Barham 25 Dec 1850; con- John G Puryear, father min- Robert Burton-

Emily & James Cliborne 23 Dec 1835; b- Giles Puryear

Franky & Joel Avery 12 Dec 1808; b- Elijah Puryear min- William Richards- 29Dec1808

Hannah & Joseph Brame 6 Jun 1815; b- John Brame

Jane C & William Kidd 15 Oct 1838; b- John G Puryear min- John B. Smith-

Jane F & David Pettus 27 Jan 1827; b- John Smith

Jane & Walter Daniel 2 May 1804; b- Benjamin Bugg con- Peter Bailey

Jane & Edward Finch 13 Mar 1775; b- John Puryear

Jane & William Hudson - Nov 1803; b- Peter Puryear min- William Creath-

Jane & David Robertson 14 Aug 1844; b- William H Ligon

Juliet Ann & Littleberry Carter 21 Dec 1835; b- William N Puryear

Letty C & James H Gregory 14 Dec 1832; b- Andrew G Elam con- Thomas B Puryear, father min- John B. Smith-

Louisa T & Thomas R Brame 14 Dec 1843; b- James H Gregory con- Thomas B Puryear, father

Lucy Ann & David W Brame 18 Feb 1850; b- Giles R Puryear

Lucy G & John H Winckler 27 Jan 1848; b- Peter Puryear min- John Bayley-

Lucy & Julius Wilburn 15 Mar 1798; b- William Powell con- Thomas Puryear, father min- William Creath-

Margaret & Edward Roffe 28 Nov 1816; b- Peter Puryear min- James Meacham-

Martha & Alford Cowan 4 Aug 1828; b- John Puryear con- Morgan Puryear, father min- Pleasant Gold- (Baptist)- 7Aug1828

Martha & James Hord 14 Nov 1803; b- Thomas Thompson James son of Thomas Hord min- William Richards- 24Nov1803

Martha & Edward Keeton 15 Nov 1813; b- William N Puryear min- John Allen-

Mary & Hillary G Burton 26 Nov 1836; b- Alexander Gillespie con- John Puryear, father

Mary & Gold Griffin 17 Nov 1823; b- Thomas B Puryear min- William Richards- 27Nov1823

Mary & James Toy Hayes 23 Dec 1791; b- Reuben Puryear min- William Creath- 29Dec1791

Mary & Thomas L Jones 16 Feb 1852; con- Peter Puryear, father min- Adam Finch- 17Feb1852

Matilda H & Andrew G Elam 17 Dec 1827; b- Littleberry Stone con- Thomas B Puryear, father min- John B. Smith- 20Dec1827

Polly & Bartlett Cole 26 Dec 1826; b- William Kersey min- William Richards- 28Dec1826

Polly & Anderson Rose 9 Jul 1804; b- Valentine McCutcheon

Sally Ann & William E Morgan 10 Jun 1852; con- R A Puryear, father min- Adam Finch- 16Jun1852

Sally O & Hiram Forlines 27 Jul 1852; con- Thomas B Puryear, father min- Robert Burton- 29Jul1852

Sally Stith & Samuel Puryear 20 Sep 1810; b- Mackintosh Puryear con- Sarah Puryear, mother of Sally

Sally W & William S Willis 15 Dec 1823; b- Peter Puryear

Sarah E F & Albert G Jeffreys 20 Feb 1843; b- Richard C Puryear

Susan E & Francis A Moody 18 Nov 1833; b- Thomas B Puryear min- William Steel- (Episcopal)- 26Nov1833

Susan G & James E Vaughan 12 Dec 1842; b- Willis Smelley con- Mary Puryear, mother min- James McAden-

Susanna & Micajah Burton 3 Jul 1791; b- Robert Burton min- James Read- (Baptist)- 18Jul1791

Quarles

Polly & Drury Pennington 6 Dec 1809; b- John Wright

Quincey

Mary E & Travis Perkinson 12 Aug 1839; b- William N Smith con- William A Quincey, brother of Mary

Quinchett

Martha & William Wilson 24 Jan 1845; b- Thomas Harris min- John B. Smith-

Quincy

Ronsey Ann & Richard T Booker 23 Dec 1829; b- William A Quincy con- Elizabeth Quincy, mother

Ragsdale

Joannah & Sherwood Harris 25 Oct 1800; b- Robert Ragsdale min- William Richards- 1Nov1800

Martha & Stephen Hudson 16 Dec 1816; b- Drury Ragsdale min- William Richards- 24Dec1816

Mary Martha & William Pettypool 10 Mar 1828; b- Hutchins F Tanner Washington Maddox test that Mary is under 21 min- James McAden- 13Mar1828

Nancy & William Gee 19 Nov 1827; b- William G Coleman min- Charles Ogburn- (Methodist) 6Dec1827

Polly & Charles Owen Hudson 15 Dec 1812; b- Young Hudson, who test Polly daughter of Drury Ragsdale, dec., and is 21 years old

Rachel & Richard Rowland 10 Dec 1781; b- Henry Robertson

Tabitha & Nicholas Mealer 12 Jul 1802; b- James Wilson min- William Richards- 5Aug1802

Rainey

Betsy M & John Kidd 16 Feb 1818; b- William Rainey con- Williamson Rainey Sr., father

Betsy W & William Rainey 17 Jun 1822; b- William Rainey Jr con- Smith Rainey, father of Mary min- Stephen Jones- (Lynchburg, Va.)- 19Jun1822

Dicy & Randal Sturdivant 27 May 1776; b- Francis Rainey

Drucilla & Mark Lambert Jackson 8 Nov 1784; b- Francis Rainey

Elizabeth H & Richard H Drumwright 6 Nov 1821; b- James Rainey con- Buckner Rainey, father min- Stephen Jones- (Lynchburg, Va.)- 8Nov1821

Elizabeth & William King 6 Sep 1815; b- Smith Rainey

Emily R & Henry R Thomas 20 Dec 1847; b- John J Rainey con- Williamson Rainey Jr, father min- Thomas Adams- (Lunenburg Co.)- 23Dec1847

Fanny & William Cook 5 May 1803; b- Buckner Rainey

Harriet C & Zachariah Curtis 11 Dec 1840; b- John Baisey con- Williamson Rainey, father min- James McAden-

Lucinda & Eli J Holtsford 13 Dec 1828; b- Thomas L Wright con- Smith Rainey, father min- James Smith- 17Dec1828

Lucinda & William Powell 21 Feb 1810; b- William Cook

Lucy A & Charles B Thompson 25 Nov 1848; b- Charles G Turner con- William Rainey, father

Margaret J & Edward S Cleaton 2 Feb 1845; b- John J Rainey con- Williamson Rainey, Jr, who test. that Margaret is 21 min- James McAden-

Martha & Nathaniel Crowder 25 Nov 1805; b- Buckner Rainey

Martha & John McNeal 22 Sep 1836; b- Phillip Rainey min- William B. Rowzee-

Mary Ann & John Pearson 30 Sep 1811; b- Smith Rainey

Mary Ann & Paschall Thomas 17 Jul 1815; b- Allen Rainey con- Williamson Rainey, father

Mary E & Thomas C Thompson 15 Sep 1853; con- Williamson Rainey, father min- Willis N. Pence-

Mary J & D'Arcy W Paul 29 Apr 1845; b- Phillip Rainey

Mary Jane & John H Walker 17 Nov 1845; b- Buckner M Rainey min- James McAden-

Mary & Richard Fox 22 Mar 1775; b- William Davis

Nancy & Isham (Jr) Nance 8 Aug 1803; b- Thomas Nance min- Matthew Dance- 11Aug1803

Narcissa A B & Edward Alexander Piller 5 Sep 1843; b- John W Piller con- Buckner M D Rainey, father min- Daniel Petty-

Polly & John House 30 Aug 1837; b- Reaman R Smith

Rebecca & Peter Bass 9 Aug 1823; b- William Rainey con- William Rainey, father min- Stephen Jones- (Lynchburg, Va.)- 14Aug1823

Sally & Robertson Thomas 22 Dec 1823; b- Williamson Rainey Jr con- Williamson Rainey Sr, father min- Stephen Jones- (Lynchburg, Va.)- 24Dec1823

Sarah W & Charles G Turner 13 Dec 1838; b- Thomas J Rainey con- Williamson Rainey, Jr, father min- Benjamin R. Duval-

Read

Catharine Thomas & Charles G Feild 11 Mar 1842; b- John S Feild con- William B Green, gdn of Catharine min- F.H. McGuire-

Martha G & Pettus Farrar 20 Nov 1826; b- James O White con- Clement Read, father min- John B. Smith- 22Nov1826

Mary J & John Langley 18 May 1833; 'Capt' John Langley b- Lewis G Meacham con- Clement Read, father

Mary & Robert Newton 8 Sep 1788; b- Elijah Graves

Susan A T & Stephen Turner 12 May 1832; Stephen from Warren Co. NC b- Lewis G Meacham con- Clement Read, father min- Stephen Turner- 18Jun1832

Reader

Bicy & John Bullington 20 Mar 1797; 'Dicy?' b- John Cox con- Grace Reader, mother min- William Richards- 23Mar1797

Patsy & James Johnson 14 Jan 1799; b- Thomas Reader min- William Richards- 31Jan1799

Reamey

Anne & Cain Coleman 9 Jan 1804; b- Richard Carter

Frances & James Mullins 18 Jan 1827; b- James Reamey min- William Richards- 25Jan1827

Mary F & John T Roberts 24 Nov 1840; b- John A Walker

Patience C & William A Richardson 29 Jul 1839; b- James Mullins

Patsy & Mastin Harris 14 Dec 1807; b- William Harris min- William Richards- 18Dec1807

Polly & Pleasant Mullins 20 Dec 1852; con- Abraham Reamey, father min- Robert Burton- 23Dec1852

Reamy

Anna & William Harris 12 Nov 1804; b- Abraham Reamy con- James Reamy, father min- Edward Almand- 20Dec1804

Reaves

Joanah & Terisha Turner 19 Dec 1785; b- John Burton con- Stephen Turner con- Thomas Rives min- John King- 22Dec1785

Redd

Eliza & George B (Jr) Hamner 1 Sep 1828; b- Samuel Young min- Allen D. Metcalf- 5Sep1828

Martha W & John T Field 20 Nov 1821; b- William M Swepson min- William Richards- 22Nov1821

Mary E & John B Scott 3 Aug 1841; b- John S Feild min- F.H. McGuire-

Nancy E & William W Swepson 12 Jun 1816; b- John Tabb con- George Redd, father min- James Meacham-

Reekes

Elizabeth C & James Roberts 30 Nov 1835; b- Thomas C Reekes, father, who also gives consent min- William B. Rowzee- 24Dec1835

Elvira E & Berryman G Tarry 5 Apr 1839; b- Thomas C Reekes min- Benjamin R. Duval-

Martha & Robert B Harris 1 Jan 1836; daughter of Capt. Thomas Reekes b- Richard C Puryear min- John B. Smith-

Mary C & Samuel H Sydnor 1 Feb 1825; b- Drury Lett con- Benjamin Reekes, father min- Charles Ogburn- (Methodist)

Sally & Thomas Jones 21 Sep 1815; b- Thomas Taylor min- Charles Ogburn- (Methodist) 5Oct1815

Sarah H & Gee Drumwright 13 Dec 1842; b- Irby Creath

Renn

Polly & Alexander Rachael 2 Jan 1819; b- Burwell Coleman con- Phillip Johnson, to whom Alexander was apprenticed min- Milton Robertson- (Warren County, N.C.) 14Jan1819

Rhodes

Fanny & Thomas Crowder 29 Mar 1785; b- John Rhodes

Richards

Mary H & James E Moseley 4 Nov 1852; con- John G Richards, father min- Robert Burton- 17Nov1852

Millicent & Lewis Toone 11 Feb 1805; b- Abraham Keen con- W W Richards, father min- James Shelburne- 4Mar1805

Rebecca & John L Jeffries 8 Sep 1806; b- William Richards

Susanna & Lemuel Moseley 17 Jul 1815; b- John Tabb con- William Richards, father

Richardson

Elizabeth A & John J Vaughan 19 May 1848; b- John Forman con- Robert Richardson, father

Elizabeth & Wilson Bottom 20 Dec 1806; b- Nathaniel Moss min- James Meacham-
Susan A & Richard W Outland 10 Aug 1839; b- William A Richardson
Susan A & John R Wright 12 Nov 1838; b- William Walden
Richeson
Mary & Thomas Jeffries 26 Feb 1798; b- James Harrison min- Edward Almand- 28Feb1798
Ricks
Dolly & John Walton 14 Oct 1798; b- Richard Brown
Ridley
Maria & George N Kennon 12 Jan 1836; 'Dr' George N Kennon b- Robert Park min- William Steel- (Episcopal)-
Riggans
Mary & John Bradley 27 Sep 1814; b- William L Taylor
Riggin
Henrietta & Willis A Nanney 14 May 1850; b- William F White con- James Riggin, father min- Robert Burton- 15May1850
Ripley
Mary Anne & William Green 10 Feb 1821; b- Edward Dodson min- Edward Almand- (Lunenburg County)- 1Mar1821
Robards
Eleanor & William Winn 18 Dec 1848; b- Howard Mallett con- E A Williams, gdn of Eleanor
Phebe & Jehu Reader 13 Jul 1801; b- James Wilson min- William Richards- 21Jul1801
Rebecca & Jesse Russell 11 Dec 1839; b- William Robards min- Benjamin R. Duval-
Roberts
Agatha & James Watson 30 Dec 1813; b- John Nance
Ann J & Lewis G Wright 24 Nov 1828; b- Isaac Watson
Ann & Francis Royster 13 Dec 1802; b- Valentine McCutcheon min- William Creath-
Betsy & Marcus Moore 3 Mar 1813; daughter of William Roberts b- Nicholas Roberts
Biddy & Ezekiel Lambert - Feb 1804; b- Robert Roberts
Brambly R & Charles Nanney 1 Aug 1846; b- William B King
Caty & Ishmael Vaughan 24 Oct 1797; b- William Roberts
Eliza M & Cleaton Jones 18 Apr 1839; b- Bennett B Goode min- Edward Wadsworth-
Eliza & Benjamin Crow 10 Dec 1853; con- Mary Roberts, mother min- George W. Andrews- 19Dec1853
Elizabeth & Thomas Robertson 16 Jun 1787; b- Thomas Roberts
Emma & Howell Mallett 18 Jul 1848; b- E A Williams con- Panby Reese, gdn of Emma
Frances & William (Jr) Roberts 21 Aug 1802; b- Phillip Roberts min- William Creath-
Lucy & Dennis Roberts 21 Dec 1798; b- William Roberts min- William Creath- 25Dec1798
Maria & Robert Peebles 24 Dec 1821; b- Edmond Roberts
Mary R & John (Jr) Nance 19 Dec 1831; b- William Pool con- John Nance Sr, father
Mary & Benjamin Freeman 26 May 1803; b- Stephen Roberts min- William Creath-
Mary & William Garrott 9 Nov 1795; b- Thomas Massey min- William Creath-

Mary & Henry Kelley 13 Mar 1793; Henry from Brunswick County b- William Nanney min- John Loyd- 14Mar1793

Mary & John Nanney 4 Nov 1822; b- James W Drumwright min- Stephen Jones- (Lynchburg, Va.)- 6Nov1822

Nancy & Robert Evans 15 Jan 1847; b- William Evans

Nancy & Stephen Hatchell 12 Nov 1792; b- William Nanney min- John Loyd- 15Nov1792

Pamela & William P Wilkerson 29 Oct 1853; con- E F Pettypool, gdn of Pamela min- John E. Montague- (Granville County, N.C.)- 2Nov1853

Patsy & Hewberry Nanney 12 Jan 1792; b- John Fowler con- William Roberts, father min- John Loyd- 13Jan1792

Rebecca W & William N Wright 19 Jul 1824; b- William Davis con- Tabitha Nanney, mother of Rebecca

Rebecca & Elijah Stone 13 Aug 1792; b- Thomas Roberts min- William Creath- 15Aug1792

Susan Ann & John Wilmoth 16 Nov 1848; b- Paschall H Bowers con- Mary Roberts, mother

Tabitha & Hugh Berry Nanney 31 Jan 1817; b- William Bennett

Tency & John Nanney 5 Oct 1835; b- Lewis G Wright con- Stephen Roberts, father

Robertson

Elizabeth E & John C Manning 18 Feb 1836; b- James B Dugger con- Hannah C Robertson, mother min- M.P. Parker-

Frances & James Kidd 8 Aug 1795; b- Mark Robertson

Mary & Richard Burns 12 Dec 1825; b- Robert Burns con- John Robertson, father min- George Petty- 13Dec1825

Mary & Wilkins Royster 13 Feb 1797; b- Samuel Hester Jr min- William Richards- 18Frb1797

Nancy & James Jones 13 Oct 1794; b- James Hudson min- William Creath- 19Oct1794

Orpy & Thomas Bailey 22 Oct 1825; b- James Robertson con- John Robertson, father min- George Petty-

Sally & William Royal 10 Jun 1799; b- Allen Robertson

Samantha Jane & William A Lowery 29 Sep 1853; con- N T Robertson, father min- P.F. August-

Robinson

Mary & William Moss 12 Oct 1809; b- Henry Royall min- James Meacham- 13Oct1809

Naomi & John Lewis 24 Mar 1818; b- Woodson Palmore con- John Robinson, father con- Benjamin Lewis, father

Roffe

Catharine & George F Hayes 28 Nov 1850; con- Jesse Roffe, father

Eliza S & William Noel 2 Mar 1814; b- Jesse Roffe min- James Meacham-

Elizabeth S & William Neal 28 Feb 1814; b- Jesse Roffe min- James Meacham- 2Mar1814

Elizabeth & Samuel Brame 21 Sep 1802; b- Ingram Roffe con- James Brame, father

Lucy A & Giles R Puryear 22 Apr 1850; b- John B Roffe con- Jesse Roffe, father

Lucy & John J Davis 2 Dec 1822; b- Bennett Goode min- James Smith- 23Dec1822

Lucy & Burwell Moss 19 Oct 1812; b- William Brown, son of James Brown con- William Brown, gdn of Lucy min- James Meacham- 10Nov1812

Mary A E & William L Eubank 19 Dec 1837; b- R J Eubank con-Samuel D Roffe, father min- James McAden-

Mary Cousins & George W Jones 20 Oct 1853; min- Adam Finch-27Oct1853

Mary E & Benjamin B Hightower 21 Nov 1842; b- Ephraim A Drumwright con- Jesse Roffe, father min- James McAden-

Nancy O & Francis Blackbourne 18 Dec 1816; b- Melchior Roffe con-Hannah O Roffe, mother min- Richard Dabbs- (Lunenburg County)-19Dec1816

Nancy & Samuel Simmons 16 Feb 1824; b- Richard H Edmonson

Permelia M & James H Phillips 3 Nov 1846; b- Joseph H Lett con-Samuel D Roffe, father min- T.W. Sydnor- 10Nov1846

Sally L & Bennett Goode 13 Jan 1818; b- Thomas Burnett con- Samuel Simmons, gdn of Sally con- Edward Deloney, gdn of Bennett min-Milton Robertson- (Warren County, N.C.) 14Jan1818

Virginia N & Joseph H Lett 4 Nov 1844; b- James Connelly con- Samuel D Roffe, father

Rogers

Ann B & Joseph Jones 7 Dec 1807; b- James Whitlow Jr

Emily A & Benjamin C Drew 6 Nov 1850; con- George Rogers, father min- William A. Smith-

Martha W & William (Jr) Davis 20 Oct 1822; b- Diggs Poynor min-James Smith- 26Oct1822

Mary C & William Blanch 16 Sep 1834; b- A C Dugger con- George Rogers, father min- William B. Rowzee-

Patsy B & William Jones 8 Dec 1810; b- Joseph Jones

Sarah M & Allison C Dugger 7 Sep 1830; b- Thomas C Dugger con-George Rogers, father min- James Smith- 9Sep1830

Rook

Elizabeth A & Richard S Vaughan 1 Jan 1850; b- B B Vaughan con-William G Rook, father min- Hartwell Arnold-

Elizabeth & Robert Roberts 20 Feb 1799; b- Starling Morgan

Hannah & Thomas Barnett 10 Jun 1790; b- William Walker con- Anna Thompson

Roper

Polly & Henry Harris 20 Oct 1809; b- Wilson Harris

Rottenberry

Lucy & Larkin Crowder 29 Sep 1789; b- Samuel Rottenberry

Mary & Noble Ladd 29 Dec 1792; b- John Ladd min- John Loyd-3Jan1793

Rottenbury

Rainey & John Griffith 14 Dec 1790; b- John Lambert con- John Griffith Sr, father min- John King- 16Dec1790

Rowlett

Cornelia S & Abraham Jackson 19 Dec 1850; min- H.G. Leigh-

Flavala A & William B Jackson 27 Feb 1838; b- Stephen Rowlett min-James McAden-

Louisa F & William M Bennett 8 Nov 1841; b- Isaiah Jackson con-Steven D Rowlett, father min- James McAden-

Sally Ann & John T Dodson 14 Jan 1834; b- Peter D Hudson

Sally & Thomas Coleman 5 Jan 1799; b- William Brown con- William Rowlett, father Thomas son of Cluverius Coleman min- William Creath-10Jan1799

Sarah J & James H Dodson 6 Dec 1844; b- William G Coleman min-John B. Smith-

Royal

Margarett B & John M Whoberry 30 Nov 1826; b- Hugh L Norvell con-Margarett Norvell, mother of Margarett B   min- Charles Ogburn- (Methodist) 21Dec1826

Mary & Samuel Allgood 4 Oct 1786; b- Edward Clarke

Sarah & William Allgood 5 Mar 1790; b- Manley Allgood

Royster

Ann W & John Stembridge 18 Dec 1837; b- Benjamin R Royster min-John B. Smith-

Eleanor & Edward A Tarwater 14 Jun 1834; b- E A Holloway min-John B. Smith-

Eliza J & Allen H Holcomb 28 Apr 1831; b- Edward B Davis con- Clark Royster, faqther

Elizabeth & John Armistead 17 Jul 1777; b- John Farrar con- William Royster, father

Elizabeth & Brown Avory 27 Jan 1810; b- Miles Hall

Frances & Starky Daniel 4 Jan 1803; b- Robert Shanks min- Balaam Ezell- 5Jan1803

Harriet & Abraham Reamey 15 Aug 1814; b- Thomas A Gillespie min-William Richards- 6Oct1814

Harriett M & Robert B Crews 13 Dec 1834; b- James Brame con-Francis Royster, father

Julia & Robert Andrews 20 Aug 1827; b- Clark Royster min- Allen D. Metcalf- 24Aug1827

Louisa & John L Scott 14 Mar 1833; b- Ruel Allen min- William Steel- (Episcopal)- 15Mar1833

Lucy Ann & Jeremiah Hardin 19 Dec 1844; b- Giles H Crowder con-Clark Royster, father

Lucy M & Joseph A Keeton 25 Apr 1848; b- John F Royster con-Francis Royster

Lucy & John Morgan 9 Mar 1801; b- John Pritchett min- William Richards- 26Mar1801

Martha S & Edward | Davis 5 Mar 1825; b- Edward Royster con- Clark Royster, father

Mary & Alexander Crews 19 Dec 1825; b- Matthew C Gill

Phebe & Abraham Greenwood 24 Nov 1825; b- William L Willis con-Dabney Collier- relation not cited min- William Richards- 29Nov1825

Rebecca L & Jechonias Yancey 15 Dec 1788; b- George Royster

Rebecca W & James Connaway 24 Dec 1816; widow of Dennis Royster, dec. b- Randolph Westbrook

Rebecca & Dennis Royster 17 Jan 1807; b- Stark Daniel min- William Richards-

Sarah & Francis Bressie 13 Apr 1778; b- Joseph Royster d of Joseph Royster s of Francis Bressie and Elizabeth Bressie

Sarah & Charles Cox 3 Nov 1845; b- Huel Stone

Sarah & Abner Hester 16 Apr 1816; b- James Hester min- William Richards- 18Apr1816

Sarah & Semour Puryear 10 Apr 1775; b- John Puryear

Susanna & John Connaway 19 Nov 1810; b- Alexander B Puryear min-William Richards- 24Nov1810

Rudd

Martha & William Parrish 19 Nov 1807; b- Augustine Smith min- Richard Dabbs- 21Nov1807

Mary B & James Thompson 16 Jun 1817; b- Matthew Walker min-Charles Ogburn- (Methodist) 3Jul1817

Nancy & Augustine (Jr) Smith 8 Feb 1790; b- William Insco

Sally & Thomas Haile 17 Dec 1804; b- Harwood Rudd min- William Richards- 19Dec1804

Sally & John Hood 8 Oct 1804; b- William Birtchett min- James Meacham- 16Oct1804

Rudder

Martha & William H Smith 19 Sep 1842; b- Thomas I Penn

Ruffin

Martha & Robert Newsom 2 Oct 1772; b- Francis Ruffin con- John Ruffin, father

Russell

Elizabeth & James Johnson 30 Oct 1780; b- Jeremiah Crowder

Henrietta M & James Burney 2 Sep 1835; con- William Hendrick, gdn of Henrietta con- John Burney of New Bern, NC

Jane Wright & Samuel Hancock Smith 24 Jul 1806; b- Thomas A Jones min- William Richards- 26Jul1806

Jane & Daniel H Jones 18 May 1824; b- William J Hightower con- Theophilus Russell, father

Lucy A & Fendall Thompson 12 Oct 1853; con- Jesse Russell, father min- James McAden-

Martha & William Wade 9 Nov 1767; b- William Robertson

Mary & John Daly 11 Mar 1782; b- Samuel Goode

Nancy & William Hendrick 24 Nov 1817; min- James Meacham-

Nancy & Edward Robards 28 Dec 1824; b- James Russell min- Charles Ogburn- (Methodist)

Patsy & Thomas Crowder 18 Dec 1787; b- Thomas Jones con- Ann Russell, mother min- Edward Almand- 14Jan1788

Prudence & Richard Jeffries 19 Jun 1797; b- Thomas Burnett min- William Richards- 22Jun1797

Sally & James Johnson 28 Feb 1786; b- John Tisdale

Sally & William McDaniel 4 Nov 1816; b- John Curtis con- John Russell, father min- Milton Robertson- (Warren County, N.C.) 6Nov1816

Sarah & Daniel Nance 13 Mar 1780; b- James Standley

Susan T & Horace Palmer 30 Jun 1827; b- Samuel Young con- William Hendrick, gdn of Susan min- James Smith- 5Jul1827

Ryland

Eliza R & James Holmes 17 Oct 1853; con- Eliza R Ryland, mother min- Adam Finch- 8Nov1853

Elizabeth H & Archer W Hanserd 21 Oct 1828; b- Thomas Ryland min- James Smith-

Julia A F & James H Sullivan 21 Dec 1829; b- Churchwell Curtis min- James Smith- 24Dec1829

Mary & Isham N Tucker 10 Sep 1817; widow b- William Insco, father of Mary min- Milton Robertson- (Warren County, N.C.)

Nancy & Wyatt B Whittemore 12 Nov 1811; b- Harrison M Ryland con- John Ryland, father min- Charles Ogburn- (Methodist) 14Nov1811

Sarah P & Alexander Smith 11 Jan 1849; b- Thomas E Ryland con- Thomas Ryland, father min- John Bagby- 17Feb1849

Sadler

Avarella & Abraham Lewis 27 Nov 1811; b- George W Holloway

Salley

Magdalene & Elisha Bowen 24 Aug 1803; b- John Turner Jr min- William Creath-

Susannah Allgood & Zachariah Shackleford 9 Oct 1797; b- John llgood min- William Creath-

Sally

    Kerenhappuck & Randolph Westbrook 10 Dec 1798; b- John Allgood min- William Creath- 26Dec1798

    Mary & John Thompson 12 Oct 1807; b- Stephen Pettypool

Sands

    Araminta N & Thomas F Drumwright - Jan 1853; min- James McAden-

Sandys

    Elizabeth & Richard J Jeffries 14 Nov 1835; b- Joseph C Brame con- A S Jeffries

    Margaret W & Thomas R McDearman 21 Jan 1840; b- James M Crowder min- John B. Smith-

    Prudence & Creed T Haskins 31 Jul 1828; min- William Richards-

    Sally & Williamson P Roberts 12 Mar 1827; b- Phillip L Sandys

Saulsberry

    Lucy & Isaac Malone 24 May 1795; b- Joseph Walker min- John Loyd-

Saunders

    Catharine & Hundley Ryland 10 Mar 1830; b- Jesse Parrish min- James Smith- 18Mar1830

    Elizabeth & William Vaughan 3 Mar 1794; b- Ambrose Vaughan of Brunswick County con- Richard Vaughan, father con- John Saunders, father min- John Loyd- 6Mar1794

    Frances P & Lunsford J Morris - Dec 1832; min- John B. Smith-

    Jane & James Greenwood 10 May 1779; b- James Hall

    Margaret & Charles L Davis - Dec 1824; b- Robert Jones con- John Saunders, father

    Mary & William (Jr) Whitlow 12 Oct 1795; b- Charles Burton min- William Richards- 17Oct1795

    Milly & Bolling Wright 30 Jul 1787; b- John Feagins con- John Saunders, father

    Nancy & Daniel Morris 15 Dec 1807; b- John Feagins con- John Saunders Sr, father

    Ora & Jesse Dortch 24 Jan 1792; b- Jacob Bugg con- Mary Saunders, mother min- John Loyd- 26Jan1792

    Polly & William Chambliss 15 Oct 1819; b- John Chambliss con- John Saunders, Sr, father

Scott

    Dolly & Wade W Daniel 4 Feb 1818; b- Drury Scott

    Mary C & Tazewell S Morton 14 Jul 1832; b- George C Scott

    Mary E & Campbell Barnett 16 Sep 1852; con- R M Scott, father min- F.N. Whaley-

    Michiel & Patrick Duffee 22 Dec 1828; b- Edmund Young min- James Smith- 25Dec1828

    Minor Parsons & William Whitehead (Jr) Johnson 29 Jul 1793; b- Samuel Scott con- William Johnson, father min- William Creath- 27Aug1793

    Pheby & Jacob Chavous 8 Dec 1800; b- Thomas A Jones con- James Mayne min- Edward Almand- 24Dec1800

    Sophia W & John S Couch 27 Jan 1829; min- John B. Smith- 27Jan1829

    Susan F & Hillary T Jeffress 24 Oct 1849; b- Robert C Scott, father, who also consents min- S. G. Mason-

Seward

    Creasy & David Holmes 1 Jan 1810; b- Lemuel Vaughan

    Lucretia J & Joseph Y Hudson 23 Dec 1817; min- James Meacham-

    Martha & Peter Thompson 18 Jul 1842; b- Joe Thompson con- Sally Deward, mother

Shackelford

Elizabeth & Jacob W Stone 19 Dec 1825; b- Benjamin W Coleman con-Zachariah Shackelford, father min- Charles Ogburn- (Methodist) 20Dec1825

Shackleford

Jane & William H Hunt 7 Oct 1828; b- Jacob W Stone con Zachariah Shackleford, father min- Charles Ogburn- (Methodist) 8Oct1828

Shaw

Mary A F & John E Lambert 15 Oct 1833; b- Richard H L Bailey con-Mary Shaw, mother min- James McAden-

Shelton

Elizabeth & Joseph F Speed 4 Mar 1812; b- John H Speed min- William Richards- 11Mar1812

Nancy A & William B Stokes 19 Jul 1813; b- Thomas Burnett min-William Richards- 24Jul1813

Short

Anne & John King 25 May 1811; b- Austin Wright Jr

Eddy & George Tucker 23 Apr 1800; b- Daniel Tucker min- Charles Ogburn- (Methodist)

Elizabeth H & Thomas Wall 30 Sep 1797; b- Freeman Short

Elizabeth & William Daniel 29 Jun 1807; b- Wyatt Short

Janey & George Finch 7 Dec 1796; b- Freeman Short min- John Loyd-21Dec1796

Martha & Samuel Daniel 13 Nov 1809; b- Henry Wall min- James Meacham- 16Nov1809

Mary Ann & Joshua Mabry 2 Jan 1818; b- William Bilbo min- James Meacham- 7Jan1818

Mary F & George Stegall 23 Jan 1799; b- Henry Finch min- John Neblett-

Nancy & John Dupree 11 Dec 1787; b- Thomas Buford con- Jacob and Mary Short, parents John Dupree from Brunswick County

Patsy & James Bing 8 Jan 1789; b- Daniel Tucker min- Thomas Scott-

Polly & Marriott House 23 Aug 1790; Marriott from Brunswick County b- Miles House con- Jacob Short, father

Rebecca J & David S Wall 3 Jul 1805; b- George Stegall

Sally & Miles House 23 Jan 1788; Miles from Brunswick County b- John Stegall con- Jacob & Mary Short, parents

Susannah & Thomas J Tucker 4 Jan 1814; b- William Marshall min-James Meacham- 6Jan1814

Simmons

Angelina E & Paschall Bracey 4 Oct 1835; d of William B Simmons, dec. b- James Holmes con- Robert Moore, guardian of Angelina min- James McAden-

Ann & James McAden 21 Feb 1821; b- William B Simmons min- James Smith-

Betsy James & Robert Moore 5 Sep 1821; b- John Simmons min- James M. Allen-

Catherine & George R Edwards 12 Jan 1797; b- Joseph Simmons

Elizabeth S & Wesley F Edmundson 7 Jan 1837; b- Samuel Simmons min- James McAden-

Elizabeth & Joseph Simmons 18 Oct 1820; min- James Smith-

Elizabeth & John Wootton 4 Dec 1841; b- James Crawford Hughes min-James McAden-

Julia G & Richard H Coleman 2 Nov 1829; b- James Holmes min- James Smith- 4Nov1829

Lucinda & Henry Bagwell 21 Mar 1818; b- Edward Simmons

Lucy A & Walter W Hite 2 Dec 1843; b- William P Drumwright con-Paschall Bracey, gdn of Lucy min- James McAden-

Lucy & Jonathon Booker 10 Aug 1795; b- Thomas Jones min- William Creath-

Martha & William Garrett 15 Dec 1828; widow b- Sanford Bowers min-James Smith- 25Dec1828

Martha & John Roffe 1 Jan 1794; b- Samuel Simmons min- William Creath- 2Jan1794

Mary & Drury Lett 6 Jan 1827; b- Isaac H Jones con- Samuel Simmons, father min- John B. Smith- 9Jan1827

Nancy W & Phillip Gill 15 Mar 1830; b- Samuel Jones min- James Smith-20Mar1830

Rebecca A & William W Curtis 18 Jan 1830; b- William N Smith con-Samuel Simmons min- Charles Ogburn- (Methodist) 20Jan1830

Sally & John C Phillips 5 Jun 1816; b- James Phillips Joseph Simmons, father min- James Meacham- 6Jun1816

Sims

Jane W & Hartwell W Hargrove 10 Nov 1837; b- Robert Chapman con-Stephen and Mary Hendrick, grandparents of Jane

Susanna & William Burt 3 Nov 1812; b- Henry Sims con- Joseph Sims, gdn for his sister

Sinclair

Gilberta M & Conway D Whittle 20 Oct 1845; 'Dr' Conway D Whittle b- S D Whittle

Singleton

Ann E & James R Callis 8 Jan 1853; con- Mary W Singleton, mother min- James McAden-

Dicey & Pleasant Chavous 28 Dec 1821; b- Henry Stewart min-Alexander M. Cowan-

Judith & Littleton Kirk 11 Mar 1813; b- Robert Singleton, father

Julia A & Benjamin Merryman 11 Apr 1848; b- Joseph C Singleton min-James McAden- 12Apr1848

Mary & Banister Thomason 25 Jul 1795; d of John and Mary Thomason b- William Thomason min- John Loyd- 30Jul1795

Nancy W & John (Jr) Evans 19 Oct 1835; b- Thomas Jones

Nancy & Robert Spilsby Edmondson 29 Jan 1803; b- Thomas Crow con-Patsy Singleton, mother

Sizemore

Avy & Alexander Cox 16 Nov 1835; b- Daniel Sizemore min- John B. Smith-

Marilla & Charles Royster 19 Aug 1839; b- Alexander Puryear con-Daniel Sizemore, father con- George Royster, father

Skelton

Patsey & Ephraim Allen 13 Feb 1792; b- Thomas Allen min- James Read- (Baptist)

Skinner

Elizabeth & Andrew Hamilton 14 Feb 1782; b- Josiah Daly Andrew from Prince George County

Skipwith

Helen & Tucker Coles 21 May 1810; b- John S Ravenscroft con- Jean Skipwith, mother Tucker from Albemarle County min- George Micklejohn-

Selina & John Cole 25 Apr 1822; b- John S Ravenscroft min- John S. Ravenscroft- (Episcopal)- (married Thursday evening, 25Apr1822, at Prestwould)

Small

Elizabeth H & Francis O D Green 20 Sep 1842; b- William S Pully

Martha & David D Taylor 17 Dec 1825; b- Isaac Taylor min- Sterling M. Fowler- 19Dec1825

Mary & Nathaniel Chambers 6 Sep 1790; b- James Chambers

Polly & Howell Collier 27 Sep 1816; b- Ranson Stroud con- George Small, father min- James Meacham- 28Sep1816

Smelley

Mary Ann & L James Thomason 20 Aug 1841; b- Willis Smelley min- James McAden-

Smith

Aggy & John Hatsell 5 Apr 1786; b- John Lollis

Ann & Thomas Vaughan 12 Oct 1772; b- Swepson Jeffries

Anne & Claiborne Curtis 23 Nov 1812; daughter of Buckner Smith b- Edward Smith min- James Meacham-

Eliza D & John D Brame 1 Dec 1831; b- John Smith con- Nancy Smith, mother min- John B. Smith-

Elizabeth G & William P Phillips 9 Nov 1841; b- Thomas D Phillips con- James Smith, father min- James McAden-

Elizabeth L & Meredith W Davis 26 Nov 1822; b- John Robinson con- Mabel Smith, mother min- William Richards-

Elizabeth & John Brame 17 Apr 1829; min- Allen D. Metcalf-

Elizabeth & Achilles Jeffries 14 Sep 1772; b- Drury Smith con- Eli Smith, father

Elizabeth & Osborne Mayo 18 Dec 1838; b- James Mayo min- John B. Smith-

Elizabeth & Henry Miller 17 Jun 1800; b- Zachariah Curtis

Elizabeth & David Thacker 7 Oct 1844; b- John W Pillar con- David Smith, father min- John C Blackwell- (Lunenburg County)-

Elizabeth & John (Jr) Wilson 12 Sep 1791; b- Thomas Burnett con- Joseph Townes, gdn of Elizabeth

Emily J L & Robert T Neathery 20 Dec 1841; b- William C Neathery con- Martha Smith, mother

Ermin E & Henry W Walker 20 Dec 1841; b- Benjamin J Walker min- James McAden-

Frances & John Finch 14 Dec 1814; b- Edward Haskins con- Robert Smith min- William Richards- 15Dec1814

Frances & William Parham 2 Jun 1851; min- J.D. Blackwell-

Louisa E & John W Waller 6 Aug 1853; con- John Smith, father min- James McAden-

Lucy & Samuel Goodwin 22 Mar 1793; b- Thomas Hord con- Mary Hord, mother and widow of Drury Smith dec.

Lucy & Richardson Puryear 16 Dec 1833; b- Giles R Smith min- William Richards- 18Dec1833

Martha C & John E Abernathy 5 Nov 1842; b- Robert Scoggin con- Henry Wilson, grandfather of Martha

Martha Jane & Andrew B Gregory 23 Oct 1843; b- William R Doggett con- J B Smith, father min- John B. Smith-

Martha & Edward Elam 13 Nov 1786; b- Edward Finch con- John Smith, father

Martha & Paschall Fagins 27 Dec 1853; min- James McAden-

Martha & John Spain 1 May 1845; b- James Smith min- John B. Smith-

Martha & William Wyatt 14 Dec 1848; b- Joseph Evans Martha test. she is 21

Mary A R & George W Mallett 22 Sep 1846; b- Redmon R Smith con- Nancy Mallett, mother

Mary E & James S Walker 20 Nov 1843; b- Phillip H Thomas min-James McAden-

Mary L & William P Cook 20 Dec 1845; b- Albert J Smith con- Sterling Smith

Mary Susan & Jesse Gee 21 Dec 1846; b- W P Haskins con- John Smith, father min- Daniel Petty- 25Dec1846

Mary & John Camp 12 May 1783; widow of Drury Smith b- George Tarry

Mary & James Garner 10 Nov 1806; b- Hume R Feild min- William Richards- 20Nov1806

Mary & William Vaughan 4 Jan 1811; b- John Lambert

Mildred & Willis Burnett 15 Apr 1821; b- John Smith min- Charles Ogburn- (Methodist)

Nancy J & Lemuel Robertson 23 Apr 1821; b- Augustine Smith min-Charles Ogburn- (Methodist) 25Apr1821

Nancy S & Charles May 16 May 1837; b- William H Smith con- John Smith, father

Nancy & John B Smith 29 Nov 1817; b- John F Finch con- Robert Smith, father of Nancy min- William Richards- 2Dec1817

Nancy & John Smith 29 Mar 1791; b- Augustine Smith

Nancy & Robert Tarry 10 Jun 1793; Robert from Halifax County d of Peartree Smith b- Joseph Townes

Pauline W & Goodwin S Overby 18 Oct 1836; b- James J Grimshaw con- John H Smith, gdn of Pauline

Peggy & James Baugh 22 Dec 1800; b- John Smith Jr. con- John Smith, Sr., father min- Ebenezer McGowan- 31Dec1800

Polly & George Tucker 29 Oct 1814; b- John Davis

Polly & Freeman Weatherford 8 Dec 1800; b- Richard Thompson con-Buckner Smith, father min- William Creath-

Pricilla & Kennon Cox 14 Mar 1803; b- John Morgan min- William Creath-

Rebecca L & William A Andrews 27 Dec 1830; Rebecca test. that she is 22 b- David Oslin min- James McAden-

Sally Burnett & George Holmes 7 Dec 1818; b- Augustine Smith min-Charles Ogburn- (Methodist) 10Dec1818

Sally G & William Nolley 11 Feb 1833; b- Jesse Perkinson con- Thomas Smith, father

Sally S & William Haskins 29 May 1817; b- Richard Russell con- Daniel Smith, father min- William Richards- 4Jun1817

Sally & Daniel Neathery 14 Feb 1816; b- Edward Smith

Sarah & Charles Allen 28 Apr 1781; b- David Royster con- Drury Smith, father

Sarah & Robert Tucker 12 Nov 1787; b- Edward Elam

Susan D & Musgrove L Pettus 25 Feb 1833; b- Giles R Smith min-William Richards- 27Feb1833

Susan M & William D Garner 20 Nov 1844; b- Asa Garner min- John B. Smith-

Susanna & John Couch 25 Oct 1799; b- Archer Smith Susanna daughter of John and Martha Smith

Susanna & Gregory Gresham 23 Jul 1806; b- Thomas Smith con- William Smith, father con- Asa Gresham Sr, father

Susanna & Dudley Haile 10 Feb 1794; b- Harrison Winn

Susanna & John Prior Smith 7 Oct 1776; d of Drury Smith b- Achilles Jeffreis

Virginia A & Robert S Barnett 22 Mar 1852; con- William Smith, father min- Adam Finch- 8Apr1852

Smithson
> Elizabeth G & William Mason 15 Dec 1831; b- Silas D Wright con-
> Sterling T Smithson, father min- Abner W. Clopton- 20Dec1831
> Martha Ann & John Forman 4 Dec 1839; b- William R Mason con-
> Sterling T Smithson, father
> Martha Ann & John Norman 24 Dec 1839; min- John B. Smith-

Somervill
> Mary B & John Y Taylor 26 Jan 1829; b- George T Taylor con- John
> Somervill, gdn
> Mary Goodloe & George T Taylor 25 Apr 1825; b- William Taylor con-
> John Somervill, father
> Susan & Francis O Markam 19 Jun 1834; b- George C Scott con-
> Eleanor H Somervill, mother

Somerville
> Catharine & Nathaniel T Green 17 Nov 1831; b- George T Taylor min-
> William Steel- (Episcopal)- 24Nov1831

Soward
> Harriett & Jesse Soward 13 Jun 1838; b- Cary J Valentine

Spain
> Jemima & Cain Coleman 30 Jan 1816; b- James Spain min- William
> Richards- 30Jan1816
> Judy & James Vaughan 11 Dec 1797; b- Sterling Spain con- Thomas
> Spain, father min- William Richards- 19Dec1797
> Louisa I & Benjamin T Lawson 2 Sep 1846; b- John Flinn con- Royal
> Spain, father min- John B. Smith-
> Louisa & John Vaughan 23 Dec 1823; b- Royall Spain min- William
> Richards- 25Dec1823
> Lucy C & Joshua Spain 16 Dec 1835; b- Royall Spain min- John B.
> Smith-
> Martha & Warner Brown 30 Mar 1846; b- Robert W Spain con- Royal
> Spain, father min- John B. Smith- 1Mar1846
> Mary C & J Alexander Pace 19 Oct 1853; J Alexander Pace from
> Petersburg, VA con- Henry M Spain, father min- S.T. Moorman-
> Mary & Daniel Graves 27 Mar 1820; b- Noel Spain con- Jemima
> Coleman, mother of Mary min- William Richards-
> Polly & James Avory 12 Dec 1808; b- Abraham Reamy min- William
> Richards- 20Dec1808

Sparks
> Martha & Benjamin Bowen 12 Sep 1803; b- Zachariah Yancey

Speed
> Eliza & John J R Spencer - Sep 1841; b- H G Speed
> Elizabeth I & William M Swepson 27 Mar 1805; b- John James Speed
> Elizabeth & Roger (Jr) Gregory 21 Oct 1791; b- Sherwood Bugg
> Elizabeth & Marshall Moody 17 Mar 1823; b- David Shelton min-
> William Richards- 19Mar1823
> Harriet & C V Lanier 16 Nov 1841; b- Henry F Speed
> Lucy & William Jeter 11 Dec 1780; b- Dabney Phillips
> Maria & William L Harris 9 Dec 1843; b- Benjamin W Leigh
> Maria & Henry G Speed 19 Nov 1838; b- John J Speed con- John J
> Speed, father min- Edward Wadsworth- 20Nov1838
> Martha & David Apperson 30 May 1778; b- Richard Hanserd
> Martha & Nathaniel Moss 19 Apr 1794; b- Lewis Dortch min- John
> Loyd- 25Apr1794
> Mary & Lewis Dortch 2 Jan 1796; b- James Speed min- John Loyd-
> 9Jan1796
> Mary & William D Jones 27 Oct 1813; b- William G Jones

Mary & Nathaniel B Nelson 23 Oct 1833; b- Edward Speed con- John J Speed, father min- Benjamin Kidd- 31Oct1833

Nancy & Edwin H Peete 8 Jan 1807; b- Charles Ogburn con- James Wilson, guardian of Nancy min- James Meacham- 13Jan1807

Sarah & Sherwood Bugg 31 Dec 1787; b- Joseph Speed min- Thomas Scott-

Sarah & Newman Dortch 29 Mar 1800; b- John Dortch min- Ebenezer McGowan- 30Mar1800

Sarah & Richard Hanserd 12 Dec 1774; b- Robert Ballard

Spence

Peggy & Beverly Averett 25 Jan 1820; b- Richard Dunson con- Thomas Spence, father min- William Richards- 25Jan1820

Spencer

Fanny J & John W Spencer 15 Apr 1850; b- Wiley N Moring con- John J R Spencer, father of Fanny

Spurlock

Aggy (Jr) & John Lollis 5 Apr 1786; b- John Hatsell

Harriett & James Royer 18 Mar 1823; b- Richard Coleman min- James Smith- 27Mar1823

Milly & John Tudor 16 Jul 1787; b- Zachariah Spurlock

Stainback

Jean & William Dugger 23 Oct 1804; b- James Stainback William from Brunswick County min- William Creath-

Martha Johnson & George Kirkland 29 Jun 1809; b- Phillip Johnson min- James Meacham- 12Jul1809

Polly & Phillip Johnson 24 Jan 1794; b- Daniel Wilson con- Laura Stainback, mother con- William Johnson, father

Sarah & William Moss 9 Dec 1805; b- James Stainback con- Susie Stainback, mother

Standley

Ann & Smith Rainey 31 Dec 1796; b- James Standley min- John Loyd- 4Jan1797

Lucy & William Giles 17 Dec 1804; b- James Standley

Mary & Coleman Young 18 Dec 1788; b- James Standley

Polly & Isaac Nance 26 Nov 1818; b- Edward Giles con- William Standley, father con- John Nance, father

Stanley

Harriet N & William C Hanbury 10 Apr 1843; b- R B Noblin

Steagall

Martha & Henry Finch 2 Jun 1794; b- Robert Pennington

Steel

Agnes M & Charles G Field 28 Oct 1828; min- William Steel- (Episcopal)-

Amelia E & Drury Feild 30 May 1832; 'Dr' Drury Feild b- Alexander Feild con- William Steel, father min- William Steel- (Episcopal)- 31May1832

Stegall

Elizabeth & Jeffrey Mustian 5 Feb 1787; b- James Chambliss

Julia & William Thompson 20 Dec 1819; b- Drury Pennington con- George Stegall, father

Stembridge

Jane & James Smith 28 Oct 1839; b- Burwell Barron min- John B. Smith-

Polly & George Roberts 15 Oct 1810; b- James Stembridge

Sterling

Ann & John Holloway 17 Dec 1793; b- Richard Hanserd con- William Starling, father

Stevens
Polly & John Carter 12 Dec 1788; b- Thomas Stevens
Stewart
Amy & Robin Evans 13 Feb 1809; b- James Chavous min- William Richards- 17Feb1809
Ann & Benjamin Baskervill 15 Sep 1851; min- Hartwell Arnold-
Betsy & John Walden 21 Apr 1804; b- Kinchen Chavous
Celey & Cuffey Mayo 2 Apr 1802; b- Daniel Mayo
Dicey & Isaac Evans 24 Dec 1792; b- William Baskervill min- William Creath- 25Dec1792
Eliza J & William Valentine 17 Aug 1846; b- Charles Stewart
Eliza & Matthew Stewart 8 Feb 1802; b- Miles Dunston
Elizabeth Jane & Thomas Harris 28 Jan 1841; b- Pettus Stewart
Elizabeth & James Allgood 13 Dec 1842; b- James Stewart con- John Stewart, father
Elizabeth & Henry Harris 30 Jul 1849; b- John Wilson min- John Bayley-
Elizabeth & Allen Nowell 14 Jul 1800; b- Frederick Nowell
Frances & John J Chavous 17 Dec 1832; b- Randolph Chavous
Frances & Emanuel Lewis 21 Jun 1819; b- Randolph Chavous min- Milton Robertson- (Warren County, N.C.) 24Jun1819
Lina & Samuel Chandler 23 Dec 1793; b- William Chandler min- William Creath- 28Dec1793
Mahala & Edwin Simpson 12 Dec 1808; b- Saunders Harris
Margaret Susanna & Alexander Quinchett 29 Mar 1845; b- G W Mallett
Mary A & Reuben Meldrum 16 Dec 1843; b- William Stewart con- Nancy Stewart, mother
Mary & Robert Cole 31 Dec 1802; b- Martin Cousins min- William Creath- 2Jan1803
Milly & Jesse Walden 8 Apr 1805; b- Frederick Ivey min- William Creath-
Nancy & James Chavous 15 Dec 1835; b- Edward Brandon min- William Steel- (Episcopal)-
Nancy & Miles Dunston 18 Feb 1802; b- Thomas Spence
Nancy & Thomas Spain 14 Aug 1801; b- Frederick Ivey
Nancy & Thomas Spence 14 Sep 1801; b- Francis Ivey min- William Creath-
Phoebe & Daniel Stone 15 Aug 1825; b- Robert Thomas
Polly & James Drew 24 Nov 1817; b- Benjamin R Pulliam min- William Richards- 27Nov1817
Polly & Frederick Hammond 14 Aug 1807; b- Frederick Dyson min- William Richards- 4Sep1807
Priscilla & Archer Bowman 8 Feb 1819; b- Charles Stewart min- Alexander M. Cowan-
Prissey & Frederick Ivey 14 Dec 1795; b- William Willis min- William Creath- 29Dec1795
Rebecca & Anthony Chavous 10 Sep 1792; b- Henry Royster min- James Read- (Baptist)
Rittah & John Harris 27 Dec 1802; b- Jeremiah Harris
Rutha & Henry Avery 9 Jan 1823; b- Thomas Spence min- John S. Ravenscroft- (Episcopal)- 15Jan1823
Sally & Hutchins Mayo 10 Feb 1806; b- Daniel Mayo Betsy mother of Sally
Sally & Thomas Valentine 18 May 1818; b- Randolph Chavous min- Milton Robertson- (Warren County, N.C.) 21May1818
Sarah & Anderson Goen 24 Dec 1838; b- Osborne Mayo

Sarah & Anderson Green 29 Dec 1838; b- Osborne Mayo min- Charles F. Burnley-

Thrudy & William Thompson 11 Nov 1805; b- Neely Stewart

Stigall

Mary & James Chambliss 10 Nov 1785; b- Mial Wall

Stiner

Eliza & Marvill W Dunnavant 29 Mar 1825; b- John V Cawthorn con- Ann Stiner, mother

Stith

Elizabeth S & Henry M Spain 10 Apr 1833; b- Francis C Spain

Lavinia & Robert D Turnbull 20 Dec 1838; b- James B Dupuy min- Thomas T. Castleman- (Lunenburg County)-

Stokes

Elizabeth B & Reps J Elam 29 Dec 1819; b- Thomas Gregory min- Silas Shelburne- (Lunenburg County)- 6Jan1820

Mary M & Leonard Claiborne 13 May 1799; b- John Powell

Stone

Catherine & John Russell 30 Mar 1801; b- Benjamin Mitchell min- John Neblett- 2Apr1801

Cecilia & Thomas Jones 20 Jan 1823; b- Jordan Stone min- Pleasant Gold- (Baptist)- 25Jan1823

Elizabeth S & James Wells 26 Dec 1850; min- S.A. Creath-

Elizabeth & Smith Y Ragsdale 4 Feb 1843; b- William G Gary con- Margaret Stone, mother min- John B. Smith-

Frances E & Robert Wells 10 Jun 1846; b- James Wells con- Jacob W Stone, father min- Daniel Petty-

Frances & Thomas E Talley 19 Feb 1821; b- Charles L Jeffries

Hannah & Robert Wilson 9 May 1808; d- of William and Tabitha Stone b- William Stone min- Richard Dabbs- 18May1808

Happy & Richard R Coleman 30 Apr 1824; b- James Royer con- Elizabeth Stone, mother

Harriett & John Manley 1 Jul 1822; b- Elijah Stone

Joanna & Thomas Cox 11 May 1813; b- Archer Cox con- Elijah Stone, father con- James Cox, father min- James Meacham- 18May1813

Martha F & William G Garey 12 Feb 1839; b- Elijah Griffin con- Margaret Stone, mother

Mary & Benjamin Mitchell 14 Dec 1795; b- William Stone

Mary & William Stovall 21 May 1832; b- Jordan Stone min- John B. Smith-

Nancy & Samuel Carpenter 7 Nov 1816; b- John Stone con- Elijah Stone, father min- James Meacham-

Nancy & William Green 2 Dec 1833; b- Eli Stone min- John B. Smith-

Nancy & John Hutcheson 9 Dec 1793; daughter of William Stone b- William Stone min- William Creath- 24Dec1793

Nancy & William Owen 20 Dec 1819; b- Hardy Stone con- Joseph Owen, father min- Pleasant Gold- (Baptist)-

Nancy & William Tucker 18 Aug 1828; b- Samuel D Roffe min- James Smith- 19Aug1828

Polly & Willis Jones 4 Nov 1803; daughter of William & Tabitha Stone b- William Stone min- William Creath-

Sally & Anderson Green 15 Nov 1819; b- Charles Yancey con- Frances Stone, mother min- Pleasant Gold- (Baptist)-

Sally & Elisha Griffin 6 Dec 1830; b- Jordan Stone min- John B. Smith-

Sally & Matthew Walker 4 Oct 1809; d of William and Tabitha Stone s of Aurelius and Nancy Walker b- William Stone min- Richard Dabbs- 19Oct1809

Susan N & Samuel Roffe 5 Jun 1815; b- Melchizedeck Roffe

Susanna & James Baugh 19 Jul 1813; b- Martin Phillips con- John Hutcheson, gdn of Susanna

Susanna & Thomas Farmer 9 Dec 1804; b- Jordan Stone

Susanna & Edmond Jones 21 Dec 1822; b- Jordan Stone min- Pleasant Gold- (Baptist)- 24Dec1822

Susannah & Samuel Puryear 28 Feb 1842; b- Alexander Puryear con- Hardy Stone, father min- Alfred Apple-

Stuart

Lucy & Billy Thomas 10 Apr 1786; b- Francis Stuart min- John Williams- 20Apr1786

Prescilla & James Stuart 14 Nov 1791; b- John Walden

Suggett

Elizabeth & Thomas Merritt 14 Dec 1785; b- Pennington Holmes con- Edgecomb Suggett, father

Lucy & Martin Phillips 5 Nov 1808; b- John Hutcheson

Molly & John Hutcheson 31 Aug 1801; b- Samuel Hutcheson min- William Creath- 1Sep1801

Sullivan

Mary A & John Gwaltney 19 Oct 1840; b- John B Sullivan

Sarah N & William T Gwaltney 13 Dec 1841; b- Robert D Sullivan

Sullivant

Mary & John Hayles 26 May 1783; b- William Baskervill

Swepson

Charity A & Alexander M Hepbourne 6 Sep 1844; b- John S Feild

Jane & John Young 24 Jan 1784; b- Enos Easter

Lucy & John James Speed 26 Jan 1801; b- G H Baskervill min- William Richards- 29Jan1801

Sarah & Leonard Sims 12 Mar 1770; b- Richard Swepson

Susanna & John (Jr) Davis 28 Mar 1786; b- Richard Swepson min- John Cameron-

Sydnor

Lucy B & Thomas P Jerman 27 Apr 1850; 'Dr' Thomas P Jerman con- B Sydnor, father

Sally B & Warren Dupree 13 Feb 1838; b- Thomas H Laird con- Ruby Sydnor, mother min- William B. Rowzee-

Tabb

Elizabeth & George H Baskervill 16 Dec 1791; b- Robert Baskervill George s of George Baskervill, Sr. min- John Loyd-

Margaret & Abraham Keen 29 Dec 1790; b- Edward L Tabb

Mary & William G Goode 2 Sep 1798; b- G H Baskervill min- Alexander Hay- (Antrim Glebe, Antrim Parish, Halifax County) 4Sep1798

Mary & Richard Swepson 12 Apr 1779; widow of John Tabb b- Achilles Jeffries

Talley

Ann & James H Puryear 15 Nov 1841; b- Burwell Barron con- William Talley, father min- John B. Smith-

Elizabeth & Spencer Pettypool 6 Feb 1844; b- William L Yancey con- Payton R Talley, father

Frances & Edmund Allgood 20 Dec 1813; b- Samuel Bugg con- Elizabeth Talley, mother

Jane & William Pettypool 15 Aug 1814; b- Stephen Pettypool con- Stephen Pettypool, gdn of Jane min- Reuben Pickett- 30Aug1814

Louisa Maria & William Bishop 22 Dec 1852; con- Robert Talley, father min- P.F. August-

Martha & William H Bugg 24 Mar 1822; b- James Crook min- Alexander M. Cowan-

Mary Ann & Edmond Creedle 11 Feb 1791; b- Drury Creedle

Mary Ann & Joseph Owen 18 Nov 1833; b- Abraham Talley min- John B. Smith-

Mary F & George W Butler 28 Jul 1847; b- Deverly Williamson con- Peyton R Talley, father

Patsy & Henry Decker 30 Dec 1791; b- William Decker

Rebecca & William D Thompson 18 Nov 1847; b- Robert Talley

Rebecca & Spencer C Vaughan 27 Dec 1844; b- Edward Davis con- Abraham Talley, father min- Thomas King- (Halifax County)- 29Jun1844

Sally & Thomas Blanks 2 Mar 1818; b- Stephen Pettypool

Tarissa Ann & Edward Pettypool 7 Nov 1843; b- Burwell Barron con- Peyton R and Jane Talley, parents min- John B. Smith-

Tandy

Ella Ann & William J Royster 23 Nov 1838; b- Samuel Watkins min- John B. Smith-

Jane & Samuel Watkins 18 Jan 1826; b- Thomas Hailey con- James Watkins, gdn of Jane, daughter of John Tandy, dec., of New Kent County min- Pleasant Gold- (Baptist)-

Tanner

Amanda C & Lafeyette Barner 12 Mar 1842; b- Tatnal Ellis con- Elizabeth Tanner, mother

Araminta M & Robert E Tanner 14 Nov 1845; b- Robert Tanner min- James McAden-

Betsy Ann & Ambrose Daly 19 Feb 1816; b- Ludwell Tanner con- Ludwell Tanner, father

Delina & Andrew Samuel 11 May 1786; b- Thomas Tanner

Elizabeth R & John P Harper 10 Nov 1832; b- Robert Tanner min- James McAden-

Julia & Joseph (Jr) Bennett 15 Oct 1827; b- Benjamin Tanner

Margaret J & Oswald M Moss 15 Nov 1841; b- Matthew Williams min- James McAden-

Mary Ann & Jordan Bennett 14 Mar 1791; b- Anthony Bennett min- John King- 17Mar1791

Mary M H & William M Tanner 21 Dec 1853; con- J B Northington, gdn of Mary min- Nathaniel Thomas-

Mary & Edmund Feild 14 Sep 1807; b- G H Baskervill min- James Meacham- 19Sep1807

Rebecca H & Evans Tanner 23 Apr 1834; b- Robert Tanner min- William B. Rowzee-

Rebecca S E & William A Jones 17 Dec 1850; daughter of Mary Tanner con- J B Northington, gdn of Rebecca min- Nathaniel Thomas-

Rebecca & William (Jr) Poole 17 Jan 1797; b- Thomas Tanner min- John Loyd- 18Jan1797

Sarah C & James M Harwell 3 Jan 1820; b- John B Harwell con- Martha Tanner

Sarah & Jonathon Bennett 17 Dec 1793; b- Thomas Tanner

Tansley

Mary & James Watkins 22 May 1822; min- Pleasant Gold- (Baptist)-

Tarry

Mary C & Samuel B Wood 18 Aug 1824; b- Thomas Ryland con- Samuel Tarry, father min- James Smith-

Mary & James Craig 19 Feb 1766; 'Rev' James Craig b- Edmund Taylor James Craig from Lunenburg County Mary daughter of Samuel Tarry

Rebecca & Samuel V Morton 19 Aug 1850; con- Edward Tarry, father

Sally & Joel T Watkins 9 Mar 1842; b- Samuel D Booker con- Edward Tarry, father

Tarwater

Louisa J & William M Puryear 1 Dec 1832; b- Edward A Tarwater con- Michael Tarwater, father min- William Steel- (Episcopal)- 4Dec1832

Tatum

Ann F & Alexander G Oliver 1 Jul 1834; b- Benjamin W Coleman con- Benjamin Tatum, gdn of Ann

Mary & Alexander Stegall 17 Nov 1845; b- Henry Coley con- Lucy L Stegall, mother con- Mary E Tatum, mother

Taylor

Ann C & William Thrower 20 Oct 1817; b- Zachariah Bugg min- Thomas Moore- 27Oct1817

Ann Eliza & William C Boswell 16 Nov 1822; b- Richard E Walker con- Thomas Taylor, father min- James Smith- 24Dec1822

Ann J & Robert Ragsdale 16 Aug 1828; min- John B. Smith-

Betsy & David Dortch 30 May 1798; b- Abel Dortch min- Ebenezer McGowan- 31May1798

Eleanor D & William Hendrick 4 Dec 1830; b- Samuel Hester con- George Taylor, father min- John B. Smith-

Elizabeth R & John F Royster 27 Aug 1853

Elizabeth Y & Spancer King 26 Jan 1829; b- David Poythress min- James Smith- 29Jan1829

Elizabeth & John Williams 26 Oct 1791; b- Samuel Holmes Jr min- John Loyd- 27Oct1791

Emily F & Robert W Bragg 21 May 1839; b- Thomas R Moss con- Martha Taylor, mother min- James McAden-

Jane & Alexander Clements 18 Jan 1820; 'Capt' Alexander Clements b- George T Taylor con- William Taylor, gdn of Jane

Joice Lark & Willis Hundley 23 Sep 1809; b- Jones Taylor min- George Micklejohn-

Judith & Archibald Green 11 Oct 1802; b- Thomas Rowlett min- F S Stewart- 9Nov1802

Louisa & Joseph H Jones 10 Dec 1840; b- John H Taylor con- Martha Taylor, mother min- James McAden-

Lucy & German B Barnett 17 Oct 1822; b- Pennington Barnett con- David Taylor, father

Lucy & Isham Cleaton 8 Mar 1809; b- William Cleaton

Martha C & Michael E Crutchfield 16 Dec 1837; b- Isaac B Watson min- James McAden-

Martha Maria & Edward S Batte 2 Dec 1819; b- George E Powell con- Thomas Taylor, father min- James Smith- 9Dec1819

Martha W & John H Pettus 15 Nov 1830; b- William W Oliver con- Martha Taylor, mother min- James Smith- 24Nov1830

Martha & James Buckner 1 May 1817; b- William Drumwright con- Goodwin Taylor, father

Martha & John Cleaton 10 Nov 1787; b- David Taylor

Martha & Henry Sandifer 14 Dec 1785; b- Samuel Durham

Mary & John Bradley 16 Nov 1772; b- Lewis Speed

Mary & John Holmes 20 Dec 1779; b- Jones Taylor John son of Isaac & Lucy Holmes

Mary & John Savage 1 May 1787; b- James Day

Nancy I & Robert Ragsdale 31 Dec 1825; b- Sherwood Harris

Nancy & Samuel Jordan 1 Dec 1811; b- Samuel Holmes min- James Meacham- 3Dec1811

Oney & William T Thomason 16 Dec 1822; b- Ludwell Evans con-
Thomas I Taylor, father min- Stephen Jones- (Lynchburg, Va.)-

Penelope & Herbert Cook 20 Dec 1802; b- John Taylor

Penelope & Drury Malone 14 Jun 1774; b- Lewis Parham

Polly Jones & James Watson 27 Jan 1796; b- Abel Dortch min- John
Loyd- 28Jan1796

Priscilla & Marriott Kirk 27 Jan 1831; b- Thomas Kirk

Rebecca B & Lewis Poythress 9 Apr 1802; b- Thomas Watson min-
James Meacham-

Rebecca J & William Watson 29 Apr 1841; b- John Wartman

Rebeccah & John Turner 8 Dec 1800; b- James Taylor, Jr min- James
Meacham- 11Dec1800

Sally & Abel Dortch 24 May 1785; b- Goodwyn Taylor

Sally & James Feild 19 Apr 1814; b- Joel Watkins con- William Taylor,
gdn of Sally, who is orphan of Anderson Taylor, dec. 'Dr' James Feild

Sarah G & Isaac B Watson 21 Mar 1825; b- William Hogan

Sarah & Ambrose Daley 30 Jan 1809; b- James Taylor

Sarah & Henry King 18 Jul 1804; Henry from Brunswick County b-
James Minge Thompson

Sarah & George Tarry 7 Dec 1790; b- Anderson Taylor

Susanna & Thomas Watson 27 Dec 1791; b- William Poole con- Abel
Dortch

Ursley & George Connell 31 Oct 1812; b- Robert Westmoreland

Temple

Frances L & Charles W Crowder 23 Jul 1849; b- James F Temple con-
Roderick Temple, father

Thellis

Mary & William Barnett 9 Jan 1844; b- Thomas Lambert con- Lucy
Thellis, mother min- James McAden-

Thomas

Elizabeth Ann & Patrick Johnson 14 Jun 1830; b- Robert A Crowder
con- William Thomas, father min- Pleasant Gold- (Baptist)- 18Jun1830

Elizabeth L & Harrison Wesson 13 Dec 1825; b- Edward Poythress con-
Winn Thomas, father

Elizabeth & Joseph Royal 11 Aug 1794; b- Matthew Clements min-
William Creath- 14Sep1794

Louisa & James A Taylor 29 Dec 1845; b- R W Thomas con- Robert
Thomas, father min- James McAden-

Martha Jane & Archer Brandon 11 Feb 1839; b- James M Chavous con-
Robert Thomas, father

Martha L & John J Thomas 5 Dec 1836; b- Martin F Lambert con-
William B Thomas, father

Mary A & Robert Cole 20 Nov 1848; b- James M Chavous con- Robert
Thomas, father

Mary Ann & John Perkinson 12 Dec 1825; b- Leonard Thomas

Mildred & Samuel Vaughan 1 Jan 1811; b- John Cheatham

Nancy & Benjamin Durham 2 Dec 1831; b- Luke Burks min- John
Wesley Childs- 15Dec1831

Nancy & James Hargrove 14 Dec 1797; b- John Thomas

Nancy & Leoderick Robertson 11 Mar 1806; b- John Allgood min-
Thomas Hardie-

Nancy & John W Wilmoth 31 Jan 1835; b- Allen G Barnes con- William
Thomas, father

Nanny & Littleberry Pearson 1 Dec 1786; b- Peter Thomas

Polly R & Isaac Webb 28 Dec 1813; b- Bushrod Webb

Polly & William Cypress 8 Feb 1816; b- Christopher Guy

Rebecca A & David W Thomas 16 Oct 1826; b- Riddick Wilson

Rebecca & Joel M Loyd 16 Aug 1819; b- Riddick Wilson

Rhoda R A & John J D Pearson 25 Nov 1846; b- R W Thomas con-
Tinsy Thomas, mother min- James McAden-

Sally & Littleberry Pearson 13 Sep 1819; b- Riddick Pearson

Sarah A & John L Foote 17 Mar 1846; b- David W Thomas

Sarah E & John J Tutor 9 Dec 1850; con- T W Thomas, father min-
Hartwell Arnold-

Tabitha & Roderick Wesson 3 Jun 1814; min- James Meacham- 7Jun1814

Tabitha & Roderick Wilson 3 Jun 1814; b- Winn Thomas, father

Tinsey Winn & Leonard Thomas 3 Nov 1824; b- Lewis Poythress

Thomason

Aggatha W & Ludwell Evans 13 Aug 1816; b- Salathiel Bowen con-
Anna Thomason, mother

Betsy & Benjamin Hatchell 17 Jul 1815; b- Thomas Taylor

Judith & William Barnett 10 Jan 1793; b- William Bowen min- John
Loyd- 15Jan1793

Lucy & Watkins L Merryman 17 Dec 1850; con- Elizabeth Thomason,
mother min- James McAden-

Polly & Robert Singleton 30 Dec 1795; d of John and Mary Thomason
b- William Barrett min- John Loyd- 31Dec1795

Rebecca & John Lambert 20 Apr 1826; b- Benjamin Evans min- John
B. Smith-

Sally & Merryman Williamson 29 Jul 1803; b- Archibald Merryman

Sukey & Bolling Chavous 25 Jan 1798; b- Banister Thomason con- Amy
Thomason, mother of Susanna min- Charles Ogburn- (Methodist)
7Feb1798

Thomerson

Elizabeth & Epps Merryman 5 Jan 1803; b- William Thomerson

Thompson

Amelia E & Allen Williams 19 Oct 1830; b- John Puryear con- Samuel
Jones, gdn of Amelia min- Pleasant Gold- (Baptist)- 21Oct1830

Amey Evans & Henry R Thompson 17 Dec 1840; b- William Evans con-
Lucy Evans, mother

Betsy & John Puryear 19 Aug 1822; b- Charles T Carter min- Pleasant
Gold- (Baptist)- 27Aug1822

Clarimore & Drury Creedle 14 Dec 1829; b- John L Hightower min-
Charles Ogburn- (Methodist) 17Dec1829

Elizabeth & Amos Lee 13 Nov 1809; b- Margarian Thompson min-
William Richards- 28Dec1809

Elizabeth & Francis Lett 21 Sep 1797; b- James Lett

Elizabeth & Marvell G Stone 7 Jan 1846; b- John W Wootton min-
John B. Smith-

Elizabeth & Cary Traylor 7 Nov 1786; b- John Johnson

Judith & William Sparks 9 Jan 1804; b- Bernard Thompson min- William
Richards- 19Jan1804

Letty & Starling Evans 12 Oct 1801; b- Bernard Thompson min- William
Richards- 15Oct1801

Martha & William Davis 17 Sep 1765; William from Brunswick County
b- Wells Thompson

Mary & John Freeman 22 Mar 1842; b- Edward R Chambers con- John
Freeman

Mary & Richard Vaughan 21 Jan 1826; b- William Stone min- Charles
Ogburn- (Methodist) 29Jan1826

Milly & Samuel Jones 19 Oct 1824; b- Edward Tillotson min- Pleasant
Gold- (Baptist)- 25Oct1824

Molly & James Thomason 4 Dec 1804; s of John and Mary Thomason b- David Hicks

Nancy & William Crow 3 Dec 1799; b- Charles Thompson con- John Crow, father min- Charles Ogburn- (Methodist)

Nancy & David Hicks 23 Jan 1795; b- George Thompson min- John Loyd- 31Jan1795

Nancy & Burwell Jackson 19 Nov 1803; b- Drury Turner

Patsy & James Harwell Barry 20 Jan 1808; b- William Crow

Polly & Job Wright 15 Jul 1811; b- Samuel Thompson min- David McCargo- (Charlotte County, Va.) 16Jul1811

Rebekah & Thomas Binford 16 Jan 1804; b- Edward Thompson

Sarah & Jeremiah Russell 21 Dec 1809; b- Theophilus Russell

Sarah & Jeremiah Russell 21 Dec 1809; b- Theophilus Russell

Sarah & John Thompson 8 May 1775; b- Asa Oliver

Susan & John S Hightower 8 Dec 1815; b- William R B Clements con- Charles Thompson, father min- Charles Ogburn- (Methodist)

Thornton

Jane & John Hodge 24 Oct 1787; b- Hugh B Nanney

Sally & Charles Anderson 11 Sep 1787; b- James Thornton Charles from Amelia County

Tibbs

Sarah & James Mayne 8 Mar 1779; b- William Tibbs

Tillotson

Ann & James Yancey 19 Nov 1825; b- Edward Tillotson min- Pleasant Gold- (Baptist)- 23Nov1825

Elizabeth & Allen Bowen 23 Jul 1829; b- James Tillotson con- Thomas Tillotson, father

Emily & William J Ragsdale 6 Oct 1834; b- James Yancey con- William Tillotson, gdn of Emily

Joyce & James Wilkerson 6 Oct 1834; b- James Yancey con- William Tillotson, gdn of Joyce min- William Steel- (Episcopal)- 9Oct1834

Lucy & Elam S Wall 27 Nov 1823; b- James Tillotson con- John Tillotson, father min- Pleasant Gold- (Baptist)- 11Dec1823

Nancy & Leonard Neal 22 May 1827; b- James Newton con- Thomas Tillotson, father min- Pleasant Gold- (Baptist)- 31May1827

Nancy & John Tillotson 19 May 1828; b- John Jones con- John Tillotson Sr, father min- Pleasant Gold- (Baptist)-

Philadelphia & John Jones 18 Dec 1822; b- John Tillotson

Rebecca & John Baynham 20 Feb 1832; b- James Yancey con- William Tillotson, gdn for Rebecca, who test. she is under 21

Sally & John Blane 2 Dec 1829; b- Edward Tillotson min- E. Hollister-

Sally & Lewis T Yancey 14 Jun 1837; b- John Tillotson

Tindal

Polly & James Griffin 14 Dec 1807; b- Overton Wiles

Tinsley

Martha & Thomas Hailey 22 Oct 1823; b- Joseph Watkins min- Pleasant Gold- (Baptist)-

Tisdale

Becky & Freeman Shell 18 Mar 1806; b- Bartlett Cox min- Charles Ogburn- (Methodist)- 21Mar1806

Levina & Bartlett Cole 27 Oct 1789; b- Edward Tisdale min- Thomas Scott-

Phebe & John Thompson 12 Jan 1795; b- William Thompson min- William Creath-

Rebecca & Stephen Draper 26 Aug 1815; b- William Tucker min- Milton Robertson- (Warren County, N.C.)

Toone

Elizabeth & Theophilus W Butler 16 Mar 1835; b- Asa Garner

Frances & Richard Nicholson 16 Nov 1840; b- George W Freeman

Joanna & George Toone 10 Oct 1814; b- Thomas Abernathy min- Milton Robertson- (Warren County, N.C.) 31Oct1814

Martha & John Johnson 27 Jan 1810; b- Thomas Johnson

Martha & John Johnson 27 Jan 1810; b- Thomas Johnson

Martha & Thomas Overton 13 Apr 1795; b- Edward Hogan min- Edward Almand- 16Apr1795

Mary M & John F Royster 10 Jul 1848; b- A Jackson Toone con- Louis and Mildred Toone, parents

Nancy S & Wylie W Collier 15 Feb 1825; b- Richard Russell

Polly & Freeman Walker 12 Jul 1789; b- Lewis Toone min- John Williams- 14Jul1789

Rebecca A & Samuel T Harris 11 Dec 1849; b- John R Toone con- Lewis Toone, father

Sarah & Joseph Clarke 14 Dec 1795; b- Bolling Clarke

Susan & Buckner Smith 15 Jan 1821; b- William Johnson con- Archibald Toone, father

Susanna & Isaac Short 12 Jan 1795; b- John Stegall

Virginia E & John W Stuart 13 Jun 1853; con- Edward F Toone, father min- James S. Kennedy- 22Jun1853

Totty

Agnes D & Hugh Rogers 14 May 1840; b- Michael H Tarwater con- Thomas E Totty, father min- D.B. Nicholson-

Rebecca P & William F Childress 22 Jul 1842; b- Hugh M T Rogers con- Thomas E Totty, father min- Charles F. Burnley-

Towler

Ann M & William A Homes 12 Nov 1844; b- Henry A Towler con- William Towler, father

Barbara J & Benjamin T Willard 24 Dec 1827; b- John A Willard con- John Winckler, gdn of Barbara con- Humphrey Willard, father min- James Smith- 26Dec1827

Elizabeth & James Garrett 17 Mar 1819; b- John Winckler min- James Meacham- 29Mar1819

Mary & Joseph Bennett 6 Sep 1821; b- Edward Deloney min- J. Nolley-

Nancy & Basil W Rice 21 May 1821; b- John Winckler

Townes

Elizabeth & Alfred Boyd 24 Aug 1836; b- William Townes min- William Steel- (Episcopal)-

Ellen F & Edward Townes 21 Dec 1844; b- William Townes

Isabella H & Francis W Boyd 2 Nov 1837; b- William Townes

Lucy Ann & John Wimbish 16 Oct 1839; b- William Townes min- A.M. Poindexter-

Martha C & Alexander G Allen 12 Aug 1822; b- William Bedford con- Joseph Townes, father

Mary J & Lewis W Wimbish 15 Apr 1842; b- Alfred Boyd con- William Townes, father min- A.M. Poindexter-

Susan & James Jones 21 Jan 1826; b- William Townes

Tucker

Amy & Gardiner Crowder 4 Dec 1788; b- David Crowder

Caroline F & Joseph H Ryland 20 Dec 1841; b- John Tucker min- John B. Smith-

Catherine & Thomas Coley 24 Feb 1800; b- Leonard Keeton

Catherine & James P Tucker 14 Dec 1772; b- Robert Williams

Charlotte Ann & Thomas A Norvell 15 Dec 1834; b- Pettus Farrar min-M.P. Parks- 18Dec1834

Eleanor F & James G Perry 25 Feb 1841; min- Charles F. Burnley-

Eleanor Frances & James G Berry 23 Feb 1841; b- William Hendrick con- William Tucker, father

Elizabeth & James Crowder 12 Dec 1810; b- Daniel Tucker Sr

Elizabeth & Osborne Evans 22 May 1838; b- Burwell Brown

Frances & John Tucker 10 Dec 1798; b- Leonard Keeton min- William Creath- 28Dec1798

Jane & James Tucker 6 Sep 1809; b- William Insco

Lucy R & John McDaniel 10 Aug 1844; b- Isaac R Watson min- James McAden-

Lucy & John Hudson 10 Dec 1804; b- Richard Walden

Martha C & Thomas Cumbia 7 Oct 1839; b- Alexander Prichett min-Benjamin R. Duval-

Martha & Merritt Tucker 6 Dec 1833; b- Usham N Tucker

Mary A & Henderson Thompson 30 Sep 1816; b- Thomas Burnett con-Daniel Tucker, father con- John Thompson Jr, father

Mary Ann & Jesse Perkinson 15 Oct 1833; b- William Smelley con-George Tucker, father min- James McAden-

Mary Ann & John Williams 15 Jan 1838; b- John Doyle min- James McAden-

Mary Thweate & Jacob Bugg 11 Sep 1798; b- Benjamin Tucker, Jr.

Mary & Zachariah Griffin 13 Aug 1849; b- W H Somervill con- William Tucker, father

Mary & Leonard Keeton 9 Mar 1801; b- Thomas Coley min- William Creath-

Nancy & William Vaughan 20 Dec 1821; min- Charles Ogburn-(Methodist)

Polly & Leonard Keeton 10 Nov 1794; b- Daniel Tucker min- William Creath- 22Nov1794

Rebecca A & William R Johnston 10 Aug 1835; b- Robert A Crowder con- S G Tucker, father min- William Steel- (Episcopal)- 13Aug1835

Sally E & Edwin Cox 16 May 1825; b- Daniel Tucker min- Charles Ogburn- (Methodist) 17May1825

Sarah G & Peterson Gwaltney 28 Jul 1846; b- Robert D Sullivan

Sarah J & Edward K Renn 18 Aug 1846; b- Robert M Hutcherson

Susan C & Thomas Mitchell 18 Apr 1851

Susan C & Thomas Pritchett 18 Apr 1851; min- J.D. Blackwell-

Tudor

Camilla & William Parrish 9 Dec 1801; b- William Roberts

Tunstall

Mary E & Allen S Mason 17 Oct 1853; con- John B Tunstall, father min- George W. Andrews- 28Oct1853

Sarah & Littleberry Watson 9 Dec 1843; b- Richard D Bugg con- John B Tunstall, father

Turner

Betsy & William Phillips 20 Dec 1799; b- Matthew Turner Jr con- John Turner, father min- William Creath-

Judith M & John Winckler 15 Apr 1816; b- Charles L Turner min-James Meacham- 17Apr1816

Lucretia & Isham Merryman 4 Apr 1787; b- Abram Merryman

Martha E J & John H Ezell 29 Nov 1841; b- James W Brame con-Judith J Turner, mother

Mary Ann & James Brame 16 Feb 1835; b- William S Pully con- Judith J Turner, mother min- M.P. Parks- 18Feb1835

Mary & John Hooper 7 Jul 1806; b- Benjamin Reekes min- Charles Ogburn- (Methodist) 10Jul1806

Mary & William Rives 1 Jan 1788; b- Nicholas Bilbo con- Thomas Rives, father con- Stephen Turner, father

Milly & John Holmes 31 Aug 1797; b- Matthew Turner Jr con- John Turner, father

Nancy & Nathaniel Jackson 24 Nov 1804; b- William Baskervill min- William Creath-

Nancy & Aurelius Walker 23 Nov 1784; d of Matthew Turner b- William Allen son of Sylvanus Walker

Polly & Bins Jackson 23 Apr 1803; b- Drury Turner min- William Creath-

Sally & Richard Hutcheson 24 Nov 1798; b- Matthew Turner min- William Creath- 29Nov1798

Wilmouth & Richard (Jr) Hutcheson 11 Oct 1804; b- Jacob Shelor Richard son of John Hutcheson min- William Creath-

Tutor

Mary J & William Fitts 18 Sep 1843; b- John J Tutor con- John G Tutor, father min- William H. Maddox- 7Oct1843

Underwood

Levinia & Baker Wells 10 Sep 1798; b- Zaccheus Ezell min- Matthew Dance- 15Sep1798

Wilhelmina & John Gwaltney 4 Dec 1806; b- William Gwaltney min- Matthew Dance- 5Dec1806

Vaden

Nancy & Abdias Gillespie 20 Jul 1818; b- Richard Apperson

Valentine

Elizabeth W & George Seward 17 Oct 1825; b- Isham Valentine

Lucy & Isaac Seward 25 Oct 1803; b- Isham Valentine

Mary C & Joseph Hutcheson 17 Nov 1835; b- Melchizedeck Roffe min- Charles Ogburn- (Methodist)

Sally & Robert Hill 15 Jan 1821; b- Randolph Chavous min- Matthew Dance- (Lunenburg County)- 30Jan1821

Vaughan

Ann J & Jones Taylor 2 Feb 1813; b- Caleb Manning no minister cited, but ceremony performed 3Feb1813

Clary & John Burton 20 Feb 1787; b- Ambrose Vaughan of Brunswick County

Dulcema & Edmund P Overby 17 Jul 1819; b- John F Carter con- Peter Z Overby, father con- S W Vaughan, father

Eliza C & George H Wells 21 Nov 1842; 'Elvira C.' according to minister return b- Pleasant Vaughan min- Daniel Petty- 28Nov1842

Elizabeth & Howard Bailey 3 Dec 1783; b- John Bell

Elizabeth & Sandefer Bowers 14 Dec 1790; b- Richard Edmondson

Elizabeth & John Cliborne 17 Dec 1849; b- David Shelton con- Peter G Vaughan, father

Elizabeth & Richard Glasscock 19 Sep 1840; b- Joseph Yancey

Elizabeth & Robert Slate 12 Nov 1802; Robert from Brunswick county b- John Saunders min- William Creath-

Elizabeth & Ledford Vaughan 20 Dec 1830; b- William Vaughan con- Priscilla Vaughan, mother of Elizabeth min- Pleasant Gold- (Baptist)- 22Dec1830

Elizabeth & Thomas Wilson 10 Nov 1789; b- Robert Birtchett min- Thomas Scott-

Ermer & James Hurt 11 Sep 1809; b- William Burton min- William Richards-

Fanny & Seymour Puryear 11 Mar 1807; b- Wiley Burrus con- Nancy Foster, aunt of Fanny

Frances E & James Wortham 14 May 1850; b- Henry Newton

Frances & Hutson Nipper 16 Nov 1792; b- Ambrose Vaughan min- John Loyd- 22Nov1792

Hannah & Jairus Vaughan 11 Jul 1796; b- Craddock Vaughan daughter of Reuben and Elizabeth Vaughan con- Richard Vaughan, father of Jairus min- Charles Ogburn- (Methodist) 3Aug1796

Jane & Samuel Dickins 25 May 1801; b- John Wilson

Jane & Peter Vaughan 24 Feb 1821; b- Atha Gregory con- S C Vaughan, father min- Pleasant Gold- (Baptist)- 10Apr1821

Louisa & Robert Newton 24 Jan 1844; b- Harman Newton con- Peter Vaughan, father min- Alfred Apple-

Lucy & Turner Saunders 20 Dec 1820; b- George Saunders con- W Vaughan, father

Martha & Starling Hood 11 Jul 1785; b- George Barnes Starling son of Robert Hood

Martha & Samuel Ingram 25 Sep 1792; b- William Green min- William Creath- 4Oct1792

Martha & John Wortham 30 Aug 1821; b- William E Wortham con- Wyatt and Maggie Vaughan, parents min- Pleasant Gold- (Baptist)- 12Sep1821

Mary B & Lewis Thompson 18 Mar 1825; b- David C Vaughan

Mary E & Lewis G Crutchfield 21 Dec 1829; b- Livingston H. Vaughan min- James McAden-

Mary & James Davis 8 Jun 1824; b- Edwin Owen con- Drusella Vaughan, mother min- Pleasant Gold- (Baptist)- 11Jun1824

Molly & Henry Green 2 Aug 1799; b- Stephen P'Pool

Molly & Henry Green 12 Aug 1799; b- Stephen Pettypool

Nancy J & Uriah Cutts 13 Dec 1847; b- William H Cutts con- Peter G Vaughan, father

Nancy & John Cheatham 23 Feb 1808; b- Ambrose Vaughan

Nancy & Mickelborough Montague 30 Jul 1798; b- Reuben Vaughan min- William Creath- 2Aug1798

Nancy & William Owen 1 Oct 1847; b- Henry H Newton con- C Vaughan, father min- Alfred Apple- 2Nov1847

Nancy & Richard H Walker 10 Jul 1798; b- Thomas Vaughan Richard son of Henry and Martha Walker

Patsy & Jesse Brown 28 May 1798; b- Thomas Vaughan

Patsy & Francis Moody 14 Sep 1789; b- William Moody con- Henry Moody, father con- Reuben Vaughan, father min- Thomas Scott-

Polly Mealer & William Wade 12 Aug 1799; b- Willis Vaughan min- Edward Almand- 15Aug1799

Polly & Peter Elam 3 Aug 1811; daughter of Willie Vaughan b- John J Norment min- William Richards- 7Aug1811

Rebecca A & Robert H Portwood 10 Jan 1845; b- Adonis M Evans con- Balaam Vaughan, father

Rebecca & William Beasley 19 May 1804; b- Reuben Vaughan

Rody & Pace Nipper 23 Oct 1792; b- Hudson Nipper min- John Loyd- 24Oct1793

Sally & Benjamin William Hudson 21 Mar 1797; b- Thomas Chappell Singleton con- Richard Vaughan, father min- John Loyd- 23Mar1797

Susan & John Chambliss 24 Dec 1835; b- Turner Saunders con- William Vaughan, father

Susan & Isham Nance 17 Aug 1835; b- Ambrose Vaughan con- Livingston H Vaughan, father

Susanna & John Arrington 30 Apr 1790; married in Granville County, N.C.

Venable

Anne & William McLin - Apr 1801; William from Greensville County b- James McLin

Mary E & Frederick E Hughes 28 Aug 1851; 'Dr' Frederick E Hughes con- P C Venable, father

Sally T & William G Venable 26 Nov 1845; b- William M Womack con- P C Venable, father

Wade

Anne & Charles H Yancey 27 Feb 1841; b- Marshall P Yancey con- Lanstat G Wade, father min- Solomon Apple-

Isabella & Joseph Townes 28 Jun 1784; Henry from Halifax County b- Henry Townes

Jane & Thomas Cannon 29 Oct 1847; b- Martin F Lambert

Judith G & Josiah Forlines 3 Nov 1838; Josiah from Halifax Co, VA b- Henderson Overby con- L G Wade, father

Margaret & William Harrison 16 Nov 1790; b- Absolom Hasting

Martha Ann & John Murray - Oct 1839; b- Richard Wood min- John B. Smith-

Nancy O & Henry G Vaughan 3 Jan 1803; b- William Wade min- William Richards- 5Jan1803

Patsy & Absolom Hastin 12 Jan 1789; b- John Wagstaff min- Edward Almand- 22Jan1789

Polly & John Speed 3 Jul 1798; b- Joseph Speed Jr con- Joseph Townes, guardian of Polly

Sarah & Jacob Hudson 8 Sep 1788; b- William Lancaster min- John Williams-

Wagstaff

Ann Freeman & William Hill 8 Jun 1789; b- Britain Wagstaff min- John Williams- 17Jun1789

Elizabeth & Benjamin Dixon 20 Nov 1800; b- John Wagstaff min- William Richards- 9Dec1800

Lilly & Peter Hutcheson 11 Dec 1797; b- John Wagstaff min- William Richards- 21Dec1797

Mary & Benjamin Duty 20 Nov 1804; b- Bazzell Wagstaff con- John Wagstaff, father min- William Richards-

Matilda & William Hunt 2 Dec 1814; b- John Tabb con- Britain Wagstaff, father min- William Richards- 15Dec1814

Polly & Jesse Hunt 8 May 1799; b- William Hunt min- Edward Almand- 30May1799

Sally & Gideon Mitchell 7 Feb 1804; b- Allen Wagstaff min- William Richards- 8Feb1804

Walden

Mary Hubbard & Samuel Whitworth 9 Mar 1778; b- Peter Burton, who test. that Mary is over 21

Milly & Elijah Bass 28 Nov 1829; b- Frederick Nowell min- William Steel- (Episcopal)-

Milly & Banister Chavous 29 Dec 1819; b- John Stewart min- Alexander M. Cowan-

Polly & Moses Stuart 20 Dec 1788; b- Eaton Walden con- JohnCharles Walden, father

Priscilla & Matthew Stewart 25 Feb 1799; b- William Chandler min- Ebenezer McGowan- 26Feb1799

Walker

Agatha & John Freeman 22 Jul 1806; b- John Johnson

Agnes & Jordan Mason 10 Oct 1808; b- Allen Walker daughter of Richard & Lucy Walker

Amanda C & John O Walker 25 Oct 1852; con- Emma F Walker, mother min- James McAden-

Ann D & Samuel E Walker 20 Jan 1845; b- Robert W Ezell con- E Walker, father min- James McAden-

Ann E & John S Clack 13 Sep 1790; b- Henry Walker d of Henry and Martha Bolling Walker

Ann E & Henry C Hayes 16 May 1838; b- Archer Hayes con- Eliza Walker, mother min- Charles F. Burnley- 18May1838

Araminta H & Thomas E Reekes 19 Dec 1846; b- George Speaks con- David A Walker, father min- James McAden-

Camilla N & James S Mason 19 Nov 1849; b- Henry C Hayes con- Eliza Walker, mother min- Robert Burton- 28Nov1849

Delilah & William O Bowler 19 Sep 1836; b- Ben F Williamson

Elizabeth A & James C Gregory 15 Jan 1851; con- Elizabeth A Walker min- George W. Andrews-

Elizabeth H & Mortimer D Tanner 21 Dec 1846; b- David D Walker con- Edward Walker, father

Elizabeth & Antilochus J Barner 20 May 1833; con- John Connell, gdn, who test. he has raised Elizabeth since childhood b- John C Jones

Elizabeth & William Cleaton 13 Dec 1817; b- Thomas Wartman min- Charles Ogburn- (Methodist) 18Dec1817

Elizabeth & John Crenshaw 14 Dec 1801; b- Thomas A Jones

Elizabeth & Tilman Elder 17 Dec 1798; b- John Holloway min- John Neblett- 24Dec1798

Elizabeth & Benjamin Ezell 15 Dec 1814; b- Robertson Ezell

Elvira F & Henry Brown 29 Sep 1853; con- David A Walker, father min- James McAden- 29Sep1853

Elvira J & John P Hudson 21 Jul 1853; con- Elizabeth Walker, mother min- James McAden-

Emma & William H Taylor 13 Dec 1830; b- James Holmes con- Wilson Walker, father min- James Smith- 16Dec1830

Fanny & John Phillips 10 Sep 1798; John from Prince George County b- Theophilus Feild min- Alexander Hay- (Antrim Glebe, Antrim Parish, Halifax County) 16Sep1798

Frances & Charles Cleaton 2 Dec 1816; b- Thomas W Walker con- Wilson Walker, father min- Charles Ogburn- (Methodist) 4Dec1816

Hannah & Thomas Farrar 22 Nov 1819; b- Zachariah H Jones con- Wilson Walker, father min- James Smith- 24Nov1819

Jane E & Noble Ladd 8 Apr 1844; b- Samuel J Vaughan min- James McAden-

Jane & Bartlett Cheatham 4 Feb 1812; b- William Davis Sr Jane daughter of Daniel Walker

Jane & John Shaw Feild 9 Jun 1788; b- Henry Walker daughter of Henry Walker min- Thomas Scott-

Janet & Diggs Poynor 14 Sep 1814; b- Phillip Rainey con- Henry Walker, father

Julia A & William Evans 22 Jun 1840; b- William E Walker con- Thomas H Walker, father min- James McAden-

Lucy F & Thomas Wartman 1 Feb 1821; b- William B Cleaton con- Henry Walker, father min- James Smith- 8Feb1821

Lucy L & Sherwood G Colley 18 Nov 1816; b- Nicholas E Walker min- Richard Dabbs- (Lunenburg County)- 22Nov1816

Lucy & John Doyle 17 Jan 1823; min- Stephen Jones- (Lynchburg, Va.)-

Margarett F & David B Kennedy 10 Dec 1839; b- William M Bennett con- Freeman Walker, father min- James McAden-

Mariah F & Thomas H Callis 28 Aug 1841; b- Richard W Turner con- Edward Walker

Martha A & Samuel Henry Holloway 7 Dec 1853; con- Edward Walker, father min- James McAden-

Martha D & Joseph W Butler 20 Dec 1847; b- Robert W Land

Martha E & Anthony Evans - Jul 1846; b- David R Walker con- Elizabeth Walker, mother min- James McAden-

Martha E & Lewis Poythress - Jul 1846; min- James McAden-

Martha P & William Nelson 16 Dec 1816; b- Thomas Blackburne con- Richard H Walker, father min- Charles Ogburn- (Methodist) 23Dec1816

Martha & Samuel J Vaughan 1 Dec 1836; b- William Cleaton

Mary T & John W Ezell 21 Sep 1853; con- Elizabeth Walker, mother min- James McAden-

Mary Williams & James Holmes 8 Dec 1835; b- William L Eubank con- Allen Walker, father min- William B. Rowzee- 16Dec1835

Mary & William H Smith 12 Feb 1808; d of Aurelius and Nancy Walker b- Matthew Walker

Nancy & Hundley Ryland 11 Jan 1802; b- John Brown

Nancy & Robert Tanner 19 Jan 1835; b- Wilson Walker min- James McAden-

Phebe & Edward Shelton 22 Dec 1803; b- Bartlett Cheatham

Polly & William Evans 8 Dec 1802; b- Wilson Walker min- James Meacham- 9Dec1802

Sally H & Edmund H Vaughan 5 Jun 1809; b- Francis E Walker min- George Micklejohn-

Sally & Herbert Cook 6 Nov 1805; b- Tilman Elder

Sally & Benjamin Evans 5 Jun 1811; b- Wilson Walker

Sarah W & Thomas C Reekes 30 Nov 1847; b- William E Dodson con- Charles P Walker, father

Susanna & James T Hayes 15 Jul 1816; b- Lewis Green

Tabitha & Robert Boyd 11 May 1803; d of Henry Walker and Martha Bolling Walker b- John Dortch min- John Cameron-

Wall

Caty & Richard Clark 20 Jan 1800; b- Richard Overby

Caty & Thomas Edwards 10 Mar 1800; b- Thomas Daniel

Elizabeth & William Vaughan 15 Dec 1818; b- Thomas Hendrick min- Reuben Pickett-

Frances & Fielding Noel 10 Dec 1823; b- Henry Wall min- James Smith-

Jane & Edward Cole 27 Nov 1817; b- Thomas B Wall con- John Wall

Jane & John Daniel 11 Feb 1820; b- James Clardy min- Abner W. Clopton-

Malvina & Daniel Reamey 2 Sep 1817; b- Mastin Harris con- Martha Wall, mother min- James Meacham- 3Sep1817

Mause Adaline & Hamlin Potts 16 May 1838; b- Benjamin T Willard con- Ann D Wall, mother

Patsy & George Thomason 2 Jan 1812; b- Thomas Benford

Rebecca & William Hendrick 11 Feb 1805; b- Howell Graves

Sally & Thomas Hendrick 12 Dec 1803; b- Charles Hamblin

Silvanah & William W Ware 10 Jan 1843; b- James Glasscock min- Alfred Apple-

Wallace

Mary & Isaac Hailey 27 Nov 1829; b- Hugh Wallace, father

Susan & Spancer Slaughter 30 Nov 1830; b- Isaac T Hailey

Waller

Caty & Henry Wilson 25 Jun 1790; b- Daniel Waller

Frances B & Marshall Nanney 19 Jan 1849; b- Charles Nanney con- John Waller, father min- James McAden- 20Jan1849

Frances B & James W Wilson 15 Jan 1827; b- Samuel H Warren con- Daniel Waller, father min- James McAden-

Lucy & Daniel Hazlewood 2 Aug 1803; b- John Waller min- William Creath-

Martha & Thomas Abernathy 4 Jan 1813; b- John Waller con- John Waller, father

Mary & Samuel Creath 19 Jan 1818; b- Thomas Abernathy con- John Waller, father

Nancy & Elisha Clark 2 Jan 1810; b- John Waller

Rebecca & Tavner Toone 16 Nov 1818; b- Isaac H Waller con- Daniel Waller, father min- Milton Robertson- (Warren County, N.C.) 19Nov1818

Walton

Ann S & William Holmes 15 Dec 1831; 'Rev' William Holmes b- John Clark

Anne & John (Jr) Hyde 16 Nov 1786; b- Edward Walton John son of John Hyde Sr min- Henry Lester- (Baptist) 21Dec1786

Barbara & Charles Barker 15 Aug 1791; b- John Walton Charles from Nottoway County min- James Read- (Baptist)- 18Aug1791

Ware

Elizabeth & James Glasscock 11 Sep 1841; b- Richard Glasscock con- Zachariah Glasscock, father con- Bartlett Tillotson, relation not mentioned min- Solomon Apple-

Warren

Ann C & John J Bugg 2 Jul 1819; b- George B Hamner con- Samuel Holmes, grandfather and gdn of Ann min- James Smith- 14Jul1819

Elizabeth & William Mitchell 22 Jul 1786; b- Richard Stone con- Thomas Marriott Sr, guardian of Elizabeth

Jane & David H Abernathy 16 Feb 1824; b- Samuel H Warren min- J. Carson- (Lunenburg County)- 16Feb1824

Polly & Robert Fox 26 Nov 1801; b- John Warren

Wartman

Ann & Thomas W Walker 18 Dec 1820; b- Diggs Poynor

Elizabeth & Thomas Smith 25 Nov 1818; b- John Wartman

Martha E F & Benjamin J Walker 15 Dec 1845; b- William N Walker min- James McAden-

Mary M & John H Walker 21 Feb 1846; b- Isaac Watson con- Thomas Wartman, father min- James J. Sledge-

Wartmen

Elizabeth & Jonathon B Northington 16 Dec 1822; b- Thomas W Walker con- Elizabeth Wartman, mother min- Stephen Jones- (Lynchburg, Va.)- 20Dec1822

Watkins

Elizabeth & Edwin Hudson 3 Jul 1830; widow b- Caphas Hudson min- William Steel- (Episcopal)-

Judith C & Samuel L Graham 22 Apr 1836; b- Charles L Read con- James Daniel, father min- P. Calhoun- 26Apr1836

Margaret E & William Morton 5 Jan 1853; con- Ann V Watkins, mother min- F.N. Whaley-

Martha & Corbin Jackson 4 Nov 1816; b- Joseph Watkins

Mary Scott & Robert C Nelson 20 Dec 1847; b- T W Venable con- Samuel V Watkins, father 'Dr' Robert C Nelson

Mary & Rowland Terry 12 Oct 1707; b- Overton Wiles

Nancy & Daniel Smith 21 Dec 1821; b- James Watkins con- Joseph Watkins, father

Polly & Archibald Loftis 17 Oct 1814; b- Joseph Watkins con- Joseph Watkins, father

Sally A & Charles E Hamilton 25 Feb 1853; min- J.W. Chesley- 2Mar1853

Sally & Jonathon Terrell 9 Dec 1830; b- James Watkins, father min- Pleasant Gold- (Baptist)- 23Dec1830

Watson

Amanda Sarah & Richard D Bugg 5 Nov 1845; b- John T Crute con- Littleberry Watson, father

Amey & Dennis Roberts 6 Mar 1821; b- John Watson min- James Smith-

Charlotte & John Barron 2 Dec 1809; b- James Standley

Frances & Thomas Lambert 18 Apr 1797; b- Richard Stone

Martha & Thomas Shelton 29 Dec 1799; b- Jordan Bennett min- Ebenezer McGowan- 31Dec1799

Mary D & George F Griffin 10 Nov 1840; b- Boswell T Crute con- Littleberry Watson, father

Nancy & Isaac Nanney 18 Apr 1821; b- James B Watson con- Isaac Watson, father min- James Smith- 19Apr1821

Phebe Malone & Anderson Wright 27 May 1793; b- William Poole Jr min- John Loyd- 30May1793

Rebecca & John Davis 11 Nov 1778; b- Michael Watson

Rebeccah & Pleasant Allen 8 Aug 1787; b- John Allen con- William Allen, Sr., father

Tabitha & Phillip Roberts 29 Dec 1802; b- Thomas Shelton

Watts

Elizabeth Hanner Barbara & Henry Ashton 31 Mar 1788; b- Richard Watts min- Thomas Scott-

Frances Anne & Richard Thompson 14 Jun 1802; b- Henry Ashton con- Anna Watts, mother min- Matthew Dance- 29Jul1802

Weatherford

Amy & Jesse Westbrook 9 Dec 1805; b- James Baker

Lucinda G & William M Gillespie 2 Dec 1844; b- George W Gillespie con- James W Dedman, gdn of Lucinda

Martha R & Alanson M Cox 6 Feb 1841; b- Henry E Weatherford min- John B. Smith-

Mary & Thomas Pritchett 3 Jun 1835; b- Alexander Pritchett

Sarah & Bartley Smithson 30 Nov 1799; b- Freeman Weatherford con- William Weatherford, father min- Matthew Dance- 4Dec1799

Webb

Betsy B & Jesse Stegall 19 Nov 1817; b- Bushrod Webb, father, who also consents

Leannah Basey & Mark L Jackson 3 Jul 1797; b- John Webb

Nancy & Thomas Cleaton 27 Nov 1787; b- Abel Dortch

Tabitha & James Harrison 5 Dec 1801; b- Abdias P Webb con- E Webb, father min- James Meacham- 8Dec1801

Weekes

Frances & Isham Coley 9 Apr 1787; b- George Tucker

Wells

Amanda E J & Henry Vaughan 4 Mar 1834; b- Ligon Wells con- Baker Wells, father min- John Wesley Childs- 5Mar1834

Anne & Anthony Ragsdale 1 Oct 1793; b- William Westbrook con- David Wells, father min- William Creath- 3Oct1793

Eliza & Alexander Crow 15 Oct 1831; b- Baker Wells min- Charles Ogburn- (Methodist) 20Oct1831

Hannah & Peter Massey 11 Mar 1802; b- William Garrott min- William Creath-

Permelia A B & George Cumbia 12 Apr 1834; b- John Gwaltney con- Henry Wells, father

Rebecca & Stephen Davis 20 Apr 1829; b- Jesse Parrish min- Charles Ogburn- (Methodist) 23Apr1829

Susan & Alexander Roberts 20 Oct 1822; b- John Garrett con- Henry Wells, father

Westbrook

Nancy & John Neathry 26 Dec 1815; b- Jesse Westbrook

Phoebe & Joseph Hawks 13 May 1799; b- Thomas Westbrook min- Charles Ogburn- (Methodist)

Westmoreland

Martha S & John Kirk 4 Feb 1828; b- Marriott Kirk con- Robert Westmoreland, father

Mary & Daniel Glover 8 Nov 1806; b- Robert Westmoreland

Whitby

Elizabeth Hill & John Hearn 18 Dec 1793; b- Nathaniel Chambers con- Mary Crowder, mother of Elizabeth min- John Loyd- 19Dec1793

White

Elanner & Joseph Medley 10 Jan 1807; b- John Dortch min- William Richards- 1Jan1807

Eliza J & Richard H Moody 20 Nov 1843; b- William White con- Jan A White, mother min- Charles F. Burnley- 22Nov1843

Elizabeth & John Dedman 11 Feb 1799; b- Henry H Dedman min- William Richards- 12Feb1799

Frances & James Tillotson 27 Nov 1823; b- Elam S Wall min- Pleasant Gold- (Baptist)- 2Dec1823

Jincy & Henry Dedman 11 May 1795; b- William White min- William Richards- 18May1795

Mary A & Thomas S Jones 5 Nov 1844; b- William T White con- Jane A White, mother

Mary & Phillip Barnes 8 Jan 1798; b- William Naish min- William Richards- 20Jan1798

Mary & Thomas Feild 11 Jan 1782; b- James Anderson

Mary & Robert Harris 10 Jan 1791; b- William White min- James Read- (Baptist)

Nancy H & Henry F Farley 21 Nov 1814; b- Henry H Dedman min- William Richards- 22Nov1814

Nancy & Samuel Hudson 8 Feb 1790; b- William White min- Edward Almand- 11Feb1790

Saluda W & James Atkins 10 Dec 1835; b- William R Mason con- Jane white, mother

Sarah & Eleazar Overby 25 May 1824; b- David Dunn min- Pleasant Gold- (Baptist)- 3Jun1824

Virginia J & John R Yancey 14 Sep 1851; con- Jane A White, mother min- Alfred Apple-

Whitehead

Elizabeth & Eleazar Clay 7 Jan 1789; b- Richard Whitehead Eleazar from Chesterfield County

Elizabeth & Clark Taylor 13 Feb 1786; b- Richard Swepson

Jane & Richard Jeffries 1 Jul 1783; b- Robert Smith

Nancy & John Gayle 23 Mar 1793; b- William Whitehead John Gayle from Halifax County min- William Creath- 26Mar1793

Sarah & James Coleman 14 Nov 1785; b- Richard Swepson James son of Cluverius Coleman

Whitlow
Anne & John Glidewell 20 Aug 1785; b- Thomas Whitlow min- John Williams- 30Sep1785
Leatha W & Henry Wright 12 Feb 1831; widow of Phillip Whitlow b- Lewis G Meacham min- Stephen Turner- 17Feb1831
Mary F & James D Throgmorton 18 Dec 1849; b- German D Dedman con- Champion Whitlow, father con- F Throgmorton, father
Tabitha W & William H Somervill 26 Sep 1849; b- Champion Whitlow
Tabitha & William Collins 28 Nov 1825; b- William Loafman min- William Richards- 29Nov1825

Whitt
Rebecca & John Curtis 9 Mar 1834; b- Alexander M Watts

Whittemore
Elizabeth T & Woodson V Johnson 22 Feb 1812; b- John Whittemore con- Buckner Whittemore, father min- Charles Ogburn- (Methodist) 24Feb1812
Martha & Anderson Copley 23 Mar 1846; b- James W Whittemore con- D Middagh, gdn of Martha min- James McAden-
Nancy & Alfred Vaughan 9 Sep 1833; b- Churchwell Curtis

Whoberry
Mary & John Hamner 22 Dec 1790; b- John Whoberry
Nancy & Robert Burnett 23 Oct 1798; b- William Whoberry con- Jacob Whoberry, father

Whobry
Sally & Benjamin Blake 3 Apr 1809; b- George B Hamner min- James Meacham- 6Apr1809

Wilborn
Nancy & Vincent Hite 14 Dec 1807; b- Thomas Wilborn con- John Wilborn, father

Wilbourn
Edith & Obadiah Overby 22 Dec 1817; b- William Wilbourn

Wilburn
Elizabeth & Henderson Wade 6 Jan 1795; b- William Harrison min- William Richards- 11Jan1795

Wiles
Amanda A & Henry H Dedman 20 Jan 1832; b- John F Yancey con- Ruth Wile, mother
Lucy Ann & George Williamson 17 Dec 1833; b- Henry H Dedman con- Ruth Wiles, mother min- John B. Smith-
Margaret & Stephen Dodson 26 May 1823; b- Thomas Rowlett
Nancy & George Wright 12 Sep 1812; b- Mastin Wiles
Tempe & William Culbreath 13 Mar 1804; b- Isaac Pinson

Wilkerson
Agnes & Robert Yancey 11 Oct 1796; b- Francis Griffin
Betsy & Thomas Matthews 22 Mar 1809; b- John Rainey
Dosha H & William L Wilkerson 21 Dec 1842; b- Ranson Elliott min- John B. Smith-
Elizabeth J & George W Wilkerson 2 Jan 1843; b- William Wilkerson con- Edward Wilkerson, father of Elizabeth con- Charles Wilkerson, father of George
Mary Ann & William E Wortham 24 Dec 1833; b- Cole Vaughan con- Amy Wilkerson, mother min- William Steel- (Episcopal)-
Mary C & Edward Overton 22 Jun 1846; b- John T Wootton min- John B. Smith-
Mary F & Miles T Hall 30 Apr 1839; b- Thomas W Owen con- Washington Wilkerson, father min- John B. Smith-

Mary & John Blanks 14 Aug 1821; min- Pleasant Gold- (Baptist)-

Sarah & Jacob Straub 4 Mar 1852; min- Thomas King- (Halifax County)-

Wilkins

Mary Ann & Obadiah Christmas 19 Jul 1853; con- James Wilkins, father min- John E. Montague- 19Jul1853

Susanna & Joseph Yancey 21 Dec 1823; b- William Wilkins min- Pleasant Gold- (Baptist)-

Wilkinson

Almiranda J & Samuel Fitts 30 Dec 1852

Frances J & Henry Ligon 16 Dec 1844; b- Stephen Williamson con- Edmond Wilkinson, father

Judith Ann & Thomas Ramsey 5 Aug 1841; b- Spencer C Wilkinson min- John B. Smith-

Martha Ann & Abner Jones 10 Jan 1853; con- Edward Wilkinson, father

Martha J & Ledford Sizemore 15 Mar 1845; b- Alexander Puryear con- Washington Wilkinson, father

Mary E & David Ligon 21 Aug 1848; b- Darrell Miles con- Edward Wilkinson, father

Williams

Dorcas & Williamson Bland 17 Nov 1806; b- James Bugg min- James Meacham-

Jane & William (Jr) Moore 8 Nov 1787; b- William Moore Sr con- Edward Williams, mother

Lucy & William Rainey 27 Nov 1817; b- Wright King con- Lewis Williams, father min- Thomas Moore- 4Dec1817

Margaret J W & William Rice 9 Aug 1815; b- Edward Travis min- Cary Syme-

Martha & Thomas (Jr) Greenwood 8 Oct 1792; b- James T Hayes min- William Creath- 25Oct1792

Mary J & Thomas Williams 22 Dec 1823; b- Matthew Williams con- Lewis Williams, Sr., father min- Stephen Jones- (Lynchburg, Va.)- 24Dec1823

Mary & Theophilus Crowder 20 Jul 1843

Mary & Joseph Thomson 18 Sep 1817; min- Charles Ogburn- (Methodist)-

Nancy & William Burnett 13 Feb 1799; b- Lewis Williams min- Ebenezer McGowan- 14Feb1799

Obedience & Samuel Colley 24 Mar 1785; b- Thomas Clark

Oslin & Thomas Drumwright 18 Jan 1804; b- Lewis Williams Sarah daughter of Lewis Williams Sr

Patsy & William Nance 4 Feb 1800; b- Lewis Williams min- Ebenezer McGowan- 6Feb1800

Polly & Josiah Thomason 17 Sep 1817; b- John Thompson James Taylor test that Polly the daughter of his sister Elizabeth Williams, and that Polly 21

Sally & James B Coleman 9 Nov 1819; b- Phillip Johnson

Sally & John Hudson 14 Jul 1800; b- Christopher Robertson min- William Creath-

Williamson

Caroline B & James J Thomas 17 Aug 1846; b- William B Greenwood con- James Williamson, father

Elizabeth & Pugh Williamson Price 4 Jul 1794; groom from Prince Edward County b- Josiah Price con- Robert Williamson, father min- William Richards- 5Jul1794

Jane & James Smith 14 Feb 1843; b- Robert A Phillips con- Ritta Williamson, mother

Jincey & Edward Barber 9 Dec 1799; b- James Greenwood con- Robert Williamson, father

Julia A & John C Gregory 13 Jul 1837; b- John Clark con- James Williamon, father

Margaret & Edward Nelson 19 Jul 1830; b- James Williamson min- Pleasant Gold- (Baptist)- 22Jul1830

Marstelle A & Byrd D Paylor 20 Apr 1850; b- Beverly Williamson con James Williamson, father

Philadelphia & Thomas Noblin 18 Oct 1813; b- Edward Tillotson con- Robert Williamson, father

Polly & John B Yancey 16 Aug 1813; b- Hepburn Wiles con- Robert Williamson, father

Sally & Eggleston Overby 17 Nov 1817; b- Thomas Noblin con- Robert Williamson, father

Willis

Ann & James Grimes 3 Jul 1832; b- Alexander Gillespie

Jane & Thomas Barnes 20 Dec 1830; b- Samuel Dedman con- Anne Willis, mother min- John B. Smith- 24Dec1830

Mary & Dudley Haile - Dec 1781; b- Thomas Haile

Nancy & Robert Lewis 22 Aug 1799; b- Edward Willis con- Edward Lewis, father William Willis, father

Sally & Pleasant Jones 10 Oct 1848; b- Bennett B Goode con- Ann Willis, mother

Susanna & Willis Royster 8 May 1811; b- Robert Shanks

Wills

Nancy M & David Wallace 22 Mar 1798; b- Larkin Crowder min- Charles Ogburn- (Methodist) 24Mar1798

Wilmoth

Mary & Elisha Wells 16 Nov 1840; b- Jesse Wilmoth

Wilson

Alice & David Gaines 27 Dec 1831; b- Ezekiel Gaines con- Drury Wilson, father min- William Steel- (Episcopal)- .

Ann & James Cheatham 9 Feb 1784; b- John Wilson

Anna & Henry Gee 10 Nov 1817; b- Henry Wilson

Elizabeth & Henry Clark 6 Jan 1801; b- Henry Wilson

Elizabeth & John Pulliam 11 Sep 1775; b- Benjamin Pulliam

Elizabeth & Thomas Smith 14 Jul 1821; b- John W Binford con- Henry Wilson, father min- Stephen Jones- (Lynchburg, Va.)- 19Jul1821

Elizabeth & Balaam Stewart 11 Mar 1839; b- John Drew

Elizabeth & Charles Taylor 23 Jul 1817; b- Lewis G Thomas Elizabeth daughter of Edward Wilson

Frances & John Jenkins 3 Jun 1816; b- William Drumwright con- Ann Wilson, mother min- Charles Ogburn- (Methodist) 6Jun1816

Jane F & Edward H Toone 11 Jul 1832; b- John S Feild min- William Steel- (Episcopal)- 12Jul1832

Judith C & Charles P Walker 30 Dec 1839; b- Thomas C Reekes min- John B. Smith-

Lucy & Burnett Marshall 13 Oct 1803; b- Frederick Watkins con- James Wilson, guardian of Lucy

Martha & George Talley 18 Oct 1813; b- John E Pettypool

Mary J & P F Pescud 27 Apr 1843; b- Wesley Whitaker Jr min- John B. Smith-

Mary & James Hardy 12 Jan 1801; b- John Boswell

Mary & Thomas Smith 28 Sep 1795; b- James Day min- Charles Ogburn- (Methodist) 1Oct1795

Nancy & Richard Hailey 26 Jan 1805; b- John E Harris min- William Creath-

Polly B & John Harris 17 Apr 1837; b- Benjamin H Harris min- James McAden-

Rebecca & Samuel Vaughan 30 May 1816; b- Charles Taylor con- E T Wilson, father

Susanna & James Waller 16 Mar 1792; b- James Wilson min- John Loyd-

Tabitha & Obadiah Smith 22 May 1798; s of Peartree Smith b- James Wilson con- Tabitha Wilson, mother and guardian min- Alexander Hay- (Antrim Glebe, Antrim Parish, Halifax County) 24May1798

Winckler

Selena K & John Rogers 6 Feb 1835; b- Richard D Bugg con- John Winckler, father

Winfield

Dolly & Joseph R Walker 6 Dec 1796; b- William Abernathy con- Joshua Winfield, father

Martha & James Robinson 2 Nov 1803; b- William Thomas con- Joshua Winfield, father min- James Meacham- 9Nov1803

Mary & Drury Robertson 4 Feb 1786; b- Matthew Turner

Nancy & Thomas Jones 26 Nov 1787; b- Joshua Winfield

Wingfield

Catharine & Reuben Wright 20 Feb 1812; b- William Bilbo

Fanny & Beverly George 2 Dec 1853

Winkfield

Rebecca & John Barnes 15 Jan 1794; b- Joshua Winkfield John from Brunswick County min- John Loyd- 23Jan1794

Winkler

Charlotte & Samuel Webster 1 Aug 1788; b- Richardson Davis

Winn

Elizabeth & Josiah Marshall 17 Feb 1802; b- Banister Winn min- William Richards- 3Mar1802

Frances & John Nance 17 Mar 1795; b- John Thomas min- John Loyd- 19Mar1795

Henrietta & Alexander Sculthorp 30 Mar 1835; b- William C Hudson con- William Winn, father min- John B. Smith-

Henriette M W & Peter Daves 4 Oct 1814; min- Charles Ogburn- (Methodist) 4Oct1814

Jane & Robert White 5 Dec 1807; b- John Dedman min- William Richards- 10Dec1807

Lucy & Nathaniel Fowlkes 1 Jul 1816; b- James Winn con- Richard Winn, father min- George Petty- 4Jul1816

Mary E & John Crews 20 Nov 1834; b- William Webb con- William Winn, father min- William Steel- (Episcopal)-

Nancy & Elijah Callis 6 Jan 1820; b- Nathaniel Fowlker con- Sally Winn, mother min- William Richards-

Prudence & William Cary 21 Jan 1822; b- Joseph B Clausel min- William Richards- 31Jan1822

Wood

Catherine H & Henry R Johnson 22 Aug 1848; b- James A Wimbish con- Henry Wood, gdn of Henry

Nancy D & Wiley W Crowder 17 Oct 1839; b- Richard Wood

Ruther & Thomas Murray 26 Dec 1832; b- William Johnson con- Richard Wood, father min- William Steel- (Episcopal)-

Woodall

Elizabeth & Thomas Ladd 16 Dec 1844; b- Jacob Woodall min- Jacob Manning-

Wootton

Elizabeth E & Lewis L Toone 14 Oct 1844; b- William R Toone min- John B. Smith-

Elizabeth & William Daniel 9 Jan 1806; b- John Winckler

Harriet W & Royall Spain 17 Dec 1838; b- John P Wootton min- John B. Smith-

Martha A & Richard Wilkerson 19 May 1835; b- John Wootton

Martha & Joseph H Keeling 8 Dec 1845; b- John W Wootton

Mary E & John L Warren 7 Dec 1838; b- Samuel Wootton Jr min- John B. Smith-

Mary & Howell Wilkerson 15 Dec 1834; b- John Wootton min- John B. Smith-

Nancy J & Charles Hutcherson 28 Feb 1818; b- John P Wootton con- Samuel Wootton Sr, father min- William Richards- 19Mar1818

Patsy H & Barrett Hughes 16 Dec 1816; b- Samuel Wootton min- James Meacham- 26Dec1816

Sarah H & Henry Brame 18 Nov 1816; b- Samuel Wootton min- William Richards- 20Nov1816

Susan P & Joseph H Keeling 15 Nov 1841; b- John Wootton min- James Delk-

Worsham

Cynthia H & Peter Overby 7 Feb 1827; b- James Keen con- S V Worsham, father min- Pleasant Gold- (Baptist)- 1May1827

Elizabeth & Thomas Glasscock 19 Nov 1821; b- Eggleston Overby min- John S. Ravenscroft- (Episcopal)- 28Nov1821

Elizabeth & Presley Hinton 10 Jan 1801; b- William Blanton min- James Meacham- 14Jan1801

Elizabeth & Reaves Neal 8 Oct 1792; b- William Neal min- James Read- (Baptist)

Larrisa & David Moore 20 Dec 1830; b- William Vaughan con- S V Worsham, father min- Pleasant Gold- (Baptist)- 23Dec1830

Letha & Lewis N Yancey 4 Jan 1827; b- John Worsham

Mary & Zachariah Glasscock 3 Dec 1850; min- Alfred Apple-

Polly & Samuel Apperson 1 Oct 1801; b- Archibald Clarke con- John Worsham, father

Rebecca & Jarrott Avory 17 Dec 1810; b- Daniel Jones

Sally & Hezekiah Yancey 10 Oct 1808; b- John Williamson

Tabitha & John Blanks 20 Feb 1815; b- Stephen Worsham

Wortham

Mary & Grandison Vaughan 28 Dec 1827; b- James Vaughan min- Pleasant Gold- (Baptist)-

Nancy & John Vaughan 29 Apr 1823; b- Pleasant Gold min- Pleasant Gold- (Baptist)- 1May1823

Parthena & Thomas Ladd 24 Oct 1836; b- James Wortham min- John B. Smith-

Wray

Sarah & Asa Oliver 1 Dec 1772; b- John Oliver

Wrenn

Martha & Daniel J Morris 31 May 1843; b- William A Homes

Wright

Ann E & William P Newton 21 Oct 1842; b- Daniel Yancey con- Nancy Wright, mother min- Alfred Apple-

Elizabeth & William (Jr) Brame 11 Apr 1834; b- John Brame Jr

Elizabeth & James Kendrick 12 Dec 1797; b- John Wright

Jane & Donaldson Potter 3 Sep 1804; b- Edmund Clements min- James Meacham- 6Sep1804

Julia C & John W Johnson 6 Nov 1843; b- John Tarpley min- Joseph Goodman- 10Nov1843

Julia C & Abner P Wright 16 May 1836; b- Horace Palmer con- John M Wright, gdn of Julia

Martha & Stephen Turner 11 Mar 1801; b- Austen Wright

Mary G & John E Wright 14 Dec 1836; b- Thomas Johnson min- Stephen Turner-

Mary & David Holloway 21 Dec 1799; b- John Holmes min- Ebenezer McGowan- 24Dec1799

Nancy & Joshua Davis 3 Jan 1805; b- William Wright

Nancy & Richard Fox 4 Oct 1792; b- Solomon Patillo

Nancy & David Wright 28 Dec 1797; David from Lunenburg County b- Roderick Wright

Nancy & Robert Wright 16 Nov 1792; b- Austin Wright Robert from Brunswick County

Polly & Reuben Dunnington 11 Jul 1798; b- William Wright con- Reuben Wright, father

Rebecca B & William H Farrar 1 Aug 1825; b- B H Bailey con- Austin Wright, Sr., father

Rebecca & Thomas Powers 19 Mar 1827; b- Christopher Haskins Jr

Sally & George Crowder 28 Oct 1803; b- Elijah Crowder

Sarah L & Edmund Clemmonds 12 Nov 1805; b- Richard Moss

Sarah L & Lewis G Meacham 18 May 1833; b- John Langley con- Mary Wright, mother

Unity A & Richard Bullock 13 Jun 1843; b- Arthur H Davis con- John M Wright, gdn of Unity min- Joseph Goodman-

Wynn

Kitty & Thomas Apperson 6 Aug 1791; b- Holeman Rice min- James Read- (Baptist)- 12Aug1791

Wynne

Mary & Richard M Allen 8 Dec 1814; widow b- Thomas Rowlett

Yancey

Avey & Martin Daniel 2 Jun 1817; b- Charles T Carter con- Zachariah Yancey, father min- Reuben Pickett- 5Jun1817

Cornelia F & Joseph T Reese 23 Jun 1842; b- James B Dupuy con- Eliza Yancey, mother

Delphia & John Tillotson 16 Jan 1801; b- Richard Murray

Dolly & Benjamin Moody 15 Nov 1813; b- William Moody con- Mary Yancey, mother min- William Richards- 16Nov1813

Elizabeth & John Griffin 11 Aug 1794; b- Robert Williamson

Elizabeth & William Leneve 1 Dec 1828; b- Stith G Yancey con- Zachariah Yancey, father min- Pleasant Gold- (Baptist)- 24Dec1828

Emily H & George W Pettypool 30 Oct 1837; b- James Yancey con- Richard Yancey, father

Harriett Pendleton & Richard Yancey 27 Feb 1832; b- John F Yancey con- Robert Yancey, Sr, father of Harriett

Jane & Peyron R Talley 30 Nov 1819; b- John B Yancey con- Zachariah Yancey, father min- Reuben Pickett- 16Dec1819

Louisa Ann & James T Jones 1 Sep 1836; b- James Yancey min- Richard Yancey min- Joseph S. Baker- 8Sep1836

Lucy & James Clark 11 Oct 1838; b- Charles H Yancey con- John Yancey, father

Lucy & Stark Daniel 19 Oct 1818; b- James Feild

Maria C & John Paris 17 Dec 1849; b- C F Harris min- C.F. Harris-

Martha & John Elam 5 Dec 1835; b- Thomas W Owen con- Charles Yancey, father min- John B. Smith-

Mary Baker & Littleberry Moore 21 Dec 1824; b- Richard Yancey min- Pleasant Gold- (Baptist)-

Mary E & Joseph M Hicks 22 Feb 1851; con- James Yancey min- William V. Wilson- 27Feb1851

Mary & Robert Williamson 25 Jan 1793; b- William Baskervill min- James Read- (Baptist) 31Jan1793

Nancy M & Samuel Williamson 30 Nov 1852; min- F.N. Whaley-

Nancy & William Clark 15 Jan 1827; b- John Yancey min- Pleasant Gold- (Baptist)- 23Jan1827

Nancy & James Green 9 Jan 1792; b- William Hendrick min- James Read- (Baptist) 11Jan1792

Nancy & Lewis Griffin 25 May 1817; b- John B Yancey min- Reuben Pickett- 5Jun1817

Parmelia & Charles Yancey 25 Feb 1828; b- Richard Yancey min- Pleasant Gold- (Baptist)- 26Feb1828

Parthena & Robert Yancey 15 Aug 1833; b- James M Yancey con- Hezekiah Yancey, father of Parthena min- John B. Smith-

Permelia & Milton Keen 10 Jul 1837; b- James M Yancey con- Hezekiah Yancey, father

Polly & Edward Clark 15 Jun 1816; b- John Culbreath

Polly & Anthony Lumpkin 14 Nov 1808; b- Charles Yancey

Rebecca & James C Lukes 4 Dec 1843; b- Leander O Yancey con- Hezekiah Yancey, father min- Alfred Apple- 7Dec1843

Selina & Lyman B Gardner 15 Oct 1838; b- Richard Yancey min- John B. Smith-

Susanna & John Williamson 3 Sep 1802; b- Richard Murray con- Robert Yancey, father min- Balaam Ezell- 4Sep1802

Susannah & William Overby 11 Jun 1804; b- Howell Graves

Temperance & James M Yancey 13 Oct 1837; b- James Yancey min- John B. Smith- 18Oct1837

Yates

Milly & Bernard Thompson 10 Dec 1804; b- John Walton

Susan R & Samuel Douglas 18 Nov 1811; b- Charles Baskervill con- John M Yates, gdn of Susan min- Matthew Dance- (Lunenburg County)- 28Nov1811

Yeargen

Elizabeth & Henry Mize 12 Jan 1807; b- John Mize Henry from Brunswick County

Nancy & John Mize 30 Dec 1805; b- Jerry Mize

Young

Ann M & John A Taylor 26 Apr 1852; con- Dianitia M Young, mother

Elanor & Clack Robinson 11 Oct 1809; b- Walter Langley min- James Meacham-

Elizabeth & George Redd 17 Sep 1812; b- James Meacham min- James Meacham-

Judith B & Walter C Langley 5 Nov 1803; b- Jesse Dortch con- Allen Young, father

Lucy & John Langley 6 Dec 1798; b- Allen Young

Martha Ann & George W Norvell 8 Aug 1840; b- Edmond Young

Mary & Jonathon Tanner 5 Jun 1798; b- Allen Young

Nancy N & Christopher (Jr) Haskins 28 Nov 1815; b- John H Hardie con- M Jones, gdn of Nancy min- James Meacham- 12Dec1815

Sarah D & Alexander S Boyd 25 Jan 1847; b- Philip Rainey, Sr. con- Dianita M Young, mother min- William A. Smith- 26Jan1847

Susanna & Howell Taylor 30 Dec 1778; b- Samuel Young

Mecklenburg County Marriages, 1765 - 1853

Date frequency of marriages by year and month

Year	Total	Jan	Feb	Mar	Apr	May	June	July	Aug	Sept	Oct	Nov
1765	2	0	0	0	0	0	0	1	0	1	0	0
1766	2	0	1	0	0	0	0	0	1	0	0	0
1767	6	0	1	1	0	0	0	0	0	1	0	2
1768	3	0	0	1	0	0	1	0	0	1	0	0
1769	3	0	0	1	1	1	0	0	0	0	0	0
1770	5	0	0	3	1	0	0	0	1	0	0	0
1771	3	0	1	0	0	0	1	0	1	0	0	0
1772	11	1	0	1	1	0	0	1	0	1	3	1
1773	6	1	1	0	1	0	1	0	0	0	0	1
1774	10	1	0	1	0	1	2	0	0	0	2	1
1775	15	1	0	2	3	2	1	0	3	2	1	0
1776	3	0	1	0	0	1	0	0	0	0	1	0
1777	5	0	0	0	0	1	0	1	1	0	1	1
1778	11	0	1	1	1	2	1	0	1	0	0	2
1779	18	0	1	2	1	5	0	0	2	1	1	2
1780	15	2	0	1	2	1	1	1	0	1	3	1
1781	14	0	0	0	1	2	0	1	1	1	2	2
1782	13	2	2	4	1	0	0	1	1	2	0	0
1783	24	1	2	0	1	3	2	2	1	2	3	2
1784	23	1	5	2	1	0	1	0	0	0	3	5
1785	52	3	1	5	3	3	2	4	7	4	2	6
1786	63	3	10	4	5	4	3	2	3	5	1	8
1787	54	8	3	5	4	1	1	5	3	2	5	10
1788	46	8	2	3	1	0	1	4	5	7	1	5
1789	42	7	4	7	1	2	4	1	1	3	3	2
1790	48	7	5	1	2	0	4	1	4	4	3	3
1791	55	4	2	4	5	3	1	4	4	2	6	5
1792	66	4	6	4	0	3	1	2	5	6	8	7
1793	43	9	0	3	0	1	3	1	2	2	3	4
1794	58	10	4	5	3	1	5	2	5	3	7	4
1795	68	12	5	2	6	6	2	2	5	5	8	3
1796	46	8	2	3	1	2	1	6	2	2	3	2
1797	68	11	5	7	2	6	4	4	3	2	6	4
1798	70	8	5	4	2	5	5	5	1	5	4	11
1799	82	5	9	9	3	5	4	9	6	3	7	4
1800	65	7	6	9	2	5	2	4	2	3	6	4
1801	68	10	1	6	4	4	5	2	5	6	7	6
1802	72	7	8	3	2	5	4	3	1	3	4	8
1803	80	11	2	2	3	6	5	3	8	4	8	9
1804	74	8	4	6	2	3	3	5	1	3	11	7
1805	49	5	7	2	4	4	0	2	1	3	1	7
1806	51	4	3	11	2	1	0	8	1	5	4	6
1807	47	8	1	3	3	3	2	3	2	4	4	4
1808	52	4	6	3	1	1	1	5	2	1	5	10
1809	54	5	2	3	1	4	4	2	4	3	5	4
1810	47	12	6	3	0	2	3	1	2	1	4	3
1811	64	6	3	3	6	8	2	4	7	7	2	5
1812	52	8	6	3	2	3	3	0	0	6	6	5
1813	50	5	6	5	1	2	2	4	4	3	4	4

Date frequency of marriages by year and month

Year	Total	Jan	Feb	Mar	Apr	May	June	July	Aug	Sept	Oct	Nov	Dec
1814	63	9	2	6	2	5	9	2	2	5	6	6	9
1815	53	2	4	4	2	4	4	3	6	5	5	6	8
1816	80	9	7	2	2	3	7	5	3	5	6	11	20
1817	70	7	2	0	2	4	4	2	6	8	5	11	19
1818	57	9	9	5	1	1	3	4	0	1	3	5	16
1819	57	4	1	3	4	4	2	4	5	4	6	8	12
1820	43	7	4	4	0	2	3	0	4	0	7	4	8
1821	72	6	6	2	5	4	3	4	4	7	3	15	13
1822	67	8	4	6	5	5	4	4	7	5	4	4	11
1823	49	5	3	4	2	1	2	1	2	1	5	8	15
1824	64	5	6	1	5	5	3	5	4	2	4	7	17
1825	72	8	7	7	4	5	4	2	4	5	5	7	14
1826	39	6	1	2	4	1	1	3	3	1	6	4	7
1827	51	12	2	4	4	2	3	1	5	3	2	3	10
1828	51	3	6	6	1	1	2	5	4	3	7	5	8
1829	52	6	4	2	3	0	1	4	1	6	3	8	14
1830	66	7	5	3	1	0	3	5	5	3	6	6	22
1831	46	4	2	1	3	1	1	2	1	1	6	6	18
1832	53	6	4	1	4	6	5	4	4	2	1	2	14
1833	57	5	3	4	2	10	1	1	1	4	8	5	13
1834	56	4	5	5	7	0	5	3	1	5	9	7	5
1835	69	7	4	6	0	3	5	2	4	4	9	8	17
1836	49	6	5	1	3	1	2	0	2	5	7	6	11
1837	41	5	2	1	1	4	2	3	3	1	6	5	8
1838	56	4	2	1	1	6	2	2	3	1	7	10	17
1839	59	3	2	3	3	2	0	8	8	2	10	3	15
1840	62	5	5	1	1	6	3	4	5	4	5	11	12
1841	63	4	12	2	3	3	4	2	6	2	3	8	14
1842	50	3	4	4	4	2	1	3	0	6	3	7	13
1843	64	6	6	4	3	3	2	1	3	6	6	9	15
1844	55	5	4	6	1	0	0	1	8	2	8	6	14
1845	65	7	4	2	7	2	1	2	3	5	6	13	13
1846	50	3	3	4	3	1	3	7	5	3	2	3	13
1847	40	5	2	1	0	3	5	3	0	1	3	5	12
1848	48	2	4	1	3	2	2	2	5	3	10	6	8
1849	48	3	1	0	3	1	2	3	5	3	9	5	13
1850	54	4	4	2	5	5	0	0	5	2	3	7	17
1851	36	2	1	1	4	0	2	2	3	4	5	6	6
1852	43	1	2	4	5	4	4	2	0	4	1	7	9
1853	57	6	3	1	2	3	6	5	3	4	7	2	15
*Tot	4105	430	297	265	201	227	204	222	252	258	375	446	928
Percent		10.5	7.2	6.5	4.9	5.5	5.0	5.4	6.1	6.3	9.1	10.9	22.6

Total marriages = 4120
* incomplete dates were not included in the table

Ministers performing ceremonies

Adams, Richard E.G.	1849	1850	2
Adams, Thomas	1815	1849	17
Allen, James M.	1821	1821	1
Allen, John	1812	1814	3
Almand, Edward	1787	1821	44
Anderson, Albert	1838	1838	1
Andrews, George W.	1850	1853	14
Apple, Alfred	1829	1851	25
Apple, Solomon	1840	1841	3
Arnold, Hartwell	1850	1852	9
August, P.F.	1851	1853	6
Bagby, John	1849	1849	1
Bain, George A.	1835	1835	1
Baker, Joseph S.	1836	1836	2
Barham, N.T.	1828	1828	1
Bayley, John	1848	1849	3
Blackwell, J.D.	1849	1851	5
Blackwell, John C	1844	1847	2
Blanch, Ezekiel	1815	1815	1
Brame, Samuel D.	1797	1797	1
Brame, Thomas R.	1823	1823	1
Brown, Aaron	1792	1792	1
Brown, Joseph A	1843	1843	2
Burnley, Charles F.	1837	1843	22
Burton, Robert	1846	1853	24
Calhoun, P.	1836	1836	2
Cameron, John	1786	1804	10
Campbell, Thomas S.	1843	1843	1
Carson, J.	1824	1824	1
Castleman, Thomas T.	1838	1838	1
Chambers, E.	1845	1846	5
Chesley, J.W.	1852	1853	4
Childs, John Wesley	1831	1834	4
Clark, John T.	1839	1839	1
Clopton, Abner W.	1820	1831	2
Compton, William	1836	1836	1
Conkling, James D.	1843	1843	1
Cowan, Alexander M.	1819	1822	16
Cox, Phillip	1789	1789	2
Creath, Joseph W.D.	1841	1841	1
Creath, S.A.	1850	1852	4
Creath, William	1788	1805	149
Crowder, Thomas	1850	1850	2
Dabbs, Richard	1807	1820	11
Dance, Matthew	1795	1848	22
Davidson, A.F.	1853	1853	2
Delk, James	1839	1841	3
Dell, John A.	1852	1852	1
Doll, John A.	1852	1852	3
Doswell, William	1853	1853	1
Dromgoole, Edward	1797	1797	1
Duncan, James A.	1851	1851	1
Duval, Benjamin R.	1838	1839	22

Ministers performing ceremonies

Easter, John	1790	1790	1
Easter, Matthew L.	1797	1798	2
Ezell, Balaam	1802	1803	6
Finch, Adam	1851	1853	10
Fowler, Sterling M.	1825	1825	1
Gold, Pleasant	1819	1833	120
Goodman, Joseph	1843	1843	2
Grigg, Lewis	1816	1816	1
Haggard, Rice	1792	1792	1
Hamersley, William	1849	1849	1
Hardie, Thomas	1805	1806	5
Harris, C.F.	1849	1849	1
Hay, Alexander	1798	1805	4
Heath, William	1790	1790	1
Hollister, E.	1829	1829	1
Jarrott, Devereaux	1785	1785	1
Jeffries, C.L.	1824	1834	2
Jeffries, Thomas M.	1822	1822	1
Jeter, James M.	1834	1836	2
Jones, Stephen	1821	1824	16
Jones, Thomas	1823	1823	1
Jordan, W.W.	1850	1850	1
Kennedy, James S.	1853	1853	4
Kidd, Benjamin	1833	1833	1
King, John	1785	1791	10
King, Thomas	1843	1852	5
Leigh, H.G.	1850	1850	1
Leigh, Joshua	1833	1833	1
Leste, Henry Y.	1785	1785	1
Lester, Henry	1784	1786	7
Ligon, John	1814	1814	1
Locke, Thomas E.	1844	1844	1
Loyd, John	1791	1797	90
Maddox, William H.	1843	1843	1
Manning, Jacob	1844	1845	3
Marshall, John	1785	1786	7
Mason, S. G.	1847	1849	3
Mason, S.G.	1846	1851	4
McAdam, James	1843	1843	1
McAden, James	1822	1853	197
McCargo, David	1810	1811	4
McGowan, Ebenezer	1798	1801	26
McGuire, F.H.	1839	1852	11
Meacham, James	1799	1819	127
Meacham, John	1802	1808	3
Metcalf, Allen D.	1826	1829	12
Micklejohn, George	1808	1811	7
Montagu, John E	1851	1851	1
Montague, John E.	1851	1853	9
Montgomery, A.D.	1834	1834	1
Moore, Thomas	1817	1817	2
Moorman, S.T.	1853	1853	1
Neblett, John	1792	1801	9

Ministers performing ceremonies

Nicholson, D.B.	1840	1840	3
Nolley, J.	1821	1821	1
Norfleet, William J.	1845	1845	1
Ogburn, Charles	1793	1835	179
Ogburn, Henry	1791	1791	3
Parker, M.P.	1836	1836	1
Parks, M.P.	1834	1835	2
Pence, Willis N.	1853	1853	2
Petty, Daniel	1831	1846	9
Petty, David	1841	1841	1
Petty, George	1816	1834	7
Phaup, John	1789	1801	2
Pickett, Reuben	1814	1819	12
Poindexter, A.M.	1839	1845	3
Ravenscroft, John S.	1817	1823	17
Read, James	17	1794	25
Richard, Richard	1815	1815	1
Richards, William	1794	1833	274
Riddick, James A.	1819	1839	2
Robertson, Milton	1812	1819	17
Robertson, William	1818	1818	1
Rowzee, William B.	1834	1845	14
Scott, Thomas	1787	1789	23
Seat, Drury	1851	1851	1
Shelburne, James	1805	1805	1
Shelburne, Silas	1819	1822	4
Slaughter, D.J.C.	1850	1850	1
Sledge, James J.	1845	1846	4
Smit, James	1823	1823	1
Smit, John B	1831	1833	2
Smith, James	1818	1830	100
Smith, John B	1828	1836	4
Smith, John B.	18	1846	135
Smith, William A	1850	1850	1
Smith, William A.	18	1853	11
Steel, William	1824	1837	81
Stewart, F S	1802	1802	1
Sydnor, T.W.	1846	1846	1
Syme, Cary	1815	1815	1
Tabb, Edward L	1825	1825	1
Terry, John	1815	1815	1
Thomas, Nathaniel	1849	1853	3
Thompson, John	1823	1823	1
Tolleson, James	1796	1796	1
Tompkins, James D.	1826	1826	1
Turner, Stephen	1827	1839	6
Wadsworth, Edward	1838	1841	10
Watkins, James	1787	1804	2
Whaley, F.N.	1852	1853	6
Williams, John	1785	1794	26
Wilson, William V.	1844	1851	10
Wood, David	1831	1832	2

Origins of Mecklenburg County

Charles City (1634)
‖
Prince George (1703)
‖
Brunswick (1732)
‖
Lunenburg (1746)
‖
Mecklenburg (1765)